being human

The Image of the Serving God

Terry Kyllo

To Jayne,
a coworker with
Christ

Blessings

Cold Tree Press

Cover Art: "Ruby," 38" by 62" oil on canvas © Alfred Currier 2004.
To see more of his work, go to www.insightsgallery.com.

The Scripture quotations contained herein, unless otherwise noted, are from the New Revised Standard Version Bible, © 1989, by the Division of Christian Education of the National Council of Churches of Christ in the U.S.A.
Used by permission. All rights reserved.

Scripture taken from THE MESSAGE. © 1993, 1994, 1995, 1996, 2000, 2001, 2002.
Used by permission of NavPress Publishing Group.

Published by Cold Tree Press
Nashville, Tennessee
www.coldtreepress.com

Who will provide the grand design
For what is yours and what is mine
'Cause there is no more new frontier
We have got to make it here

– Eagles, from "The Last Resort"

See, I am making all things new.

– Revelation 21:5

Acknowledgements

Had I grown up in a different town, gone to a different church, married a different person, gone to school elsewhere, or been at a different church these last six years, this book would not be the same. We have a profound impact on each other, and we miss out when we ignore the power of relationship.

As early as high school I learned that I loved to talk theology. My English teacher, Dorothy Smith, shoved books at me and allowed me to debate them with her. Oh, Dorothy, how patient you were!

This work has gone through three feedback editions. The task of translating Lutheran theology from its historical and present usage into a form that is both readable and understandable in our current context has taken much trial and error. Many people have helped me along the way.

My thanks go out to Dan Erlander, who was my pastor while I was attending college and who patiently helped me to reconnect my life to my latent faith. I am grateful for his feedback on all the drafts of this book.

I want to thank those who read earlier drafts and gave me thoughtful feedback: Catherine Harmon, Richard Treston, Paul Sundberg, Dick Wendt, Kathryn Buffum, Gary Delanius, Kevin

Bates, David Greenlee, Tim Sexton, Sanford Hampton, Vicki Wesen, Mark Nelson, Kevin Bates, Dave Sharkey, Cathie Carlisle, Steve Purcer, Mary Campbell, Dan August, and Debbie Exley. I also thank Jeannine Honey for proofreading, research, and helpful editorial work on the second edition as well as Sherri Shavers for proofreading as we neared publication.

Chara Curtis is my friend and has been my editor on this book. Without her fierce and loving hard work this book would not be what it is. I am grateful for our ongoing conversation.

I want to thank my dear friend Andy Rutrough for our friendship and many late-night conversations about what this Christian thing is all about. He has been a great help, suggesting many changes for the drafts that have led to this current book.

I wish to thank Bishop Don Maier and Bishop David Wold, who, after hearing a presentation of some of this material, encouraged me to write it down.

The people of Celebration Lutheran Church have been significant in changing me, both as a person and as a pastor. They give me the freedom to say what I think and let me know when my thoughts are crazy. We search for the truth as a playful and engaged congregation, and I am grateful to be among them.

A great deal of my theology, and therefore this book, comes from the experience of reading Douglas John Hall, one of the great theologians of our time. If I were to footnote each idea in this book that I can connect to his writings, I would have hundreds of footnotes. Hall's answers to life's tough questions and his humility in dealing with both God and the readers of his books have influenced me deeply.

My parents, Bruce and Ruth Kyllo, have formed me deeply through their struggles and their joys. I am proud to be their child.

Lauren and Shelby, my daughters, were a great source of fun and inspiration as I wrote this book. Their questions and their joy for life have often made me re-think many things.

My wife, Sheryl, is especially deserving of my appreciation. I thank her for supporting my decision to get away for three weeks in order to get this book started and for her patience as I wrote morning and night. Above all, she loves me—the best gift of all.

Table of Contents

~

being human

The Image of the Serving God

Terry Kyllo

Introduction

How To Read This Book

I imagine three audiences for this book:

- People with little or no church experience who want to hear what Christians say about being human
- Those who want a reintroduction to Christianity after a painful experience with aggressive Christians or who find the media's portrayal of Christianity to lack depth and substance
- Active Christians who want a fresh perspective on Christianity

Foremost in my mind as I wrote this book were people with little or no experience with Christianity. In this book I endeavor to explain Christian terminology and ways Christians think. Yes, Christians do think, and we question things too. I don't claim to speak for all Christians, or even for my own faith community; rather, I speak for what I have learned so far from life, from Lutheran Christianity, and from many other forms of Christianity. Mostly though, I seek to write about what it means to be human, for that is really what this whole Christian thing is about.

I have spent a lot of time with people who have had painful experiences with Christians and their churches. I hope that your healing process will be helped by reading this book. For those who find media Christianity lacking in depth, I hope this book might serve either as an introduction or a re-introduction to a Christian way of life. Take your time. God loves you regardless of whether or not you attend church.

For active Christians, I hope to provide a fresh perspective on what the whole Christian enterprise is about. You may occasionally find that I explain things you already know. When I am explaining something basic, try to think through how you would say it. I want to be a partner with you in learning how to express the depth of the Christian way of life in ways non-churchy people can appreciate. I would love to hear how you would have said it differently, more eloquently, or with greater clarity.

Finally, I want to make it clear that in ten years I will probably not like some of what I wrote here. You may not like, for many good reasons, what I wrote here. But let's make a deal. Let's read and write so as to reflect on what it means to be human, and not try to corner the market on truth. Okay? *Deal!*

Chapter One

Faith Communities: What and Why

"You seem kinda normal to me," Joan remarked. "Why do you do this church thing?"

I took this as a compliment.

We were at a wedding reception. I was the pastor and she was the maid of honor. She told me that the worship service was nice, "not too churchy." We sat down to eat.

"I take it you don't belong to a church," I said.

"Oh, no! Why would I? I guess I believe in Joan's religion: Love myself and love other people. It isn't as if I don't believe in God. But, Terry, you seem like a normal guy. Why do you bother with Christianity?"

It seemed as though she was saying I was wasting my "kinda normalness" on Christianity.

I answered this way: "If you had to build a car in your lifetime, by yourself, getting your own raw materials, with no textbooks on engineering, could you do it?"

"No, there's too much I don't know," she said.

"Neither could I," I said. "I would have to experiment with mining, refining of metals, and molding all the various materials. I would have to learn how to engineer an engine, a drive train, and a body so that together they would stand up to use. As one person, I just don't think I have all that ability in me. Yet normal human beings do build cars. How do they do that?"

"I guess they learn from each other."

"Yes," I said. "They learn *directly* from each other—what I call an *engineering community*. But they also learn *indirectly* from people who are no longer alive through an *engineering tradition*. They combine what they learn from the engineering community and the engineering tradition and then add their own spark of creativity to build the cars of today. Faith communities and faith traditions work in the same way. In community we learn directly from each other, and through tradition we learn indirectly from people who lived long ago."

Joan toyed with the food on her plate, as if summoning an appetite for what I had just said.

"Since God loves us just as we are, why not just live life and not worry about it?" She took another bite.

It was my turn to rearrange the food on my plate.

"What you say is true," I finally said, "and that's what a great many people do. We know that if you build a car and it doesn't work right, then you simply build another car. The thing is, we don't get "do-overs" with our lives, so it makes sense to learn from others. When we cut ourselves off from other people, living or past, we cut ourselves off from much of the depth of our own lives. Imagine an engineer putting square wheels on a car when her textbooks—a part of her engineering tradition—and her design team—a part of her engineering community—tell her square wheels won't work."

"Living the human life isn't as cut and dried as designing a wheel."

"All the more reason to learn from others. My faith tradition lets me learn from thousands of human beings who have left behind what they learned over a lifetime. Listening to the tradition allows me to be challenged in ways I would not challenge myself and comforts me in ways I could not comfort myself. The tradition doesn't define what being human is, but it gives me tools with which to explore being human. And if I come up with a new set of tools along the way or learn something from a different custom, then that will be added to the tradition if others find it useful. That is what religion is at its best—understanding what it means to be a human being and how to live as one."

"And be challenged, huh?"

Joan seemed to want to think that over for a bit, and we finished our meal in silence.

After dessert I asked, "So, after talking about this stuff, do I still seem normal?"

She chuckled. "Well, kinda."

Later, as the reception drew to a close, Joan told me she had a new appreciation for faith traditions and would think about exploring Judaism, her own tradition, more deeply. We parted on warm terms.

Understanding Faith Communities and Faith Traditions

It is important to be clear at this point about what I mean by the terms "faith community" and "faith tradition." A faith community is comprised of people gathered around a tradition that helps them to understand what it means to be human. Faith communities usually have a local expression, i.e., churches or congregations. Faith communities also have a national or even worldwide expression, i.e., denominations or associations. For the purposes of this book I will use the term to refer to the national or worldwide faith community unless I indicate otherwise.

A faith tradition consists of the core teachings, practices, and history of the community that are passed down from one generation to another and that form the character of that faith community. Faith traditions have both particular and worldwide expressions. For instance, I am a Lutheran Christian and, while I have come to my present understanding of Christianity while being in Lutheran churches, I also consider myself to be a part of the entire Christian community and have learned much from others. As you read, you will notice that this book contains quotes from many different faith traditions. A part of the Lutheran tradition teaches us to understand ourselves as one faithful expression of the Christian faith as we love, live, and learn with others.

Now you may ask: Which comes first, a faith tradition or a faith community? The answer is they usually emerge together. It's the chicken *and* the egg. Communities of people always have some basic understanding of who they are as a group and how they see the world. As faith communities face new situations, they test how well their way of seeing the world actually fits the world they experience. While faith communities may not use scientific equipment to test their tradition, over time they do test it to see if it helps them understand their world and themselves.

Faith traditions are not static things written in stone for all time. Faith traditions hold basic views of the world that are adapted and sometimes changed to address the life-situation of the community while remaining in tension with the basic character of earlier teachings. (I will talk about this basic character or core teaching in chapter seven.)

Imagine a group of backpackers who want to hike north to a particular mountain. Rivers, hills, trees, and other mountains lie between them and this mountain. To get to the mountain they must do two things: adjust to the local terrain, and keep moving toward their goal.

A faith community must distinguish between its core understandings (the mountain) and its changeable practices (responses to local terrain). Sometimes, of course, people have a hard time telling the difference—often a source of conflict in faith communities. This is where the history of the faith community is important. We can remember earlier times when the faith community was trying to faithfully respond to the local terrain. Previous generations in the faith community have had their challenges, and we can learn not only from what they have ultimately come up with but from their struggle. We learn that it is okay to struggle to understand what it means to be human.

In the 4th century, the pastors of the major congregations got together because they faced a difficult challenge: How could they express the essence of the Christian faith, which had emerged from the Jewish culture, in the very different world of Roman culture? After working four years to write the Nicene Creed, the pastors were tired and wanted to go home. They agreed on a version of the creed, but for many it raised as many questions as it answered. It wasn't until 60 years later, in Constantinople, that many of these questions reached a level of resolution.

The history of the creed teaches us two important lessons: Christians have the freedom to try to express what it means to be human in our own time, and we should never be too satisfied with how we express it.

Finding Meaning in Our Lives

Faith communities and faith traditions emerge together and continue over time because human beings desire to understand what it means to be human. Many philosophers and theologians, people who think about God, have said that wondering what it means to be a human being is what makes us human.

"Where was I when you were married?" my six-year-old daughter, Lauren, asked as we were looking at wedding pictures.

"You weren't born yet," I said—knowing that, while true, this answer hardly does justice to the mystery.

We talked about the people at the wedding, some of whom had died before Lauren and her sister, Shelby, could meet them.

Lauren asked the inevitable question. "Daddy, why do we die?"

"I'm not sure, Sweetie," I said."But I know that life is a gift."

Our mortality raises important questions. People who learn they have only a few months to live often find that they live more intensely and more consciously than they had before. Impending death helps them to focus on and seek out life's most meaningful and enjoyable experiences.

However inspired we may be by people who find meaningful life in the face of impending death, most of us don't choose to grapple with the question of what brings meaning to our lives until we have to. We often choose to avoid the inevitability of our mortality—and thus the importance of depth in our lives— by choosing instead to skim life's surface in devoted adherence to the first commandment of our culture, succinctly stated in this advertising slogan for Sprite™: Obey your thirst.™

How thirsty we must be!

Obeying this cultural commandment, which implies that what is most important is the amount we have and consume, we Americans spend ten percent of our time (the equivalent of 5.2 weeks per year, day and night) assessing and purchasing new merchandise: on the hunt for the new house, the latest techno device, or the perfect motor vehicle that suits our needs and strokes our public identity. Like people happy and exhausted after some prehistoric hunt, we come home with the meat (stuff) today, and tomorrow when we are hungry again, we break out the club (credit card) and go hunting (shopping) for more.

But if consuming more and better stuff really can bring us peace, why are so many of us—after so much consumption—still in so much pain?

In the Midst of Two Famines

Two famines are at work in our world. One is the *famine of basic needs* we see in those late-night TV hunger appeals that ironically appear right after the super-sized fast food commercial. Although famine is experienced in America, this lack of food, clothing, and shelter is mostly suffered in other countries.

The other famine hits us right at home. In fact, it hits us in our very soul. I am talking about *a famine of meaning and community* that steals the deep pleasure of life away from us.

The great malady of the twentieth century, implicated in all of our troubles affecting us individually and socially, is "loss of soul." When soul is neglected, it doesn't just go away; it appears symptomatically in obsessions, addictions, violence, and loss of meaning. Our temptation is to isolate these symptoms or to try to eradicate them one by one; but the root problem is that we have lost our wisdom about the soul, even our interest in it. [1] *(Thomas Moore)*

Instead of paying attention to the depth of human life, we seek to find meaning and satisfaction in stuff.[2] Yet even with all the stuff in our homes, garages, and rented storage spaces, we are hurting. We are lonely.

I have walked at night and gone into your homes and found people dying unloved. Here in the West you have a different kind of poverty—a poverty of the spirit, of loneliness, of being unwanted. And that is the worst disease in the world today.[3] *(Mother Theresa)*

Twenty-six hundred years ago in the land of Israel, a truth teller named Amos found a similar situation brewing. He said that if people continued to live the way they were living, they would suffer the consequences of their way of life.

The time is surely coming, says the Lord GOD, when I will send a famine on the land; not a famine of bread, or a thirst for water, but of hearing the words of the LORD. They shall wander from sea to sea, and from north to east; they shall run to and fro, seeking the word of the LORD, but they shall not find it. *(Amos 8:11-12)*

We are experiencing a famine such as this. It is as if the nourishment we need is not available—a sense of truth and love and relationship is missing. Even those who work to restore "family values" are hard pressed when it comes to the "value of family." Inside, we are suffering. Like the children of some Third World country we see on late-night TV, we are hungry with no food and little hope of food. No triple cheeseburger, even with deluxe fries and a cola, can fill this hunger.

Addressing Famine with Faith

I believe that God calls faith communities and faith traditions to address both of these famines.

In faith communities, people can develop deep and lasting relationships with each other. In studying, praying, serving, and worshiping together, the famine of community is eased. We realize that we have traveling companions who respect our differences and our commonalities as we seek to learn the truth about ourselves and our world and attempt to realize the meaning and depth of the life we have been given.

Faith traditions also ease the famine for meaning and community by reminding us that we are part of a faith community that has endured through time. People who lived long ago have walked the journey of life and have left us some of their best writing and practices to assist us as we find our way.

Faith communities and their traditions help us to face our mortality. Genuine faith communities gather to face the limited nature of life, helping to attune the community to the precious and often delicate nature of life. Together, we explore the depth of the human experience and remind one another that our lives are valuable and meaningful and that we are called to serve others.

My faith community continues to teach me to trust God in a life that is a holy and precious gift—a gift that I am called upon to share with others. I see this gift in action as my faith community explores the life Jesus lived 2000 years ago. In this exploration, I begin to find out who I am and why I'm here. With others, I begin to sense God, in whose presence I live and move and have my being. And so, for me, my faith community provides a place for both meaning and community.

There are times when I don't want either meaning or community. There are times when being a part of a faith community is hard work, and I don't feel like doing it. Sometimes my faith tradition confuses me; sometimes it even makes me angry. Yet even my anger (or confusion) helps me to learn, as my anger reveals as much about me as it does the objects of my anger. My faith community, along with the tradition we are learning and living, gives ample food for the journey of life—maybe not a sugar high, but food that sticks to my bones.

This solid and nutritious spiritual food helps us to address the famine of basic needs as well. Faith communities have gathered to start hospitals, social service organizations, and world hunger programs that specifically address the needs of human beings around the world. Given opportunities to serve and develop relationships with those experiencing the famine of basic needs, we learn that despite those experiential differences we may have, what we share is far more powerful: a common humanity living in one world.

Faith communities address the twin famines in many different ways. We use rituals—that is, repeated words and actions—in worship to help our deepest selves understand the value and meaning of our lives. We gather to study the Scriptures, to ask questions and to seek answers. We gather to serve others in need. We support each other in times of crisis.

The Value of Community

John died of a brain hemorrhage while working at the City's wastewater treatment plant. The mayor of our small town called me because he knew John was a member of our congregation. He told me what had happened and asked where to find Ruth, John's wife. I told him that she had gone on a trip and had left only minutes before.

Knowing where she hid her key, I let myself into her house to find more information about her itinerary. I located a member of the church who knew which shuttle service Ruth was taking to the airport. We drove to a neighboring town, intercepted the shuttle, and brought Ruth back home.

By the time we returned, the food had already started to come in. Another member of the church was shopping for things Ruth would need in the coming days. We all prayed and consoled one another. We also gave each other time and space to be alone.

As a local faith community, we had talked about death many times. Other deaths had occurred in our congregation. We had planned other funerals. We knew the territory. Grateful that we could rely on tradition to get us through many aspects of the process, we were equally grateful to one another for contributing time and care, and for sharing both in sorrow and in comfort. Several times during the ensuing painful weeks, Ruth said, "I don't know what I would do without my faith and without all of you."

People gave money in John's name to the church. A year later, Ruth arranged for the donations to help a school in Africa install a septic system. In life, John had served other people; how fitting that he should serve others in his death too. Imagine a "dead" wastewater treatment plant worker helping to create a living septic system—how John would have laughed at that!

By living out our relationships with each other in service to the world, faith communities in both their local and larger expressions address the famine of basic needs and the famine of meaning and community. God is present and active in our lives. This is something that people in my faith community celebrate and try to describe and live out in daily life.

While faith communities can be great, faith communities can also have their problems.

Chapter Two

Faith Communities Aren't Perfect

You might ask, "If there are so many faith communities around, how come the famines exist in the first place?" I would respond by saying that many faith communities don't major in the meaning and depth of life, and so they neglect the twin famines of our time.

Churches can become social clubs designed to please the people in them, or churches can become museums that represent the thought and customs of centuries-old religion. Both can neglect the issues of the day. Sometimes churches try so hard to fit into the culture around them that they become nothing more than mouthpieces for the culture, losing the capacity to speak to the ways in which culture, as it is, destroys people. Sometimes people with powerful personalities lead worshipers to worship the leader more than worship God. Some churches are simply too boring for us to put up with; others, while understandably desiring to attract and serve our 21st-century population, ride the pendulum into modernity so far that it becomes awkward to make that swing back to the depth of their teaching.

But there is something more: Local faith communities can be hurtful to people. Theology (i.e., the study of thought about God) can be used to bind and gag people with shame and guilt.

People in churches, like those in any human organization, can get into power struggles and crush people who are just trying to figure out how to live. Leaders sometimes misuse their positions of power and trust in exploitation of others to satisfy their own ego, sexual, or economic needs.

I do not believe that all faith communities are great. All of them have their faults, and some of them can be downright destructive. Yet the capacity of faith communities to hurt people is also a sign of their potential to lift the human spirit to greater things. In both their local and worldwide expressions, faith communities are very powerful, and that power can be used for good or ill.

The Problem of Desiring People-Perfect Churches

People often set themselves up for disappointment when they naïvely expect people in churches to be perfect. When they see disappointing, albeit normal, human tendencies exhibited in churches, they become disenchanted. They had not expected such behavior from "good church people."

Christians and their communities have hurt thousands of people. Yet ignorance, misunderstanding, conflict, and hurtful conversations are expected parts of human interaction here on planet Earth. When one person at our work place is rude to us, we don't stop going to work. While we may not like conflict, we accept it as a normal part of life.

Many people, upon experiencing ignorance, misunderstanding, conflict, and hurtful conversations in a church, never want to be a part of a church again. "Those church people are all hypocrites," they say. Behind this is the assumption that to be in a church is to claim to be morally or relationally better than people not in a church. While some traditions may teach this, the Lutheran faith tradition does not.

Perfection-seeking people are those who demand perfection

of themselves and deny their own humanity. They hope that by hanging around supposedly "perfect church people" long enough they will become perfect, too. *Thus, their church-going is actually a powerful self-judgment.* As this perfection fails to materialize and they see flaws in the people in the church, they often blame the church or the pastor for not producing their desired results, and *their self-judgment turns into judgment of others.* Then, the search for the "right church" begins again.

My faith tradition teaches us that we can have both love for ourselves and others and realistic expectations at the same time. We teach that all of us are capable of hurting each other all the time. Even our best qualities can, without our intent or knowing, become a source of pain for other people. My faith tradition also teaches that we are simultaneously "saints and sinners"—not either/or, but both. This means that *we are beloved children of God in both our "saintly" moments and in our times of discord.* Consciously accepting that we are capable of both good and bad, we are not surprised when there is conflict or hurt in a church— which, after all, is made up of people.

This teaching reminds us to be on the lookout for the ways our behavior in the faith community is doing damage, additionally reminding us that we can expect to be hurt sometimes, too. The absence of hurtful things is not what marks a genuine faith community; it is marked by what we do after hurtful things happen.

> My friends, if anyone is detected in a transgression, you who have received the Spirit should restore such a one in a spirit of gentleness. Take care that you yourselves are not tempted. Bear one another's burdens, and in this way you will fulfill the law of Christ. *(Galatians 6:1-2)*

To be a part of a faith community is to accept that none of us gets it right. In learning to accept the failings and foibles of

our brothers and sisters in the community, we can begin to accept
our own.

> And forgive us our sins, as we forgive those who sin
> against us. *(Lord's Prayer)*

Junk-Food "Christianity"

Televangelists (I beg your pardon in using this blanket label;
certainly, there are televangelists who are exceptions to what I
write here) may make Christianity look appealing to a few, but to
most people they look ridiculous. Some preach that the Bible
gives you the right tools to become socially successful, financially
rich, and therefore happy—their lives are living proof. Others
preach fear: The world is ending soon, so please send in your
check now to ensure your salvation. Others tell you that if you
don't believe exactly what and as they do, you are not acceptable
to God.

Even more disturbing are fringe groups, such as the Ku Klux
Klan and Aryan Nations, who claim to be Christian but preach
and act out of hatred and fear of others. These groups, as well as
their counterparts in other faiths, usually use their religion to
express their fears and to exercise control over fearful followers
who don't want to deal with the ambiguities of life.

Genuine religion, from the perspective of my faith community:

- Is not a method for getting into heaven
- Is not a way to possess certainty or gain control of
  the world or God
- Is not a way of knowing the secret knowledge
- Is not a way to escape the tensions of life
- Is not a way to be right and tell others they are wrong

Yet these are precisely the things militant extremists and
most televangelists would have us believe religion is supposed to

do. The Apostle Paul warned the first-century community of faith at Ephesus that people often use religion to get these things:

> You can be sure that using people or religion or things just for what you get out of them—the usual variations on idolatry—will get you nowhere, and certainly nowhere near the kingdom of Christ. Don't let yourself be taken in by religious smooth-talk. God gets furious with people who are full of religious sales talk but want nothing to do with him.[4] *(Ephesians 5)*

To use religion to gain a ticket to heaven, certainty, secret knowledge, or to be right is nothing less than idolatry—putting something in the place of God. Humans love to have an idol, such as a statue, because we determine where it sits, what it looks like, and how big it is. We can use our ideas about God—even those we can back up with quotes from the Bible—as idols too. Humans have a tendency to make idols because we like control: what better way to control the world than to control God?

Each of these uses of religion is a way for us to gain more control of our lives and pretend that we are not limited and mortal. This approach to religion may seem great to many who are hungry from the famine of meaning and community, but in reality this approach is a kind of spiritual junk food. It tastes great for a while, but soon after we eat it, we realize we don't feel so good.

Why? Trying to gain control of everything, we lose our capacity for wonder—every surprise is seen as a threat to our control. Trying to maintain control, we see each new person, idea, or experience as something we need to dominate instead of as something to be learned from and savored. Trying to deny that we are limited and mortal, we become very serious and lose the playfulness that makes life worth living. All of us are "living life, facing death." Doing so consciously enables us to embrace the important things, let the small stuff go, and laugh once in a while.

Spiritual Abuse

A couple came to my congregation one Sunday. I noticed that they were not too comfortable with me. They kept their distance, and so I did not force contact with them. I wondered if I had said something in my sermon that bothered them. I found out later, after many weeks of careful communication, that they were just a bit nervous around pastors. They had good reason to be.

Suffering the loss of a stillborn child, they had gone to their previous pastor for comfort. Instead of comforting them, he told them that God was punishing them for not doing God's will in some part of their lives.

The implications of his theology were that the miscarriage was their fault and that God was justified in taking their child away. This increased the reactive guilt that couples experience with a stillbirth. It complicated their relationship as each wondered which one of them had "sinned." The pastor's theology eroded their trust in themselves, in each other, and in God.

Ironically, shortly thereafter the former pastor's wife had a miscarriage. The pastor applied the theology with which he had wounded this couple to himself. He decided that he was being too permissive in letting certain people, "the sinners," be in his church. At least he was consistent! By the next Sunday he had changed the locks on the church doors and equipped ushers with clipboards, telling them to turn the "bad people" away from worship. It wasn't until a few years later that he began to question his authority to determine who the "bad people" were.

The couple told me this story as we were seated around their dinner table.

"It's a miracle that you ever went to a church again," I said.

They looked at each other, and then she replied, "After we thought about it for a while, we realized that God was not responsible for what this pastor had said. We just hoped not everyone believed like him."

After many hours of conversation, the couple came to understand that I was not going to blame either them or God for the stillbirth. It took time, coupled with the warm welcome of a faith community, for them to see that God had not punished them. Rather, God loved them and grieved with them.

The wounds we receive in churches can be healed. The hurt experienced by this couple in one church could only be completely healed by becoming a part of another one. They otherwise would have given their painful experience power of control over them, keeping them from being a part of a local faith community when they wanted to be. It is important to face our painful experiences so that they do not control us.

Misuse of Power and Trust

Recently, examples of religious leaders using their position of trust within local faith communities to sexually exploit others have made the headlines. Local churches and denominations don't always handle these things well.

We know that clergy are not the only ones to misuse their positions of trust. It is estimated that ten percent of all doctors, lawyers, teachers, therapists, and others in positions of authority cross a sexual boundary with a client at some point in their careers. Most of these professions, and the institutions that support them, create ways to limit such occurrences and respond to help the victims after an abuse.

I have served at two congregations that previously had suffered sexual misconduct. Although my denomination has clear guidelines for how to handle clergy sexual misconduct, deciding how to respond for the benefit of all was very difficult. We had to consider the congregation, the victims who had come forward, and the legal issues of libel.

I used to wonder, "Why did I have two congregations that experienced this?"

A co-worker helped me to understand. Not until the late 1980s did we begin to understand the difference between an *affair* (which can be plenty devastating to relationships) and the *abuse of trust* that is clergy sexual misconduct (which can be especially devastating to a person's relationship with God). As this distinction became well known, many people came to understand that they had not had "an affair with the pastor." Rather, the pastor had abused the power of his or her position.

That we are hearing of so many cases of sexual misconduct is actually much better than having them remain covered up. The fact that we now understand and have language to describe such abuse reveals important growth in the church and in our culture. Hopefully, this growth will lead to better ways to prevent abuse and will aid in the healing of both the victims and the victimizers.

Many churches and denominations have a lot to learn about how to prevent and respond to such situations. To be fair, however, many churches and denominations do handle abuse allegations well—we just don't hear about it on the six o'clock news. Good news doesn't often make headlines.

When Personal Salvation Is the Goal

Sometimes churches have far too small a vision of what life is about. Sometimes people are "converted" only to store themselves on pews one hour per week.

> There is a tradition within at least two of the major religions in this country, American Protestantism and Roman Catholicism, of emphasis upon salvation of

the individual. Once that happens, then what? Often
very little. Frequently churches are not set up with
the vision to provide anything more. We need to recognize that therapy, recovery, or conversion isn't
enough. As a man gets personally stronger, he must
find things that relate him back to the world. He
needs to take responsibility for making changes in the
world, and not only in himself. Because once you consider the state our society is in, you must recognize
that we have no choice.[5] *(Moore and Gillette)*

Moore and Gillette, in a book written to men, are expressing
the world's need for positive male energy, and how faith communities often do not call forth this gift from men. Faith communities and the traditions with which they interact are meant to help
people engage in the meaning and purpose of their lives in the
real world of beauty, pain, evil, and compassion. Our culture generally makes this kind of engagement difficult. The default setting
in our culture, as Moore and Gillette point out, is the singular focus
of faith communities on the individual's salvation. Interestingly
enough, this is just as true of many New Age religions as it is of
many forms of Christianity—hence the continuous workshops
about how to gain "inner peace." But this personal salvation or
inner peace without a deep connection to and practical work
(engagement) on behalf of the rest of the world is just another
form of "me-first" consumerism.

One could argue that this "spiritual consumerism," Christian or
otherwise, is more damaging than regular consumerism, because
it inoculates us from the language and symbols of faith traditions
that might address the famine of meaning and community.
Thus, after the failure of so many workshops on enlightenment
or our third altar call to bring us peace, we say, "I tried it and it
didn't work for me." Well, of course it didn't "work for *you*,"
because the point of the Christian faith tradition is not only to

bring healing to you, but also to call you to work for the healing of world (more later).

An old farmer I worked for used to say about people who talk big but don't get much done, "That boy has a big motor, but he ain't got no transmission." Unfortunately, churches don't always remind people that they have a transmission.

Courage to Take Another Shot

Faith communities are not perfect. Faith traditions do not get it right all the time. But then, neither do you and I. If we wait for the perfect faith community to come down out of heaven before we can join it, we really are making a decision that we can't participate in the meaning and depth of life until we become perfect.

I was a pretty good high-school basketball player. One day I missed a last-second shot, and we lost the game. Afterward, my coach took me aside. I told him how bad I felt and that I didn't want to take the last-second shot ever again.

"Terry," he said, "to take the last shot in a game, you have to accept the fact that you might miss. But that is the price of playing the game—everybody misses the shot sometimes. It isn't whether you make or miss the shot that I am most interested in. What matters is having the courage to take the best shot you can and accepting what happens."

To be human, to do theology, or to be a part of the church is to accept not only our own mistakes but also the mistakes of others. When churches and their participants are conscious of their potential for both good and ill, we have the chance to lessen the damage and increase the good. This is why my faith tradition so strongly emphasizes that we are "saints and sinners." Joining a church is not all that different from any other human relationship—the joy of the relationship includes and in part flows out of our mutual vulnerability to the other.

Not every church serves junk food of control, ill-treats people with hurtful theology, has abusive pastors, or has too small a vision for what life is about. Many try to address the twin famines afflicting humanity. Many are able to accept their capacity to heal and to hurt, accept criticism from others, and look at themselves honestly and with humor.

Of course, a lot of this capacity for self-reflection and perspective depends on how "truth" is understood.

Chapter Three

Our Search for Truth

Seeking the depth held within our experiences requires that we question the events in our lives. As we question, we need to be clear about what kinds of answers we expect or are prepared to find. Are we seeking answers that will reveal the truth, or truths, for all time? Is there such a thing as ultimate, forever truth?

Three Views of Truth

Depending on our view of truth, we deal with it in different ways. I find that most people in our time understand truth to be one of (or a mixture of) the following:

- Truth as a puzzle
- Truth as a waste of time
- Truth as a glorious mystery

Truth As a Puzzle

Some people see truth as a puzzle, believing that if you get the right pieces, you can put them all together and have a perfectly clear picture of the truth. While it is true that humankind accepts certain ideas as true, serious theologians and scientists throughout history have known that truth is bigger than the sum of its parts. Knowing this, they usually present their ideas as "theories."

Nevertheless, some Christians view truth as a puzzle that can be solved, saying that the Bible provides the "pieces" that together comprise the picture of perfect understanding. For them, reading the Bible is a search for certainty. Putting the Biblical pieces together in countless ways and at countless times, these people believe that the picture they arrive at is the revelation of truth and—make no mistake!—the only correct one.

The problem is that who we are and what we know deeply affects how we interpret the Bible (or any other kind of experience) and how we put the pieces together.

> We do not see things as they are; we see things as we are. *(ancient Jewish saying)*

When a Christian claims to read the Bible "literally," he or she is usually reflecting a tendency to see truth as a puzzle. My faith community sees this approach as very dangerous, because what is really being claimed is an ability to have perfect understanding. This claim usually indicates a quest for power and control—*our* power and *our* control, not God's.

The writers of the Hebrew Bible (often referred to as the Old Testament) seemed to believe that anyone seeing God's face would die because we are limited and God is not. To be exposed to God directly would be like filling a water balloon (us) with a fire hydrant (God). This is why they portrayed God as speaking through an "angel," meaning "messenger," human or otherwise.

The Hebrew people held God in awe. To respect God, they did not speak their name for God, "Yahweh," aloud. They did not want to become so familiar with God's name that they took it for granted.

> Familiarity breeds contempt. *(Publius Syrus, 42 B.C.E.)*

The Hebrew people understood that something even more was involved in speaking God's name: to name and speak the name of a thing, they thought, was to exercise control over it. By not saying the name they used to mean "God," they were consciously acknowledging that they did not have control over God.

Even more central to the Hebrew understanding of God, was the prohibition against idolatry, i.e., making a picture or a statue to represent God. (Exodus 20:4) From the perspective of my faith tradition, some Christians run the risk of idolatry, not with statues or paintings, but with their images and concepts of God, even if these images and concepts are Biblical ones. Idolatry can refer to any human claim to define or control God.

How far is the literalists' claim from the Hebrew recognition that our words do not control God! This misunderstanding, however, is not the fault of the writers of the Bible. It is vital to remember that the Bible was written and edited over the course of more than one thousand years, and that it was written by many people whose perspectives reflect cultures and times different from our own. To read the Bible with respect—that is, to respect the messages and intentions of its writers and editors—we must recognize that we are engaged in cross-cultural work. Unfortunately, many people in our 21st century take ideas expressed in first-century culture and understanding, bring them "literally" to our century, and think they know what is meant. This not only leads to strange interpretations of the Bible, it is disrespectful of the Bible, of those who wrote it, and of the communities of faith that selected these writings.[6]

Biblical literalists forget that the Bible is a collection of writings from people who did not always agree with each other on important issues yet remained within one faith community. The editors of the Hebrew Scriptures were wise enough to represent these diverse, yet related, schools of thought in the writings they accepted as a part of the core teachings of the faith. The editors of the Christian Scriptures followed this tradition by having four authors describe their views of the life and teachings of Jesus, additionally including many other writings. Keeping a variety of perspectives in the Bible was yet another way, and a time-honored one, to acknowledge the limitation of human language and understanding and to respect the mystery of God.

Other Christians believe that modern scholarship is capable of finding the "real words of Jesus." Once found, these would supposedly give us the definitive teachings by which to live. Yet after almost a century of study, scholars do not all agree about which words Jesus actually said. My faith community believes this approach can also be dangerous, as it is a search for an impossible certainty whose inherent failure often leads people to despair. While fundamentalist Christians (those who see truth as a puzzle) seek to gain control by using the Bible, real-words-of-Jesus Christians seek to gain control over the Bible so that it can no longer change them.

Tertullian, a frequently quoted theologian of the second century, experienced this same phenomenon in his day:

> Heretics either wrest plain and simple words to any sense they choose by their conjectures, or else they violently resolve by a literal interpretation words which are incapable of a simple solution.[7] *(Tertullian)*

Truth As a Waste of Time

Some people in our culture believe truth is simply one's opinion. They therefore see trying to arrive at shared truth, or truth as understood by a community, as a waste of time.

For these people, doubt is the *only* trustworthy partner in any search for truth. Having been disappointed by many people, ways of thinking, and institutions that have claimed to have the truth for all time, these people naturally guard themselves against being misled again. The problem with this is that doubt can only nudge us toward what not to believe; it cannot help us choose how best to live.

> Today, people not only have to choose what to
> believe, they have to choose if belief itself is possible.
> Belief in anything means the choice to make oneself
> the object of ridicule. To believe in the truth today is,
> therefore, a matter of courage.[8] *(Thomas Merton)*

Doubt has an important role in the search for truth, but by itself it is not enough. Thomas Merton, a leader of a Roman Catholic monastic order, worked with many young people as they wrestled with doubt and faith and how both played a role in informing decisions about what to do with their lives. Merton came to see in them, as well as in himself, that the meaningful life cannot be won by choosing *either* the safety of certitude *or* the refuge of doubt. Meaningful life embraces the "and" of risking belief even when in doubt.

Meaningful life also embraces risking relationship with people, both individuals and communities. A woman I know told me that every Sunday morning she goes out to "talk with her church" as she walks in the woods. I affirmed her desire for some quiet time, a regular connection to the natural world, and the peace it gave her. I, too, take walks in the woods and find myself changed by the experience. But I asked her an important question: "Do the trees talk back?" Communion with trees without conscious and regular communion with a faith community can be a form of self-protection. It is important to affirm our connection to the natural world, but it is also important to affirm and strengthen our connection to other humans. In a faith community we learn from one another's questions, struggles, and insights. Together, we try to understand what it means to be human. But more than any insight I might gain *from* people, it is my relationship *with* people I value. In those relationships I am affirmed in ways that trees can never affirm me. In those relationships I am challenged in ways that trees would never challenge me.

My faith community understands that God is bigger than our

doubts and is open to our questions. God welcomes our questions and doubts, because they show us the gap between our limited understanding expressed in words and the reality of God's presence in our lives. We explore God's presence together because we can learn much from and by being in relationship with each other.

Truth as a Glorious Mystery

My faith community tends to teach that shared truth is attainable, yet truth about anything, especially about God, is a glorious mystery. Human beings are not capable of *defining* the truth, but we can *describe* it. When we try to define the truth—in an attempt to gain certainty, perhaps—we are simply fooling ourselves. We can describe our experience of God to the best of our ability today, knowing that tomorrow we may well find our words of yesterday strangely lacking.

Imagine that your mother is sitting beside you and I ask you to define her. Could you do it? Would you even try? You could offer a physical description, recount her family history, talk about facets of her personality, and muse about her likes and dislikes. But if you talked for an entire day, would you even have begun to define her? Of course not. And if you tried, how would she feel? Probably ill-respected and remarkably little known.

Human beings are limited in what we can know simply because we are mortal and limited, as are our language, experience, and culture. Fortunately, this is not the end of the story. We can come to some common understandings of God despite our limitations. We would do well to remember, however, that God is "in the room." Just as we would be careful and, perhaps, a bit hesitant to even describe, let alone define, our mother if she were in the room, so we should be with God.

This hesitancy arises not because we are fearful, but because we are respectful. God is not some concept or philosophy that we are discussing—although we do use concepts and philosophy to help us. God is the creator of all that exists. Our wildest imaginings and our most sublime thoughts fall short when we try to describe God.

To see truth as a mystery is to recognize that we must be humble in speaking about anything. Like a child who can only partially describe, but can in no way define, his or her mother, we have neither the words nor the knowledge to define our Maker. Yet as we offer our descriptions, we sense that they are pointing far beyond themselves toward the reality of God.

To see truth as a mystery is also to recognize that doubt and faith are friends. When truth is seen as a puzzle or as a waste of time, doubt and faith are opposites, even enemies. My faith community believes that faith can only happen in the midst of some doubt.

Who trusts her balance more: a woman walking on dry, smooth cement or a woman walking on a tightrope 100 feet above the cement? Although the woman who walks the tightrope obviously trusts her balance more, she also has more reason to doubt. Faith in God, understood as trust in God, takes place in the same way. Just as the woman might misjudge her ability to trust balance, we might be wrong in our ideas about God. And like the woman whose doubt leads her to exercise caution while relying on balance, we have found that doubt is helpful in strengthening faith.

People drew pictures of dragons, monsters, and the edge of the world on ancient maps to symbolize what was outside their knowledge. But mystery does not lie only at the edge of our knowledge; it is inherent in all our knowing, at every level of our knowing. Although a map may serve as a guide to the world, it does not fully describe or define the world; and just as the world is always "beyond" the map, the truth is always "beyond" our words. Because we trust God, we can embrace this mystery instead of fighting it. The Apostle Paul recognized and celebrated this mystery in a letter to the Corinthians.

> When I came to you, brothers and sisters, I did not
> come proclaiming the mystery of God to you in lofty
> words or wisdom. For I decided to know nothing
> among you except Jesus Christ, and him crucified.
> *(1 Corinthians 2:1-2)*

Doubt has an important place in conversation about God. It plays the role of reminding us that our best words and concepts fall short of defining God. Yet even as our words and concepts fall short, they point to new questions and new ways of describing our wonder of God. Doubt expressed in questions can help us to see how our ideas about God fall short and help to us to delve more deeply into our understanding of God's relationship to us and our relationship to God.

Far from being enemies, doubt and faith are partners in our exploration of God's glorious mystery.

The Truth of God: Hidden and Revealed

Doubt and faith are partners as we try to understand the glorious mystery of God. Because God is not available to us in such a way that we can measure and question God directly, the Christian faith tradition understands God as both hidden and revealed.

Hidden God

Jewish and Christian faith traditions believe that God's inner nature is hidden from us. In Latin this is called *Deus Absconditus*, or "hidden God." God's inner nature is not hidden because God is playing hide-and-seek, but because we are limited in what we are able to know and understand.

The story of Moses at the burning bush is an example of the Hebrew writer's awareness of human limitation in understanding God. Moses sees the bush, talks to the angel in it, and asks to know God's name. The angel's voice comes from the bush and says, "I am who I am." In other words, God is saying, "You don't know everything about me, but I'm asking you to trust me." "I am who I am" is not a name that describes God's inner nature, but a name that describes the relationship between God and humans.

Rooted in these traditions, Paul[9] used the metaphor of mirrors to talk about the mystery of God. In Paul's day, mirrors were made out of polished metal and so were quite dim.

> For now we see in a mirror, dimly, but then we will
> see face to face. Now I know only in part; then I will
> know fully, even as I have been fully known.
> (1 Corinthians 13:12)

This theme of respecting the mystery of God continued through the early centuries of Christianity. Gregory of Nyssa, a highly influential Christian thinker, said, "Following the instructions of the Holy Scripture, we have been taught that the nature of God is beyond human speech."[10]

To see truth as a mystery allows us to realize that we cannot know God's nature because God is beyond our comprehension. This, then, is the screen on which we project everything we say about God.

Revealed God

We may see dimly, but we can see a little. Throughout history, God has acted in such a way that we can glimpse the character of God and the nature of God's intentions toward the world. In Latin, this is called *Deus Revalatus*, or "revealed God." "Revealed" is perhaps too strong a word. A better way might be to say that God has acted in such a way as to give us a reliable "sneak peak" at who God is.

Jewish people believe that the heart of God was (and remains) revealed in the act of freeing their ancestors from slavery in Egypt. While believing this, Christians further believe that the ultimate

revelation of God's relationship to the world is Jesus Christ. In
Jesus' love for, service to, and "hands-on" relationship with the
world, we see God revealed.

The Christian Scriptures are central for us because they
contain writings of people who shared experiences with Jesus.
The books included in the Christian Scriptures, or New
Testament, were chosen from among many writings because
they express something essential about Jesus, and therefore
about God, to their readers. We respect and use these
Scriptures because they continue to express God's revelation
in Jesus to us. Paul, in 1 Corinthians 13:12, wasn't trying to
introduce a set of ideas about God, but rather introduce Jesus
as one in whom we are able to see a mirror-like reflection of
how God relates to us and the world. Scriptures are important
because they "carry Christ" to us, valuable because of whom
they introduce.

Because of this, my faith community respects, studies, and
reads the Bible. We believe it is inspired by, but not written by,
God. We don't believe that its writers intended it to define our
knowledge of science or history; and while we are willing to use
modern scholarship to understand the Bible, we tend not to chop
whole parts out of it because of historical contradiction or scientific disproval. We read it as a collection of theological works that
express the reliable sneak peak God has given us. Though we do
not believe God wrote the Bible, we have a very high view of
what happens when we read it together: We are re-imagined by
God into a new humanity.

My faith community has learned a lot from Martin Luther, a
Roman Catholic monk and professor of Theology who lived in
Germany in the 16th century. Luther led a movement to reform
the Roman Catholic Church and its teachings[11] and was, according
to many historians, one of the most influential people in the
Western world. Part of his legacy is his insight into the role and
importance of Scripture:

> Here [in the Scriptures] you will find the swaddling clothes and the manger in which Christ lies, and to which the angel points the shepherds. Simple and lowly are these swaddling clothes, but dear is the treasure, Christ, who lies in them. [12] *(Martin Luther)*

The Bible is a collection of writings by people who had powerful experiences of God and who shared them with their faith community. These writings are like the manger in which Jesus lay: although made with old boards, these writings bring to us the message of God's love that helps provide a new vision of our life and of our world.

We further believe that God communicates with us in two ways when we read the Bible together: as challenge and as comfort. God challenges us and helps us to change our self-destructive and world-destroying ways. God comforts us in our pain and sorrow. God comforts us and challenges us because God loves us.

Many people ask about some of the terrible things that happen in the Bible—the killings, sacrifices, and wars. Without denying the horror of some of these stories, we see in them a fundamental truth: God always begins with us based upon who we are now. God does not wait for us to be perfect (or even "not bad") before God interacts with us. God starts with us where we are because God is so committed to people that God is willing to continue relating with us when we do ugly, even horrible, things in God's name. Why? So that God can help us to change.

> And as he sat at dinner in the house, many tax collectors and sinners came and were sitting with him and his disciples. When the Pharisees saw this, they said to his disciples, "Why does your teacher eat with tax collectors and sinners?" But when he heard this, he said, "Those who are well have no need of a physician, but those who are sick." *(Matthew 9:10-13)*

Here, Jesus talks about God's interaction with the world as that of healer. God desires that we come to relate to God and all of God's creation. As a physician must begin with the patient's true condition, so God continually begins with humans and human culture where and as we are.

To initiate this, God carefully reveals who God is so that human beings can begin to understand in whose image we are made. My faith tradition uses words to express God's revelation in Jesus to future generations. We understand, however, that our words about this revelation, even the Biblical words, can only point to God; they cannot define God. God is the only ultimate.[13] No book, pastor, or church can claim to be ultimate. We therefore make a distinction between the *Living Word*, God's living presence in our lives, and the words we use to describe God.

We don't have to define God with words any more than we need to define our mothers, because we are in a living, changing, growing relationship with God. Instead, we tell the story of how our mother has loved us, struggled with us, and laughed with us. The Scriptures are just such a story about our relationship with each other and with God.

God is present and active in our lives. This is something that people in my faith community celebrate and try to describe. God is also a mystery, a glorious mystery that is bigger than our best words on our best day. Yet we dare to speak because we trust that God will accept our hesitant attempts to describe God, like a loving parent who joyously accepts the portrait colored by his or her child.

Chapter Four

Anything But Human

Christianity is a faith tradition learned, questioned, and taught by a faith community that seeks to understand what it means to be human. That we don't always like to be human is one of the key insights offered by the Christian tradition about the human condition.

Human beings were created to have healthy, loving, joyful relationships with:

- God
- Ourselves
- Other people
- The world and its creatures

We were created to enjoy these relationships:

- As part of the creation
- As limited beings
- With a special role of caring for the creation as a part of it

God made humans for relationships.

What We Mean When We Say "Sin"

When we use the word *sin*, we mean breaking the relationships
we were created to have. We believe that humans do this by trying
to be God or less than human. Seeking to be more or less than we
were created to be, we break the relationships that we were
meant to have.

I feel compelled to say that many people understand the
word "sin" to mean that people are bad, and so, interpreting the
word in this way, when they read it they feel bad. This is not
what I mean, nor is it what my faith tradition teaches. Yet this is
a word—and I hope you will understand as we go on—and a
description of human nature that is essential if we are to understand ourselves. To make this a descriptive word and not a shaming
word, try to understand sin as "broken relationship" as we continue,
and I will remind you of this meaning from time to time.

The second story of creation, found in Genesis, chapters 2
and 3, helps to describe this aspect of our humanity. Before we
begin to read parts of this story, I must tell you that when we are
speaking of the man and woman in the story, we are not talking
about two people who lived long ago whom we should blame for
all human problems. The man and the woman in this story represent
every human being, male and female. In other words, the writer
of this story describes what you and I do everyday.

Desiring to Be More Than We Are (Pride)

The man is made out of the mud (the same thing all the rest
of life is made from) to tend the garden. God asks the man to be
careful, though, for there is danger in the world. God tells the
man what he can do safely and what he cannot:

> And the LORD God commanded the man, "You
> may freely eat of every tree of the garden; but of the
> tree of the knowledge of good and evil you shall not

eat, for in the day that you eat of it you shall die."
(Genesis 2:16-17)

God asks the man to name all the animals: and while that
feels great, the man still misses the company of an equal. So God
creates another human being out of the man's flesh.[14] Now the
man is complete, having an equal to relate to. The two are naked,
a symbol for their vulnerability, and they are not ashamed.

Then a crafty animal[15] comes and asks some difficult questions. He asks whether God had really said that there was a
dangerous tree in the Garden. The woman answers that they
should not eat of the tree in the middle of the garden or they
will die.

> But the serpent said to the woman, "You will not
> die; for God knows that when you eat of it your
> eyes will be opened, and you will be like God, know-
> ing good and evil." So when the woman saw that the
> tree was good for food, and that it was a delight to the
> eyes, and that the tree was to be desired to make one
> wise, she took of its fruit and ate; and she also gave
> some to her husband, who was with her, and he ate.
> *(Genesis 3:4-6)*

Why did the two eat the fruit of the tree after they had been
warned that if they ate it they would die? In this story God is like
a parent telling a child not to touch the burner on the stove, yet
the child touches it anyway.

The woman and the man ate the fruit because they wanted
to "be like God." They were not satisfied with creaturely existence and limitation. They didn't like the fact that they couldn't
eat from one tree even though they had all the others from which
to eat. They wanted to be freed from the anxiety of not knowing
and not being in control of everything.

The man and the woman represent us. We are the ones who are not satisfied with our creaturely existence and limitation. Even though we would benefit from recognizing the limitations given by God, we refuse. And even though we can trust this God, we desire to control everything ourselves.

This is one-half of our understanding of sin: human beings want to be God and have everything revolve around us. In the language of theology, this form of sin is called "pride."

Desiring to Be Less Than We Are (Self-Negation)

The story continues with the man and the woman trying to cover up their nakedness[16] and then hiding from God.

> Then the eyes of both were opened, and they knew that they were naked; and they sewed fig leaves together and made loincloths for themselves. They heard the sound of the LORD God walking in the garden at the time of the evening breeze, and the man and his wife hid themselves from the presence of the LORD God among the trees of the garden. But the LORD God called to the man, and said to him, "Where are you?" He said, "I heard the sound of you in the garden, and I was afraid, because I was naked; and I hid myself." *(Genesis 3:7-10)*

The man and woman, in trying to be God, become anxious. Eating the fruit to become like God, they eat something that they knew will hurt them. By eating it, they are consciously choosing to not care for themselves. Furthermore, by eating the fruit not made for eating, they misuse the creation. They try to escape their God-given role as caretakers of the world and of themselves, becoming less than they were created to be.

In the language of theology, this form of sin is called "self-negation."[17]

At this point in the story, the man and the woman seem, for the most part, to have hurt only themselves. However, breaking one relationship usually leads to breaking others. The story continues as God finds them hiding in the bushes. Now the blame game begins.

> God said, "Who told you that you were naked? Have you eaten from the tree of which I commanded you not to eat?" The man said, "The woman whom you gave to be with me, she gave me fruit from the tree, and I ate." Then the LORD God said to the woman, "What is this that you have done?" The woman said, "The serpent tricked me, and I ate." *(Genesis 3:11-13)*

Here, the man and the woman each try to minimize their personal responsibility by blaming another for the self-destructive choices each has made. To refuse responsibility for our actions is to deny the fullness of what God made us to be. Refusing our responsibility also leads us to behave in ways that lead to the destruction of others and our created world. Because of this, a saddened God tells the human beings that the consequences for denying their God-given identity will be pain, suffering, and harm—both for human beings and for the creation they have misused.

Denying Who We Are Causes Pain

In trying to deny who we are made to be (i.e., trying to be God or be less than human), we break our God-given relationships by:

- Turning away from God by trying to take God's place (be "in control")
- Hurting ourselves by doing things we know will hurt us; then, not taking responsibility for our actions
- Hurting others by giving them things that will hurt them
- Blaming others for our actions

- Hurting the creation by misusing it, and then blaming somebody else
- Engaging in meaningless work and activities

No wonder we feel famished for meaning and community. We do what the man and the woman did: deny who we were created to be! The reason we feel anxiety, meaninglessness, and isolation is that we deny who we are.

Sin (understood as breaking a relationship that we were created to enjoy and nurture), like breaking a bone, causes us pain.

A modern example comes from a friend of mine:

> The image that comes to mind is the overworked soccer mom who lives at wit's end accommodating her children and her husband. She strives for an image of perfection: the ideal mother who can hold down a full-time successful career, look beautiful (by the culture's standards), keep a perfect house, have intelligent and well-behaved children, and have an idyllic intimate relationship with her husband. Under this image she suffers and complains, "If only [fill in the blank], life would be better." In her drive to do and be the impossible, she drives herself and her family to misery.[18]

This woman, like all of us, is engaging in both self-negation and pride at the same time. Pride is her belief that she can realize a perfectionist vision for herself and her family. Self-negation is her lack of acceptance of her own and her family's limitations and imperfections. This hard and unforgiving vision leads to despair when it cannot be fulfilled, followed by promises to try harder. Like a hamster on a wheel, she runs harder but stays in the same place. It is no wonder that, as we do similar things in our own lives, we so often seek to relieve the pain through addictions, consumerism, and overwork.

Morals, Ethics, and Sin

That we understand sin as breaking a relationship does not mean that we believe morals and ethics have no place. We all have to learn, from very early ages, what it means to care for ourselves and for other people. Morals and ethics, as Martin Luther taught us, serve three purposes:

- To help humans live together
- To convince us of our tendency to break relationships (sin)
- To teach Christians how to begin to love God, ourselves, others, and the creation[19]

God's Response to Sin Is Love and Truth in Love

Many fundamentalist Christians, believing that sin is the breaking of a rule set down by God, feel that our tradition doesn't take sin seriously. Beneath this is the belief that when you break one of these rules, God will punish you because God can't stand sin.

My faith tradition says that God's response to sin arises directly from God's love for the world, not from God's allergy to rule breaking. Because God loves me, I know that God also loves my neighbor. If I act in such a way that I hurt my neighbor, God's love for that neighbor demands that God take my neighbor's hurt seriously. But God's anger, arising out of God's love for my neighbor, does not negate the love that God has for me. God will seek to help me see how I hurt my neighbor—all the while staying in relationship with me! I may not like facing the truth that I have hurt my neighbor; I might even get defensive or angry. But my reaction to the truth does not deter God. God's love for me remains secure, even as God's love for others is secure.

Love Fulfills the Law

Fundamentalist Christians tend to think that God's primary response through Jesus to sin is to give to give the right rules to

live by. The problem is, Jesus didn't give many rules. When asked
what was necessary to obey God, he answered that what God
desires for us is love:

> When the Pharisees heard that he had silenced the
> Sadducees, they gathered together, and one of them,
> a lawyer, asked him a question to test him. "Teacher,
> which commandment in the law is the greatest?" He
> said to him, "'You shall love the Lord your God with
> all your heart, and with all your soul, and with all
> your mind.' This is the greatest and first commandment.
> And a second is like it: 'You shall love your neighbor
> as yourself.' On these two commandments hang all
> the law and the prophets." *(Matthew 22:34-40)*

In this interaction with a rule-oriented Pharisee, Jesus indicates
that love for God and love for our neighbor are the heart and core
of morals and ethics. Morals and ethics are the practical working
out of love. Morals, however, can sometimes serve to distract us
from the love they are meant facilitate by leading us to focus on
rule-keeping instead of neighbor-keeping.

We believe God's response to sin asks something far more
difficult and compelling than obedience to a list of rules. God
asks us to be about the business of love for the other citizens (and
creatures) of the world. Paul echoes this in his writing as well:

> Love does no wrong to a neighbor; therefore, love is
> the fulfilling of the law. *(Romans 13: 10)*

Jesus Calls Us to the Rigors of Love

Many non-Christians assume that fundamentalist Christianity
is "more Christian" than other forms of Christianity. They assume
fundamentalists are right about God's response to sin, and so
assume that fundamental Christianity is more rigorous or more

faithful than other forms of Christianity. At the same time, most people reject what they often perceive to be the legalistic and judgment-centered attitudes of fundamentalists. They therefore, often with some sadness, reject Christianity as a whole.

Fundamentalists are picking up a theme from the Hebrew Scriptures. But that is not the only theme. Nor is it the central theme. We believe that Jesus had many opportunities to affirm the rule-orientation of some parts of the tradition, but he chose instead to call people to rigorous and thoughtful love of God and neighbor.

My faith tradition has taught me that Jesus taught a love-orientation, not a rule-orientation. Moral and ethical conversations are not ends in themselves but are necessary to help us live out the relationships we were meant to have as we learn what it means to love, learn that we don't always love, and learn that we don't always love well.

God's Steadfast Love: The Gift That Heals

Sin reveals itself in all human relationships—in our personal lives, as members of faith communities, and as members of a country. We believe that no one is immune from sin as broken relationships.

> For there is no distinction, since all have sinned and fall short of the glory of God. *(Romans 3:23)*

At first this verse may sound strange. What does Paul mean by human beings falling short of the "glory of God?" If humans can't come close to describing God, how can we even be expected to take aim at God's glory? But the writers of the Christian Scriptures transform the image of God's glory, formerly understood as "power," to the glory of God as the self-giving love of Jesus' birth, life, death and resurrection. God's glory is now understood as relationship with us through self-giving love. With this as the definition of glory, Paul's statement that we fall short of this glory is not only true, but an understatement.

This verse in Romans does not mean that human beings are "bad." God's blessing[20] of human beings as part of a "very good" creation still holds true, even if we obscure this blessing by our desire to be more or less than we are, thus falling short of the glory of self-giving love. But this verse does mean that all humans share in sin together. Thus, our tradition teaches us that we all play a part in the famine of meaning and community whose consequences are devastating.

We are indeed in great pain! We can neither stand the strain of godhood nor endure being less than human.

In chapter two I wrote that the Christian faith tradition calls us to work for the world. Now I can explain a little more of what I meant. Humans are trapped in either trying to be God or less than human, both of which reveal a profound, blinding focus on the self. Somehow, someone must help us out of this blindfolded, straitjacketed condition. Someone must let us out of the squirrel cage. Someone must help us to see that to be fully human is be so grounded in God's love for us that we are able to give ourselves to the world. We experience peace when we become committed to the world's peace.

God does not abandon us to our situation. The creator of the universe joins us where we hurt the most to transform us, fill our true hunger, and heal us for new life.[21] How Christians understand this depends on the tradition of Christianity with which they most agree.

Chapter Five

Three Kinds of Christianity

Chances are, the Christianity of my faith community is not the Christianity you grew up with, see on television, or read about in newspapers and magazines (unless you grew up watching Davey and Goliath). My faith tradition has been "under the radar" of our popular culture. We represent another Christianity. But you might be surprised at the number of Christians from many denominations who would say that what I have written here is "not a bad beginning"—and, to be sure, this book is intended as only a beginning, an introduction to our theology and worldview.

For the purposes of this book, I will talk about three kinds of Christianity practiced in our country. Each understands God's relationship with the world, and therefore us, in a different way.[22]

I call these three forms of Christianity:

- Don't Worry, Be Happy
- God of the Gun
- God of Grace

I will describe the logic of each form of Christianity and compare it to what I have learned from my faith tradition.

Before I go on, I want to make it clear that no church, including my own, perfectly follows Jesus' teachings. I am not claiming to be right for all time. While attempting to express what my faith community has taught me to this point, I admit to having much more to learn. Every faith community falls short—in many ways—of the depth and breadth of Jesus' vision for us.

Don't Worry, Be Happy

One popular way to be a Christian in America is to Don't Worry, Be Happy. God is love and God loves everyone, so don't worry too much about what you do or think. Just be nice to people, go to church occasionally (or not), and everything will be fine. If there is injustice in the world, don't worry about it; God will fix it later. In the meantime sip a latté and just be happy! The logic of this way of doing Christianity is:

God loves everyone; therefore, don't worry, be happy.

Don't-Worry-Be-Happy Christianity reveals a God who seems to be rather disinterested in the everyday sufferings and joys of human beings in this life, a God who is mostly interested in what happens after we die. God will take all people to heaven and will make everything okay. God is like a nice, disinterested parent who lets you do what you want and is vaguely sorry when you suffer for your decisions. But this begs the question: Is a "love" this disinterested in the real hopes and hurts of people really love?

> Love doesn't just accept everything. If it's love, it cares about the real condition of the beloved; and if the beloved is in fact a distortion of the person that he or she could be, then the only role that true love can [take] is one of truth and the intention to change. "Jesus loves me" does not mean that Jesus likes me, accepts me, and makes no great demands upon me. Jesus loves me—therefore I had better be prepared

for some embarrassing moment of truth and some
hard work![23] *(Douglas John Hall)*

Don't-Worry-Be-Happy Christianity presents a God who
does not really love us—at least, not enough to bother calling us
to respect who we are. Here, permissiveness is substituted for
love. This is not the God revealed in Jesus when he called the tax
collector, an outcast from Jewish society, to be his disciple (Luke
5:27). This is not the God revealed in Jesus when he healed the
blind man (Luke 18:35) or saved a woman from being stoned to
death (John 8:3). Jesus was passionate about the well-being of
people in this life. God's love means calling people to change so
that they can be what they were created to be—even though that
change may be uncomfortable or difficult.

In Don't-Worry-Be-Happy Christianity, we seek to procure a
kind of eternal life insurance policy with a cheap monthly rate,
and we usually end up treating eternal life insurance the same
way we treat the earthly kind—pay the bill and forget about it.

This form of theology has these characteristics:

Understanding Sin	What sin? Humans are all nice—they just need more education. I'm fine the way I am. I am enlightened.
What Jesus Does	He is a nice guy who was misunderstood.
How This Theology Makes Us Feel	Warm and fuzzy—God is so nice! Neglected—God seems to have no capacity or need to understand and deal with our pain.
Our Motivation for Loving God	We are nice, and so, of course, we love God.

Don't-Worry-Be-Happy Christianity does not reflect the life and teachings of Jesus very well. It twists the teachings of Jesus and turns God into a permissive God who leaves us in pain-filled meaninglessness but promises a good dessert after this crummy life is over. Christianity is so much more than this!

God of the Gun

Another popular form of Christianity in America is God of the Gun. It is constantly publicized in the media and may be the most common form. It is certainly loudest! This understanding of God can best be explained by a story:

> You are walking on a downtown street when you hear footsteps behind you. You turn around to see a stranger pointing a gun at your head. The stranger demands, "Love me, do what I tell you, and you will live. If you don't, you will die!"

Could you love this person? You might choose to pretend to, but in your heart, you will be angry and hope to get away as quickly as possible.

Strangely enough, many Christians see God's relationship to us in the same way, only it's God who is holding the gun. Here is the logic of God-of-the-Gun Christianity:

> If you love God and do what God wants,
> then God will love you and take you to heaven;
> otherwise, you will be rejected, unhappy in life,
> and sent to hell.

The major problem with this kind of Christianity is this: It is not possible to love or trust a God who threatens us.

The God of the Gun creates a conditional relationship with

us. If we obey the rules and fulfill the conditions, then God accepts us. If we don't, we are sentenced to death. Conditional relationships always imply that one person must do something before the other will fulfill his or her part of the bargain. This understanding of Christianity says that human beings must change *before* God accepts us. Most people faced with this kind of situation simply try to escape.

Conditional relationships are not always bad. When you pay for milk at the grocery store, you participate in a conditional relationship. Conditional relationships are only destructive when the two people are in an unequal power relationship. The person with the gun has more power than you do, so you must "love" him, or at least act like you do, in order to stay alive.

Certainly, any relationship between humans and God is an unequal power relationship; therefore, if God's relationship to us is conditional, we can only respond out of fear. Trust and love are simply not possible in a conditional relationship of unequal power.

The way God-of-the-Gun Christianity understands sin implies that we must live by an ever-expanding list of rules. But when we are honest with ourselves, we see that no human being can live by these rules all the time. Although we can do well for a short while, we eventually begin to see that we have not lived up to the rules. This causes us to live with constant guilt and/or to minimize the rules and take the path of hypocrisy in order to cope with such stringent controls being placed on our lives.

God-of-the-Gun Christianity leads to an even bigger problem: When we believe that God does not love us as we are, that something is so horribly wrong with us that God cannot possibly love us now, we feel a great deal of shame.

Guilt and shame lead to the motivators that this theology creates: self-preservation and fear. If we have to change to be accepted by God, then we had better change, or we will end up in hell. We have to love God and follow the rules so that we can make God love us back. However, it is no more possible for us to love a God who threatens us than it is possible for us to love a person who puts a gun to our head. The only goal we have at gunpoint is to survive.

While this kind of Christianity may provide instant motivation (fear) for change, the change is short-lived and rarely brings joy and peace. Once the initial change wears off—say, after three or four weeks—people often feel like a failure. Furthermore, they wonder if God has failed them. This leaves many people in a worse condition than when they first knelt at the altar rail.

Worse is that this form of Christianity makes God inherently violent. God is angry at our rule-breaking, has no capacity for real forgiveness, and must punish someone. Instead of pointing the gun at us, God points it at Jesus and kills him. How nice of God to take out anger on God's son instead of on us! (Note the irony here.) Further, Jesus' death apparently didn't quite satisfy God. We are forced to wonder whether God has more bullets in the gun and what will happen if we don't obey God. We know that even though Jesus died for our sin, we have to "shape up" now or we will burn in hell.

This form of theology has these characteristics:

Understanding Sin	Sin is breaking a rule, and there are lots of rules to keep.
What Jesus Does	He took the punishment that God planned to give all humans for sin (breaking the rules), but we had better keep those rules from now on.
How This Theology Makes Us Feel	We feel a crippling guilt from breaking the rules that we are supposed to keep, and we feel the shame of not being loved.
Our Motivation for Loving God	Fear and self-preservation.

Since this is the primary image of Christianity in our country, no wonder so many people have looked elsewhere for spiritual teaching.

I am not saying that God does not love people who believe or even preach this view of Christianity. No doubt we have things to learn from them. I am simply saying that I have been taught, and try to practice, a different understanding of Christianity that also deserves a hearing.

Martin Luther lived in a time when this form of theology was the only option. He realized that if he was honest with himself, he could not obey the rules perfectly, or even very well. He realized, in a moment of deep despair, that if his relationship with God were left up to him, he was doomed. In that moment he began to understand God's love differently. This rediscovery is at the heart of what it means to be a Christian from a Lutheran perspective.

God of Grace

My faith community reflects a third way to be Christian: God of Grace. We find it to be deeper and more meaningful than the insurance policy of Don't-Worry-Be-Happy, and it helps us to see that God is not holding a gun to our heads. Once again, let's begin with a story:

> You are walking down the street, when you hear foot-
> steps behind you. You turn around. You see an estranged
> friend from years ago who greets you with a smile
> and says, "Hi. I'm wondering if we could talk. I know
> it didn't work out so well before. I would like to try
> again, if that's okay with you."

How would you respond to this situation? You might have feelings to work through, issues to clear between the two of you, and forgiveness to give and receive. That can be hard work. Nevertheless, you would probably be tempted to give it a try.

Your estranged friend obviously still cares for you—enough even
to risk rejection. While the request may bring up old painful feelings,
if you are like me, you would probably feel honored and valued.

There is a logical structure (albeit surprising and unconven-
tional) beneath this old friend's words:

> Because I love you, I desire a new relationship with you.

This is the logic of God-of-Grace Christianity. God not only
created us, God also deeply values us. God became a human in
Jesus and radically, unconditionally affirms all life. Through his
death on the cross, Jesus experienced what God's absence feels
like. This means that God meets us where we need God most—
in our pain and brokenness. While we are in great pain trying to be
God or less than human, God responds by being lovingly present
with us so as to renew God's relationship with us.

> Now God has us where he wants us, with all the time
> in this world and the next to shower grace and kind-
> ness upon us in Christ Jesus. Saving is all his idea, and
> all his work. All we do is trust him enough to let
> him do it. It is God's gift from start to finish! We
> don't play the major role. If we did, we'd probably go
> around bragging that we'd done the whole thing! No,
> we neither make nor save ourselves. God does both
> the making and the saving. He creates each of us by
> Christ Jesus to join him in the work he does, the good
> work he has gotten ready for us to do, work we had
> better be doing.[25] *(Ephesians 2)*

This form of theology has these characteristics:

Understanding Sin	Sin is breaking relationship by trying to be more or less than human.

What Jesus Does	He joins us in our pain and shows us God's unconditional love, giving us hope for renewed life.
How This Theology Makes Us Feel	Forgiven: God loves us and wants a new relationship with us. Accepted: God likes us. Challenged to change: God wants us to be the people we were created to be.
Our Motivation for Loving God	We are motivated by sheer gratitude, not only for life but also for the way God loves and likes us. We trust a life that is in God's hands.

The apostle Paul had lived under a rule-keeping system in his early years. Following Jesus, he began to live the "gift life": all in life is a gift, and we respond to that gift out of gratitude.

> Christ has set you free to live a free life. So, take your stand! Never again let anyone put a harness of slavery on you. I am emphatic about this. The moment any one of you submits to circumcision or any other rule-keeping system, at that same moment Christ's hard-won gift of freedom is squandered.[26]
> (Galatians 5)

Paul had lived a God-of-the-Gun religion and found it did not work. But he also found, both in himself and in the churches he founded, that human beings tend to resist simply trusting God's love. We want to earn it the old-fashioned way. In his letter to the Galatians, Paul warns them that they are "squandering" this gift of freedom by trying to change the logic of Christianity from the God of Grace to the God of the Gun, from unconditional love to conditional love.

> I suspect you would never intend this, but this is what happens. When you attempt to live by your own religious plans and projects, you are cut off from Christ, you fall out of grace. Meanwhile, we expectantly wait for a satisfying relationship with the Spirit. For in Christ, neither our most conscientious religion nor disregard for religion amounts to anything. What matters is something far more interior: Faith expressed in love.[27]
> (Galatians 5)

The mere fact that God-of-the-Gun Christianity has more TV stations and publishing companies is not what makes it the most common form of Christianity. Human nature does that. Human nature is to trust our own religious and moral accomplishments instead of trusting God's free gift of love that we call "grace." This is actually just another expression of sin. Trying to be God by being in control of our relationship with God is clearly trusting in ourselves rather than in God. Paul says that in trying to earn God's love, we teach ourselves that we cannot trust God to love us now. This is what he means when he says that we "fall out of grace." Essentially, our human tendency is to trade in grace for slavery to a bunch of rules. In Paul's words, to live in God-of-Grace Christianity, "all we do is trust God enough to let him do it."

For us, faith is trust in God's love as revealed in Jesus Christ. We trust that, even in our worst moments, God both loves and likes us and calls us to a new life. We trust that, even in our best moments, God both loves and likes us and still calls us to change. Wherever life finds us at the moment—in doubt, in fear, in courage, in grief, or in love—faith is simply the trust that God loves and likes us right now.

We trust this love because of what our faith community sees in Jesus Christ.

Chapter Six

What Jesus Does

I once asked a class of junior high students what they would do in the following story: Imagine you are God and you create a colony of intelligent ants so that they could enjoy you and each other. Instead, they chose to fight with each other over small plots of the colony, ignore you, and pretty much make a mess of the whole thing.

One of the students, with an evil grin on his face, said, "I would take a gallon of gasoline and blow them up. I made them, and they don't even appreciate it."

"The problem with that," I said, "is that the creator wouldn't have an ant colony any more. Doesn't the creator have a responsibility or better yet a desire to 'hang in there' with even an ungrateful creation?"

A second student told me that he would "stand over the ant colony and tell them, 'STRAIGHTEN UP, OR I WILL DESTROY YOU.'"

"That's an interesting idea," I replied, "but your goal in creating them was to have them love you. Now that you have threatened them, they are only going to fear and secretly hate you."

A third student said something quite different. "I would become an ant, so I could speak in ant language and try to tell them what they are missing."

"What would you do if they rejected you, even killed you?" I asked.

"I would be like Jesus and make myself alive again."

"Why?"

The first student answered, "So they could see you won't give up on them!"

The students' responses illustrate some of the differing views we hold regarding how God responds to our human tendency to be anything but human. Two theoretical views of God's response, both centuries-old, have become so commonplace that they are often considered facts. Formed within a specific time and a particular worldview, these theories were offered by authors who were attempting to answer questions and respond to the fears and anxieties of their day. The first of these theories I will call "Anselm's theory," and the second, the "Payment-to-the-Devil theory." These theories that have led to the following views:

- (Anselm's theory) When human beings sinned, God was going to punish us, but Jesus took the punishment we deserved from God, and so now we can get to heaven when we die.

- (Payment-to-the-Devil theory) When human beings sinned, we became the property of the devil, but Jesus was punished as ransom to buy us back, and so now we can get to heaven when we die.

Anselm's Theory – 11th Century

I must preface this section by saying that Anselm's theory has so dominated popular Christian thought that many people would not know how to talk about God's love and forgiveness in any other way. Many people, including Lutherans, will continue to use Anselm's theory to express God's love, and it is not my intention to belittle or undervalue any person who finds this understanding helpful. I affirm that God does offer forgiveness and love in Jesus Christ. Further, I seek to offer an increasingly popular view that holds Anselm's theory does not adequately express the God we see revealed in Jesus. I will suggest other views that can better express this God in our time.

Anselm's theory has its roots in early Christianity, but it became increasingly popular after Anselm of Canterbury in the 11th century. Like Internet Explorer in Microsoft Windows™, this view has become the default setting in our culture and is what most people think Christian belief is all about. The scenario goes like this:

- We owe the Creator obedience.
- We do not obey and so incur a debt of sin to God.
- We cannot make up for our debt of sin.
- God is "just" and requires payment for this debt.
- God sends Jesus who pays our sin debt.
- Now the sin bookkeeping department is happy.
- We can get in on this amnesty if we take Jesus as our personal Lord and Savior.

In Anselm's day, the Middle Ages, this made a lot of sense to people who were struggling with a common anxiety: How can we find forgiveness in a God that is angry at human sin? Anselm's theory gave them a way to understand that Jesus took care of their debt of sin, and the church gave them ways to experience this forgiveness. This theory worked for them. It helped them to understand one of the things the church had always said Jesus did: "offer forgiveness to human beings."

However well it worked to relieve the "sin problem" for the people of the Middle Ages, there are many problems with his theory, some of which did not go unnoticed even in Anselm's day. Most problematical are the inherent implications that run counter to Jesus' own teachings, which include:

- God cannot forgive.
- God is violent.
- The books don't balance.
- Jesus saved you, you bad person, you.
- Sacrifice changes God, not humans.
- It's just between "me and Jesus."

God Cannot Forgive

If you owe me $20 and I forgive you the debt but ask your brother or sister to pay it, have I really forgiven the debt? Of course not! Yet Anselm's theory would have us believe that this is how God understands forgiveness.

Both the Hebrew Scriptures and the teachings of Jesus, however, tell us something quite different:

> For I desire steadfast love and not sacrifice, the knowledge of God rather than burnt offerings.[28] *(Hosea 6:6)*

> "Go and learn what this means, 'I desire mercy, not sacrifice.' For I have come to call not the righteous but sinners." *(Matthew 9:10-13)*

It is not logically consistent for God to desire us to give mercy freely to each other *and* for God to demand payment in the form of a sacrifice *before* God gives mercy to us. If God demanded payment before our relationship with God could be renewed, then "merciful" would not be the right word to describe God; a better word might be "mercenary." Anselm's vision of Christianity paints a portrait of a God who is only willing to show mercy when God is paid for mercy.

God Is Violent

At first it might sound nice that Jesus took our punishment, but what kind of God would require the punishment? It would have to be a God who, at some level, really does need or like violence. If you sell a chair at a garage sale, you are hardly going to accept a bunch of shattered glass in payment; you will trade the chair for something you want, namely money. If God receives Jesus' suffering and pain as payment, then God wants or needs that suffering and pain the same way we need money. My faith community has taught me a different way.

> You are walking down the street near your home. You see a child run out into the street after a ball. Time slows down. You see a truck speeding down the street. The driver's attention is distracted as he tries to read the address numbers on the houses. The child will be hit unless you do something. You run out, grab the child, and throw her onto the grass. A second later you are hit. [29]

Did you pay for the girl's life? Did you pay for the truck driver's inattention? Yes, you did. But you didn't pay anyone. You paid the consequences of your love for both of them with damage to your body. It is in this sense that Jesus paid for our sin (broken relationship). In Jesus God pays the consequences of God's love for us.

The Books Don't Balance

Even if God must be "paid for our debt of sin," how can one man's punishment and death at the hands of Roman soldiers for one night and part of one day make up for all the sin, pain, and destruction in human history? Perhaps time slows down for Jesus and so that he suffers almost an eternity. Maybe he goes to hell for all people and takes our place there. People have suggested these and other ideas in an attempt to patch this hole in Anselm's theory. None of these ideas is based in Scripture, and the mere existence of these ideas reveals people's awareness of this major flaw in Anselm's theory.

Jesus Saved You, You Bad Person, You

Anselm's theory implies that while Jesus took the big hit for all of us and we all should be grateful, we must also be careful to remember that Jesus died a horrible death for which you and I are to blame. The not-so-subtle message is that we should feel guilty and forgiven at the same time—which, of course, is no forgiveness at all. This is like a husband who says he forgives his wife, but takes every opportunity to remind her of what she did wrong and what a good husband he is to have forgiven her. So God is no better than a passive-aggressive spouse?

Sacrifice Changes God

Anselm misunderstood sacrifice and this misunderstanding has been passed down to most people today. Sacrifice was a ritual used to express gratitude. It also was used to express remorse and a desire for reconciliation between people and people, and between people and God. Some religions in the Middle East thought sacrifice brought the gods to act in a certain way, but not the Jewish religion.[30] In the Jewish religion sacrifice was meant to change human beings, not God. In fact, many prophets and Jesus himself said that God did not want sacrifices, but rather God wanted people to be humble, merciful to others, and to enact peace and justice in their communities. When sacrifices were not helping people to reform their lives to live in love with each other, sacrifices were cast aside as useless, or they were cast aside as something worse: rituals misused by people to insulate themselves from the pain of their way of life.

As the truth teller Amos wrote on God's behalf:

I hate, I despise your festivals, and I take no delight in

your solemn assemblies. Even though you offer me your burnt offerings and grain offerings, I will not accept them; and the offerings of well being of your fatted animals I will not look upon. Take away from me the noise of your songs; I will not listen to the melody of your harps. But let justice roll down like waters, and righteousness like an ever-flowing stream. *(Amos 5:21-24)*

Jesus' death was not a sacrifice to God as debt payment for sin. God did not need a sacrifice in order to be able to forgive us.

If we had been able to enter heaven without an outward thing, there would be no necessity for God to send Jesus.[31] *(Martin Luther)*

Here, Luther reminds us that we are the ones who need the "outward thing" of God becoming a human in Jesus. God gave because of our need, not because of God's incapacity to forgive.

Just Me and Jesus

People tend to apply Anselm's view in such a way that all that matters is "me and Jesus." Believing that Jesus was interested only in rescuing individuals from hell when they die, they lean toward being interested only in that same goal. The fate of creation and the suffering of others are small matters by compare, and all that really matters in life is "ME getting to heaven when I die." This view overlooks the original definition of "salvation", which includes the inseparable healing of individual and community. God created the world as one world; God heals the world as one world.

The Payment-to-the-Devil Theory – Early Christian Centuries

The second but not nearly so popular view of Jesus' death and resurrection is the Payment-to-the-Devil theory. It emerged early in Christianity and it made sense to many people in its day because their major anxiety was: How can we be saved from evil spirits and the devil? Just as an alcoholic's life is held captive by alcohol, so they thought the world was held captive by the devil. Here is the basic logic to this understanding:

- God and the devil are at war.
- We sinned and gave the devil ownership of us.
- Jesus paid the devil for all the sins.
- The devil had to give us back to God.
- We can be freed from the devil if we take Jesus as our personal Lord and Savior.

A lot of debate took place in the early church about this theory, but most were not willing to grant the devil this much power. They did, however, see this as one possible explanation:

> To whom is God paying the ransom? Certainly not God!
> Therefore, why not the Devil?[32] *(Origen of Alexandria)*

While it is clear from Origen's comment that he was hardly certain of it, this and variant forms of this idea (that the devil was causing lots of problems and that Jesus death and resurrection gave us power over those problems), helped people to claim, from their perspective on the world, God's power in their lives and world. That God responds to and overcomes evil in Jesus has always been a central part of Christian teaching. This theory gave them a way to see that Jesus was giving them release from these dark powers.

There are, however, several problems with this view:

- This view is not Biblical.
- This view fosters dualism.
- Sacrifice was never dedicated to the devil, but only to God.
- We no longer view the world this way.

This View Is Not Biblical

There are only five references to the word "ransom" in the Christian Scripture (New Testament). None of these verses mention to whom the "ransom" is paid. It would have been easy for Jesus to make this clear by simply adding "to the devil" or "to God," but he does not do this (Matthew 20:28, Mark 10:45). Paul, in 1 Timothy 2:6, mentions Jesus as a "ransom for all," but he, too, does not clarify to whom the ransom is paid. Why? Because the word "ransom" had changed in its Greek usage and had lost its specific meaning of a payment to release a prisoner, and becoming a word meaning "simply 'rescue,' 'deliver' as an act of God's power."[33] Peter, in 1 Peter 1:18, says Jesus ransomed humanity "from futility." Jesus was rescuing us, not paying off some captor.

This View Fosters Dualism

While Christians do believe that evil is alive and well in our lives and in our world, most Christian teaching has rejected dualism, which divides the world into two camps, one evil and one good. First, it gives the devil too much credit. As a created being, the devil simply doesn't have what it takes to be at war with God—war happens between people who are on the same level, and the devil and God are not on the same level. Evil is the good creation twisted and hurting, not the property of the devil. Second, this understanding doesn't recognize the way that good and evil are intermingled in our lives and in the life of the world. At its worst, this view creates people who think they are totally on God's side and can do whatever they want to those who they think are on the devil's side.

Sacrifice Was Never Dedicated to the Devil, but Only to God

A Hebrew person in the first or any century would never imagine a sacrifice dedicated to the devil. The Hebrew people believed in one God in a time when most people believed in many gods. What others attributed to many gods, the Hebrew people attributed to one. There was simply no other worth sacrificing to. For Christians to claim that God sacrificed Jesus to the devil is not only a transformation of the Jewish practice of sacrifice, but a rejection of it.

We No Longer View the World This Way

People today do not believe that the devil or evil spirits are behind every bush. What first century people attributed to evil spirits we understand as disease, mental illness, the evil that humans do unconsciously, and the systemic evil that emerges from governments and organizations that destroy the environment and oppress people. (For a modern re-interpretation of this view, see: *The Powers That Be: a Theology For a New Millennium* by Walter Wink. Ironically, after Wink's re-interpretation, this view has a lot to say to us.) While modern people sense that evil is bigger than the sum of its parts, we tend not see evil in terms of evil spirits.

Answers for Other Times

Both of these views made sense in their day and helped people to understand the power of Jesus' life, death, and resurrection. But neither of these views speaks to most people today—witnessed, in part, by the large number of people who are leaving the Christian church for other religions or for the religion of Sunday morning sports.

These two ways of understanding what Jesus does simply do not address the questions, the pain, and the fears of 21st century people. They do not have the same interpretive power for our time that they once had. To accept either view, people in our time must adopt a worldview from a long time ago. To adopt Anselm's view, we have to take fear of punishment from God as our primary anxiety, even though meaninglessness and loneliness are even deeper anxieties. To adopt the Payment-to-the-Devil theory, we have to see the devil everywhere, even though we now know about the cause of the common cold. Although some do adopt these worldviews (at least, on Sunday morning), many more simply say, "This stuff doesn't make sense," and assume that all Christianity is a museum religion—an interesting place to visit, but you wouldn't want to live there.

A View for the 21st Century

There are other views of what Jesus does. The Christian Scriptures provide many metaphors for the meaning of Jesus' life, death, and resurrection, including:

- Passover lamb *(John 1:29, Hebrews 11:28)*
- Reconciler of all things *(Colossians 1:19-23)*
- Sacrifice of atonement, reconciliation *(Romans 3:21-26)*
- Word become flesh *(John 1)*
- Innocent victim who becomes conqueror of death *(Acts 2:15)*
- Serpent lifted up to bring healing *(John 3:14, Numbers 21:5-9)*
- Mediator between God and humans *(Galatians 3:20)*
- Ransom *(1 Timothy 2:3-6)*
- Shepherd who dies to protect the sheep *(John 10:11)*
- Fulfiller of God's promise to make Abraham and his children a blessing to all nations *(Acts 2:25)*

Why so many metaphors? The idea of God becoming a human—living as we live and suffering and dying to be reconciled to us—was, and still is, so radical that it was hard for early Christians to find ways to talk about it. One of the reasons the earliest gospel (Mark, written around 55 C.E.) took so long was because time was needed to even begin to put this heretofore unthinkable concept into words.

In the most popular understandings of Christianity, the

many-hued set of metaphors we find in Scripture have been inappropriately reduced to one: Jesus as sacrifice for sin, either to God or the devil. Coupled with a complete misunderstanding (a payment meant to change God) of what Hebrew sacrifice meant, we are left with an incomplete, twisted understanding of Jesus and thus a twisted understanding of God.

In Luke, chapter 15, Jesus tells the story of the prodigal son. The younger son asked for his share of the father's money, land, and animals. In doing so, he basically said to his father, "I wish you were dead." He went off to another country and wasted his money on sex, drugs, and rock and roll. A famine hit that land, and when he was out of money, he was out of friends. He made his living feeding pigs—which, in the Jewish world, was the bottom of the bottom of the barrel.

He came to himself and returned home thinking that he could be hired on as one of his father's servants. But the father saw him coming and sent for a ring and a robe: signs of his acceptance back into the family.

If Anselm's were the correct view, Jesus might have told the story this way:

> The father sees the younger son coming and sends for the older son, saying, "Well, I can't take him back unless I give you 15 lashes because I need to be paid for the sin he committed against me."

If the Payment-to-the-Devil theory were correct, Jesus might have told the story this way:

> The father sees the younger son coming, but before he gets there the devil shows up saying, "When he sinned he became my property. You can't have him back until I get paid for the sins he committed. I need you to give 15 lashes to your older son before you can have him back."

But Jesus does not tell the story in either of these ways. The father accepts the son back into the family and rejoices that he has returned. Can God do no less? No, God does more: God comes and finds us!

> But God, who is rich in mercy, out of the great love with which he loved us even when we were dead through our trespasses, made us alive together with Christ—by grace you have been saved. *(Ephesians 2:4-5)*

Both Anselm's theory and the Payment-to-the-Devil theory *place the main action somewhere else.* Anselm's view places the key action in God (who is in heaven); the Payment-to-the-Devil theory places the key action between God and the devil (in hell). But the point of Jesus' birth, teaching, death, and resurrection is to reveal that God is radically with, and unconditionally for all human beings. *All the action takes place right here, right now.*

Jesus is born into a very poor and powerless family in an unimportant part of Palestine, showing God's presence with all people. He preached that the Kingdom of God was near. (Mark 1:15) He ate with and accepted those most people assumed were not acceptable to God. (Matthew 8:5-13, 9:10-13, John 4:1-42) He taught us to love our enemies and that our enemies were capable of love. (Luke 6:27-36) In the night leading up to his arrest, Jesus refuses armed conflict to save himself; fighting is not an expression of God's love. On the cross, he prays to God, "Father forgive them, they don't know what they are doing." (Luke 23:34) He gives a comforting promise to a thief who is crucified beside him. He even joins us in experiencing the absence of God, while still trusting God, by quoting the 22nd Psalm, "My God, my God, why have you forsaken me?" (Matt. 27:46) Only a short while later, in an act of supreme trust, he says, "Into your hands I give my spirit." (Luke 23:46)

The Power of the Resurrection

If this is the end of it, then it was a nice gesture by God—a nice try, but no cigar! God does not let the death of Jesus be the last word. God is not content to simply join us in pain and suffering. God wishes to bring this beautiful and good, but hurting and lonely, creation into renewed life.

God makes Jesus alive again. God does this not to show off or simply because Jesus had been a "good boy" and deserves his dessert. God does this, in the words of one of my junior high students, "So we can see that [God] isn't giving up on us." God meets us in death and pain, but does not leave us there. God seeks to reconcile Godself to the world.

> He is the image of the invisible God, the firstborn of all creation; for in him all things in heaven and on earth were created, things visible and invisible, whether thrones or dominions or rulers or powers— all things have been created through him and for him. He himself is before all things, and in him all things hold together. He is the head of the body, the church; he is the beginning, the firstborn from the dead, so that he might come to have first place in everything. For in him all the fullness of God was pleased to dwell, and through him God was pleased to reconcile to himself all things, whether on earth or in heaven, by making peace through the blood of his cross. *(Colossians 1:15-20)*

What we see in Jesus' death and resurrection is not a *strategy*, like a football coach calling a Hail Mary pass at the end of the game. Jesus' death and resurrection shows God's *stance* toward human beings. In Jesus we see how God plays the game. In other words, *the way we see God working in Jesus is how God works in our lives!* This is the whole point of the early church's teaching that Jesus was both God and human at the same time. God joins each of us in our lives. God meets us in our weakness, vulnerability, loneliness, meaninglessness, and greatest pain. God brings new life out of death. We call this the Theology of the Cross.

> The theology of the cross declares God is with you—
> Emmanuel. He is alongside you in your suffering. He
> is in the darkest place of your dark night. You do not
> have to look for him in the sky, beyond the stars, in
> infinite light, in glory unimaginable. He is incarnate
> (in flesh). This means he has been crucified. For to
> become flesh, to become one of us means not only to
> be born, but also to die, to fail.[34] *(Douglas John Hall)*

The resurrection, then, is not simply the power of God to raise one man from the dead, but the power and promise of God to enter into our world, suffering with us and bringing us to healing. By entering our darkness and meeting us in our pain in Jesus, God announces that we are not alone. Our lives, though small in an ever-expanding, cold universe with billions of people and thousands of cultures, are not meaningless. God affirms all life by joining us in Jesus. God brings healing to us in his cross and new life.

In Jesus' death we see something else too—something we don't like to see: our own pain due to our separation from God, self, others, and the world. His gruesome death shows us not just the consequences of some political decisions by a few first-century Jews and Romans. His death on the cross reflects human (yes, this includes us!) rejection of God and the suffering we both bear and inflict when we cut ourselves off from the source of our life. Seeing Jesus' death, we see our own; witnessing his feelings of despair and loneliness, we come to experience our own.

We don't like to acknowledge the terror our broken relationships bring us to, and we spend a lot of energy avoiding this terror.

Consciously looking at this terror is worth the trouble, however, because the story does not end there. In Jesus' resurrection we come to realize that the God who joins us in death, despair, and loneliness is a God to be trusted—a God who loves us before we know that love.

> The question for Luther's doctrine of atonement is thus not that of abstract payment to God but rather how God can succeed in giving himself to us so as to actually take away our sins, to destroy the barrier between us and God.[35] *(Gerhard Forde)*

God is not trying to seek a loan from Jesus to cover up a problem in heaven's sin bookkeeping department. In Jesus the creator of the universe reaches out to bridge the separation that we experience between us and God. God's presence in our suffering, and God's participation in it, changes our lives and changes the world. God brings us new life. God is radically with and unconditionally for all people.

The Meaning of Sacrifice

This is not to say that the metaphor of Jesus as sacrifice is wrong and should be dismissed, but that Anselm and our culture have understood the Jewish practice of sacrifice wrongly.

Let me be clear: no one understanding of Jesus' life, death, and resurrection will be able to contain or adequately explain the implications of God-with-us, Emmanuel. We humans often seek to insulate ourselves from the life-changing reality of God's radical participation in our lives and unconditional love for us. One way we do this is by trying to seal God in the box of our theories. Both Anselm's theory and the Payment-to-the-Devil theory have been used this way. No matter how old and ornate the box is or how many preachers pound the pulpit about it, no box is capable of containing God.

Jesus' transformation of the tradition of sacrifice is a great example of God's capacity to lovingly and playfully show us the futility of boxing up God.

Shortly before Jesus death, he was in a room with his disciples eating a Passover meal. (Luke 22:7-23) In this meal, he took the Hebrew idea of sacrifice and put it on its head. Jesus offers himself, and therefore God, to his disciples in bread and wine. His disciples had a hard time with this (John 6:22-65), because Jesus was changing an understanding that they had held their entire lives. Traditionally, sacrifice had been understood as a human offering something to God. In Jesus, God does just the opposite: God offers Godself to us so that we might come to trust God's love, mercy, and compassion. God is radically with us. God is unconditionally for us. God offers us Godself so that we might be reconciled.

Jesus' death was not God taking out God's anger with human sin on Jesus, but rather Jesus was God's attempt to save us from the truck that was bearing down on us, to show how much God desires a relationship with us. Jesus is God's sacrifice *to* us.[36]

> God sacrificed Jesus on the altar of the world to clear that world of sin. Having faith in him (trusting in him) sets us in the clear.[37]

God Seeks Reconciliation

The most common form of theology in our country falls short of this understanding by making God into someone who accepts a payment of pain and violence to balance the bookkeeping-of-sin department account rather than meeting a God who seeks true reconciliation. Jesus did not die in our place, but he died on our behalf—for *our* benefit so that the consequences of sin (broken relationship) might be healed. This is what is meant by the phrase, "Jesus died for us."[38] In this sense saying, "Jesus died for us" or "for our sin" is very appropriate. Jesus accepted the risk that humanity would reject God's offer of love. Jesus paid the price of God's love for the world, but he didn't "pay" anyone. To use the word "pay" here is simply to use a figure of speech.

God seeks to be reconciled with us, even though we are the ones who misuse our lives, other people, and God's world. God seeks to heal us, even though our lives are marked by the loneliness, the addiction, and the violence arising from our self-negation and self-idolatry. God seeks to bring healing to a world, even though the power of evil threatens to overwhelm all that is good. It is this healing of people and the world that is meant by the word "salvation."

God is willing to pay the consequences of God's love for the world. This is what Jesus did on the cross. God became a human in Jesus and, by doing so, paid the consequences of God's love for us.

Willing to Risk in Expressing Unconditional Love

In Jesus, God accepted the risk of pain and death because God is radically with and unconditionally for all people.

What difference does this make?

I was working at an alternative school with an eleven-year-old boy who had been raped by two men. His mother admitted that, although she was in the next room, she did nothing as these two "friends" raped him. Understandably, the boy was angry and distrustful of all adults. In so much pain, he was a real pain to teachers and so disruptive that he had been kicked out of four different schools. Then he came to us.

I was in college and was a big guy, as I threw shot put and discus. Of all the people working at this school, the boy hated me the most because I looked like one of the men who had hurt him. I truly scared him! Ironically, this was why I was assigned to work with him.

"He has got to face his fears," my supervisor said, "and you are going to face his fears with him."

While the idea frightened me, it held the familiar ring of a story I had heard somewhere before.

At first, all I did was sit next to him in class. He responded by hitting me on an arm over and over again. I switched sides occasionally so that neither arm would get too sore. Knowing that he wasn't really trying to hurt me, I remained patient. After a few months, he began to trust me. I was even able to tickle him, wrestle with him, and joke with him about all kinds of things. My supervisor had told me to do this so that the boy could face his fears and learn that not all men were going to hurt him.

One day as I was playing with him, I lightly hit his solar plexus by mistake. He screamed and ran out of the building. Three blocks later I caught up to him.

"What happened?" I asked, catching my breath. "I didn't mean to hurt you!"

"I know," he said. "I'm sorry I ran.It's just that one of the guys who raped me hit me there that day."

We both stood on the sidewalk beside that busy street and wept. It was the first time he admitted to being raped.

A few months later, after many conversations about what he had experienced, he was back at regular school and was a good student.

I believe this is what God does with us by joining us in our humanity and sharing our pain on the cross of Jesus. Years after my interaction with the boy, I was able to link that "familiar ring" to the story that held its song. It was this story I had heard in my faith community as a child about how God faces our fears with us.

Although my faith community sometimes told this story in a confused or disjointed way, I had learned that Jesus enters the pain caused by our desire to be anything but human, helps us to become conscious of it, and then brings us to new life in relationship with God. I could dare to serve this hurting boy, unsure that I would be able to help, because in this story I had learned that death and defeat were not to be the last word for me or for the whole of the human race.

God is a serving and healing God who is present in our pain. Being made in the image of this serving and healing God, we are most deeply human when we are serving and healing others.

Chapter Seven

The Core of Christianity

God created the world out of love. God reveals God's love for us in Jesus Christ and offers connection to our purpose for life. But what does this all add up to? What does this say about the purpose and meaning of human life? Key to these questions is our understanding of God's relationship to the universe.

I have learned much from reading the books of Douglas John Hall, a theologian who teaches at McGill University in Canada. In his writings[39] he states the core of Christianity in a profound way: God is committed to loving the world.

The Scripture story—from God's creation of the world and the revelation of God's love in freeing the slaves from Egypt to God's joining us in human life in Jesus Christ—tells of this commitment.

When God calls Abraham and Sarah to leave their families, God makes a promise to them.

> Now the LORD said to Abra[ha]m, "Go from your country and your kindred and your father's house to the land that I will show you. I will make of you a great nation, and I will bless you, and make your name great, so that you will be a blessing. *(Genesis 12:1-3)*

The intent of this promise to Abraham and Sarah is that God, through them, will bless all the people of the earth so that they will become blessings. God expresses this continuously kept promise (despite Abraham's, Sarah's, and their children's lack of faithfulness to the work of being a blessing) by God's activity with and through the people of Israel and Jesus' life, death, and resurrection. God is committed to the world, and God wants partners to help God express this commitment.

This understanding of the core of Christianity has many implications. Here are a few.

God Loves All That God Made

Many people think that all God is interested in is saving people from the creation and taking them to heaven. In this understanding, Jesus is like the movie character, Rambo, who goes into a Viet Cong prison camp, blows up everything, and saves the prisoners. This may be sufficient for a movie script, but God is not content with this storyline. Rather, God wants to bring healing to the *entire* situation which, by definition, must include the Viet Cong.

If God is committed to the world, just taking a few people to heaven is not enough. We must remember that in the first creation story, God did not call the creation "good, very good" until the entire creation was complete. God is committed to *all* of creation and will bring it to wholeness one day. Care for the creation (being a blessing) is one of our highest responsibilities. Jesus asked his disciples to preach the good news of God's love to the whole creation.

> And he said to them, "Go into all the world and proclaim
> the good news to the whole creation." *(Mark 16:15)*

God Forever Loves All That God Has Made

God not only loves us while we are alive but also continues to love us when we die. God's promise in Jesus is that death is not the last word in our existence; rather, God's intention is to make us alive again to live with God in the creation. This is an important promise of God, according to my faith community.

Unfortunately, new life after death has often been understood as a promise that leads Christians to devalue our present life. This is a profound misunderstanding. God promises resurrection precisely because God values our lives! Jesus was the first person to believe in his resurrection—he believed in it before his death. (Mark 9:31) It was his deep understanding of God's promise of life that gave him courage to face his likely death. Simply stated, resurrection by God means that we cannot lose, so we are free to live as God calls us to live, even if that leads us to great risk.

This Life Is Good

Many people think that bodily existence is second-rate to a more out-of-body kind. They believe that Earth is just a training ground for the afterlife. Many further believe that humans are separate from the creation. However, if God created us as human and as a part of this world on purpose, to believe our existence is second-rate and separate from the creation is to tell God that God messed up.

> Then the LORD God formed man from the dust of the ground, and breathed into his nostrils the breath of life; and the man became a living being. And the LORD God planted a garden in Eden, in the east; and there he put the man whom he had formed. (Genesis 2:7-8)

> The LORD God took the man and put him in the Garden of Eden to till it and keep it. (Genesis 2:15)

First, God forms the man of the dust of the ground (a part of creation) and then places him in the garden. Second, God tells him of his role in the creation: a part of creation, caring for creation. We were created as a part of this world, from the stuff of this world. Without the world, we could not exist. Without us, the world would not be whole, like a word with a key letter missing (is that "ours" or "yours"?). But what is the value of one part (y) without the rest (ours)? Without the earth and all its creatures, we could not exist and would not be whole. Far from being separate from the earth, we have a role of responsibility within it. God did not make a mistake in making us of the dust of the ground. Even the dust was considered good.

We Are Called into Partnership with God, Individually and in Community

Because God is committed to loving the world, God called Abraham and Sarah to leave their homeland and learn what it means to trust God. God intended for them to be a blessing to all the families of the earth by helping to bring greater meaning and community so that the lives of all might be more joyous.

Abraham and Sarah celebrated God's love for the world simply by trusting God enough to listen to God. By leaving their home, they willingly (if imperfectly) joined God in love for the world. They generated a whole community of people to join them in being a blessing.

A descendant of Abraham and Sarah, Jesus was a part of God's promise to bless all nations. Jesus gathered a community of people to join him in his work of being a blessing. As Jesus gathers us to join him, we are asked to continue the blessing—a tradition established by God. Jesus continues to call together a community of people on his behalf to do two things:

- Celebrate God's commitment to the world
- Join God in commitment to the world

I am not claiming that this is the purpose of the church only. It is the purpose of human beings. We are here to celebrate a God who gave us this gift of life, and to join God in caring for this world. Read again this quote from Ephesians:

> God does both the making and the saving. He creates each of us by Christ Jesus to join him in the work he does, the good work he has gotten ready for us to do, work we had better be doing.[40] *(Ephesians 2)*

Celebrating and joining God in commitment to the world is what human beings are here to do. When we do not form our lives around doing these two things, we create the famine of meaning and community from which we suffer.

Celebrating God's Commitment to the World

Christian faith communities gather to celebrate God's love for all people and the world. We thank God for God's creation. We thank God for our lives, for the lives of our loved ones, and for all life that sustains us here. We do this in many ways:

- Worship
- Education classes
- Social gatherings
- Small groups
- Playing together
- Individual prayer and praying together

We remind each other of God's gift of love for all creation. We also remind each other of God's love for each person. Martin Luther taught that the most important words in the Lord's

Supper are "the body of Christ given *for you*." As we receive the
bread and wine, we remind each other that God's love is specific.
God knows my name and God knows yours. God became a
human being with you in mind. Jesus lived and died for you. We
don't believe that God only has a blanket of love for the whole
world, but that God has love for each particular thing and person.
What cause for celebration!

There are times, of course, when people in faith communities
don't feel like celebrating. We often don't feel grateful and thankful.
Sometimes we just don't feel like getting up and participating in
worship. On the other hand, we often find that the act of going
to worship and thanking God even (or especially) when we don't
feel like it helps us to become more grateful. This is because
sometimes our actions lead to our feelings.

Celebrating God's love for the world is our response to God,
as Jesus reminded his disciples:

> 'You shall love the Lord your God with all your
> heart, and with all your soul, and with all your mind.'
> (Matthew 22:37)

Joining God in Commitment to the World

God's love for the world, and for each part of it, began before
the world did. God's love for the world is deeper than the universe
and more passionate than we can imagine. My faith community has
taught me that God calls people *to join God in love for the world*.

Jesus not only reminded us to love God with all our might,
he also said:

> 'You shall love your neighbor as yourself.'
> (Matthew 22:39)

The good news of God's love must be "embodied" for people
to see and feel. All the theology books in the world and all the

Bibles in hotel rooms would be meaningless were it not for people who in their everyday lives enact God's love for the world.

> So, if anyone is in Christ, there is a new creation: everything old has passed away; see, everything has become new! All this is from God, who reconciled us to himself through Christ, and has given us the ministry of reconciliation; that is, in Christ, God was reconciling the world to himself, not counting their trespasses against them, and entrusting the message of reconciliation to us. So, we are ambassadors for Christ, since God is making his appeal through us; we entreat you on behalf of Christ, be reconciled to God. *(2 Corinthians 5:17-20)*

We are ambassadors for Christ in this world, entrusted with the ministry of reconciling all things. The church joins God in commitment to the world in many ways, including:

- Giving money and bringing services to the poor
- Recognizing our common humanity with all people
- Advocating for the marginalized
- Giving time to serve people in local communities
- Pointing out the injustices in the world
- Imagining new ways to live without doing damage to the created world
- Sponsoring thousands of hospitals and social ministries

Motivated by Gratitude and Compassion

To serve in these and other ways is not a way to earn God's love. God's love is a gift, just as life itself is a gift. Not only committed to loving and healing the world, God is also committed to loving and healing us. Though we can but glimpse the fullness of God's love, its presence fills us with awe and gratitude, and it is this gratitude that forms the motivation to join God in loving and healing the world. Unlike the motivation of fear that invites self-preservation as our ultimate goal, motivation brought through gratitude provides the potential wherein real love of other can be expressed and realized.

> Do nothing from selfish ambition or conceit, but in humility regard others as better than yourselves. Let each of you look not to your own interests, but to the interests of others. Let the same mind be in you that was in Christ Jesus, who, though he was in the form of God, did not regard equality with God as something to be exploited, but emptied himself, taking the form of a slave, being born in human likeness. And being found in human form, he humbled himself and became obedient to the point of death—even death on a cross. *(Philippians 2:3-8)*

We often fall short of having the same mind that was in Jesus; we continue to be saint and sinner at the same time. But our faith tradition is clear that God seeks to motivate not with guilt or shame, but by loving us so outrageously that we cannot help but respond, even if we respond imperfectly.

In the Image of the Serving God

In this letter to the faith community at Philippi, Paul writes that we are called, just as Jesus was, to serve the world because of God's love for us. The deeper meaning of his message arises when we consider God's revelation of Godself in Jesus. We see *a God who is a servant, and we are made in the image of that God!*

> Then God said, "Let us make humankind in our image, according to our likeness." *(Genesis 1:26)*

A serving God made the universe. We have been made in the image of a serving God. When we ignore this, we ignore the purpose for our existence. Without knowing and actualizing our purpose, we hunger and hurt. This is not where "ignorance is bliss"; this is ignorance *of* bliss.

Chapter Eight

The Problem of Evil

Certainly, the problem of evil is a topic too large to be fully explored here, and any attempt to do so would be outside the purposes of this book. Yet I would like to address the two most common questions associated with this problem. The first is a basic human question: Why do bad things happen to good people? This question has to do with the relationship between a good God and a world in which people suffer. The second is another, but related, human question: How do we name, understand, and respond to evil in the world? This question is about the capacity of individuals and communities to engage in war, terrorism, slavery, economic inequity, and exploitation of the weak.

Bad Things Happen

It doesn't take too much observation to see that many things are not fair in this world. Good people die in car crashes on the way to the food bank while others who are selfishly preoccupied with pleasure and money seemingly live happily ever after. What do we make of this?

Is God in Control?

A common answer, given by those in our culture who believe

in God, is that God is in the reward and punishment business: you obey the rules and you get some goodies; you disobey and you get hurt. This belief is often expressed in the words (or indictment) we hear spoken after something bad happens to someone else: "They must have had it coming."

When confronted with the randomness and injustice of what happens to people, some will argue that God's ways are "mysterious," and that while God is controlling everything, even the bad things that happen will "be for the best in the end."

This sounds great—at first. That is, until we ask what possible good can come of famines in which millions die, the rapes of women and children, and the ethnic "cleansing" of entire populations in eastern Europe and elsewhere. Even if these events were to lead to some good down the road, on some cosmic good-versus-bad scale, who would want to trust or love a God who would choose to sacrifice human lives for the sake of some cosmic balance? Furthermore, why couldn't a God who is all-powerful make a universe in which such choices never need to be made?

Living with Chance

If God is in the business of reward and punishment, then God does, at least by appearances, a very poor job of it. I can certainly find no discernable pattern behind what happens to people. My faith tradition records the thoughts of many people about why bad things happen to good people, and why bad things happen at all. Key to our understanding is chance.

> Again I saw that under the sun the race is not to the swift, nor the battle to the strong, nor bread to the wise, nor riches to the intelligent, nor favor to the skillful; but time and chance happen to them all. (*Ecclesiastes 9:11*)

The writer of Ecclesiastes says that our personal experience is heavily influenced by chance. Our place of birth, the family we are born into, our body, our basic personality, and our intelligence are all given by chance. How many experiences in our lives are determined not by our decisions or by what we do, but by what seems to happen to us?

In more recent times (1926), Max Born, the leading atomic researcher at the University of Göttingen who gave quantum mechanics its name, showed that identical experiments can have different outcomes, concluding that in any single collision it is impossible to predict which way the particle will go.

Certainly, people who lived before the age of science often attributed many things to "the gods." Today, without denying God's activity in the world, my faith community takes a different approach.

A friend of mine was riding his motorcycle to work when a horse in a nearby stall jumped the fence and ran out in front of him. There was nothing he could do. Curiously, the horse was just the right height to allow for my friend's whole weight to hit the horse instead of the pavement. The horse took the majority of the impact and died. My friend suffered a broken wrist and a banged-up knee. If the horse had been shorter, my friend could have easily died.

He later asked, "What is God trying to tell me?"

After a wisecrack about motorcycles, I answered that I didn't believe that God made the horse jump out at him to teach him some lesson. If God were in the business of controlling all such events, then why couldn't God do a better job of it? Certainly, God could teach us lessons without hurting us or killing horses.

"If you attribute this event to God," I said, "then the holocaust is God's doing too. Do you believe that God did that?"

He shook his head.

"Neither do I," I said. "But I do believe that God is present and active in our lives. God may not have made the horse jump out in front of you to teach you a lesson, but God will work with you so as to bring the most life out of this situation."

"I don't think God likes it when we get hurt in this world of chance," I said, "but I think God respects chance."

"Why would God let chance happen, when so many things hurt or kill people?" he asked.

"We don't know," I said. "But without chance, there is no freedom."

Choice within the Context of Chance

Imagine a world where you are perfectly free to decide what to do, but someone who wants to manipulate you controls everything around you. How free would you be?

This theme was explored wonderfully in the movie, *The Truman Show*.[41] Truman grew up in a fake city filled with actors and video cameras. His life was recorded for people to watch from the outside. His first step, first bike ride, first kiss—all were choreographed for the audience to see. As he grew up, he began to see the cracks in his fake world, and he almost died attempting to escape it. Finally, at the edge of the dome that had been his sky, he found a door and exited his fake-but-safe world to find the real-but-risky life beyond.

If even a 100% loving person controlled all things in our lives, wouldn't we make the same choice that the character Truman did? Wouldn't we try to escape the controlled world in order to find a world where both our choices and the chance of the world make up our future?

We all would like a "better" world—one without death, pain, and limitation. But how many of us would want to give up our freedom in return? It is interesting that many people want God to safely control all the things around them, yet these same people will become very upset when their ability to choose is threatened.

A respected teacher in my tradition, Joseph Sittler, taught that we do not have an answer to the problem of evil,[42] but we do have a response: God desires our freedom. Freedom to love or hate, hurt or heal. To make this possible, God must, for the most part, allow the world to respond to chance and the laws that govern our material world. Otherwise, we would not be human; we would merely be puppets of God, forever manipulated and forever clamoring for our freedom.

Chance means that we can make decisions, both individually and collectively, that can destroy or build our world. We can choose to serve life, but we often take the opportunity that chance provides to kill and destroy.

Still, God does not abandon us to chance. God joins us in all the choices and chances of existence and promises new life, in this life and the next. God created the world for creatures that could love God, ourselves, each other, and the world. Chance, choice, and risk are necessary ingredients to that world.

Collective Sin

My faith community has taught me not only to take sin (broken relationship) seriously but also to take evil seriously. Evil happens when people join together in expressing personal sin (self-idolatry and self-negation), either consciously or unconsciously.

God is committed to *this* world, not to a make-believe-best-of-all-possible-it's-a-small-world-after-all world. God is committed to the real world, where some little girls are celebrated in love with $150 worth of useless birthday party favors *and* where other little girls are sold into sexual slavery for $50. In this real world, we are willing to pay a lot of money for landscaping and yet are unwilling to change what or how much we consume in order to protect our forests. Seeing the disregard for life in his day, the truth teller Amos said:

> Hear this, you that trample on the needy, and bring to ruin the poor of the land, and practice deceit with

false balances, buying the poor for silver and the
needy for a pair of sandals, and selling the sweepings
of the wheat. *(Amos 8:4)*

In Amos' day, as in our own, people were cheating the poor
and the helpless and bribing judges so that they could win their
court cases. A bribe was the price of a pair of sandals—life was
that cheap to them! However, God sent truth tellers to bring the
people of Israel back to the purpose for their lives. These
prophets used warnings in the hope that people would change,
seeing the pain that their collective evil was causing.

The Example of Nazi Germany

A classic case of collective evil is Nazi Germany. Hitler grew
up feeling that he was a failure, born in a country broken by
World War I. He answered these feelings of self-negation by going
exactly in the opposite direction, self-idolatry. Read the League of
German Girls' version of the Lord's Prayer:

Adolph Hitler, you are our great leader. Thy name
makes the enemy tremble. Thy Third Reich comes; thy
will alone is law upon earth. Let us hear daily thy voice
and order us by thy leadership, for we will obey to the
end even with our lives. We praise thee! Heil Hitler.[43]

What would this self-idolatry of Hitler's and his hatred of
Jews have amounted to if the German people had not wanted to
believe they were the center of God's plans? Hitler told them:

God has created this people and it has grown according
to His will. And according to our will it shall remain
and never shall it pass away.[44]

He saw Germany as the army of light against all the dark

forces of the world. Robert Waite writes in his book, *The Psychopathic God, Adolph Hitler:*

> His version of human history was essentially one of religious mythology. He believed that a pure German people had lived in an early Garden of Eden. But this pure race had been attacked by the Devil, made incarnate in the form of the Jew. Indeed, he said explicitly "the Jew is the personification of the Devil and of all evil." Thus, he reached his conclusion that in fighting the devil, he was doing the work of the Almighty God.[45]

What happened? The self-idolatry of a man with intelligence and a talent for leadership called people out of their self-negation to join him in his self-idolatry. He taught that the Jewish people were the source of all evil and if they were exterminated, all evil would be too. His idolatry was expressed in his belief that evil was totally outside himself. Together they projected all their rage at Jewish people who, they believed, personified all evil.

It started slowly. First came the registration of Jews, followed by the night when many of the synagogues were burned. Next, the Jews were moved from their homes into ghettos, and then from ghettos into death camps.

An avalanche starts slowly, but once it gets going it is hard to stop. This is what happened to the German people. All of the feelings of helplessness after World War I and the desire for power of a whole people were twisted around the hatred of one man and became collective sin, or evil, here expressed in the scapegoating of an ethnic group.[46] Because many participated in this evil together it gained a power that one person's sin could never attain.

Collective sin usually takes something that is in itself good and warps it into something that is not good. Certainly, the

German people had reason to love their country. To support their leaders, within reason, is good for a people. However, Hitler's regime twisted reasonable love of country into the highest value in the world. Over time, it became clear many would do anything their leaders asked of them.

To make your leader into an unquestioned leader, ordained by God, is to give away your responsibility to do what is right.

> You shall not follow a majority in wrongdoing.
> (Exodus 23:2)

Many of the people felt they were doing the right thing, or they felt powerless to stop it. Their leaders deceived them, and they deceived themselves. For some, following Hitler gave them the opportunity to fulfill the needs of their self-idolatry and the urge to dominate other human beings. For others, going along with Hitler gave them the ability to hand over their own personal power and escape their own responsibility (self-negation).

This is not to say that evil is only the sum of its parts; it is more than what human beings do consciously. D.H. Lawrence was in Germany in 1923 and sensed early on that something destructive was being birthed.

> It is as if life had retreated eastwards. As if German life were slowly ebbing away from contact with western Europe, ebbing to the deserts of the east, . . . Returning again to the fascination of the destructive east, that produced Attila. . . At night you feel strange things stirring the darkness, strange feelings stirring out of this still unconquered Black Forest. You stiffen your backbone and you listen to the night. There is a sense of danger. It is not the people. They don't seem dangerous. Out of the very air comes a sense of danger, a queer, bristling feeling of uncanny danger. . .

Something has happened to the human soul, beyond all help. . . It is fate; nobody can alter it. . . At the same time, we have brought it upon ourselves. . . .[47]

The Domination System

New Testament writers used many words to indicate that evil has a life of its own. In his books on the language of evil in the New Testament, Walter Wink says that these words refer to what he calls the "Domination System." The Domination System teaches us what to believe, what to see, and what to value, based on the premise that power and life come through domination and control of other humans and the world. The Domination System twists human beings, organizations, governments, economic systems, and whole cultures to serve the most self-centered and destructive potentials of human nature. It is hard to discern when all of us are participating in it—evil seems to come from the "air."

But it is important to remember that those who perpetuate the Domination System are held captive to it, as are its victims. The Christian Scriptures use the words "devil" or "Satan" (among others words) to refer to the idea that people who do evil, are themselves held captive by it:

> And the Lord's servant must not be quarrelsome but kindly to everyone, an apt teacher, patient, correcting opponents with gentleness. God may perhaps grant that they will repent and come to know the truth, and that they may escape from the snare of the devil, having been held captive by him to do his will.
> (2 Timothy 2:24-26)

Some Christians, including some elected officials, believe that the job of the Christian is to "destroy evil" and "kill the evildoers." But this view denies both the potential and the real power of evil in our own lives (Romans 7:19) and the inherent created good-

ness of those held captive by evil. Trying to "destroy evil" leads us
to falsely believe that we are both capable of discerning evil
(Matthew 7:1-4) and totally different from those who practice it
(Romans 3:23). Destroying evil and killing the evildoers is not
what Jesus tells us to do:

> "But I say to you that listen, Love your enemies, do
> good to those who hate you, bless those who curse
> you, pray for those who abuse you." *(Luke 6:27-28)*

Love is Jesus' response to evil. Love is the response he asks of
his disciples. We are to love the victims and love the victimizers.
We are to love our friends and love our enemies. While love's
expression may be different for different people, love is what
Jesus teaches. For some, this love, offered in God's forgiveness,
may bring consciousness of their participation in evil, leading to
repentance and reconciliation. For others, this love may bring
recognition of the lie of their powerlessness, reconciling them to
the true power given them by God. All need and receive healing
from God. Loving our enemies is the act of remembering that the
vision of another as enemy is a lie. The deepest reality is that we
are brothers and sisters, children of one God. To love our enemies
is to embody the radical love of God for all.

Earlier, I use the example of Nazi Germany because it is
something with which we are all familiar. Nazi Germany was not
the first time the personal sin of individuals joined together to
become collective sin, or evil; nor has it been the last.

It is much harder for us to see the ways that we participate,
often unconsciously, in world-destroying, life-negating activities.
Though we are not putting people into forced labor camps at
gunpoint, our collective desire for inexpensive clothing often
creates the conditions in which business owners operate brutal
child labor factories in other countries—cheap clothing at such
a price!

The owners of these companies certainly have personal responsibility, as do government leaders, for these child labor factories. We, however, share in this responsibility. The American belief that the key to happiness is having more and more stuff and our reluctance (or laziness) to check out the conditions in which our goods are made make us responsible too.[48]

Won't future generations look back at us and say, "Couldn't they have done more to help?" Yet, if future historians choose to be fair, they will also have to see how generous Americans are, how much money we give to the poor among us and to the needy around the world.

"Total giving to charitable organizations of all kinds, both in absolute figures and as a proportion of income, is higher in the United States than in virtually any other advanced industrial society," writes Robert Wuthnow in *God and Mammon in America*.[49] A report, entitled "Philanthropy in the American Economy," by the White House Council of Economic Advisers states that "[g]iving to charity hit a record $190 billion in 1999—an increase of 41% since 1995."[50] (Of course, the level of giving changed quite a bit after the economic downturn that began in 2001.)

Acknowledging Our Part in Collective Sin

We do not line up in a black-and-white cartoon world with bad people (them) against eternally virtuous heroes (us). To engage the collective sin of our time is to recognize that, to some degree, all of us are a part of it. Simply purchasing the clothes made by children in child labor factories makes us a part, even if only a small part, of making child labor possible.

Don't we know this? Don't we avoid thinking about it?

Yet this is only the start.

An estimated one billion people in the world suffer from hunger and malnutrition. About 24,000 people die every day from hunger.[51] Six million children under the age of five die every year as a result of hunger.[52]

Forty million people around the world are infected with the human immunodeficiency virus (HIV) which causes AIDS.[53] Ninety percent of people living with AIDS (36,000,000) live in developing countries; 75 percent of them (30,000,000) live in sub-Saharan Africa, and just over seven percent (2,900,000) are children under the age of 14.[54]

The richest five percent of the world's people have incomes 114 times that of the poorest five percent. Twelve million people die each year from lack of water, and one billion people lack access to clean water with an estimated 1.7 million deaths per year.[55]

Approximately one million children (mainly girls) are exploited in the multi-billion dollar commercial sex trade every year. Children suffer from all sorts of harm: diseases such as diarrhea from malnutrition; respiratory illnesses caused by tobacco use; repetition injuries such as those suffered in sweat-shops; sexually transmitted diseases such as HIV/AIDS acquired in the sexual slave industry; recruitment as soldiers; amputation of limbs, death, or rape from armed conflict; death, trauma, and illness from landmines, guns, drugs, and pollution; and torture and ill-treatment.[56]

Without going into similar details, we know it is foolhardy to believe that we can continue to consume our natural resources at the current rate and not cause irreversible damage to the ecosystem that makes our life possible.

Could it be that our famine of meaning and community is connected with the famine of basic needs that creates and fur-thers these conditions? Perhaps we seek to run away from this knowledge by preoccupying ourselves excessively with work, sex, consumerism, obsessive recreation, and drugs. Perhaps by devaluing the human beings who make our cheap jeans, we devalue ourselves too. No wonder we seek to cover our pain with all our addictions!

In a wonderful introduction to Buddhism, Thick Nack Hanh

writes about our responsibility to care for our planet with the following story:

> The Buddha said: "A young couple and their two-year-old child were trying to cross a desert, and they ran out of food. After deep reflection, the parents realized that in order to survive they had to kill their son and eat his flesh. But with every morsel of their baby's flesh they ate, the young couple cried and cried."
>
> If, while we eat, we destroy living beings or the environment, we are eating the flesh of or own sons and daughters. We need to look deeply together and discuss how to eat, what to eat, and what to resist.[57]
> (Thick Nack Hanh)

God has placed this planet and its creatures in our care, and we need to remember that our lives will end one day. The world we leave behind will be our blessing or our curse to future generations. God has given us a wonderful world. We need to preserve, restore, and cherish it. To be a servant of the earth is at the heart of what it means to be human.

Can we do more to lessen the pain and suffering of the world?

Collective sin is hard to see when we are submerged in it. Evil seems so natural, it seems "that's just the way things are." Life is certainly difficult enough without engaging such questions. Even when we do see some of the injustices in the world, figuring out how to respond without becoming defeated, guilt-ridden, or self-righteous is even harder.

The key to engaging in this discussion is to remember that God always starts with us where we are. God loves and accepts us now. We do not need to change for God to love us. God seeks to bring change in us not only for another's good but for our own good as well.

Confronting Evil

Jesus taught about and lived something he called the "kingdom of God." His idea of that kingdom was rather radical. Simply put, the kingdom of God is God's power to bring us to live the way that God intends humanity to live: in an attitude actively reflecting value and enjoyment of all life and all people.

The first radical part of Jesus' understanding of the kingdom was when and where it is. Many people in his day thought the kingdom of God would come at the re-creation of the world (often referred to today as the "end of the world"). As such, it could be looked forward to; essentially, however, it could be ignored until later. Jesus had a different understanding:

> Once Jesus was asked by the Pharisees when the kingdom of God was coming, and he answered, "The kingdom of God is not coming with things that can be observed; nor will they say, 'Look, here it is!' or 'There it is!' For, in fact, the kingdom of God is among you." *(Luke 17:20-21)*

Participating in God's Kingdom

Jesus taught that the kingdom of God would not be a reality only at some later date, but that the kingdom of God is eternal (encompassing past, present, and future) and, as such, is among us now, even if not yet fully realized. In this kingdom, pain from sin is continuously offered comfort and healing. Moreover, he offered his disciples, while yet living in their human culture, entrance into the kingdom, would they but accept and adopt a new way of being human: celebrating and joining God's commitment to the world. God's kingdom is breaking into the kingdom of the world and its Domination System, seeking to free people, governments, economic systems, and cultures from its life-warping hold.

Because the kingdom of God is among us, as Jesus taught, we need not wait around for some cosmic alarm clock to begin living this way. But Jesus was clear that living the kingdom life would lead to conflict with the Domination System ("Domination System" is one understanding of what the Christian Scriptures refer to as the kingdom of the world or of Satan).

> "A disciple is not above the teacher, nor a slave above the master; it is enough for the disciple to be like the teacher, and the slave like the master. If they have called the master of the house Beelzebul (the Devil), how much more will they malign those of his house-hold!" *(Matthew 10:24-25)*

Jesus' practices of eating with tax collectors and publicly judged sinners, talking in public with women, and confronting the Pharisees' divorce practices[58] were all ways in which he confronted the collective evil around him while announcing God's way to live. Sometimes he confronted collective sin head-on:

> Early in the morning he came again to the temple. All the people came to him and he sat down and began to teach them. The scribes and the Pharisees brought a woman who had been caught in adultery; and making her stand before all of them, they said to him, "Teacher, this woman was caught in the very act of committing adultery. Now in the law Moses commanded us to stone such women. Now what do you say?" They said this to test him, so that they might have some charge to bring against him. Jesus bent down and wrote with his finger on the ground. When they kept on questioning him, he straightened up and said to them, "Let anyone among you who is without sin be the first to throw a stone at her." And

once again he bent down and wrote on the ground.
When they heard it, they went away, one by one,
beginning with the elders; and Jesus was left alone
with the woman standing before him. Jesus straight-
ened up and said to her, "Woman, where are they?
Has no one condemned you?" She said, "No one, sir."
And Jesus said, "Neither do I condemn you. Go your
way, and from now on do not sin again." *(John 8:2-11)*

In this story, the crowd has gathered to stone a woman
accused of adultery. We don't know if her accusers were correct
or not. She could have been forced to have sex. She could have
been forced into prostitution to eat. She could have been completely innocent. The writer of John doesn't tell us, and what's
more important, the crowd doesn't care. They would all take part
in her killing, all the while the man with whom she had sinned
was apparently free to go. The whole culture was taking part in
the oppression of women, and all present were accessories to
these crimes. For them this was "just the way it was." They were
going to take out their anger, and perhaps their guilt, on her.
They wanted Jesus to bless this arrangement.

They came to Jesus and asked what he would say. First, he
stalled to slow them down by writing in the dirt. He then short-
circuited their desire to scapegoat her by stating that anyone who
had not sinned should throw the first stone. He made them recognize
that they shared something with the woman: they all had sinned.
Further, if the correct response to sin is to stone the sinner, they
might well be next. Stunned into silence, the crowd melted away,
leaving only Jesus and the woman. Here Jesus confronted the
same kind of collective evil that happened in Germany and was
able to diffuse it.

Daring to Value the Under-Valued

More often, though, Jesus confronted collective sin by simply

valuing the people his culture de-valued. The very act of valuing
the poor, women, and other outcast people challenged the entire
culture that was held in the grips of the Domination System. His
act of valuing the "wrong" people made a lot of people angry. At
times this even disturbed those whom he was valuing:

> Now as they went on their way, he entered a cer-
> tain village, where a woman named Martha wel-
> comed him into her home. She had a sister named
> Mary, who sat at the Lord's feet and listened to
> what he was saying. But Martha was distracted by
> her many tasks; so she came to him and asked,
> "Lord, do you not care that my sister has left me to
> do all the work by myself? Tell her then to help
> me." But the Lord answered her, "Martha, Martha,
> you are worried and distracted by many things;
> there is need of only one thing. Mary has chosen
> the better part, which will not be taken away from
> her." *(Luke 10:38-42)*

While many people think that Martha was upset because
Mary was not helping to make dinner, it seems highly unlikely
that Luke would bother to write about such a minor family
squabble. What is more plausible is that Martha was upset
because Mary was sitting at Jesus' feet. *To sit at the feet of a teacher
was to be accepted as an official student or disciple of that teacher.*[59]
In Jesus' day, women were not allowed to study scriptures, nor
could they talk to a man who was not a member of their family.
Martha was disturbed by the fact that Jesus accepted Mary as a
disciple. She tried to interrupt this dangerous relationship by
calling Mary back to her traditional role as a woman. She had
reason to fear that others would see this and punish Jesus and
Mary for this unacceptable behavior, for which the penalty could
have been death by stoning.

Jesus was punished. Many Bible scholars believe that his confrontation with collective sin, the evil of the Domination System, and his valuing of women and other marginalized people were the main reasons for his imprisonment and death. Jesus himself became the scapegoat for the people (John 18:14), but his resurrection would reveal that he was innocent and that all such scapegoating is nothing more than a destructive lie.[60]

In the midst of all risk, Jesus trusted in God, believing that the last word would be neither the destruction of people by the culture nor his own death. Just as God had spoken the first word of abundant creation, so would God speak a word of abundant re-creation.

> Then I saw a new heaven and a new earth; for the first heaven and the first earth had passed away, and the sea was no more. And I saw the holy city, the new Jerusalem, coming down out of heaven from God, prepared as a bride adorned for her husband. And I heard a loud voice from the throne saying, "See, the home of God is among mortals. He will dwell with them as their God; they will be his peoples, and God himself will be with them; he will wipe every tear from their eyes. Death will be no more; mourning and crying and pain will be no more, for the first things have passed away." *(Rev. 21:1-4)*

We, too, without being paranoid or seeking some religious Purple Heart, must expect that living a kingdom life will not only bring great joy, but may also entail painful conflict. The disciple is not above the teacher.

God sees, with no illusions, the reality of sin and collective sin in the world, and with tears streaming down God's face, reaches into the devastation to bring new life again. This is the mystery and wonder of God's commitment to the world. God joins us and becomes vulnerable, just as we are vulnerable, to all the problems of the world.

Jesus declares God's love and value for the health and healing of all people, communities, corporations, governments, and cultures; and he is willing to die rather than soft-peddle that message. When we use the words "gospel" and "good news," we refer to this message of God's love and value for all people. When my faith community uses the word "salvation," we mean the healing and restoration of all of these aspects of human life to their proper place in God's kingdom.

God calls us to gather together to join God in responding to the hurt and pain of the creation (which includes humans) and so risk playing our part in God's promise to renew all things. We dare to trust because we see in Jesus a way of trusting a God who is the maker and re-maker of all.

The Church and Evil

There are many examples of how Christian faith communities have not lived up to God's purposes for them. In the Middle Ages, the church and the kings in Europe sent thousands of soldiers to kill Muslims and Jews throughout Europe and the Middle East. Many leaders of the church, as well as the rulers, said that if a Christian died on one of these Crusades, he or she would get a great reward in heaven.

In Martin Luther's day, the church in Europe needed a lot of money to build some buildings in Rome. To help raise the funds, they told people that if they wanted forgiveness for sins, they should buy a piece of paper called an "indulgence." With this paper, a person could skip purgatory and go straight to heaven. This taught people that forgiveness is financially expensive yet cheap in terms of our relationship with God and others, requiring some change *from* us but little change *in* us.

Outraged by this practice, and after intensive study, Martin Luther sought to reform the church. Ultimately, although he didn't want to leave the church, he was excommunicated (thrown out), whereupon he began his own church.

As Hitler came to power in Germany, some Lutherans resisted and fought against him, but many more Lutherans got deeper and deeper into the life-destroying goals of his government.

In our own country, some Christians believe that the world is going to end soon so it doesn't matter what we do to the world—"It's going to burn anyway."[61] Others try to fit human history into their theories of the "end of the world" and support the oppression of the Palestinian people by the Government of Israel so that Jesus will come again. Some Christians feel that America is a blessed nation and interpret that to mean that God cares more about us than people in other countries. Still other Christians spend all their time and energy raising funds for elaborate church buildings and beautiful prayer chapels, while their neighbors, blocks away, live in dire poverty.

We must also be honest about the times Christians in the church have stood, at their own risk, against the powers of destruction. That over a ten-year period otherwise good people went along with a tyrant's slow brainwashing of a nation isn't amazing; it has happened before and it will happen again. What is amazing is that there were people like Dietrich Bonhoeffer[62] who fought against the avalanche of hatred in Germany at that time. (Many of these historical stories are not so well known because it is often "sexier" for historians to write about the times Christians have failed than to write about the times Christians have done well.)

There is no doubt that Christians have not always lived up to the purpose for the church. Christians have done life-destroying things. We have at times allowed our call to love as Christ loved to be twisted into collective evil in service of the Domination System. The key question is: Is Christianity the problem?

I don't believe Christianity is the source of the problem, although far too often Christians have participated in the problem.

The source of evil is our universal human capacity to use our freedom to be less than human or try to be God. While Christianity (and, indeed, other religions) tries to become conscious of, limit, and transform this capacity for evil, churches sometimes become the servant of evil in the world and lose their life-valuing perspective. Christians and their churches are not immune from the human tendency to sin. We all break our created relationships either by trying to be God or by being less than human. The ways the church has fallen short of God's vision for us are the result of human sin. The church needs to be honest about this and attempt to change. We dare to change because we trust God's love.

Valuing Our Created Humanity

God, who is committed to the universe and to us, created all things. Limited, mortal, and living in a world of natural law and chance, all humans tend to misuse their freedom by trying to be God" or less than human, and we find ourselves blinded by and trapped in our focus on ourselves. The consequences of human sin and collective sin are devastating both to humans and to the world of which we are a part. Despite being warped by the Domination System, God considers us a part of the "very good" of creation.

Jesus confronts both our personal sin (broken relationship) and our collective evil so that the world might be healed. God reveals in Jesus Christ that God is radically with us, loving humans unconditionally, both individually and collectively. In Jesus, God draws us into the fullness of our created identity. Jesus helps us see that humans are neither God nor less than human, yet what we are is "very good."

At the heart of being human is celebrating God's love for the world and joining God in love for our selves, for each other, and for the created world. Created to be servants of God in the world, we derive our highest joy and pleasure from being the image of the Serving God, in joyful service to all life.

Chapter Nine

About Being Human

Celebrating God's love and joining God in commitment to the world—this is the purpose of human beings. We have been made in the image of the Serving God who gives Godself to us in Jesus Christ. But the world we are called to join God in loving is a world that is in great pain.

Being Human Gives us Strength to Face Pain

To love something that is hurting is to open ourselves to some of its pain. To love something that is so big and complex as the world is to face our own limitation and powerlessness—even as we learn to trust our God-given strength.

Joining God in commitment to the world requires that we look at the modern realities that have amplified human impact on the creation. While our individual capacity for sin has not changed, the sheer numbers of human beings now living on the planet, together with our ever-expanding technology, have dramatically increased human capacity for effecting both good and ill.

We cannot go back to some perfect starting place. Neither are we called to abandon the world to the life-destroying personal and collective sin of humanity. We ache to do something, but what is it, and where do we find the strength?

In this context, perhaps we can now begin to understand the daring of God who gives of Godself to heal the world—the God in whose image we are made:

> "For God so loved the world that he gave his only Son, so that everyone who believes in him may not perish but may have eternal life." *(John 3:16)*

While our commitment to loving and healing is personal, responding to the pain of the world is not some personal crusade. Each of us can only be one small part of a larger community of people who seek to be fully human in a hurting world. We realize that God has been responding to the world's pain longer than we have and that, ultimately, this world is in God's loving and compassionate hands. And so, as we join God in commitment to the world, we take our cue from our Serving God. God awakens us to the power of God's love, filling and grounding the universe. In response to this deepest reality, we learn to trust and find our strength.

Being Human Provides a New Vision to Life

The famines discussed earlier in this book are nothing new. Through our faith tradition, Christians remember how the human tendency to sin has played itself out in other times. As the writer of Ecclesiastes wrote:

> What has been is what will be, and what has been done is what will be done; there is nothing new under the sun. *(Ecclesiastes 1:9)*

We try to understand our human tendency to try to be God or less than human and the ways these tendencies deform our lives. Out of this God-inspired awareness, the Jewish people wrote the story of the man and the woman in the garden. They wrote it so that others could gain insight into why human beings feel so much pain. We read it and ponder its meaning for us so that each of us can begin to see himself, herself, each other, and the world in a new way. We read this story to unveil the lies that deprive us of the best of our humanity.

I believe that being a part of a Christian faith community can help us, as individuals, to recover from the famine of meaning and community. I also believe that being part of a Christian faith community can increase our ability to *live out* an alternative vision of being human—valuing those devalued by the culture and thereby valuing ourselves, all people and, indeed, the whole creation.

Being Human Means Ongoing Personal Transformation

God continuously calls us to change. God wants us to experience the immeasurable joy found in dedicating our lives to celebrating God's love for the world and joining God in loving commitment to this world. We are called to give up both our life-destroying desires to be God and our cowardly desires to find safety in being less than we are. We must strive to overcome our tendencies to sin in these two ways, die to these tendencies each day, so that a new life might emerge in which we more fully appreciate and share the awe-inspiring gifts of God's creation. Such change is painful, to say the least. This is a part of what Jesus means in saying:

> Whoever does not carry the cross and follow me cannot be my disciple. *(Luke 14:27)*

God's gift of Jesus reveals to us what it is to be human. Although created in the image of God, humanity tends to reject its true nature and finds itself despairing in the kingdom of the Domination System rather than celebrating in God's kingdom. Jesus taught that nothing less than a personal transformation is needed to return us to the truth of who we are. He did not mean that we should carry around big, wooden crosses or make-believe persecution complexes. He wasn't saying that we should go out and find some way to kill ourselves or have others do it for us. In asking us to "take up our cross," Jesus is telling us that the hard work of daily change is at the heart of what it means to be human. It is this transformation that is celebrated in Baptism, where, in water and words, God again pledges God's love for us and asks us to die to our sin and receive our rightful place in creation.

Some Christian traditions say that we must be "born again," using the conversation of Jesus with Nicodemus in John 3 (which is, by the way, a poor translation; "born from above" is a better one). People who use this phrase often seem to feel that it means "a once-and-forever-life-changing experience of God." While my faith tradition certainly affirms positive life change, we tend to distrust the term "born again" because it is too easily twisted to infer that once this particular change has been realized, no more change is needed, sought, or desirable. One might as well say, "I am now right with God, and so I can forevermore claim ownership of righteousness." Unfortunately, the descriptor "born again" is frequently utilized as protection against the hard work of making further changes. From a Lutheran perspective, we are born again every day, not because we make ourselves so, but because God births us into a new life in God's kingdom. Being a Christian is not as much about having been changed as it is about being committed to a process of change in which we learn to adapt from living "the best life I know for me" to "living the life God has prepared for me."

This change is not an easy process. It can be likened to the process of overcoming addiction: the source of the temptation is ever near even as our resistance to the temptation is strengthened.

Dying to our tendency to sin requires daily effort, the support of a faith community, and courage. It can only be done "one day at a time," and even more realistically, "one moment at a time."

A faith community can bear a vital role in this daily change. It is a great comfort to be in the company of people who are also consciously embracing such continual change. The encouragement that comes from simply being with each other, let alone from what we learn from each other, is vital to ongoing life change. Accepting one another's struggles and failures and celebrating new life, we come to accept and celebrate our own.

Not grounded in fear of punishment, this process is grounded in trust in God, a God who loves us unconditionally and who cares about our "real condition." We trust that even God's challenging words to us are spoken in abiding love. Relying on God all the way, we also receive the gift of peace and life. Jesus said:

> I came that they may have life, and have it abundantly.
> (John 10:10)

Receiving both the comfort of God's love and God's continual challenge to us, we relax, secure in God's love, and become able to be in service to the world and its people without fear.

Being Human Means Engaging Cultural Transformation

As we allow our own personal transformation, we gain tools with which to participate in the cultural transformation that God seeks to bring. God's loving hand seeks to heal broken relationships within and among human beings, organizations, governments, and economic systems.

I am learning that as we are parts of a larger whole, we cannot focus only on healing our own personal sin; we must also partner with God in unmasking and bringing to healing the collective sin in which we participate. We do not further cultural transformation by pointing a judgmental finger at others and calling *them* "sinners." Honesty asks that we work to become more conscious of how *our* decisions contribute to the destruction of our natural world and the suffering of other people. We may come to realize that we need to change many things about the way we live and our attitudes concerning what is vital to our lifestyle. We may be led, over time, to confront our culture in its life-destroying habits even as we support its positive ones. Motivated by our desire to embody God's love for the world, we find that we are able to transform our "tried and untrue" tools of self-punishment and derision of others into the most effective implement of change: love.

> Jesus came to Galilee, proclaiming the good news of God, and saying, "The time is fulfilled, and the kingdom of God has come near; repent, and believe in the good news." *(Mark 1:14-15)*

From the outset of Jesus' ministry, we see that he did not come to announce an after-life insurance policy or some novel philosophy for us to tinker with, either of which might distract us from living a meaningful life. He came to proclaim a new way to live *now*—the kingdom of God. God's kingdom—that is, a world in which human life is a reflection of God's purpose in love—is breaking into the life-destroying way of sin. To "repent" means to turn around. It means a total reorientation to life in God's kingdom. In this kingdom we value ourselves, others, and the world. Jesus teaches us how to live in this kingdom and what we are here to live for. This is good news.

Yet there are times when this good news is hard to bear in light of all the bad news that surrounds us. Some have said that being human in this world can be like flying into the wind all the time. Conflict is hard to bear alone. Here again, the faith community can offer support and encouragement. Knowing that others are engaged in the same work helps us to continue when we otherwise might quit. This is not easy to see when our culture values the supposedly independent individual above all else.

> I am a rock, I am an island. *(Simon & Garfunkel, from "I Am a Rock)*

Being a rock and an island gets pretty lonely. Walking against the wind of culture is hard enough to require that others sometimes take the lead: there are benefits to flying in formation with a group going in the same general direction. This doesn't lessen our individuality; being an individual includes being in relationship with others. Throughout history, agents of change have been strong individuals who rely on the support of close friends, advisors, and co-workers. We have come to see that this ability to rely on others is, in fact, a part of personal strength.

My faith tradition reminds us that neither personal transformation nor cultural transformation is completed by us. The kingdom of God is among us, yet there remain other kingdoms—that is, other ways in which humans live—that are world- and life-destroying. The ultimate healing of the world is in God's hands. Until ultimate healing comes, we work and wait in hope and in faith, celebrating and joining God in commitment to the world. We may not see the completion of our work in our lifetime, but we trust that the maker of all *is* the re-maker of all, in whose hands the creation is made very, very good.

Being Human Means Finding Meaning in Enjoyment

After all this discussion of personal and cultural transformation, it is important to remind ourselves that being made in the image of the Serving God means serving our deepest selves as well. Doing is only one part of being. A key part of the purpose for our lives is enjoyment of life's fullness, realized through work, rest, relationship, depth, and care for our bodies.

In Luther's day, many people felt that the only "calling" was to serve as a priest or a monk. Contrary to this unfortunate view, Luther taught that everyone had a calling. Your calling might be to serve as a teacher, a gardener, a programmer, a nurse, or a sales associate. Engaging in meaningful work that contributes to society is a great source of enjoyment. Recognizing that each patient, student, client, or product of our work is worth our time and effort, instead of waiting for the weekend to deliver up its promise of pleasure, we savor each moment and activity as one that holds both personal satisfaction and community value.

But without rest and time with loved ones, work, even meaningful work, can become a form of slavery. The Hebrew teaching of the Sabbath—a day of rest, worship, prayer, and play—is important because it affirms human life and relationship as meaningful apart from what we accomplish through work. This teaching has long reminded us that God calls us to live as the image of the Serving God, who, according to the story in Genesis, rested after completing the creation. Undeniably, joyful, vibrant, playful servants are more effective than gloomy, exhausted servaholics (something I am still learning!).

Attending to our interior lives is vital to being human. Prayer, contemplation, and meditation are key to our enjoyment of being human. These and other practices help us to rediscover that each moment can be filled with depth and meaning because God is present with us.

While affirming the depth of our experience, we also affirm that we are physical beings whose bodies need and deserve care, exercise, good food, rest, play, and enjoyment.

> Go, eat your bread with enjoyment, and drink your wine with a merry heart; for God has long ago approved what you do. Let your garments always be white; do not let oil be lacking on your head. Enjoy life with the wife whom you love, all the days of your

vain life that are given you under the sun, because
that is your portion in life and in your toil at which
you toil under the sun. Whatever your hand finds to
do, do with your might. *(Ecclesiastes 9:7-10)*

Our current cultural tendency is to get these necessities out
of the way: we gobble fast food and multitask as we strive toward
ever-increasing productivity. But at the end of life, what has this
gotten us but lives half-lived, partially experienced, and dimly
remembered?

And do not keep striving for what you are to eat and
what you are to drink, and do not keep worrying. For
it is the nations of the world that strive after all these
things, and your Father knows that you need them.
Instead, strive for his kingdom, and these things will
be given to you as well. *(Luke 12:29-31)*

Being human does include personal and cultural transformation, yet these transformations need to happen precisely so that
we can receive with joy the life that God has so freely given. To
be so serious about the business of transformation that we forget
the joy of being alive is to miss the point entirely.

One pastor I know has a collage of pictures on her office
wall, mostly of Jesus laughing. The only words on the wall: Joy is
the surest sign of the presence of God. It is a wonderful reminder
that Jesus joins, suffers, dies, and rises so that he can include us
in the loving, creative laughter of God.

Being Human Reconnects Us to Meaning and Depth in Relationship

I've sat with many people who were preparing to die.
Impending death has a way of clarifying many issues for people;

it is in some ways a gift. While listening to these people talk about their lives, I have not heard them talk about the big houses they had, the nice cars they did or did not buy, or the overtime hours they wish they had worked. I have heard them talk about the people they love and the people who love them. I have heard them celebrate the things they share with people, things they find meaningful as a part of something larger than themselves. This has shown me that human beings find the meaning and depth of life in relationship.

Jesus wishes to teach us now what many learn only at the end of life. Being a Christian isn't about having some stale ideas about God; it is about who we are and what we value. Relating to God in Jesus, we come to glimpse who we are in all our relationships. Paul wrote about this to the Christian faith community:

> It is in Christ that we find out who we are and what we are living for. . . . It is in Christ that you, once you heard the truth and believed the message of salvation, found yourselves home free—signed, sealed, and delivered by the Holy Spirit. This signet from God is the first installment on what's coming, a reminder that we'll get everything God has planned for us, a praising and glorious life.[63] *(Ephesians 1)*

In Jesus Christ, we find out how to be who we are: beings created in the image of the Serving God. To respond to the famine of meaning and community, we begin by healing and deepening our relationships, knowing that God does love us now. People often imagine that the teachings of Jesus ask us to attend to an otherworldly set of priorities. While Jesus does call us to attend to the depth, meaning, and purpose of life through prayer, study, service to neighbor, relationships in the faith community, and worship, these spiritual disciplines are meant to help us more deeply relate to those whom God has put in our lives.

If you have a spouse, find practical ways to love him or her. If you have children, serve their best future interests as well as letting them have fun. If you are estranged from a family member, let him or her know that you are open to renewed conversation.

Every day, every activity, and every relationship is part of our truest worship of God:

> So here's what I want you to do, God helping you: Take your everyday ordinary life—your sleeping, eating, going to work life—and place it before God as an offering. *(Romans 12)*

Every relationship, no matter how trivial, holds the potential for meaning and depth. But this is especially true in our relationships with our family. House cleaning, family meals, caring for our family members when they are ill—all the menial and relational aspect of your life with your family are holy because God is there with you. These are the people you have been given to care for. No task is too menial if it nourishes your family.[64] Even those things that bother us about family are holy, as these annoyances often become the jokes and exaggerated stories of later years, having taught us about ourselves.

Where to Start

When relief workers feed those who have been starving for some time, they don't serve a seven-course meal on the first day. They start with some bread soaked in water. The bodies of starving people shut down the digestive process in order to conserve energy. To recover the ability to eat regularly takes the better part of a week.

So many of us have been starved for meaning and community for so long that we, too, must start slowly. We must expect some "digestive problems" as we begin to take nourishment.

To begin hearing the Living Word of God, we make ourselves available to and aware of the presence of God in each other. This is challenging work, but we don't have to start from scratch, and we don't have go it alone. Our tradition holds many writings and practices that help us to recognize and respond to the kingdom of God. We explore our tradition, question it, and even add to it.

More than just exploring a tradition, though, we have come to trust the God our tradition reveals. God is committed to loving and healing this world, as revealed to us in the life of Jesus Christ.

In the first chapter, I wrote that being a part of a faith community holds benefits for us—such as learning in relationship with people alive today and, through tradition, from those who lived in the past—in addition to the gift of accompaniment in our life journey. But I am not a Christian because I have done a cost-benefit analysis and found the benefit to be greater than the cost. I am a Christian because God called me to remember my identity as one who is made in the image of the Serving God. I continue to discover what that means.

Perhaps you hear God calling you to celebrate and join God's love and healing work for the world. We invite you to discover with us what this means.

Just as God always starts with us as we are now, we start with ourselves as we are now. And so, in our midst, you will find people who, just like you, make mistakes and sometimes get off on the wrong track. Yet our worth is not measured by some readiness checklist; our call is not to some spiritual Mt. Everest where perfection is required or attained. We are invited to relax into the Serving God's love.

We are loved and liked by God right here and right now—loved and liked just as we are, even when we may not love and like ourselves. So deeply touched by God's love for and commitment to all that God has made, we are moved to celebrate being human in the image of the Serving God.

Notes

1 Thomas Moore, *Care of the Soul* (New York: Harper Collins, 1992) i.

2 Evy McDonald, *Simpler Living, Compassionate Life*, Michael Schut, ed (Denver: Living the Good News, 1999) 60. "As the United States got back on its feet the American Boom Era began. Leading economists felt that perpetual economic growth was possible. We, the public, only needed to be taught to want and consume more and more. In 1955 economist Victor Lebow wrote, "We seek our spiritual satisfaction or ego satisfaction in consumption. . . . We need things consumed, burned up, worn out, replaced and discarded at an ever increasing rate.""

3 Michael Schut, *Simpler Living, Compassionate Life*, Michael Schut, Ed (Denver: Living the Good News, 1999) 24.

4 Eugene Peterson, *The Message*. (Colorado Springs: NavPress, 1996) 483.

5 Robert Moore and Douglas Gillette, *The King Within* (New York: W. Morrow, 1992) 242.

6 The Hebrew Scriptures were written, selected, and edited out of the verbal tradition between the 7th century B.C.E. and the 1st century C.E. The Christian Scriptures were written in the latter part of the 1st century, but were selected

starting about 150 C.E. and ending around 350 C.E.)

7   Jaroslav Pelikan, *The Christian Tradition: A History of the Development of Doctrine* (Alternate title: *The Emergence of the Catholic Tradition* (Chicago: University of Chicago Press, 1971) 61. It is interesting to note that Tertullian became a heretic, by his own definition (someone who teaches outside of the bounds of Christian theology), later in his career.

8   Thomas Merton, *Contemplation in a World of Action* (New York: Doubleday, 1971) 36.

9   Paul lived in the first century, and was the primary person who started churches in the non-Jewish world. Many of his letters to the churches he started are included in the Christian Bible.

10 Jaroslav Pelikan, *The Christian Tradition: A History of the Development of Doctrine* (Alternate title: *The Emergence of the Catholic Tradition*) (Chicago: University of Chicago Press, 1971) 222.

11 Luther did not want to create a new church, but due to many factors (including political ones) he and his followers found they had no choice.

12 J. J. Pelikan, H. C. Oswald, and H. T. Lehmann, eds, *Martin Luther, Luther's Works, Word, and Sacrament*, Vol. 35 (Philadelphia: Fortress Press) 236.

13 Paul Tillich, *Systematic Theology* (Chicago: University of Chicago Press, 1957) 37.

14 The Hebrew word used by the man to describe the woman is "ezer." This word is used in the Hebrew Bible only a few times and is often used to describe the help that God gives to humans. Thus, the word "ezer" in Genesis 2:20-22 means "strong partner" and does not imply a subservient position for the woman. From Dr. Walter Michel, class notes 1990, Lutheran School of Theology at Chicago.

15 Walter Bruggemann, *Genesis*, Gerald May, ed. (Atlanta: John Knox, 1982) 40-52. The serpent was not understood by the

Hebrew people to be Satan or the devil. Rather, it was simply a talking animal like those used in many theological stories of the day.

16 Covering up their "nakedness" has to do with their vulnerability and limitedness, and probably has little to do with sex.

17 Judith Plaskow, *Sex, Sin, and Grace* (University Press of America, 1980), 154.

18 From my friend Ken Nakata.

19 *The Book of Concord*, Theodore G. Tappert, ed. and trans., (Philadelphia: Fortress Press, 1959) 479.

20 The word "blessing" means "to speak well of" and refers to God empowering humans to do what we were made to do.

21 Christians often confuse limitation, grumpiness, or just plain stupidity as sin. If you are sick and get grumpy toward a family member, that is not sin; it is simply a human limitation. Sin would only enter into the picture if you failed to apologize, or used your illness as an opportunity to be mean and nasty.

22 I realize there are many more than three ways that people understand Christianity, and many subsets of these three. I find these three to be the most popular in our culture.

23 http://www.livingpulpit.org/ Douglas John Hall, *The Living Pulpit*, Copyright © 2000.

24 Many in my faith community understand "hell" to be more a way of being, than a place with devils with red-hot pokers. "Hell" is when you and I are separated from God and our true selves. In this section I am using the word "hell" in its usual way, a place the bad people go when they die, because this is the way it is often used in God-of-the-Gun Christianity.

25 Eugene Peterson, *The Message* (Colorado Springs: NavPress, 1996) 476.

26 Eugene Peterson, *The Message* (Colorado Springs: NavPress, 1996) 476.

27 Eugene Peterson, *The Message* (Colorado Springs: NavPress, 1996) 476.

28 Jesus also quotes this passage on several occasions: see Matthew 9:13 and 12:7.

29 Gerhard Forde, *Christian Dogmatics Vol. 2*, Bratten and Jenson, ed (Philadelphia; Fortress Press, 1984), 88.

30 Laurence Boadt, *Reading the Old Testament* (New York: Paulist Press, 1984), 272-273. This book has been a standard textbook for colleges and seminaries for years.

31 J. J. Pelikan, H. C. Oswald & H. T. Lehmann, eds, *Luther, M. Luther's Works, Vol. 29: Lectures on Titus, Philemon, and Hebrews* (Saint Louis: Concordia Publishing House 1999, ©1968).

32 Jaroslav Pelikan, *The Christian Tradition: A History of the Development of Doctrine* (Alternate title: *The Emergence of the Catholic Tradition* (Chicago: University of Chicago Press, 1971) 148.

33 M. Eugene Boring, Neil M. Alexander, ed., *The New Interpreter's Bible, Vol. VIII*, (Nashville: Abingdon Press, 1995) 399. The Hebrew Bible is written in Hebrew, but there was a translation of it called the Septuagint that was done around the year 350 B.C.E. The Greek word "lypton" was used in Exodus 6:6 and Deuteronomy 7:8 in the sense of rescue of the people from Egypt's Pharaoh. It is clear from both versions of the story that God certainly offered no ransom to the Pharaoh, who in that context was considered the embodiment of God's rival god. Some may notice the use of the word "ransom" in the Psalm referring to God ransoming us from the power of Sheol. Sheol was not understood by the Hebrew people to be "hell." It was a euphemism for death and a waiting room in which the dead waited for the Day of the Lord. See the Hebrew poetry in Hosea 13:14 in which Sheol is understood as death.

34 Douglas John Hall, *Lighten Our Darkness* (Philadelphia: Westminster Press, 1976) 149.

35 Gerhard Forde, *Christian Dogmatics Vol. 2*, Bratten and

Jenson, ed (Philadelphia; Fortress Press, 1984), 52. Here the word "atonement "means "how God reconciles us to God."

36 James Allison, *Raising Abel* (Also published under: *Living in the End Times: The Last Things Reimagined*, (London, SPCK 1996) 45-48.

37 Eugene Peterson, *The Message*. (Colorado Springs: NavPress, 2002) 2036.

38 Gerhard Forde, *Christian Dogmatics Vol. 2*, Bratten and Jenson, ed (Philadelphia; Fortress Press, 1984), 16.

39 Douglas John Hall, *Thinking the Faith, Professing the Faith, Confessing the Faith* (Minneapolis: Fortress Press, 1989, 1991, 1993).

40 Eugene Peterson, *The Message* (Colorado Springs: NavPress, 1996) 476.

41 *The Truman Show*, Paramount Studios, written by Andrew Niccol, Directed by Peter Weir, 1998.

42 Joseph Sittler, *Gravity and Grace*, ed. Linda M. Dellof (Augsburg Fortress Publishers, 1986) 99-100.

43 Robert G. L, Waite, *The Psychopathic God: Adolph Hitler* (New York: Basic Books, 1977) 31.

44 Robert G. L, Waite, *The Psychopathic God: Adolph Hitler* (New York: Basic Books, 1977) 16 – speech delivered 31 July 1937, Breslau.

45 Robert G. L, Waite, *The Psychopathic God: Adolph Hitler* (New York: Basic Books, 1977) 29.

46 René Girard, *I See Satan Fall Like Lightning*, trans. by James G. Williams (Maryknoll; Orbis Books, 2001) 158-159.

47 D. H. Lawrence, "Letter from Germany," in Pheonix, 2 Vols. (London: William Heinemann, 1936) 1:107-110

48 http://www.childlabournews.info ("Trafficking in Children to be Focused on June," and "Funding Call for Child Labour, Garment Workers" Child Labor News Service, 12 June 2003).

49 http://www.christianitytoday.com/ ("Anatomy of a Giver" (Parts 1 and 2) Christianity Today Magazine, May 19, 1997)

compare with Storm Batters Philanthropic Sector," Philanthropy News Digest, January 5, 2003, found at http://www.charitynavigator.org).

50 http://www.globalassignment.com/ ("Philanthropy in the US" Global Assignment Americans Abroad. The Adams Report 4-12-01).

51 http://www.thehungersite.com/ ("Hunger: Do Your Know The Facts?" and "Hunger and Poverty Facts." The Hunger Site, 2000-2003).

52 http://www.unicef.org/newsline/ ("UNICEF calls for eradication of commercial sexual exploitation of children" UNICEF Press Centre, 2003).

53 http://www.hillconnections.org/ ("Children at Risk" Hill Connections: Contemplation—Linking Faith with Action, May 2003).

54 http://www.who.int/nhr/information ("Health and the Fifty-Eighth Session of the United Nations Commission on Human Rights, 18 March to 26 April 2002." Palais des Nations, Geneva, World Health Organization).

55 World Heath Organization, "The Right to Water, 2003," found at http://www.who.int/water_sanitation_health/rightowater/en/

56 http://globalmarch.org/worstformsreport/global.html

57 Thich Nhat Hanh, The Heart of the Buddha's Teaching, (New York: Broadway Books) 32-33.

58 Tax collectors were outcast because they were Roman collaborators; to eat with them implied that you accepted them. "Sinners" were not necessarily people of poor moral character. Rather, they were simply economically poor and could not afford to pay the temple tax and purchase the correct animals to sacrifice to God. Pharisees believed that God was punishing the people of Israel, through Roman occupation, because the tax collectors and sinners where not faithful to God. Of course, the Pharisees thought they themselves were. By pointing to the sin of their divorce practices, Jesus points out

that they were not faithful. The divorce practices allowed rich men to perpetually divorce older wives in order to acquire younger wives. The divorced women were often forced into either prostitution or slavery.

59 From a speech by the Apostle Paul as recorded in Acts 22:3: "I am a Jew, born in Tarsus in Cilicia, but brought up in this city at the feet of Gamaliel, educated strictly according to our ancestral law, being zealous for God, just as all of you are today."

60 René Girard, *I See Satan Fall Like Lightning,* trans. by James G. Williams (Maryknoll; Orbis Books, 2001) See the Introduction by James G. Williams, but read the whole thing.

61 This means that, from the perspective of my faith community, a preoccupation with the "end of the world" is beside the point. When Luther was asked what he would do if he knew that Jesus was coming tomorrow, he replied, "I would plant an apple tree." Some Christians view the world as a "throw-away" world because of their theories regarding the end times. My faith community believes that God is committed to the life and health of this world. For ancient peoples, stories of the "end times" were used much in the same way as creation stories: stories used to talk about our current situation, and about the meaning of life. Nevertheless, we do believe that God will one day make the world whole. See Revelation 21:1-5

62 Dietrich Bonhoeffer was a Lutheran Pastor in Germany who could have escaped to America but chose to go back to Germany and resist the Nazis. He was part of a plot to kill Hitler. He was killed a few days before his prison was liberated by the Allied troops.

63 Eugene Peterson, *The Message* (Colorado Springs: NavPress, 1996) 476.

64 I do not mean to say that doing degrading things or being physically or emotionally abused is of God. God intends us

to live in mutually loving relationships. Those in such abusive relationships have a responsibility to themselves and to God to work to heal the family's way of relating; and failing that, to leave it. I do mean that cleaning bathrooms and caring for the physical needs of family members is of God.

Selected Bibliography

General Audiences

- *Why Christian,* Douglas John Hall (Minneapolis, Fortress Press, 2001)
- *Biblical Authority or Biblical Tyranny? Scripture and the Christian Pilgrimage,* L. William Countryman (Boston, Cowley Publications, 1994)
- *The Bible Makes Sense,* Walter Bruggemann (Winona, St.Mary's Press, 1997)
- *Luther the Reformer:The Story of the Man and His Career,* James M. Kittelson (Minneapolis, Augsburg, 1986)
- *Amazing Grace: A Vocabulary of Faith,* Kathleen Norris (New York, Riverhead Books, 1998)
- *The Message: The Bible in Contemporary Language,* Eugene S. Peterson (Colorado Springs, Navpress, 2002)
- *The New Oxford Annotated Bible,* New Revised Standard Version, (New York, Oxford University Press, 2001)
- *Simpler Living, Compassionate Life: A Christian Perspective,* Michael Schut (Denver, Living the Good News, 1999)
- *The Powers That Be: Theology for a New Millennium,* Walter Wink (New York, Galilee, Doubleday, 1998)
- *For Common Things: Irony, Trust, and Commitment in America Today,* Jedediah Purdy (New York, Vintage Books, 2000)

- *The New Interpreter's Bible: A Commentary in Twelve Volumes*, Leander E. Keck, Ed. (Nashville, Abingdon Press, 1995)
- *The Overspent American: Why We Want What We Don't Need*, Juliet B. Schor (New York, Harper Perennial, 1998)
- *The Book of God*, Walter Wangerin Jr. (Nashville, Zondervan, 1998)
- *Celebration of Discipline*, Richard Foster (San Francisco HarpersSanfrancisco, 1988)
- *Prayer: Finding the Hearts True Home*, Richard Foster (San Francisco, HarpersSanfrancisco, 1992)
- *Life of the Beloved*, Henri Nouwen (New York, Crossroads, 2002)
- *In Search of God: Meditation in the Christian Tradition*, W. Herbstrith (New York, New City Press, 1989)
- Any of the books in the Lutheran Voices series: see www.augsburgfortress.org
- Any of the books in The New Church's Teaching Series (Episcopalian): see www.cowley.org
- *The Rapture Exposed*, Barbara Rossing (Boulder, Westview Press, 2004)

Pastors and Leaders
- *Thinking the Faith*, Douglas John Hall (Minneapolis, Augsburg Fortress, 1989)
- *Professing the Faith*, Douglas John Hall (Minneapolis, Augsburg Fortress, 1993)
- *Confessing the Faith*, Douglas John Hall (Minneapolis, Augsburg Fortress, 1996)
- *Prepare a Road: Preaching Vocation*, Community Voice, Marketplace Vision, Kim L. Beckman (Cambridge, Cowley, 2002)
- *The Unnecessary Pastor: Rediscovering the Call*, Marva Dawn and Eugene Peterson (Vancouver, Regent College Publishing, 2000)
- *The Wolf Shall Dwell with the Lamb: A Spirituality for Leadership in a Multicultural Community*, Eric H. F. Law (St. Louis, Chalice Press, 1993)
- *Raising Abel*, James Allison (London, SPCK, 1996)

- *I See Satan Fall Like Lightning*, René Girard (Maryknoll, Orbis, 2002)
- *The Powers That Be: Theology for a New Millennium*, Walter Wink (Minneapolis, Augsburg Fortress, 1999)
- *Naming the Powers: The Language of Power in the New Testament*, Walter Wink (Minneapolis, Augsburg Fortress, 1983)
- *When the Powers Fall: Reconciliation in the Healing of Nations*, Walter Wink (Minneapolis, Augsburg Fortress, 1998)
- *Engaging the Powers: Discernment and Resistance in a World of Domination*, Walter Wink (Minneapolis, Augsburg Fortress, 1986)
- *Unmasking the Powers: The Invisible Forces That Determine Human Existence*, Walter Wink (Minneapolis, Augsburg Fortress, 1986)
- *The New Testament World: Insights from Cultural Anthropology*, Bruce J. Malina (Louisville, Westminster John Knox Press, 2001)
- *Battle For God*, Karen Armstrong (New York, Ballentine, 2000)
- *Is Nothing Sacred? When Sex Invades the Pastoral Relationship*, Marie M Fortune (San Francisco, Harper and Row, 1989)
- *Lutheranism: The Theological Movement and Its Confessional Writings*, Eric W. Gritsch (Philadelphia, Fortress Press, 1976)
- *The Creed*, Luke Timothy Johnson (New York, Doubleday, 2003)
- *Religion and Public Life in the Northwest: the None Zone*, Patricia O'Connell Killen and Mark Silk, Ed. (Walnut Creek, AltaMira Press, 2004)
- *Rise of Christianity*, Rodney Stark (New York, HarperCollins, 1997)

About The Author

Terry Kyllo attended seminary at the Lutheran School of Theology at Chicago, receiving his Masters of Divinity (a four-year degree required for Lutheran ordination) in 1991. Having served two previous congregations, he is now Pastor of Celebration Lutheran Church in Anacortes, Washington. Celebration is engaged in an ecumenical partnership with four Episcopal congregations, and Terry serves on a team of pastors who attend to each of these congregations.

Terry's path to pastoral vocation began when in high school he was told that he could not accept evolutionary theory and be a Christian. This created a tension in his life between Christianity and the modern world that ultimately led him away from Christianity for a time. Eventually realizing that it must be possible to both be a Christian and live in today's world, he passionately engaged in conversation and study to discover the underlying bases for these seemingly contradictory viewpoints and to reconcile those ideas. Being Human has grown out of this passion.

Terry grew up in Lacrosse, Washington, a wheat-farming town of 300 people in southeastern corner of the state. His father was a custodian at the school, and his mother was a homemaker who was diagnosed with Multiple Sclerosis when Terry was five. From the experience of his mother's illness, Terry learned that life is fragile and is to be honored. He is still learning from his father's faithfulness in the midst of illness.

Terry lives in Anacortes, Washington, with his wife and two children.

Printed in the United States
202177BV00002B/139/A

W9-BAT-110

At a Glance

Color Atlas
of Human Anatomy

in 3 volumes

Volume 2: Internal Organs
by Helga Fritsch and Wolfgang Kuehnel

Volume 3: Nervous System and Sensory Organs
by Werner Kahle and Michael Frotscher

Volume 1

Locomotor System

Werner Platzer, MD

Professor Emeritus
Former Chairman, Institute for Anatomy
University of Innsbruck
Innsbruck, Austria

Doctor of Science
Wake Forest University
Winston-Salem
North Carolina, USA

6th revised and enlarged edition

215 color plates
Illustrations by Professor Gerhard Spitzer

Thieme
Stuttgart · New York

Library of Congress Cataloging-in-Publication Data is available from the publisher

1st Bulgarian edition 2005
1st Chinese edition 2000
1st Czech edition 1996

1st German edition 1976
2nd German edition 1978
3rd German edition 1979
4th German edition 1984
5th German edition 1986
6th German edition 1991
7th German edition 1999
8th German edition 2003
9th German edition 2005

1st English edition 1978
2nd English edition 1984
3rd English edition 1986
4th English edition 1992
5th English edition 2004

1st Dutch edition 1978
2nd Dutch edition 1981
3rd Dutch edition 1990
4th Dutch edition 2000
5th Dutch edition 2006
1st French edition 1979
2nd French edition 1983
3rd French edition 2001
4th French edition 2006
1st Hungarian edition 1996
1st Greek edition 1985
1st Indonesian edition 1983
2nd Indonesian edition 2000
1st Italian edition 1979
2nd Italian edition 1987
3rd Italian edition 2000
4th Italian edition 2007
1st Japanese edition 1979
2nd Japanese edition 1981
3rd Japanese edition 1984
4th Japanese edition 1990
5th Japanese edition 2002
1st Polish edition 1998
1st Portuguese edition 1988
2nd Portuguese edition 2007
1st Serbo-Croatian edition 1991
2nd Croatian edition 2003
1st Spanish edition 1977
2nd Spanish edition 1988
3rd Spanish edition 2001
4th Spanish edition 2007
1st Turkish edition 1987

© 2009 Georg Thieme Verlag,
Rüdigerstrasse 14, 70469 Stuttgart, Germany
http://www.thieme.de
Thieme New York, 333 Seventh Avenue,
New York, NY 10001, USA
http://www.thieme.com

Cover design: Thieme Publishing Group
Typesetting by Druckhaus Götz GmbH, Ludwigsburg
Printed in China by Everbest Printing Co Ltd

ISBN 978-3-13-533306-9   1 2 3 4 5 6

Important note: Medicine is an ever-changing science undergoing continual development. Research and clinical experience are continually expanding our knowledge, in particular our knowledge of proper treatment and drug therapy. Insofar as this book mentions any dosage or application, readers may rest assured that the authors, editors, and publishers have made every effort to ensure that such references are in accordance with **the state of knowledge at the time of production of the book.**

Nevertheless, this does not involve, imply, or express any guarantee or responsibility on the part of the publishers in respect to any dosage instructions and forms of applications stated in the book. **Every user is requested to examine carefully** the manufacturers' leaflets accompanying each drug and to check, if necessary in consultation with a physician or specialist, whether the dosage schedules mentioned therein or the contraindications stated by the manufacturers differ from the statements made in the present book. Such examination is particularly important with drugs that are either rarely used or have been newly released on the market. Every dosage schedule or every form of application used is entirely at the user's own risk and responsibility. The authors and publishers request every user to report to the publishers any discrepancies or inaccuracies noticed. If errors in this work are found after publication, errata will be posted at www.thieme.com on the product description page.

Some of the product names, patents, and registered designs referred to in this book are in fact registered trademarks or proprietary names even though specific reference to this fact is not always made in the text. Therefore, the appearance of a name without designation as proprietary is not to be construed as a representation by the publisher that it is in the public domain.

This book is an authorized and revised translation of the 9th German edition published and copyrighted 2005 by Georg Thieme Verlag, Stuttgart, Germany. Title of the German edition: Taschenatlas der Anatomie, Band 1: Bewegungsapparat.

Translator: Terry C. Telger, Fort Worth, Texas, USA
(Parts from previous English edition.)

Illustrations: Professor Gerhard Spitzer, with contributions by Stefanie Gay, Lothar Schnellbächer, and Stefan Spitzer

Preface to the Sixth Edition of Volume 1

It is with great joy that I thank all those who have purchased this book during the past three decades. Your interest has prompted the creation of a sixth edition, which contains new material as well as corrections of minor errors that have entered the text over time. Without you, dear readers, these refinements would not have been possible.

Since the fifth edition was published, we have gradually rediscovered the importance of morphology, recognizing that **morphology is essential in patient care**. As a result, much of the new material in the sixth edition is presented in the form of Clinical Tips.

A "Latin Equivalents" page has been added to each chapter for interested readers. I have also included more eponyms in this edition, in recognition of the growing but regrettable trend toward the more frequent use of proper names in anatomical terms.

The new edition also has color-keyed borders, making it easier to locate specific chapters, and it includes references to certain Latin terms that are essential for international communication. Finally, I have added an Index of Proper Names that are used in anatomical eponyms, while noting that a number of terms are associated with more than one name.

I am grateful to Thieme Medical Publishers and especially to Dr. Clifford Bergman, Mr. Stephan Konnry, and Ms Elisabeth Kurz, who readily agreed to my wishes and did an outstanding job in the production of this edition.

First and foremost, I dedicate this edition to my wife, Liselotte Platzer, MD, who has stood by my side for many years, and to our daughters, Beatrix Volc-Platzer, MD, Associate Professor, and Ulrike Dapunt, MD Secondly, I dedicate this book to Wake Forest University in Winston-Salem, North Carolina, for conferring upon me an honorary Doctor of Science degree.

Werner Platzer

Preface to the First Edition of Volume 1

This volume provides a concise outline of the locomotor apparatus and of the topography of the peripheral pathways related to the musculoskeletal system. It is meant to complement and not to replace larger textbooks of anatomy. Anatomy is best brought to life by visualizing it, so a particularly large number of illustrations has been included. They have been made from *specially* prepared specimens and, whenever possible, variants have been shown as they appeared in original dissection. For greater clarity the illustrations have been supplemented by schematic drawings, some of which have been taken from other monographs.

The publisher's artists deserve special thanks because it is only their skill that has allowed the author's intentions to be realized. *G. S. Spitzer* drew the most difficult preparations with sympathy and clarity, *L. Schnellbächer* was responsible for the skilled reproduction of the majority of the systematic illustrations, and *D. Klittich* undertook the legends and the production of some drawings.

The illustrators were dependent on skilled anatomical dissections for which the author wishes particularly to thank Dr. *H. Maurer.* The format of the publication has demanded some reduction in the scale of their endeavors, but for their experience, corrections and many hours of discussion I am most grateful to my indefatigable assistants, Docent Dr. *S. Poisel* and Dr. *R. Putz.*

I wish to thank Prof. *A. Ravelli,* Head of the Department of Radiological Anatomy of our Institute, for the radiographs which have been used as the basis for many illustrations. Similarly, many others not mentioned here made great efforts to help this book to success, and I am grateful to all of them. First and foremost, this book is intended for medical students, but it will also provide information on human morphology for the interested layman. If there are a few mistakes of omission, I would appreciate suggestions and criticism from all my colleagues.

Particular mention must be made, too, of Dr. h.c. *G. Hauff* and his assistants, notably *A. Menge,* for their understanding and support. The publishers afforded all possible aid to further production of the book.

This volume is dedicated to my wife, whom I must thank for reading the proofs of the German Edition, and to my daughters *Beatrix* and *Ulrike.*

Innsbruck, September 1975   Werner Platzer

Contents

viii   Contents

Topography of Peripheral Nerves and Vessels 333

General Anatomy

The Body

Parts of the Body (A, B)

The body is divided into the main part of the body (*trunk in the wider sense*) and the upper and lower limbs, *extremities.* The trunk is divided into the head, the neck, and the torso (*trunk in the narrower sense*). The torso consists of the *thorax, abdomen,* and *pelvis.*

The upper extremity is joined to the trunk by the shoulder girdle and the lower extremity by the pelvic girdle. The shoulder girdle consists of the clavicles (**1**) and the scapulas (**2**), which lie on the trunk and move on it. The pelvic girdle, which consists of the two hip (coxal) bones (**3**) and the sacrum (**4**), forms an integral part of the trunk.

General Terms (A–G)

Principal Axes

The *longitudinal (vertical) axis,* long axis (**5**) of the body, is vertical when the body is held in an upright posture.

The *transverse (horizontal) axis* (**6**) is perpendicular to the long axis and runs from left to right.

The *sagittal axis* (**7**) runs from the back to the front surface of the body in the direction of an arrow (sagittal) and is perpendicular to the other two axes.

Principal Planes

Median plane, the plane through the longitudinal axis and the sagittal axis; it is also called the *median sagittal* or *midsagittal plane* (**8**). It divides the body into two almost equal halves, or *antimeres* (hence also called *plane of symmetry*). It includes the longitudinal and sagittal axes.

Sagittal or *paramedian plane* (**9**), any plane which is parallel to the median sagittal plane.

Frontal or *coronal plane* (**10**), any plane which contains the transverse and longitudinal axes and is parallel to the forehead and perpendicular to the sagittal planes.

Transverse planes (**11**) lie perpendicular to the sagittal planes and to the coronal planes. They are horizontal in the upright posture and contain the sagittal and transverse axes.

Directions in Space

cranial = toward the head (**12**)
superior = upward with the body erect (**12**)
caudal = toward the buttocks (**13**)
inferior = downward with the body erect (**13**)
medial = toward the middle, toward the median plane (**14**)
lateral = away from the middle, away from the median plane (**15**)
medius = in the midline (**16**)
median = in the median plane
deep (profundus) = toward the inner body (**17**)
peripheral, superficial = toward the body surface (**18**)
rostral = toward the rostrum (beak), towards the oral and nasal region
anterior = toward the front (**19**)
ventral = toward the abdomen (**19**)
posterior = toward the back (**20**)
dorsal = toward the back (**20**)
proximal = toward the trunk (**21**)
distal = farther away from the trunk (**22**)
ulnar = toward the ulna (**23**)
radial = toward the radius (**24**)
tibial = toward the tibia (**25**)
fibular = toward the fibula (**26**)
palmar (volar) = on or toward the palm of the hand (**27**)
plantar = on or toward the sole of the foot (**28**)

Directions of Movement

flexion = the act of bending
extension = the act of straightening
abduction = movement away from the median plane
adduction = movement toward the median plane
rotation = movement around an axis
circumduction = circular (circumferential) movement

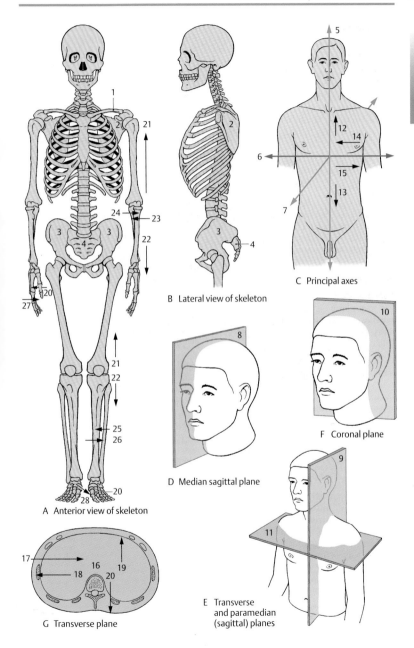

C Principal axes

B Lateral view of skeleton

D Median sagittal plane

F Coronal plane

A Anterior view of skeleton

E Transverse and paramedian (sagittal) planes

G Transverse plane

The Cell (A)

The smallest living entity is the *cell*. There are unicellular organisms, *protozoa*, and multicellular organisms, *metazoa*. Human cells range in size from 5 to 200 µm. They live for different lengths of time. Some cells survive for only a few days, e.g., granular leukocytes of the blood, and others survive the whole of the human life span, e.g., nerve cells.

Cells differ in shape depending on their function (for example, muscle cells are elongated).

Each cell consists of the cell body, *cytoplasm* (**1**), and the nucleus, *karyoplasm* (**2**), containing one or more *nucleoli* (**3**). The nucleus is separated from the cytoplasm by the double membrane, *nuclear envelope* (**4**).

Cytoplasm

The cytoplasm is subdivided into **organelles**, **cytoskeleton**, and **cell inclusions**. These structures are contained in a fluid component, the **cytosol**.

The cell membrane, *plasma membrane* or *plasmalemma* (**5**), appears as a trilamellar structure in electron micrographs. The cell surface is irregular and may exhibit fine processes, *microvilli*. The cell membrane is covered by a thick coat, the *glycocalyx*, of about 20 nm. The glycocalyx is species-specific as well as cell-specific, thus facilitating cell–cell recognition.

Organelles

The *endoplasmic reticulum* (*ER*) (**6**) consists of a system of interconnected cisterns; it may be granular (rough ER) (**6**) or agranular (smooth ER). The rough ER has small granules, *ribosomes*, attached to the cytoplasmic side of its membrane. The ribosomes are approximately 15–25 nm in diameter and are made up of ribonucleic acid and protein molecules. The rough ER is involved in protein synthesis, while the smooth ER fulfills various other functions (it plays a role, for example, in lipid metabolism of hepatocytes).

The *mitochondria* (**7**) are of special importance as they provide the cell with energy. They are long flexible, rod-shaped organelles which move about in the cytoplasm. They vary in number and size depending on the type and functional state of the cell.

The *Golgi apparatus* (**8**) consists of several *dictyosomes*, or *Golgi stacks*. Each dictyosome consists of a stack of disc-shaped cisterns. The Golgi apparatus is responsible the formation and supplementation of the glycocalyx but is also involved in the synthesis and modification of carbohydrates and polypeptides produced in the ER.

Other organelles are the *lysosomes* (**9**) and *peroxisomes* (microbodies).

Cytoskeleton

The cytoskeleton consists of *microtubules* (including the *centrioles*, **10**, and *basal bodies*), *actin filaments* (microfilaments), and various cell-specific *intermediate filaments*. The two centrioles usually lie near the nucleus; together with the specialized cytoplasm surrounding them, the *centroplasm*, they form the *centrosome* (microtubule-organizing center). The cytoskeleton plays a major role in cell movement as well as intracellular movement (see page 6).

Cell Inclusions

These include ribosomes, *lipids* (**11**), *glycogen* (**12**), *pigments* (**13**), *crystals*, and other insoluble components.

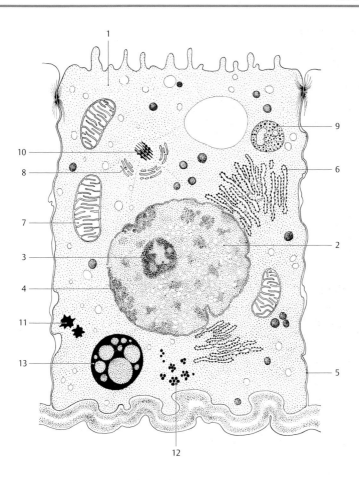

A Diagram of a cell according to electron-
microscopic findings
(from Faller, A.: Der Körper des Menschen,
13th Ed. Thieme, Stuttgart 1999)

Cell Nucleus (A, B)

The **nucleus** (**A**), karyoplasm, is essential for the life of the cell. Its size does depend on the size of the cell. Normally cells possess one or more nuclei. The nucleus is usually visible in living cells because it is more refractive than the cytoplasm; it is separated from the cytoplasm by the delicate birefringent nuclear membrane (**1**). Upon fixation, a network-like structure, *chromatin* (**2**), becomes visible in the *interphase nucleus* (resting nucleus between cell divisions). The chromatin carries the genetic material; it condenses in the *dividing nucleus* to form the *chromosomes*.

The micronucleus, *nucleolus* (**3**), consists of proteins and is rich in ribonucleic acid (RNA). The number and size of the nucleoli varies a great deal among different cells. In the cells of females, each active nucleus contains a clump of chromatin (Barr body), the *sex chromatin* (**4**), which is attached to the nuclear membrane or the nucleolus. It is used to determine the sex of a cell and hence of an individual. The sex chromatin is particularly easy to see in white blood cells (granulocytes) where it assumes the shape of a drumstick. In order to make the diagnosis of female sex, at least 6 drumsticks must be seen in 500 granulocytes.

Vital Cell Functions (C—H)

Every cell displays **metabolic activity** which can be divided into *structural metabolism* and *functional metabolism*. Structural metabolism is the ability of a cell to assimilate ingested material to build up cellular structures, while functional metabolism serves cellular functions.

The uptake of particular material is called *phagocytosis*, that of liquids *pinocytosis*. The release of substances by glandular cells is called *secretion*. The sum of oxidative processes within the cell is called *cell respiration*.

Among cellular **movements**, the *cytoplasmic movement* is the most important one and includes movements of mitochondria, vesicles, and inclusions. More pronounced movements occur during each cell division. The cells themselves move by *ameboid movement* initiated by cytoplasmic processes called *pseudopodia*. Ameboid movement is especially pronounced in white blood cells (such as granulocytes and monocytes). Certain cells move by means of *cilia*, or *kinocilia*, which arise from basal bodies (kinetosomes). When joined together, ciliated cells form a **ciliated epithelium** and create *ciliary movement*. A cell with only one prominent cilium (*flagellum*) is called a *flagellated cell*.

Reproduction of cells takes place by cell division. We distinguish between *mitosis, meiosis,* and *amitosis*. Each cell division requires division of the nucleus. The interphase nucleus changes into the dividing nucleus, and the chromosomes become visible and perform characteristic movements (*karyokinesis*) toward the two poles of the *mitotic spindle*.

The process of **mitosis** is subdivided into different phases, namely, *prophase* (**C**), *prometaphase* (**D**), *metaphase* (**E**), *anaphase* (**F, G**), and *telophase* (**H**). The nuclei of the two daughter cells are subsequently reorganized into interphase nuclei (*reconstruction phase*).

During **meiosis** (*reductional division*) the number of chromosomes per cell is reduced by half from the diploid to the haploid complement. The reduction takes place in both male and female germ cells during the first (or second) meiotic division and is required in preparation for fertilization.

During **amitosis** (*direct nuclear division*) the nucleus is divided by simple cleavage without chromosomal condensation and without the formation of a mitotic spindle. The distribution of chromosomes is therefore at random. The nuclear division may or may not be followed by division of the cytoplasm.

For more details, see *Histologie, Zytologie und Mikroanatomie des Menschen* by Leonhardt, H., 8th edition, Thieme, Stuttgart, 1990; Taschenatlas der Zytologie, Histologie und mikroskopischen Anatomie by Kühnel, W., 11th edition, Thieme, Stuttgart, 2002.

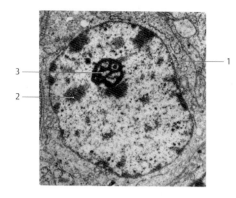

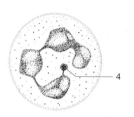

A Cell nucleus, ×12 000; electron micrograph

B White blood cells with sex chromatin attached to the segmented nucleus, ×1000
(Figs. A and B taken from Leonhardt, H.: Human Histology and Cytology, 8th Ed. Thieme, Stuttgart 1990)

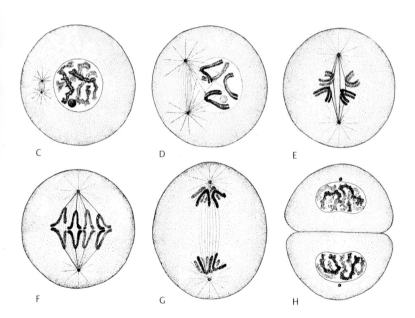

C–H Diagram of mitosis
(from Leonhardt, H.: Human Histology, Cytology, and Microanatomy, 8th Ed. Thieme, Stuttgart 1990)

Tissues

Tissues are aggregations of similarly differentiated cells and their derivatives. Several tissues may be associated to form an **organ**. The manner in which different cells are associated determines the different types of tissues. A more common system of classifying tissues is based not on the manner of association of cells but on their histological structure and physiological functions. **Epithelial, supportive,** and **muscular tissues** are described in this volume. Nervous tissue is discussed in volume 3.

Epithelia (A–G)

Epithelial tissues are associations of closely adjoining cells. They can be classified according to **function**, as well as to the **organization** and **shape** of their epithelial cells.

On the basis of their **functions**, superficial, glandular and sensory epithelia can be distinguished. **Superficial epithelium** is, first of all, *a protective epithelium* which forms a covering over the external and internal body surfaces and prevents bacteria from entering the body or the body from drying up. Moreover, the epithelia, for example, the *secretory and absorptive types*, bring about the exchange of materials, that is, they can, on the one hand, take up substances (absorption) and, on the other hand, eliminate different substances (secretion). Epithelial tissue also takes up stimuli. This reception of stimuli takes place in superficial epithelium in which different, specialized epithelial cells become induced.

Glandular epithelium represents all epithelial cells which form a secretion and release it to an external or internal surface by an excretory duct (**exocrine glands**) or release it directly into the vascular system as a hormone (**endocrine glands**).

Exocrine glands can be classified as *endoepithelial* or *exoepithelial* depending upon their relationship to the superficial epithelium. Likewise, these glands can be divided into *eccrine, apocrine* and *holocrine* glands on the basis of the amount and manner of their secretions.

Eccrine cells are always ready to secrete and occur within the respiratory, digestive and genital tracts (see vol. 2). Apocrine glands are represented by the mammary and the odoriferous, axillary sweat glands; holocrine glands are represented by the sebaceous glands.

The **sensory epithelia** represent specialized epithelia within the individual sense organs and are discussed with them.

All epithelia rest on a basement membrane *(basal membrane)* which represents the boundary layer to the underlying connective tissue.

On the basis of their **organization**, epithelia can be divided into **simple** (single-layered, **A, B, C**), **stratified** (multilayered, **D**), or **pseudostratified** (**F**) epithelia. In the stratified epithelium only the deepest layer of cells makes contact with the basement membrane, whereas in the pseudostratified epithelium all cells contact the basement membrane, but not all the cells reach the surface.

On the basis of the **shape** of the epithelial cells, epithelia can be classified as **squamous** (**A**), **cuboidal** (**B**), or **columnar** (**C**) **epithelia**.

Squamous epithelium, a markedly protective epithelium, can be *nonkeratinized* or *keratinized*. The epithelium of the skin is keratinized squamous epithelium, whereas nonkeratinized squamous epithelium (**E**) is found in parts of the inner surfaces of the body which are particularly vulnerable to mechanical stress, for example, the oral cavity. Simple nonkeratinized squamous epithelium consists of attenuated, pavement-like cells which include serous membranes (**mesothelium**) and the lining epithelium of blood and lymphatic vessels (**endothelium**). Columnar and cuboidal cells can possess processes, cilia, in which case one can speak of a **ciliated epithelium** (**F**), for example, that which lines the respiratory tract.

Cuboidal and columnar epithelia possess secretory and absorptive properties. They are found, for example, in the renal tubules (cuboidal) and in the intestinal tract (columnar). **Transitional epithelium** (**G**) is a special form of epithelium. Its cells can adapt themselves to different conditions of tension (distension and contraction) and make up the epithelium which lines the efferent urinary tract.

A Simple squamous epithelium
(pavement epithelium)

B Simple cuboidal epithelium

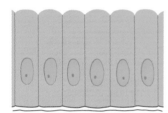

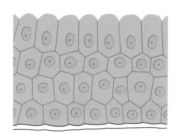

C Simple columnar epithelium

D Stratified columnar epithelium

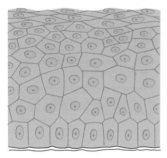

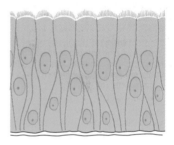

E Squamous stratified epithelium
(nonkeratinized)

F Pseudostratified ciliated epithelium

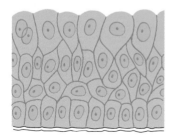

G Transitional epithelium

Connective Tissue and Supporting Tissues

These tissues consist of complex combinations of cells, including **fixed** and **free cells**, and **intercellular substance**. The fixed cells are named according to the type of tissue, for example, connective tissue cells, cartilage cells, bone cells, etc. The intercellular substance in mature supporting tissue consists of *ground substance* and *differentiated fibers*.

Some of the principal types are:

Connective tissue: embryonic, reticular, interstitial, and rigid connective tissue and fatty (adipose) tissue.

Cartilage tissue: hyaline, elastic, and fibrous cartilage.

Bone.

Connective Tissue (A, B)

In addition to fixed and free cells, the intercellular substance contains reticular, collagen, and elastic fibers, ground substance, proteoglycans and glycoproteins.

Fixed cells: **Fibrocytes** (highly branched cells; their precursors, the fibroblasts, are able to produce intercellular substance and fibers), **mesenchymal cells**, **reticulum cells**, **pigment cells**, and **fat cells**.

Free cells: **histiocytes** (polymorphic cells), **mast cells** (capable of ameboid movement) and, less commonly, **lymphocytes, plasma cells, monocytes,** and **granulocytes**.

The **intercellular substance** contains fibers—*reticular (lattice) fibers*—which resemble collagen in their structure (see below). They form fiber networks around capillaries, in basement membranes, around renal tubules, and elsewhere. The second group of *collagen* fibers consist of fibrils held together by an amorphous adhesive substance. They are found in all kinds of supporting tissues. They are wavy, almost unstretchable and always occur grouped in bundles. This type is found particularly in tendons, the tympanic membrane, etc. Different types of collagen (I and III) are found in connective tissue, and these are dependent on the structure of the collagen molecules. Finally, there are the (yellowish) *elastic fibers*, which are also arranged in networks. They occur in arteries near the heart, certain

ligaments (ligamenta flava, see p. 56) and elsewhere. The intercellular substance also includes the **ground substance**, which is partly produced by the tissue cells. It is involved in the exchange of materials between tissue cells and the blood.

Embryonic connective tissue: contains mesenchymal cells and the most important type is mesenchyme.

Reticular connective tissue (**A**) contains reticular fibers and *reticular cells* which are able to phagocytize and store material. They have a remarkably active metabolism. This type of connective tissue can be divided into *lymphoreticular* (in lymph nodes, etc.) and *myeloreticular* (bone marrow) connective tissue.

Interstitial connective tissue is a loose tissue with no particular structure. Its main purpose is to fill gaps between individual structures (muscles, etc.) and it also forms a displacement layer. In addition to these functions, interstitial connective tissue takes part in general metabolism and regeneration. As well as cells (fibrocytes, fat cells) it contains collagen, elastic and lattice fibers, and ground substance.

Rigid connective tissue (**B**) contains a high proportion of collagen fibers and fewer cells and less ground substance than interstitial connective tissue. It is found in the palmar and plantar aponeuroses, in tendons, etc.

Fatty tissue contains large cells with a flattened nucleus lying at the cell margin. *Monovacuolar white fatty* (adipose) *tissue* should be distinguished from *plurivacuolar brown fat*. The latter is more common in infants than in adults, e.g., in the fatty capsule around the kidney. In addition to fat cells, it contains interstitial connective tissue and shows some lobular structure. There is **storage fatty tissue**, which is dependent on the nutritional state, and **structural fatty tissue**, which is independent of nutrition. The latter occurs in joints, bone marrow, the fat pads in the cheeks, etc. The storage type is most common in the subcutaneous fat layer. It is broken down according to requirements and the cells take on the form of reticular cells. After very marked weight loss (cachexia), their cytoplasm fills up with fluidserous fat cells.

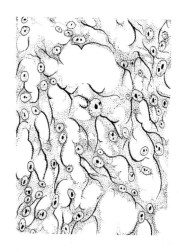

A Reticular connective tissue, ×300

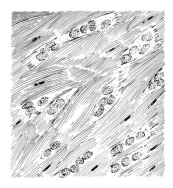

B Dense connective tissue in the corium, ×300
(Figs. A and B taken from Leonhardt, H.:
Human Histology, Cytology, and Micro-
anatomy, 8th Ed. Thieme, Stuttgart 1990)

Cartilage (A–C)

Cartilage is compressible as well as flexible, yet **resistant to pressure and to bending**, and soft enough to be cut. It consists of cells and intercellular substance, which is almost free of vessels and nerves. The nature of the intercellular substance determines the type of cartilage, which can be subdivided into **hyaline, elastic**, and **fibrous** forms.

Cartilage cells, *chondrocytes*, are fixed cells rich in water, glycogen, and fat. They have a vesicular appearance, a spherical shape and a similarly shaped nucleus. The *intercellular substance*, which is very rich in water (up to 70%), forms the basis of the protective function of cartilage. Cartilage is almost avascular and free of nerves; it is formed of fibrils or fibers and an amorphous ground substance containing proteoglycans, glycoproteins, lipids, and electrolytes.

Hyaline Cartilage (A)

Hyaline cartilage is slightly **bluish** and milky and contains abundant collagenous fibrils (converted to gelatin by boiling) and scattered elastic networks within its intercellular substance. In articular cartilage, the collagenous fibrils always course in the direction of the strongest stress. The cells occupying the cartilaginous lacunae are surrounded by a capsule which is separated from the remaining intercellular substance by the *cellular halo*. The cells, which can be organized more or less into rows or columns (p. 16), form, together with the cellular halo, a *chondrone* or *territory*. In this case it always concerns several daughter cells arising from one cell. Externally, the cartilage is surrounded by a connective tissue covering, the *perichondrium*, which blends into the cartilage more or less continuously.

Hyaline cartilage exposed to pressure (joint surfaces at the lower limb) contains more glycosaminoglycans (chondroitin sulfate) than less stressed hyaline cartilage (e.g., joint surfaces of the upper limb).

The lack of sufficient blood vessels may favor degenerative processes inside the cartilage. These are initiated by the "unmasking" of collagenous fibers, i.e., the collagenous fibrils become visible in the microscope. Since the content of water and chrondroitin sulfate decreases with age, the stress capacity of hyaline (articular) cartilage decreases.

Calcification of hyaline cartilage occurs very early in life.

Hyaline cartilage is found in joint cartilage, and rib cartilage, in respiratory tract cartilage, in epiphysial disks and in the precursors of those parts of the skeleton that undergo chondral ossification. **Epiphysial disk cartilage** contains columns or rows of cartilage cells, a structure which enables growth of cartilage (p. 16) and subsequently of the bone that follows it.

Elastic Cartilage (B)

In contrast to the bluish hyaline cartilage, elastic cartilage is **yellowish** in color. Its intercellular substance is rich in elastic fibers and contains fewer collagen fibrils. The large proportion of elastic fibers makes this type of cartilage particularly pliable and elastic. It does not contain calcified deposits. It is found in the auricle, the epiglottis, etc.

Fibrous Cartilage (C)

Fibrous cartilage, also known as connective tissue cartilage, contains fewer cells than the other types but has many *bundles of collagen fibers*. It is found particularly in parts of the intervertebral disks (p. 54) and of the symphysis pubis (p. 22).

General Anatomy

A Hyaline cartilage (rib cartilage),
   ×180

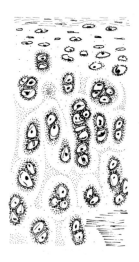

B Elastic cartilage (ear cartilage),
   ×180

C Fibrocartilage (intervertebral
   disk), ×180
   (Figs. A–C taken from Leonhardt,
   H.: Human Histology, Cytology,
   and Microanatomy, 8th Ed.
   Thieme, Stuttgart 1990)

Bone (A–B)

Bone tissue (osseous tissue) consists of bones cells (*osteocytes*), *ground substance*, *collagenous fibrils*, a *cement substance*, and *different salts*. The ground substance and collagenous fibrils form the intercellular substance, the *osteoid*. The fibrils belong to the organic part, the salts to the inorganic part. The most important salts are calcium phosphate, magnesium phosphate, and calcium carbonate. In addition, compounds of calcium, potassium, and sodium with chlorine and fluorine are also found.

The salts confer hardness and strength. A salt-free or "decalcified" bone is pliable. A deficiency in calcification can result from a lack of vitamins, as well as from hormonal disturbances. A lack of vitamins can arise, for example, when there is an absence of ultraviolet irradiation to the body resulting in a failure to convert provitamins into vitamins. Inadequate calcification leads to a softening of the bone, e.g., in rickets.

The organic constituents, like the salts, are also responsible for the strength of a bone. When there is inadequate organic material, the elasticity of the bone is lost, and as a result the bone becomes brittle and can no longer handle stress. The relationship between inorganic salts and collagenous fibrils becomes altered during life. In the newborn the content of inorganic salts amounts to about 50% and rises to 70% in the elderly along with a loss of elasticity, i.e., flexibility and resistance to shock decrease. Destruction of the organic matter can also be attained artificially by the use of heat.

Two types of bone can be distinguished on the basis of the arrangement of its fibrils: **woven bone** (reticulated) and **lamellar bone**. Nonlamellar, woven bone corresponds structurally to ossified connective tissue and in humans primarily occurs only during development. In the adult it is found only in the capsule of the inner ear and adjoining the sutures of the cranial bones.

The substantially more common and more important **lamellar bones** (A–B) exhibit a distinct stratification produced by layers of parallel-running collagenous fibrils which are designated as *lamellae* (**1**). These lamellae alternate with layers of *osteocytes* (**2**). The lamellar arrangement takes place around a vascular canal, the *central canal*, or *haversian canal* (**3**), which, together with its lamellae, constitutes an osteon or *haversian system* (**A**). The collagenous fibers are about 2–3 μm thick and are arranged spirally in such a way that a right (**4**) and a left spiral (**5**) lamella (5–10 μm thick) appear alternately with one another, thus bringing about an increase in stability.

Between the osteons are *interstitial lamellae* (**6**) which represent the remains of previous osteons. The vascular canals in the osteons are in communication with smaller *oblique canals*, the so-called *Volkmann's canals* (**7**). The structure and the organization of the osteons are dependent on the stress of the bone. When there is a change in stress, the osteons become reconstructed, as evidenced by macroscopic observation. In this case, attention should be especially paid to the behavior, within the femur, of the *trajectories*, the lines of tension, which are developed in response to the stresses.

The nourishment of bone takes place from the periosteum (p. 20). Bone marrow is nourished via the nutrient foramina (nutrient arteries).

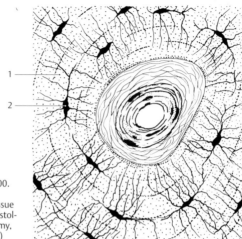

A Haversian system (osteon), ×400.
In the center a haversian vessel
with perivascular connective tissue
(from Leonhardt, H.: Human Histology, Cytology, and Microanatomy,
8th Ed. Thieme, Stuttgart 1990)

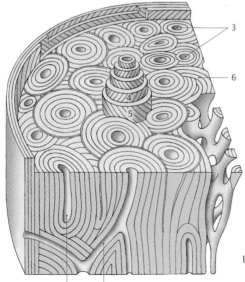

B Diagram of the compact part
of the diaphysis of a long bone

Development of Bone (A—C)

Bone formation (*osteogenesis*) is based on the activity of *osteoblasts* (**1**) which are specialized mesenchymal cells. Osteoblasts secrete an intercellular substance, the *osteoid*, which consists initially of soft ground substance and collagen fibers. Osteoblasts develop into *osteocytes*, the definitive bone cells. At the same time multinucleated *osteoclasts* (**2**) develop; these bone-degrading cells are associated with the absorption and remodeling of bone.

We distinguish *direct bone formation (intramembranous ossification)* (**A**) from *indirect bone formation (chondral ossification)* (**B, C**).

Intramembranous ossification, *osteogenesis membranacea* (**A**), is the development of bone from connective tissue. The latter contains many mesenchymal cells which develop via osteoblasts (**1**) into osteocytes. At the same time, osteoclasts (**2**) develop and collagen fibers also appear. The original bone is a membrane bone and is later remodeled into lamellar bone. The skull cap, the facial bones, and the clavicles develop as intramembranous bones.

Chondral ossification, *osteogenesis cartilaginea* (**B, C**), requires preformed parts of skeletal cartilage (cartilage models) which will then become replaced by bone. Growth is possible only as long as cartilage still remains. Prerequisite for replacement bone formation is the presence of *chondroclasts*; these are differentiated connective tissue cells that degrade cartilage and thus enable the osteoblasts to form bone. Two types of replacement bone formation are recognized—*endochondral* (**C**) and *perichondral ossification*.

Endochondral ossification (**3**) begins inside the cartilage, and occurs predominantly in the epiphyses. The **epiphyses** are the ends of the long bones (see p. 20), while the shafts are called **diaphyses**. *Perichondral ossification* (**4**), which originates in the perichondrium (**5**), is confined to the diaphysis. The *epiphysial disk* (growth plate) (**6**), which is necessary for growth in length, forms a layer between the epiphysis and the diaphysis. That part of the shaft adjacent to the epiphysial disk is called the **metaphysis** and develops first on an endochondral basis (see below).

Note: An *apophysis* is a bony outgrowth that does not arise from its own ossification center. An example is the mastoid process (pp. 288, 290), which originated purely in response to tendon traction.

Within the epiphysial cartilage, the processes of ossification occur in separate zones. In the epiphysis there is the *zone of reserve cartilage*, a capping of hyaline cartilage that is not affected by bone formation in the epiphysial plate. Next to this inactive cartilage is the *zone of growth* (**7**) where the cartilage cells form columns. Here the cartilage cells divide, thus increasing in number. The next layer closer to the shaft is the *zone of maturation* (**8**); it contains vesicular cartilage, and calcification is already occurring. It is followed by the *zone of ossification* where cartilage is degraded by chondroclasts and replaced with bone by osteoblasts. Some remnants of cartilage remain, so that the endochondral bone (**9**) of the diaphysis can be distinguished from the perichondral bone. It will later be replaced by perichondral bone. The endochondral bone is destroyed by the invading osteoclasts.

The increase in bone diameter in the region of the diaphysis is brought about by deposition of new bony material on the outer surface beneath the cellular layer of the periosteum. The *bone marrow cavity* (**10**) becomes larger as a result of bone destruction. All growth processes are regulated by hormones.

The bony anlagen in the epiphyses first appear after birth, except for those in the distal femoral epiphysis and the proximal tibial epiphysis. In both of these epiphyses, and in the cuboid bone, osteogenesis begins just before birth in the tenth intrauterine month (a sign of maturity).

Clinical tip: After closure of the epiphysial disk X-rays show a fine line, later, in adolescence, known as the **epiphysial disk scar**.

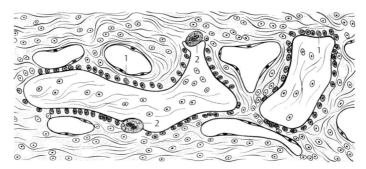

A Intramembranous ossification

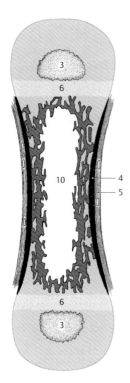

B Chondral ossification of a long bone
(diagram). Endochondral ossification
in the epiphyses and perichondral
ossification in the diaphysis

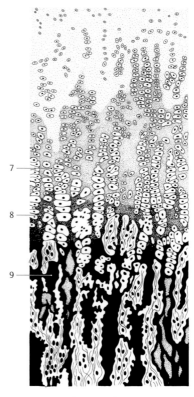

C Ossification in the region of
the epiphyseal disk cartilage

Muscular Tissue (A—D)

Muscular tissue is characterized by elongated cells containing myofibrils formed from myofilaments. These myofibrils are responsible for the contractility of the muscle cells. Three types of muscular tissue can be distinguished on the basis of fine structure and physiological characteristics: smooth (**A**), striated (**B, D**) and cardiac muscle (**C**).

Smooth Muscle (A)

Smooth muscle consists of spindle-shaped cells, each being 40–200 μm long and 4–20 μm thick, with a central nucleus. These myofibrils are difficult to demonstrate and do not have transverse striations. Transverse reticular fibers join adjacent muscle cells and bind groups into functional units. Smooth muscle is not under voluntary control; axons synapse directly with the muscle cells (see vol. 3).

Hormonal influences may cause smooth muscle to increase in length and to proliferate, i.e., there may not only be an increase in the size of the cells but cells may also be newly formed. An example is the uterus, the muscle fibers of which may reach a length of 800 μm.

Striated Muscle (B, D)

Striated muscle consists of muscle cells (muscle fibers) which may be 10–100 μm thick and up to 15 cm long. The nuclei lie immediately beneath the surface of the cells in the direction of the long axis of the muscle fibers. The myofibrils are easily visible and are responsible for the longitudinal striations. The transverse striations are due to the periodic alternation of smaller, lighter, singly refractive (isotropic) zones (I bands) and wider, darker, double-refractive (anisotropic) zones (A bands). The A bands contain a light zone (H band) with a fine, dark middle line (M band), and the I bands show a delicate, anisotropic intermediate line (Z band). The myofibrillar segment which lies between two Z bands is called a **sarcomere**.

Each skeletal muscle cell contains several nuclei. The cytoplasm (*sarcoplasm*) contains a variable number of mitochondria (*sarcosomes*). According to their function, a distinction is made between *twitch* muscle fibers and *tonic* muscle fibers. The twitch muscle fibers include red (fast twitch) muscle fibers with high myoglobin and mitochondria content (for long-term stress performance) and white muscle fibers with high myofibril content (for short-term maximum stress performance).

The color of a muscle is due to its blood supply and the myoglobin in solution in the sarcoplasm. In addition, the color is determined also by the water content and the abundance of fibrils. This explains why different muscles differ in color. Thinner fibers with less fibrils and water content are light in color, while thicker fibers appear darker.

The *sarcolemma* encloses individual muscle fibers as a connective tissue sheath. There is a delicate layer of connective tissue, the *endomysium*, between the fibers. Several muscle fibers are surrounded by the *internal perimysium*, and together they form the primary muscle bundle (fascicle).

The *external perimysium* is a connective tissue layer which combines several primary bundles to form a muscle.

Striated skeletal muscles are voluntary muscles, and they are innervated via motor endplates (neuromuscular junctions) (see vol. 3).

Striated Cardiac Muscle (C)

The muscle fibers of the heart contain a large amount of sarcoplasm and form networks. Transverse striations are present, but the sarcomeres are shorter and the I band is narrower than in skeletal muscle. In cardiac muscle fibers the nuclei lie centrally. *Sarcosomes* are far more numerous than in skeletal muscle. In addition, cardiac muscle tissue contains highly refractile, transverse *intercalated disks*, which lie at the position of a Z band. Further details are given in volume 2.

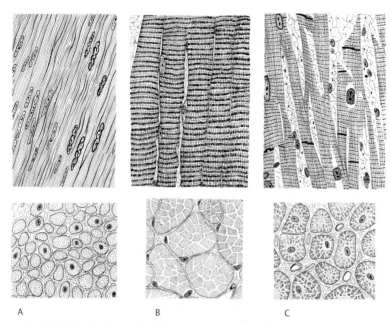

A   B   C

Longitudinal section (top row) and transverse section (bottom row) of smooth muscle (A), striated muscle (B), and cardiac muscle (C), ×400 (from Leonhardt, H.: Human Histology, Cytology, and Microanatomy. 8th Ed. Thieme, Stuttgart 1990)

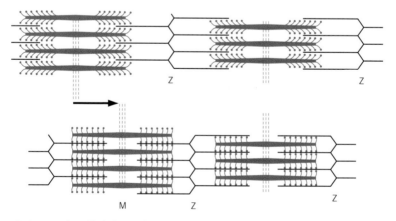

D Diagram of myofibrils during relaxation (top) and contraction (bottom)

General Features of the Skeleton

Classification of Bones (A–F)

The **bones** form the bony **skeleton**, and with the joints, they represent the passive locomotor system which is controlled by the active locomotor apparatus, the musculature. The different shapes of bones are dependent on their function and their position in the body. Macroscopically two differently constructed portions can be distinguished. A rather *dense compact* or *cortical bone* (**1**) is generally observed on the surface. Within the short and flat bones and in the epiphyses and metaphyses of the long bones, there is a spongelike meshwork formed of individual bony trabeculae, *trabecular* or *spongy bone* (**2**). Between the meshes is the bone marrow or medulla. In the flat bones of the skull, the compact material is called the *external* (**3**) and *internal* (**4**) *laminae* and in between them is the *diploe* (**5**), corresponding to the spongy bone.

Long Bones (A–C)

A long bone as, for instance, the humerus (**A**), consists of a *body* (**6**) and two *ends* (**7**). In the center of the shaft (body) of a long bone (**B**, **C**) is the bone marrow or *medullary cavity* (**8**), which contains red or yellow bone marrow. This cavity is the reason for the name "tubular bones." Tubular bones grow mainly in *one* direction.

Flat Bones (D)

Flat bones consist of two layers of compact bone between which there may be found spongy material. Flat bones include the scapula and several bones of the skull, e.g., the parietal bone (**D**). Basically, growth in flat bones proceeds in *two main* directions.

Short Bones (E)

The short bones, which include, for instance, the small bones of the wrist (e.g., the capitate bone [**E**]), have a spongy core surrounded by compact bone.

Irregular Bones

These include all those bones, such as vertebrae, which do not belong to any of the preceding groups.

Pneumatized Bones (F)

These bones contain air-filled cavities lined by mucous membrane (**9**). They are found in the skull (ethmoid, maxilla [**F**] etc.).

Sesamoid Bones

These mostly occur in the skeleton of the hands and feet. They may also be found in tendons, e.g., the *patella*, the largest sesamoid bone in the body.

Periosteum

The **periosteum** covers all parts of the bone which are not joint surfaces. It consists of a *fibrous layer* and an *osteogenetic layer* forming the cambium layer. It contains many blood and lymph vessels and nerves. The latter account for the pain felt after a blow to a bone. Larger blood vessels in the outer layer send numerous capillaries to the inner cell-rich layer. This is the site of the osteoblasts, which build up bone. After fractures, formation of new bone starts in the periosteum.

Blood vessels and nerves reach the bone through nutrient foramina. Some bones have canals which also serve for the passage of vessels, usually only veins, which are known as emissary veins. They are found, for example, in the vault of the skull.

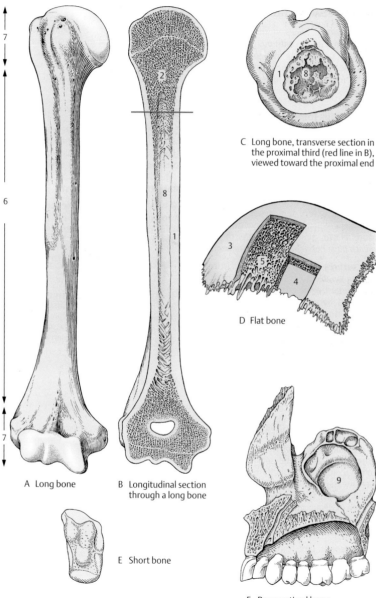

A Long bone

B Longitudinal section
through a long bone

C Long bone, transverse section in
the proximal third (red line in B),
viewed toward the proximal end

D Flat bone

E Short bone

F Pneumatized bone

Joints between Bones

The individual bones of the skeleton are connected either *continuously* or *discontinuously*. Continuous bony joints comprise the large group of **synarthroses**, in which two bones are joined directly by various tissues.

Continuous Joints between Bones (A–H)

Fibrous Joint (A–E) Syndesmosis

In a syndesmosis two bones are joined by collagenous or elastic connective tissue. The union may be expansive or narrow. The *interosseous membrane* (**A1**) in the forearm is a very taut syndesmosis consisting of collagenous connective tissue. More elastic syndesmoses are the *ligamenta flava* between the vertebral arches.

The **sutures of the skull** are a particular type of syndesmosis (**B, C, D, E**). These sutures retain connective tissue, which has persisted between the bones developing from connective tissue. Only when the connective tissue has completely disappeared does the growth of the skull cease and the sutures fuse. The sutures of the skull are classified according to their shape: *serrate suture* (**B**) with sawlike edges, as in the sagittal suture; *squamous suture* (**C, D**) where one bone overlaps another, as between the parietal bone and the temporal bone; and last, *plane suture* (**E**) as between the nasal bones.

A specialized type of fibrous joint is the **gomphosis**, a peg-and-socket joint found in the fixation of the teeth in the alveoli of the jaw. Here, the tooth is joined to the jaw by connective tissue which permits a slight degree of displacement.

Cartilaginous Joint (F) Synchondrosis

The second, large group of continuous bony joints is formed by the synchondroses (**F2**), which are joints of hyaline cartilage between two bones. During adolescence, these are always found in the *epiphysial disks*. Hyaline cartilage material is also present between the first, sixth, and seventh ribs and the sternum. The cartilaginous material disappears from those sites where it only permits growth. Epiphysial disks or cartilage are subsequently completely replaced by bony material.

Symphysis (G)

Symphyses are also cartilaginous joints in which two bones are bound by fibrocartilage and connective tissue, e.g., between the two pubic bones, *pubic symphysis* (**G**).

Bony Union (H), Synostosis

This is the firmest possible joint between two bones, e.g., between the parts of hip bone, or between epiphyses and diaphyses after growth has ceased.

> **Clinical tip:** Synovial joints may sometimes become synostotic. However, they are then not called synostoses, but ankyloses (stiffened joint). An **ankylosis** presupposes that the joint was previously movable, and the alteration is usually the result of a disease process. Physiological ankylosis is regarded as the fusion of the articular processes of the sacral vertebrae.

A Interosseous membrane

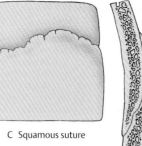

B Serrate suture

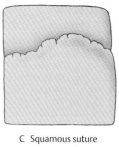

C Squamous suture

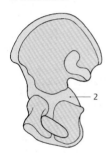

D Squamous suture
   in cross section

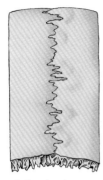

E Internasal suture

F Hip bone, medial view; cartilaginous interstices still present

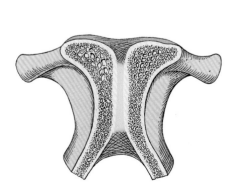

G Symphysis

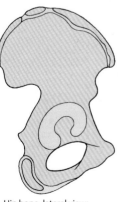

H Hip bone, lateral view;
   cartilaginous interstices closed

Discontinuous Joints between Bones (A–C)

These joints, **diarthroses** or **synovial joints**, consist of *articular surfaces* (**1**), an *articular capsule* (**2**), a *joint cavity* (**3**) between the articular surfaces, and, according to need, some *additional features* (strengthening ligaments, intercalated disks, articular lips [labra], and bursae).

In a joint with two articular surfaces or bodies, that articular body which is moved is the *movable segment*; the one at comparative rest is the stationary or *fixed segment*.

To assess the degree of mobility of a joint, it is necessary to determine the *angle of excursion* (**4**), i.e., the angle between its *initial* and *final* positions. The angle of excursion of a joint may be reduced by various factors. They include, in addition to the tension of the articular capsule, additional ligaments which restrict movement (*ligamentous limitation*, see p. 26), bony processes (*bony limitation*) and limiting surrounding soft tissues (*soft tissue limitation*). The *midposition* (**5**) is that position between the initial and final positions in which all parts of the joint capsule are under equal tension.

> **Clinical tip:** The range of movement of a joint is now given in terms of the neutral-0-position of the SFTR method of *Russe* and *Gerhardt* (**C**). The neutral-0-position of all joints is that found in the erect position, with straight hanging arms and the palms facing forward. There is a difference between anatomical and anthropological methods of measurement which must be taken into account. Movements are measured in the **S**agittal plane, **F**rontal plane, and **T**ransverse plane and during **R**otation (SFTR). In the numbers given, it should be remembered that the first figure always refers to extension, retroversion, abduction, external rotation, supination, or a movement to the left corresponding to the function of the joint, the second is the neutral-0 position and the third is the final position in opposition to that of the first movement.

Articular Surfaces

A joint possesses at least two articular surfaces. They are usually covered by hyaline cartilage (**6**) and occasionally by fibrous cartilage or connective tissue interspersed with fibrocartilage.

The cartilage is tightly interlocked with the bone and the superficial surface is shiny and smooth. The thickness of the cartilage layer varies from 2 to 5 mm, though the patella has some very thick areas, up to 6 mm. The cartilage is nourished via the synovial fluid as well as by diffusion from the capillaries in the synovial membrane.

Joint Capsule

The joint capsule may be taut or loose and is attached to the bone near the cartilage-covered surfaces. It consists of two layers, the inner *synovial membrane* (**7**) and an *outer fibrous membrane* (**8**). The synovial membrane contains elastic fibers, blood vessels and nerves. The amount of blood supply is directly related to the degree of activity so that very active joints are more richly vascularized than the less active ones. The synovial membrane possesses inward-facing processes containing fat, the *plicae synoviales* (**9**), synovial folds, and *synovial villi*. The fibrous membrane is of variable thickness and contains a large quantity of collagen fibers and very few elastic ones. Irregularities in the thickness of the fibrous membrane may result in weak spots through which the synovial membrane may protrude; these cyst-like protrusions are called *ganglia* by the surgeon.

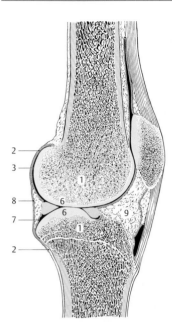

2
3

8
7
2

6
6
1
1
9

A Section through knee joint

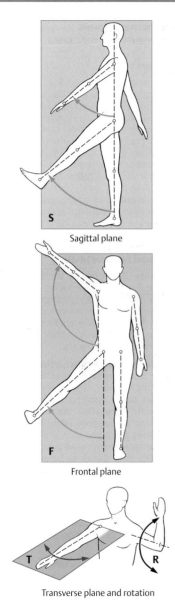

S
Sagittal plane

F
Frontal plane

T

R

Transverse plane and rotation

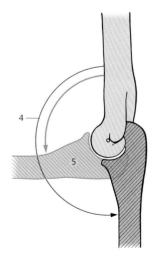

4

5

B Angle of excursion and middle position

C Neutral-0-method and SFTR recording

General Anatomy

Discontinuous Joints between Bones, continued

Joint Cavity (A, C)

A joint or articular cavity (**1**) is a cleftlike capillary space which contains *synovial fluid*. This is a clear, viscous, mucin-containing fluid resembling albumin. The fluid acts as a lubricant and aids nutrition of the articular cartilage. Its viscosity, which is determined by its content of hyaluronic acid is temperature dependent—the lower the temperature, the higher the viscosity of the synovial fluid. Since synovial fluid may also be regarded as a dialysate of blood plasma, its constitution, i.e., its chemical and physical features, can be of diagnostic value in a variety of diseases.

Additional Features (A–D)

Ligaments (**2**). Ligaments are designated by their function as *reinforcing ligaments* (for the joint capsule), *guiding ligaments* (in movements), or *restrictive ligaments* (to restrict movements). According to their position there are *extracapsular*, *capsular*, and *intracapsular* ligaments.

Articular disks or **menisci articulares** (**3**) consist of collagenous connective tissue containing fibrocartilage. A disk divides the joint cavity completely; a meniscus, only partly. They affect the direction of movement, ensure good contact between the moving parts, and may, under certain circumstances, produce two completely independent joint spaces, as, for instance, in the mandibular and sternoclavicular joints. Regeneration of disks after injury or removal is possible.

Articular lips (**4**), Labra articularia, consist of collagenous connective tissue with scattered cartilage cells and serve to enlarge the joint surface.

Bursae and **synovial pockets** may communicate with the joint cavity (**5**). They form large or small, thin-walled sacs lined by synovial membrane (**6**), which repre-

sent a weak point in a joint but which produce an enlargement of the joint space.

Maintenance of Contact

There are various forces that act on the two articular surfaces and maintain contact between them. First, there are the muscles that span the joint and guarantee a certain degree of contact between the articular surfaces. Next, there may be accessory capsular ligaments to increase the degree of contact. In addition, there is a certain degree of surface adhesion, and, as another important factor, atmospheric pressure. Atmospheric pressure holds the articular surfaces together with a force equal to the product of the area of the smaller joint surface and the air pressure.

Clinical tip: Joints are subject to **age alterations**; the avascular articular cartilage (**7**) loses its elasticity.
Surfaces covered by cartilage undergo age alterations (**8**) and may degenerate. Outgrowths from the cartilage margins may occur, which are sometimes invaded by bone-forming cells. In such instances the cartilage becomes ossified and restricts joint mobility. Such processes may affect small joints such as intervertebral joints and they may occur in young people if the joints in question are overstressed.
The "vacuum phenomenon," first described by Fick, refers to linear or crescent-shaped lucencies that appear in radiographs of joints and are caused by tissue gases entering the joint.

General Anatomy

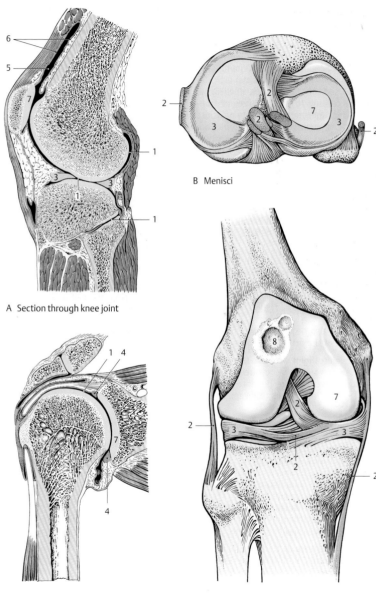

A Section through knee joint

B Menisci

C Section through shoulder joint

D Knee joint, frontal view

Types of Discontinuous (Synovial) Joints (A–F)

Joints may be classified from various points of view. One classification is related to the **axes** and subdivides joints into monaxial, biaxial, and multiaxial articulations. A second classification divides the joints according to their **degrees of freedom**, which indicate the mobility of articular surfaces against each other. Joints are therefore divided into those with one, two, or three degrees of freedom. Another classification makes use of the **number of articular surfaces** and so separates simple from complex joints. A *simple joint* consists of only two surfaces lying in one capsule. If more than two surfaces are present in the articular capsule, the joint is called a *complex joint* (e.g., elbow joint, **B**).

Different types of joints may be combined. *Joints combined of necessity* are found at different points on two bones (e.g., proximal and distal radioulnar joints). *Forcibly combined joints* are activated by one or more muscles that span several joints, e.g., hand and finger joints by the flexors of the fingers (see p. 173).

Joints may also be classified according to the **shape of the articular surfaces**:

A *plane joint*, a joint with two flat surfaces, possesses two degrees of freedom, and gliding movements are possible (e.g., the small vertebral joints, zygapophyseal joints).

A *hinge joint* or *ginglymus* (**A**) consists of a convex and a concave articular surface. The concave articular surface often has a ledge-shaped elevation which fits into a groove of the convex one. Tense lateral ligaments (**1**) help to fix the joint more firmly. Hinge joints have one degree of freedom (e.g., the humero-ulnar articulation **B**). Ginglymus and trochoid articulation (below) are collectively known as *cylindrical joints*.

Trochoid joints include the pivot joints and the rotary joints. Both have one axis and one degree of freedom, and both have one convex cylindrical surface and a corre-

sponding concave joint surface. The joint axis runs through the cylindrical surface. In a pivot joint the convex (peglike) surface rotates within the concave surface, which is enlarged by ligaments (annular ligament, **2**; e.g., in the proximal radio-ulnar joint, **B**). In a rotary joint the concave articular surface rotates around the convex surface (e.g., the distal radio-ulnar joint).

Ellipsoidal or condylar joints have a convex and a concave elliptical joint surface. They have two degrees of freedom and are multiaxial, with two principal axes. When the movements are combined, a circumduction is possible, e.g., the radiocarpal joint.

A *saddle joint* (**C**) consists of two saddle-shaped articular surfaces each having a convex and a concave curvature. It has two degrees of freedom and two main axes, but is in fact multiaxial. Circumduction is possible (e.g., the carpometacarpal joint of the thumb, **D**).

Ball-and-socket or *spheroidal joints* (**E**) are multiaxial and consist of a globular bony head within a cup or socket. There are three degrees of freedom and three principal axes (e.g., shoulder joint **F**). A special type of ball-and-socket joint is the *enarthrosis* in which the socket extends beyond the equator of the head. The hip joint is usually an enarthrosis which, however, has an enlarged cavity due to the articular labrum.

A special type of joint is the fixed joint or *amphiarthrosis*. This has very limited mobility since both the ligaments and the capsule are taut and the articular surfaces are rough, e.g., the sacroiliac joint.

General Anatomy

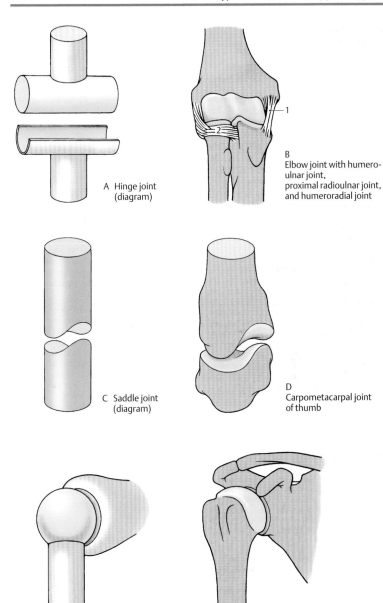

A Hinge joint
   (diagram)

B
Elbow joint with humero-
ulnar joint,
proximal radioulnar joint,
and humeroradial joint

C Saddle joint
   (diagram)

D
Carpometacarpal joint
of thumb

E Ball-and-socket
   joint (diagram)

F Shoulder joint

General Features of the Muscles

Classification of Skeletal Muscles (A–F)

In all skeletal muscles we distinguish an *origin* and an *attachment* (*insertion*). The origin is always on the less mobile bone (fixed end) and the attachment on the more mobile bone (mobile end). In the limb, the origin is always proximal and the attachment distal. At the point of origin there is often a *muscle head*, which merges into the *belly* (**1**) and ends in a *tendon* (**2**). Muscle power is dependent on the physiological cross section, which is the sum of the cross sections of all the fibers. From this the absolute muscular strength is calculated.

The location of the muscle belly depends on the space available. An important factor for the muscle's activity is its effective terminal part. The tendon of a muscle may, for example, be bent around a portion of the skeleton, *muscular trochlea*, as a fulcrum (*hypomochlion*). A long tendon may prove advantageous if there is a shortage of space. The best example of this are the long finger muscles, whose muscle bellies are situated in the forearm but whose effect shows only in the fingers.

According to the relationship between the muscle fibers and the tendons, we distinguish between various muscle types. **Fusiform muscles** (**A**) have long fibers and produce extensive but not forceful movements. Fusiform muscles have relatively short tendons. Another type is the **unipennate muscle** (**B**), which has a long tendon through the muscle to which the short muscle fibers are attached. This ensures a relatively large physiological cross section and consequently more muscle power. A **bipennate muscle** (**C**) has the same structure as a unipennate muscle, but the fibers are attached to both sides of the tendon. There are also **multipennate muscles**.

There are several forms of muscle origin, for example two-, three-, and four-headed muscles, in which the individual heads fuse into a single muscle belly and terminate in a common tendon. Examples of this muscle type include the biceps (**D**) and the triceps brachii.

If a muscle has only one head but one or more *intermediate tendons* (**3**), we speak of a digastric or **multigastric muscle** (**E**). One such muscle with two bellies, **digastric muscle**, has two successive, almost identical large muscle segments. A **flat muscle** (**F**) of a triangular shape, *triangular muscle* with a flat tendon or *aponeurosis* (**4**), is distinguishable from a quadrangular flat muscle, *quadrate muscle*.

Muscles may extend over one or more joints and are then called *uniarticular, biarticular,* or *multiarticular* muscles. They may produce different and in some cases even opposing movements at the various joints. Examples are the interossei muscles of the hand, which flex at the proximal joint but extend at the middle and terminal joints of the fingers.

The muscles which work together to produce one movement are called **synergists**, and those that produce opposing movements are called **antagonists**. The combination of synergists and antagonists can vary in different movements. In flexion of the wrist, for instance, several muscles are synergists which in radial abduction become antagonists.

It is essential for their function that muscles have a *tone*, even at rest. In a muscle we find either *active* or *passive insufficiency*. In active insufficiency, a muscle becomes exhausted when it has attained its maximal shortening. In passive insufficiency, from another position the end point is reached prematurely, for example, in the impossibility of forming a fist when the hand is flexed. In muscle action we distinguish an *active moving* and a *passive halting function*. Thus, a muscle may function passively to halt and actively to produce movement.

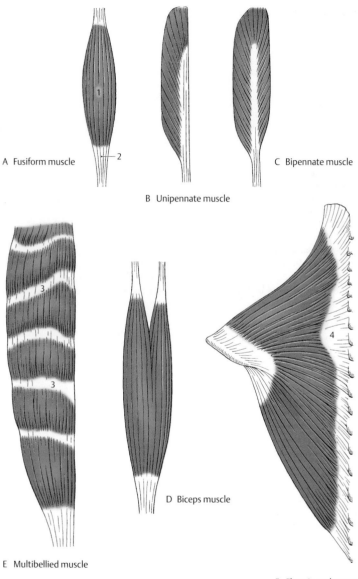

A Fusiform muscle

B Unipennate muscle

C Bipennate muscle

D Biceps muscle

E Multibellied muscle

F Flat triangular muscle

Auxiliary Features of Muscles (A–D)

A number of auxiliary structures are essential for muscle function. They include:

(a) Connective tissue coverings, **fascias**, which surround individual muscles or muscle groups and allow them to move one against the other.

(b) **Tendon sheaths** (**A**, **B**), which increase the gliding capacity of tendons. The inner or *synovial layer* has an inner visceral layer (**1**), which lies in immediate contact with the tendon (**2**), and a parietal layer (**3**), which is connected via the *mesotendon* (**4**). The synovial fluid, which is present between the visceral and parietal layers, acts as a lubricant to aid movement of the tendon. The outside of the vaginal sheath is covered by a *fibrous layer* (**5**).

(c) A **synovial bursa** (**C**, **6**) protects a muscle where it lies directly against a bone.

(d) **Sesamoid cartilages** or **bones** (**D**) are found where tendons are subjected to pressure. The largest sesamoid bone is the patella (**7**), which is part of the knee joint and is also connected via the patellar ligament (**8**) and the tendon of the quadriceps (**9**) to the tibia.

(e) Fatty bodies, **corpora adiposa**, lie between individual muscles and may reduce friction. Such fatty bodies (e. g., the axillary fatty body) are found in variable numbers throughout the body.

Investigation of Muscle Function

Muscle function can be judged in a variety of ways. The simplest are *palpation* and *inspection*. The shape of a muscle may be demonstrated by particular movements.

Anatomical methods permit the demonstration of individual muscles in preparations. The origin, course and insertion of a muscle can be determined, but an exact evaluation of its function cannot be obtained from a cadaver. Thus, dissection is an indirect method which only allows inferences and does not take into account the cooperation of individual muscles.

Electrical stimulation may be used to investigate muscle function, the stimuli being applied where the nerve enters the muscle ("motor point"). This method has the disadvantages, first, that it is useful only for superficial muscles, and second, that it produces maximal contraction without making allowances for the fact that other muscles may affect or reduce this maximal contraction.

Electromyography is another method of investigation of muscle function, in which action potentials of fibers are recorded by an electrode placed directly in the muscle. With the help of this method, it has been shown that, with an increase in effort, more and more motor units (muscle fibers with their motor end plates and nerves, see vol. 3) become activated. Electromyography has demonstrated that all fibers are never active at the same time. While some fibers are at rest, others contract, so that there is an even increase or decrease in tension.

A limiting factor, even with this method, is the difficulty of determining the extent to which an individual muscle contributes to any given movement.

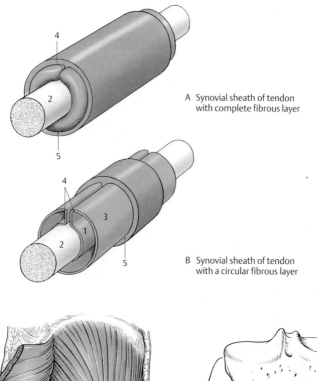

A Synovial sheath of tendon with complete fibrous layer

B Synovial sheath of tendon with a circular fibrous layer

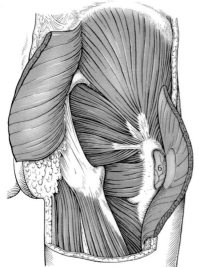

C Synovial bursa

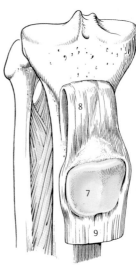

D Sesamoid bone (patella)

Anatomical Terms and their Latin Equivalents

General Anatomy	Anatomia generalis
Articular surface	Facies articularis
Ball and socket joint	Articulatio sphaeroidea
Bony union	Junctura ossea
Cartilage tissue	Textus cartilaginous
Cartilaginous joint	Junctura cartilaginea
Connective tissue	Textus connectivus
Ellipsoidal or condylar joint	Articulatio ellipsoidea
Fatty tissue	Textus adiposus
Fibrous joint	Juncutra fibrosa
Flat bones	Ossa plana
Hinge joint	Gynglimus
Joint capsule (cavity)	Capsula (cavitas) articularis
Lamellar bone	Os compactum (lamellare)
Long bones	Ossa longa
Medullary cavity	Cavitas medullaris
Plane (pivot) joint	Articulatio plana (trochoidea)
Pneumatized (sesamoid) bones	Ossa pneumatica (sesamoidea)
Saddle joint	Articulatio sellaris
Short (irregular) bones	Ossa brevia (irregularia)
Simple (complex) joint	Articulatio simplex (composita)
Smooth muscle	Musculus nonstriatus
Striated muscle	Musculus striatus
Synovial fluid	Synovia
Woven bone	Os spongioisum (primitivum)

Systematic Anatomy of the Locomotor System

Trunk

Vertebral Column

The **vertebral column** forms the basic structure of the trunk. It consists of 33–34 *vertebrae* and *intervertebral disks*.

The vertebrae are divided into
- 7 cervical
- 12 thoracic
- 5 lumbar
- 5 sacral
- 4–5 coccygeal vertebrae

The sacral vertebrae fuse to form the *sacrum* and the coccygeal vertebrae fuse to form the *coccyx*. Thus the sacral and coccygeal vertebrae are false vertebrae, while the others are true vertebrae.

Cervical Vertebrae (A–G)

Of the seven vertebrae comprising the cervical vertebral column, three can be readily distinguished: the first, or **atlas**, the second, or **axis**, and the seventh, the **vertebra prominens**. Only small differences characterize the third, fourth, fifth, and sixth cervical vertebrae. The *vertebral body* (**1**) is continued backward into the *vertebral arches* (**2**), each of which comprises two portions, an anterior *pedicle* (**3**) and a posterior *lamina* (**4**). At the junction of these two parts, a *superior articular process* (**5**) projects cranially and an *inferior articular process* (**6**) extends caudally. A recession, the *superior vertebral notch* (**7**), is evident between the superior articular process and the vertebral body, whereas a larger *inferior vertebral notch* (**8**) is found between the inferior articular process and the body. The articular processes bear *articular surfaces* or *facets* (**9**); the superior articular facet is directed dorsally, the inferior articular facet ventrally. The vertebral arches terminate in a *spinous process* (**10**), which is directed dorsally and which, in the third to sixth cervical vertebrae, is bifid at its end. In cervical vertebrae the vertebral body and its arches enclose a relatively large *vertebral foramen* (**11**). The *transverse process* (**12**) extends laterally and includes a vertebral and costal element (p. 52)

which incompletely fuse during development so that a *foramen transversarium* (**13**) is preserved. The transverse process is distinguished by an *anterior tubercle* (**14**) and a *posterior tubercle* (**15**) connected by a grooved bridge of bone serving as the *sulcus for a spinal nerve* (**16**).

In the **third cervical vertebra**, the articular facets on the superior articular processes form an angle of 142° to each other open posteriorly (angular aperture, *Putz*), whereas in the fourth to seventh cervical vertebrae, this angle amounts to about 180°.

The anterior tubercle of the **sixth cervical vertebra** can be especially prominent and is designated as the *carotid tubercle* (**17**). The upper plates of the bodies of the third to seventh cervical vertebrae exhibit raised lateral margins, the *uncal processes* or *unci* (**18**, p. 58).

The **seventh cervical vertebra** possesses a large spinous process which is significant as the uppermost palpable spinous process of the vertebral column. It is consequently designated as the *vertebra prominens*. However, its transverse process usually lacks an anterior tubercle (**E**).

▬ **Variants:** The transverse process of C 7 (**G**) is incompletely developed and the costal element has incompletely fused (**19**) so that the part arising from this anlage can be distinctly differentiated from the vertebra. If the costal element is preserved independently, a **cervical rib** develops (**20**). Cervical ribs customarily appear bilaterally. When they appear only on one side, they are more frequently found on the left than on the right. The foramen transversarium can be bipartite in different vertebrae.

> **Clinical tip:** The presence of a cervical rib may cause a triad of disorders, known also as **Naffziger syndrome:**
> 1. Pain due to distortion of vessels.
> 2. Pain related to the brachial plexus (sensory disturbances, especially of the ulnar nerve).
> 3. Palpable abnormalities in the greater supraclavicular fossa.

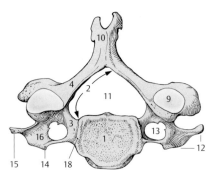

A Fourth and fifth cervical vertebrae from above

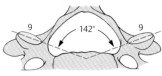

B Third cervical vertebra from above (section)

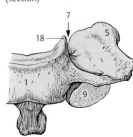

C Sixth cervical vertebra from front (section)

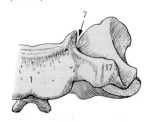

E Vertebra prominens from front (section)

D Vertebra prominens from above

F Cervical vertebra from side

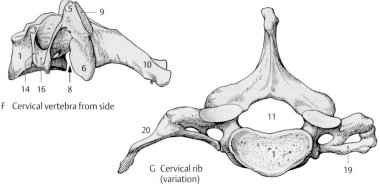

G Cervical rib (variation)

Cervical Vertebrae, continued

First Cervical Vertebra (A–C)

The **atlas** differs basically from the other vertebrae in that it lacks a vertebral body. In the atlas we therefore describe a smaller *anterior* (**1**) and a *larger posterior arch* (**2**). Both arches have small protuberances in the median plane, the *anterior* (**3**) *and posterior tubercles* (**4**). The posterior tubercle may sometimes be very poorly developed. Lateral to the large *vertebral foramen* (**5**) of the atlas lie the *lateral masses* (**6**), each of which has a *superior* (**7**) and an *inferior articular facet* (**8**). The upper articular facet is concave and its medial margin is often indrawn. Sometimes a superior, articular facet may be subdivided. The lower articular facet is flat or may be very slightly deepened and almost circular. On the inner side of the anterior arch is the articular facet for the dens, *fovea dentis* (**9**). From the *foramen* transversarium (**11**), which is located in the *transverse process* (**10**), a groove, the *sulcus of vertebral artery* (**12**), extends across the posterior arch for the reception of the vertebral artery.

▰▰ **Variants:** The sulcus for the vertebral artery may be replaced by a *canal* (**13**). Rarely, the atlas is divided into two halves joined by cartilage. Equally rarely, unilateral or bilateral assimilation of the atlas, i.e., bony fusion with the skull, may be observed.

Second Cervical Vertebra (D–F)

The **axis** differs from C3–6 because of the *dens* or *odontoid process* (**14**). On the cranial surface of the body the axis carries a toothlike process, the *dens axis*, which ends in a rounded point, the *apex dentis* (**15**). The anterior surface of the dens has a definite articular surface—the *anterior articular facet* (**16**). The posterior surface may have a smaller articular facet—the *posterior articular facet* (**17**).

The lateral articular facets slope laterally. The poorly developed *transverse process* (**18**) contains the *foramen transversarium.*

The shape of the lateral articular facets is somewhat complex. Although they may appear almost flat in a bony (macerated) preparation, they are more ridged when their cartilaginous covering is present. This covering is important in the joint between the atlas and the axis (see p. 60). The *spinous process* (**19**) is large and often, though not always, it has a bifurcated tip. It develops from the joined parts of the *vertebral arch* (**20**), which in common with the *vertebral body* (**21**), encompass the *vertebral foramen* (**22**).

> **Clinical tip:** Isolated fractures of the arch of the atlas may occur, especially after car accidents, and should be differentiated from congenital variations of the atlas (p. 44). A fracture of the dens is the typical axis fracture. Care is required because free proatlas segments (p. 52) may rarely be found within atlanto-occipital membrane.
>
> The position of the axis of the dens relative to the body of second cervical vertebra depends on the curvature of the cervical spine. In the absence of a lordosis (p. 62) it faces slightly backward. Its longitudinal axis then makes an angle with the vertical through the body of the second cervical vertebra.

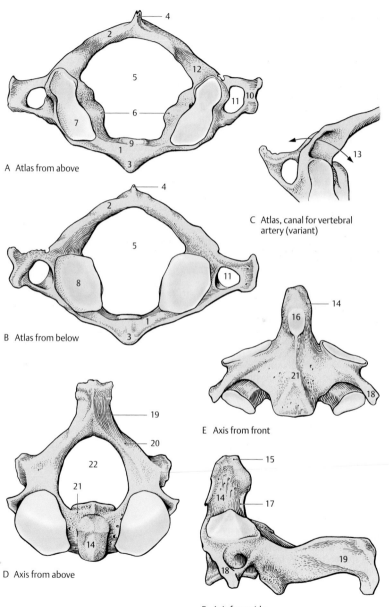

Trunk

A Atlas from above

C Atlas, canal for vertebral artery (variant)

B Atlas from below

E Axis from front

D Axis from above

F Axis from side

Trunk

Thoracic Vertebrae (A–D)

The 12 **thoracic vertebrae** each have a *vertebral body* (**1**), which has incompletely ossified cranial and caudal plates of compact bone and, on the dorsal surface, openings for the exit of the basivertebral veins. Laterally, the vertebral body usually has two *costal facets* (**2**), each of which is half of an articular facet (**D**) for articulation with the head of a rib. The first, tenth, eleventh, and twelfth thoracic vertebrae are exceptions.

The first thoracic vertebra (**D**) has a complete articular facet (**3**) at the cranial border of its body and a half facet (**4**) at the caudal border. The tenth vertebra (**D**) has only a half articular facet (**5**), while the eleventh (**D**) has a complete articular facet (**6**) at its cranial border. The twelfth thoracic vertebra (**D**) has the articular facet for the head of the rib in the middle of the lateral surface of the body (**7**).

From the posterior surface of the body arises the *vertebral arch* with its *pedicles* (**8**) that continue on each side into the laminae *of the vertebral arch* (**9**). The two laminae unite to form the *spinous process* (**10**). The spinous processes of the first to ninth thoracic vertebrae overlap each other like roof tiles, so that their tips lie one to one and a half vertebrae lower than the corresponding vertebral bodies. They are triangular in cross section, in contrast to the spinous processes of the last three thoracic vertebrae, which are vertically oriented plates. They do not descend but extend directly dorsally. On the upper margin of the pedicle of the arch is the poorly developed superior *vertebral notch* (**11**), and on the lower margin, the deeper *inferior vertebral notch* (**12**). The *vertebral foramen* (**13**) lies between the vertebral arch and the posterior surface of the body.

Cranially, where the pedicle of the vertebral arch becomes the lamina, there are the *superior articular process* (**14**) and caudally the *inferior articular process* (**15**). Laterally and a little posteriorly lie the *transverse processes* (**16**), which in the first to tenth thoracic vertebrae carry a *costal facet* (**17**) for articulation with the costal tubercle. The facets are concave only in the second to fifth thoracic vertebrae. On the first, sixth to ninth and tenth thoracic vertebrae, the facet is flattened. The shape of the facet imparts a differing mobility to the ribs (see p. 68).

Special Features: Like the cervical vertebrae, the first thoracic vertebra often has an *uncus corporis* (*Putz;* uncal process) on each side of its body. In the eleventh and twelfth thoracic vertebrae, the transverse processes may already be rudimentary. In this case, as occurs in the lumbar vertebrae (p. 42), there may be an *accessory process* and a *mamillary process* on each side.

> **Clinical tip:** The vertebral notches, one caudal and one cranial, together form the *intervertebral foramen* (**18**), which serves for the passage of the spinal nerves. Processes affecting the bones in this area may produce a narrowing which in turn may cause **nerve lesions**.

Trunk

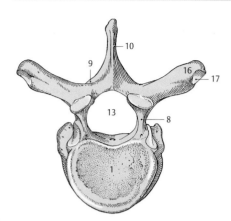

A Thoracic vertebra from above

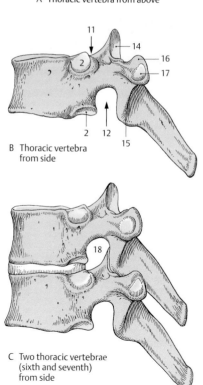

B Thoracic vertebra
from side

C Two thoracic vertebrae
(sixth and seventh)
from side

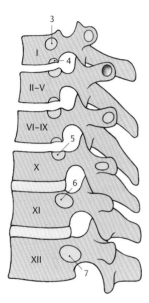

D Diagram of articular facets
of costovertebral joints

Lumbar Vertebrae (A–D)

The *bodies* (**1**) of the five **lumbar vertebrae** are much larger than those of the other vertebrae. The *spinous process* (**2**) is flat and is directed sagitally. The *lamina of the arch* (**3**) is short and sturdy, and the *pedicles of the vertebral arch* (**4**) are very thick, corresponding in size to those of the lumbar vertebra. The flattened lateral processes of the lumbar vertebrae may be called *costal processes* (**5**), and since they originate from rib anlagen, they are fused with the vertebrae. Behind the costal process is an *accessory process* (**6**) of variable size. Together with the *superior articular process* (**7**) and the *mamillary process* (**8**) resting on it, it represents the remnant of the *transverse process*. The *inferior articular process* (**9**) extends caudally. In essence, the articular facets face medially (**10**) on the superior articular processes and laterally (**11**) on the inferior articular processes. There is always a more or less marked angulation of these articular surfaces.

Between the superior and inferior articular processes there is a region which is almost bereft of spongiosa. Clinically, it is known as the interarticular part (**12**).

As in all other vertebrae, there is a small *superior vertebral notch* (**13**) between the body of the vertebra and the superior articular process. The much larger *inferior vertebral notch* (**14**) extends from the posterior surface of the body as far as the root of the inferior articular process. The *intervertebral foramina* formed by the corresponding notches are relatively large in the lumbar vertebrae, whereas the *vertebral foramen* (**15**) is relatively small. At the posterior surface of the vertebral body inside the vertebral foramen, there is a large opening for the exit of a vein. The outer margins or the upper and lower surfaces (*intervertebral surfaces*) of the vertebral bodies of lumbar, as well as other, vertebrae exhibit a distinctly visible, ring-shaped, compact, bony lamella, the marginal ridge or *ring epiphysis* (**16**). Spongy bone occupies the central area of the vertebral body (**17**).

The compact ring corresponds to the ossified portion of the vertebral body epiphysis (p. 52). Among the five lumbar vertebrae, the fifth lumbar vertebra can be distinguished from the others in that its vertebral body decreases in height from front to back.

■■■ **Variants:** Fairly often in the first lumbar vertebra and less commonly in the second lumbar vertebrae, the costal process does not fuse with the bone and instead forms a so-called **lumbar rib** (**18**). The last lumbar vertebra may fuse with the sacrum. This is called **sacralization** of the vertebra.

> **Clinical tip:** Lumbar ribs may cause pain because of their proximity to the kidney.
> Spondylolysis (p. 44) may occur in the region of the interarticular part.
> An important diagnostic and therapeutic procedure is **lumbar puncture**, in which cerebrospinal fluid is withdrawn from the subarachnoid space with a spinal needle introduced in the midline between the spinous processes of the third and fourth lumbar vertebrae.

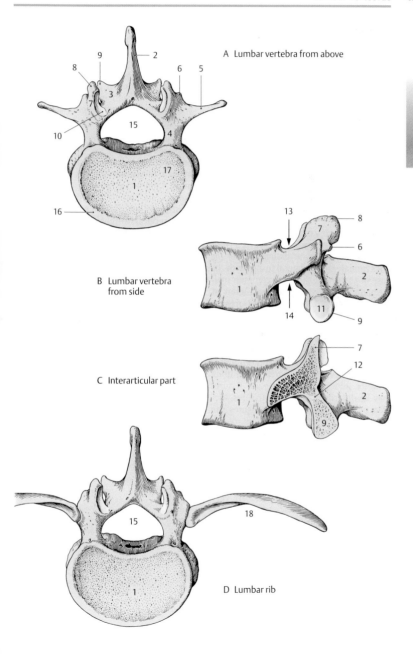

A Lumbar vertebra from above

B Lumbar vertebra from side

C Interarticular part

D Lumbar rib

▨ Malformations and Variations of the presacral vertebral Column (A–E)

Malformations of the vertebrae may be associated with more or less severe changes in the spinal cord. Various fissures or other abnormalities which may not have caused any symptoms can sometimes be detected by chance on x-rays, ultrasound, CT, or MRI studies. Since these are developmental defects, some grouping will be done here. Moreover, only the free vertebrae will be considered—variations of the os sacrum are described on page 50. Likewise, cervical ribs (see p. 36) and lumbar ribs (see p. 42) will not be mentioned here.

Apart from such variations as the presence of a *vertebral artery canal* (see p. 38), or such malformations as *assimilation of the atlas* (unilateral or bilateral fusion with the base of the skull), the most common malformations are **fissures in the region of the vertebral arches**. *Posterior fissures* must be distinguished from *lateral* ones and from *fissures at the root of the vertebral arches*, as well as from those *between the body and the arch*, as described by *Töndury*. In addition, there is the rare anterior *fissure of the anterior vertebral arch of the atlas*. Anterior and posterior vertebral fissures may be described as median fissures. Median posterior vertebral arch fissures can be associated with malformations of the spinal cord. According to *Töndury*, they arise during the mesenchymal phase of vertebral development.

Posterior fissures are quite common in the atlas (**A, B**) but they occur less often in the lower cervical vertebrae (**E**) and are very rare in the upper thoracic vertebrae. They are not uncommon in the lower thoracic and upper lumbar vertebrae and are most frequent in the sacrum (spina bifida, see p. 50).

Very infrequently the atlas has an **anterior median fissure** and in the example illustrated here there is also a posterior median fissure (**B**).

Lateral vertebral arch fissures (**C**) occur immediately posterior to the superior articular process (**1**), with the result that the inferior articular processes (**2**), together with the arch and the spinous process, are separated from the other parts of the vertebra. This bony division is called *spondylolysis* and may lead to true slipping of the vertebra (*spondylolisthesis*).

Another malformation is the occurrence of **fused vertebrae** (**D**), i.e., the fusion of two or more vertebral bodies, as happens normally in the sacrum. Fused vertebrae occur most commonly in the neck, upper thoracic and lumbar regions. The example illustrated shows fusion of the second and third cervical vertebrae (**D**). Fused vertebrae may be caused by a number of things, but the disturbance is always in the mesenchymal phase of development of the vertebral column.

Clinical tip: The fusion of vertebrae may also result from various diseases and from spinal trauma (e.g., motor vehicle injuries).

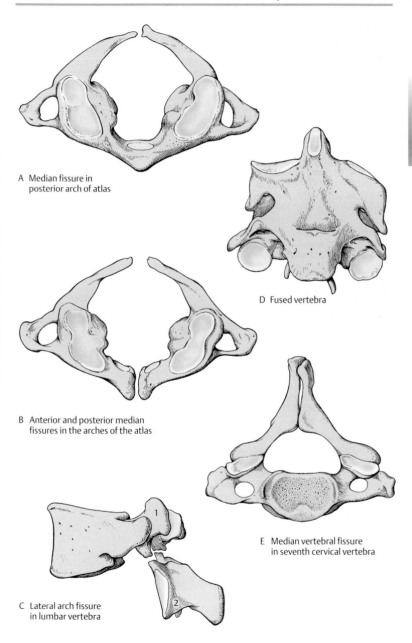

A Median fissure in
   posterior arch of atlas

B Anterior and posterior median
   fissures in the arches of the atlas

C Lateral arch fissure
   in lumbar vertebra

D Fused vertebra

E Median vertebral fissure
   in seventh cervical vertebra

Trunk

Sacrum (A, B)

The **sacrum** consists of the five sacral vertebrae and the intervertebral disks that lie between them. It has a concave anterior or **pelvic surface** (**A**) and a convex **dorsal surface** (**B**). The *base of the sacrum* (**1**) has a surface which faces the last lumbar vertebra. The *apex of the sacrum* (**2**) faces downward and lies opposite to the adjoining coccyx.

Usually, the concave curvature of the **pelvic surface** (**A**) is not uniform but has its greatest depth approximately at the level of the third vertebra. Here the sacrum may even appear angulated. The pelvic surface has four paired pelvic *anterior sacral foramina* (**3**) as exits for the ventral branches of the spinal nerves (see vol. 3). These foramina are not equivalent to the intervertebral foramina found in other vertebrae, which here lie directly next to the sacral canal, but are surrounded both by vertebral and rib anlagen (see p. 52). They correspond to those foramina that are formed by vertebrae, ribs (or rib anlagen), and superior costotransverse ligaments. Between the right and left anterior sacral foramina lie the *transverse ridges* (**4**), which are due to fusion of the adjacent surfaces of the vertebrae and intervertebral disks. That part of the sacral bone which lies lateral to the pelvic foramina is called the *lateral part* (**5**, p. 48).

The **dorsal surface** (**B**) is regularly convex. Five longitudinal ridges, not always clearly developed, have their origin in fusion of the corresponding processes of the vertebrae. The *median sacral crest* (**6**) is formed in the midline by the fused spinous processes. Lateral to it, but medial to the *posterior sacral foramina* (**7**) is the *intermediate sacral crest* (**8**), which is usually the most poorly developed. It represents the fused remnants of the articular processes of the vertebrae. Lateral to the dorsal foramina the *lateral sacral crest* (**9**) can be seen, which represents remnants of the transverse processes.

In the cranial prolongation of the intermediate sacral crest at the upper end, the *superior articular processes* (**10**) are found which articulate with the last lumbar vertebra. Like the anterior sacral foramina, the eight dorsal sacral foramina are not equivalent to the intervertebral foramina of other vertebrae. They correspond to those openings which are formed in common by the vertebra, rib (or rib anlagen), and the costotransverse ligament. They are the exits for the dorsal branches of the spinal nerves.

The median sacral crest terminates just above the *sacral hiatus* (**11**), which represents the inferior aperture of the vertebral canal at the level of the fourth sacral vertebra. It is bounded laterally by the *two sacral horns* (**12**).

> **Clinical tip:** Local anesthetic can be injected into the sacral hiatus for treatment of chronic low back pain. This therapy can anesthetize the pelvic region and lower limbs without affecting cardiac or respiratory function. Note that the needle must be angled on reaching the third sacral vertebra!

Trunk

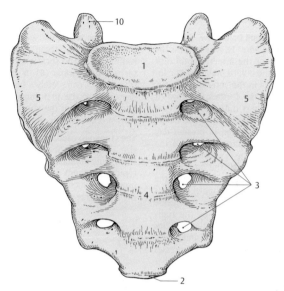

A Sacrum from front

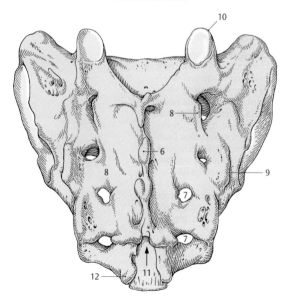

B Sacrum from back

Sacrum, continued (A–D)

A view of the **sacrum from above** (**A**) shows in the middle the *base* (**1**), which forms the contact surface of the intervertebral disk with the last lumbar vertebra. Of all the intervertebral disks in the vertebral column, this one extends the furthest forward. It also projects furthest into the pelvis (see p. 62) and should by definition be called the promontory. However, in present-day usage, the most prominent point of the base of the sacral bone is called the **promontory**. On either side of the base lie the wings, *alae sacrales* (**2**). They form the upper surface of the *lateral part*, which is formed on one side by the transverse processes and on the other by the rudiments of the ribs. Posterior to the base lies the entrance to the sacral canal and lateral to it are the two *superior articular processes* (**3**), which articulate with the last lumbar vertebra.

In a **lateral** view (**B**) of the sacrum, the *auricular surface* (**4**) for the articulation with the hip bone can be seen. Posterior to it lies the *sacral tuberosity* (**5**), a roughened area for the attachment of ligaments.

The *sacral canal* lies within the sacrum and, corresponding in shape to the sacrum, is irregularly curved and of uneven width. At about the level of the third sacral vertebra the canal is narrowed. Channels which correspond to the intervertebral foramina and are formed from the fused superior and inferior vertebral notches open laterally from the sacral canal. The corresponding sacral foramina open ventrally and dorsally from these short channels (p. 46).

Sex Differences: Males (**D**) have a longer sacrum with more marked curvature. Females (**C**) have a shorter but broader sacrum, which is less curved.

> **Clinical tip:** The promontory angle as described by Schmorl and Junghanns is normally in the range of 120° to135°. It is measured at the most prominent point where lines tangent to the lower border of L4 and the upper border of S2 intersect.

Coccyx (E, F)

The **coccyx**, which is usually formed from three to four vertebrae, is normally only rudimentary. The surface which faces the sacrum has *cornua* (**6**) or *horns*, formed from the completely fused articular processes of the first coccygeal vertebra. The remainder of the coccygeal vertebrae consist only of small, round bones.

The cranial to caudal vertebrae decrease in size. Only the first coccygeal vertebra shows any similarity to the structure of a typical vertebra. It shows two lateral processes which represent the remnants of the transverse processes.

Trunk

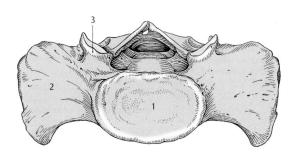

A Superior view of sacrum

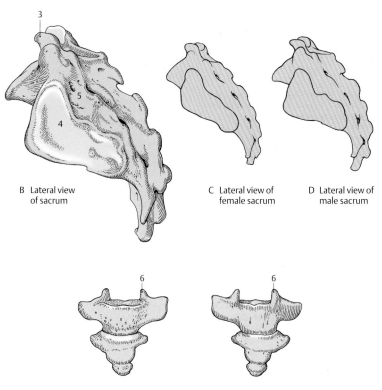

B Lateral view of sacrum

C Lateral view of female sacrum

D Lateral view of male sacrum

E Anterior view of coccyx

F Posterior view of coccyx

Trunk

▦ Variations in the Sacral Region (A–D)

The vertebral column usually consists of **24 presacral vertebrae**, the remainder being arranged into five fused sacral vertebrae and three to four coccygeal vertebrae. About one-third of individuals have an additional sacral vertebra, so that the sacrum consists of six vertebrae. Either one lumbar vertebra may be included in the sacrum (**A**), or the first coccygeal vertebra may be fused with it (**B**).

Situation (**A**) is called **sacralization** of a lumbar vertebra, and (**B**) is called sacralization of the coccyx or the first coccygeal vertebra, If either a lumbar or a coccygeal vertebra is fused with the sacrum, there are five sacral foramina on each side and the sacrum appears larger than in its typical form.

Fusion of the last lumbar vertebra may be unilateral, producing a **lumbo-sacral transitional vertebra**, which may lead to scoliosis of the spine (see p. 62). A lumbosacral transitional vertebra occurs also when there is **lumbalization** of the first sacral vertebra. In this case, dorsally there is incomplete fusion of the first sacral vertebra with the rest of the vertebrae and there is no bony union in the region of the lateral parts, i.e., in those areas that originated from remnants of ribs.

It should be noted that when lumbalization of a sacral vertebra occurs, there may nevertheless be five vertebrae if the first coccygeal vertebra is fused with the sacrum. An increased number of sacral vertebrae, i.e., sacralization of a lumbar or coccygeal vertebra, is more common in males than in females.

Quite often an incomplete medial sacral crest is found (according to *Hintze* in 44% at 15 and 10% at 50 years of age). In these cases the posterior wall of the sacral canal appears to be defective (**C**). Apart from this, incomplete fusion of the spinous process of the first sacral vertebra with the spinous processes of the other sacral vertebrae produces a vertebral arch in the first sacral segment and so the medial sacral crest starts from the second vertebra.

Lastly, sometimes none of the vertebral arches are fused, so that there is no posterior bony wall in the sacral canal. This malformation is called **spina bifida** (**D**).

Clinical tip: When the spinal cord is intact and the skin of the area is undamaged the condition is called **spina bifida "occulta".** It occurs in 2% of males and 0.3% of females. It is usually of no clinical importance.

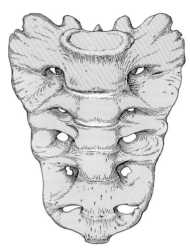

A Sacralization of fifth lumbar vertebra

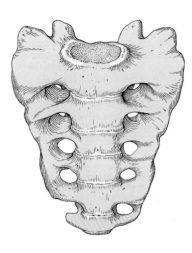

B Sacralization of first coccygeal vertebra

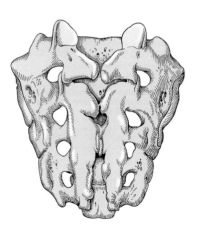

C Incomplete medial sacral crest

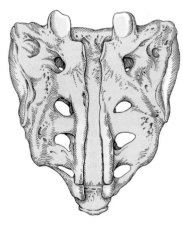

D Spina bifida

Ossification of the Vertebrae (A–I)

Basically all vertebrae possess *three bony anlagen*, from which two develop perichondrally and one endochrondrally. The perichondral cuffs (**1**) lie at the roots of the vertebral arches (pedicles), while the bony nucleus (**2**) is found in the body of the vertebra. Apart from these centers of ossification, individual vertebrae have *secondary epiphysial bony anlagen* which appear on the surface of the vertebral body, as well as in the transverse and spinous processes.

The **atlas** (**A**) develops from two lateral bony anlagen (**1**), but in the 1st year of life the ventral arch may develop its own bony center (hypochordal bar), which fuses with the other two between the ages of 5 and 9 years. The transverse processes of the atlas and axis contain rudimentary rib anlagen (**3**).

In addition to the three bony anlagen and the secondary epiphyses, the **axis** (**B, C**) has further ossification centers. The dens (**4**) is usually considered to arise from the bony anlage of the body of the atlas, although, according to another theory (*Ludwig*), it is formed from the dental processes. Relatively late a bony center (*ossiculum terminale*) develops in the *apex of the dens* (**5**), corresponding to the body of the proatlas, and it does not fuse with the dens until the 25th year of life.

In the **other cervical vertebrae** (**D**) *three typical bony anlagen* develop toward the end of the 2nd intrauterine month. Bony anlagen appear in the transverse processes (**6**), which develop from the rib precursors (parietal bars), and from which the anterior tubercles and parts of the posterior tubercles are formed. The bony arches fuse in the 1st year. The fusion between the body and arches at the *neurocentral junction* occurs between the 3rd and 6th years of life. *Secondary epiphysial anlagen* appear at the ends of the transverse processes and the spinous processes between 12 and 14 years, and fuse with them at about 20 years. The *epiphyses of the vertebral bodies*, a cranial and a caudal cartilaginous plate, ossify from the 8th year onward in ring form (*anular epiphysis*) and fuse with the body from about the age of 18.

In the **thoracic region** (**E**) the bony anlagen of the *pedicles* (**1**) develop first in the upper thoracic vertebrae. The endochondral center (**2**) of the

vertebral body develops during the 10th week of intrauterine life, at first in the lower thoracic vertebrae. Fusion of the bony halves of the arches commences in the 1st year of life, and between the arch and the body it starts between the ages of 3 and 6. The *epiphyses of the vertebral bodies* ossify in a ringlike fashion.

The **lumbar vertebrae** (**F, G, K**), also, ossify from *three bony anlagen*; the bony centers (**2**) in the vertebral bodies appear first in the upper lumbar vertebrae (about the same time as in the bodies of the lower thoracic vertebrae) and the bony anlagen in the vertebral arches (**1**) appear somewhat later. The costal processes (**7**) develop from the *rib anlagen*.

The *secondary epiphyses* are represented by a bony anlage at the spinous process, as well as the ring ossified *anular epiphysis* (**8**) of the vertebral body which is found both at its upper and lower surfaces.

In each of its segments the **sacrum** (**H, I**), develops, like the rest of the vertebrae, from three bony anlagen, and, in addition, from a rib anlage (**9**) in the region of the lateral mass on each side. Thus, *each segment* of the sacrum has *five ossification anlagen*. In the region of the lineae transversae there is an additional bony fusion of the margin with the intervertebral disks, the ossification of which begins at 15–16 years of age. The nuclei that arise from the rib rudiments appear in the 5th–7th fetal month and fuse with the remaining ossific centers in the 2nd–5th postnatal year. The sacral vertebrae fuse with one another in a caudocranial sequence up to the age of 25–35 years.

The **coccygeal vertebrae** develop from bony centers that appear in the 1st year and fuse between the ages of 20 and 30 years.

Trunk

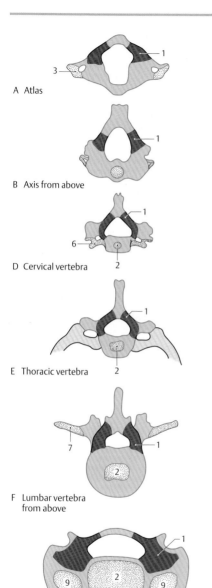

A Atlas

B Axis from above

D Cervical vertebra

E Thoracic vertebra

F Lumbar vertebra
from above

H Sacrum
from above

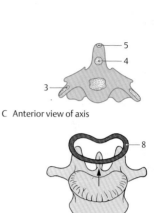

C Anterior view of axis

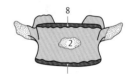

K Lumbar vertebra
with anular epiphysis

G Anterior view
of lumbar vertebra

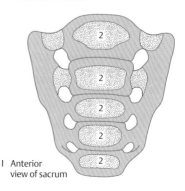

I Anterior
view of sacrum

Intervertebral Disks (A–D)

Each **intervertebral disk** consists of an outer tense *anulus fibrosus* (**1**) and a soft jellylike nucleus, the *nucleus pulposus* (**2**), which contains remnants of the notochord (chorda dorsalis). The anulus fibrosus consists of concentrically arranged collagen fibers and fibrocartilage which keep the nucleus pulposus under tension. The intervertebral disks lie between the bodies of the individual vertebrae. In a sagittal section they appear conical. In the cervical and lumbar region they are higher in front and lower behind. The reverse is true in the thoracic region, where disks are lower in front and higher behind. Basically, the thickness of the intervertebral disks increases from the cranial to the caudal region.

The intervertebral disks include the *hyaline cartilage plates* (**3**) derived from the epiphyses of the vertebral bodies. This functional unit represents an important part of a segment of motion (see p. 62). In addition, the intervertebral disks are also held in position by the longitudinal ligaments (**4**). The posterior longitudinal ligament is fused with the disks (see p. 56) over a broad surface, while the anterior longitudinal ligament is only loosely attached to them.

The intervertebral disks and the longitudinal ligaments form a functional entity and together are known as the **intervertebral joint**.

Function: The intervertebral disks act as shock absorbers. The nucleus pulposus distributes the pressure. Loading compresses them, and when it is released, they regain their original shape after some time. In movements within the vertebral column (**C, D**) the intervertebral disks, as elastic elements, are compressed or stretched unilaterally.

Clinical tip: With increasing age, a reduction in internal pressure may result in shrinkage of the nucleus pulposus. This causes lessening of tension in the anulus fibrosus so it becomes torn more easily. Basically, each tear begins in the region of the nucleus pulposus (*Schlüter*). Radially running tears (caused by excessive loads even in the young) should be distinguished from concentric tears. The latter are associated with degenerative processes. Finally, parts of the intervertebral disk may be displaced.

Displacement with invasion of the adjacent vertebral body is known as a **"Schmorl's nodule"**. It is clearly visible in radiographs. **Pulposus herniation** occurs if the jellylike nucleus is pushed dorsally and laterally into the vertebral canal after damage to the anulus fibrosus. This may endanger the spinal cord, or individual spinal roots or spinal nerves.

Herniation of the nucleus pulposus is most common between the third and fourth lumbar vertebrae, as well as the fourth and fifth lumbar vertebrae. In addition, it often affects the lowest two cervical intervertebral disks between the fifth and sixth, or sixth and seventh cervical vertebrae.

Prolapse of a disk (i.e., of the nucleus) develops from a complete rupture of the anulus fibrosus. Reduction in the tension of the anulus fibrosus may lead to a loss of elasticity, followed by invasion of osteoblasts and ossification of parts of the disk.

A Intervertebral disk from above

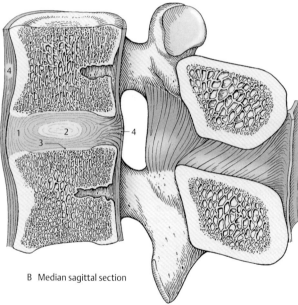

B Median sagittal section

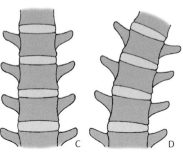

C Diagram of part of
vertebral column in
upright position

D Diagram of part of
vertebral column,
bent sideways

Trunk

Ligaments of the Vertebral Column (A–D)

The **anterior and posterior longitudinal ligaments:** the ligaments run anterior or posterior to the vertebral bodies.

The **anterior longitudinal ligament** (**1**) originates from the anterior tubercle of the atlas, and extends downward along the anterior surface of the vertebral bodies as far as the sacrum. It broadens out caudally and is **always firmly bound to the vertebral bodies**, but not to the intervertebral disks.

The **posterior longitudinal ligament** (**2**) is divided into a superficial and deep layer and courses along the posterior surface of the vertebral body. The superficial layer arises as a continuation of the tectorial membrane (p. 60) at the body of the axis and extends up to the intervertebral disk between L3 and L4 (*Prestar* and *Putz*). The deep layer represents the continuation of the cruciform ligament of the atlas and extends into the sacral canal. In the cervical region the superficial layer is broad, whereas it becomes narrower in the thoracic and lumbar regions and fuses with the deep layer below L3/L4. The deep layer is very thin in the cervical region, whereas in the thoracic and lumbar segments it forms a rhombic expansion (**3**) at the intervertebral disks (**4**) and the upper marginal ridges of the vertebral bodies. In these regions a **firm union is established with the intervertebral disks**, thus affording them extensive protection. A narrow space is present between the vertebral body and the deep layer of the ligament for veins exiting from the vertebral body.

The longitudinal ligaments increase the stability of the vertebral column, particularly during flexion and extension movements. They have therefore two functions, namely to restrict movement and to protect the intervertebral disks.

The **ligamenta flava** (**5**) extend segmentally between the vertebral arches (**6**). They border the medial and dorsal sides of the intervertebral foramina. Their yellow color is due to an interrupted latticework arrangement of elastic fibers which form most of the bands. Even at rest these ligaments are under tension. During flexion of the spine they become more extended and **help the return of the vertebral column to the erect position.**

The **ligamentum nuchae** (not shown) extends from the external occipital crest to the spinous processes of the cervical vertebrae. The sagittal position provides attachment for muscles, and it continues beyond the neck as the interspinal and supraspinal ligaments.

The **intertransverse ligaments** (**7**) are short ligaments between the transverse processes.

The interspinous ligaments (**8**) are also short ligaments that extend between the spinal processes (**9**).

The **supraspinous ligament** (**10**) begin on the spinal process of the seventh cervical vertebra and extend as far as the sacrum to provide a continuous connection between the vertebrae and the sacrum.

Long and short *perivertebral bands* occur lateral to the anterior longitudinal ligament, particularly in the lumbar and thoracic regions. These short bands (**11**), which extend parallel to the anterior longitudinal band, join adjacent intervertebral disks. Longer bands may arch over one disk.

12 Superior costotransverse ligament (p. 68)
13 Lateral costotransverse ligament (p. 68)
14 Radiate ligament of the head of rib (p. 68)

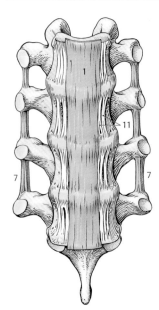

A Anterior longitudinal ligament

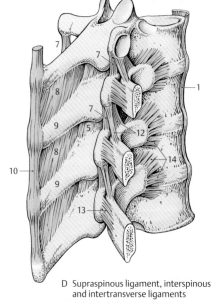

D Supraspinous ligament, interspinous and intertransverse ligaments

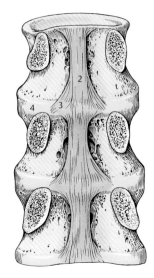

B Posterior longitudinal ligament

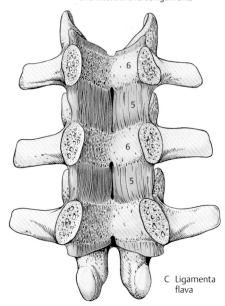

C Ligamenta flava

Joints of the Vertebral Column (A–E)

Zygapophyseal Joints (A–B)

These are the vertebral synovial joints between the articular processes (**A**). Clinically, they are also referred to as vertebral arch joints or "small vertebral joints". The *articular capsules* become tenser in the craniocaudal direction. In the cervical region they are broad and lax with *meniscus-like infoldings*. These *plicae synoviales* (**B**), enable the joints to bear a greater load. However, there is relatively little movement between any two adjacent vertebrae. It is only the combined action of all the participants (vertebrae and intervertebral disks) which results in corresponding movements. In the **cervical** region there is *lateral*, *forward*, and *backward flexion*, and a limited *rotation*. In the **thoracic** region mainly *rotation*, but to some extent also *flexion* and *extension* are possible. In the **lumbar** region *flexion* and *extension* essentially occur, although *slight rotation* is sometimes possible.

Movement in the individual segments of the vertebral column is dependent upon the position of the articular surfaces. With regard to the cervical vertebrae, the joint surfaces assume an approximately frontal position. To be sure, the joint surfaces of the third cervical vertebrae exhibit a different position (see p. 37, Fig. B) in that they form an angle of 142° with one another (*Putz*). In the case of the thoracic vertebrae they describe sectors of a cylindrical mantle and in the lumbar vertebrae most of the articular facets lie rather parallel to the sagittal plane. The locations of these facets in the lumbar vertebrae, however, can exhibit a great variation (*Putz*).

"Uncovertebral Joints" (C–E)

The "uncovertebral" joints are found in the **cervical** region. The *uncinate processes*, which are flat at first, begin to elevate in childhood. Between the ages of 5 and 10 years, fissures appear in the cartilage which assume an articular character; thus "uncovertebral" joints are not present initially but develop *secondarily*. Approximately between the ages of 9 and 10 years, these structures extend as gaps into the disks. This initially confers functional advantages, but later in life the fissure may develop into a complete tear through the disk (**E**), with a risk of **pulposus herniation** (see p. 54). Although uncovertebral joints are initially physiological structures, later they may become pathological due to rupture of the disk.

> **Clinical tip:** Clinically, the differential diagnosis between "uncovertebral joints" and traumatic or pathological changes is very difficult. Damage to the disk is most common at C5, where it may be visible in a lateral radiograph as the **"lordotic crack"**.

Lumbosacral Joint

The lumbosacral joint is the articulation of the last lumbar vertebra with the sacral bone. There is a very variable relationship between the articular surfaces and the superior articular processes of the sacral bone. It is asymmetrical in 60% of people. The iliolumbar ligament (p. 188) joins the costal process of L4 and L5 to the iliac crest and protects the lumbosacral joint from overloading during flexion and rotation (*Niethard*).

Sacrococcygeal Joint

The connection between the sacrum and the coccyx is often a *synovial joint*. It is strengthened by a superficial ligament and a deep posterior sacrococcygeal ligament, an anterior sacrococcygeal ligament and a lateral sacrococcygeal ligament.

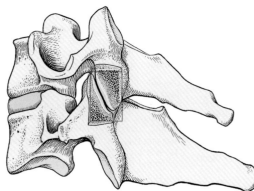

A Zygapophyseal joint (sagittal section)

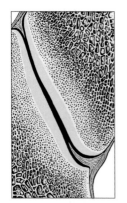

B Meniscoid folds in (small)
   vertebral joint (enlarged)

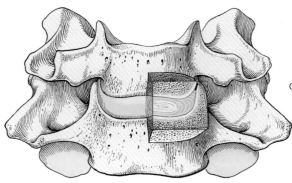

C Uncovertebral joint
   between C 6 and C 7
   (frontal section)

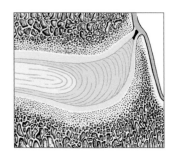

D Uncovertebral joint (enlarged)

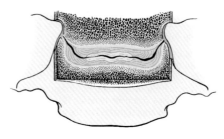

E Frontal section of split intervertebral disk
   in cervical spine region

Trunk

Joints of the Vertebral Column, continued

Atlanto-occipital Joint (A, D, E)

The right and left **atlanto-occipital articulation** is a combined joint between the atlas and the occipital bone, which in shape corresponds to an ellipsoid joint (**A, D**). The articular surfaces are the *superior articular facets* of the atlas and the *occipital condyles* (**1**). The joint capsules are lax and permit sideways bending and forward and backward movements. This **"upper head joint"** is secured by ligaments, just like the **"lower head joint"**.

Atlanto-axial Joints (B–E)

The so-called **"lower head joint"** consists of the conjoined **median** and **lateral atlanto-axial joints**. Functionally it is a *rotary joint* in which movement of 26° to each side is possible from the midposition. In the lateral joints the articular facets are the *inferior articular facets of the atlas* (**2**) and the *superior articular facets of the axis* (**3**). The incongruity of the articular surfaces is reduced by the cartilaginous covering and *meniscoid synovial folds* (**4**). The folds appear triangular in sagittal section (**C**). The articular facets of the median atlanto-axial joints include the *anterior articular facet of the dens of the axis* (**5**), and the *facet for dens on the posterior surface of the anterior arch of atlas* (**6**). In addition, in the region of the *transverse ligament of atlas* (**7**), which extends behind the dens, there is another articular surface on the dens. The "lower head joint", like the upper one, is secured by ligaments.

The **ligaments of both "head joints"** are the *apical ligament of dens* (**8**), which extends from the apex of the dens to the anterior margin of the foramen magnum. The *transverse ligament of atlas* (**7**) connects the two lateral masses of the atlas. It passes posterior to the dens and stabilizes it. The transverse ligament is strengthened by *longitudinal bands* (**9**) which run up-

ward to the anterior margin of the foramen magnum and downward to the posterior surface of the body of the second cervical vertebra. The longitudinal bands and the transverse ligament of the atlas together form the *cruciate ligament of atlas.*

The *alar ligaments* (**10**) are paired ligaments that arise on the dens and ascend to the lateral margin of the foramen magnum. They have a protective function, preventing excessive rotation between the atlas and the axis. The *tectorial membrane* (**11**) is a broad band which arises on the clivus and descends to join the posterior longitudinal ligament.

The *anterior* (**12**) *and posterior* (**13**) *atlanto-occipital membranes* consist of broad connective tissue fiber bands extending between the anterior and the posterior arches of the atlas, respectively, and the occipital bone.

14 Ligamenta flava
15 Nuchal ligament
16 Zygapophysial joint
17 Dura mater
18 Hypoglossal canal

I–III   Cervical vertebrae 1 to 3

> **Clinical tip:** Nerve lesions are more common in the cervical spine (55%) than in any other vertebral region. Note, however, that lesions of the atlas and axis are fundamentally different from lesions of other cervical vertebrae.

Trunk

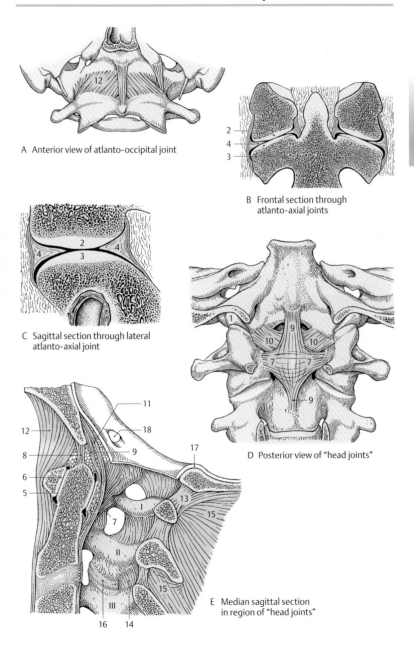

A Anterior view of atlanto-occipital joint

B Frontal section through atlanto-axial joints

C Sagittal section through lateral atlanto-axial joint

D Posterior view of "head joints"

E Median sagittal section in region of "head joints"

The Vertebral Column, Curvatures and Movements (A–H)

Curvatures of the Vertebral Column

In the sagittal plane the vertebral column of the adult shows two anteriorly convex secondary curvatures, **lordoses**, and two posteriorly convex primary curvatures, **kyphoses**.

The lordoses are in the cervical and lumbar regions (**1**) and the kyphoses in the thoracic and sacral regions (**2**). The intervertebral disk between the fifth lumbar vertebra and the sacrum is sometimes called the promontory (see p. 48).

> **Clinical tip:** The curvature in the cervical region is quite variable. Three types occur between the ages of 20 and 30 years. The **"true lordosis"** (**A**) is actually very uncommon. A double lordosis (**B**), also called a **lordotic bend** (p. 58), is the most common and is typical of adults in the 3rd decade of life. In addition, there may be almost a complete absence of lordosis, the **"attenuated form"**, (**C**). Investigation of differences between the sexes has shown that true lordosis is least common in females, that double lordosis occurs with equal frequency in both sexes, and that the attenuated type is more common in females than in males (*Drexler*).
>
> A lateral curvature is known as **scoliosis**. A slight degree of scoliosis is often present in radiographs, deviation to the right of the median sagittal plane being more common than to the left. The most common pathological finding is increased kyphosis (adolescent kyphosis, kyphosis of old age).

The curvatures of the vertebral column develop as a result of the stresses of sitting and standing. Its load capacity is dependent on the degree of ossification of the vertebrae, so that the final posture (**D**) is not achieved until after puberty. The line of the center of gravity lies partly in front of and partly behind the vertebral column. In a child of 10 months (**E**), the curvatures are already present, but the line of the center of gravity (**3**) lies behind the vertebral column. In infants of 3 months (**F**), the curvatures are only indicated.

In adults the vertebral column is like an elastic rod, the mobility of which is restricted by ligaments. During the aging process the vertebral column undergoes various changes, so that in the elderly a reduction in the thickness of the disks produces a rather uniform kyphosis of the entire vertebral column, and so reduces its mobility.

Movements of the Vertebral Column

Forward and backward bending (flexion and extension) occur primarily in the cervical and lumbar spine. Backward bendings particularly marked between the lower cervical vertebrae, the eleventh thoracic and second lumbar vertebrae and the lower lumbar vertebrae. Because of the greater mobility in this region, damage and injury to the spinal column due to overstrain is more frequent here than at other levels. In forward bending (blue) and backward bending (yellow) of the cervical (**G**) and lumbar (**H**) spine, changes are seen in the intervertebral disks which are subject to considerable stress. The degree of *lateral flexion* in the cervical and lumbar regions is approximately equal, but it is greatest in the thoracic region.

Rotation is possible in the thoracic and cervical region and particularly in the "lower head joint" area. Head rotation always goes hand in hand with movement of the "lower head joint", movement of the cervical and slight movement of the thoracic spine. New research (*Putz*) has shown that rotation is also possible in the lumbar region. Movement of 3° to 7° may occur between two vertebrae.

Movements take place in "segments of motion" (*Junghanns*) which are combined into "zones of motion" (*Putz*). A segment of motion is the range of movement between two vertebrae. This includes the intervertebral disks with superior and inferior hyaline cartilage plate, vertebral joints, and ligaments, including all spaces.

Functional zones of motion:
- Craniovertebral joints–C3 –
- C3 –T1(T2)
- T1 (T2)–(T11) T12
- (T11) T12 –Sacrum

Or:

Craniovertebral joints – 3rd cervical vertebra
3rd cervical – 1st (2nd) thoracic vertebra
1st (2nd)–(11th) 12th thoracic vertebra
11th (12 thoracic vertebra–sacrum

> **Clinical tip:** Limitations of vertebral motion, called **restrictions**, most commonly affect the third cervical vertebra due to the position of the joint surfaces. They are also common in the lower cervical and lumbar spine. Restrictions cause significant pain due to nerve irritation, with neuralgia and muscle pain often radiating to the limbs. Spinal restrictions can usually be relieved by manual manipulation. Untreated restriction may eventually cause irreversible damage to the articular cartilage.

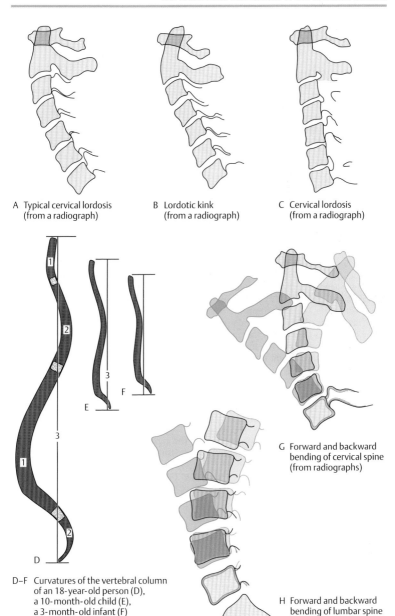

A Typical cervical lordosis
   (from a radiograph)

B Lordotic kink
   (from a radiograph)

C Cervical lordosis
   (from a radiograph)

Trunk

D–F Curvatures of the vertebral column
      of an 18-year-old person (D),
      a 10-month-old child (E),
      a 3-month-old infant (F)
      (from radiographs)

G Forward and backward
   bending of cervical spine
   (from radiographs)

H Forward and backward
   bending of lumbar spine
   (from radiographs)

Thoracic Cage

Ribs (A–F)

In each **rib** we distinguish a bony part, the **os costale**, and at the anterior end the **costal cartilage**.

There are 12 pairs of ribs, of which the upper seven are normally connected directly to the sternum and are called **true ribs**. The lower five ribs, **false ribs**, are joined indirectly (8th–10th) or not at all (11th–12th) to the sternum. The 11th and 12th ribs can be distinguished from the others as **floating ribs**.

Each **rib** has a *head* (**1**), *neck* (**2**), and a *body* (**3**). The border between the neck and the body is defined by the *tubercle* (**4**). The head and the tubercle (*articular facet of the tubercle*, **5**) each have an articular surface. From the 2nd to the 10th rib, the *articular facet of the head* (**6**) is divided in two by the *crest of the head of the rib* (**7**). On the upper margin of the neck of most ribs is the *crest of the neck of the rib* (**8**). Lateral and ventral to the tubercle is the *angle of the rib*. With the exception of the 1st, 11th and 12th, all ribs have a *costal sulcus* on the lower surface.

Curvatures. There are three curvatures—of the edge, the flat surface, and a torsion curvature. Although the *edge curvature*, which is the principal one in the 1st rib, is readily apparent, the *flat surface curvature* can only be seen on close inspection. It is present from the 3rd rib on. If the upper surface of a rib is viewed near its anterior end and is followed toward the back, it will be seen that the surface slowly turns dorsally. In addition to this curvature, there is a longitudinal twist in the rib, which is most marked in the middle ribs and is called torsion. It is not present in the 1st, 2nd or 12th ribs.

The **hyaline costal cartilage** begins to calcify with increasing age, more in males than in females. This reduces mobility of the thorax (see p. 70).

Individual Features of Particular Ribs

The **1st rib** (**A**) is small and flattened. On the inner circumference of its cranial surface is an area of roughness, the *scalene tubercle* (**9**), to which the anterior scalenus is attached. Posterior to it lies the *groove for subclavian artery* (**10**), and in front of it is the *groove for subclavian vein* (**11**), which is not always clearly visible.

The **2nd rib** (**B**) has a rough area on its upper surface, the *tuberosity for the serratus anterior muscle* (**12**), from which one part of the serratus anterior originates.

The costal tubercle and costal sulcus are absent from **ribs 11 and 12** (**D**), and the costal angle is only indicated.

In two-thirds of cases the 10th rib ends freely, i.e., it is not connected with the 9th rib and with the sternum. The first seven ribs are usually directly connected to the sternum, although sometimes the first eight may be so associated, and less commonly only the first six.

■■■ **Variants:** The number of pairs of ribs is variable. There are usually 12 pairs, but sometimes 11 or 13 are found. When there are 13 pairs, cervical (see p. 36) or lumbar ribs (see p. 42) may be present.

Malformations may lead to **fenestrated** or **forked ribs** (**E**). Most commonly they affect the 4th rib.

Ossification (F)

The cartilage anlagen begin to ossify, progressing from dorsal to ventral by the end of the 2nd intrauterine month. By the end of the 4th intrauterine month, ossification ceases and the ventral part is preserved as the rib cartilage.

Trunk

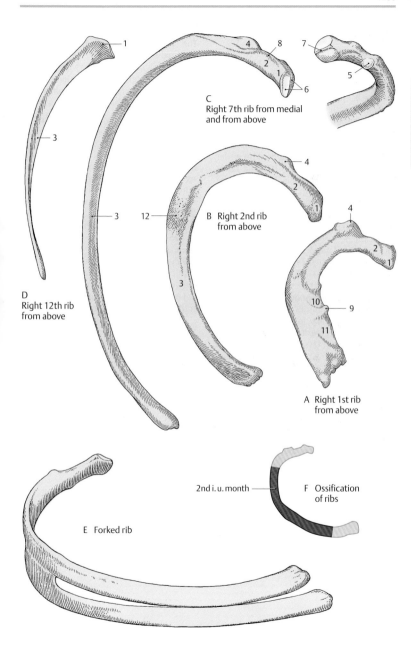

C Right 7th rib from medial and from above

D Right 12th rib from above

B Right 2nd rib from above

A Right 1st rib from above

E Forked rib

2nd i.u. month

F Ossification of ribs

Sternum (A–F)

The **sternum** consists of the *manubrium* (**1**), the *body* (**2**) and the *xiphoid process* (**3**). Between the manubrium and the body lies the *sternal angle* (**4**), which is open toward the back. The xiphoid process is cartilaginous until maturity; with advancing age it may become ossified completely or remain partially cartilaginous. At the cranial end of the manubrium sterni is the *jugular notch* (**5**) and lateral to it on either side the *clavicular notches* (**6**). The latter articulate with the clavicle. Just below the clavicular notch, the manubrium again has an additional paired *costal notch* (**7**) for a continuous cartilaginous joint with the 1st rib. At the sternal angle is a *notch* (**8**) for articulation between the sternum and the 2nd rib. The lateral borders of the body have costal-notches for continuous connections with ribs 3–7. The costal notch for the 7th rib lies just at the point of transition between the body and the xiphoid process. The manubrium and body of the sternum are usually joined by the *manubriosternal joint* (*synchondrosis* see p. 68). A *xiphosternal joint* (*synchondrosis*) between the body and the xiphoid process is much less common.

The xiphoid process varies in shape. It may consist of one piece or it may be forked. Sometimes it contains a foramen and it may be bent forward or backward.

Sex Differences: The body of the sternum is longer in males than in females, and, for sterna of the same length, that of the male is narrower and slimmer than that of the female.

■ **Variants:** Very rarely there are **suprasternal bones** (**9**), also called the episternum, at the cranial end of the manubrium near the jugular notch. Sometimes there is an opening within the sternum, a **congenital sternal fissure** (**D 10**), which arises during development.

Ossification (E, F)

The sternum develops from *paired sternal bands* which are formed by longitudinal fusion of individual rib anlagen, followed by fusion of the sternal bands. In the region of the jugular notch a *paired suprasternal body* forms and subsequently regresses.

In the preformed cartilaginous part of the sternum, ossification starts from several bony centers. The first center usually appears in the manubrium between the 3rd and 6th intrauterine months. The remaining centers, usually paired, but partly unpaired, five to seven in number, then arise in the body of the sternum, the most caudal appearing in the 1st year. Fusion of the centers occurs between the ages of 6 to 20 (25) years. Secondary epiphyseal anlagen may appear in the region of the clavicular notch which, however, only fuse with the manubrium between the ages of 25 and 30 years. Between the ages of 5 and 10 years, two osseous centers may develop in the region of the xiphoid process.

Clinical tip: Sternal puncture is performed by introducing a sternal puncture needle through the body of the sternum in the midline between the attachments of the second and third ribs. It must never be made at the level of the costosternal connections since synchondroses can be present here. Likewise, the lower two-thirds of the body of the sternum should **never** be punctured since a congenital sternal fissure (see above) conditioned by the paired ossific centers can be present.

Trunk

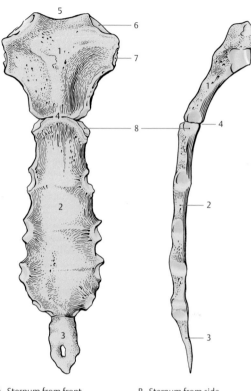

A Sternum from front

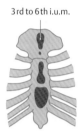

B Sternum from side

3rd to 6th i.u.m.

E Sternal ossification before birth

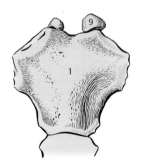

C Suprasternal bones

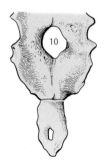

D Congenital sternal fissure

3rd to 6th g.m.

5th to 10th year

F Sternal ossification between 5 and 10 years

Joints of the Ribs (A–C)

Mobility of the ribs is a precondition for respiration. There are connections between the ribs and vertebral column (joints) and also between the ribs and the sternum (diarthroses and synchondroses).

Costovertebral Joints (A, B)

Joints of the heads of ribs (1). Apart from the 1st, 11th, and 12th ribs, the joints of the heads of the ribs with the vertebral column represent double-chambered joints. Each rib articulates with the upper or lower borders of two neighboring vertebrae, and the intervertebral disk is connected by an *intra-articular ligament of head of rib* to the crest of the head of the rib. The capsule is strengthened by the *radiate ligament of head of rib* (**2**).

Costotransverse joints (3). With the exception of ribs 11 and 12, all ribs also articulate with the transverse processes of the vertebrae, so that here the two joints, head of rib and *costotransverse joints*, are obligatorily combined. The articular surfaces of the costotransverse joints are the *articular facet of the costal tubercle* and the *costal fovea of the transverse process*. The capsules of these joints are delicate and are strengthened by ligaments, the *costotransverse ligament* (**4**), including the *lateral costotransverse ligament* (**5**) and the *superior costotransverse ligament* (**6**).

In the region of the 12th rib there is, in addition, the *lumbocostal ligament*, which extends from the costal process of the 1st lumbar vertebra to the 12th rib.

Movements. Sliding movements are possible for the 1st rib and ribs 6–9, and rotary motion about the neck is possible for ribs 2–5.

Sternocostal Joints (C)

Only some of the junctions between the ribs and the sternum are synovial joints. They are always present between the sternum and ribs 2–5, but ribs 1, 6, and 7 are joined to the sternum by *cartilaginous joints*, or *synchondroses* (**7**). The sternocostal joints are strengthened by ligaments which continue into the *sternal membrane* (**8**). An *intra-articular sternocostal ligament* (**9**) is always present at the 2nd sternocostal joint. The other strengthening ligaments are the *radiate sternocostal ligaments* (**10**). In the sternocostal articulations one must keep in mind that the ribs (see p. 64) consist of bone and cartilage. The joints between the sternum and the ribs are formed by the cartilaginous part of the rib. This costal cartilage loses its elasticity at an early age due to calcium deposition.

The **interchondral joints** are a special type of articulation which occurs between the cartilages of the 6th– 9th ribs.

11 Manubriosternal symphysis (joint)
12 Clavicle
13 Xiphoid process

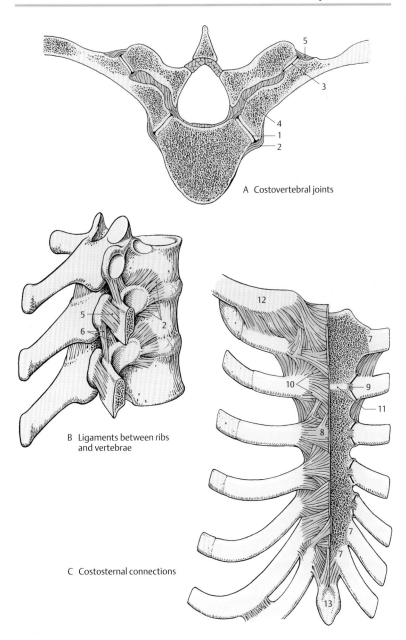

A Costovertebral joints

B Ligaments between ribs and vertebrae

C Costosternal connections

Trunk

Structure of the Thoracic Cage (A–D)

The **thorax** consists of *12 thoracic vertebrae and their intervertebral disks, 12 pairs of ribs and the sternum.* The thorax encloses the **thoracic cavity**, which has a *superior* (**1**) and an *inferior* (**2**) *aperture*. While the superior aperture is relatively narrow, the inferior one is very wide. The inferior thoracic aperture is limited by the *costal arch* (**3**) and the *xiphoid process* (**4**) the superior one by the two first ribs. The angle between the right and left costal arches is called the *infrasternal angle* (**5**).

The marked curvature of the ribs in the dorsal region and their posteriorly directed course between the transverse processes of the thoracic vertebrae and the costal angle makes the posterior thoracic wall project dorsally. This space, which lies lateral to and behind the vertebral column, is called the *pulmonary groove* of the thorax.

Movements of the Thoracic Cage (A–D)

Its elasticity makes for great resistance to stress. Movements of the thorax result from a summation of individual movements. As limiting positions we distinguish **maximal expiration** (**A, B**) on the one hand and **maximal inspiration** (**C, D**) on the other. During inspiration there is a widening of the thorax both in the ventrodorsal and in the lateral directions. The expansion is made possible (1) by the mobility in the costovertebral joints, (2) by elasticity of the costal cartilages which permit twisting, and (3) to a slight extent by increased kyphosis of the thoracic column.

During expiration the ribs are depressed, thus diminishing the size of the thorax in the ventrodorsal and lateral direction. At the same time there is some decrease in the thoracic kyphosis. The infrasternal angle increases, becoming less acute during inspiration, while during expiration it becomes more acute.

The mobility of the thorax is reduced by calcification of the costal cartilages. The shape of the thorax is not decisive in determining respiratory capacity. The essential factor is its mobility, i.e., the difference in volume between maximal expiration and maximal inspiration. Disorders not only of the cartilage but also of the joints cause reduction of total thoracic function.

The **forces which move the thorax** are generated by the *intercostal* (see p. 82) and *scalenus muscles* (see p. 80). The intercostal muscles occupy the intercostal spaces. They are primitive metameric muscles, which must be included in the autochthonous thoracic musculature. The latter also include the transversus thoracis and subcostal muscles. The musculature is innervated by ventral rami of the spinal nerves, the intercostal nerves.

Clinical tip: Erb's point is a left parasternal auscultation point located in the third intercostal space in the plane of the cardiac valves (*red dot* in the diagrams).

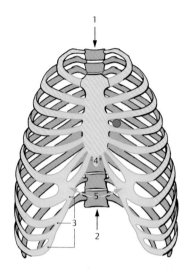

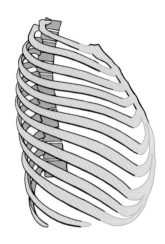

A Thorax – expiratory position
 from front

B Thorax – expiratory position
 from side

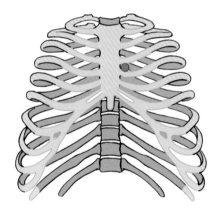

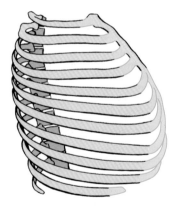

C Thorax – inspiratory position
 from front

D Thorax – inspiratory position
 from side

Trunk

Intrinsic Muscles of the Back

This group includes *all the muscles inner-vated by the dorsal rami of the spinal nerves*. Together they are called the **erector spinae**. In the living body there are two longitudinal columns lateral to the spinous processes, which are most marked in the lumbar region. The muscles lie in an osteo-fibrous canal formed by the bones of the vertebral arches, the costal processes and the spinous processes. Posteriorly and laterally this canal is limited by the thora-columbar fascia (p. 78). Because these muscles are difficult to demonstrate and are subject to considerable variation, cur-rently they classified without regard for their embryonic origins. Thus, we no longer speak in terms of a "lateral tract" and "medial tract" but divide the muscles into three parts:

Erector spinae
- iliocostalis
- longissimus
- spinalis

At the origin of all three muscles is the erector spinae aponeurosis (erroneously called the "sacrospinalis" in older publica-tions), the
spinotransversales
- splenii
interspinales (p. 74)
intertransversarii (p. 74) and the
transversospinales (p. 74)
- rotatores
- multifidus
- semispinalis

Erector Spinae Muscles

The **iliocostalis** (**1, 2, 3**) consists of the ilio-costalis lumborum, the iliocostalis thoracis and the iliocostalis cervicis. The **iliocostalis lumborum** (**1**) *extends from the sacrum, ex-ternal lip of the iliac crest and the thora-columbar fascia to the costal processes of the upper lumbar vertebrae and the lower 6–9 ribs*. The **iliocostalis thoracis** (**2**) *stretches from the lower six to the upper six ribs*, and the **iliocostalis cervicis** (**3**) *arises from the 6th–3rd ribs and inserts on the transverse processes of the sixth to fourth cervical vertebrae*.
Nerve supply: dorsal rami (C4–L3).

The **longissimus** (**4, 5, 6**) is subdivided into the longissimus thoracis (**4**) and cervicis (**5**) and the longissimus capitis (**6**). The **longissimus thoracis** *arises from the sacrum, the spinous processes of the lumbar verte-brae and the transverse processes of the lower thoracic vertebrae and extends to the 1st or 2nd ribs*. It is attached medially and laterally; medially to the accessory processes (**7**) of the lumbar vertebrae and to the transverse processes (**8**) of the thoracic vertebrae, and laterally to the ribs, the costal processes (**9**) of the lumbar vertebra and the deep lamina of the thora-columbar fascia. The **longissimus cervicis** *arises from the transverse processes of the upper six thoracic vertebrae and extends to the posterior tubercles of the transverse processes of the second to fifth cervical vertebrae*. The **longissimus capitis** *originates from the transverse processes of the three to five upper thoracic and the three lower cer-vical vertebrae and ends on the mastoid process* (**10**).
Nerve supply: dorsal rami (C2–L5).

Spinotransversal Muscles

The **splenius cervicis** (**11**) *extends from the spinous processes of the (third) fourth to (fifth) sixth thoracic vertebrae to the trans-verse processes of the first and second cervi-cal vertebrae*.

The **splenius capitis** (**12**) *arises from the spinous processes of the upper three thoracic and the lower four cervical verte-brae and ends in the region of the mastoid process* (**10**).
Nerve supply: dorsal rami (C1–C8).

The actions of all these muscle supplement each other. The first two are largely responsible for the erect posture of the body and then the two splenii, when contracted on one side, produce rotation of the head to the same side. They have an additional supporting function for the other intrinsic muscles of the back. In the thoracic and lumbar regions the intrinsic muscles of the back are held in place by the thoracolumbar fascia.

▬ Variants: Variations in the number of muscle slips is common.

I–XII: 1st to 12th ribs
13 Aponeurosis of the erector spinae muscle

The **levatores costarum** on page 78.

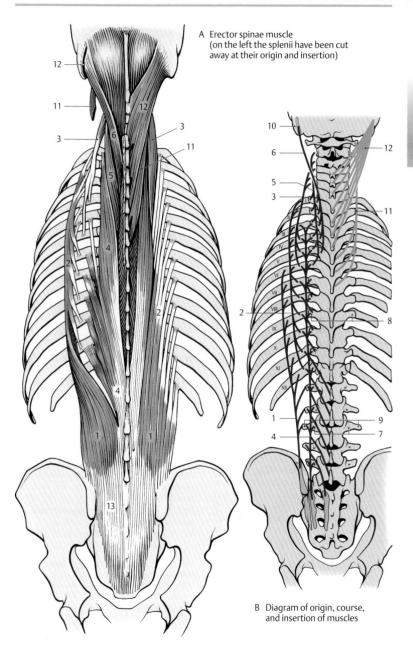

A Erector spinae muscle
(on the left the splenii have been cut
away at their origin and insertion)

B Diagram of origin, course,
and insertion of muscles

Intrinsic Muscles of the Back, continued (A—C)

Interspinales

The **interspinales** are arranged segmentally and are present in the cervical and lumbar regions. They are absent from the thoracic region, except between the first and second, second and third, and eleventh and twelfth thoracic vertebrae, and between the twelfth thoracic and first lumbar vertebrae. *They link adjacent spinous processes.* On either side there are **6 interspinales cervicis** (**1**), **4 interspinales thoracis** (**2**), and **5 interspinales lumborum** (**3**). Nerve supply: dorsal rami (C1 –T3 and T11 – L5).

Intertransversarii

The **intertransversarii** lie lateral to the interspinales. The **6 posterior intertransversarii cervicis** (**4**) connect the *adjacent posterior tubercles of the transverse processes of cervical vertebrae 2-7.* Nerve supply: dorsal rami (C1 –C6). The **4 medial intertransversarii lumborum** (**5**) connect the *mamillary* and *accessory processes of adjacent lumbar vertebrae.* Nerve supply: dorsal rami (L1 –L4).

Erector Spinae

The **spinalis** is divided into the spinalis thoracis, cervicis and capitis. The latter is only occasionally present. The fibers of the **spinalis thoracis** (**6**) *arise from the spinous processes of the third lumbar through tenth thoracic vertebrae. They are inserted on the* spinous processes of thoracic vertebrae 8–2; the innermost fibers (from the tenth to eighth thoracic vertebrae) are the shortest. The fibers of the **spinalis cervicis** (**7**) *arise from the spinous processes of the second thoracic through the sixth cervical vertebrae and insert on the* spinous processes of the fourth to second cervical vertebrae. Nerve supply: dorsal rami (C2 –T10).

Transversospinales

The **rotatores breves** (**8**) and **longi** (**cervicis**), **thoracis** (**9**) (**et lumborum**) are most prominent in the thoracic region. *Each arises from a transverse process and runs to the next higher spinous process, or the one after, where it is inserted into the base.* Nerve supply: dorsal rami (T1 –T11).

The **multifidus** (**10**) consists of a number of small fasciculi (**M. multifidus, lumborum, thoracis** and **cervicis**) which extend from the sacrum to the second cervical vertebra. It is best developed in the lumbar region. The individual fascicles *arise from the superficial aponeurosis of the longissimus muscle, the dorsal surface of the sacrum, the mamillary processes of the lumbar vertebrae, the transverse processes of the thoracic vertebrae and the articular processes of the seventh to fourth cervical vertebrae. The muscle bundles cross two to four vertebrae and are inserted in the spinous processes of the appropriate higher vertebrae.* Nerve supply: dorsal rami (C3 –S4).

The **semispinalis**, which overlies the multifidus laterally, is divided into thoracic, cervical and cephalic (*capitis*) parts. Individual muscle bundles cross five or more vertebrae. The fibers of the **semispinalis thoracis** and **cervicis** (**11**) *arise from the transverse processes of all thoracic vertebrae. They are inserted in the spinous processes of the upper six thoracic and lower four cervical vertebrae.* The **semispinalis capitis** (**12**), which is one of the strongest muscles of the neck, *arises from the transverse processes of the upper four to seven thoracic vertebrae and the articular processes of the five lower cervical vertebrae. It is inserted between the superior and inferior nuchal lines of the skull.* Nerve supply: dorsal rami (T4 –T6, C3 –C6 and C1 –C5).

The straight muscles function as extensors when both sides are innervated and unilaterally as lateral flexors when only one side is innervated. Oblique muscles function when unilaterally innervated as rotators and bilaterally innervated as extensors.

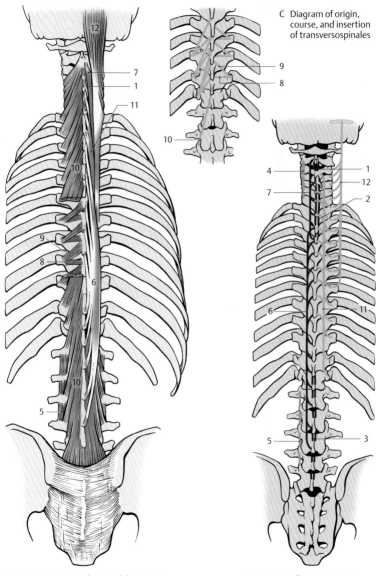

C Diagram of origin, course, and insertion of transversospinales

A Erector spinae muscle, multifidus muscle partially removed to make the rotator muscles visible)

B Diagram of origin, course, and insertion of straight muscle system

Trunk

Suboccipital Muscles (A, B)

The paired short nape muscles, the rectus capitis posterior minor and major and the obliquus capitis superior and inferior, are part of the intrinsic muscles of the back, and, except for the inferior obliquus capitis, they, too, belong to the straight system of the medial tract. Both recti originate from interspinal muscles and the obliquus capitis superior from an intertransverse muscle.

Two other short neck muscles, the rectus capitis lateralis and the rectus capitis anterior, do not belong to the intrinsic muscles of the back. The former is one of the muscles that have migrated from the ventrolateral body wall: it is described on page 78. The anterior rectus capitis, a prevertebral muscle, is described on page 80.

The **rectus capitis posterior minor** (**1**) *arises* from the *posterior tubercle of the atlas* and ascends upward in a fan shape. It *inserts* in the medial region of the *inferior nuchal line*. It is covered at the lateral aspect of its insertion by the rectus capitis posterior major muscle.

The **rectus capitis posterior major** (**2**) takes its *origin* from the *spinous process of the second cervical vertebra* and *inserts* at the *inferior nuchal line* lateral to the rectus capitis posterior minor muscle. It also widens out in the direction of its insertion in a similar fashion as the rectus capitis posterior minor.

The **obliquus capitis superior** (**3**) *originates from the transverse process of the atlas*. It is inserted on the occipital bone somewhat above and lateral to the rectus capitis posterior major.

The **obliquus capitis inferior** (**4**) *runs from the spinous process of the second cervical vertebra to the transverse process of the atlas*.

All the short nape muscles act on the head joints. Bilateral contraction causes the straight and oblique muscles to bend the head backward and unilateral contraction of the obliquus capitis superior turns the head sideways. Lateral rotation of the head is caused by synergistic contraction of the rectus capitis posterior major and obliquus capitis inferior.

Nerve supply: suboccipital nerve (C1).

> **Clinical tip:** The rectus capitis posterior major and the obliquus capitis superior and inferior form the **suboccipital triangle** (trigonum a. vertebralis). Here the vertebral artery (see p. 346) can be located, lying on the posterior arch of the atlas. Between the artery and the posterior arch of the atlas lies the first cervical nerve, whose dorsal ramus, the suboccipital nerve (see p. 346 and vol. 3) innervates these muscles. Suboccipital puncture is described on p. 346.

■■ **Variants:** The rectus capitis posterior minor can be absent or very small on one side. The rectus capitis posterior major is rarely absent. Sometimes it can be divided into two muscles.

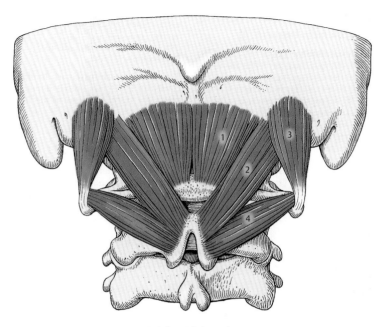

A   Suboccipital muscles

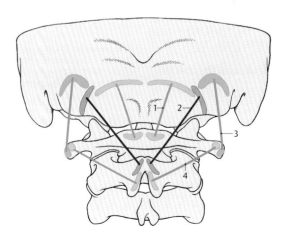

B   Diagram of origin, course, and insertion of muscles

Trunk

Body Wall

Thoracolumbar Fascia (A, B)

The **thoracolumbar fascia** (**1**) completes the osteofibrous canal formed by the vertebral column and the dorsal surfaces of the ribs. *It invests all intrinsic muscles of the back* (**2**) *and consists of three layers.* The **superficial = posterior layer** (**3**) is firmly bound to the erector spinae aponeurosis in the sacral region. Ascending in the body it becomes somewhat thinner and serves as an origin for the latissimus dorsi (**4**) and posterior inferior serratus (**5**). In the cervical region, where it has become very thin, it separates the splenius capitis and splenius cervicis from the trapezius (**6**) and becomes the nuchal fascia (**7**).

The **deep = anterior layer** (**8**) arises from the costal processes (**9**) of the lumbar vertebrae and separates the intrinsic back muscles (**2**) from those of the ventrolateral body wall.

The internal abdominal oblique (**10**) and the transversus abdominis (**11**) arise from the deep layer which extends as far as the iliac crest. The **middle layer** lies within the intrinsic back muscles.

The **nuchal fascia** (**7**) continues laterally forward into the superficial cervical fascia (see p. 331). The nuchal ligament lies in the middle of the nuchal fascia.

Extrinsic Ventrolateral Muscles (A)

The muscles described are innervated by the ventral rami of the spinal nerves, and in the course of development have migrated into the dorsal body wall.

The **rectus capitis lateralis** *runs from the transverse process of the atlas to the jugular process of the occipital bone* and corresponds developmentally to an anterior intertransverse muscle. Its action produces lateral head flexion.
Nerve supply: C1.

The **anterior intertransversarii cervicis** are six small bundles running *between the ventral protuberances on the transverse processes of the cervical vertebrae.*
Nerve supply: C2–C6.

The **lateral intertransversarii lumborum** consist of five to six muscle bundles *between the costal processes of the lumbar vertebrae.*
Nerve supply: L1–L4.

The **levatores costarum** *arise from the transverse processes of the seventh cervical and the first to eleventh thoracic vertebrae. They reach the costal angles* of the next rib below as the **short levatores costarum**, or the second rib below as the **long levatores costarum**. They are involved in spinal rotation.
According to *Steubl* these muscles are innervated by the dorsal rami of the spinal nerves and so belong to the lateral tract of the intrinsic back muscles.
Nerve supply: dorsal rami of the spinal nerves.

The **posterior superior serratus** (12) *originates from the spinous processes of the last two cervical and the first two thoracic vertebrae and is inserted on ribs 2–5*, which it elevates.
Nerve supply: intercostal nerves (T1–T4).

The **posterior inferior serratus** (**5**) *arises from the thoracolumbar fascia* in the region of the twelfth thoracic and first to third lumbar vertebrae *and usually extends* with four digitations *to the 12th–9th ribs*. It lowers the ribs.
Nerve supply: intercostal nerves (T9–T12).

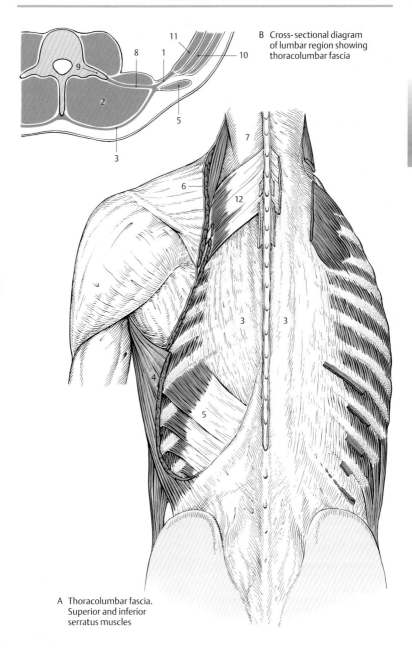

B Cross-sectional diagram of lumbar region showing thoracolumbar fascia

A Thoracolumbar fascia. Superior and inferior serratus muscles

Prevertebral Muscles (A, B)

The prevertebral muscles include the rectus capitis anterior, longus capitis, and longus colli.

The **rectus capitis anterior** (**1**) *extends from the lateral mass of the atlas* (**2**) *to the basal part of the occipital bone* (**3**). It helps to flex the head.
Nerve supply: cervical plexus (C1).

The **longus capitis** (**4**) *arises from the anterior tubercles of the transverse processes of the third to sixth cervical vertebrae* (**5**). It runs upward and is *attached to the basal part of the occipital bone* (**6**). The two longi capitis muscles bend the head forward. Unilateral action of the muscle helps to tilt the head sideways.
Nerve supply: cervical plexus (C1–C4).

The **longus colli** (**7**) is roughly triangular in shape because it consists of three groups of fibers. The **superior oblique fibers** (**8**) *arise from the anterior tubercles on the transverse processes of the fifth to second cervical vertebrae* (**9**) *and are inserted on the anterior tubercle of the atlas* (**10**). The **inferior oblique fibers** (**11**) *run from the bodies of the first to third thoracic vertebrae* (**12**) *to the anterior tubercle on the transverse process of the sixth cervical vertebra* (**13**). The **medial fibers** (**14**) *extend from the bodies of the upper thoracic and lower cervical vertebrae* (**15**) *to the bodies of the upper cervical vertebrae* (**16**). Unilateral contraction of the muscle bends and turns the cervical vertebral column to the side. Together, both longi colli muscles bend the cervical spine forward. Electromyographic studies have shown that the homolateral muscle is also involved in lateral flexion and rotation of the cervical vertebral column.
Nerve supply: cervical and brachial plexus (C2–C8).

Scalene Muscles (A, B)

The **scalene muscles** represent the cranial continuation of the intercostal muscles. They arise from the vestigial ribs of the cervical vertebrae. They are the most important muscles for quiet inhalation, as they lift the first two pairs of ribs and thus the superior part of the thorax. Their action is increased when the head is bent backward. Unilateral contraction tilts the cervical column to one side. Occasionally there is a scalenus minimus which arises from the seventh cervical vertebra and joins the scalenus medius. It is attached to the apex of the pleura.

The **scalenus anterior** (**17**) *arises from the anterior tubercles of the transverse processes of the (third) fourth to sixth cervical vertebrae* (**18**) *and is inserted on the anterior scalene tubercle* (**19**) *of the first rib*.
Nerve supply: brachial plexus (C5–C7).

The **scalenus medius** (**20**) *arises from the posterior tubercles of the transverse processes of the (first) second to seventh cervical vertebrae* (**21**). It is *inserted into the 1st rib behind the subclavian artery groove and into the external intercostal membrane of the 1st intercostal space* (**22**). In this way it can reach the 2nd rib. The attachment at the 1st rib is located behind the groove for the subclavian artery.
Nerve supply: cervical and brachial plexus (C4–C8).

The **scalenus posterior** (**23**) *runs from the posterior tubercles on the transverse processes of the fifth to seventh cervical vertebrae* (**24**) *to the 2nd (3rd) rib* (**25**). It can be absent.
Nerve supply: brachial plexus (C7–C8).

A **scalenus minimus muscle** may be present in about one-third of cases. It arises from the *anterior tubercle* of the transverse process of the seventh *cervical vertebra* and *reaches the fibrous vault of the pleura and the 1st rib*. If the muscle is absent, a *transverse cupular ligament (Hayek)* replaces it.
Nerve supply: brachial plexus (C8).

Clinical tip: Between the scalenus anterior and scalenus medius lies the **scalene opening** (**26**), through which pass the brachial plexus (see p. 360 and vol. 3) and the subclavian artery. Retroversion of the arm may occlude the subclavian artery between the rib and the clavicle. Together with the longus colli, the scalenus anterior forms the medial wall of the **scalenovertebral triangle** (**27**; see p. 366).

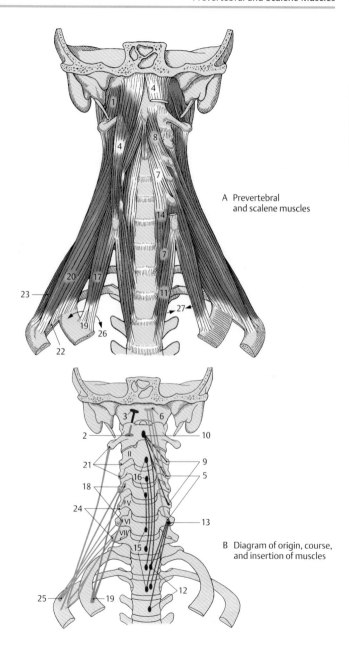

A Prevertebral
   and scalene muscles

B Diagram of origin, course,
   and insertion of muscles

Trunk

Muscles of the Thoracic Cage

Intercostal Muscles (A–D)

In addition to the scalene muscles, the intercostals are necessary for movements of the chest wall. These are divided into
- **external intercostal**
- **internal intercostal**
- **subcostal and**
- **transverse thoracic muscles**

The outermost intercostal muscles, the **external intercostals** (**1**), *extend from the costal tubercle to the beginning of the rib cartilage* and continue in every intercostal space into the **external intercostal membrane** where the rib bone merges with the costal cartilage. Each of these muscles *originate from the lower margin of a rib* and are *inserts at the upper margin of a rib*. The external intercostals run from superoposterior to the inferoanterior. According to their function they are known as inspiratory muscles (*Fick*). Recently electromyography has shown that the external intercostals are active only during forced inspiration and that quiet breathing depends on the action of the scalene muscles alone (see p. 80).
Nerve supply: intercostal nerves (T1 –T11).

The **internal intercostals** (**2**) *run from the costal angle to the sternum* in every intercostal space. *They arise from the superior margin of the inner surface of the rib and are inserted in the region of the costal groove.* From the costal angle medially toward the vertebrae, the internal intercostals are replaced by ligamentous fibers, which are known as the **internal intercostal membrane**.

In the region of the costal cartilages they may be referred to as **intercartilaginous muscles** (**3**).

A portion of each inner intercostal muscle is separated to form the intercostales intimi, also called the **innermost intercostal muscles.** Between them and the internal intercostals lie the intercostal nerve and vessels.

The direction of the internal intercostals is opposite to that of the external muscles, i.e., they run from inferoposterior to superoanterior.

According to *Fick* they are expiratory muscles, i.e., they are activated only when the ribs are lowered. The intercartilaginous muscles, particularly those of the 4th– 6th intercostal spaces, act as inspiratory muscles by virtue of their position in relation to the sternum.
Nerve supply: intercostal nerves (T1 –T11).

The **subcostals** (**4**), which lie in the region of the costal angles, consist mainly of fibers of the internal intercostal muscles that extend over several segments. They have the same function as the internal intercostals.
Nerve supply: intercostal nerves (T4 –T11).

The **transversus thoracis** (**5**) *arises from the internal surface of the xiphoid process and the body of the sternum.* Its fibers run in a laterocranial direction and *are attached to the lower border of the 2nd– 6th costal cartilages.*

The direction of the muscle slips fans out, i.e., the uppermost slip ascends steeply upward, whereas the lowermost slip courses parallel to the transversus abdominis muscle. A sharp boundary between the transversus thoracis and the transversus abdominis is only then attained when the origin of the costal part of the diaphragm (p. 102) is well developed from the 7th rib. The transversus thoracis functions in expiration.
Nerve supply: intercostal nerves (T2 –T6).

▬ **Variants:** Numerous variations are known. Right and left muscles are frequently formed asymmetrically. Sometimes it can be absent. The number of slips can vary.

Clinical tip: The internal thoracic artery and vein course ventral to the transversus thoracis. When the muscle is strongly developed, the artery is difficult to expose during coronary bypass operations.

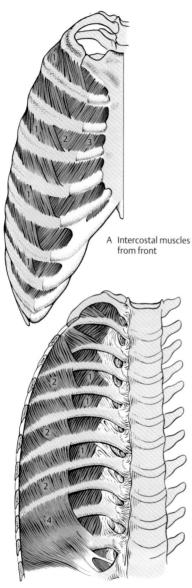

A Intercostal muscles from front

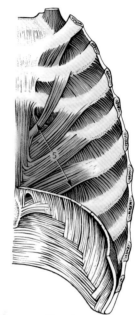

B Transversus thoracis, viewed from inside anterior thoracic wall

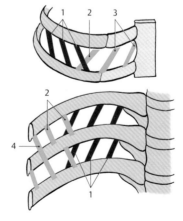

C View from inside posterior thoracic wall

D Diagram of origin, course, and insertion of muscles

Trunk

Abdominal Wall

The abdominal wall is limited superiorly by the infrasternal angle and inferiorly by the iliac crest, the inguinal sulcus, and the pubic sulcus. Under the abdominal skin lies the more or less extensive subcutaneous fatty tissue, which is separated from the muscles by the superficial abdominal fascia. The framework of the abdominal wall is provided by the abdominal muscles. The superficial abdominal muscles are so arranged as to produce the greatest possible degree of effectiveness. Individual abdominal muscles develop from several myotomes and are therefore innervated by several segmental nerves. This makes possible regional contraction of the ventral muscles.

Superficial Abdominal Muscles:

Lateral group:
- **External abdominal oblique**
- **Internal abdominal oblique**
- **Transversus abdominis**

Medial group:
- **Rectus abdominis**
- **Pyramidalis**

Deep Abdominal Muscles:

- **Quadratus lumborum**
- **Psoas major**

Flattened ligaments, the aponeuroses of the lateral abdominal muscles, enclose the rectus abdominis to form the **rectus sheath** (see p. 88).

Superficial Abdominal Muscles

Lateral Group (A–C)

The **external abdominal oblique** (**1**) *arises with eight slips on the outer surface of the 5th–12th ribs* (**2**). Between the 5th and (8th) 9th ribs it interdigitates with the slips of the serratus anterior (**3**) and between the 10th and 12th ribs with those of the latissimus dorsi (**4**).

Fundamentally, the direction of its fibers is from superolaterally and posterior toward inferomedially and anterior. The fibers which come from the three lowest ribs extend almost vertically down to the iliac crest and its labium externum (**5**), and the remainder run obliquely from superolaterally to inferomedially, where they merge into a flat aponeurosis (**6**). The transition of the muscle fibers into the aponeurosis follows an almost vertical line which is covered by the margin between the cartilage and bone of the 6th rib. Barely above the anterior superior iliac spine, the transition of the muscle fibers into the aponeurosis takes place in a transverse plane. One speaks here of a "muscle edge." The lowermost portion of this aponeurosis is continuous with the inguinal ligament (**Lig. of Vesal**).

The **superficial inguinal ring** lies in the medial region directly above the **inguinal ligament** and is bordered by the *medial* (**7**) and *lateral* (**8**) *crus* as well as by *intercrural fibers* (**9**; p. 96). The attachment of the external abdominal oblique is located in the midline. Here, the aponeuroses of the right and left muscles are interwoven with one another and with those of the other lateral abdominal muscles to form a fibrous raphe, the **linea alba** (**10**).
Nerve supply: intercostal nerves (T5 –T12).

▬ **Variants:** The muscle may have more or fewer slips of origin. Tendinous intersections may be present. There may also be connections with the nearby latissimus dorsi and serratus anterior.

Clinical tip: Up to 15 different terms, most of them antiquated, have been applied to the inguinal ligament over the years, ranging from crural arch and superficial crural arch to Poupart's ligament. Several of the terms have nothing to do with the actual inguinal ligament (see also Kremer et al., Chirurgische Operationslehre, Volume 7/1; p. 62–63).

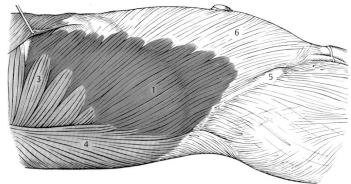

A   Abdominal wall from side: external abdominal oblique

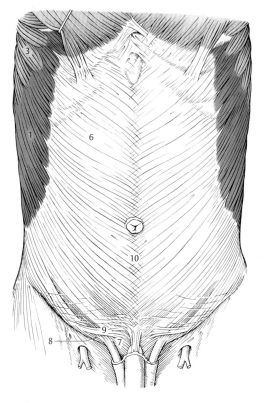

B   Abdominal wall from front: external abdominal oblique

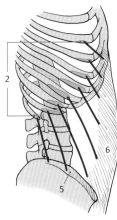

C   Diagram of origin, course, and insertion of muscles

Trunk

Superficial Abdominal Muscles

Lateral Group (continued) (A, B)

The **internal abdominal oblique** (**1**) *originates* at the *intermediate line of the iliac crest* (**2**), at the *deep layer of the thoracolumbar fascia* and at the *anterior superior iliac spine* (**3**). Individual fibers can also arise from the *inguinal ligament* (**4**).

The muscle takes a fan-shaped, predominantly ascending course, and thus, **three parts** can be distinguished on the basis of their attachments.

Its **cranial portion** *inserts* at the *lower margins of the last three ribs* (**5**).

The **middle part** (**6**) *continues medially into the aponeurosis, which is divided into anterior and posterior layers.* These layers form the framework of the *rectus sheath* (see p. 88), and they reunite in the linea alba. The anterior layer completely covers the rectus abdominis, but the posterior layer ends about 5 cm below the navel as a cranially convex line, the arcuate line. As this margin is not always sharply defined, it is more correct to speak of an *area arcuata* (*Lanz*).

Its **caudal part** is continued in the male into the spermatic cord as the *cremaster muscle* (**7**). The development of the cremaster muscle is subjected to great variation. In the female the muscle bundles which reach the round ligament of the uterus are distinctly weaker and are designated as the round ligament part of the internal abdominal oblique.

Nerve supply:
Internal abdominal oblique: intercostal nerves (T10 –T12 and L1).
Cremaster muscle: genital ramus of the genitofemoral nerve (L1 –L2).

■■■ **Variants:** Reduction or increase in the number of slips inserting on the ribs as well as of tendinous intersections may occur.

The **transversus abdominis** (**8**) *arises by six slips from the inner surface of the cartilage of ribs 7–12* (**9**); its slips interdigitate with those of the costal part of the diaphragm. They are attached directly to the origins of the transversus thoracis muscle. *It also takes its origin from the deep layer of the thoracolumbar fascia, the inner lip of the iliac crest* (**10**), *the anterior superior iliac spine* (**11**) *and the inguinal ligament* (**12**). Its fibers run transversely to a medially concave line which is known as the *semilunar line*. The aponeurosis begins at this line. It is cranial to the lines or area arcuata and participates in the formation of the posterior layer of the rectus sheath.

Caudal to the area arcuata (see above), the aponeurosis only forms the anterior layer of the rectus sheath. The transversus abdominis participates via its aponeurosis in the linea alba. The **inguinal falx**, also called the conjoined tendon or ligament of Henle (see p. 92), a band which is concave laterally, runs from the aponeurosis to the lateral margin of the attachment of the rectus abdominis muscle.

Nerve supply: intercostal nerves (T7 –T12) and L1.

■■■ **Variants:** The transversus abdominis may fuse completely in its lower region with the internal abdominal oblique, and because of this it is sometimes called the *complex muscle*. There are reports in the literature of its complete absence. The number of bands of origin may be increased or decreased.

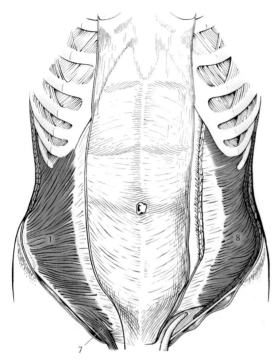

A Abdominal wall from front,
   internal abdominal oblique muscle
   and transversus abdominis

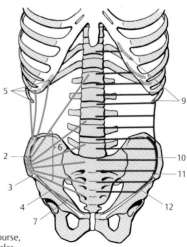

B Diagram of origin, course,
   and insertion of muscles

Trunk

Superficial Abdominal Muscles, continued

Medial Group (A–D)

The **rectus abdominis** (**1**) arises by three slips from the *outer surface of the cartilages of the 5th–7th ribs* (**2**), the *xiphoid process* (**3**), and the *intervening ligaments. It descends to the pubic crest* (see p. 186). In its course down near the level of the umbilicus there are three tendinous intersections; sometimes there are another one or two below it.

Nerve supply: intercostal nerves (T5–T12).

▰▰ Variants: The muscle may arise from more ribs or, rarely, may be entirely absent.

The rectus abdominis lies within the **rectus sheath**. This is formed by the aponeuroses of the three lateral abdominal muscles coming together in such a way that above the *arcuate line* (**4**) the aponeurosis of the internal abdominal oblique (**5**) divides into an *anterior* (**6**) and *a posterior lamina* (**7**). The aponeurosis of the external abdominal oblique (**8**) strengthens the anterior lamina and that of the transversus abdominis (**9**) strengthens the posterior lamina of the sheath. In the region of the **linea alba** (**10**) there is partial intertwining of the fibers (**B**).

Between the individual aponeurotic fibers there is a fatty infiltrate. The linea alba extends as far as the symphysis and is strengthened at the superior margin of the pelvis (**11**). Below the arcuate line the rectus sheath is incomplete, since the aponeuroses of all the lateral abdominal muscles run in front of both rectus muscles, and the inner side of these muscles is covered only by the transversalis fascia (**12**; see p. 92) and the peritoneum (**C**). In the region of the origin of the rectus abdominis, the rectus sheath is a thin fascial structure representing a continuation of the pectoral fascia.

> **Clinical tip:** Separation of the rectus muscles and an abnormal increase in the width of the linea alba is of clinical importance (**rectus diastasis**; see p. 96).
> Only the anterior surface of the rectus abdominis muscle is fused to the rectus sheath in the region of the intersecting tendons. Therefore abscesses or collections of pus can only form between two intersections on the anterior surface, while on the posterior surface they may extend along the entire rectus muscle.

The small, triangular **pyramidalis** (**13**) *arises from the pubis, radiates into the linea alba* and lies within the aponeurosis of the three lateral abdominal muscles. It is supposed to be absent in 16–25% of cases.

Careful examination reveals that the pyramidalis is present in most cases, although variable in its development. We have found it in 90% of cases, so that in only 10% of cases no muscle fibers were seen. The sole function of the pyramidalis is to tense the linea alba.

Nerve supply: T12–L1.

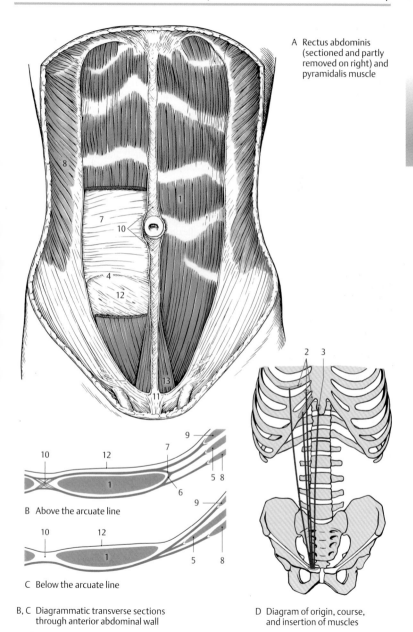

A Rectus abdominis
(sectioned and partly
removed on right) and
pyramidalis muscle

B Above the arcuate line

C Below the arcuate line

B, C Diagrammatic transverse sections
through anterior abdominal wall

D Diagram of origin, course,
and insertion of muscles

Function of the Superficial Abdominal Musculature (A–D)

The superficial abdominal muscles with their aponeuroses form the basis of the anterior and lateral abdominal wall.

Together with the deep muscles, the psoas major and the quadratus lumborum, they are necessary for movement of the trunk. In addition, the anterior and lateral abdominal muscles act on the intra-abdominal space. Their contraction produces an increase in intra-abdominal pressure. The diaphragm and the pelvic floor are also involved. This is necessary, for example, when the bowels are opened. Finally, they may be important during respiration, when the rectus abdominis contracts in forced expiration.

Basically, all the superficial muscles act together to produce the different movements conditional on the tension of the aponeuroses within the linea alba. The direction of tension (**A**) in the individual muscle fibers is such that they supplement one another.

The rectus abdominis (green) runs craniocaudally and is subdivided into several segments. Most of the fibers of the external oblique abdominal (red) run obliquely from superolaterally to inferomedially, while those of the internal oblique abdominal (blue) extend inferolaterally to superomedially. The transverse abdominal muscle (violet) runs transversely from lateral to medial.

In individual movements the function of each muscle may vary.

Flexion (**B**) of the trunk is essentially a movement of the rectus muscles (green). They are assisted by the oblique muscles (not shown).

Lateral flexion (**C**) is achieved by contraction of the external oblique muscle of the abdomen (red), the internal oblique abdominal muscle (blue) of the same side, the quadratus lumborum muscle (not shown) and the intrinsic muscles of the back (not shown) of the same side.

Rotation (**D**) follows contraction of the internal oblique abdominal (blue) on the same side (i.e., the side toward which the body is rotated) and the external oblique abdominal of the opposite side.

It should be understood that the external oblique abdominal (red) and the internal oblique abdominal (blue) of the same side sometimes act synergistically (in lateral flexion) (**C**), and sometimes are antagonists (**D**).

The transverse abdominal (violet) is mainly active in abdominal pressure, so that both transverse muscles may constrict the abdominal cavity. In addition, during expiration, their contraction may pull the diaphragm upward.

Clinical tip: During contraction of the abdominal muscles, particularly in reaching the upright posture from the supine position, it should be noted that the iliopsoas muscle (p. 94) plays an essential part. In a thin person, the tendinous intersections (p. 88) of the rectus muscles and the strands of origin of the external oblique muscles may be clearly seen. Any damage to the rectus muscles, such as a **rectus diastasis** (p. 96), can be seen. In addition, reflex contractions of the superficial abdominal muscles in intraperitoneal inflammations (reflex contraction of the abdominal muscles) may be observed.

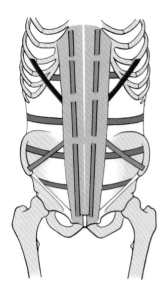

A   Direction of tension of the muscle fibers

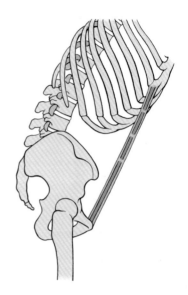

B   Anterior flexion

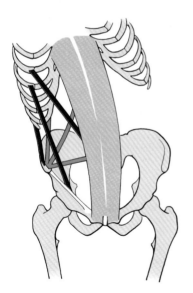

C   Lateral flexion

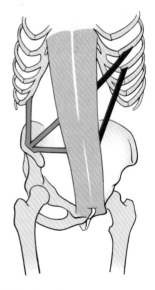

D   Lateral rotation

Trunk

Fascias of Abdominal Wall (A, B)

The abdominal wall can be divided into:
- The **skin**
- The **subcutaneous fatty tissue**
- The **connective tissue lamellae**
- The **superficial abdominal fascia**
- The **muscles and their fascias**
- The **transverse fascia**
- The **peritoneum**

The connective tissue lamellae permeating the subcutaneous fatty tissue form the **membranous layer of the subcutaneous tissue of abdomen** or **Scarpa's fascia** (**1**) which is arranged in the caudal region of the abdominal wall in the inguinal regions and in the pubic region. The fatty tissue in this region is called the **fatty layer of the abdomen, the abdominal fat pad**, or **Camper fascia**. Both structures together form the **subcutaneous tissue of abdomen**. The membranous abdominal layer, which continuous onto the thigh, is of significance to the surgeon because the larger subcutaneous vascular trunks are situated between it and the true superficial abdominal fascia. A portion of the connective tissue lamellae which is continued in the direction of the sexual organs is also designated as the **fundiform ligament of the penis** (**2**) **or clitoris**.

The **abdominal fascia** (**3**) represents a thin plate which is strengthened only in the region of the linea alba (p. 96) and covers the entire anterior abdominal musculature and its aponeuroses. The portion of the fascia situated in the midline continues into the elastic-rich fibers of the **suspensory ligament of the penis** (**4**) **or clitoris**. This ligament embraces the corpus cavernosum penis or clitoris with two crura.

In the region of the superficial inguinal ring the fascia fuses with the extension of the aponeurosis of the external abdominal oblique to form the **external spermatic fascia** (**5**), which provides the outer covering of the spermatic cord. With the aponeurosis of the external abdominal oblique it is more firmly bound also in the region of the inguinal ligament and then continues in the fascia of the thigh (**6**).

The inner loose abdominal wall fascia, the **transversalis fascia** (**7**), covers the inner surface of the abdominal muscles. It is taut in the umbilical region, where it may be called the **umbilical fascia** (**8**).

This fascia is also reached by connective tissue lamellae with embedded fat cells which pass upward from the apex of the urinary bladder. They contain the urachal cord and the cords of the umbilical arteries and can be designated as the vesicoumbilical fibrous septum. This septum strengthens the transversalis fascia.

In caudal direction the transversalis fascia fuses with the inguinal ligament to form the **iliopubic tract** (**9**), thus constituting the posterior wall of the inguinal canal (see p. 96 ff.). It extends from the inguinal ligament into the **iliac part** of the iliopsoas fascia, which covers the iliac muscle (**10**). Superiorly it covers the diaphragm and posteriorly the quadratus lumborum and psoas major as **iliopsoas fascia**.

In the region of the inguinal canal the transversalis fascia, strengthened by aponeurotic fibers of the transversus abdominis, thickens to form the **interfoveolar ligament** (**11**; see p. 98). Attached medially to the rectus abdominis (**12**), the transversalis fascia extends as a band covering a radiation of the aponeurosis of the transverse abdominal muscle and is firmly attached to it. This band, which is laterally concave, extends behind the reflex ligament (p. 96) to the lacunate ligament (p. 100), where it is in close contact with the inguinal ligament, and is called the **inguinal falx** (**13**) or conjunctival tendon.

Lateral to the interfoveolar ligament the transversalis fascia evaginates at the deep inguinal ring (**14**) to form the **internal spermatic fascia**. Below the inguinal ligament lies the femoral canal (**15**).

16 Cord of umbilical artery
17 Urachal cord

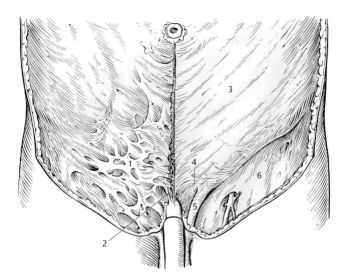

A Right: subcutaneous tissue of abdomen;
   left: (external) superficial abdominal fascia

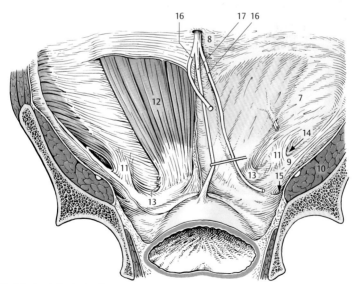

B Anterior abdominal wall
   from inside with transverse fascia on the right

Trunk

Deep Abdominal Muscles (A, B)

The **psoas major** (**1**) is subdivided into a **superficial** and a **deep part**. *The superficial part arises from the lateral surfaces of the twelfth thoracic and the first to fourth lumbar vertebrae* (**2**) *as well as their intervertebral disks. The deep part arises from the costal processes of the first to fifth lumbar vertebrae* (**3**).

The psoas major joins the iliacus and, surrounded by the iliac fascia, extends as the **iliopsoas** (**4**) through the lacuna musculorum to the *trochanter minor* (**5**). The lumbar plexus runs between the two layers of the psoas major (see also p. 234). Nerve supply: direct branches from the lumbar plexus and the femoral nerve (L1–L3).

The psoas major extends over several joints and is capable of considerable elevation of the leg. The iliacus muscle (see p. 234), with which it joins to form the iliopsoas muscle, is a powerful flexor and thus supplements the action of the psoas major. In the recumbent position both psoas muscles help to lift the upper or lower half of the body. In addition, the psoas major can give slight assistance in lateral flexion of the vertebral column.

Sometimes a **psoas minor** is found, *split off from the psoas major*, which enters into the iliac fascia and *inserts on the iliopubic eminence*. It acts as a tensor of the fascia (see p. 234).
Nerve supply: direct branch from the lumbar plexus (L1–L3).

> **Clinical tip:** The fascia surrounds the psoas major as a tube, *psoas fascia*, stretching from the medial lumbocostal arch (see p. 102) to the thigh. Thus, any inflammatory processes in the thoracic region can extend within the fascial tube to appear as **psoas (wandering) abscesses** as far down as the thigh.

The **quadratus lumborum** (**6**) *extends to the 12th rib* (**7**) *and to the costal processes of the first to third (fourth) lumbar vertebrae* (**8**). *It arises from the inner lip of the iliac crest* (**9**). This muscle consists of two incompletely separated layers. The ventral layer reaches to the 12th rib and the dorsal layer is attached to the costal processes.

The quadratus lumborum muscle lowers the 12th rib and aids lateral flexion of the body.
Nerve supply: T12 and L1–L3.

10 Median arcuate ligament
11 Medial arcuate ligament
12 Lateral arcuate ligament
13 Diaphragm (costal part)
14 External abdominal oblique
15 Pectineus

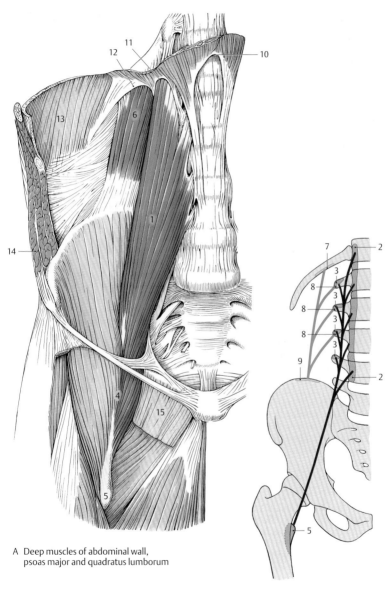

A Deep muscles of abdominal wall,
psoas major and quadratus lumborum

B Diagram of origin, course,
and insertion of muscles

Sites of Weakness in the Abdominal Wall (A–D)

Sites of weakness in the musculoapo-neurotic abdominal wall are the sites at which **hernias** tend to develop. A hernia is the escape of abdominal contents from the original body cavity. These contents lie in a *hernial* sac, a secondary protrusion of the peritoneum which comes through the *hernial orifice* in the abdominal wall. **Sites of weakness in the abdominal wall** are: the *linea alba, umbilicus, inguinal region, femoral canal, lumbar triangle, and surgical scars.*

Linea alba

The linea alba (**1**) is formed by interlacing of the aponeuroses of the lateral abdominal muscles and is a tendinous raphe lying between the rectus sheaths. It ends at the upper margin of the symphysis. On the dorsal surface it widens near its attachment and ends as a triangular plate, the **posterior attachment of linea alba (adminiculum of the linea alba)**. Above the umbilicus (**2**) it is 1–2 cm wide, while below the recti muscles (**3**) lie closer to each other and the linea alba is narrower. Under pathological conditions when there is a fat pendulous abdomen, or during pregnancy, the two recti may separate, producing **rectus diastasis** (**A**). A relatively small **epigastric hernia** (**4**) may develop in the linea alba. It develops from an enlargement of a small hole within the linea alba. An epigastric hernia may expand into a ventral abdominal wall hernia.

Umbilicus (2)

It is produced by fusion of the structures that originally protruded from the umbilicus with the adjacent tissues, and is reinforced by connective tissue. If the umbilical ring is stretched, as during pregnancy, an **umbilical hernia** (**5**) may occur.

Scars

Incisional hernias (**6**) may develop at the site of surgical scars.

Inguinal canal

The inguinal canal is produced by apposition of the lateral abdominal wall muscles and it extends obliquely through the abdominal wall. The **anterior wall** of the canal is formed by the *aponeurosis of the external abdominal oblique* (**7**) and the **floor** by the *inguinal ligament*. The **posterior wall** consists of the *transversalis fascia*, while the **roof** is formed by the caudal margin of the *transversus abdominis* . The **deep inguinal ring** (see p. 98) is the internal opening and the **superficial inguinal ring** (**8**) is a slit-like opening in the aponeurosis of the external abdominal oblique. The superficial inguinal ring (**8**) is only visible after dissecting off the external spermatic fascia (**9**) away from the external abdominal oblique. It is bounded by concentrated fiber bundles of the aponeurosis, the *medial crus* (**10**), the *lateral crus* (**11**), and the *intercrural fibers* (**12**). Posteriorly, the superficial inguinal ring is reinforced by the *reflected inguinal ligament* (**13**) which represents a division of the inguinal ligament.

In the male, the spermatic cord, which is enclosed by the *cremasteric fascia* and *cremaster muscle* (**14**), runs through the inguinal canal. In the female, the *round ligament of the uterus* and *lymphatics* run through the inguinal canal (see vol. 2). These lymphatic vessels arise from the uterine fundus and drain into the superior superficial inguinal lymph nodes (p. 414).

15 Femoral hernia (p. 100)
16 Indirect inguinal hernia (p. 100)

Trunk

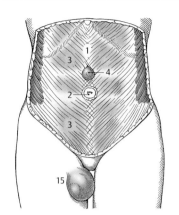

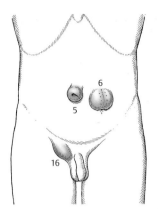

A Hernias of the anterolateral abdominal wall and the femoral region

B Hernias of the anterolateral abdominal wall

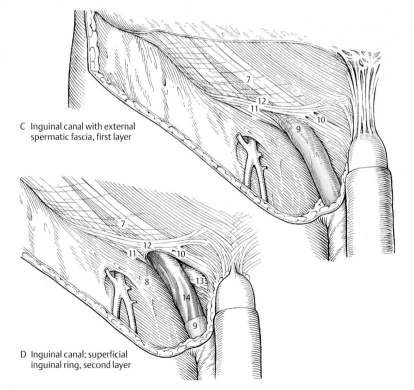

C Inguinal canal with external spermatic fascia, first layer

D Inguinal canal; superficial inguinal ring, second layer

Sites of Weakness in the Abdominal Wall, continued

Inguinal Canal, continued (A, B)

Incising the *aponeurosis* (**1**) of the external abdominal oblique reveals the *internal abdominal oblique* (**2**). In the male, several of its fibers continue into the spermatic cord as the *cremaster muscle* (**3**). Another portion (**4**) of the fibers of the cremaster muscle originates from the inguinal ligament. Since the muscle fibers are developed very differently, the entire middle covering of the spermatic cord has been designated as the *cremasteric fascia with its accompanying cremaster muscle* (**5**), also called the Cooper fascia. In the female, these few muscle fibers are referred to as the round ligament part of the internal oblique.

The *transversus abdominis* (**6**) forms the roof of the inguinal canal and is rendered visible only after cutting through the internal abdominal oblique (**2**) and the cremasteric fascia (**5**). The **deep inguinal ring** (**7**) is formed by the evagination of the *transversalis fascia* (**8**) which continues as the *internal spermatic fascia* (**9**), the innermost covering of the spermatic cord.

Abdominal Wall from Inside (C)

Both openings of the inguinal canal, the deep and superficial inguinal rings, represent sites of weakness in the abdominal wall. By examination of the abdominal wall from the inside (**C**), where the innermost layer, the peritoneum, is preserved, we see that it is depressed in two places, described as the **lateral inguinal fossa** (**10**), corresponding to the deep inguinal ring that lies beneath it, and the **medial inguinal fossa** (**11**), corresponding to the superficial inguinal ring.

Removal of the perineum reveals the *transversalis fascia* (**8**) which exhibits various strengthening tracts. Along the inguinal ligament is the *iliopubic tract* (**12**), and between medial inguinal fossa and lateral inguinal fossa is the *interfoveolar ligament* (**13**). This band, called also the **ligament of Hesselbach**, is highly variable in its development. Caudally, it is interwoven with the iliopubic tract. Cranially, it may radiate over a wide area and may participate in *semilunar fold* in forming the medial boundary of the deep inguinal ring (**7**).

The interfoveolar ligament may sometimes contain muscle fibers and is then known as *interfoveolar muscle*. In this region the *inferior epigastric artery* and *vein* (**14**) are found, which create a peritoneal fold that is called the *epigastric fold* (**15**). Erroneously, it is also known as lateral umbilical fold, although it does not reach the umbilicus.

When examining the abdominal wall from the inside, we find the **supravesical fossa** (**16**) in addition to the lateral and medial inguinal fossae; it is medial to the latter and separated from it only by the *cord of the umbilical artery* (**17**). Hernias may develop at any of these three sites (see p. 100).

Clinical tip: The *inguinal triangle*, or **Hesselbach's triangle**, is the region delimited *medially* by the lateral margin of the rectus abdominis muscle, *caudally* by the pectineal ligament (p. 100), and *laterally* by the external iliac artery and vein and inferior epigastric artery and vein. The triangle carries three weak sites of the abdominal wall, namely, the *medial inguinal fossa* (**11**), the *supravesical fossa* (**16**), and the *femoral canal* (**18**, p. 100). It has recently regained importance in connection with minimally invasive surgery.

---

19 Reflected (inguinal) ligament
20 External spermatic fascia
21 Cut margin of the peritoneum
22 Medial umbilical fold (cord of umbilical artery)

Trunk

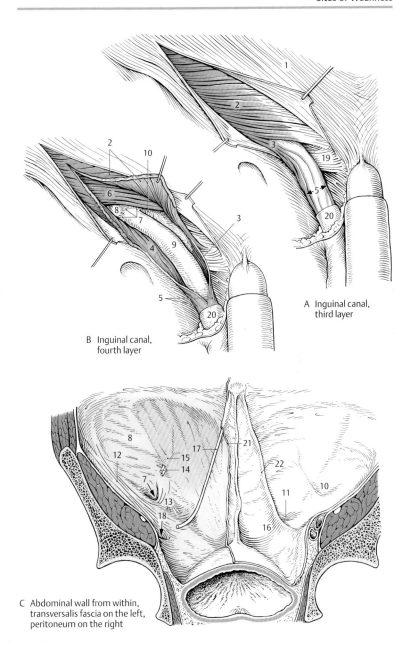

A Inguinal canal,
third layer

B Inguinal canal,
fourth layer

C Abdominal wall from within,
transversalis fascia on the left,
peritoneum on the right

Sites of Weakness in the Abdominal Wall, continued

Hernias in the inguinal region (A)

The lateral, medial inguinal and supravesicular fossae are regions of minimal resistance. Under certain circumstances they become stretched, bulge out and **inguinal hernias** may occur. Two types of inguinal hernias are distinguished—direct and indirect—and *both traverse the superficial inguinal ring*. The **direct inguinal hernia** (**1**) *has its hernial orifice in the medial inguinal fossa*. An **indirect inguinal hernia** (**2**) *passes through the inguinal canal* (and is therefore also known clinically as *hernia of the canal*). It uses as *points of exit* the *lateral inguinal fossa* and the *deep inguinal ring*. Another type of hernia, the **supravesical hernia** (**3**), leaves the abdomen through the *supravesical fossa*; its hernial orifice, therefore, lies medial to the obliterated umbilical artery (**4**). The point of passage of this hernia through the abdominal wall is also the superficial inguinal ring.

The direct inguinal hernia and the supravesical hernia are difficult to distinguish from the outside. They are always **acquired hernias**, while indirect inguinal hernias may be acquired or **congenital**. During the descent of the testis in males, *the processus vaginalis*, an evagination of the serosa, is carried along into the scrotum. It later becomes obliterated and loses all previous connection with the peritoneal cavity, so that only a closed serous sac, the cavum serosum scroti, remains. In some cases, however, a connection persists and there may be then a congenital inguinal hernia with a patent processus vaginalis.

Femoral canal (B)

The femoral canal (**5**) represents an additional possible site for herniation. The femoral canal *lies behind the inguinal ligament* (**6**), within the vascular space (**7**), the medial femoral aperture. Laterally this is separated from the *muscular space* (**8**) by

the *iliopectineal arch* (**9**). In the medial part of the vascular space, medial to the large femoral vessels, lies the femoral canal (**5**). It is **bordered medially** by the **lacunar ligament** (**10**), which merges with the **dorsal border** of the **pectineal ligament** (i.e., Cooper's ligament) across a ligamentous arch, the processus falciformis lacunaris. The canal is closed by loose connective tissues, the **femoral septum** (**11**).

The lymphatics pass through this femoral canal. It also contains the *deep inguinal lymph node* (**12**), also known as Cloquet's or Rosenmüller's node. In cases of excessive intra-abdominal pressure combined with weak connective tissue, a femoral hernia may result.

> **Clinical tip:** A **femoral hernia** can be differentiated from an inguinal hernia by its position in relation to the inguinal ligament and to the scrotum or the labium majus. Only an inguinal hernia can reach the scrotum or labia majora, while a femoral hernia appears in the thigh. Femoral hernias occur three times more often in women than in men.

Lumbar triangle

Between the iliac crest, the dorsal margin of the external oblique muscle of the abdomen and the lateral margin of the latissimus dorsi muscle (see p. 140) there is often a triangular interval, the lumbar triangle. It contains fatty tissue and the internal oblique muscle of the abdomen. It is uncommon for **lumbar hernias** to occur through the triangle but it happens more often in males than females.

13 Femoral vein
14 Femoral artery
15 Femoral nerve
16 Iliopsoas
17 Iliopectineal bursa
18 Lateral femoral cutaneous nerve
19 Pectineal muscle

Trunk

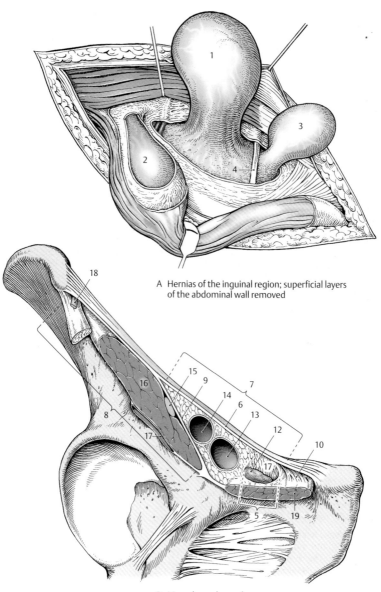

A Hernias of the inguinal region; superficial layers
of the abdominal wall removed

B Muscular and vascular spaces
with femoral canal

Diaphragm (A, B)

The **diaphragm** separates the thoracic and abdominal cavities. It consists of a **central tendon** (**1**) and a muscular portion, which can be divided into **sternal** (**2**), **costal** (**3**), and **lumbar** (**4**) **parts**.

Current nomenclature describes the lumbar part of the diaphragm as a uniform structure. Nevertheless, it is subdivided into a **left crus** and a **right crus** with three origins each, namely, at the lumbar vertebrae, the medial arcuate ligament, and the lateral arcuate ligament.

The **sternal part** (**2**), which *arises from the inner surface of the xiphoid process* (**5**), consists of muscle that is rather lighter in color than the rest and which radiates into the central tendon.

The **costal part** (**3**) *arises from the inner surfaces of the cartilage of ribs 7–12 by means of individual slips* which alternate with the slips of origin of the transversus abdominis.

The **lumbar part** (**4**) has a **medial** and a **lateral crus** and occasionally an **intermediate crus** splits off from the medial crus. The **right medial crus** (**6**) *arises from the bodies of the first to fourth lumbar vertebrae, and the* **left medial crus** (**7**) *from the bodies of the first to third lumbar vertebrae*. The **lateral crus** (**8**) *originates from two arches, formed by the medial arcuate ligament* (**9**)*, the psoas arcade or medial lumbocostal arch, and the lateral arcuate ligament* (**10**)*, quadratus arcade or lateral lumbocostal arch. The psoas arcade extends from the lateral surface of first (second) lumbar vertebral bodies to the costal process* (**11**) *of the first lumbar vertebra. The lateral arcuate ligament extends from this process to the apex of the 12th rib.*

Below these tendinous arches the psoas major (**12**) and quadratus lumborum (**13**) are visible. There are gaps between the lumbar, costal and sternal parts of the diaphragm, which are points of minimal resistance. Between the lumbar and costal components lies the **lumbocostal triangle** (**14**), and between the sternal and costal parts is the **sternocostal triangle** (**15**).

The double-domed diaphragm, which is slightly depressed in the middle by the heart, is pierced by openings for the passage of various structures. Between the medial crura lies the **aortic hiatus** (**16**), which is limited by tendons (median arcuate ligament). Through it passes the aorta and posteriorly to it the thoracic duct. The right medial crus (**6**) consists of three muscle bundles, of which that arising from the lumbar vertebrae is the largest and it reaches the central tendon (**1**) directly. A *second* bundle (**17**) arises from the *median arcuate ligament* (**18**), the tendinous border of the aortic hiatus (**16**), and forms the right border of the **esophageal hiatus** (**19**). The third bundle (**20**) also arises from the median arcuate ligament, but dorsally, and forms the left border of the esophageal opening as the **"hiatus sling"**. Only in exceptional cases does the left medial crus (**7**) participate in the formation of the border of the esophageal opening. The esophageal hiatus is bordered by muscle, and through it pass the esophagus and the anterior and posterior vagal trunks.

The **caval opening** (**21**) lies in the central tendon, and through it pass the inferior vena cava and a branch of the right phrenic nerve. The greater and lesser splanchnic nerves, on the right the azygos vein and on the left the hemiazygos vein, pass through unnamed openings in the medial crus, or between it and the intermediate crus if present. The sympathetic trunk runs between the intermediate and lateral crura. Nerve supply: phrenic nerves ([C3] C4 [C5]).

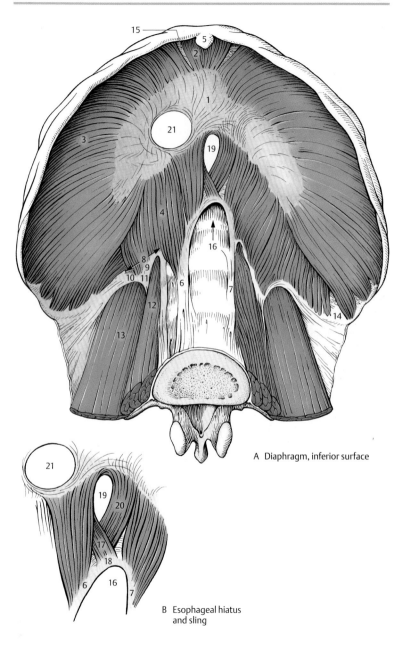

A Diaphragm, inferior surface

B Esophageal hiatus
and sling

Trunk

Position and Function of the Diaphragm (A)

In life the position and shape of the diaphragm depend on the phases of respiration, the position of the body and the degree of distension of the viscera.

As the principal respiratory muscle, the shape of the diaphragm changes greatly during the various phases of respiration. In the midposition between maximal expiration and inspiration, in the upright posture, the right dome of the diaphragm reaches the 4th intercostal space, and the left dome the 5th intercostal space. In *maximal expiration* (blue) *the projection on the anterior chest wall on the right lies at the upper margin of the 4th rib, and on the left in the 4th intercostal space. During maximal inspiration* (red), *the diaphragm sinks to about the 1st to 2nd intercostal space.* The sternal part and its origin act as a fixed point. During expiration the muscle fibers rise and during maximal inspiration they descend toward the center of the tendon.

The **costodiaphragmatic recess** between the upper surface of the diaphragm and the ribs is flattened during maximal inspiration.

In the recumbent position convolutions of the abdominal viscera push the diaphragm upward and backward.

Clinical tip: Dyspneic patients prefer to sit rather than to lie and so relieve the thorax of the pressure of the abdominal contents.

Sites of Diaphragmatic Hernias (B)

Diaphragmatic hernias occur when the contents of the abdominal cavity enter the thorax. They may be congenital or acquired. True diaphragmatic defects (blue) must be distinguished from enlargement of preexisting weak spots (red), such as the *esophageal hiatus* (**1**), the *lumbocostal triangle* (**2**) and *sternocostal triangle* (**3**). True diaphragmatic hernias usually occur in the *central tendon* (**4**) or the *costal part* (**5**). The majority of diaphragmatic hernias are prolapses, as they lack a hernial sac. They are known as **false diaphragmatic hernias**. **True hernias** with a sac are uncommon and occur only as para-esophageal hernias.

The commonest congenital hernia is due to enlargement of the lumbocostal triangle (**2**). Another type of congenital hernia is **para-esophageal** in position and always occurs on the right side of the esophagus. It is a type of **hiatus hernia,** which, however, in the great majority of cases is an acquired sliding hernia. Sliding hernias have no hernial sac and develop through enlargement of the esophageal hiatus (**1**).

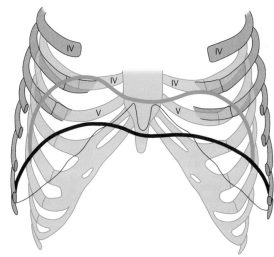

A Position of diaphragm during maximal inspiration (red) and maximal expiration (blue)

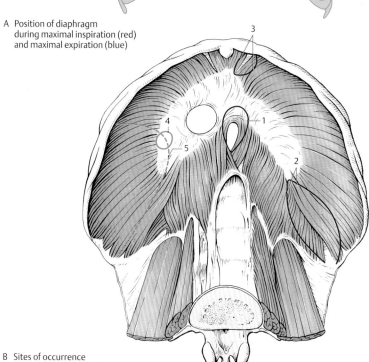

B Sites of occurrence of diaphragmatic hernias

Trunk

Pelvic Floor (A, B)

The pelvic floor is the closure of the trunk inferiorly and posteriorly. It is formed by the **pelvic diaphragm** and the **urogenital diaphragm**.

Pelvic Diaphragm

This consists of the **levator ani** and **coccygeus muscles**.

The **levator ani** (**1**) *arises from the pubic* bone (**2**), *the tendinous arch of the levator ani muscle* (**3**) *and the ischial spine* (**4**). Its fibers are divisible into the **puborectalis muscle** (**5**), the **puboperinealis = ** prerectal fibers (**6**), the **pubococcygeal** (**7**) and the **iliococcygeal muscles** (**8**). The medial fibers of the puboperinealis form the *crura of the levator,* between which is enclosed the *urogenital hiatus.* The puboperinealis muscles extend into the perineum and thereby separate the urogenital tract from the anal tract. The urogenital hiatus is limited laterally by the levator crura and posteriorly by the puboperineal muscles. Through the urogenital hiatus pass the urethra and the genital canal, while behind the prerectal fibers only the rectum (anal canal) passes. Some of the fibers of the puborectalis end pararectally in the *external anal sphincter* (**9**), some run on to form a retrorectal sling behind the rectum. The fibers of the pubococcygeal and the iliococcygeal muscles extend laterally onto the *anococcygeal ligament* (**10**) and insert on this or directly onto the coccyx (**11**).

The genital hiatus is narrower in the male and broader in the female. Due to the width of the aperture of the genital hiatus a second closure mechanism—the urogenital diaphragm—is essential.

The **coccygeus** (**12**) *arises by means of a tendon from the ischial spine and ends on the coccyx.* It may be absent.

Function: The levator ani is concerned with intra-abdominal pressure. It bears the weight of the pelvic contents and thus has a supporting function. In its dynamic function it participates in closure of the rectum.

Urogenital Diaphragm

This consists mainly of the **deep transverse perineal muscle** (**13**). *It arises from the ramus of the ischium and from the inferior pubic ramus and extends to the urogenital hiatus.* The posterior part of the diaphragm is reinforced by the **superficial transverse perineal muscle** (**14**). *This arises from the ischial tuberosity* (**15**) *and radiates into the perineal body.* Anteriorly the urogenital diaphragm is completed by the **transverse perineal ligament** (**16**).

Both the urogenital diaphragm and the pelvic diaphragm are covered on their upper and lower surfaces by fascia appropriately termed the *superior* and *inferior urogenital diaphragmatic fascia (perineal membrane)* and the *superior* and *inferior pelvic diaphragmatic fascia,* respectively. The ischiorectal (ischioanal) fossa lies between the pelvic and urogenital diaphragm and is open posteriorly.

Nerve supply: The pelvic diaphragm is innervated, as a rule, by a long branch from the sacral plexus, the urogenital diaphragm by twigs from the pudendal nerve.

The term "urogenital diaphragm," which is a meaningful term, has been mostly discarded from the anatomical nomenclature (but not from clinical parlance) and has been replaced by the terms *perineal membrane with transverse perineal ligament* and *deep transverse perineal muscle.*

> **Clinical tip:** Overstretching of the pelvic diaphragm in women leads to a prolapse of their internal sexual organs, which can occur especially after childbirth. It is important to keep in mind that childbirth can also result in a laceration of the levator ani with a concomitant traumatic injury to the pelvic diaphragm. **Perineal hernias** rarely emerge through muscle-weak locations in the pelvic floor, although they are substantially more frequent in women.

For further details of the pelvic floor, see volume 2.

17 Sacrospinal ligament
18 Sacrotuberal ligament

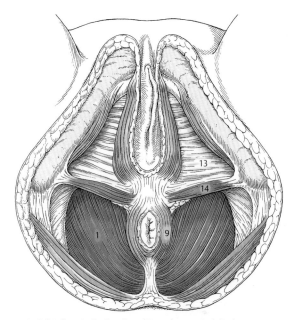

A Pelvic floor in the female, pelvic and urogenital diaphragm

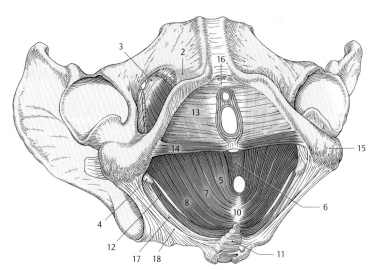

B Pelvic floor in the female, diagram of musculature

Anatomical Terms and their Latin Equivalents

Trunk	Truncus
Alar ligaments	Ligamenta alaria
Caval opening	Foramen venae cavae
Conjoint tendon	Tendo conjunctivus
Costal notch	Incisura costalis
Esophageal (aortic) hiatus	Hiatus oesophageus (aorticus)
False (true) ribs	Costae spuriae (verae)
Floating ribs	Costae fluctantes
Iliopectineal arch	Arcus iliopectineus
Innermost intercostal muscles	Musculi intercostales intimi
Intervertebral joint	Symphysis intervertebralis
Joint of head of rib	Articulatio capitis costae
Nuchal fascia	Fascia nuchae
Pelvic (urogenital) diaphragm	Diaphragma pelvis (urogenitalis)
Rectus sheath	Vagina musculi recti abdominis
Scalene tubercle	Tuberculum musculi scaleni anterioris
Superficial (deep) inguinal ring	Anulus inguinalis superficialis (profundus)

Systematic Anatomy of the Locomotor System

Upper Limb

Bones, Ligaments and Joints

In the upper limb we distinguish the **shoulder girdle** and the **free upper limb.** The shoulder girdle is formed by the scapulae and the clavicles.

Shoulder Girdle

Scapula (A–E)

The shoulder blade or **scapula** (A–E) is a flat, triangular bone. It has a *medial border* (**1**), a *lateral border* (**2**) and a *superior border* (**3**), which are separated from each other by the *superior* (**4**) and *inferior* (**5**) *angles* and the truncate *lateral angle* (**6**). The anterior or *costal surface* is flat and slightly concave (*subscapular fossa*). It sometimes shows clear lines of muscle attachments. The *posterior surface* is divided by the *spine of scapula* (**7**) into a smaller *supraspinous fossa* (**8**) and a larger *infraspinous fossa* (**9**). The spine of the scapula has a triangular base medially, which rises laterally to terminate in a flattened process, the *acromion* (**10**). Near the lateral end lies an oval *articular facet* (**11**) for articulation with the clavicle, the *clavicular facet.*

The *acromial angle* (**12**) is a readily palpable bony point, which marks the place where the lateral acromial margin continues into the spine of scapula. The lateral angle bears the *glenoid cavity* (**13**). At its upper border is a small projection, the *supraglenoid tubercle* (**14**). Below the glenoid cavity lies the *infraglenoid tubercle* (**15**). The *neck of scapula* (**16**) is adjacent to the glenoid cavity.

The *coracoid process* (**17**) lies above the glenoid cavity. It is bent at a right angle lateroventrally and its tip is flattened. Together with the acromion it protects the joint which lies beneath it. Medial to the base of the coracoid process, on the upper margin of the scapula, lies the *suprascapular notch* (**18**).

The scapula lies on the thorax with the base of its spine at the level of the third thoracic vertebra. The inferior angle of the scapula should lie between ribs 7 and 8 and, when the arm hangs down, its medial margin should be parallel to the row of spinous processes. The **scapular plane** is the plane in which the scapular plate lies. It forms an angle of 60° with the plane of symmetry (median sagittal). The glenoid cavity faces laterally and anteriorly.

▨▨ **Variants:** The scapular notch may be transformed into a *scapular foramen* (**19**). The medial margin of the scapula is sometimes concave and the scapula is then called a **scaphoid scapula.**

Ossification: The scapula develops (E) from several ossification centers. In the 3rd intrauterine month a large bony center develops in the region of the supraspinous and infraspinous fossae and the spine of the scapula. In the 1st year of life a center develops in the coracoid process, and between the ages of 11 and 18 years smaller centers may appear throughout the scapula. All the centers fuse with each other between the ages of 16 and 22 years. The center which develops in the acromion between 15 and 18 years of age may, in rare instances, remain unfused (os acromiale).

Ligaments of the Scapula

The **coracoacromial ligament** crosses the shoulder joint and extends between the coracoid process and the acromion. The **superior transverse scapular ligament** bridges the scapular notch. (Only in rare cases is there an inferior transverse scapular ligament, which extends from the margin of the spine of the scapula to the glenoid cavity.)

Upper Limb

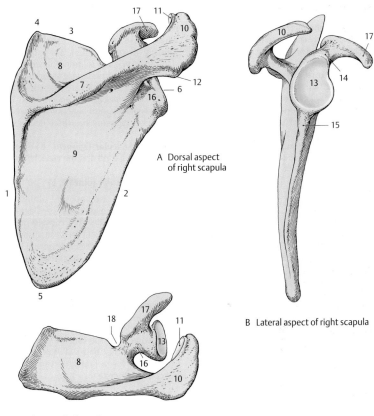

A Dorsal aspect of right scapula

B Lateral aspect of right scapula

C Right scapula from above

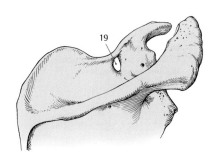

D Foramen scapulae (variant)

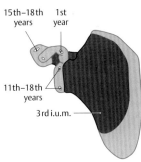

15th–18th years   1st year

11th–18th years

3rd i.u.m.

E Ossification of scapula

Clavicle (A, B, F)

The collar bone or **clavicle** is an S-shaped bone, anteriorly convex in the medial two-thirds of its length, while the lateral third is concave anteriorly. Toward the sternum is the stout **sternal end** (**1**) and toward the scapula the flat **acromial end** (**2**), and between the two lies the **body of the clavicle**. At the sternal end we find a triangular *sternal articular facet* (**3**). The *acromial articular facet* (**4**) is almost oval. Near the sternal end, on the lower surface of the clavicle, is the *impression for the costoclavicular ligament* (**5**). The groove for the subclavian muscle lies on the undersurface of the *clavicular body*. The prominent *conoid tubercle* (**6**) lies near the acromial end close to the *trapezoid line* (**7**).

Ossification: The clavicle develops in connective tissue, and ossification begins in the 6th intrauterine week. The ends are performed in cartilage but an ossification center does not appear in the sternal end until 16–20 years of age. It synostoses with the rest of the clavicle between the ages of 21 and 24 years.

> **Clinical tip:** Cleidocranial dysostosis is a malformation due to maldevelopment or non-development of the connective tissue part of the clavicle. It is associated with defects of those bones of the skull that are preformed in connective tissue.

Joints of the Shoulder Girdle (C–E)

Connections with the trunk are made through a continuous fibrous (costoclavicular ligament, **8**) and discontinuous synovial joints (sternoclavicular joint). In the same way, the parts of the shoulder girdle are connected to each other by continuous fibrous (coracoclavicular ligament) and discontinuous synovial joints (acromioclavicular joint).

Sternoclavicular Joint (C)

This is a joint with an *articular disk* (**9**) which divides the space of joint cavity in two. The socket is a shallow concave indentation in the sternum, and the head is formed by the sternal end of the clavicle.

The incongruity is adjusted by the cartilage-like fibrous tissue, which covers both articular facets, and by the disk, which is fixed cranially to the clavicle and caudally to the sternum. The capsule is slack and thick and is strengthened by the *anterior* (**10**) and *posterior sternoclavicular ligaments*. The clavicles are interconnected by the *interclavicular ligament* (**11**). The sternoclavicular joint functions as a ball-and-socket type and has three degrees of freedom.

The **costoclavicular ligament** (**8**) extends between the 1st rib and the clavicle.

Acromioclavicular Joint (D, E)

This consists of two apposing, almost flat joints surfaces covered by cartilage-like fibrous tissue (**12**). The capsule has a strengthening ligament on its superior surface, the *acromioclavicular ligament* (**13**).

The **coracoclavicular ligament** extends between the coracoid process and the clavicle. It can be divided into anterolateral and posteromedial parts. The lateral part, the **trapezoid ligament** (**14**), arises from the upper medial margin of the coracoid process and extends to the trapezoid line. The medial part, the **conoid ligament** (**15**), arises from the base of the coracoid process and has a fanlike termination on the conoid tubercle.

> **Clinical tip:** Marked posterior and inferior displacement of the clavicle may compress the subclavian artery, as can be detected by a weakening of the radial pulse.

16 Superior transverse scapular ligament
17 Coraco-acromial ligament
18 Subclavius muscle

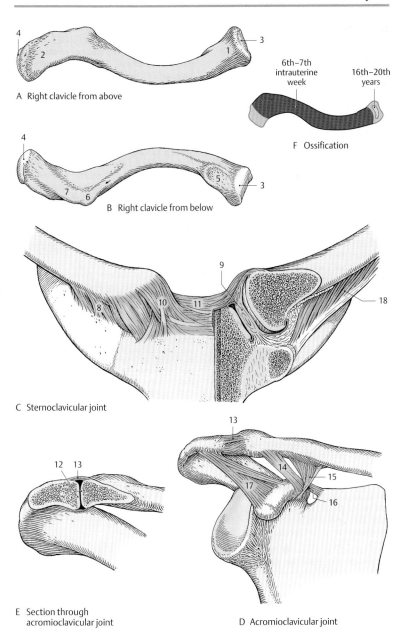

A Right clavicle from above

F Ossification

6th–7th
intrauterine
week

16th–20th
years

B Right clavicle from below

C Sternoclavicular joint

E Section through
acromioclavicular joint

D Acromioclavicular joint

The Free Upper Limb

The bones of the **free upper limb** are
 – The **humerus**
 – The **radius** and **ulna**
 – The **carpal bones**
 – The **metacarpal bones**
 – The **phalanges**

Bone of the Arm
Humerus (A–H)

The **humerus** articulates with the scapula
and the radius and ulna. It consists of the
body and **upper (proximal)** and **lower (distal)
ends**. The proximal end is formed by the
head (**1**), adjoining the *anatomical neck* (**2**).
On the anterolateral surface of the proxi-
mal end lies laterally the greater tubercle
(**3**), and medially is the *lesser tubercle* (**4**).
Between these tubercles begins the *intertubercular sulcus* (**5**), which is bounded distally by the *crests of the lesser* (**6**) and
greater (**7**) *tubercles*. The *surgical neck* (**8**)
lies proximally on the body of the
humerus. In the middle of the body lies
laterally the *deltoid tuberosity* (**9**). The body
may be divided into an *anteromedial surface* (**10**) with a *medial border* (**11**), and an
anterolateral surface (**12**) with a *lateral
border* (**13**), which becomes sharpened distally and is called the *lateral supracondylar
ridge*. The *groove for the radial nerve* (**14**)
lies on the posterior surface of the body.
The distal end of the humerus bears on its
medial side the large *medial epicondyle*
(**15**) and on the lateral side the smaller
lateral epicondyle (**16**).

The *trochlea* (**17**) and the *capitulum* (**18**) of
the humerus form the *humeral condyles* for
articulation with the bones of the forearm.
The *radial fossa* (**19**) lies proximal to the
capitulum and proximal to the trochlea is
the somewhat larger *coronoid fossa* (**20**).

Medial to the trochlea (**D**) there is a shallow groove, the *groove for ulnar nerve* (**21**).
On the posterior surface above the trochlea
is a deep pit, the *olecranon fossa* (**22**).

The humerus is twisted at its proximal end,
i.e., the head is posteriorly rotated at about
20° in relation to the transverse axis of the
distal end (**torsion**). The angle between the
long axis of the humerus and that of the
head averages 130°, and at the distal end,
between the transverse axis of the joint
and the long axis of the shaft of the
humerus, there is an angle of 76° to 89°.

The **proximal epiphysial line** (**23**) runs transversely through the lesser tubercle and inferior to the greater tubercle. It crosses the
zone of attachment of the capsule (see
p. 117) in such a way that a small part of the
shaft comes to lie within the capsule. At
the **distal end** there are two epiphyses and
two epiphysial lines (**24**). One epiphysis carries the medial epicondyle and the other
the joint surfaces and the lateral epicondyle.

Ossification: In general, development of the
ossification centers and fusion of the epiphyses
occur somewhat earlier in females than in males.
The perichondral bone anlage in the shaft appears in the 2nd– 3rd intrauterine month. The
endochondral ossification centers in the
epiphyses appear between the 2nd week of life
and the 12th year. Three centers appear proximally soon after birth, and distally four ossification centers develop later. The distal epiphysial
disks fuse during puberty and the proximal disks
at the end of puberty.

▬ **Variants:** Just above the medial epicondyle a
supracondylar process (**25**) is occasionally found,
and above the trochlea there may be a *supratrochlear foramen* (**26**).

Clinical tip: 50% of fractures of the humerus
occur in the **shaft**. There is a risk of damage to
the radial nerve!

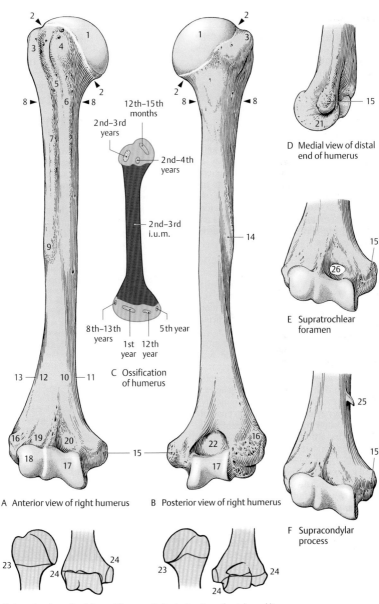

C Ossification of humerus

12th–15th months

2nd–3rd years

2nd–4th years

2nd–3rd i.u.m.

8th–13th years

1st year

12th year

5th year

D Medial view of distal end of humerus

E Supratrochlear foramen

F Supracondylar process

A Anterior view of right humerus

B Posterior view of right humerus

G Anterior view of epiphyseal lines

H Posterior view of epiphyseal lines

Upper Limb

Upper Limb

Shoulder Joint (A–G)

The bony socket, the **glenoid cavity**, of the ball-and-socket **shoulder joint** is much smaller than the **head of the humerus**. The hyaline cartilage covering (**1**) of the glenoid cavity is thicker at the margins than in the center. The socket is enlarged by a fibrocartilaginous lip, the **glenoidal lip** (**2**).

The socket is perpendicular to the plane of the scapula, and the position of the scapula determines the attitude of the entire joint. The surface of the glenoid cavity has an area of 6 cm^2 to withstand an atmospheric pressure of 6 kp (approx. 60 N) on the joint. The upper limb weighs about 4 kg. As there are no strong ligaments, the shoulder joint is maintained by the action of the enveloping muscles. It is known as a **"muscle-dependent joint."**

The head of humerus (**3**) is ball-shaped. Its hyaline cartilage covering begins at the anatomical neck and extends somewhat farther distally at the intertubercular sulcus. The cartilage gives the head a more oval shape. The **synovial layer of the articular capsule** is attached to the glenoid lip. It is evaginated pouchlike (**C**) along the intracapsularly coursing tendon of the long head of the biceps (**4**) and surrounds it as the *synovial sheath of the intertubercular groove* (**5**). The **fibrous layer of the joint capsule** in the upper arm forms a connective tissue layer across the intertubercular sulcus and converts it into on osteofibrous canal. The **articular capsule** is slack and when the arm hangs down it has a pendent pouchlike part on its medial surface, the *axillary recess* (**6**). The upper portion of the capsule is partly strengthened by the *coracohumeral ligament* (**7**) and three weak *glenohumeral ligaments*. The coracohumeral ligament arises from the base of the coracoid process (**8**) and radiates into the capsule, extending to the greater and lesser tubercles. When the arm is hanging in its normal anatomic position, the upper half of the head of the humerus is in contact with the joint capsule and the lower half with the glenoid cavity.

The shoulder joint is associated with a number of synovial sacs. As a rule, it communicates *with the subcoracoid bursa, the subtendinous bursa of the subscapular muscle* (beneath the tendon of the *subscapular muscle*, **9**), *the intertubercular synovial sac* and the *coracobrachial bursa*.

Movements of the Shoulder Joint (D–F)

The shoulder joint has **three degrees of freedom of movement**. **Abduction** and **adduction** refer to movements away from the position of rest (**D**) of the head of the humerus in the scapular plane (see p. 110). Purely lateral abduction (**E**) always produces **retroversion** and slight **rotation**, while abduction from the scapular plane is anteriorly directed (frontal abduction).

Flexion (**anteversion**) is forward lifting of the arm. Because of rotary components associated with these other movements, a compound movement, **circumduction**, occurs in which the arm traces the surface of a cone. Abduction (**E**) is *always* associated with movement of the scapula: excessive associated scapular movement occurs with abduction of more than 90° (**F**; elevation), because then the movement of the joint is restricted by the coracoacromial ligament (**10**; see p. 110).

Clinical tip: **Dislocation** is more common in the shoulder than in any other joint. If associated with a torn capsule, it usually occurs low and in front.

The palpable and visible **prominence of the shoulder joint** is produced by the greater tubercle, the location of which indicates the position of the head of the humerus. The protuberance disappears when the shoulder is dislocated, as the head of the humerus is no longer in its socket. When palpating a dislocated shoulder the finger enters an empty cavity (G) below the acromion.

A fracture of the (intracapsular) anatomical neck is uncommon and the prognosis is very poor.

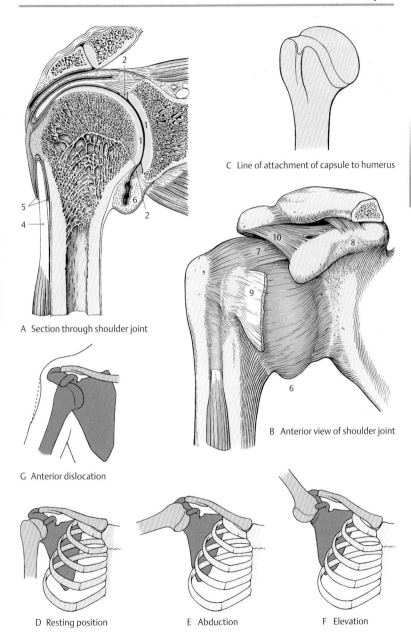

C Line of attachment of capsule to humerus

B Anterior view of shoulder joint

A Section through shoulder joint

G Anterior dislocation

D Resting position

E Abduction

F Elevation

Bones of the Forearm

In the **forearm**, the shorter **radius** lies laterally, the longer **ulna**, medially.

Radius (A–E)

The **radius** comprises a **shaft** (1) and a **proximal** and a **distal extremity**. The proximal extremity contains the *head* (2) with its *articular facet* (3) which continues into the *articular circumference* (4). Medially, at the transition between the *neck* (5) and its shaft, lies the *radial tuberosity* (6). The shaft has an approximately triangular shape in cross section with a medially directed *interosseous border* (7), an *anterior surface* (8), an *anterior border* (9), a *lateral surface* (10) and a *posterior border* (11) which represents the boundary between the lateral and *posterior surfaces* (12). The lateral surface of the shaft at approximately its middle third exhibits a distinct, well developed roughened area, the *pronator tuberosity* (13). At the distal end of the radius is the *suprastyloid crest* with the *styloid process* (14) and medial to it, the *ulnar notch* (15). The *carpal articular surface* (16) is directed distally.

Dorsally are found various distinctly developed **grooves** in which course the tendons of the long extensors. From lateral (radial) to medial (ulnar), the *first groove* (17) resides on the styloid process and contains the tendons of the abductor pollicis longus and extensor pollicis brevis muscles. The *second groove* (18) serves for the passage of the tendons of the extensor carpi radialis longus and brevis, whereas the *third groove* (19) courses obliquely and houses the tendon of the extensor pollicis longus. In the *fourth groove* (20) lie the tendons of the extensor digitorum and extensor indicis muscles. The lateral bony ridge lying by the third groove is usually palpable and is also designated as the **dorsal tubercle** (21).

Clinical tip: The styloid process of the radius extends about 1 cm, farther distally than that of the ulna. This is an important detail to remember when setting fractures.

Ossification: Perichondral ossification of the radial shaft begins in the 7th intrauterine week. The epiphyses are formed endochondrally and postnatally, the distal epiphysis in the 1st and 2nd, the styloid process in the 10th–12th and the proximal epiphysis in the 4th–7th year. Epiphysial fusion occurs proximally between ages 14 and 17 years, distally between the 20th and 25th years of life.

Ulna (F–L)

The **ulna** possesses a **shaft** (22) and a **proximal** and a **distal extremity**. The proximal end exhibits a hook-shaped, curved process, the *olecranon* (23), which has a roughened surface. In front is the *trochlear notch* (24), which extends up to the *coronoid process* (25).

The *radial notch* (26) lies laterally and articulates with the articular circumference of the radial head. The *ulnar tuberosity* (27) is located at the transition to the shaft. Lateral to it lies the *supinator crest* (28), which appears as an inferior prolongation of the radial notch. The shaft of the ulna is three-sided. The *interosseous border* (29) is directed laterally and the *anterior surface* (30), which faces anteriorly, is separated from the *medial surface* (32) by the *anterior border* (31). The medial surface is separated from the *posterior surface* (33) by the *posterior border* (34). The anterior surface at about the middle of the ulna presents a *nutrient foramen* (35) and the *head* (36) contains the *articular circumference* (37) and the small *styloid process* (38) projecting distally.

Ossification: Perichondral ossification of the shaft of the ulna begins in the 7th intrauterine week. The ossific centers in the epiphyses are endochondral in origin and appear distally between the 4th and 7th postnatal years, in the styloid process between the 7th and 8th years, and proximally between the 9th and 11th years of life. Epiphysial fusion takes place earlier proximally, later distally.

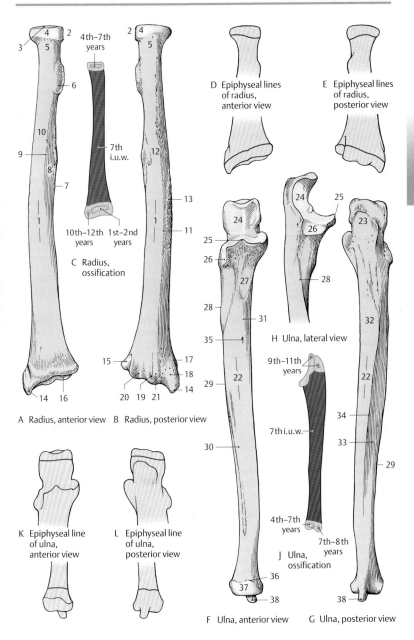

4th–7th years

7th i.u.w.

10th–12th years   1st–2nd years

C Radius, ossification

A Radius, anterior view   B Radius, posterior view

D Epiphyseal lines of radius, anterior view

E Epiphyseal lines of radius, posterior view

H Ulna, lateral view

9th–11th years

7th i.u.w.

4th–7th years

7th–8th years

J Ulna, ossification

F Ulna, anterior view   G Ulna, posterior view

K Epiphyseal line of ulna, anterior view

L Epiphyseal line of ulna, posterior view

Elbow Joint (A–D)

The **elbow joint** is a **compound joint** with the three articulating surfaces of the bones within the joint capsule. It really consists of three joints:
- The **humeroradial joint**
- The **humero-ulnar joint**
- The **proximal radio-ulnar joint**

It is secured by *bone* and *ligament*. Bony stability is provided by the trochlea of the humerus and the trochlear notch of the ulna into which it fits. Ligamentous stability is due to the annular ligament of the radius and the collateral ligaments.

The thin, lax **joint capsule** (**1**) encloses the joint surfaces. In order to prevent pinching of the capsule between these surfaces during movement of the joint, fibers from the brachialis and triceps brachii muscles act as *articular muscles* and radiate into the capsule in order to tense it. Both *humeral epicondyles* (**2**) are outside the capsule (**D**). The synovial membrane surrounds the olecranon fossa and both fossae on the anterior side of the humerus (**D**). Between the **synovial** (**3**) and **fibrous** (**4**) **membranes** of the capsule in the region of the fossa is a large amount of fatty tissue (**5**), which may help to limit extreme movements of the joint. In the ulnar region, the line of attachment of the capsule (**D**) follows the margin of the trochlear notch, so that the tips of the *olecranon* (**6**) and the *coronoid process* (**7**) still project within the capsule. On the radius the capsule extends as a sac below the *anular ligament of radius* (**8**), the *superior sacciform recess* (**9**). This extension of the capsule makes rotation of the radius possible.

The very strong collateral ligaments are embedded in the sides of the joint capsule. The **ulnar collateral ligament** (**10**) arises from the medial epicondyle of the humerus and usually possesses *two strong fiber bundles*, an *anterior one* (**11**) which is directed to the coronoid process, and a *posterior one* (**12**) which extends to the lateral margin of the olecranon. The ulnar nerve runs under the latter bundle in the groove for ulnar nerve. Between these two fibrous bundles lies loose connective tissue, which is limited on the ulnar side by *oblique fibers* (**13**).

The **radial collateral ligament** (**14**) extends from the lateral epicondyle of the humerus to the anular ligament of radius and proximal to the latter radiates into the ulna. The radial collateral ligament fuses with the superficial extensors. The **quadrate ligament** connects the neck of the radius to the radial notch of the ulna.

Finally, there is the **anular ligament of radius** (**8**) which is attached at both ends onto the ulna and encircles the head of the radius. There is often cartilaginous tissue on its inner surface, which acts as a moveable buttress for the radius during pronation and supination (see p. 122).

Because of the interaction of these three joints in any flexed or extended position, a simultaneous rotation of the radius around the ulna is possible.

The following movements are possible: flexion, extension, supination and **pronation** (see p. 122).

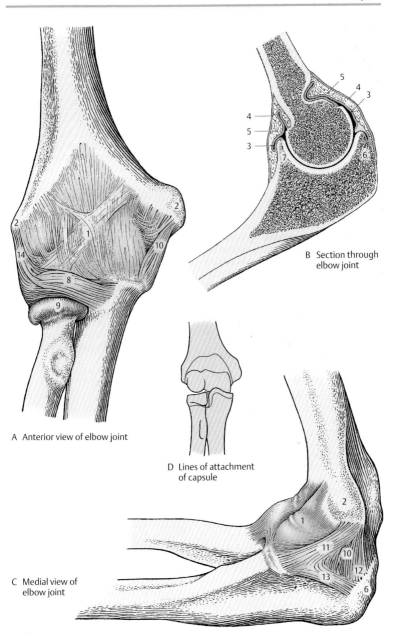

B Section through elbow joint

A Anterior view of elbow joint

D Lines of attachment of capsule

C Medial view of elbow joint

Elbow Joint, continued (A–C)

The **humeroradial joint** (**1**) is formed by the **capitulum of the humerus** and the **articular facet** on the **head of the radius**. It corresponds in form to a ball-and-socket joint. The **humero-ulnar joint** (**2**), a hinge joint, occurs between the **trochlea of the humerus** and the **trochlear notch of ulna**. On the trochlea there is a *channel* (**3**) which accommodates the leading edge of the trochlear notch. Flexion and extension movements between the upper arm and forearm occur at the humeroradial and humero-ulnar joints. The axis of movement corresponds to the axis of the trochlea of the humerus and its extension through the capitulum of the humerus. The **proximal radio-ulnar joint** (**4**) is formed between the **articular circumference of the head of radius** and the **radial notch of ulna**, together with the **anular ligament** (**5**). This is a pivot joint and it permits movements of the radius around the ulna together with the distal radio-ulnar joint. Rotation of the radius around the ulna is called **pronation** (**B**; bones cross over each other) or **supination** (**C**; bones lies parallel to one another). The axis of this movement runs from the center of the fovea on the head of the radius to the styloid process of the ulna.

The **"angle of excursion"**, i.e., the anteriorly measured angle between the upper arm and forearm at maximal extension is insignificantly greater in females (180°) than in males (175°). Hyperextension is possible in children. At maximal flexion the upper arm and forearm forms an angle of about 35° (soft tissue restraint). The **"carrying angle"**, i.e., the angle, open to the lateral side, between the upper arm and forearm when the limb is fully extended (abduction angle) varies between 158°– 180°, with an average of about 168.5°.

Distal Radio-ulnar Joint (D)

The **distal radio-ulnar joint** (**6**), a pivot joint, is formed by the **head of ulna** and the **ulnar notch of radius**. Between the radius and the styloid process of the ulna lies an *articular disk*, which separates the distal radio-ulnar from the radiocarpal joint. The **capsule** is lax and extends from the *inferior sacciform recess* (**7**) up to the shaft of the ulna. The **proximal** and **distal radio-ulnar joints** are **necessarily combined joints** to permit pronation and supination.

Continuous Fibrous Joint between Radius and Ulna (D)

The **interosseous membrane of the forearm** (**8**) stretches between the radius and the ulna. Its fibers run from proximal laterally to the medial side of the ulna distally. Fibers of the *oblique cord* (**9**) run in the opposite direction to those of the interosseous membrane. It strengthens the interosseous membrane proximally. The cord begins approximately at the ulnar tuberosity and extends to the interosseous border of the radius distal to the radial tuberosity.

> **Clinical tip:** The interosseous membrane not only prevents parallel displacement of the radius and ulna but also allows pulling and pressure stresses to be transmitted from one bone to the other. It is so strong that during overstrain of the forearm the bones tend to fracture before the fibers are torn.
>
> The most common of all fractures (first described by *Colles* in 1814) is at **a classic site on the radius**, and is due to a fall on the palm of the hand with the arm extended. The weight of the body is transmitted through the humerus and the ulna and then passes through the interosseous membrane to the radius. The distal end of the radius resists the counter-pressure, so that maximal stress develops and causes a fracture of the lower radius. The distal fragment is displaced radially and dorsally as the fibers of the interosseous membrane fix the shaft of the radius to the ulna (bayonet position).

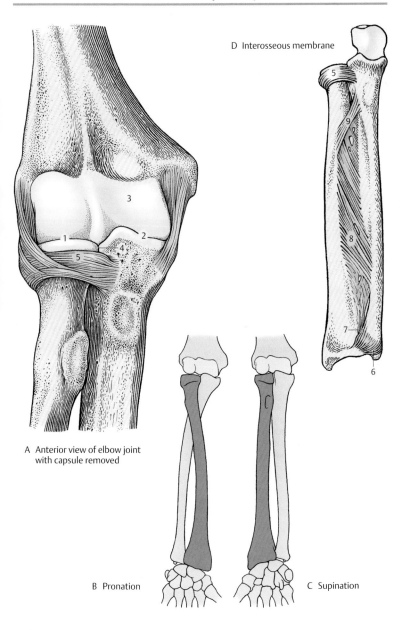

D Interosseous membrane

Upper Limb

A Anterior view of elbow joint
   with capsule removed

B Pronation

C Supination

Carpus (A–C)

The **carpus** consists of eight **carpal bones** arranged in two rows of four.

In the *proximal row* from lateral to medial are
- The **scaphoid** (**1**)
- The **lunate** (**2**)
- The **triquetrum** (**3**) and, superimposed on it,
- The **pisiform** (**4**).

In the *distal row* from the lateral to the medial side are
- The **trapezium** (**5**)
- The **trapezoid** (**6**)
- The **capitate** (**7**) and
- The **hamate** (**8**)

Each carpal bone has several facets for articulation with the neighboring bones.

Both rows of bones together, i.e., the entire carpus, form an arch which is convex proximally and concave distally. The palmar surface of the carpus is also concave and is spanned by the *flexor retinaculum*, which forms the osteofibrous **carpal tunnel**.
The flexor retinaculum stretches from the scaphoid and trapezium to the hamate and triquetrum. Projections on these named bones are palpable through the skin. With the hand pendent the pisiform is easily moved and is readily palpable, as is the tendon of flexor carpi ulnaris, which inserts into the pisiform. The scaphoid and trapezium form the floor of the radial notch, erroneously called the "anatomical snuffbox" (see p. 392).

Clinical tip: The scaphoid (**1**) is of particular interest clinically since it is the most frequently fractured carpal bone. Ulnar abduction (p. 132) brings about a divergence of the fragments, whereas with radial abduction (p. 132) the fragments are compressed. Palmar and dorsal flexion (p. 132) open the fracture cleft toward the dorsal or palmar aspect, respectively.
Inadequate treatment of a scaphoid fracture can lead to a pseudoarthrosis or necrosis of a fragment. Seventy percent of all scaphoid fractures occur in its middle third. **Carpal tunnel syndrome** is described on p. 388.

▬ **Variants:** Sometimes small accessory bones are found between the carpal bones. More than 20 of such accessory bones have been described so far. However, apart from the **central bone** (**9**), only the **styloid** (**10**), the **secondary trapezoid** (**11**), and the **secondary pisiform** (**12**) are considered to be proven accessory bones.

The possibility of the presence of such accessory carpal bones must always be borne in mind when examining radiographs of the wrist. The most common accessory bone is the os centrale (**9**). Its cartilagenous anlage is nearly always found in humans, but it almost always synostoses with the scaphoid (**1**). Fusion of carpal bones has also been described; the most frequent fusion is between the lunate and triquetrum.

The scaphoid, triquetrum and pisiform bones may also be divided in two. This may be confused with fractures of these bones.

Upper Limb

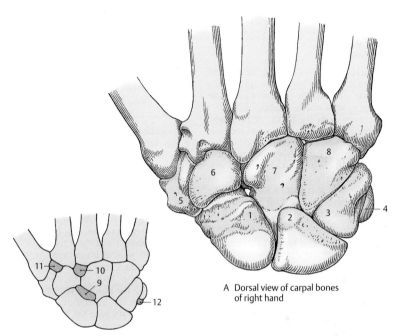

A Dorsal view of carpal bones of right hand

C Accessory carpal bones

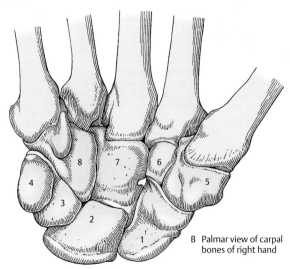

B Palmar view of carpal bones of right hand

Individual Bones of the Carpus (A, B)

Proximal Row

The **scaphoid** (**1**) is the largest bone in the proximal row. On its palmar surface is a *tubercle* (**2**), which is easily palpable through the skin. The scaphoid articulates proximally with the radius, distally with the trapezium and trapezoid, and medially with the lunate and capitate. Blood vessels enter along the entire roughened surface of the bone. In one-third of cases, blood vessels reach the scaphoid bone only on its distal face; in this case, a fracture of the scaphoid bone (see p. 124) may be followed by necrosis of the proximal fragment.

The crescent-shaped **lunate** (**3**) articulates proximally with the radius and the articular disk, medially with the triquetrum, laterally with the scaphoid and distally with the capitate and sometimes also with the hamate.

The **triquetrum** (**4**) is almost pyramidal in shape with its apex pointing medially. The base faces laterally and articulates with the lunate. Proximally it articulates with the articular disk and distally with the hamate. The palmar surface has a small articular facet (**5**) for the pisiform.

The **pisiform** (**6**), the smallest carpal bone, is round and possesses on its dorsal surface an articular surface for the triquetrum. It is readily palpable and is inserted as a sesamoid bone in the tendon of the flexor carpi ulnaris.

Distal Row

The **trapezium** (**7**) possesses a *tubercle* (**8**) which is palpable on dorsiflexion on the hand, and medial to it there is a groove (**9**) for the tendon of the flexor carpi radialis. Distally it has a saddle-shaped articular facet (**10**) for the first metacarpal bone. A facet for articulation with the trapezoid lies medially, and between the distal and medial articular facets there is a further small facet for the joint with the second metacarpal bone. Proximally the trapezium articulates with the scaphoid.

The **trapezoid** (**11**) is wider dorsally than on its palmar surface. It articulates proximally with the scaphoid, distally with the second metacarpal, laterally with the trapezium and medially with the capitate.

The **capitate** (**12**) is the largest carpal bone. It has facets proximally for articulation with the scaphoid and the lunate, laterally for the trapezoid, medially for the hamate and distally mainly for the third metacarpal bone, as well as partly for the second and fourth metacarpals.

The **hamate** (**13**) is readily palpable. On its palmar aspect is the *hamulus* (**14**), which is curved laterally. The latter is related to the flexor digiti minimi brevis and the **pisohamate ligament**. It articulates distally with the fourth and fifth metacarpal bones, laterally with the capitate, proximally and medially with the triquetrum, and proximally and laterally with the lunate.

Ossification: The ossific centers arise endochondrally and appear only after birth. In the 1st year of life (usually in the 3rd month) they develop in the capitate and hamate, in the 2nd to 3rd years in the triquetrum. In girls, the bony center appears in the triquetrum at the beginning of the 2nd year, whereas in boys the earliest appearance is seen only after $2^{1}/_{2}$ years. The center of ossification for the lunate develops between the 3rd and 6th years, that for the scaphoid between the 4th and 6th years, those for the trapezium and trapezoid between the 3rd and 6th years. The pisiform arises between years 8 and 12.

Upper Limb

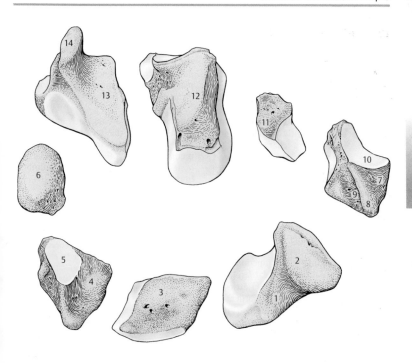

A Carpal bones of right hand, anterior (palmar) view

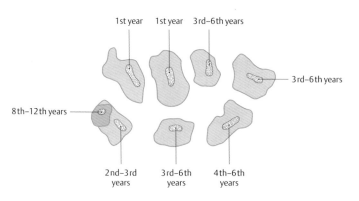

B Development of carpal bones

Bones of the Metacarpus and Digits (A–C)

The five **metacarpals** of the hand each have a *head* (**1**), a *shaft* (**2**), and a *base* (**3**). On all of these there are articular facets at one end (base) for articulation with the carpals and at the other (head) for the phalanges. The palmar surface is slightly concave and the dorsal surface slightly convex. The dorsal surface exhibits a characteristic triangular configuration toward the head. The proximal articular facet of the **first metacarpal** is saddle-shaped; the **second metacarpal** has a notched base proximally for articulation with the carpus, and on the medial side the third metacarpal. On the dorso-radial side of the base of the **third metacarpal** is a *styloid process* (**4**) and radially an articular facet for the second metacarpal. Proximally, for junction with the carpus, there is one articular facet, and on the ulnar side there are two articular facets for articulation with the **fourth metacarpal.** The fourth metacarpal has two articular facets radially but only one on its ulnar side for articulation with the **fifth metacarpal.**

The **bones of the digits**: Each digit (i.e., the index, middle, ring and little finger) consists of more than one bone, namely, a **proximal** (**5**), a **medial** (**6**), and a **distal phalanx** (**7**). The sole exception is the **thumb**, which has only two phalanges.

Each **proximal phalanx** has a flattened palmar surface, dorsally and transversally it is convex and has roughened sharpened borders for the attachment of the fibrous tendon sheaths of the flexor muscles. It has a *shaft* (**8**), a distal *phalangeal head* (also called a "trochlea") (**9**), and a *proximal* base (**10**). The base has a transverse oval socket, an articular facet for the metacarpals.

The base of the **middle phalanx** has two convex facets separated by a smooth ridge to conform to the shape of the head of the proximal phalanx.

The base of the **distal phalanx** also bears a ridge. At the distal end there is a rough palmar surface for insertion of the tendon of the flexor digitorum profundus as well as a palmar-facing roughened, spade-shaped *plate* (**11**) at its terminus, *the tuberosity of distal phalanx.*

Sesamoid bones are regularly found in the joints between the metacarpals and the proximal phalanx of the thumb, one lying medially and the other laterally. Sesamoid bones are also found in variable numbers in the other fingers.

Ossification: In both the metacarpals and the phalanges there is only one epiphysial center of ossification in addition to the perichondral diaphysis (3rd intrauterine month). In the metacarpals the distal epiphysial centers develop in the 2nd year of life, except for the 1st metacarpal, in whose proximal end the center appears in the 2nd–3rd year. In the phalanges epiphysial ossification centers occur only proximally.

> **Clinical tip: Pseudoepiphyses** may develop in the metacarpal bones. In radiographs they may be distinguished from true epiphyses, as they are attached to the diaphysis by a piece of bone. The 1st metacarpal bone may have a pseudoepiphysis at its distal end, but all other metacarpal bones have them at the proximal end: they must be distinguished from fractures. Pseudoepiphyses are found more commonly in certain diseases.

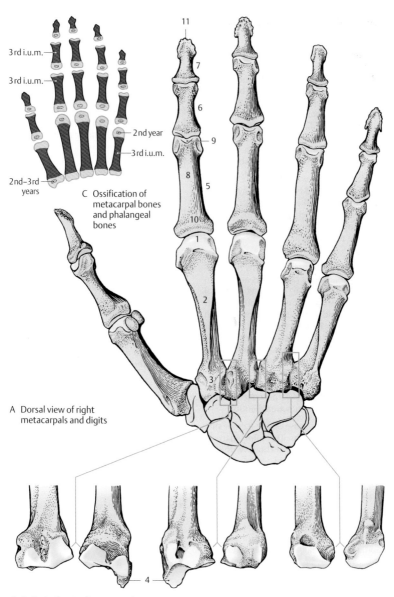

3rd i.u.m.

3rd i.u.m.

— 2nd year

— 3rd i.u.m.

2nd–3rd
years

C Ossification of
metacarpal bones
and phalangeal
bones

A Dorsal view of right
metacarpals and digits

B Articular facets of metacarpals
on their opposing surfaces

Upper Limb

Radiocarpal and Midcarpal Joints (A–E)

The **radiocarpal** or **wrist joint** is an ellipsoid joint formed on one side by the **radius** (**1**) and the **articular disk** (**2**) and on the other by the **proximal row of carpal bones**. Not all the carpal bones of the proximal row are in continual contact with the socket-shaped articular facet of the radius and the disk. The *triquetrum* (**3**), only makes close contact with the disk during ulnar abduction and loses contact on radial abduction.

The **capsule** of the wrist joint is lax, dorsally relatively thin, and is reinforced by numerous ligaments. The joint space is unbranched and sometimes contains *synovial folds*. Often the wrist joint is in continuity with the midcarpal joint.

The **midcarpal joint** is formed by the **proximal** and **distal row of carpal bones** and has an S-shaped joint space. Each row of carpal bones can be considered as a single articular body, and they interlock with each other. Although there is a certain limited degree of mobility between members of the proximal row of carpal bones, this is not true of the distal row because they are joined one to another (**4**), as well as to the metacarpal bones by strong ligaments. Thus, the distal row of carpal bones and the metacarpals form a functional entity.

The **joint capsule** is tense on the palmar surface and lax dorsally. The joint space is branched and has connections with the radiocarpal joint, and around the *trapezium* (**5**) and *trapezoid* (**6**) there are also connections with adjacent carpometacarpal joints.

Sometimes the joint space contains numerous *synovial folds* (**7**). The space between the lunate and triquetrum and the capitate and hamate is padded by synovial folds which may be visible in radiographs.

Ligaments in the Region of the Wrist (A–E)

Four groups of ligaments can be distinguished:

Ligaments which unite the forearm bones with the carpal bones (violet). These include the *ulnar collateral ligament* (**8**), the *radial collateral ligament* (**9**), the *palmar radiocarpal ligament* (**10**), the *dorsal radiocarpal ligament* (**11**), and the *palmar ulnocarpal ligament* (**12**).

Ligaments which unite the carpal bones with one another, or **intercarpal ligaments** (red). These comprise the *radiate carpal ligament* (**13**), the *pisohamate ligament* (**14**), and the *palmar intercarpal* (**15**), *dorsal intercarpal* (**16**), and *interosseous intercarpal ligaments* (**4**).

Ligaments between the carpal and metacarpal bones, or **carpometacarpal ligaments** (blue). To this group belongs the *pisometacarpal ligament* (**17**), the *palmar carpometacarpal ligaments* (**18**), and the *dorsal carpometacarpal ligaments* (**19**).

Ligaments between the metacarpal bones, or **metacarpal ligaments** (yellow). These are organized into *dorsal* (**20**), *interosseous* (**21**), and *palmar* (**22**) *metacarpal ligaments.*

Almost all of these ligaments strengthen the joint capsules and partly guide the movements of the joints of hand.

The joints between the carpal bones of a row are designated as **intercarpal joints**. Only the joint between the triquetrum and the *pisiform*, the **pisiform joint** deserves special attention.

Clinical tip: Several more ligaments are described in hand surgery. They are important in cases of surgical intervention.

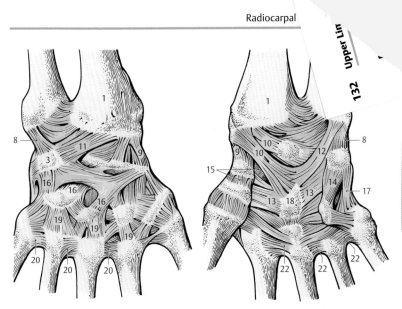

A Ligaments of right wrist,
   dorsal surface

B Ligaments of right wrist,
   palmar surface

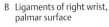

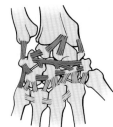

D Diagram of ligaments
   of right wrist, dorsal surface

C Section through right wrist,
   dorsal view

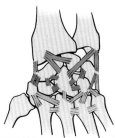

E Diagram of ligaments
   of right wrist, palmar surface

ovements in the Radiocarpal and Midcarpal Joints (A–C)

Starting from the midposition (**A**), we distinguish
  – **Marginal movements** of **radial deviation** (**abduction**; **B**) and **ulnar deviation** (**adduction**; **C**)
    from
  – **Movements in the plane of the hand**, i.e., **flexion (palmar flexion)** and **extension (dorsiflexion)** as well as
  – **Intermediate or combined movements**

Marginal Movements

Pure radial abduction: Radial abduction is carried out by the synergistic cooperation of the following muscles: extensor carpi radialis longus, abductor pollicis longus, extensor pollicis longus, flexor carpi radialis, and flexor pollicis longus. *The scaphoid* (red) *is tilted toward the palmar surface*, where it becomes palpable through the skin. Tilting of this bone allows the *trapezium* (blue) and *trapezoid* (green) to approach the radius. Since the *trapezoid* and the second *metacarpal bone* are rigidly joined together and the flexor carpi radialis and extensor carpi radialis longus are inserted into the second metacarpal bone, radial abduction represents a pulling action on this functional unit. The trapezoid glides along the scaphoid and, as the latter bone is not fixed, it can be moved, and since it cannot free itself from its other articulations, it is forced to tilt.

This tilting movement occurs along a radio-ulnar transverse axis. In addition to tilting of the scaphoid, there is palmar displacement of the other proximal carpal bones. **Radial abduction occurs around a dorsopalmar axis**, which runs through the *head of the capitate* (violet). In this movement the *pisiform* (dotted line) traverses the greatest path, as can be seen in radiographs.

Pure ulnar deviation: *Ulnar adduction involves a tilting or dorsal shifting of the proximal row of carpal bones.* The muscles collaborating in this action are especially the extensor carpi ulnaris and the flexor carpi ulnaris, in addition to the extensor digitorum and extensor digiti minimi. **Movement toward the ulnar side takes place around a dorsopalmar axis** through the head of the capitate, *the tilting movement around a radio-ulnar axis.*

Extent of Movements of Deviation

Movements of deviation are equally possible on either side of the **midposition**. The midposition corresponds to an ulnar deviation of 12° and must not be confused with the straight position of the hand.

The **straight position** is one in which the long axis of the third finger runs over the capitate bone and is in a straight line with the long axis of the forearm. Starting from the straight position radial deviation is smaller, namely 15°, while ulnar deviation is about 40°. These values are only true when the arm is in strict supination; in strict pronation they are slightly greater. The angle is much larger if the forearm is pronated and the humerus rotated around the elbow joint. Possibly the various muscles are able to function more effectively in the latter position.

The radiographs from which Figures **A–C** were drawn were taken with the arm in pronation.

hamate	Orange
lunate	Black
triquetrum	Yellow

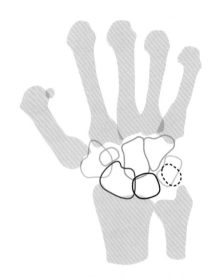

A Straight position of right hand
   (from a radiograph)

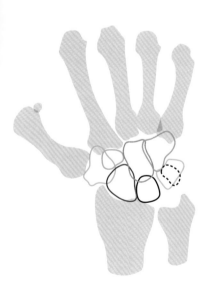

B Radial abduction of right hand
   (from a radiograph)

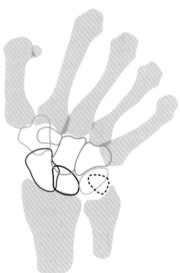

C Ulnar adduction of right hand
   (from a radiograph)

Movements in the Radiocarpal and Midcarpal Joints, continued (A–C)

Movements in the Plane of the Hand

Palmar flexion and dorsiflexion: The *proximal carpal bones are displaced toward the palmar side during dorsiflexion, toward the dorsal side during palmar flexion.* This becomes particularly evident at the scaphoid (red) which protrudes toward the palmar side during dorsiflexion and is palpable through the skin. *The axes of movements course transversely, through the lunate* (black) *for the proximal row and through the capitate* (violet) *for the distal row.* **Flexion and extension consist of movements which take place around both these axes.** The magnitude of the angle between maximum dorsiflexion and palmar flexion is about 170°. **Palmar flexion** *occurs mainly at the radiocarpal (wrist) joint,* **dorsiflexion** *predominantly at the midcarpal joint.* Palmar flexion takes place by the action of the long flexors of the fingers, as well as by the flexors of the wrist and the abductor pollicis longus. Dorsiflexion is carried out by the radial extensors of the wrist and by the extensors of the fingers (p. 172).

Intermediate or Combined Movements

These result from the directions in which the involved muscles work, and through them and the movements of the various joints, including the elbow and the shoulder, it is possible to produce movements which approximate those of a ball-and-socket joint. One focus of all joint and movement axes runs through the capitate. The structure of the wrist necessitates certain restrictions of mobility; for example, it is not possible to produce abduction during maximum palmar flexion, because in the latter position the proximal row of carpal bones cannot be either displaced or tilted.

Carpometacarpal and Intermetacarpal joints

Carpometacarpal Joint of the Thumb

This joint is a **saddle joint**, which allows *abduction* and *adduction* of the thumb, as well as *opposition, reposition,* and *circumduction.*

Carpometacarpal Joints

All other joints between the carpal and metacarpal bones are **amphiarthroses.** They are fixed by tense ligaments, the palmar and dorsal carpometacarpal ligaments.

Intermetacarpal Joints

These, too, are **rigid joints** and are fixed by dorsal, palmar, and interosseous ligaments.

Metacarpophalangeal and Digital Joints (D–E)

The **metacarpophalangeal joints** are **ball-and-socket joints in shape** with *lax capsules. The palmar side of the capsule is strengthened by palmar ligaments and fibrous cartilage.* The articulation is between the head of the metacarpal (**1**) and the base of the proximal phalanx (**2**). Restriction of movements is caused by the *collateral ligaments* (**3**), whose origin (**4**) is dorsal to the axis of motion of the joint of the heads of the metacarpals. The greater the movement, the tighter the ligaments become. In flexion, movements of abduction are almost impossible. The joints may be rotated passively by up to 50°. The joints between the bones of the fingers, the **interphalangeal joints of the hand**, are **hinge joints**, which may be flexed and extended. They, too, have collateral (**5**) and palmar ligaments.

trapezoid	Green
triquetrum	Yellow
trapezium	Dark blue
hamate	Orange
pisiform	Black dotted line

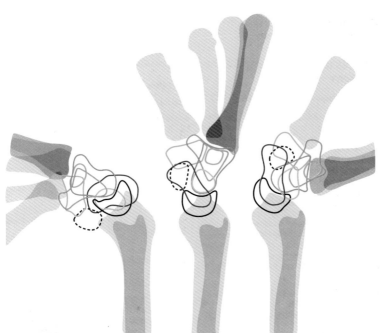

B Palmar flexion of right hand (from a radiograph)

A Mid-position of right hand, seen from side (from a radiograph)

C Dorsiflexion of right hand (from a radiograph)

D Lateral view of digital joints

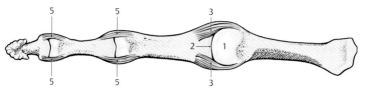

E Palmar view of metacarpophalangeal and digital joints with capsules removed

Muscles, Fascias, and Special Features

Muscles of the Shoulder Girdle and Arm

Classification of the Muscles (A–C)

Ontogenetically the limb muscles stem from the ventral body wall musculature. Their division into dorsal and ventral muscle groups results from consideration of their topography and innervation. The nerves arise from ventral or dorsal parts of the plexus (see vol. 3). The immigration into the shoulder girdle region of various muscles which ontogenetically stem from other regions, for instance, from the branchial musculature, has obscured the simple principle underlying this classification. Further information should be sought in textbooks of embryology. In any description of the musculature, it is important to retain the genetic principle as far as possible and by this to prove the relationship of the individual muscles.

Another method of classification is that of functional relationship. Here muscles are grouped together according to their actions on individual joints.

Shoulder Girdle Muscles

The shoulder girdle muscles may be grouped ontogenetically into those which have migrated from the trunk into the upper limb, those which extend secondarily from the arm into the trunk, and those which have immigrated as craniothoracic muscles from the head to the shoulder girdle.

Shoulder Girdle Muscles with Insertions on the Humerus

Dorsal Muscle Group (see p. 138)

- Supraspinatus (**1**)
- Infraspinatus (**2**)
- Teres minor (**3**)
- Deltoid (**4**)
- Subscapularis (**5**)
- Teres major (**6**)
- Latissimus dorsi (**7**)

Ventral Muscle Group (see p. 142)

- Coracobrachialis (**8**)
- Pectoralis minor
  (exception: insertion on the scapula)
- Pectoralis major (**9**)

Trunk Muscles which Insert on the Shoulder Girdle

Dorsal Muscle Group (see p. 144)

- Rhomboideus major
- Rhomboideus minor
- Levator scapulae
- Serratus anterior

Ventral Muscle Group (see p. 146)

- Subclavius
- Omohyoid

Cranial Muscles which Insert on the Shoulder Girdle
(see p. 146)

- Trapezius
- Sternocleidomastoid

Muscles of Arm

The muscles of the limb are separated according to their position into those of the arm and those of the forearm (see p. 158). The arm muscles are divided into ventral and dorsal groups, which are separated by intermuscular septa.

Ventral Muscle Group (see p. 154)

- Brachialis (**10**)
- Biceps brachii (**11**) with its long (**12**) and short (**13**) heads

Dorsal Muscle Group (see p. 156)

- Triceps brachii with its long (**14**), medial (**15**) and lateral heads (**16**)
- Anconeus

17 Axillary artery and vein
18 Brachial artery
19 Brachial veins
20 Basilic vein
21 Cephalic vein
22 Radial nerve
23 Median nerve
24 Ulnar nerve
25 Medial antebrachial cutaneous nerve
26 Musculocutaneous nerve
27 Axillary or circumflex nerve

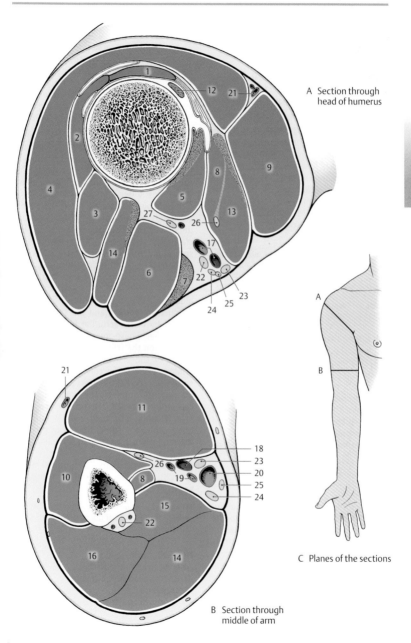

Upper Limb

A Section through head of humerus

B Section through middle of arm

C Planes of the sections

Upper Limb

Shoulder Muscles Inserted on the Humerus

Dorsal Group of Muscles (A–C)

Insertion on the greater tubercle of the humerus as well as the crest of the greater tubercle and its continuation (the supraspinatus, infraspinatus, teres minor, and deltoid).

The **supraspinatus** (**1**) *arises from the supraspinous fascia and the supraspinous fossa* (**2**). It passes over the joint capsule, with which it is fused, to reach the *upper facet of the greater tubercle* (**3**). It holds the humerus in its socket, tenses the capsule, and abducts the arm. Sometimes there is a synovial bursa near the glenoid cavity.
Nerve supply: suprascapular nerve (C4–C6).

> **Clinical tip: Tendonopathy of the supraspinatus** caused by excessive strain or trauma is common. It is associated with calcification in the tendon near the greater tubercle and causes severe pain on abduction. Tendon ruptures also occur and are most common after 40 years of age.

The **infraspinatus** (**4**) *arises from the infraspinous fossa* (**5**), *the spine of scapula* (**6**), *and the infraspinous fascia, and runs to the greater tubercle* (**7**; middle facet). The infraspinatus reinforces the capsule of the shoulder joint. Its main function is external rotation of the arm. Near the joint socket there is often the subtendinous bursa of the infraspinatus muscle.
Nerve supply: suprascapular nerve (C4–C6).

▰▰ **Variant:** It is frequently fused with the teres minor.

The **teres minor** (**8**) *arises from the lateral border of the scapula* (**9**) superior to the origin of the teres major, and is *inserted on the lower facet of the greater tubercle* (**10**). It acts as a weak lateral rotator of the arm.
Nerve supply: axillary (circumflex) nerve (C5–C6).

▰▰ **Variant:** It may be fused with the infraspinatus.

The **deltoid** (**11**) is divided into three parts, **clavicular** (**12**), **acromial** (**13**), and **spinal** (**14**). The **clavicular part** arises from the *lateral third of the clavicle* (**15**), the **acromial part** from *the acromion* (**16**), and the **spinal part** from the *lower border of the spine of the scapula* (**17**). *All three parts are attached to the deltoid tuberosity* (**18**). In the region of the greater tubercle of the humerus, there is a subdeltoid bursa.

The three sections of the deltoid muscle act partly as synergists and partly as antagonists. It is the most important **abductor** of the shoulder joint. Abduction up to about 90° is mostly performed by the deltoid, at first only by the acromial fibers. Only after the first two-thirds of the movement of abduction have been completed do the clavicular and spinal fibers become responsible for the movement. The clavicular and spinal fibers are able to **adduct** the arm after it has been lowered to a third of its range of movement. The clavicular fibers, aided by some of the acromial fibers, can produce **anteversion**, and the spinal fibers, helped by other acromial fibers, produce **retroversion**. These movements are superimposed on the framework of basic movements of the arm (swinging of the arm while walking). The clavicular and spinal sections of the deltoid exert a rotary action on these movements. The clavicular fibers can produce **medial** (**internal**) **rotation** in an arm which is adducted and laterally rotated, while the spinal fibers can produce (**lateral**) (**external**) **rotation** in a medially rotated arm.
Nerve supply: axillary (circumflex) nerve (C4–C6); clavicular fibers also by pectoral branches (C4–C5).

▰▰ **Variant:** Fusion with neighboring muscles; absence of the acromial fibers; occurrence of supernumary groups of muscle fibers.

19 Teres major
20 Long head of the triceps
21 Lateral head of the triceps
22 Trapezius
23 Levator scapulae

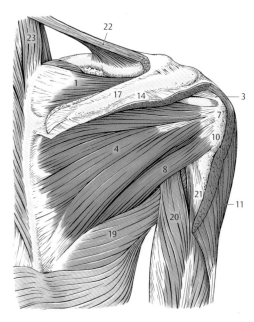

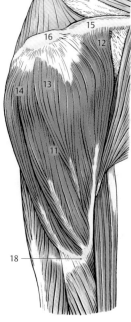

A Dorsal shoulder muscles inserting
on greater tubercle and its crest,
view from back

B Deltoid muscle seen from side

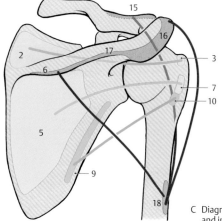

C Diagram of origin, course,
and insertion of muscles

Upper Limb

Shoulder Muscles
Inserted on the Humerus

Dorsal Muscle Group, continued (A–D)

Insertion on the lesser tubercle and its crest subscapularis, teres major and latissimus dorsi

The **subscapularis** (1) arises in the *subscapular fossa* (2) *and is inserted on the lesser tubercle* (3) *and the proximal part of its crest.* Near to its attachment between the subscapularis and the joint capsule occurs the subtendinous bursa of the *subscapularis* (4), and between it and the base of the coracoid process lies the *subcoracoid bursa* (5). Both bursae are connected with the joint space. It produces medial (internal) rotation of the arm.
Nerve supply: subscapular nerve (C5–C8).

■■ **Variant:** The occurrence of accessory bundles.

> **Clinical tip: Paralysis** of the subscapularis produces maximal lateral (external) rotation of the upper limb, which indicates that it is a particularly strong medial rotator of the arm.
> The term **"rotator cuff"** is often incorrectly used for the subscapularis, supraspinatus (6), infraspinatus (7), and teres minor (8) muscles. It is more correct to use the term "muscle-tendon cuff" or "tendon hood."

The **teres major** (9), which *arises from the lateral border* (10) *of the scapula near the inferior angle, is inserted on the crest of the lesser tubercle* (11), near the subtendinous bursa of the teres major. Its main function is retroversion of the arm toward the midline, a movement requiring retroversion and simultaneously a small medial rotation. It is particularly prominent if the arm has previously been anteverted and slightly abducted. The muscle also helps in adduction.
Nerve supply: thoracodorsal nerve (C6–C7).

■■ **Variant:** Fusion with the latissimus dorsi or complete absence of the muscle.

The **latissimus dorsi** (12) is broad and flat, and is the largest muscle in humans. *It arises from the spinous processes of the seventh to twelfth thoracic vertebrae* (13) as the *thoracolumbar fascia* (14) *and the posterior third of the iliac crest* (15) as the **iliac part**, *from the 10th–12th ribs* (16) as the **costal part**, and, in addition, very often from the *inferior angle of the scapula* as the **scapular part** (17). The latissimus dorsi thus usually arises in four parts which have different functions. It develops embryologically with the teres major, with which it is inserted on the *crest of the lesser tubercle* (18). The subtendinous bursa of the latissimus dorsi lies immediately before the junction of both muscles. The latissimus dorsi provides the muscular basis of the posterior axillary fold. It lowers the raised arm and adducts it. When the arm is adducted, it pulls it backward and medially, and rotates it so far medially that the back of the hand can cover the buttock. The latissimus dorsi is often called the "dress coat pocket" muscle. Both latissimi can act together to pull the shoulders backward and downward. They function, too, during forced expiration and in coughing (coughing muscle).
Nerve supply: thoracodorsal nerve (C6–C8).

■■ **Variant:** The occurrence of aberrant muscle fibers that run into the pectoralis major as a muscular arch across the axilla.

19 Long head of triceps muscle
20 Long head of biceps muscle
21 Coracoacromial ligament
22 Glenoid cavity
23 Glenoid lip
24 Joint capsule
25 Bursa of supraspinatus muscle
26 External oblique abdominal muscle
27 Trapezius muscle (partly resected)

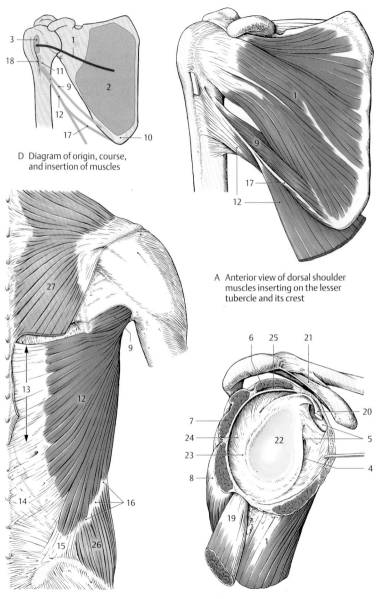

D Diagram of origin, course, and insertion of muscles

A Anterior view of dorsal shoulder muscles inserting on the lesser tubercle and its crest

B Posterior view of latissimus dorsi muscle

C Muscle-tendon cuff

Upper Limb

Shoulder Muscles Inserted on the Humerus, continued

Ventral Muscle Group (A, B)

The **coracobrachialis** (**1**) *arises from the coracoid process* (**2**) together with the short head of the biceps brachii. *It is inserted on the medial surface of the humerus on the continuation of the crest of the lesser tubercle* (**3**). It anteverts the arm and also holds the head of the humerus in its joints socket.
Nerve supply: musculocutaneous nerve (C6–C7).

The **pectoralis minor** (**4**) is the only shoulder girdle muscle which is not inserted on bone in the free limb. *It arises from the 3rd– 5th ribs* (**5**) *and is inserted on the coracoid process* (**6**). It lowers and rotates the scapula.
Nerve supply: pectoral nerves (C6–C8).

▰ **Variant:** More or fewer slips of origin.

The **pectoralis major** (**7**) is divided into three parts, i.e., the **clavicular**, **sternocostal** and **abdominal parts**.

The **clavicular part** *arises from the medial half of the anterior surface of the clavicle* (**8**), while the **sternocostal part** *comes from the sternal membrane and the cartilages of the 2nd– 6th ribs* (**9**). There are additional deep origins (**10**) of the sternocostal part from the 3rd (4th)– 5th costal cartilages. The weaker **abdominal part** *stems from the anterior layer of the uppermost part* (**11**) *of the rectus sheath. The pectoralis major is inserted on the crest of the greater tubercle* (**12**) in such a manner that the fibers are twisted, so that the abdominal part is attached most proximally and forms a pocket which is open above.

It is a strong muscle, four-sided when the arm hangs down; when the arm is raised, its borders form a triangle. It forms the muscular basis of the anterior axillary fold.

With the arm abducted, the clavicular and sternal parts can produce anteversion, a movement which is familiar from swimming. All parts of the pectoralis major act together, and forcibly and rapidly lower the raised arm. In addition, the whole muscle can adduct the arm and rotate it medially. The sternocostal and abdominal parts together lower the shoulder anteriorly.

Finally, the muscle can act as an accessory muscle during inspiration if the arms are fixed. Exhausted athletes after a race may be seen to prop up their arms on their trunk, so that the pectorales majores can be brought into action as accessory muscles of respiration to move the thorax.
Nerve supply: pectoral nerves (C5–T1).

▰ **Variants:** Individual sections may be absent. The sternocostal part may be divided into a sternal and a costal part. Sometimes the clavicular part is in direct contact with the deltoid muscle when there is no clavipectoral trigone (p. 370). A muscular axillary arch may be formed which is related to the latissimus dorsi muscle. There is a variant form in about 7 % of cases.

13 Short head of the biceps
14 Long head of the biceps
15 Deltoid (partly resected)

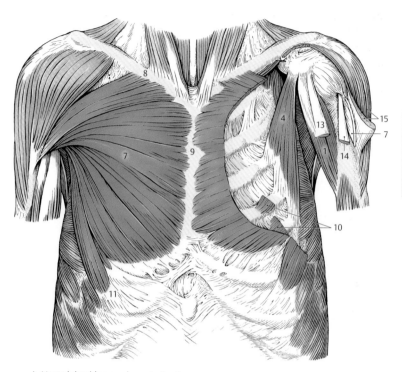

A Ventral shoulder muscles, anterior view

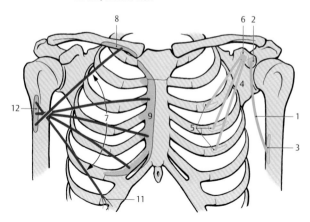

B Diagram of origin, course, and insertion of muscles

Upper Limb

Trunk Muscles
Inserting on the Shoulder Girdle

Dorsal Muscle Group (A–D)

The **rhomboid minor** (**1**) *originates from the spinous processes of the sixth to seventh cervical vertebrae* (**2**) *and inserts at the medial border of the scapula* (**3**).

The **rhomboid major** (**4**), situated caudal to the rhomboid minor, *arises from the spinous processes of the first to fourth thoracic vertebrae* (**5**) and likewise *inserts at the medial margin of the scapula* (**3**), caudal to the insertion of the rhomboid minor.

Both muscles have the same function, namely to press the scapula onto the thoracic wall, and they can retract the scapula toward the vertebral column.

The two muscles are sometimes fused to form a single rhomboid muscle.
Nerve supply: dorsal scapular nerve (C4–C5).

The **levator scapulae** (**6**) *arises from the dorsal tubercles of the transverse processes of the first to fourth cervical vertebrae* (**7**) and *is inserted on the superior angle of the scapula and the adjacent part of the medial border* (**8**). It elevates the scapula while rotating the inferior angle medially.
Nerve supply: dorsal scapular nerve (C4–C5).

The **serratus anterior** (**9**) *usually arises by nine (ten) slips from the 1st–9th ribs* (**10**) but sometimes from ribs 1–8. The number of slips is greater than the number of ribs from which they arise, as there are usually two slips from the 2nd rib. *The insertion of the muscle extends from the superior to the inferior angles along the entire medial border of the scapula* (**3**). The muscle is divided into three sections according to the points of insertion, namely a **superior part** (**11**), inserted near the superior angle of the scapula, an **intermediate part** (**12**), inserted along the medial border of the scapula, and

an **inferior part** (**13**) which is attached near to or at the inferior angle of the scapula.

All three parts pull the scapula toward the front, a movement essential for anteversion of the arm. It is the opposite of that produced by its antagonists, the rhomboid muscles. The superior and inferior parts together press the scapula onto the thorax, and in this movement they act synergistically with the rhomboid muscles. The inferior part rotates the scapula laterally and pulls the inferior angle lateral and forward. This movement makes elevation of the arm possible. All three parts may act to lift the ribs when the shoulder girdle is fixed, and so can act as an accessory muscle of respiration.
Nerve supply: the long thoracic nerve (C5–C7).

Variants: An increased or decreased number of slips of origin.

> **Clinical tip:** Paralysis of the serratus anterior caused by damage to the long thoracic nerve produces a **winged scapula** on the affected side, making it impossible to raise the arm laterally past 90° ("**rucksack paralysis**").
> The possibility of damage to the rhomboid muscles must be considered in the differential diagnosis, as this may also produce a winged scapula, although without interfering with arm elevation (see also pp. 148 and 150).

14 Subscapular
15 Teres major
16 Teres minor
17 Infraspinatus
18 Supraspinatus
19 Clavicle
20 Subclavius
21 External oblique muscle of the abdomen
22 Section through the scapula

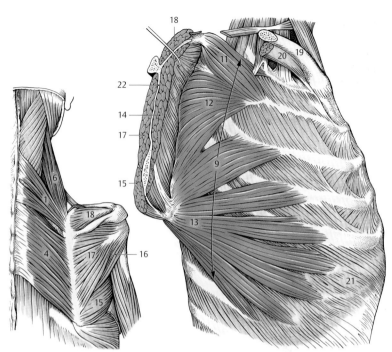

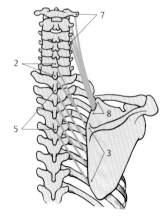

A Rhomboid muscles and levator scapulae muscle, posterior view

C Serratus anterior muscle, lateral view

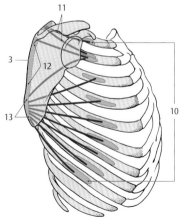

B Diagram of origin, course, and insertion of muscles

D Diagram of origin, course, and insertion of serratus anterior muscle

Trunk Muscles Inserting on the Shoulder Girdle, continued

Ventral Muscle Group (A–C)

The **subclavius** (**1**) *arises from the junction of bone and cartilage of the 1st rib* and is inserted into the *subclavian groove on the lower surface of the clavicle*. It pulls the clavicle toward the sternum and so stabilizes the sternoclavicular joint.

Nerve supply: subclavian nerve (C5–C6).

▬▬ **Variants:** This muscle may be absent.

The **omohyoid** is a two-bellied muscle; its **inferior belly** (**2**) *arises from the upper margin* (*border*) *of the scapula* near the scapular notch (**3**), and its **superior belly** (**4**) *inserts at the lateral one-third of the lower border of the hyoid bone* (**5**). It is, among others, a fascia tenser and, as a vascular muscle, dilates the internal jugular vein lying beneath it (see also p. 326).

Nerve supply: ansa cervicalis "profunda" (C1–C3).

▬▬ **Variant:** The muscle may arise from the clavicle instead of the scapula, in which case it is known as the **cleidohyoid muscle**.

Cranial Muscles Inserted on the Shoulder Girdle (A–C)

The **trapezius** (**6**) is divided into **descending**, **transverse** and **ascending parts**.

The **descending part** *arises from the superior nuchal line, the external occipital protuberance and the nuchal ligament* and is inserted on the *lateral third of the clavicle* (**7**). The **transverse part** *arises from the seventh cervical third thoracic vertebrae* (from their spinous processes and supraspinous ligaments) and *is inserted on the acromial end of the clavicle, the acromion* (**8**) *and part of the spine of the scapula* (**9**). The **ascending part** *arises from the second or third to twelfth thoracic vertebrae* (from the spinous processes and supraspinous ligaments) and *is inserted on the triangular portion of the spine or the adjacent part of the scapula* (**10**; see also figures on. p. 329).

The primary action of the trapezius is a static one, namely to stabilize the scapula and thus to fix the shoulder girdle. In its active function, when it contracts, it pulls the scapula and the clavicle backward toward the vertebral column. The descending and ascending parts rotate the scapula, and the former, in addition to adduction, also produces a slight elevation of the shoulder and so assists the serratus anterior. If the latter is paralyzed, the action of the descending part of the trapezius may still permit some elevation of the arm above the horizontal.

Nerve supply: accessory nerve and trapezius branch (cervical plexus C2–C4).

▬▬ **Variants:** The attachment to the clavicle may be widened to extend to the origin of the sternocleidomastoid muscle. In these cases there is a tendinous arch for the passage of the supraclavicular nerves (p. 358).

One head of the **sternocleidomastoid** (**11**) *arises from the sternum* (**12**) and the other *from the clavicle* (**13**). *It is inserted on the mastoid process* (**14**) and *the superior nuchal line* (**15**), where there is a tendinous junction with the origin of the trapezius.

As its action on the shoulder girdle is of minor importance, it is not discussed here, but subsequently with the muscles of the head (see p. 328).

Nerve supply: accessory nerve and cervical plexus (C1–C2).

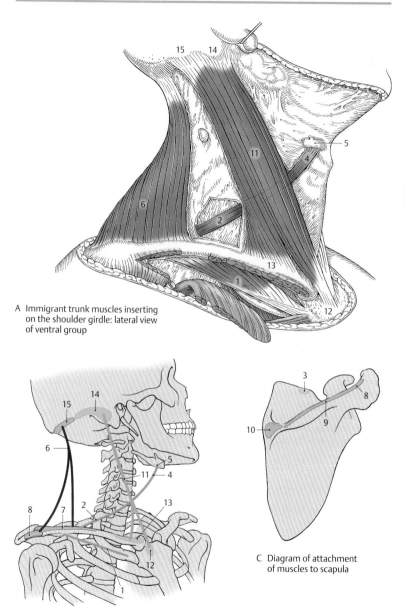

A Immigrant trunk muscles inserting
on the shoulder girdle: lateral view
of ventral group

B Diagram of origin, course, and insertion of muscles

C Diagram of attachment
of muscles to scapula

Function of the Shoulder Girdle Muscles (A–C)

We distinguish **adduction**, drawing of the arm toward the body, and **abduction,** lateral raising of the arm through 90° around a **sagittal axis** which runs through the head of the humerus. **Elevation** which may be a continuation of abduction, is not due to movement within the shoulder joint but is produced by **rotation of the scapula**, the inferior angle of which is moved forward and laterally.

In addition, there is **anteversion** or forward lifting of the arm, and **retroversion** or backward lifting of the arm. Both movements occur around a **frontal axis** which runs through the head of the humerus.

Finally there is **rotation** of the upper limb. This is due to pivoting of the arm (hanging down by the side) around an **axis which runs from the head of the humerus through the ulnar styloid process.** It corresponds to the axis of pronation and supination of the forearm, so that we may say that rotation leads to reinforcement of the movements of pronation and supination. We distinguish between **lateral** (external) and **medial** (internal) **rotation**. The compound movement of **circumduction** may also be either a **lateral or medial circumduction**. In it, the movement of the humerus is cone-shaped. Obviously, the same muscles which are active in rotation of the arm also function in circumduction.

Adductors (**A**) include
- The pectoralis major (red, pectoral nerves)
- The long head of the triceps brachii (blue, radial nerve, see p. 156)
- The teres major (yellow, thoracodorsal nerve)
- The latissimus dorsi (orange, thoracodorsal nerve)
- The short head of the biceps brachii (green, musculocutaneous nerve)
- The clavicular and spinal parts of the deltoid (brown, broken line, pectoral branches and axillary nerve)

Abduction (**B**) is produced by
- The deltoid (red, axillary nerve and pectoral branches)
- The supraspinatus (blue, suprascapular nerve)
- The long head of the biceps brachii (yellow, musculocutaneous nerve)

The serratus anterior and trapezius may aid this movement by producing slight rotation of the scapula.

Elevation (**C**) of the upper limb is produced by
- The serratus anterior (red, long thoracic nerve)

Before the arm can be elevated, it must be abducted by the deltoid, the long head of the biceps brachii and the supraspinatus. In the transition from abduction to elevation, the trapezius (blue, accessory nerve) supports the action of the serratus anterior. The effect of the latter depends on its action on the clavicular joints (acromioclavicular and sternoclavicular joints).

Clinical tip: If the **serratus muscle is paralyzed**, elevation of the arm is limited to the 15° produced by action of the trapezius.
In **fractures of the humerus**, the level is an important determinant of the displacement of the bony fragments. If the fracture is proximal to the insertion of the deltoid muscle, the greater adductor force causes the proximal bony fragment to be pulled medially. If the bone is broken distally to the deltoid insertion, the overpowering force of the deltoid muscle pulls the proximal part laterally and anteriorly (p. 380).

The color of the arrows shows the order of importance of the muscles in individual movements:

red
blue
yellow
orange
green
brown

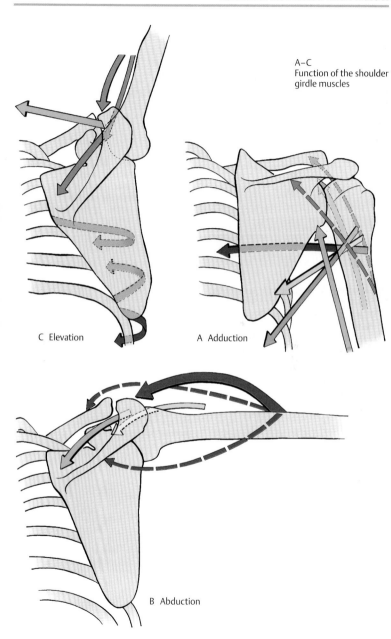

A–C
Function of the shoulder
girdle muscles

C Elevation

A Adduction

B Abduction

Upper Limb

Function of the Shoulder Girdle Muscles, continued (A–D)

The muscles which produce **Anteversion** (flexion; **A**) include
- The clavicular and some of the acromial fibers of the deltoid (red, pectoral branches and axillary nerve)
- The biceps brachii (blue, musculocutaneous nerve, see p. 154)
- The pectoralis major (yellow, pectoral nerves)
- The coracobrachialis (orange, musculocutaneous nerve)
- The serratus anterior (green, long thoracic nerve)

Clinical tip: Anteversion is still possible in paralysis of the serratus anterior, but it is accompanied by marked elevation of the scapula from the thoracic wall (winged scapula).

Retroversion (extension; **B**) is brought about by
- The teres major (red, thoracodorsal nerve)
- The latissimus dorsi (blue, thoracodorsal nerve)
- The long head of the triceps brachii (yellow, radial nerve)
- The deltoid (orange, axillary nerve)

There is always some associated movement at the acromioclavicular joint.

Lateral (external) rotation (**C**) is produced by
- The infraspinatus (red, suprascapular nerve),
  the teres minor (blue, axillary nerve)
- The spinal part of the deltoid (yellow, axillary nerve)

The strongest lateral rotator, the infraspinatus, performs much more work than all the others combined. With lateral rotation, the scapula and clavicle are simultaneously pulled backward by the trapezius and rhomboid muscles. Thus, this action also involves movements at the sternoclavicular and acromioclavicular joints.

Clinical tip: During sudden lateral rotation, the antagonistic pulling force of the most powerful medial rotator, the subscapularis, may result in avulsion of the lesser tubercle.

Medial (internal) rotation (**D**) is carried out by
- The subscapularis (red, subscapular nerve)
- The pectoralis major (blue, pectoral nerves)
- The long head of the biceps (yellow, musculocutaneous nerve)
- The clavicular part of the deltoid (orange, pectoral branches)
- The teres major (green, thoracodorsal nerve)
- The latissimus dorsi (brown, thoracodorsal nerve)

By far the strongest action is produced by the subscapularis and the weakest by the latissimus dorsi. When the elbow is extended, the short head of the biceps (not illustrated) also contributes slightly.

The cited movements, however, do not occur exclusively at the shoulder joint. In the living person, an associated movement of the shoulder girdle always takes place, as well as that of the trunk with certain movements.

The color of the arrows shows the order of importance of the muscles in the individual movements:

red
blue
yellow
orange
green
brown

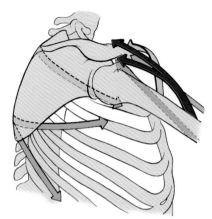

A Anteversion

A–D
Function of the shoulder
girdle muscles
(continued)

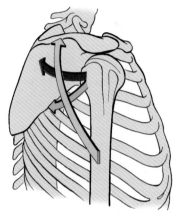

C Lateral rotation

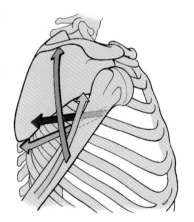

B Retroversion

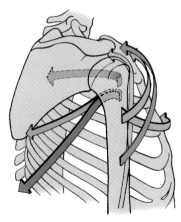

D Medial rotation

Fascias and Spaces in the Shoulder Girdle Region

Fascias (A, B)

Each shoulder girdle muscle is surrounded by its own fascia to permit free movement of the muscles against each other. Particularly strong fascias are the **deltoid fascia** (**1**), the **pectoral fascia** (**2**), and the **clavipectoral fascia** (**3**).

The **deltoid fascia** covers the deltoid muscle and sends numerous septa deeply between the individual muscle bundles. Anteriorly it is attached to the pectoral fascia and posteriorly, where it is especially strong, it merges into the fascia which covers the infraspinatus muscle. Distally it continues as the *brachial fascia* (p. 180). Additionally it is fixed to the spine of the scapula, the acromion and the clavicle.

The **pectoral fascia** covers the superficial surface of the pectoralis major muscle and extends from there over the *deltoideopectoral sulcus* (**4**) to the deltoid muscle. It is attached to the **axillary fascia** (**5**), which is partly loose and partly dense.

The **clavipectoral fascia** surrounds the subclavius, the pectoralis minor, and partly extends over the coracobrachialis. It separates the pectoralis major from the pectoralis minor. At the lateral border of the latter it radiates into the axillary fascia.

A special feature of the remaining fascias is that in the region of the infraspinatus and teres minor they may become aponeurotic and muscle fibers may actually arise from them.

The **axillary fascia** forms the continuation of the pectoral fascia as far as the fascia covering the latissimus dorsi. It does not consist of regularly arranged, dense connective tissue, but instead there are zones of loose tissue which may easily be removed. After removal of the loose part of the axillary fascia, an oval zone may be seen, the proximal fascial border of which is called the axillary arch of *Langer*.

Special Spaces in the Shoulder Girdle Region (Axillary Spaces and Axilla)

Axillary spaces (see p. 374). There is a **medial** and a **lateral axillary space**. These spaces are called the *triangular* and *quadrangular* spaces, respectively, because of their shapes. The medial or triangular is bounded by the teres minor, the teres major and the long head of the triceps brachii, the lateral or quadrangular space by the long head of the triceps brachii, the teres minor, the teres major, and the humerus.

Axilla. The axilla is *pyramidal* in shape. Anteriorly it is limited by the *anterior axillary fold* (**6**), the muscular basis of which is the pectoralis major, and also deep in the anterior wall are the pectoralis minor and the clavipectoral fascia. The posterior wall of the axilla consists of the *posterior axillary fold* (**7**), which is basically formed by the latissimus dorsi. Moreover, the subscapularis, with the scapula and teres major also participate in the formation of the dorsal wall. The medial wall is formed by the thorax and the serratus anterior covered by a fascia. The lateral wall consists of the upper part of the arm. (The contents of the axilla are described on p. 372.)

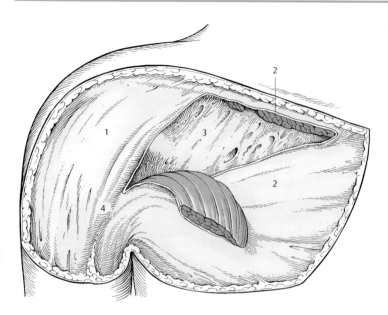

A Fascias in region of the clavipectoral triangle

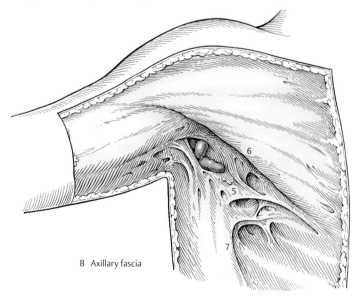

B Axillary fascia

Upper Limb

Arm Muscles

According to their position the muscles of the upper limb may be divided into arm and forearm muscles. In the arm, the ventral group is divided from the dorsal group by the intermuscular septa.

Ventral Muscle Group (A–C)

The **brachialis** (**1**) *arises from the distal half of the anterior surface of the humerus* (**2**) *and the intermuscular septa. It is inserted into the ulnar tuberosity* (**3**) *and the joint capsule* (as the articular muscle). It is a single joint muscle and is the most important flexor of the elbow joint independent of pronation or supination of the forearm. Its full power is exerted in lifting a heavy load. In such a movement there is also slight retroversion at the shoulder joint.

Nerve supply: musculocutaneous nerve (C5 –C6). A small, lateral part of the muscle is supplied by the radial nerve (C5 –C6).

▰▰ **Variant:** Insertion into the oblique cord or into the radius.

The **biceps brachii** (**4**) arises with its **long head** (**5**) from the *supraglenoid tubercle* (**6**) and with its **short head** (**7**) from the *coracoid process* (**8**). Both heads usually join, at the level of insertion of the deltoid, into the biceps muscle, which again terminates with two tendons. The stronger tendon is *inserted into the radial tuberosity* (**9**), with a bicipitoradial bursa enclosed. The other flattened tendon, the *bicipital aponeurosis* (**10**), whose fibers form the continuation of part of the short head, *radiates into the antebrachial fascia on the ulnar side*. The long head traverses the shoulder joint and, covered by a synovial sheath, it extends along the intertubercular groove (**11**) of the humerus. In its action it uses the head of the humerus as a fulcrum.

The biceps brachii acts on two joints. With its long head it abducts the arm and rotates it medially. The short head is an adductor.

Both heads are active in anteversion of the shoulder joint. The biceps brachii is also a flexor and strong supinator of the elbow joint. Its supinator action is increased during flexion of the elbow joint. It should be pointed out that, on the whole, the supinators are more strongly developed than the pronators. Therefore, the most essential rotary movements of the forearm are supinator movements (e.g., turning a screw). Its aponeurosis spans the fascia of the forearm.

Nerve supply: musculocutaneous nerve (C5–C6).

▰▰ **Variant:** In 10% of cases a third head may arise from the humerus to join to the belly of the biceps.

> **Clinical tip:** The tendon of the long head of the biceps is especially susceptible to muscle or tendon tears. When this tendon is ruptured, the head of the humerus stands high.

12 Long head of the triceps brachii
13 Lateral head of the triceps brachii
14 Medial head of the triceps brachii
15 Lateral intermuscular septum
16 Medial intermuscular septum
17 Latissimus dorsi
18 Subscapularis
19 Pectoralis minor
20 Coracobrachialis

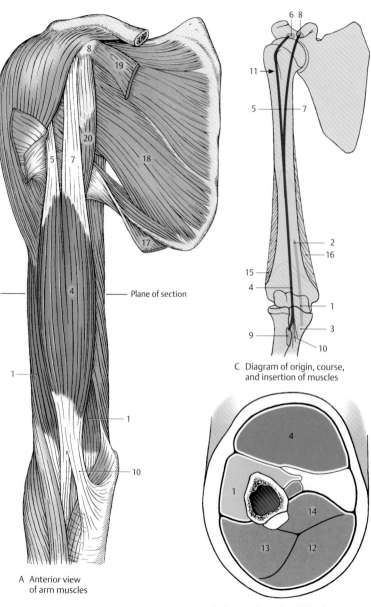

C Diagram of origin, course, and insertion of muscles

A Anterior view of arm muscles

B Section through middle of arm

Arm Muscles, continued

Dorsal Muscle Group (A–C)

The **triceps brachii** (**1**) has three heads, **long** (**2**), **medial** (**3**) and **lateral** (**4**).

The **long head** (**2**) *arises from the infraglenoid tubercle of the scapula* (**5**) and extends distally in front of the teres minor (**6**) and behind the teres major (**7**). The **medial head** (**3**) *arises distally from the groove for the radial nerve* (**8**), *from the dorsal surface of the humerus* (**9**), from the *medial intermuscular septum* (**10**), and, in its distal part, also from the *lateral intermuscular septum* (**11**). The medial head is largely covered by the long and lateral heads. It is only visible distally as it lies flattened against the humerus. The **lateral head** (**4**) *arises from the dorsal surface of the humerus lateral and proximal to the groove for the radial nerve* (**12**). *Proximally it originates just beneath the greater tubercle* (**13**) *and ends distally in the region of the lateral intermuscular septum* (**11**).

The three heads fuse in a flat common-end tendon, which is *inserted on the olecranon of the ulna* (**14**) *and the posterior wall of the capsule*. The long head of the triceps brachii acts on two joints, while with the other heads it acts only on one joint. It is **the** extensor of the elbow joint. At the shoulder the long head is involved in retroversion and adduction of the arm.

Part of the tendon of the triceps brachii radiates into the forearm fascia and may almost completely cover the anconeus. In the region of its attachment to the olecranon there are often bursae; the subcutaneous olecranon bursa and subtendinous bursa of the triceps brachii. Sometimes an intratendinous olecranon bursa can be seen.

Nerve supply: radial nerve (C6 –C8).

Variants: A tendinous arch is very frequently found between the origin of the long head and the tendon of insertion of the latissimus dorsi. Very rarely the long head can arise additionally from the lateral margin of the scapula and from the articular capsule of the shoulder joint.

The **anconeus** (**15**) *arises from the dorsal surface of the lateral epicondyle* (**16**) *and the radial collateral ligament and is inserted into the proximal one fourth of the dorsal side of the ulna* (**17**), close to the medial head of the triceps brachii. Its function is to assist the triceps brachii in producing the movement of extension, and it also tenses the capsule of the elbow joint.

Nerve supply: radial nerve (C7–C8).

18 Trapezius
19 Deltoid
20 Infraspinatus
21 Biceps brachii
22 Brachialis
23 Coracobrachialis
24 Humerus

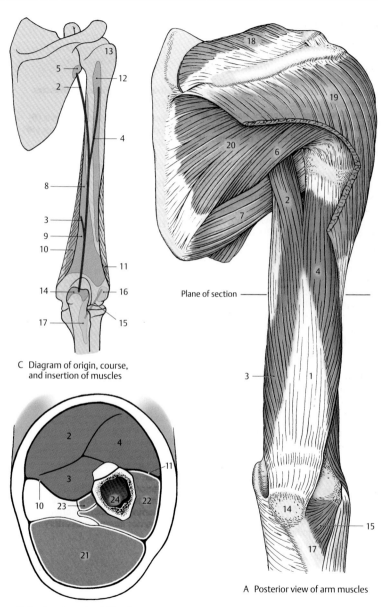

C Diagram of origin, course, and insertion of muscles

B Section through middle of arm

A Posterior view of arm muscles

Muscles of the Forearm

Classification of the Muscles (A–D)

The forearm muscles are divided into three groups according to their relationship to the various joints, their attachments and their mode of action.

- **The first group** comprises muscles attached to the radius, which are only involved in movements of the bones of the forearm.
- **The second group** of forearm muscles extends to the metacarpus and produces movement at the wrist.
- **The third group** comprises those muscles that extend to the phalanges and are responsible for finger movements.

Another system of classification is based on the position of the muscles in relation to each other. The ulna and radius with the interosseous membrane separate a ventral muscle group, the flexors, from a dorsal group of extensors. Connective tissue septa between the ventral and dorsal muscles separate a radial group. The flexors and extensors can be divided into superficial and deep muscles.

Finally, the muscles of the forearm may also be divided into two groups according to their innervation—from either the ventral or dorsal portions of the plexus.

From the practical point of view, the muscles will be classified according to their positions relative to one another. This also provides the most comprehensive functional subdivision.

Ventral Group of Forearm Muscles

Superficial Layer (see p. 160)

- Pronator teres (**1**)
- Flexor digitorum superficialis (**2**)
- Flexor carpi radialis (**3**)
- Palmaris longus (**4**)
- Flexor carpi ulnaris (**5**)

Deep Layer (see p. 162)

- Pronator quadratus (**6**)
- Flexor digitorum profundus (**7**)
- Flexor pollicis longus (**8**)

Radial Group of Forearm Muscles (see p. 164)

- Extensor carpi radialis brevis (**9**)
- Extensor carpi radialis longus (**10**)
- Brachioradialis (**11**)

Dorsal Group of Forearm Muscles

Superficial Layer (see p. 166)

- Extensor digitorum (**12**)
- Extensor digiti minimi (**13**)
- Extensor carpi ulnaris (**14**).

Deep Layer (see p. 168)

- Supinator (**15**)
- Abductor pollicis longus (**16**)
- Extensor pollicis brevis (**17**)
- Extensor pollicis longus (**18**)
- Extensor indicis (**19**)

20 Median nerve
21 Ulnar nerve
22 Superficial branch of radial nerve
23 Deep branch of radial nerve
24 Muscular branch of median nerve
25 Brachialis artery
26 Radial artery
27 Ulnar artery
28 Basilic vein
29 Cephalic vein
30 Radius
31 Ulna
32 Interosseous membrane
33 Common interosseous artery and vein
34 Anterior interosseous artery
35 Posterior interosseous artery

Upper Limb

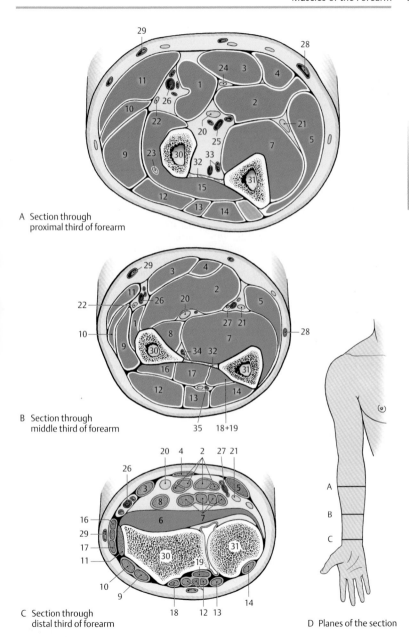

A Section through
proximal third of forearm

B Section through
middle third of forearm

C Section through
distal third of forearm

D Planes of the section

Ventral Forearm Muscles

Superficial Layer (A–D)

The **pronator teres** (**1**) *originates with its* **humeral head** *from the medial epicondyle of the humerus* (**2**) *and from the medial intermuscular septum* and with its **ulnar head** *from the coronoid process of the ulna* (**3**). It inserts at the pronator tuberosity (**4**) of the radius. Together with the pronator quadratus, it pronates the forearm and contributes to flexion at the elbow joint.
Nerve supply: median nerve (C6–C7).

▓▓ **Variants:** The ulnar head may be absent. If a supracondylar process is present (see p. 114), the humeral head will also arise from it.

The **flexor digitorum superficialis** (**5**) *arises by its* **humeral head** *from the medial epicondyle of the humerus* (**6**), by its **ulnar head** *from the coronoid process of the ulna* (**7**), and by its **radial** *head from the radius* (**8**). Between the heads stretches a tendinous arch which is crossed below by the median nerve and the ulnar artery and vein. Its tendons run in a common sheath (see p. 182) through the carpal tunnel. The muscle ends in four tendons, each inserted onto the lateral *bony crests* (**9**) *in the center of the middle phalanges of the second—fifth fingers*. At this point the tendons divide into two slips (**10**, **perforated muscle**). The tendons of the *flexor digitorum profundus* (**11**) glide between and through them. It is a very weak flexor of the elbow, but a strong flexor of the wrist and the finger joints. Its action on the digits is impaired when the wrist is maximally flexed.
Nerve supply: median nerve (C7–T1).

The **flexor carpi radialis** (**12**) *arises from the medial epicondyle of the humerus* (**6**) *and from the superficial fascia of the forearm. It inserts into the palmar surface of the base of the second metacarpal* (**13**) and also in some cases on the third metacarpal. It runs in the carpal tunnel in a groove in the trapezium, which is closed to form an osteofibrous canal. It is a weak flexor and pronator of the elbow joint and partici-

pates in palmar flexion of the wrist, and, together with the extensor carpi radialis longus (see p. 164), it produces radial abduction.
Nerve supply: median nerve (C6–C7).

The **palmaris longus** (**14**) *arises from the medial epicondyle of the humerus and radiates into the palmar surface of the hand* with the **palmar aponeurosis** (15; see also p. 178). It flexes the hand toward the palm and tenses the palmar aponeurosis.
Nerve supply: median nerve (C7–T1).

▓▓ **Variant:** It may be absent, but even then the palmar aponeurosis is always present.

The **flexor carpi ulnaris** (**16**) *lies on the medial side. Its* **humeral head** *arises from the medial epicondyle of the humerus* (**6**) and its **ulnar head** *from the olecranon and the upper two-thirds of the posterior margin of the ulna* (**17**). *It is inserted onto the pisiform bone* (**18**) and extends by the *pisohamate ligament* as far as the *hamate* (**19**) and by the *pisometacarpal ligament* to the *fifth metacarpal* (**20**). Proximal to its attachment to the pisiform bone, the muscle usually gives off descending tendon fibers which pass obliquely distally and radiate into the antebrachial fascia. It runs outside the carpal tunnel. It participates in palmar flexion, where it is more effective than the flexor carpi radialis and also helps in ulnar adduction of the hand.
Nerve supply: ulnar nerve (C7–C8).

21 Brachioradialis
22 Flexor pollicis longus
23 Pronator quadratus
24 Biceps brachii
25 Flexor retinaculum
26 Lumbricales
27 Abductor pollices brevis
28 Flexor pollices brevis
29 Palmaris brevis
30 Ulna
31 Radius
32 Vinculum longum
33 Vinculum breve

Upper Limb

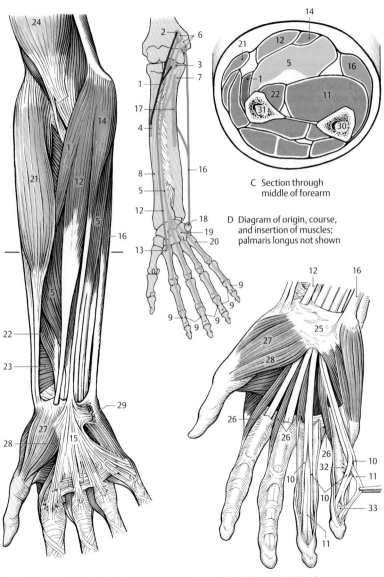

C Section through middle of forearm

D Diagram of origin, course, and insertion of muscles; palmaris longus not shown

A Superficial flexors of ventral group of forearm muscles (plane of section indicated)

B Superficial flexors in the hand, palmar aponeurosis removed

Ventral Forearm Muscles, continued

Deep Layer (A–C)

The **pronator quadratus** (**1**) *arises from the distal quarter of the palmar surface of the ulna* (**2**) and is *inserted on the distal quarter of the palmar surface of the radius* (**3**). It pronates the forearm assisted by the pronator teres.

Nerve supply: anterior interosseous branch of the median nerve (C8–T1).

■■■ **Variants:** The muscle can reach further proximally. It can also reach different carpal bones and rarely the muscles of the thenar eminence. The muscle is sometimes absent.

The **flexor digitorum profundus** (**4**) *arises from the proximal two thirds of the palmar surface of the ulna* (**5**) *and the interosseous membrane*. In its course through the carpal tunnel, its tendons and those of the superficial flexors of the fingers (see p. 160) are surrounded by a common tendon sheath (see p. 182). *It is attached by four tendons to the base of the terminal phalanges of the second to fifth fingers* (**6**). Because of its relationship to the flexor digitorum superficialis whose terminal tendon it pierces, it is also called the **perforating muscle**. In addition, the *lumbrical muscles* (**7**) arise from the radial side of its tendons. It is a flexor of the wrist, midcarpal, metacarpophalangeal and phalangeal joints.

Nerve supply: anterior interosseous branch of the median nerve and the ulnar nerve (C7–T1).

■■■ **Variant:** The tendon which reaches the index finger often has a belly of its own (see Fig. A).

The **flexor pollicis longus** (**8**) *arises from the anterior surface of the radius, distal to the radial tuberosity, and from the interosseous membrane* (**9**). Surrounded by its own tendon sheath (see p. 182), it extends through the carpaltunnel, then lies between the heads of the flexor pollicis brevis and *continues onto the base of the terminal phalanx of the thumb* (**10**). It is a flexor of

the terminal phalanx of the thumb and it is also able to abduct it a little in the radial direction.

Nerve supply: anterior interosseous branch of the median nerve (C7–C8).

■■■ **Variant:** In 40% of cases there is also a humeral head arising from the medial epicondyle of the humerus. In these cases there is a tendinous connection with the humeral head of the flexor digitorum superficialis muscle.

11 Brachioradialis
12 Flexor retinaculum
13 Abductor pollicis brevis
14 Flexor pollicis brevis
15 Flexor carpi radialis
16 Palmaris longus
17 Flexor digitorum superficialis
18 Flexor carpi ulnaris
19 Pronator teres
20 Radius
21 Ulna

Upper Limb

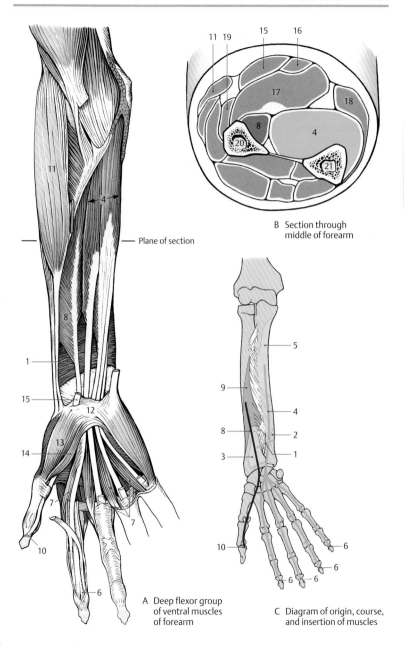

B Section through middle of forearm

— Plane of section

A Deep flexor group of ventral muscles of forearm

C Diagram of origin, course, and insertion of muscles

Upper Limb

Radial Forearm Muscles (A–D)

The radial group includes three muscles which act as flexors at the elbow joint.

The **extensor carpi radialis brevis** (**1**) *arises from the common head of the lateral epicondyle of the humerus* (**2**), *from the radial collateral ligament and from the anular radial ligament, and is inserted on the base of the third metacarpal* (**3**). It runs through the second tendon compartment (p. 182) on the dorsum of the wrist. The extensor carpi radialis brevis is a weak flexor of the elbow joint. It brings the arm to the midposition from ulnar abduction and flexes dorsally.
Nerve supply: deep branch of the radial nerve (C7).

The **extensor carpi radialis longus muscle** (**4**) *arises from the lateral supracondylar crest of the humerus* (**5**) and the *lateral intermuscular septum* as far as the lateral epicondyle and runs with the extensor carpi radialis brevis through the second tendon compartment. *It is inserted on the base of the second metacarpal* (**6**). It is a weak flexor at the elbow joint, a weak pronator in the flexed arm and a supinator in the outstretched arm. At the carpal joints it acts with the extensor carpi ulnaris in dorsiflexion and with the flexor carpi radialis in radial abduction.
Nerve supply: deep branch of the radial nerve (C6–C7).

The two muscles just described are called **"fist clenchers"**, as during clenching the hand must be slightly flexed dorsally to permit maximal action by the flexors.

Clinical tip: Pain may occur in the lateral epicondyle of the humerus when the fist is clenched. This is called **epicondylitis of the humerus** and is thought to result from periosteal irritation in the region of origin of the two radial extensors due to overuse (tennis elbow).

The **brachioradialis** (**7**) *arises from the lateral supracondylar crest of the humerus* (**8**) *and the lateral intermuscular septum. It is inserted into the radial surface of the styloid process of the radius* (**9**). Unlike the muscles of the forearm described above, this muscle acts only on a single joint. It brings the forearm into the midposition between pronation and supination. In this position it acts as a flexor. It has a minimal flexor action in slow movements and in the supinated forearm.
Nerve supply: radial nerve (C5–C6).

Clinical tip: Immediately proximal to its insertion, between its tendon and the tendon of the flexor carpi radialis (p. 160), is the place where the pulse of the radial artery mey be felt (see also p. 386).

10 Extensor digitorum
11 Extensor digiti minimi
12 Extensor carpi ulnaris
13 Extensor pollicis longus
14 Extensor pollicis brevis
15 Abductor pollicis longus
16 Ulna
17 Radius

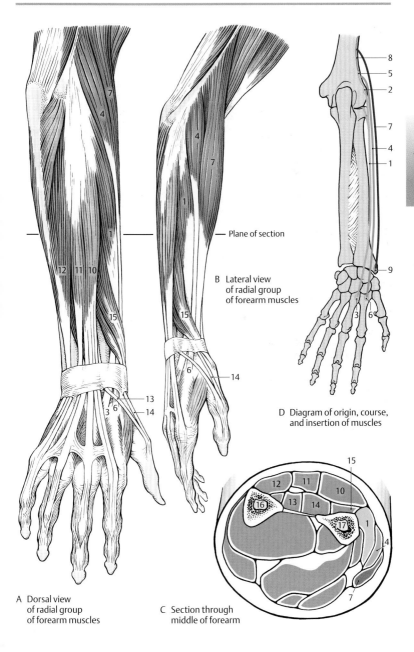

— Plane of section

B Lateral view
of radial group
of forearm muscles

D Diagram of origin, course,
and insertion of muscles

A Dorsal view
of radial group
of forearm muscles

C Section through
middle of forearm

Dorsal Forearm Muscles

Superficial (Ulnar) Layer (A–C)

The **extensor digitorum** (**1**) *has a flattened origin from the lateral epicondyle of the humerus* (**2**), *the radial collateral ligament, the anular radial ligament and the antebrachial fascia.* It runs through the fourth compartment of tendons (p. 182). *With its tendons it forms the dorsal aponeurosis* (**3**) *of the second to fifth fingers.* In addition, slips of the tendons run to the bases of the proximal phalanges (**4**) and to the capsules of the metacarpophalangeal joints.

Between the individual tendons **intertendinous connections** (**5**) are always present, starting from the fourth to the third and fifth fingers. The extensor digitorum extends and spreads the fingers. It is the strongest dorsiflexor of the wrist and the midcarpal joints and it acts, too, as an ulnar abductor.

Nerve supply: deep branch of the radial nerve (C6–C8).

▓▓ **Variants:** The muscle belly for the tendon of the second finger can be independent. The tendon to the fifth finger can be absent. In contrast, the tendons to the individual fingers also can be doubled.

The **extensor digiti minimi** (**6**) *arises together with the extensor digitorum in a common head* (**2**) and extends through the fifth tendon compartment of the dorsum of the wrist, usually as two tendons, *to the dorsal aponeurosis of the fifth finger.* Sometimes it is absent and then the extensor digitorum takes over its function with an additional tendon. It extends the fifth digit and helps in dorsiflexion and ulnar abduction of the hand.

Nerve supply: deep branch of the radial nerve (C6–C8).

The **extensor carpi ulnaris** (**7**) *arises from the common head* (**2**), together with the extensor digitorum, *and from the ulna* (**8**) and runs on the mediodorsal side of the ulna

through the sixth tendon compartment *to the base of the fifth metacarpal* (**9**).

It is really misnamed because it acts as a strong ulnar abductor, an action that is most easily understood from the course of its tendon in relation to its axis of movement (p. 134); the tendon runs dorsally to the radiocarpal joint and palmarly to the midcarpal joint. This leads to dorsiflexion of the radiocarpal joint and palmar flexion in the midcarpal joint, i.e., the two functions balance one another. Hence the principal action of the muscle is as an abductor. Its antagonist is the abductor pollicis longus.

Nerve supply: deep branch of the radial nerve (C7–C8).

▓▓ **Variant:** An additional tendon which extends to the proximal phalanx is frequently found on the radial side.

10 Extensor carpi radialis longus
11 Extensor carpi radialis brevis
12 Abductor pollicis longus
13 Extensor pollicis brevis
14 Extensor pollicis longus
15 Extensor indicis
16 Radius
17 Ulna
18 Anconeus

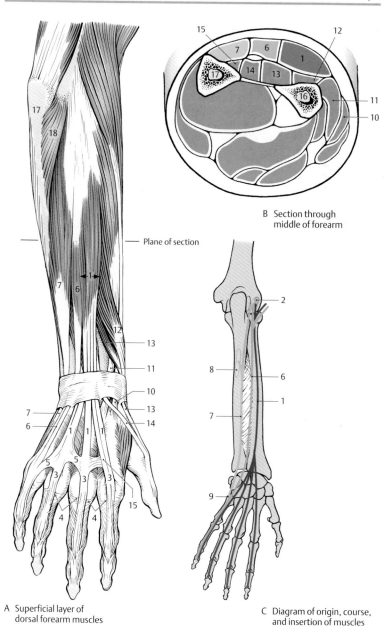

B Section through middle of forearm

Plane of section

A Superficial layer of dorsal forearm muscles

C Diagram of origin, course, and insertion of muscles

Upper Limb

Dorsal Forearm Muscles, continued

Deep Layer (A–C)

The surfaces from which the **supinator** (**3**) *originates include the supinator crest of the ulna* (**1**)*, the lateral epicondyle of the humerus* (**2**)*, the radial collateral ligament, and the anular radial ligament.* Those fibers originating from the most posterior portion of the radial collateral ligament run superficially and form a distally convex tendinous arch. *The muscle inserts on the radius* (**4**) between the radial tuberosity and the attachment of the pronator teres. It encircles the radius and supinates the forearm, in contrast to the biceps brachii, in every position of flexion and extension.
Nerve supply: deep branch of the radial nerve (C5–C6).

The **abductor pollicis longus** (**5**) *arises from the dorsal surface of the ulna* (**6**) distal to the supinator crest of the ulna, *from the interosseous membrane* (**7**)*, and from the dorsal surface of the radius* (**8**). It runs through the first tendon compartment (see p. 182) and is *inserted on the base of the first metacarpal* (**9**). Part of the tendon reaches the trapezium and another part often fuses with the tendon of the extensor pollicis brevis and abductor pollicis brevis.

Due to its position it flexes the hand toward the palm and abducts it radially. The main function of this muscle is abduction of the thumb.
Nerve supply: deep branch of the radial nerve (C7–C8).

The **extensor pollicis brevis** (**10**) *arises from the ulna* (**11**) distal to the abductor pollicis longus, *from the interosseous membrane* (**12**)*, and from the dorsal surface of the radius* (**13**)*, and extends to the base of the proximal phalanx of the thumb* (**14**). It extends and abducts the thumb because of its close relationship to the abductor pollicis longus, with which it runs in the first tendon compartment.

Nerve supply: deep branch of the radial nerve (C7–T1).

■ **Variant:** Its terminal tendon is frequently doubled. In rare cases it can be absent.

The **extensor pollicis longus** (**15**) *arises from the dorsal surface of the ulna* (**16**) *and the interosseous membrane* (**17**). It runs on the dorsal side of the wrist through the third tendon compartment. *It is inserted on the base of the distal phalanx* (**18**) *of the thumb.* It uses the dorsal tubercle on the radius, which is situated lateral to the third tendon compartment, as a fulcrum and extends the thumb. At the wrist it dorsiflexes and abducts the hand radially.
Nerve supply: deep branch of the radial nerve (C7–C8).

The distal third of the *dorsal surface of the ulna* (**19**) *and the interosseous membrane* (**20**) *are the sites of origin* of the **extensor indicis** (**21**). It runs with the extensor digitorum muscle, through the fourth tendon compartment and *projects its tendon into the dorsal aponeurosis of the index finger.* It extends the index finger and participates in dorsiflexion at the wrist and midcarpal joints.
Nerve supply: deep branch of the radial nerve (C6–C8).

■ **Variant:** Two or three tendons are frequent observed. The muscle is sometimes absent.

22 Extensor digitorum
23 Extensor digiti minimi
24 Extensor carpi ulnaris
25 Ulna
26 Radius

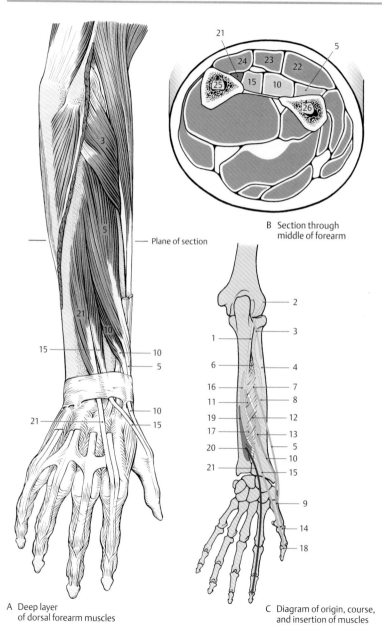

B Section through
middle of forearm

— Plane of section

A Deep layer
of dorsal forearm muscles

C Diagram of origin, course,
and insertion of muscles

Function of Muscles of the Elbow Joint and Forearm (A–D)

The movements at the elbow joint are **flexion** and **extension. The axis of movement runs through the epicondyles of the humerus.** All muscles which pass in front of the axis act as flexors and all those which pass behind it act as extensors at the elbow joint. Since many of the muscles act on several joints, their names are not always appropriate for their function in relation to the elbow joint. In addition, their action at the elbow joint is dependent on the attitude of the neighboring joints.

The **flexors (A)** include
- Biceps brachii (red, musculocutaneous nerve)
- Brachialis (blue, musculocutaneous nerve)
- Brachioradialis (yellow, radial nerve)
- Extensor carpi radialis longus (orange, radial nerve)
- Pronator teres (green, median nerve)

Less important are (not shown): the flexor carpi radialis, extensor carpi radialis brevis and palmaris longus. Flexion in the position of pronation, performed by contraction of almost all the flexors, is strongest. The exceptions are the brachialis muscle which is equally strong in all positions and the biceps brachii muscle whose flexor power is reduced in pronation.

The only important **extensor (B)** is the triceps brachii (red, radial nerve). The most effective parts of it are the medial and lateral heads, while the long head of the triceps is only of secondary importance. The anconeus may be disregarded as an extensor.

The movements of the forearm are **reversing movements** at the proximal and distal radio-ulnar joints, with associated movements at the humeroradial joint.

These reversing movements are **pronation** and **supination** (see p. 122) and **they occur around an axis which runs from the fovea on the head of the radius to the styloid process of the ulna.**
Pronation and supination are executed with almost equal force but with greater strength if the elbow joint is flexed. The preponderance of pronation is a false impression due to a medial rotation in the shoulder joint (*Lanz* and *Wachsmuth*).

The muscles which act as **supinators (C)** are
- Supinator (red, radial nerve)
- Biceps brachii (blue, musculocutaneous nerve)
- Abductor pollicis longus (yellow, radial nerve)
- Extensor pollicis longus (orange, radial nerve)
- Brachioradialis (not shown)

In the outstretched arm, the extensor carpi radialis longus also works as a supinator.

Pronation (D) is produced by
- Pronator quadratus (red, median nerve)
- Pronator teres (blue, median nerve)
- Flexor carpi radialis (yellow, median nerve)
- Extensor carpi radialis longus (orange, radial nerve) in the flexed arm
- Brachioradialis (not shown)
- Palmaris longus (not shown)

The color of the arrows shows the order of importance of the muscles in each movement:

red
blue
yellow
orange
green

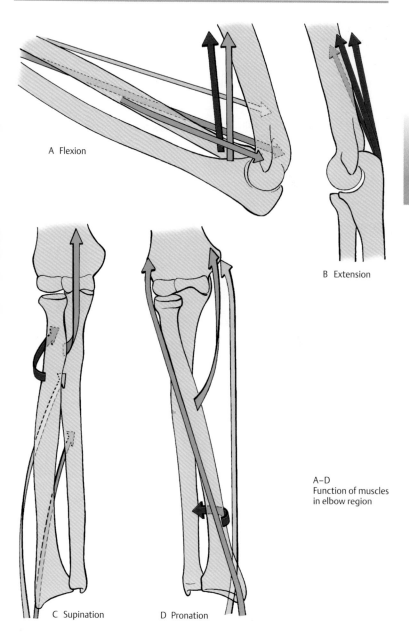

A Flexion

B Extension

C Supination

D Pronation

A–D
Function of muscles
in elbow region

Function of Muscles of the Wrist and the Midcarpal Joint (A–D)

We distinguish **dorsiflexion** (**A**), lifting of the back of the hand, and **palmar flexion** (**B**), lowering of the back of the hand.

These movements take place at the radiocarpal and midcarpal joints **through an imaginary transverse axis which runs through the capitate bone.** We also distinguish **radial abduction** (**C**) and **ulnar abduction** (**D**) about a dorsopalmar axis through the capitate bone.

It should be noted here that, in the resting position of the hand, the long axis through the 3rd metacarpal bone, the axis through the capitate, and the main axis of the forearm run parallel to one another. The main axis of the forearm runs from the middle of the radial head to the styloid process of the ulna. This axis corresponds to the axis of movements during pronation and supination.

Palmar flexion is the most powerful of the movements described above. The flexors are considerably stronger than the extensors and among them, the flexors of the fingers are the most powerful.

> **Clinical tip:** The predominance of the flexors causes the hand to assume a position of palmar flexion after a longer period of rest (healing of a fracture). Thus, the hand should be set in slight dorsiflexion.

The muscles which take part in **dorsiflexion** are
- Extensor digitorum (red, radial nerve)
- Extensor carpi radialis longus (blue, radial nerve)
- Extensor carpi radialis brevis (yellow, radial nerve)
- Extensor indicis (orange, radial nerve)
- Extensor pollicis longus (green, radial nerve)
- Extensor digiti minimi (not shown)

Palmar flexion can be produced by
- Flexor digitorum superficialis (red, median nerve)
- Flexor digitorum profundus (blue, median nerve and ulnar nerve)
- Flexor carpi ulnaris (yellow, ulnar nerve)
- Flexor pollicis longus (orange, median nerve)
- Flexor carpi radialis (green, median nerve)
- Abductor pollicis longus (brown, radial nerve)

Both flexors of the fingers are the strongest flexors at the wrist joint.

Radial abduction is produced by
- Extensor carpi radialis longus (red, radial nerve)
- Abductor pollicis longus (blue, radial nerve)
- Extensor pollicis longus (yellow, radial nerve)
- Flexor carpi radialis (orange, median nerve)
- Flexor pollicis longus (green, median nerve)

Ulnar abduction is produced by
- Extensor carpi ulnaris (red, radial nerve)
- Flexor carpi ulnaris (blue, ulnar nerve)
- Extensor digitorum (yellow, radial nerve)
- Extensor digiti minimi (not shown)

The color of the arrows shows the order of importance of the muscles in each movement:

red
blue
yellow
orange
green
brown

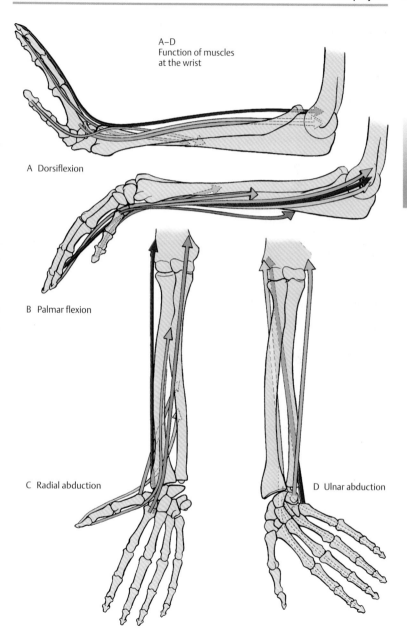

A–D
Function of muscles
at the wrist

A Dorsiflexion

B Palmar flexion

C Radial abduction

D Ulnar abduction

Intrinsic Muscles of the Hand

The intrinsic muscles of the hand may be divided into three palmar groups. We distinguish
- The **central muscles** of the **hand**
- The **thenar muscles** of the thumb
- The **hypothenar muscles** of the little finger

The extensor aponeurosis lies on the dorsum of the digits.

Central muscles of the hand (A–D)

The seven short, pennate **interossei** may be divided into **three palmar single-headed** and **four dorsal double-headed muscles**.

The **palmar interossei** (**1**) *arise from the second, fourth, and fifth metacarpal bones* (**2**). *They insert by short tendons on the corresponding proximal phalanges* (**3**) *and they also radiate into the corresponding tendons of the dorsal aponeurosis* (**4**).

Their tendons run dorsal to the *deep transverse metacarpal ligaments* (**5**) and palmar to the axis of the metacarpophalangeal joints. Thus, they flex at the metacarpophalangeal joints, and by their radiations into the dorsal aponeurosis they are able to extend at the interphalangeal joints. Through their relationship to the metacarpal and phalangeal bones, they also adduct in relation to an axis which passes longitudinally through the middle finger; they move the second, fourth, and fifth fingers toward the middle finger.

The **dorsal interossei** (**6**) *arise by two heads from the adjacent sides of the five metacarpal bones* (**2**, **7**). Like the palmar interosseous muscles, *they extend to the proximal phalanges and radiate into the dorsal aponeurosis* (**4**). The first dorsal interosseous extends to the proximal phalanx of the second finger on the radial side, the second and third interosseous muscles reach the proximal phalanx of the middle finger on both the radial and ulnar

sides, and the fourth dorsal interosseous muscle extends to the proximal phalanx of the fourth finger on the ulnar side.

Like the palmar interosseous muscles, they flex at the metacarpophalangeal joints and extend at the interphalangeal joints. They function as abductors in relation to the axis of the middle finger (stretching of the finger).

Nerve supply: deep branch of the ulnar nerve (C8–T1).

The four **lumbricales** (**8**) *arise from the radial sides of the tendons of the flexor digitorum profundus* (**9**). As these tendons are mobile, the sites of origin of the lumbricales are not fixed. Covered by the palmar aponeurosis and palmar to the deep transverse metacarpal ligaments (**5**), *they run to the extensor aponeurosis* (**4**) *and to the joint capsules of the metacarpophalangeal joints.* They flex at the metacarpophalangeal joints and extend at the interphalangeal joints.

Nerve supply: the two radial lumbricales are supplied by the median nerve and the two ulnar ones by the deep branch of the ulnar nerve (C8–T1).

10 Flexor retinaculum
11 Abductor pollicis brevis
12 Flexor pollicis brevis
13 Transverse head of the abductor pollicis
14 Abductor digiti minimi
15 Flexor carpi ulnaris
16 Flexor carpi radialis

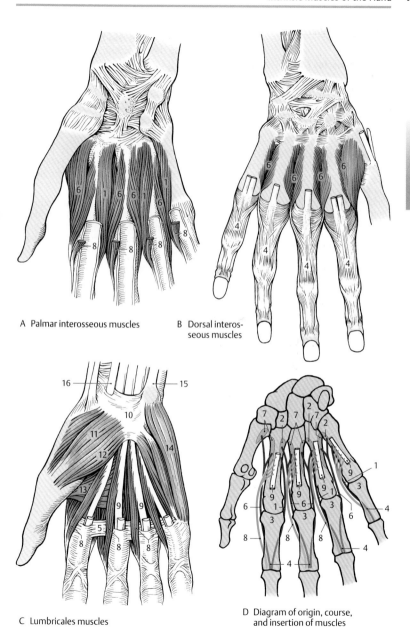

A Palmar interosseous muscles

B Dorsal interosseous muscles

C Lumbricales muscles

D Diagram of origin, course, and insertion of muscles

Intrinsic Muscles of the Hand, continued

Thenar Muscles (A–D)

These include
- Abductor pollicis brevis
- Flexor pollicis brevis
- Adductor pollicis
- Opponens pollicis

The **abductor pollicis brevis** (**1**) *arises from the scaphoid tubercle* (**2**) *and the flexor retinaculum* (**3**). *It is inserted into the radial sesamoid bone* (**4**) *and to the proximal phalanx* (**5**) *of the thumb*. It abducts the thumb.
Nerve supply: median nerve (C8–T1).

The **flexor pollicis brevis** has a **superficial head** (**6**) and a **deep head** (**7**). *The former arises from the flexor retinaculum* (**3**) *and the latter from the trapezium* (**8**), *trapezoid* (**9**), *and capitate* (**10**). It is *inserted into the radial sesamoid bone* (**4**) *of the metacarpophalangeal joint of the thumb*. It flexes, adducts and abducts the thumb and is able to bring the thumb into opposition.
Nerve supply: the superficial head is supplied by the median nerve and the deep head by the ulnar nerve (C8–T1).

The **adductor pollicis** *also has two heads of origin*, the **transverse head** (**11**) *originating from the entire length of the third metacarpal* (**12**), and the **oblique head** (**13**) *originating from the adjacent carpal bones*. It is *inserted into the ulnar sesamoid bone* (**14**) *of the metacarpophalangeal joint of the thumb*. It produces adduction and assists in the opposition and flexion of the thumb.
Nerve supply: deep branch of the ulnar nerve (C8–T1).

The **opponens pollicis** (**15**) *arises from the tubercle of the trapezium* (**16**) *and the flexor retinaculum* (**3**), *and is inserted into the radial margin of the first metacarpal* (**17**). It produces opposition of the thumb and assists in adduction.
Nerve supply: median nerve (C6–C7).

In summary, the muscles of the thenar eminence may also be classified according to their function:

Adduction of the thumb is produced by the adductor pollicis with the help of the flexor pollicis brevis and the opponens pollicis.

Abduction is produced by the abductor pollicis brevis and partly by the flexor pollicis brevis.

The position of **opposition** is produced principally by the opponens pollicis, assisted by the flexor pollicis brevis and adductor pollicis.

Reposition (return to the neutral position) is effected by the long muscles of the dorsal side, namely the extensor pollicis brevis, extensor pollicis longus and abductor pollicis longus.

Clinical tip: The so-called **"reticular bands"** (*Landsmeer*) run from the attachments of the abductor pollicis brevis and the adductor pollicis; they reach to the extensor tendons and insert together with these on the terminal phalanges. They are important for hand surgery.

Upper Limb

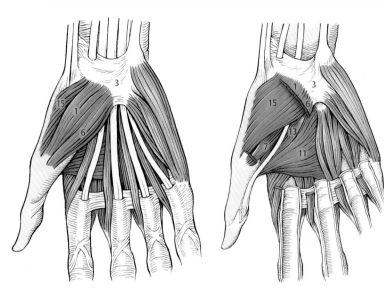

A Thenar muscles, first layer

B Thenar muscles, second layer

C Thenar muscles, third layer

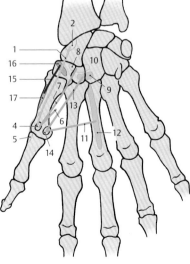

D Diagram of origin, course,
   and insertion of muscles

Intrinsic Muscles of the Hand, continued

Palmar Aponeurosis (A)

The **palmar aponeurosis** (also see p. 388) consists of *longitudinal* (**1**) and *transverse* (**2**) fascicles. The longitudinal fibers run to the tendon sheaths of the flexor tendons (**3**), the deep transverse metacarpal ligaments (**4**), and the ligaments of the metacarpophalangeal joints. They also radiate into the corium of the palm of the hand (**5**). The palmar aponeurosis is connected to the deep palmar fascia (p. 180) by nine septa (**6**). Eight of the septa border both sides of the tendons of the superficial and deep flexors of the digits, while the ninth septum lies on the radial side of the first lumbrical muscle (p. 174). The septa arise both from the longitudinal and transverse fasciculi.

The connection of the deep palmar fascia with the carpal bones corresponds to the anchoring of the palmar aponeurosis to the skeleton of the hand. The longitudinal fasciculi reach the second through the fifth finger and radiate mostly in the hand and in the fibrous layer of the synovial sheaths (p. 182). A few of the fibers join the superficial transverse metacarpal ligament. The transverse fasciculi lie proximally deeper than the longitudinal fasciculi. Distally, the transverse fasciculi (**2**) are visible, lying in the same layer as the longitudinal fibers.

The palmar aponeurosis makes a functional entity with the ligaments, septa and fascias. It is firmly fixed to the skin of the palm of the hand over the carpal bones.

In the hypothenar eminence lies the **palmaris brevis** (**7**), which may be in the process of involution *and whose fibers connect the palmar aponeurosis and the flexor retinaculum* (**8**) *to the skin of the ulnar border of the hand.*
Nerve supply: superficial branch of the ulnar nerve (C8–T1).

Hypothenar Muscles (B–D)

The muscles of the hypothenar eminence consist of
   – Abductor digiti minimi (**9**)
   – Flexor digiti minimi brevis (**10**)
   – Opponens digiti minimi (**11**)

The **abductor digiti minimi** (**9**) *arises from the pisiform* (**12**), *the pisohamate ligament* (**13**), *and the flexor retinaculum* (**8**) and is *inserted into the ulnar margin of the base of the proximal phalanx of the fifth digit* (**14**). In part it also radiates into the extensor aponeurosis of the little finger. It functions as a pure abductor.
Nerve supply: deep branch of the ulnar nerve (C8–T1).

The **flexor digiti minimi brevis** (**10**) *arises from the flexor retinaculum* (**8**) *and also from the hamulus of the hamate* (**15**). At its insertion it fuses with the tendon of the abductor digiti minimi and *ends on the palmar surface of the base of the proximal phalanx* (**16**). It flexes at the metacarpophalangeal joint.
Nerve supply: deep branch of the ulnar nerve (C8–T1).

▬ **Variant:** Very often, the muscle is absent.

The **opponens digiti minimi** (**11**), like the flexor digiti minimi brevis, *arises from the hamulus of the hamate* (**15**) *and from the flexor retinaculum* (**8**). *It is inserted into the ulnar margin of the fifth metacarpal* (**17**). It brings the little finger into the position for opposition.
Nerve supply: deep branch of the ulnar nerve (C8–T1).

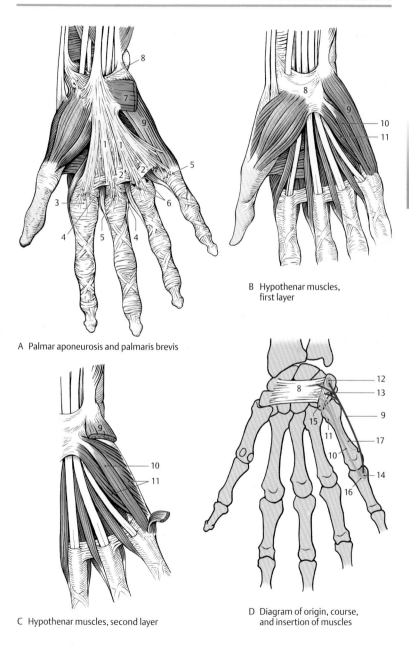

A Palmar aponeurosis and palmaris brevis

B Hypothenar muscles,
   first layer

C Hypothenar muscles, second layer

D Diagram of origin, course,
   and insertion of muscles

Upper Limb

Fascias and Special Features of the Free Upper Limb

Fascias (A–D)

In the arm the **brachial fascia** (**1**) surrounds the flexors and extensors. Between the flexor and extensor groups of muscles on the medial and lateral sides of the humerus are the *medial* (**2**) and *lateral* (**3**) *brachial intermuscular septa*. These septa connect the brachial fascia with the humerus. The medial intermuscular septum begins proximally at the level of the insertion of the coracobrachialis muscle, while the lateral septum begins just distal to the deltoid tuberosity. Both septa are attached to the margins of the humerus and extend to the corresponding epicondyles. The fascia of the arm is continuous with the *axillary fascia* (**4**) and with the *antebrachial fascia* (**5**). On the anterior surface of the arm just above the elbow there is an aperture, the *hiatus basilicus* (**6**; see p. 376).

The **antebrachial fascia** (**5**) is tightly attached to the dorsal surface of the ulna. The *bicipital aponeurosis* (**7**) radiates into the forearm fascia, and the latter sends strong septa (**8**) deep between the individual muscle groups (see p. 158).
At the distal end of the forearm the fascia is strengthened by transverse bands to form the extensor retinaculum on the dorsal surface which provides conduits for the tendons of various muscles. Deep to the extensor retinaculum there are six compartments for passage of the extensor tendons. On the palmar surface, descending tendon fibers of the flexor carpi ulnaris muscle spread radially and distally near to the wrist into the antebrachial fascia. A separate space (**Guyon's box,** see p. 388) is formed by these fiber bundles and the fascia which covers the deep muscles.

The **dorsal fascia of hand** (**9**) superficially forms a close, dense extension of the extensor retinaculum (p. 182), composed of strong transverse fibers. Distally, it becomes the dorsal aponeurosis of the fingers. In addition it is more or less tightly connected to the intertendinous connections (p. 166). The dorsal fascia of hand is attached to the metacarpal bones on the ulnar and radial margins of the back of the hand. Between the tendons of the long extensors of the fingers and the dorsal interosseous muscles (p. 174) there is a deep, delicate leaf (**10**) of this fascia.

The **palmar aponeurosis** (**11**, p. 178) on the palmar side forms a continuation of the flexor retinaculum (p. 182), the superficial and lateral boundaries of the central midhand compartment. Via nine septa, it is connected to the **deep palmar fascia** (**12**), which covers the palmar interosseous muscles. The adductor pollicis muscle (**14**) is covered by its own delicate **adductor fascia** (**13**).

The superficial transverse metacarpal ligament is found at the roots of the fingers. It is a thin, transverse ligament into which some of the longitudinal fasciculi of the palmar aponeurosis radiate. There is close contact between this ligament and the subcutis.

15 Palmar interosseous muscles
16 Dorsal interosseous muscles

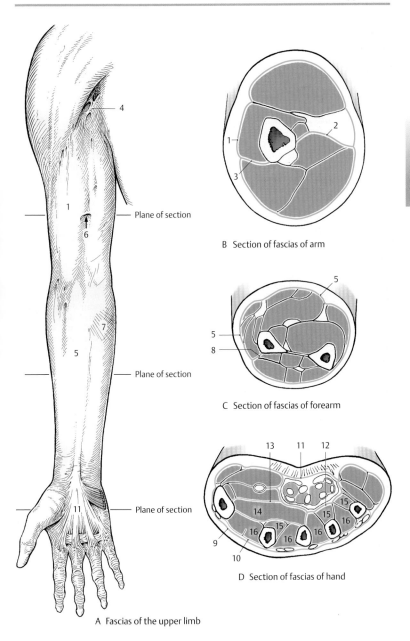

B Section of fascias of arm

C Section of fascias of forearm

D Section of fascias of hand

A Fascias of the upper limb

Plane of section

Plane of section

Plane of section

Upper Limb

Carpal Tendinous Sheaths (A–E)

There are dorsal carpal tendinous sheaths, palmar carpal tendinous sheaths, and palmar digital tendinous sheaths.

Dorsal Carpal Tendinous Sheaths (A)

The **dorsal synovial sheaths** lie in six tendon compartments formed by the *extensor retinaculum* (**1**) and *septa* (**2**), which arise from the undersurface of the retinaculum and are attached to bony ridges on the radius and ulna. These six osteofibrous compartments contain the synovial sheaths of variable length for nine tendons. They are counted from the radial to the ulnar side. In the *first compartment* lie the *sheaths containing the tendons of the abductor pollicis longus and the extensor pollicis brevis* (**3**). In the *second compartment* lie the tendon sheaths for the tendons of the extensor carpi radialis longus and brevis, the *vagina tendinum musculorum extensorum carpi radialium* (**4**). In the *third compartment*, the slightly obliquely lying *canal* contains the *sheath with the tendon of the extensor pollicis longus* (**5**). The *fourth compartment*, the last compartment attached to the radius, contains the sheath of the *extensor digitorum* and the *extensor indicis* (**6**). The *fifth compartment* carries the *tendon* of the extensors of the little finger in the *tendon sheath of the extensor digiti minimi* (**7**), and the *sixth compartment* contains the *tendon sheath of the extensor carpi ulnaris muscle* (**8**).

Palmar Carpal Tendinous Sheaths (B)

The *flexor retinaculum* (**9**) completes the carpal tunnel (p. 124) through which the median nerve runs and the tendons of various flexor muscles run in three **palmar synovial tendon sheaths**. Most radially, the tendon of the flexor carpi radialis runs in the *synovial tendon sheath for the flexor carpi radialis* (**10**) in its own groove in the trapezium bone, thereby dividing the radial attachment of the flexor retinaculum into two parts. Adjacent to it lies the *syn-ovial sheath of the flexor pollicis longus muscle* (**11**), through which runs the digital tendon sheath of the thumb. The flexor digitorum superficialis and flexor digitorum profundus muscles run together in a *common synovial sheath of the flexor muscles* (**12**).

Digital Tendinous Sheaths (B)

The five **synovial sheaths of the digits of the hand** are surrounded by **fibrous sheaths**, which consist of *anular* (**13**) and *cruciate* (**14**) fibers. Between the parietal and visceral layers of the synovial sheath (p. 32) there is a mesotendon with blood vessels and nerves. A *mesotendon* in the region of the digital tendon sheaths is called a *vinculum longum* (p. 160) and *vinculum breve* (p. 160).

▆▆ **Variants (C–E):** In about 72% of people the *digital tendon sheath of the little finger* (**15**) is directly connected to the carpal tendon sheath (**12**), while the other tendon sheaths usually extend from the metacarpophalangeal joint to the base of the terminal phalanx. In about 18% of cases there is no connection between the tendon sheath of the little finger (**15**) and the carpal tendon sheaths. In addition to a direct connection of the tendon sheath of the fifth finger to the carpal tendon sheath, the *tendon sheath of the index finger* (**16**) (in 2.5%) or the *tendon sheath of the ring finger* (**17**) (in about 3%) may communicate directly with the carpal tendon sheaths.

> **Clinical tip:** Inflammation of the sheath for the tendons of the abductor pollicis longus and the extensor pollicis brevis occurs frequently and causes pain in the region of the styloid process of the radius.

18 Intertendinous connection

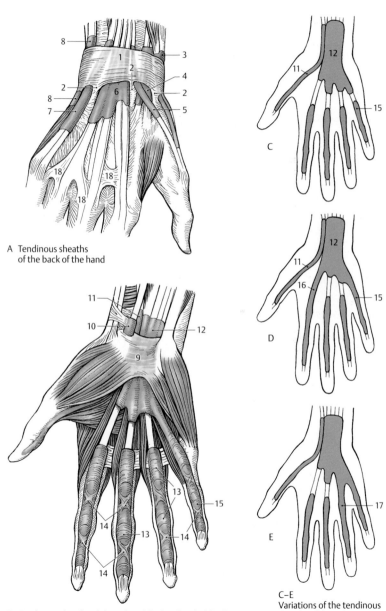

A Tendinous sheaths
of the back of the hand

B Tendinous sheaths of the palm of the hand and of the fingers

C–E
Variations of the tendinous
sheaths of the palm

Anatomical Terms and their Latin Equivalents

Upper Limb	Membrum superius
Carpal tunnel	Canalis carpi
Elbow joint	Articulatio cubiti
Flexor retinaculum	Retinaculum musculorum flexorum
Forearm	Antebrachium
Humeroradial joint	Articulatio humeroradialis
Humero-ulnar joint	Articulatio humeroulnaris
Index finger	Index or digitus secundus
Little finger	Digitus minimus or quintus
Midcarpal joint	Articulatio mediocarprlis
Middle finger	Digitus medius or tertius
Neck of radius	Collum radii
Oblique cord	Chorda oblique
Palmar (dorsal) carpal tendinous sheaths	Vaginae tendinum carpales palmares (dorsales)
Proximal radio-ulnar joint	Articulatio radioulnaris proximalis
Ring finger	Digitus anularis or quartus
Shaft of radius	Corpus radii
Shoulder girdle	Cingulum membri superioris
Shoulder joint	Articulatio humeri
Sternal end	Extremitas sternalis claviculae
Thumb	Pollex
Ulnar notch	Incisura ulnaris
Wrist joint	Articulario radiocarpalis

Systematic Anatomy of the Locomotor System

Lower Limb

Bones, Ligaments, Joints

Pelvis

The bony **pelvis** consists of:
- The two hip bones
- The sacrum
- The coccyx (see p. 48)

Hip Bone (A–C)

The **hip bone** consists of three parts, the **pubis,** the **ilium** and the **ischium,** which synostose in the *acetabular fossa* (**2**), which is bordered by the *acetabular margin* (**1**) and is surrounded by the *lunate surface* (**3**). The *acetabular notch* (**4**) opens the acetabulum inferiorly and thus limits the *obturator foramen* (**5**).

The **pubis** consists of a *body* (**6**), a *superior ramus* (**7**), and an *inferior ramus* (**8**). The two rami border the obturator foramen anteriorly and inferiorly. Near to the superior end of the medially orientated *symphysial surface* (**9**) lies the *pubic tubercle* (**10**), from which the *pubic crest* (**11**) extends medially and the *pecten pubic* (**12**) runs laterally toward the *arcuate line of the ilium* (**13**). At the transition of the superior ramus of the pubis into the ilium, there is the elevation of the *iliopubic eminence* (**14**). The *obturator groove* (**15**) lies inferior to the pubic tubercle and is bordered internally by the *anterior obturator tubercle* (**16**) and the *posterior obturator tubercle* (**17**), which is not always present.

The **ilium** is divided into the *body* (**18**) and the *wing of ilium*. The body forms part of the acetabulum and is delimited externally by the *supra-acetabular groove* (**19**) and internally by the arcuate line (**13**). External to the wing lies the *gluteal surface* (**20**) and internal to it the *iliac fossa* (**21**) is visible. Behind the iliac fossa there is the sacropelvic surface with the *iliac tuberosity* (**22**) and the *auricular surface* (**23**). The *iliac crest* (**24**) starts anteriorly at the *superior anterior iliac spine* (**25**) and divides into the *outer* (**26**) and *inner* (**27**) *lips*, and an *inter-mediate zone* (**28**), which extends upward and backward. There, the outer lip bulges laterally as the *iliac tubercle* (**29**). The iliac crest ends in the *posterior superior iliac spine* (**30**). Beneath the latter lies the *posterior inferior iliac spine* (**31**), while anteriorly beneath the anterior superior iliac spine lies the *anterior inferior iliac spine* (**32**). The *inferior gluteal* (**33**), *anterior gluteal* (**34**), and *posterior gluteal* (**35**) lines lie on the gluteal surface. In addition, there are various vascular canals among which at least one corresponds functionally to an emissary vessel.

The **ischium** is divided into the *body* (**36**) and the *ramus of the ischium* (**37**), which together with the inferior ramus of the pubis forms the inferior border of the obturator foramen. The ischium bears the *ischial spine* (**38**), which separates the *greater sciatic notch* (**39**) from the *lesser sciatic notch* (**40**). The greater sciatic notch is formed partly by the ischium and partly by the ilium, and it extends to the inferior surface of the auricular facies. The *ischial tuberosity* (**41**) develops on the ramus of the ischium.

Ossification: Three anlagen appear: in the 3rd intrauterine month (ilium), 4th–5th intrauterine month (ischium), and the 5th–6th intrauterine month (pubis). They fuse in the center of the acetabulum in a Y-shaped junction. Within the acetabulum one or more individual ossification centers develop between the ages of 10 and 12 years. Synostosis of the three bones occurs between the ages of 5 and 7 years, but within the acetabulum itself not until between the ages of 15 and 16 years. Epiphysial centers of ossification occur in the spines at the age of 16, in the ischial tuberosity and in the iliac crest between the ages of 13 and 15 years.

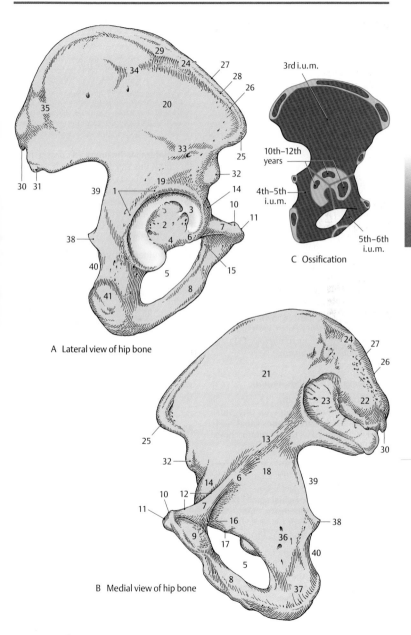

C Ossification

3rd i.u.m.

10th–12th years

4th–5th i.u.m.

5th–6th i.u.m.

A Lateral view of hip bone

B Medial view of hip bone

Junctions between the Bones of the Pelvis (A, B)

Symphysis

The two hip bones are joined at the *pubic symphysis* (**1**) by a fibrous cartilage with a hyaline cartilage covering, the *interpubic disk*. Within the disk a small nonsynovial cavity may be present. Cranially and caudally the junction is reinforced by the **superior** (**2**) and the **inferior** (**3**) *pubic ligaments*, respectively.

Sacroiliac Joint

This articulation (**4**) is formed by the auricular surface of the hip bone and the auricular surface of the sacrum. Both are covered by fibrous cartilage. A very taut joint capsule encloses in male the almost immobile joint, in female partly moveable joint which is an amphiarthrosis. The capsule is strengthened by the *ventral* (**5**), *interosseous* (**6**), and *dorsal* (**7**) *sacroiliac ligaments*. The joint is reinforced indirectly by the *iliolumbar ligament* (**8**), which connects the ilium (**9**) to the lumbar vertebrae (**10**), as well as by the *sacrotuberous* (**11**) and *sacrospinous* (**12**) *ligaments*.

Ligaments in the Pelvic Region

The **obturator membrane** (**13**) closes the obturator foramen, except for the small opening of the **obturator canal** (**14**), through which pass the obturator blood vessels and nerve.

The **sacrospinous** (**12**) and **sacrotuberous** (**11**) **ligaments** extend like a fan from the lateral margin of the sacral bone (**15**) and the coccyx (**16**) to the ischial spine (**17**) and to the ischial tuberosity (**18**). The sacrotuberous ligament is stronger and longer than the sacrospinous ligament.

Owing to these two ligaments, the greater sciatic notch is converted into the *greater sciatic foramen* (**19**), the lesser sciatic notch into the *lesser sciatic foramen* (**20**). In addition to the sacrospinous ligament, the sacrotuberous ligament also takes part in the delimitation of the greater sciatic foramen.

> **Clinical tip:** Although rare (more frequent in females than males), an **obturator hernia** of the thigh can extend through the obturator canal covered by the pectineus muscle. Likewise of rare occurrence are **sciatic hernias** which pass through the sciatic foramina and protrude caudal to the lower margin of the gluteus maximus.

The **iliolumbar ligament** (**8**) passes from the costal processes of the fourth and fifth lumbar vertebrae (**21**) to the iliac crest (**22**) and to the adjacent region of the iliac tuberosity (**23**). The **transverse acetabular ligament** bridges the acetabular notch and completes the articular surface for the head of the femur.

The **inguinal ligament** (lig. of Vesalius) (**24**) is formed by the inferior border of the aponeurosis of the external abdominal oblique. It extends between the anterior superior iliac spine (**25**) and the pubic tubercle (**26**). At the latter point of attachment it spreads out along a broad surface in the form of the **lacunar ligament** (**27**). Between the inguinal ligament and the anterior margin of the hip bone are the *muscular* (**28**) and the *vascular* (**29**) *spaces*, which are separated from each other by the **iliopectineal arch** (**30**).

Morphology of the Bony Pelvis
(see p. 190)

We distinguish a true and a false, or a lesser and greater pelvis. The region inferior to the terminal line is called the lesser pelvis. The *pelvic inlet* (superior pelvic aperture) leads into the lesser pelvis, which is bordered by the promontory, the arcuate line, the iliopubic eminence, the pecten of the pubis, and the upper edge of the symphysis (*terminal line*). The *pelvic outlet*, the inferior pelvic aperture, is the region between the subpubic angle or pubic arch, the ischial tuberosities and the coccyx.

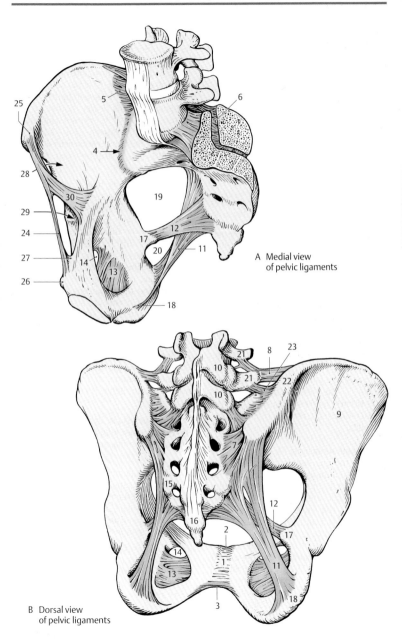

A Medial view
   of pelvic ligaments

B Dorsal view
   of pelvic ligaments

Morphology of the Bony Pelvis, continued

Orientation of the Pelvis and Sex Differences (A–F)

An angle of about 60° is enclosed between the plane of the pelvic inlet and the horizontal plane. It is known as the **pelvic inclination**. In the upright posture the anterior superior iliac spines and the pubic tubercles are in the same frontal (coronal) plane.

Classification of Pelvic Types

In females we distinguish various pelvic shapes, of which the most common (50%) is the gynecoid type. Other forms are the android, anthropoid, and platypeloid types. Classification into four main types is achieved by measuring certain pelvic diameters. The pelvic **diameters** or **conjugates** are measured at the pelvic inlet and outlet and as oblique diameters.

Diameters and External Pelvic Measurements (A–C)

The **transverse diameter** (**1**) (13.5–14 cm) joins the extreme lateral points of the pelvic inlet. The **oblique diameter I** (**2**) (12–12.5 cm) is the line drawn between the right sacroiliac joint and the left iliopubic eminence. The **oblique diameter II** (**3**) (11.5–12 cm) represents a line between the left sacroiliac joint and the right iliopubic eminence.

The **anatomical conjugate** (**4**; approximately 12 cm) is the line between the symphysis and the promontory. The **true conjugate** (**5**) joins the posterior surface of the symphysis (retropubic eminence) to the promontory. It is the shortest diameter of the pelvic inlet (11.5 cm); because it is of particular importance in parturition, it is also known as the *obstetric conjugate*. As the true conjugate cannot be measured directly, it is deduced from the **diagonal conjugate** as the oblique diameter (13 cm). The diagonal conjugate (**6**) extends from the inferior pubic ligament to the promontory and is measured through the vagina.

The **straight conjugate** (**7**) at the pelvic outlet represents the connection between the lower border of the symphysis and the tip of the coccyx (9.5–10 cm). As its length is variable due to the flexibility of the coccyx, the **median conjugate** (**8**) of the pelvic outlet, which connects the lower border of the symphysis to the lower border of the sacrum (11.5 cm), is a more important longitudinal diameter. An additional measure is the **transverse diameter of the pelvic outlet** (10–11 cm) between the two ischial tuberosities.

Using a pelvimeter, two distances on the pelvis may be measured, the **interspinous distance** (**9**) between the anterior superior iliac spines is approximately 26 cm in the female, and the **intercristal distance** (**10**) between the furthest lateral points of the two iliac crests is 29 cm in the female. The **external conjugate,** the distance between the spinous process of the fifth lumbar vertebra and the upper edge of the symphysis (about 20 cm), can also be measured with a pelvimeter. In some instances the **intertrochanteric distance** (31 cm) between the two femurs is also measured.

The **female pelvis** (**D**, red) has wider projecting iliac wings, transversely directed obturator foramina, and a definite **pubic arch**. The lesser pelvis is larger than in the male.

The **male pelvis** (**D**, light gray), has more erect iliac wings, longitudinally orientated obturator foramina, and a **subpubic angle**.

E *Pubic arch* demonstrated by placing the hand on it; the arch lies between the thumb and the index finger.

F *Subpubic angle*, demonstrated by placing the hand on it; the angle lies between the index and middle fingers.

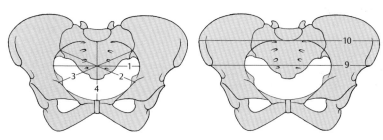

B Pelvic diameters

C External pelvic measurements

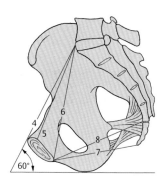

A Pelvic inclination

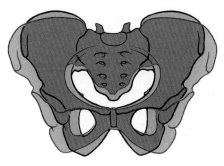

D Comparison between a male pelvis and a female pelvis

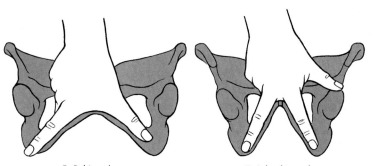

E Pubic arch

F Subpubic angle

The Free Part of the Lower Limb

Femur (A–C)

The thigh bone, or **femur,** is the largest tubular bone of the body and comprises a **shaft** (**1**) with a **neck** (**2**) and **two ends, proximal** and **distal.** An angle is formed between the shaft and neck, the **angle of inclination** (neck–shaft angle, also erroneously called the collodiaphysial angle; see also p. 196).

The shaft exhibits three surfaces: *anterior* (**3**), *lateral* (**4**), and *medial* (**5**). The lateral and medial surfaces are separated on the dorsal side by a two-lipped roughened line, the *linea aspera* (**6**) which represents a thickening of the compacta. A nutrient foramen is found near this line. The *medial* (**7**) and *lateral* (**8**) *lips* of the linea aspera diverge proximally and distally, the lateral lip becoming continuous proximally with the *gluteal tuberosity* (**9**). This tuberosity can often develop very strongly and is then designated as the *third trochanter* (**10**). The medial lip extends up to the undersurface of the femoral neck.

Somewhat lateral to this lip is a ridge, the *pectineal line* (**11**), descending from the lesser trochanter. Both proximally and distally the femoral shaft loses its triangular form and becomes rather four-sided.

The *head of the femur* (**12**) with its umbilicate pit *or fovea* (**13**), presents an irregular border with the neck. The transition of the neck into the shaft is marked at the anterior surface by the *intertrochanteric line* (**14**) and at the posterior surface by the *intertrochanteric crest* (**15**). At the boundary between the middle and proximal third of the intertrochanteric crest is a slight elevation, the *quadrate tubercle* (**16**). Directly below the *greater trochanter* (**17**) is a pit-like depression, the *trochanteric fossa* (**18**). The *lesser trochanter* (**19**) protrudes backward and medially.

The *medial* (**20**) and *lateral* (**21**) *condyles* form the distal end of the femur. Both are united on the anterior surface by the *patellar surface* (**22**), whereas they are separated on the posterior surface by the *intercondylar fossa* (**23**). This fossa is delimited from the posterior surface of the shaft by the *intercondylar line* (**24**), which forms the base of a triangle (*popliteal surface,* **25**). The sides of this triangle represent the continuation of the lips of the linea aspera and are also designated as the *medial* and *lateral supracondylar lines.*

The *medial epicondyle* (**26**) protrudes medially above the medial condyle and bears an elevation, the *adductor tubercle* (**27**). The *lateral epicondyle* (**28**), situated on the lateral side, is demarcated from the lateral condyle by the *popliteal groove* (**29**).

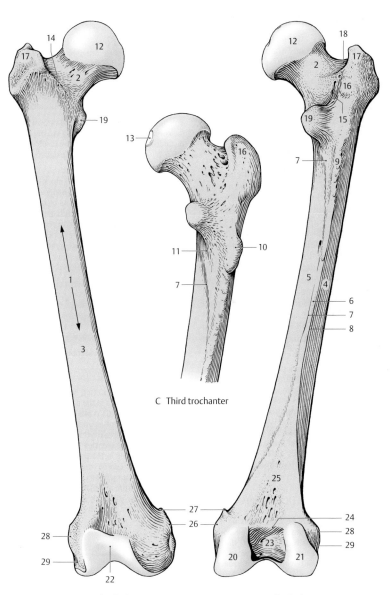

C Third trochanter

A Anterior view of right femur   B Posterior view of right femur

Femur, continued (A–C)

The *medial* (**1**) and *lateral* (**2**) *condyles* differ both in size and shape. They diverge distally and posteriorly. The lateral condyle is wider in front than at the back, while the medial condyle is of uniform width. The oblique position of the shaft of the femur means that in the upright position both condyles are in the horizontal plane despite their different sizes.

In the transverse plane both condyles are only slightly and almost equally curved (**3**) about the *sagittal axis* and in the sagittal plane there is a curvature (**4**) which increases posteriorly. This means that the radius of curvature decreases posteriorly. The midpoints of the curve thus lies on a spiral line (an involute), i.e., on a curve the midpoints of which follow another curve. This produces not but innumerable *transverse axes*, which permits the typical flexion of the knee joint (p. 212) that consists of sliding and rolling motion. At the same time, it ensures that the collateral ligaments become sufficiently lax to permit rotation of the knee joint. The medial condyle has an additional curvature about a *vertical axis*, the "rotatory curvature" (**5**).

Ossification: The perichondral bony cuff of the shaft appears in the 7th intrauterine week. In the 10th month of fetal life an endochondral center becomes visible in the distal epiphysis (**sign of maturity**). Further ossification centers develop in the head of the femur in the 1st year of life, in the greater trochanter in the 3rd year, and in the lesser trochanter at about the age of 11–12 years. The proximal epiphysis fuses earlier (17–19 years) than the distal (19–20 years).

Patella (D–H)

The patella is the largest sesamoid bone of the human body. It is triangular in shape with its base facing proximally and its tip, the *apex patellae* (**6**), facing distally. It has two surfaces, one toward the joint with the femur and the other directed anteriorly. These two surfaces join at a lateral (thinner) and a medial (thicker) margin. The anterior surface may be divided into

three parts and incorporates the tendon of the quadriceps femoris muscle.

In the upper third there is a coarse, flattened, rough surface which often has exostoses and serves largely for the attachment of the tendon of the quadriceps muscle. The middle third is characterized by numerous vascular canaliculi, while the lower third includes the apex, which serves as the origin of the patellar ligament.

The inner surface may be divided into an articular surface covering about three-quarters and a distal surface with vascular canaliculi. This is filled by fatty tissue, the infrapatellar adipose body.

The articular surface is divided into a lateral (**7**) and a medial (**8**) facet by a variably developed vertical ledge. Four types may be distinguished: Type 1, the most common, has a larger lateral and a smaller medial articular surface; Type 2 has two almost equally large articular facets; Type 3 has a particularly small, hypoplastic medial articular face, and in Type 4 the ledge which divides the facets is only indicated.

The whole articular surface area of the patella in the adult is about 12 cm^2 and, especially in the center, is covered by cartilage of up to 6 mm thickness. Maximal cartilage thickness is found at about 30 years of age and then continually decreases with increasing age.

Ossification (F): An ossification center develops in the 3rd–4th year.

▉▉ **Variants:** There is often emargination of the lateral proximal edge of the patella. This is called a **patella emarginata** (**G**). A **patella bipartita** is the result of ossification of an additional cartilaginous layer in the same area in which there has been an emargination. The old idea that several ossification centers occur in the patella which then fail to fuse is not accepted today (*Olbrich*). In addition to a bipartite patella (**H**) there are **multipartite patellas**. Partite patellas occur almost exclusively in males. They may be distinguished from fractures by their position and their shape.

Plane of section
in Fig. B

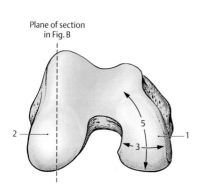

A Distal view of the condyle of the femur

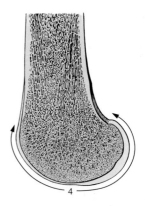

B Section through the lateral condyle

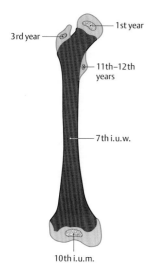

1st year

3rd year

11th–12th
years

7th i.u.w.

10th i.u.m.

C Ossification of the femur

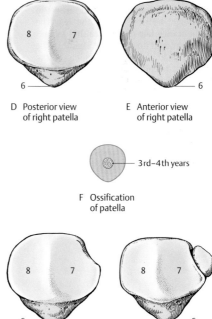

D Posterior view
of right patella

E Anterior view
of right patella

3rd–4th years

F Ossification
of patella

G Patella emarginata

H Bipartite patella

Positions of the Femur (A–G)

The angle formed between the neck and the shaft of the femur is often erroneously called the **collodiaphyseal angle** or, more correctly the **neck–shaft angle**, i.e., **the angle of inclination**. In the newborn it is about 150°, decreasing at the age of 3 years (**A**) to 145°. In adults (**B**) the angle varies between 126° and 128°, and in old age (**C**) it reaches 120°.

> **Clinical tip:** In **disease of bone** (e.g., rickets), the angle of inclination may be reduced to 90°. The angle of inclination is decisive for the strength and stability of the femur; the smaller the angle the greater the risk of transcervical fracture. The incidence of **transcervical fractures** in the elderly is related to the loss of elasticity of the bony tissues as well as to the reduction in the angle of inclination.

The angle of inclination influences the relation of the femoral shaft with respect to the weight-bearing line of the leg. The **weight-bearing line of the** (healthy) **leg** lies along a straight line from the middle of the femoral head through the middle of the knee joint to the middle of the calcaneus. The plane which passes through the lower surface of the femoral condyles is at right angles to this vertical line. This produces an angle between the axis of the shaft of the femur and the weight-bearing line. This angle is related inter alia to the angle of inclination and is important in relation to the correct position of the lower limb (see also p. 214).

> **Clinical tip:** Pathologic changes in the angle of inclination result in abnormal posture of the legs. An abnormally small angle of inclination produces **coxa vara** (**D**), and an abnormally large angle **coxa valga** (**E**). The latter is usually combined with genu varum or bowleggedness (see p. 214), as any change in the shape of the femur naturally must affect the knee joint. A coxa vara leads to genu valgum (see p. 214).

The femur also has a **torsion** (**F**). If a line drawn through the neck of the femur is superimposed on a line drawn transversely through the condyles, an angle will be produced. In a European the mean angle is 12°, with a range from 4° to 20°. The torsion angle, which is associated with the inclination of the pelvis, makes it possible for flexion movements of the hip joint to be transposed into rotatory movements of the head of the femur.

Abnormal values for the torsion angle result in atypical postures of the lower limbs. If the torsion angle is increased, the limb is turned inward, and if it is decreased or absent, the limb is turned out; both postures result in a reduced range of mobility to one side.

> **Clinical tip:** In the moderately flexed hip, the tip of the greater trochanter does not rise above a line which joins the superior anterior iliac spine to the ischial tuberosity. This theoretical line is known as the **Roser–Nélaton line** (**G**). In a case of fracture of the neck of the femur, or a dislocation, these three points no longer lie on a straight line. Thus, the Roser–Nélaton line may be of help in the diagnosis of fractures, although its practical value is disputed.

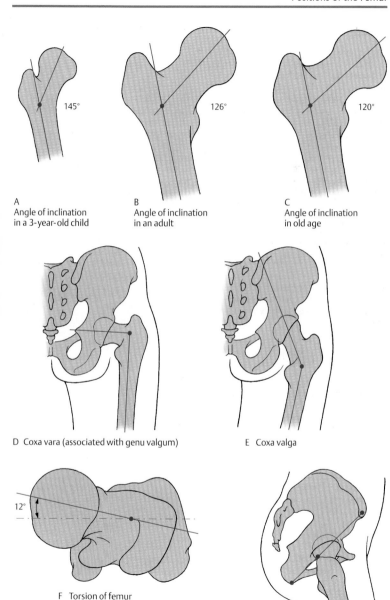

A
Angle of inclination
in a 3-year-old child

B
Angle of inclination
in an adult

C
Angle of inclination
in old age

D Coxa vara (associated with genu valgum)

E Coxa valga

F Torsion of femur

G Roser-Nélaton line

Hip Joint (A–D)

The articular surfaces of the **hip joint** are formed by the **lunate surface of the acetabulum** (**1**) and the **femoral head** (**2**). The lunate surface of the joint cavity presents a section of a hollow sphere and is extended beyond the equator by the **acetabular lip** (**3**). The acetabular lip consists of fibrocartilaginous material. The lunate surface and the lip cover two-thirds of the femoral head. The bony socket is incomplete and closed inferiorly by the **transverse acetabular ligament** (**4**). The acetabular labrum is found on the free margin of this ligament. The *ligament of the head of the femur* (**6**), which is covered by a synovial membrane, extends from the acetabular fossa, where there is a fatty cushion (**5**), to the head of the femur. This ligament contains the artery to the head of the femur, which comes from the acetabular branch of the obturator artery. The head of the femur is also supplied with blood branches of the medial and lateral circumflex femoral arteries.

The middle part of the upper rim of the acetabulum appears thickened in radiographs and may be called the **roof of the socket**.

The **joint capsule** is attached to the hip bone outside the acetabular lip, so that the latter projects freely into the capsular space. The capsular attachment (**8**) at the circumference of the head of the femur lies at about the same distance from the cartilaginous rim of the head of the femur. Therefore, the extracapsular part of the neck is shorter in front than at the back. Anteriorly the line of attachment is in the region of the *intertrochanteric line* (**7**), while posteriorly line of attachment (**8**) is a fingerbreadth away from the *intertrochanteric crest* (**9**).

Hip joint ligaments. Among these ligaments is the strongest in the human body, the *iliofemoral ligament* (**10**), which has a tensile strength of 350 kg. Often this ligament is incorrectly termed the **Bertini ligament**, but actually it was first described by **Bellini.**

There are five ligaments, of which four are extracapsular and one is intracapsular.

The **extracapsular ligaments** are the *zona orbicularis* (**11**), the *iliofemoral ligament* (**10**), the *ischiofemoral ligament* (**12**), and the *pubofemoral ligament* (**13**). The last three ligaments strengthen the capsule and, at the same time, prevent an excessive range of movement. The zona orbicularis lies like a collar around the narrowest part of the neck of the femur. On the inner surface of the capsule it is to be seen as a distinct circular elevation, and externally it is covered by the other ligaments, which partly radiate into it. The head of the femur projects into the zona orbicularis like a button in a buttonhole. Together with the acetabular lip and atmospheric pressure, the zone orbicularis serves as an additional arrangement to maintain contact between the head and the socket.

The ligament of the head of the femur runs **within the capsule**.

Those regions of the capsule which are not strengthened by ligaments represent areas of weakness. The *iliopectineal bursa* lies between the capsule and the iliopsoas muscle. In 10–15 % of people it communicates with the hip joint.

Clinical tip: During inflammatory processes, e.g., **effusions into the joint**, the weaker areas are pushed outward and become very pressure-sensitive.
Luxations tear the capsule, and the ligament of the head of the femur with the artery of the head of the femur may be severed. This may produce nutritional deficiencies in the head of the femur. **Femoral neck fractures** are classified as **medial** or **lateral**. Medial fracture lines are within the joint capsule, while lateral fracture lines are extracapsular.

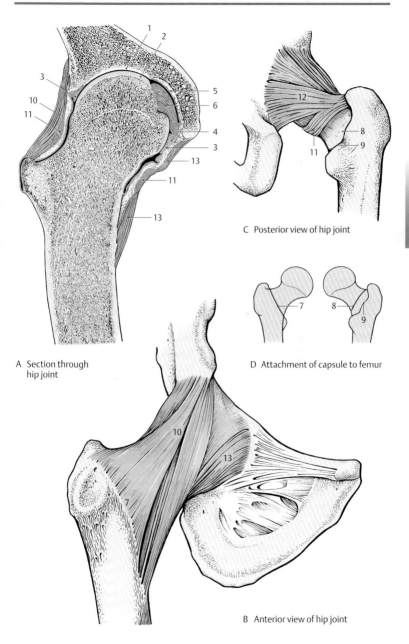

A Section through hip joint

C Posterior view of hip joint

D Attachment of capsule to femur

B Anterior view of hip joint

Hip Joint, continued

Ligaments of the Hip Joint (A, B)

The **iliofemoral ligament** (**1**) arises from the *anterior inferior iliac spine* (**2**) and the *rim of the acetabulum* and extends to the *intertrochanteric line* (**3**). It has a strong **transverse part** (**4**), which lies further cranially and runs parallel to the axis of the neck, and a weaker **descending part** (**5**) lying further caudally and running parallel to the axis of the shaft.

The two parts, of which the lateral portion is twisted like a screw, act differently and form roughly the outline of an inverted Y. In the upright position, with the pelvis tilted posteriorly, the twist and tension of this ligament permits the stance to be maintained without muscular activity and prevents the trunk from falling backward. In addition, the iliofemoral ligament keeps the head of the femur in contact with the socket. When the thighs are flexed, there is a reduction in tension in both iliofemoral ligaments, which allows the pelvis to tilt a little further back, so that the sitting posture becomes possible.

The thicker, transverse (lateral) part of the ligament prevents lateral rotation and adduction of the femur. The descending (medial) part restricts medial rotation. When the thigh is flexed, the entire ligament becomes lax, so that a much greater degree of rotation is possible.

The **ischiofemoral ligament** (**6**) arises from the *ischium* below the acetabulum and runs almost horizontally over the neck of the femur to the attachment of the lateral part of the iliofemoral ligament. In addition it radiates into the **zona orbicularis** (**7**). It prevents medial rotation of the thigh.

The **pubofemoral ligament** (**8**), the weakest of the three ligaments, arises from the *obturator crest* and the adjacent part of the *obturator membrane* (**9**). It radiates into the capsule, specifically into the **zona orbicularis** (**7**), and continues by way of this into the femur. It restricts movements of abduction.

The intracapsular **ligament of the head of the femur** extends from the *acetabular notch to the fovea for ligament of the head.* It does not serve to maintain contact between these structures. When the hip is dislocated, it may prevent further displacement to a certain degree, since only then does it become stretched.

Movements of the Hip Joint

In life, muscle tone restricts joint movement, most noticeably when the extended limb is anteriorly elevated.

Movements of the hip joint include **flexion (anteversion)** and **extension (retroversion)**, **abduction** and **adduction**, **circumduction** and **rotation**. **Flexion** and **extension** occur about a **transverse axis through the head of the femur.** With the knee bent, the thigh may be raised against the abdomen. This movement of flexion is much greater than that of extension, which can only be executed slightly beyond the vertical.

Abduction and **adduction** occur about an **anterior-posterior axis through the femoral head.**

Rotation of the femur occurs around a **(vertical) axis through the head of the femur and the medial femoral condyle**. With the leg extended, a rotation of 60° is possible.

Circumduction is a compound movement in which the leg describes the surface of an irregular cone, the apex of which lies in the head of the femur.

10 Acetabular lip
11 Ischial tuberosity
12 Greater trochanter

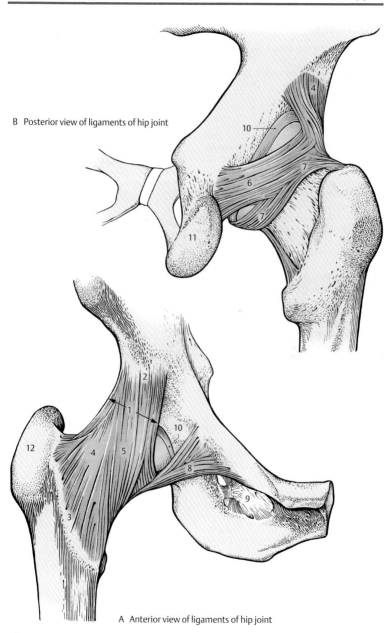

Lower Limb

B Posterior view of ligaments of hip joint

A Anterior view of ligaments of hip joint

Bones of the Leg

The bones of the leg are the tibia, or shin-bone, and fibula. The tibia is the stronger bone which alone provides the connection between the femur and the bones of the ankle and foot.

Tibia (A–D)

The **tibia** has a somewhat triangular **shaft** (**1**) and **proximal** and **distal ends**. At the **proximal end lie** the *medial* (**2**) and *lateral* (**3**) *condyles.* The proximal surface, the *superior articular surface* is interrupted by the *intercondylar eminence* (**4**). This elevation is subdivided into a *medial* (**5**) and a *lateral* (**6**) *intercondylar tubercle.* In front of and behind the eminence lie the *anterior* (**7**) and *posterior* (**8**) *intercondylar area.* On the outward-facing overhang of the lateral condyle there is a small *articular facet*, directed laterally and distally, for articulation with the fibula (**9**).

The three-sided **shaft of the tibia** has a sharp *anterior border* (**10**), which proximally becomes the *tibial tuberosity* (**11**) and is flattened distally. It separates the *medial surface* (**12**) from the *lateral surface* (**13**). The lateral surface joins the *posterior surface* (**15**) at the *interosseous border* (**14**). The posterior surface is separated from the medial surface by the *medial border* (**16**). Proximally on the posterior surface of the shaft of the tibia is a slightly roughened area, the *soleal line* (**17**), extending obliquely from the distomedial side to the proximolateral side. Lateral to this there is a *nutrient foramen* (**18**) of varying size.

The **distal end** is prolonged medially to form the *medial malleolus* (**19**) with its *malleolar articular facet.* The *malleolar groove* (**20**) runs along its posterior surface. The *inferior articular surface of the tibia*, which lies on the lower surface of the distal end of the tibia, articulates with the talus. On the lateral side, in the *fibular notch* (**21**), there is a syndesmotic connection, i.e., a fibrous joint, with the fibula.

In the adult the proximal end of the tibia is bent slightly backward. We speak of **retroversion** or an actual backward tilting of the tibia. The angle between the superior articular facet of the tibial condyle and the horizontal averages 4° to 6°. In the last gestational months this initially very small angle increases to about 30°. In the first months after birth, and more especially when learning to stand upright, the angle becomes smaller.

The superior articular surface lies behind the long axis of the tibia. This means that the proximal end of the tibia is shifted posteriorly. This shift is referred to as **retroposition**.

The tibia also shows **torsion**, i.e., rotation between its proximal and distal ends. This is often present in adults and is attributed to increased growth of the medial tibial condyle.

Ossification: In the shaft of the tibia perichondral ossification begins in the 7th intrauterine week, an endochondral ossification center develops at the proximal end in the 10th intrauterine month or in the 1st year, and an endochondral osseous center in the distal epiphysis appears at the beginning of the 2nd year. The distal epiphysis fuses first, between the ages of 17 and 19 years, and the proximal epiphysis fuses later, between the ages of 19 and 20 years.

Lower Limb

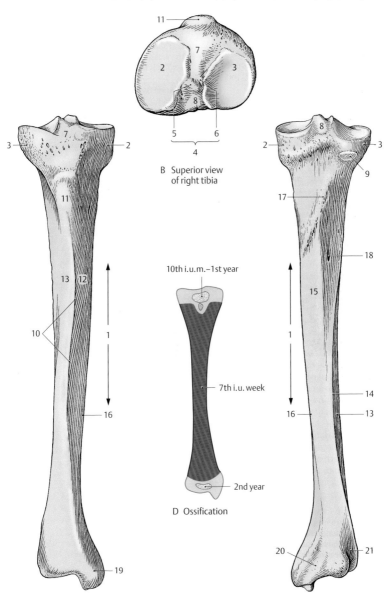

B Superior view
of right tibia

10th i.u.m.–1st year

7th i.u. week

2nd year

D Ossification

A Anterior view of right tibia

C Posterior view of right tibia

Bones of the Leg, continued

Fibula (A–D)

The **fibula** corresponds approximately in length to the tibia, but is a slimmer and therefore more flexible bone. It, too, consists of **two extremities and a shaft**.

The **proximal end** is the *head of the fibula* (**1**) with its *articular facet* (**2**) and a small protuberance, the *apex of the fibular head* (**3**).

The **shaft of the fibula** (**4**) is approximately triangular in its middle part and has three borders and three surfaces. In the distal third there is a fourth broder. The sharpest edge is the forward-facing *anterior border* (**5**), which separates the *lateral* (**6**) from the *medial* (**7**) *surface*. The *medial crest* (**8**) separates the medial surface from the *posterior surface* (**9**). It is separated from the *lateral surface* (**6**) by the *posterior border* (**10**). On the medial surface there is a low but very sharp bony ridge, the *interosseous border* (**11**), to which the *interosseous membrane* (**12**) is attached. Approximately in the center of the posterior surface or on the posterior border, there is a nutrient foramen.

On the lateral surface of the **distal end**, which expands distally, there is the large, flat *lateral malleolus* (**13**) with a *facet for articulation with the talus on its inner surface* (**14**). Behind it there is a deep groove, the *lateral malleolar fossa* (**15**), to which the posterior talofibular ligament is attached. A variable, well-developed groove, the *malleolar groove* (**16**), is present on the lateral surface behind the lateral malleolus. The tendons of the peronei muscles (p. 260) course in this groove.

Ossification: The perichondral bony cuff develops in the region of the shaft in the 2nd intrauterine month. An endochondral ossification center develops in the malleolus in the 2nd year and in the head of the fibula in the 4th year.

The distal epiphysis fuses earlier, between the ages of 16 and 19 years, and the proximal somewhat later, between 17 and 20 years. The junction line of the proximal epiphysis runs below the head of the fibula, and that of the distal epiphysis above the malleolus.

> **Clincal tip:** Clinically, care must be taken not to confuse these epiphysial disks, particularly that of the distal epiphysis, with fracture lines.

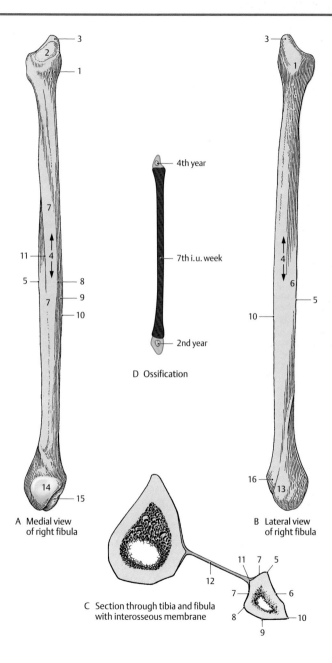

A Medial view
of right fibula

D Ossification

4th year

7th i.u. week

2nd year

B Lateral view
of right fibula

C Section through tibia and fibula
with interosseous membrane

Knee Joint (A–C)

The **knee joint** is the largest joint in the human body. It is a hinge joint, a special type of mobile trochoginglymus. Flexion of it combines rolling and gliding movements. In the flexed position some rotation is possible.

The articular bodies of the knee joint consist of the **femoral condyles** and the **tibial condyles**. The incongruence of these joint surfaces is compensated by a relatively thick cartilaginous covering and by the **menisci**. In addition to the tibia and femur, the **patella** also forms part of the knee joint. The clinician also uses the term *femoropatellar joint*, meaning that region of the knee joint in which the patella is in contact with the femur.

The femoral condyles diverge to some extent distally and posteriorly. The *lateral condyle* is wider in front than at the back, while the *medial condyle* is of more constant width. In the transverse plane the condyles are only slightly bent on a sagittal axis. In the sagittal plane, the curvature increases toward the back, i.e., the radius of curvature becomes smaller (p. 194). In addition, the medial condyle curves about a vertical axis (curvature of rotation). The *superior tibial articular surface* is formed by the condyles, which are separated by the intercondylar eminence and both intercondylar areas.

The wide, lax **capsule** (**1**) is thin in front and at the side and is strengthened by ligaments. The patella is inserted into the anterior wall of the capsule.

At various points the knee joint possesses **ligaments**, **menisci**, and **communicating bursae**.

Ligaments. The **patellar ligament** (**2**) is a continuation of the *quadriceps tendon* (**3**), which extends from the *patella* to the *tibial tuberosity* (**4**). The **lateral patellar retinaculum** (**5**) is formed by fibers of the vastus lateralis muscle and some fibers from the rectus femoris muscle. Some fibers of the ilio-

tibial tract also radiate into it. Laterally, it joins the tibial tuberosity of the tibia. The **medial patellar retinaculum** (**6**) is formed to a large extent by fibers from the vastus medialis muscle, which runs distally, medial to the patellar ligament and is attached to the tibia in front of the medial collateral ligament. Transverse fibers (**8**), which arise from the *medial epicondyle* (**7**) radiate into the medial patellar retinaculum. Two lateral ligaments act as guidance ligaments for flexion and extension of the joint. The **tibial collateral ligament** (**9**) is a flattened, triangular ligament, which is built into the fibrous membrane of the capsule, and is fused with the medial meniscus (p. 208). It contains three groups of fibers. The *anterior long fibers* (**10**) extend from the medial epicondyle (**7**) to the *medial border of the tibia* (**11**). The *short, upper, posterior fibers* (**12**) radiate into the medial meniscus, and the *inferior, posterior fibers* (**13**) extend from the medial meniscus to the tibia. It is covered partly by the superficial pes anserinus and is crossed inferiorly by that part of the *tendon of the semimembranosus* (**14**) which is attached to the tibia. The round **fibular collateral ligament** (**15**) is not fused with the capsule nor with the lateral meniscus. It arises from the *lateral epicondyle* (**16**) and is attached to the *head of the fibula* (**17**).

On the dorsal surface, the **oblique popliteal ligament** (**18**) comprises the lateral radiation of the tendon of the semimembranosus (**14**). It extends laterally and proximally. The **arcuate popliteal ligament** (**19**) arises from the *apex of the head of the fibula* (**20**) and passes into the capsule, crossed by the tendon of the *popliteus* (**21**).

22 Suprapatellar bursa
23 Medial bursa subtendinous of gastrocnemius
24 Medial head of gastrocnemius
25 Lateral head of gastrocnemius

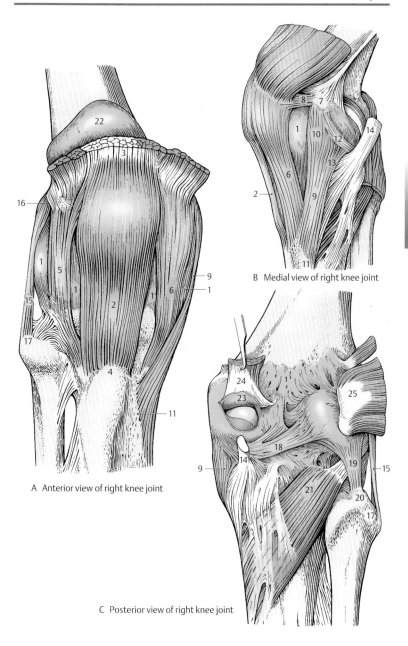

Lower Limb

B Medial view of right knee joint

A Anterior view of right knee joint

C Posterior view of right knee joint

Lower Limb

Knee Joint, continued (A–C)

A further group of **ligaments** of the knee joint is that of the *cruciate ligaments*. They serve in particular to maintain contact during rotary movements. They are intracapsular but extra-articular ligaments (p. 210).

The **anterior cruciate ligament** (**1**) runs from the anterior intercondylar area of the tibia to the inner surface of the lateral condyle of the femur. Fibers arising from the lateral side extend further dorsally than those from the medial side.

The **posterior cruciate ligament** (**2**) is stronger than the anterior cruciate ligament. It passes from the lateral surface of the medial condyle of the femur to the posterior intercondylar area.

The **menisci** consist of connective tissue with extensive collagen fiber material, infiltrated with cartilage-like cells. The collagen fibers run in two principal directions. The strong fibers follow the shape of the menisci between their attachments, while weaker fibers pass radially to an imaginary midpoint and interlace between the longitudinally running fibers. This arrangement means that curved longitudinal tears (see below) can occur more easily than transverse tears. The cartilage-like cells mostly lie near the superficial surface of the menisci.

In transverse section the menisci are seen to be flattened medially. On the external surface they fuse with the synovial membrane of the joint capsule. They may move over the underlying tibia. They are supplied with blood from the middle genicular and inferior lateral and medial genicular arteries of the knee, which together form the perimeniscal marginal arterial arcades.

The **medial meniscus** (**3**) is semicircular in shape and is fused with the *tibial collateral ligament* (**4**). Their points of attachment are relatively widely separated. The medial meniscus is wider posteriorly than anteriorly, so the *anterior crus* (**5**) is much thin-

ner than the *posterior crus* (**6**). Its attachment makes it far less mobile than the lateral meniscus. External rotation of the leg causes the greatest displacement and pulling stress on it. Internal rotation relaxes it.

The **lateral meniscus** (**7**) is almost circular; its points of attachment lie close together, and it is of uniform width. It is more mobile than the medial meniscus, as it does not fuse with the *fibular collateral ligament* (**8**), and therefore it is less stressed by the different movements. From its posterior horn arise one or two ligaments. The **anterior meniscofemoral ligament** (**9**) anteriorly and the **posterior meniscofemoral ligament** (**10**) posteriorly pass behind the posterior cruciate ligament to the medial femoral condyle. The posterior meniscofemoral ligament is present more often than the anterior (about 30%). Less often (see Fig. **C**) both ligaments are present. The **transverse ligament of knee** (**11**) joins the two menisci in front. In 10% of cases it is divided into several strips.

> **Clinical tip:** Clinicians distinguish an **anterior** and a **posterior horn** in each meniscus. Menisci may be torn by continuous excessive force or by uncoordinated movements (e.g., flexion in external rotation with a fixed foot).
> **Damage to the medial meniscus is about 20 times more frequent than to the lateral meniscus**, because of its more limited mobility and its thin anterior crus. *Longitudinal ruptures* (*bucket handle tear*) or *fractures of the anterior or posterior horn* may occur. After surgical removal of a meniscus, with preservation of the marginal zone of the capsule, meniscoid tissue may be formed which takes over the function of the meniscus. The meniscofemoral ligaments may cause difficulties during operations on the posterior horn.

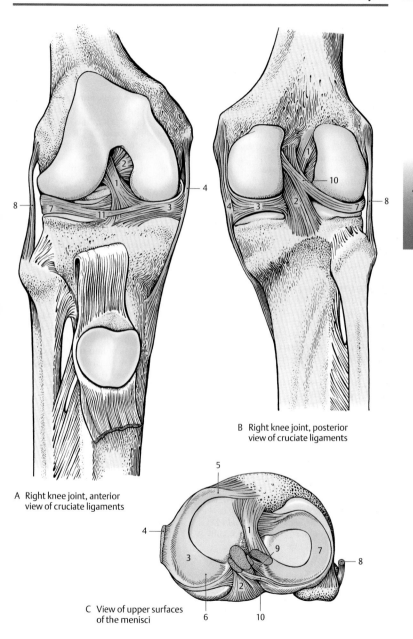

B Right knee joint, posterior view of cruciate ligaments

A Right knee joint, anterior view of cruciate ligaments

C View of upper surfaces of the menisci

Knee Joint, continued (A–D)

The *synovial* (**1**) and *fibrous* (**2**) *membranes* of the **articular capsule** are separated by fatty deposits on their anterior and posterior surfaces. The reflection of the **synovial membrane** anteriorly lies on the *femur* (**3**), usually at some distance from the margin of the cartilage where the synovial membrane arises (**4**). This is due to the presence of the *suprapatellar bursa* (**5**), which communicates with the joint space. It should be noted that at this site of reflection (**6**), the synovial membrane appears slightly lifted from the bone by periosteal connective tissue (**7**). On the *tibia* (**8**) the attachment and the reflection of the synovial membrane anteriorly lie close to the cartilaginous margin. Posteriorly, the attachment of the synovial membrane to the femur is at the *cartilage margin* (**9**) of the *femoral condyles*, which produce two dorsally directed extensions (**10**) in the joint space. In the center, the synovial membrane passes in front of the *anterior cruciate* (**11**) and *posterior cruciate* (**12**) ligaments, so that although the ligaments are intracapsular they lie extra-articularly between the synovial (**1**) membranes. Their posterior attachment to the tibia is exactly on the cartilage margin (**13**). The *menisci* (**14**) are incorporated into the synovial membrane.

The **joint space** itself has a complicated structure. Anteriorly, in the exposed joint, there is a wide fatty pad, the *infrapatellar fat pad* (**15**), inserted between the synovial and fibrous membranes. This extends from the lower margin of the *patella* (**16**), which is enclosed in the anterior wall of the capsule, to the *infrapatellar synovial fold* (**17**) dividing the remnant of the original subdivision of the joint into two chambers.

The infrapatellar synovial fold extends through the joint space with a free upper margin and continues on the cruciate ligaments, which it surrounds from the front (see above). The *alar folds* (**18**) lie lateral to the infrapatellar fat pad and to the infrapatellar synovial fold.

There are numerous **bursae** around the knee joint, some of which communicate with the joint cavity. The largest of the **communicating bursae** is the *suprapatellar bursa* (**5**), which lies anteriorly and increases the joint space proximally. Posteriorly lie the *subpopliteal recess* and the *semimembranosus bursa*, which are much smaller. At the origin of the two heads of the gastrocnemius muscle are the *lateral* and *medial subtendinous bursae of gastrocnemius*.

The **noncommunicating synovial bursae** include the *subcutaneous prepatellar bursa*, which is located directly in front of the patella, as well as the *deep infrapatellar bursa* (**19**), which is situated between the *patellar ligament* (**20**) and the fibrous membrane of the joint capsule. In particular cases, the latter bursa can also be in communication with the articular cavity. Additional smaller bursae which are not regularly present include the *subfascial prepatellar bursa*, the *subtendinous prepatellar bursa*, and the *subcutaneous prepatellar bursa*.

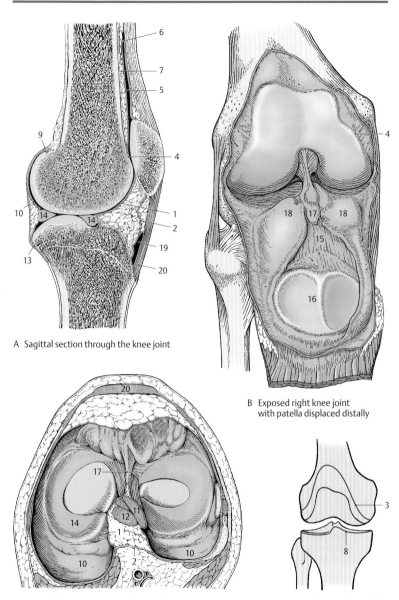

Lower Limb

A Sagittal section through the knee joint

B Exposed right knee joint
with patella displaced distally

C Transverse section through knee joint,
proximal view of distal part

D Attachment of capsule

Movements of the Knee Joint (A–E)

The knee may be **flexed** and **extended** about an almost transverse axis, and in the flexed position **rotation** is possible about the axis of the lower leg.

In the **extended knee** (**A**) both *collateral ligaments* (**1, 2**) and the *anterior part of the anterior cruciate ligament* (**3**) are taut. During extension the femoral condyles glide into the almost extreme position in which the *tibial collateral ligament* (**1**) is completely unfolded. During the last 10° of movement before complete extension there is an **obligatory terminal rotation** of about 5° (**the joint is "screwed home"**). *This is caused by stretching of the anterior cruciate ligament and is permitted by the shape of the medial femoral condyle (p. 194), assisted by the iliotibial tract (p. 254).* Both lateral ligaments become taut and at the same time there is a slight unwinding of the cruciate ligaments (**3, 4**). Final rotation of the non-weight-bearing active leg is produced by lateral rotation of the tibia, and in the weight-bearing (standing) leg by medial rotation of the thigh. In the position of extreme extension the collateral (**1, 2**) and cruciate ligaments are tensed (**A**).

Normal extension is to 180°, although in children and adolescents the leg may be overextended by about 5°. In the newborn, maximal extension is impossible because of the physiological occurrence of tibial retroversion (p. 202).

In the **flexed knee** (**B**) the *fibular collateral ligament* (**2**) is completely relaxed, and the *tibial collateral ligament* (**1**) is largely lax, while the *anterior* (**3**) and *posterior* (**4**) cruciate ligaments are taut. In flexion, rotation is possible under the control of the cruciate ligaments. The extent of **medial rotation** (**C**) **of the leg** is less than of **lateral rotation**. *During medial rotation of the tibia on the femur, the cruciate ligaments are twisted around each other and so prevent any appreciable medial rotation. In the same way, the dorsal fibers of the tibial collateral ligament* (**1**) *are tensed at extreme medial rotation. During lateral rotation, the cruciate ligaments become unwound.* The limit of lateral rotation is primarily determined by the *tibial collateral ligament* (**2**); its maximal extent is 45° to 60°. The amount of rotation can be verified by movement of the head of the fibula (**5**) when the leg is lifted from the ground.

Because of the oblique position of the cruciate ligaments, in every position one cruciate ligament or part of one is always tense. In any case, these ligaments come to control the joint as soon as the collateral ligaments become inadequate, i.e., the cruciates maintain stability when the collaterals relax.

During rotation the femur and *menisci* (**6**) move over the tibia, and during flexion and extension the femur rolls and glides on the menisci, so that we may consider the knee to be a **"mobile joint"**.

Clinical tip: The relatively large and incongruent joint surfaces are subject to considerable stress and they often show damage to the cartilaginous covering in old age, as well as bony changes. In a case of ruptured anterior cruciate ligament (**D**), the so-called **anterior drawer sign** (**E**) is observed, i.e., in the flexed position (with the collateral ligaments relaxed) the lower leg can be pulled forward 2–3 cm (arrow).

Rupture of the posterior cruciate ligament and the fibular collateral ligament results in the **posterior drawer sign**, i.e., the lower leg may be pushed backward. Abnormal lateral movements occur if there is a torn lateral ligament (**wobbly joint**).

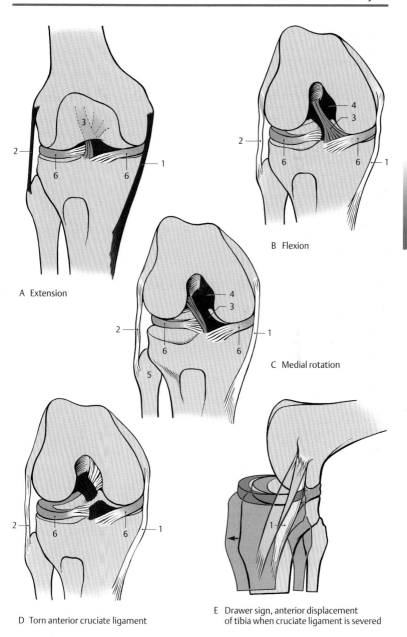

A Extension

B Flexion

C Medial rotation

D Torn anterior cruciate ligament

E Drawer sign, anterior displacement of tibia when cruciate ligament is severed

Lower Limb

Lower Limb

Alignment of the Lower Limb (A–C)

Irrespective of the angle of inclination of the femur (see p. 196), the alignment or shape of the lower extremity depends on the correct development of the knee joint. A misalignment of the lower limb will cause abnormal loading and early signs of deterioration of the knee joint.

If the knee joint is developed normally, the limb is straight (**genu rectum, A**). In that case the *weight-bearing line* (**1**) runs *through the middle of the head of the femur* (**2**), the *middle of the knee joint*, and, when extended, also through the *middle of the calcaneus* (**3**).

When the *weight-bearing line* is displaced laterally (**1**), i.e., it runs *through the lateral femoral condyle* (**4**) or *the head of the fibula* (**5**), the condition is known as **genu valgum** or *"knock-knee"* (**B**). In this case the tibial collateral ligament (**6**) will be overstretched and there is excessive stress on the lateral meniscus (**7**), the cartilage-covered articular surface of the lateral femoral condyle (**4**) and the lateral condyle of the tibia (**8**). The joint space is larger on the medial than on the lateral side. In genu valgum we have increased end rotation. In a case of knock-knees the medial surfaces of the legs near the knee joints touch, while the medial malleoli elsewhere have no contact.

When the *weight-bearing line* (**1**) runs *through the medial femoral condyle* (**9**) or medial to it, the condition is known as **genu varum** (**C**) or *"bowleggedness"*. The fibular collateral ligament (**10**) is overextended, and there is increased stress and wear and tear on the medial meniscus (**11**) and on the cartilage covering of the articular surfaces. In the region of the knee joint the legs cannot be made to touch. In genu varum the legs cannot be completely extended, so terminal rotation cannot occur.

Connections between the Tibia and the Fibula (D)

The **tibiofibular joint** (**12**) is an almost immobile synovial joint (**amphiarthrosis**) between the *head of the fibula* (**13**) and the *fibular articular facet of the lateral tibial condyle* (**14**). It possesses a **tense capsule** which is reinforced by the *anterior and posterior ligaments of the head of the fibula*. It is also known as a **compensation joint** because, during maximal forward dorsiflexion in the ankle (talocrural) joint, there is expansion of the malleolar mortise, and this results in a compensatory movement in the tibiofibular joint.

In addition to the synovial joint between the leg bones, the **interosseous membrane of leg** (**15**), as a **fibrous joint**, fixes the two bones. The fibers in the interosseous membrane run inferiorly from the tibia to the fibula and are very tense.

At the distal end of the two bones is the **tibiofibular syndesmosis** (**16**). This consists of an *anterior tibiofibular ligament*, a relatively flat ligament which runs obliquely over the anterior surfaces of the distal ends of both bones, and the *posterior tibiofibular ligament* on their posterior surfaces. The fiber direction of the posterior ligament is more horizontal. Both ligaments are only very slightly extensible, so that during dorsiflexion slight displacement of the leg bones from each other is possible.

17 Semitendinosus, gracilis, and sartorius, strongly loaded
18 Biceps femoris and iliotibial tract, strongly loaded

Lower Limb

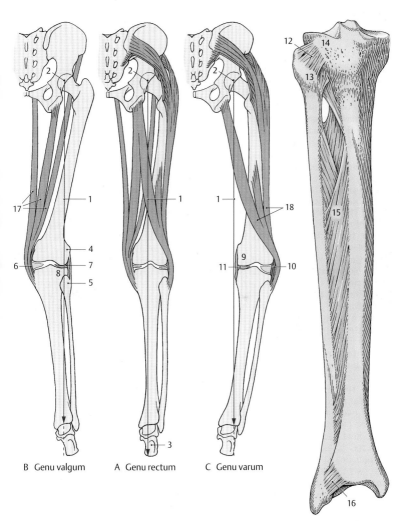

B Genu valgum   A Genu rectum   C Genu varum

A–C Positions of the lower limb and knee joint
      (according to *Lanz–Wachsmuth*)

D Connections between
    tibia and fibula

Bones of the Foot (A–G)

The skeleton of the foot may be divided into:
- The **tarsus** (ankle)
- The **metatarsus**
- The **digits** (toes)

The **tarsus** consists of seven bones, the **talus, calcaneus, navicular, cuboid** and the three **cuneiform bones**. The **metatarsus** consists of **five metatarsals**, and the **digits** are formed by the **phalanges**.

Tarsal Bones

The **talus** (A–C) transmits the weight of the entire body to the foot. We distinguish in it a **head** (**1**), a **body** (**2**), and a **neck** (**3**). The head of the talus carries the *navicular articular surface* for articulation with the navicular bone, and the neck of the talus has small vascular channels and roughened areas. On the body of the talus we distinguish the *trochlea* (**4**) and behind this a *posterior talar process* with *lateral* (**5**) and *medial* (**6**) tubercles. Immediately adjacent to the medial tubercle is the *groove for the tendon of the flexor hallucis longus* (**7**). The trochlea of the talus and its superior surface are wider in front than at the back. This is more pronounced in right tali than in left tali. On the lateral side, the superior surface blends with the *lateral malleolar facet* (**8**), which extends onto the *lateral talar process* (**9**). Medially lies the smaller *medial malleolar facet* (**10**). The three joint surfaces serve for articulation with the malleolar mortise. As an inferior continuation of the navicular articular surface, we find the *anterior facet for calcaneus* (**11**). Continuous with the anterior calcaneal facet (infrequently there is an intermediate cartilage-free zone) lies the *middle calcaneal facet* (**12**). Posterior to the latter, the *talar sulcus* (**13**) and the large *posterior calcaneal articular facet* (**14**) are found.

The talus also articulates with ligaments that have cartilage depositions (see p. 224). Variably developed articular surfaces are therefore present on its inferior surface. These are referred to as the (larger) *articular facet for the plantar calcaneonavicular ligament* and the (smaller) *articular surface for the calcaneonavicular part of the bifurcate ligament*.

Ossification: An ossification center appears in the talus in the 7th–8th intrauterine month.

■ **Variant:** In exceptional cases, the lateral tubercle of the posterior talar process forms an independent bone, the **os trigonum** or **accessory talus**.

The **calcaneus** (**D–G**) is the largest tarsal bone. Posteriorly it bears the large calcaneal tuberosity, **tuber calcanei** (**15**) which has two forward-facing processes at the point of transition onto its lower surface, the *lateral* and *medial processes of the tuber calcanei*. The Achilles tendon is inserted into the roughened area on the tuber calcanei. Anteriorly there is the *surface for articulation with the cuboid bone* (**16**). On the upper surface of the calcaneus, there are normally three articular surfaces, the *anterior* (**17**), *middle* (**18**), and *posterior* (**19**) *talar articular surfaces*. Between the latter two lies the *calcaneal sulcus* (**20**), which, together with the talar sulcus (see above), forms the **tarsal sinus**. The two anterior articular surfaces may be joined together. On the medial surface, the **talar shelf, sustentaculum tali** (**21**) projects outward. It bears the middle talar articular facet. Inferiorly lies the *groove for the tendon of flexor hallucis longus* (**22**). In most cases there is a slightly elevated bony tubercle on the lateral surface of the talus, the *peroneal trochlea* (**23**), under which runs the *groove for the tendon of peroneus longus* (**24**).

Ossification: A bony center develops in the calcaneus in the 4th–7th intrauterine month.

Clinical tip: In some cases there is an anteriorly directed bony process, the **calcaneal spur**, arising from the medial tuberal process, from which various muscles of the sole of the foot arise. A calcaneal spur may be very painful.

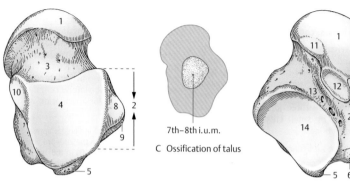

A Superior view of right talus

C Ossification of talus

7th–8th i.u.m.

B Inferior view of right talus

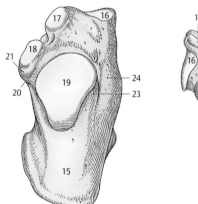

D Superior view of right calcaneus

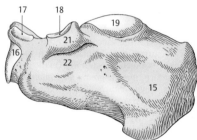

E Medial view of right calcaneus

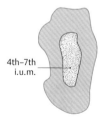

4th–7th
i.u.m.

G Ossification of calcaneus

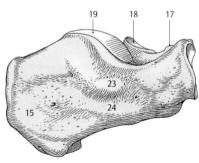

F Lateral view of right calcaneus

Bones of the Foot

Tarsal Bones, continued (A–P)

The **navicular** (**A–C**) articulates with the talus and with the three cuneiform bones. A concave articular surface faces the head of the talus. The *tuberosity of the navicular* (**1**) is directed *plantarly* and medially. Distally there are three joint surfaces separated only by small crests for the three cuneiform bones.

Ossification: An ossification center develops in the 3rd–4th year.

The **cuboid** (**D–F**) is shorter laterally than medially. Distally there are joint surfaces for the fourth and fifth metatarsal bones separated by a ridge. Medially lies the joint surface for articulation with the lateral cuneiform bone, and sometimes, behind it, we find a small area for articulation with the navicular. The *calcaneal process* (**2**), with its surface for articulation with the calcaneus, is directed posteriorly. On the inferior surface runs the *groove for tendon of peroneus longus muscle* (**3**), posterior to which is a transverse ridge, the *tuberosity of cuboid* (**4**).

Ossification: The ossification center in the cuboid develops in the 10th intrauterine month (**sign of maturity**).

The three **cuneiform bones** (**G–P**) differ from each other in size and position in the skeleton of the foot. The **medial** (**G, H**) is the largest and the **intermediate** (**J, K**) is the smallest of the cuneiform bones. The broad surface of the medial cuneiform faces the sole of the foot, while the intermediate and **lateral** (**L, M**) cuneiform have their sharp edges directed plantarly.

All three cuneiform bones have articular surfaces proximally for articulation with the navicular (**5**). Distally and directed toward the digits are articulations for the metatarsals. The medial cuneiform articulates with the first metatarsal and, to a small extent, with the second metatarsal (**6**), while the lateral cuneiform has joint surfaces for articulation with the third metatarsal, a small facet for the second metatarsal (**7**) and sometimes an equally small facet for the fourth metatarsal. The intermediate cuneiform articulates distally only with the second metatarsal. The three cuneiform bones also articulate with each other. In addition, the lateral cuneiform has a joint surface (**8**) for articulation with the cuboid.

Ossification: Ossification centers appear in the medial cuneiform (**N**) in the 2nd–3rd year, in the intermediate cuneiform (**O**) in the 3rd year, and in the lateral cuneiform (**P**) in the 1st–2nd year.

A Posterior view
of right navicular

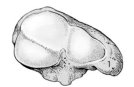

B Anterior view
of right navicular

3rd–4th years

C Ossification
of navicular

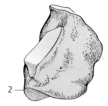

D Dorsal view
of right cuboid

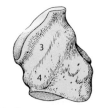

E Plantar view
of right cuboid

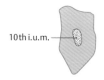

10th i.u.m.

F Ossification
of cuboid bone

G Medial view of right
medial cuneiform

J Medial view of right
intermediate cuneiform

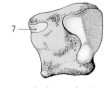

7

L Medical view of right
lateral cuneiform

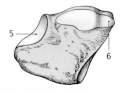

5

6

H Lateral view of right
medial cuneiform

K Lateral view of right
intermediate cuneiform

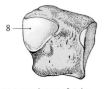

8

M Lateral view of right
lateral cuneiform

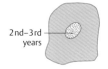

2nd–3rd
years

N Ossification of medial
cuneiform

3rd year

O Ossification of inter-
mediate cuneiform

1st–2nd
years

P Ossification of lateral
cuneiform

Bones of the Foot, continued

Metatarsals (Ossa metatarsi) (A, B)

The five **metatarsals** are long bones and are convex dorsally. All of them possess a *base* (**1**), a *shaft* (**2**), and a *head* (**3**). The **first metatarsal** is the shortest and thickest. There is a *tuberosity* at the base of the first metatarsal on its plantar surface. In the region of this tuberosity and lateral to it, the bone articulates laterally with the base of the second metatarsal and posteriorly via a curved surface with the medial cuneiform (**4**). On its anterior end the head carries, on its plantar surface, a small ridge, and on either side of it there are two small grooves. In these are regularly found two small **sesamoid bones** (**5**). The **second, third, and fourth metatarsals** are slimmer and their bases are wider dorsally than on their plantar sides. On the facing sides there are joint surfaces for articulation with each other, and posteriorly proximally for the cuneiform and the cuboid bones. The heads of these three metatarsal bones are compressed laterally so that they resemble rollers. The **fifth metatarsal** bone differs in that it has a *tuberosity* (**6**) on the lateral side of its base.

Bones of the Toes

The second–fifth digits each have a **proximal, middle** and **distal phalanx,** while the first digit has only two phalanges. Each phalanx has a *base* (**7**), a *shaft* (**8**), and a *head* (**9**). The distal phalanx (**10**) has a *distal tuberosity*. There are small grooves on the proximal and middle phalanges.

■■ **Variant:** Occasionally, in the fifth digit the middle and distal phalanges may be joined. This may already be the case in the cartilaginous stage before birth.

Sesamoid Bones

Near the metatarsophalangeal joints there may be many sesamoid bones, although they are only present regularly in the region of the head of the first metatarsal.

Ossification: The cartilaginous metatarsal anlagen develop a perichondral bony cuff in the shaft in the 2nd–3rd intrauterine month, and occasionally there is also an epiphysial ossification center. Like the metacarpals, the epiphysial bony center of the first metatarsal is in its base, in the other metatarsals it is always in the head. The epiphysial endochondral ossification centers develop in the 2nd–4th years. In some instances there may be additionally a second epiphysial anlage in the first and fifth metatarsal bones.

Epiphysial centers appear in the base of the phalanges in the 1st–5th year, while perichondral ossification in the shaft develops in the 2nd–8th intrauterine month. They fuse during puberty. The individual bony anlagen are relatively variable and their times of appearance can be different, so the figures quoted here should only be taken as a general guide.

11 Intermediate cuneiform bone
12 Lateral cuneiform bone
13 Cuboid bone
14 Navicular bone

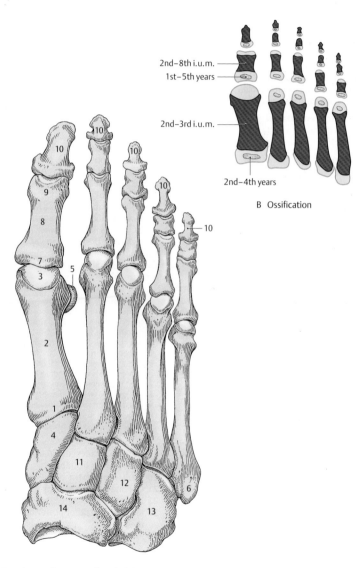

2nd–8th i.u.m.

1st–5th years

2nd–3rd i.u.m.

2nd–4th years

B Ossification

Lower Limb

A Dorsal view of metatarsals and phalanges of right foot

Lower Limb

Joints of the Foot (A–C)

The **joints of the foot** include the upper ankle joint, or **talocrural joint**, and the lower ankle joint, or **subtalar** and **talocalcaneonavicular joints**.

In addition we have **cuneonavicular, calcaneocuboid, cuneocuboid,** and **intercuneiform articulations**.

The **tarsometatarsal joints** are articulations between the tarsal and metatarsal bones.

Articular connections between the bases of the metatarsals are the **intermetatarsal joints** and those between the metatarsals and the phalanges of the foot are the **metatarsophalangeal joints**.

Also present are joints between the phalanges, or **interphalangeal articulations** of the foot.

Ankle Joint

The **articular surfaces** of the talocrural joint are formed by the *malleolar mortise* (**1**) and the superior surface of the *talar trochlea* along with its medial and lateral malleolar facets. The tibia and fibula form a mortise, or clasp, for the roll of the talus (see p. 216). The joint surface of the fibula extends further distally than the tibia.

The **joint capsule** (**2**) is attached to the margins of the cartilaginous layer of the articular surfaces. The joint cavity contains anterior and posterior synovial folds.

Ligaments of the ankle joint. The largest ligament on the medial side is the *deltoid (or medial) ligament* (**3**), which consists of tibionavicular (**4**), tibiocalcaneal (**5**), and anterior and posterior (**6**) tibiotalar parts. The tibionavicular part (**4**) extends from the tibia (**7**) to the navicular (**8**) and covers the anterior tibiotalar part. The tibiocalcaneal part (**5**) runs to the sustentaculum tali (**9**) and partly covers the tibionavicular part (**4**). Other ligaments include the *anterior talofibular ligaments* (**10**), the *posterior talofibular ligament* and the *calcaneofibular*

ligament (**11**). The anterior talofibular ligament connects the lateral malleolus to the neck of the talus. The posterior talofibular ligament runs almost horizontally from the lateral malleolar fossa to the posterior talar process. The joint capsule bulges distal and proximal to this ligament. The malleolar mortise is fixed by the *anterior* (**12**) and *posterior tibiofibular ligaments*. These bands and the calcaneofibular ligament are collectively known as the lateral collateral ligaments.

Movements. Both **plantarflexion** and **dorsiflexion** are possible. In plantarflexion, as the trochlea of the talus is narrower posteriorly, which leaves more free play in the mortise, slight side-to-side movement is possible. The ankle joint is a **hinge joint** with a **transverse axis**, *beginning just beneath the tip of the medial malleolus and running through the thickest part of the lateral malleolus*. The range of movement between maximal dorsal and plantar flexion is up to 70°.

> **Clinical tip:** Two joint lines permit amputation of the forefoot or of the forefoot and midfoot. **Chopart's joint line** (**C**, red) is incorrectly called the "transverse tarsal joint." It first runs between the talus (**13**) and calcaneus (**14**) and then between the navicular (**8**) and cuboid (**15**). The *bifurcate ligament* (Chopart ligament) (**16**, see p. 226) is a key landmark, as it must be divided in opening the Chopart joint line. **Lisfranc's joint line** (**C**, blue) lies between the tarsals and the metatarsals. It should be noted that the second metatarsal (**17**) projects proximally, so the line is not straight.

18 Plantar calcaneocuboid ligament
19 Long plantar ligament
20 Medial cuneiform
21 Intermediate cuneiform
22 Lateral cuneiform
23 Medial tubercle of posterior process of the talus
24 Plantar calcaneonavicular ligament

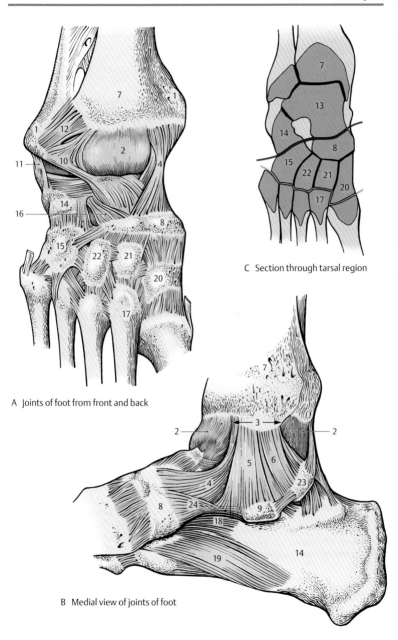

A Joints of foot from front and back

C Section through tarsal region

B Medial view of joints of foot

Joints of the Foot, continued

Subtalar and Talocalcaneonavicular Joints (A, B)

Although separate, these joints act in unison. The **subtalar joint** (**1**) forms the posterior part and the **talocalcaneonavicular joint** (**2**) forms the anterior part of the joint. The **articular surfaces of the subtalar joint** are formed by the *talus* (**3**) and the *calcaneus* (**4**). The **capsule** is loose and thin and is strengthened by the *medial* and *lateral* (**5**) *talocalcaneal ligaments*.

The **talocalcaneonavicular joint** is made up of three bones. In addition to the **joint surfaces** of the *talus*, *calcaneus*, and the *navicular* (**6**), there is an additional articular surface covered by cartilage on the *plantar calcaneonavicular ligament* (**7**). This ligament connects the calcaneus in the region of the medial articular surface with the navicular bone, and together with the latter forms the articular cavity for the head of the talus (**spring ligament**).

The **capsule** of the talocalcaneonavicular joint (anterior part) is attached immediately at the edge of the cartilage or it extends as far as the plantar calcaneonavicular ligament. The tense *bifurcate ligament* (see **8**, p. 226), which binds the calcaneus (**4**), navicular (**6**), and cuboid (**9**) together, strengthens the capsule. The *interosseous talocalcaneal ligament* (**10**), lying in the tarsal sinus, divides the subtalar from the talocalcaneonavicular joint.

In summary, the ankle joint permits **hinge movements** while the subtalar and the talocalcaneonavicular joints permit **rotation**. The ankle joint is a hinge joint, a **ginglymus**, and the others are pivot joints, **trochi**, and together they function as a **trochginglymus**. Movements of rotation are known as **pronation (eversion)** and **supination (inversion)**, corresponding to the pronating and supinating movements of the hand.

Supination is the elevation of the medial (inner) edge of the foot, and pronation is the elevation of the lateral edge of the foot with simultaneous lateral rotation. The full range of movement of pronation and supination between their extreme limits amounts to 60°.

Joints between the Other Tarsal and Metatarsal Bones (A, B)

The **calcaneocuboid joint** (**11**) is an amphiarthrosis. The joint cavity is a part of the so-called Chopart's joint line (see p. 222). The **cuneonavicular** and the **tarsometatarsal joints** as well as the **cuneocuboid joint** are also amphiarthroses. The ligaments which reinforce the joint capsules will be discussed on page 226. To these amphiarthroses belong the **intertarsal joints** and the **intermetatarsal joints,** which lie between the adjacent sides of the bases of the second–fifth metatarsal bones.

Joints of the Toes

The **metatarsophalangeal joints** and the **interphalangeal joints** of the foot may be divided into the proximal and the middle and distal joints. The proximal metatarsophalangeal joints are ball-and-socket joints, although their mobility is restricted by collateral ligaments. The middle and distal joints are pure hinge joints.

12 Dorsal calcaneocuboid ligament
13 Dorsal cuboideonavicular ligament
14 Talonavicular ligament
15 Dorsal tarsometatarsal ligaments
16 Dorsal metatarsal ligaments
17 Long plantar ligament
18 Plantar metatarsal ligaments
19 Tendon of the peroneus longus
20 Tendon of the tibialis anterior
21 Tendon of the tibialis posterior
22 Tendon of the peroneus brevis
23 Plantar calcaneocuboid ligament
24 Plantar cuboideonavicular ligament

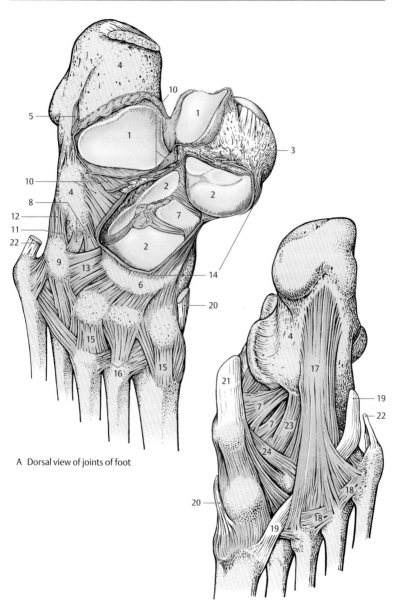

A Dorsal view of joints of foot

B Plantar view of joints of foot

Ligaments of the Joints of the Foot (A, B)

The ligaments of the tarsus are divided into several groups.

Ligaments which join the leg bones to each other and to the tarsals (red) include the *deltoid ligament* (**1**), the lateral ligament consisting of the *anterior talofibular ligament* (**2**) and the *posterior talofibular ligament* (**3**), the *calcaneofibular ligament* (**4**), the *anterior tibiofibular ligament* (**5**), and the *posterior tibiofibular ligament* (**6**).

Ligaments which join the talus to the other tarsals (green) include the *talonavicular ligament* (**7**), the *interosseous talocalcaneal ligament* (**8**), the *lateral* (**9**), and *medial* (**10**) *talocalcaneal ligaments* and the *posterior talocalcaneal ligament* (**11**).

The remaining dorsal tarsal ligaments (yellow) include the *bifurcate ligament* (**12**) with its calcaneonavicular and calcaneocuboid fibers, the *dorsal intercuneiform ligaments* (**13**), the *dorsal cuneocuboid ligament* (**14**), the *dorsal cuboideonavicular ligament* (**15**), the *dorsal cuneonavicular ligaments* (**16**), and the *dorsal calcaneocuboid ligaments* (**17**).

The plantar tarsal ligaments (blue) **connect the individual tarsals on their plantar surfaces.** They include the *long plantar ligament* (**18**) extending from the calcaneal tuberosity to the cuboid and metatarsal bones. The *plantar calcaneonavicular or spring ligament* (**19**, see p. 228) is important for the stability of the foot. The medial part of the long plantar ligament, the *plantar calcaneocuboid ligament* (**20**), is particularly important. In addition, there are the *plantar cuneonavicular ligaments*, the *plantar cuboideonavicular ligament*, the *plantar intercuneiform ligaments*, the *plantar cuneocuboid ligament*, and the interosseous ligaments, namely, the *interosseous cuneocuboid ligament* and the *interosseous intercuneiform ligaments*.

Ligaments between tarsus and metatarsus (violet). These may be divided into the *dorsal* and *plantar tarsometatarsal ligaments* and the *interosseous cuneometatarsal ligaments*.

Ligaments between the metatarsals (pink). They include the *dorsal* and *plantar interosseous metatarsal ligaments*, all of which lie near the bases of the metatarsals.

Morphology and Function of the Skeleton of the Foot (C, D)

Examination of the skeleton of the foot reveals that in the posterior segment the bones lie over one another, whereas in the middle and anterior regions they lie side by side. By this means the foot becomes arched with the formation of **sagittal** (longitudinal) and **transverse arches**.

It is incorrect to describe the foot as having a longitudinal or transverse "vault." All types of vault (barrel, cloister, cross) have a **keystone-type** construction that makes them *inherently* stable. An arch does not possess this property.

Starting from the talus, a medial series of bones (light gray) continues straight on, while a lateral series (dark gray) fans out from the calcaneus toward the front. The **medial series** consists of the *talus* (**21**), the *navicular* (**22**), and the *cuneiform bones* (**23**), and the *three medial metatarsals* with their *associated phalanges*. The **lateral series** contains the *calcaneus* (**24**), the *cuboid* (**25**), and the *two lateral metatarsals* with their *corresponding phalanges*.

This results in the foot being wide in front and narrower at the back; it is also higher behind than in front. Finally, the foot also has an arch which faces medially and is curved both longitudinally and transversely. The longitudinal curvature is more marked on the medial than the lateral edge of the foot. The transverse arch is well developed only in the midfoot and forefoot.

Clinical tip: Clinically the talus and calcaneus are considered the back foot, while the other tarsals are regarded as the middle foot and the metatarsal and phalangeal bones as the forefoot.

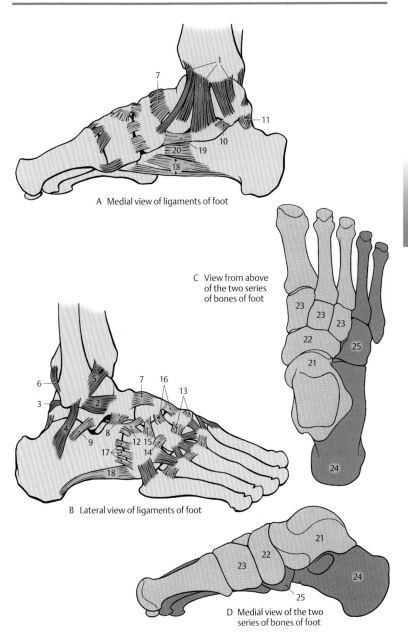

A Medial view of ligaments of foot

C View from above of the two series of bones of foot

B Lateral view of ligaments of foot

D Medial view of the two series of bones of foot

The Plantar Arch and Its Function (A–C)

The plantar arch is normally in a position of supporting the weight of the body. The **bony points of support of the arch** on a level ground surface are the *calcaneal tuberosity* (**1**), the *head of the first metatarsal* (**2**), and the *head of the fifth metatarsal* (**3**). Thus, the supporting surface is in the form of a triangle (**A**, dotted red). If a **footprint** (**B**) is examined, a somewhat larger supporting surface is found, which is produced by the soft tissues. The **line of transmission** of the weight of the body runs from the *tibia* (**4**) to the *calcaneus* (**5**) and to the *midfoot* and *forefoot* (**6**). The transmission of pressure to the arch in both directions tends to flatten its curvature, and this is opposed by the ligaments and the plantar muscles.

Ligaments. *Ligaments cannot fatigue and have a greater resistance to stress than muscles.* Their resistance does not vary, but if they are overstretched they are unable to return to their previous shape.

The ligaments may be divided into the **plantar aponeurosis** (**7**), the **long plantar ligament** (**8**, **9**), the **plantar calcaneonavicular ligament** (**10**), and the **short plantar ligaments**.

The **superficial plantar aponeurosis** (**7**) joins the calcaneal tuberosity to the plantar surface of the digits. It acts especially in the standing (static) position. In the metatarsal part of the foot, tension in the transverse fibers of the aponeurosis supports both the longitudinal and the transverse arches.

The **long plantar ligament** (**8**, **9**) braces the lateral series of the tarsals. It arises from the plantar side of the calcaneus, becomes wider distally and extends as a *long, superficial fibrous layer* (**8**) inferior to the tendon of the peroneus longus to the bases of the metatarsals. Short fibers reach the tuberosity of the cuboid as the *plantar calcaneocuboid ligament* (**9**).

The **plantar calcaneonavicular ligament** (**10**) and the **short plantar ligaments** together form the deepest layer of ligaments. *It increases the size of the socket for the head of the talus.* On the inner surface it is covered by fibrocartilage, which sometimes may be calcified. This ligament may be up to 5 mm thick.

Plantar muscles. They also resist the effect of the weight of the body in spreading the foot, and they surround the arches like a clamp. *They are subject to fatigue and are weaker than the ligaments.* However, muscle tension can be regulated according to stress, and recent investigations have shown that it is brought into play under conditions of great stress. The action of the medial abductors is superior to that of the lateral abductors.

The plantar muscles are divided into the **intrinsic muscles of the foot** (**11**), which stretch between the tarsals and the metatarsals and phalanges, and the **tendons of the extrinsic muscles of the foot**, which descend from the leg and are inserted on the various tarsals, metatarsals, and phalanges. The intrinsic muscles of the foot permit movements of the digits with respect to the metatarsals and tarsals. In the standing or static position, the digits and metatarsals are pressed onto the ground, and the intrinsic muscles of the foot function as tensor muscles of the plantar arch, as they counteract the sagging tendency of the metatarsals.

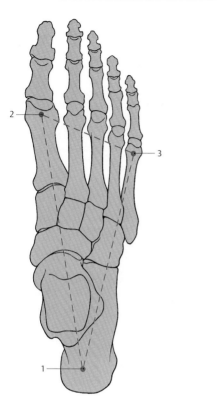

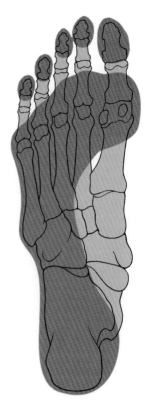

A Skeleton of foot, showing
   weight-bearing points;
   view from above

B Footprint of right foot with outline
   of the bony skeleton; view from below

C Medial view of plantar
   arch of foot

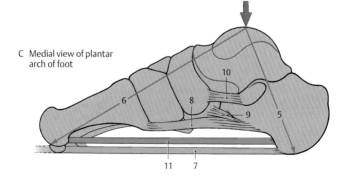

Foot Types (A–J)

The normal posture of the foot in the living may be determined by taking a footprint. In the **healthy foot**, **pes rectus** (A) the *print should show impressions of five digits, anterior and posterior parts of the sole, and a strip joining them.* The *main load* on the healthy foot (E) *lies medially on the calcaneus* (1) *and the head of the first metatarsal* (2).

> **Clinical tip:** If the print shows a *wide, flattened impression* (B) of the entire sole, then the subject has a **flatfoot**, **pes planus**. Flat feet are caused by inadequacy of the intrinsic plantar muscles, which leads to an overextension of the ligaments and thus to a collapse of the plantar arch. When this occurs, there is a pronation of the talus, and this may then slide medially over the calcaneus (F). The end result is a remodeling of all the involved tarsals (calcaneus, talus, navicular, and cuboid).
>
> During development of flatfoot, severe pain in the foot and leg occurs, due to overstretching of the long muscles of the sole.
>
> A *footprint in two parts* (C) represents a **high longitudinal arch, pes cavus** (C). Here the calcaneus is supinated, while the other skeletal parts of the foot are pronated.
>
> A **pes planovalgus** has a *footprint that bulges medially* (D). It represents the combination of a flatfoot and **pes valgus** (H); the calcaneus is pronated.

In the **healthy foot** (G), *the weight-bearing line of the lower limb* (see also p. 214) *runs through the middle of the calcaneus to its undersurface.*

> **Clinical tip:** In **pes valgus** (H), *the vertical axis through the talus and calcaneus is sharply angulated with respect to the longitudinal axis of the lower limb, thus forming an obtuse angle, open externally.* The foot is everted (pronated). This posture of the foot may be caused by paralysis of the muscles of supination—triceps surae, tibialis posterior, flexor hallucis longus, flexor digitorum longus, and tibialis anterior.

> **Clubfoot, pes varus** (J), shows the exact opposite. *Here the long axis through the talus and calcaneus and the axis of the lower limb form an angle which is open medially.* This may be caused, for instance, by paralysis of the pronators, the peroneal muscles, extensor digitorum longus, and the extensor hallucis longus, resulting in supination.

> In **pes rectus** (G) the lateral malleolus is lower than the medial malleolus. In **pes valgus** (H) this difference in height is increased, while in **clubfoot** (J) the difference is absent or may even be reversed.

> **Other abnormal postures of the foot** include **pes equinus** and **pes calcaneus**. Pes equinus is the result of a paralysis of the extensors, and pes calcaneus is caused by paralysis of the flexor muscles.

> A combination of pes varus and pes equinus is represented by a **pes equinovarus**, which occurs after paralysis of the peroneal nerve and injury to the tibialis anterior.

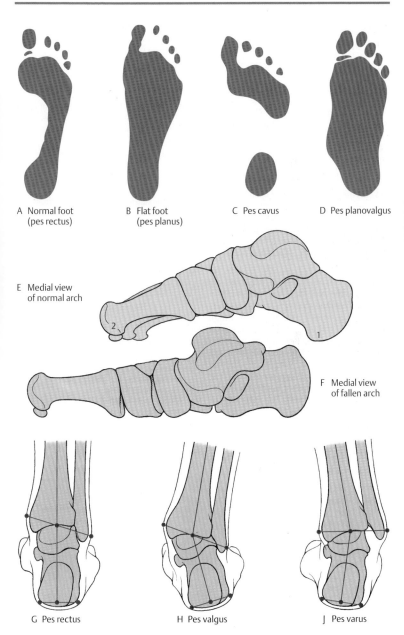

A Normal foot (pes rectus)

B Flat foot (pes planus)

C Pes cavus

D Pes planovalgus

E Medial view of normal arch

F Medial view of fallen arch

G Pes rectus

H Pes valgus

J Pes varus

Muscles, Fascias, and Special Features

Muscles of the Hip and Thigh

Classification of the Muscles (A–C)

The hip muscles may be classified in several ways. Like the muscles of the shoulder girdle, they may be subdivided according to their locations or innervation from the ventral and dorsal divisions of the plexus layers (see vol. 3). Further, they may also be grouped according to their development on the basis of their points of insertion. In this classification we distinguish between dorsal muscles with an anterior and posterior group, and ventral hip muscles. It is also possible to classify the muscles of the hip joint according to their function.

Thigh muscles may also be classified according to their location, function or innervation. According to their location, we distinguish anterior and posterior thigh muscles and adductors. With the exception of the gracilis, all the adductors act solely on the hip joint and therefore insert on the femur. The true thigh muscles act primarily on the knee joint and are inserted into the leg. Here the extensors must be distinguished from the flexors. The extensors of the knee joint lie on the anterior surface of the femur and the flexors are on its posterior surface. Ontogenetically the sartorius is considered an extensor, since it has only been displaced secondarily and now flexes at the knee joint.

Discussion of the hip muscles will take into consideration their sites of insertion as well as their functions. The thigh muscles will be discussed first in terms of their location and then according to their function.

Dorsal Hip Muscles (see p. 234)

The anterior group, which is inserted in the region of the lesser trochanter, includes

Psoas major and iliacus, together forming the iliopsoas (**1**)
Psoas minor

The posterior group, which is inserted in the region of the greater trochanter region and its continuation, includes

Piriformis (**2**)
Gluteus minimus (**3**)
Gluteus medius (**4**)
Tensor fasciae latae (**5**)
Gluteus maximus (**6**)

Ventral Hip Muscles and Adductors of the Thigh (see p. 238)

Obturator internus (**7**)
Gemelli (**8**)
Quadratus femoris (**9**)
Obturator externus (**10**)
Pectineus (**11**)
Gracilis (**12**)
Adductor brevis (**13**)
Adductor longus (**14**)
Adductor magnus (**15**)
Adductor minimus (**16**)

Anterior Thigh Muscles (see p. 248)

Quadriceps femoris, consisting of
– Rectus femoris (**17**)
– Vastus intermedius (**18**)
– Vastus medialis (**19**)
– Vastus lateralis (**20**)
Sartorius (**21**)

Posterior Thigh Muscles (see p. 250)

Biceps femoris (**22**)
Semitendinosus (**23**)
Semimembranosus (**24**)
Popliteus (see p. 264)

25 Fascia lata
26 Anteromedial intermuscular septum
27 Lateral femoral intermuscular septum
28 Neck of the femur
29 Femoral artery
30 Femoral vein
31 Saphenous nerve
32 Great saphenous vein
33 Sciatic nerve
34 Deep femoral artery
35 Femoral nerve

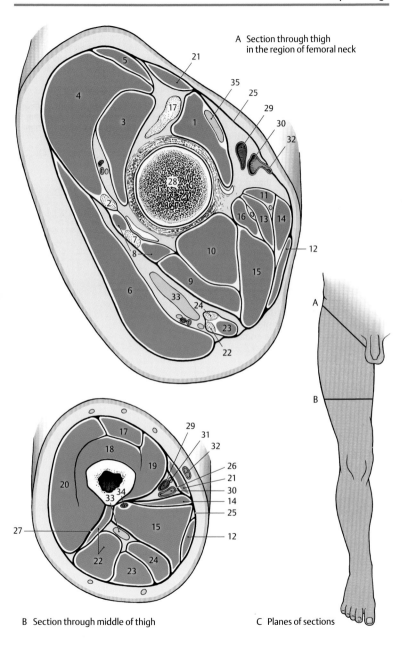

A Section through thigh
in the region of femoral neck

A

B

B Section through middle of thigh

C Planes of sections

Dorsal Hip Muscles

Anterior Group Inserted in the Region of the Lesser Trochanter (A, B)

The **psoas major** (**1**) is divided into a superficial and a deep part. The **superficial part** *arises from the lateral surfaces of the twelfth thoracic vertebra and first to fourth lumbar vertebrae* (**2**) *as well as from their intervertebral disks.* The **deep part** *arises from the costal processes of the first to fifth lumbar vertebrae* (**3**).

The psoas major joins the iliacus (**4**) and, surrounded by the iliac fascia, proceeds as the **iliopsoas** (**5**) across the iliopubic eminence through the muscular lacuna to be inserted on the *lesser trochanter* (**6**). In the region of the iliopubic eminence, the iliopectineal bursa lies between the muscle and the bone and extends as far as the anterior surface of the capsule of the hip joint with which it communicates. Between the lesser trochanter and the attachment of the iliopsoas lies the iliac subtendinous bursa. The lumbar plexus lies between the two layers of the psoas major (see also p. 404).

The **iliacus** (**4**) *arises in the iliac fossa* (**7**) *and also from the region of the anterior inferior iliac spine.* It joins the psoas major (**1**) to form the **iliopsoas** (**5**). *The fibers of the iliacus are regularly inserted in front of the fibers of the psoas major and extend distally over the lesser trochanter.*
The iliopsoas is the most important muscle for lifting (flexing) the leg forward and makes walking possible. It also serves to bend the trunk forward and to lift the trunk when lying down.
The iliopsoas is also a lateral rotator of the hip joint. In contrast to the iliacus, the psoas major acts on a number of joints, since it crosses vertebral and sacroiliac joints. It is therefore also involved in lateral bending.
Nerve supply: lumbar plexus and femoral nerve. Psoas major (L1–L3), iliac muscle (L2–L4).

▪▪ **Variants: The psoas minor** is present in less than 50% of subjects. *It arises from the twelfth thoracic and first lumbar vertebra and projects into the iliac fascia.* It is either inserted on the iliopubic eminence or radiates into the iliopectineal arch.
Nerve supply: lumbar plexus (L1–L3).

The psoas major may also arise from the head of the 12th rib and the iliacus may arise from the capsule of the hip joint and from the sacrum.

Clinical tip: Wandering (hypostatic) abscesses, see p. 94.

8   Pectineus
9   Adductor minimus
10 Adductor longus
11 Iliopectineal arch
12 Inguinal ligament

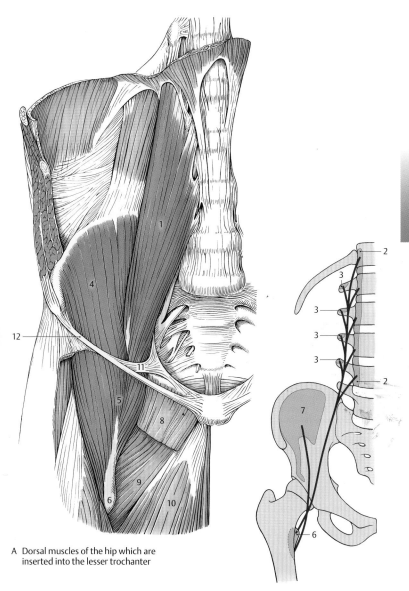

A Dorsal muscles of the hip which are
  inserted into the lesser trochanter

B Diagram of origin, course,
  and insertion of muscles

Dorsal Hip Muscles, continued

Posterior Group Inserted in the Region of the Greater Trochanter (A–D)

The **tensor fasciae latae** (**1**) *arises in the region of the anterior superior iliac spine* (**2**) *and extends distal to the greater trochanter into the iliotibial tract* (**3**), *which is inserted on the lateral tibial condyle.* It presses the head of the femur into the acetabulum. It is also a flexor, medial rotator and abductor, and assists the anterior bundles of the gluteus medius and minimus.
Nerve supply: superior gluteal nerve (L4–L5).

The powerful **gluteus maximus** (**4**) has a **superficial** and a **deep origin**. The **superficial fibers** *arise from the iliac crest* (**5**), *the posterior superior iliac spine* (**6**), *the thoracolumbar fascia, the sacrum* (**7**), *and the coccyx* (**8**). The **deep fibers** *arise from the ala of the ilium* (**9**) behind the posterior gluteal line, *from the sacrotuberal ligament* (**10**) *and the fascia of the gluteus medius (Aponeurosis glutealis).* The **proximal part** *radiates into the iliotibial tract* (**3**) and the **distal part** *inserts into the gluteal tuberosity* (**11**). Between the latter and the greater trochanter lies the large trochanteric bursa of gluteus maximus (**12**). Its relationship to the ischial tuberosity is dependent on the posture of the body. In the upright posture the muscle covers the ischial tuberosity but leaves it free in the seated position.

It is primarily an extensor and lateral rotator at the hip joint and represents a muscular defense against excessive forward tilting of the pelvis. It comes into action when climbing stairs and when changing from the sitting to the upright posture. With its different sites of insertion it is able to act as an abductor as well as an abductor. That part which tenses the fascia lata abducts, while the part inserted on the gluteal tuberosity adducts. Both glutei maximi may assist in contraction of the external sphincter ani.
Nerve supply: inferior gluteal nerve (L5–S2).

The **gluteus medius** (**13**) *arises from the gluteal surface of the ala of the ilium* (**14**), between the anterior and posterior gluteal lines, *from the iliac crest* (**15**) *and its fascia (Aponeurosis glutealis). It is inserted on the greater trochanter* (**16**) *like a cap.* Between the tendon of attachment and the greater trochanter lies the trochanteric bursa of the gluteus medius. The anterior fibers of the gluteus medius act as a medial rotator and flexor, and the posterior part as a lateral rotator and extensor of the hip, while the entire muscle can function as an abductor (for instance in dancing).
Nerve supply: superior gluteal nerve (L4–L5).

The **gluteus minimus** (**17**) *arises from the gluteal area on the ala of the ilium* (**18**) between the anterior and inferior gluteal lines *and is inserted into the greater trochanter* (**19**). There is its trochanteric bursa at its insertion. It corresponds in function to the gluteus medius, although it is a weaker abductor.
Nerve supply: superior gluteal nerve (L4–S1).

The **piriformis** (**20**) *originates as several slips from the pelvic surface of the sacrum,* lateral to the pelvic sacral foramina (**21**), *and from the margin of the greater sciatic notch.* It passes through the greater sciatic foramen *and is inserted on the anteromedial aspect of the tip of the greater trochanter* (**22**). In the upright posture it functions as a lateral rotator and abductor, and it also plays a part in producing extension of the thigh.
Nerve supply: sacral plexus (L5–2).

■■ **Variants:** The muscle may be divided into several parts by the sciatic nerve or other branches of the sacral plexus. Sometimes it may be partly or completely absent.

23 Obturator internus
24 Quadratus femoris

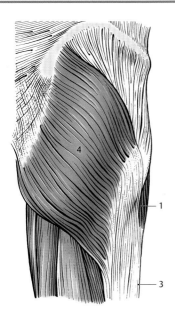

A Posterior group of hip muscles: tensor of fascia lata and gluteus maximus

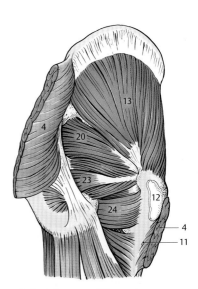

B Posterior group of hip muscles: piriformis and gluteus medius

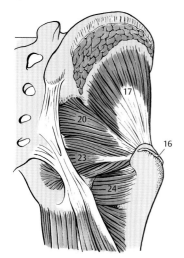

C Posterior group of hip muscles: piriformis and gluteus minimus

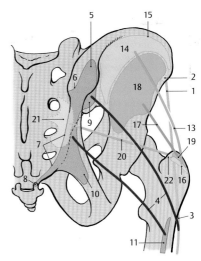

D Diagram of origin, course, and insertion of muscles

Ventral Hip Muscles (A–D)

The ventral muscles, which are innervated by the ventral branches of the nerve plexus layer, function as lateral rotators. They are important in the control of the body's balance. Basically, the lateral rotators are stronger than the medial rotators, and therefore, in the normal position of the limb, the apex of the foot points slightly outward to achieve better support for the body.

The **obturator internus** (**1**) *arises from the inner surface of the hip bone around the obturator foramen and from the obturator membrane*. It passes through the lesser sciatic foramen, almost filling it, and *is inserted into the trochanteric fossa* (**2**). The sciatic bursa of the obturator internus is found near the lesser sciatic notch. The bone acts as a fulcrum for this muscle. With the gluteus maximus and quadratus femoris it forms the strongest lateral rotator of the hip joint. In the sitting position, with the limb flexed in front, it acts as an abductor.

The two **gemelli** represent, as it were, marginal heads of the obturator internus. According to *Lanz* all three muscles together may be termed the **triceps coxae**. The **superior gemellus** (**3**) *arises from the ischial spine* (**4**), and the **inferior gemellus** (**5**) *from the ischial tuberosity* (**6**). *Both reach the trochanteric fossa* (**2**). Their function is to assist the obturator internus.
Nerve supply: inferior gluteal nerve, sacral plexus (L5–S2).

Variants: It is quite common for one or the other gemellus. and sometimes both, to be absent. Occasionally the obturator internus receives extra bundles of muscle fibers arising from nearby ligaments.

The **quadratus femoris** (**7**) *arises from the ischial tuberosity* (**6**) and runs as a four-sided flattened muscle *to the intertrochanteric crest* (**8**). It acts as a strong lateral rotator and adductor of the thigh.
Nerve supply: inferior gluteal nerve, sacral plexus (L5–S2).

Variants: It may be absent or it may fuse with the adductor magnus.

The **obturator externus** (**9**) *arises from the external surface of the medial bony margin of the obturator foramen and the obturator membrane. It extends to the trochanteric fossa* (**2**) *and* (rarely) *to the capsule of the hip joint.*
This muscle lies deep and it only becomes visible when the adjacent muscles have been removed. At its origin it is covered by the adductors and in the thigh by the quadratus femoris. It is a lateral rotator and a weak adductor.
Nerve supply: obturator nerve (L1–L4).

10 Piriformis
11 Sacrum

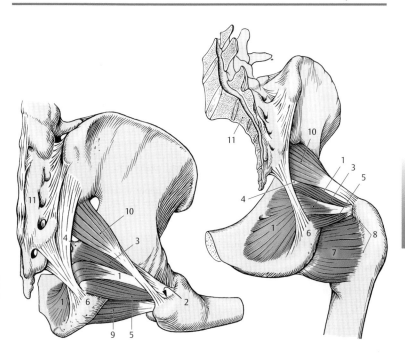

A Dorsal view of ventral muscles
   of hip with thigh flexed

B Dorsal view of ventral muscles
   of hip with thigh extended

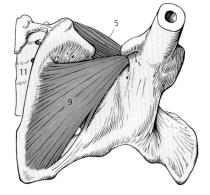

C Distal view of obturator
   externus muscle

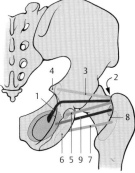

D Diagram of origin, course,
   and insertion of muscles

Adductors of the Thigh (A–D)

The **functional** adductors of the thigh include
- The obturator externus (see p. 238)
- The gracilis
- The pectineus
- The adductor brevis
- The adductor longus (see p. 242)
- The adductor magnus (see p. 242)
- The adductor minimus (see p. 242)

All the adductors are innervated by the obturator nerve, but some receive additional fibers from the femoral nerve (pectineus) and tibial nerve (adductor magnus).

The **gracilis** (**1**) *arises near the symphysis from the inferior ramus of the pubis* (**2**), and, as the only muscle of the adductor group to act on two joints, it *extends as far as the medial surface of the tibia* (**3**), onto which it is inserted together with the semitendinosus and sartorius *as the pes anserinus superficialis* (**4**). It is the most medial muscle directly beneath the surface, and when the thigh is abducted, its origin can clearly be seen arching beneath the skin.

When the knee is extended, it acts as an adductor of the thigh and a flexor of the hip joint. It also flexes at the knee joint. In the region of the pes anserinus, between the three tendons of insertion of the muscles mentioned and the tibia, there is always a bursa, the anserine bursa.
Nerve supply: anterior branch of the obturator nerve (L2–L4).

The **pectineus** (**5**) *arises from the iliopubic eminence, along the pecten of the pubis* (**6**), as far as the pubic tubercle (**7**). It extends obliquely distalward and has an elongated rectangular shape. The proximal fibers run immediately behind the lesser trochanter. *It is inserted into the pectineal line* (**8**) *and into the proximal part of the linea aspera* (**9**). The pectineus and iliopsoas (see p. 234) together form the floor of the iliopectineal fossa. The pectineus flexes at the hip joint (anteversion), adducts the thigh

and according to electromyographic investigations acts as a weak medial rotator.
Nerve supply: femoral nerve (L2–L3) and the anterior branch of the obturator nerve (L2–L4).

The **adductor brevis** (**10**) *arises from the inferior ramus of the pubis* (**11**) near the symphysis and *reaches the upper third of the medial lip of the linea aspera* (**9**). It lies very close to the adductor longus. In addition to its function as an adductor, it also acts as a lateral rotator and weak flexor at the hip joint.
Nerve supply: anterior branch of the obturator nerve (L2–L4).

12 Adductor longus
13 Adductor magnus
14 Adductor minimus
15 Obturator externus
16 Quadratus femoris
17 Semitendinosus
18 Sartorius
19 Iliopsoas

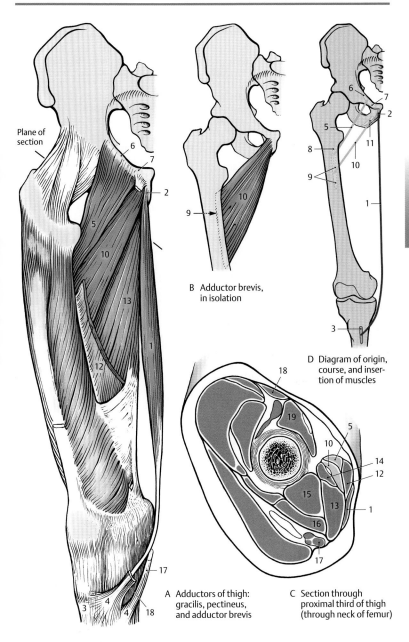

Plane of section

B Adductor brevis, in isolation

D Diagram of origin, course, and insertion of muscles

A Adductors of thigh: gracilis, pectineus, and adductor brevis

C Section through proximal third of thigh (through neck of femur)

Adductors of the Thigh, continued (A–D)

The **adductor longus** (**1**) *arises from the superior ramus of the pubis* (**2**) *and is inserted into the middle third of the medial lip of the linea aspera* (**3**). The adductor longus lies ventrally on the adductor magnus (**4**). Proximally and close to the femur, the adductor brevis (**5**) is interposed between them. The fibers of the adductor longus extend distally into the adductor canal (see below). It is primarily an adductor and a lateral rotator, but may also produce some degree of flexion (anteversion).
Nerve supply: anterior branch of the obturator nerve (L2–L4).

The **adductor magnus** (**4**) *arises from the anterior surface of the inferior ramus of the pubis* (**6**) *and the inferior ramus of the ischium* (**7**) *as far as the ischial tuberosity* (**8**). The large muscle belly passes downward on the medial side of the thigh and divides into **two parts**. **One part** (**9**) *is attached directly by its muscle fibers to the medial lip of the linea aspera* (**10**) and **the other** (**11**) *is attached by a tendon to the adductor tubercle* (**12**) *of the medial epicondyle.* The tendinous part forms an intermuscular septum and on the medial side it separates the flexors from the extensors.

Between these insertions of the adductor magnus, there is a slit-like opening, the **adductor hiatus** (**13**). The tendinous portion may be palpated through the skin behind the vastus medialis and in front of the medial dimple of the knee.

The adductor magnus is a powerful adductor, which is particularly active when crossing the legs. The part attached to the linea aspera acts as a lateral rotator. Only the part which reaches the medial epicondyle acts as a medial rotator of the outwardly rotated and flexed leg, as well as an extensor of the hip joint.

The **adductor minimus** (**14**) is an incompletely separated division of the adductor magnus. *Its fibers arise from the inferior ramus of the pubis* (**6**) *as the most anterior part of the adductor magnus and run to the medial lip of the linea aspera* (**10**), crossing over the upper part of the fibers of the true adductor magnus. It adducts and laterally rotates the femur.

Nerve supply: is common to both muscles. The obturator nerve supplies the part that is attached to the linea aspera, and the tibial nerve supplies the part inserted on the adductor tubercle (L3–L5).

Aponeurotic tendon fibers split off from the muscular part (**9**) of the adductor magnus (**4**) and pass over onto the tendinous surface of the vastus medialis (**15**; see p. 248). This is known as the **anteromedial intermuscular septum = subsatorial fascia = vasto-adductor membrane** (**16**). Some fibers of the adductor longus (**1**) may radiate into this membrane. *Between the vastoadductor membrane and the adductor magnus, adductor longus and vastus medialis, there is a tunnel*, the **adductor canal**, which opens through the **adductor hiatus** (see above) into the popliteal fossa.

17 Gracilis
18 Sartorius
19 Femur

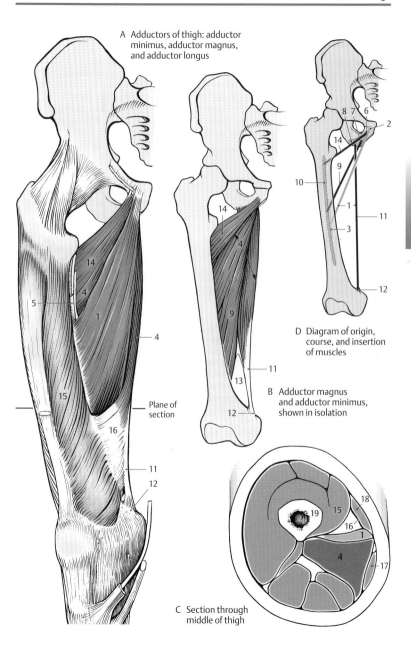

A Adductors of thigh: adductor minimus, adductor magnus, and adductor longus

D Diagram of origin, course, and insertion of muscles

B Adductor magnus and adductor minimus, shown in isolation

Plane of section

C Section through middle of thigh

Lower Limb *(sidebar)*

Function of the Hip Muscles and Adductors of Thigh (A, B)

As some hip muscles have extensive areas of origin and insertion, the various parts of the muscle may produce very different movements. It must also be noted that some of the muscles span not only the hip joint but also vertebral joints and the knee joint

Further influence on the vertebral joints by
– Psoas major

Further influence on the knee joint by
– Gracilis
– Tensor fasciae latae
– Sartorius
– Rectus femoris
– Semimembranosus
– Semitendinosus and
– Long head of biceps femoris

As such, muscles of the thigh also act upon the hip joint, in addition to the muscles of the hip.

We distinguish **lateral** and **medial rotation** movements which occur around the **longitudinal axis of the limb**. With the hip extended, medial rotation is more extensive than lateral rotation. With the hip flexed, the restrictive ligaments are tensed, so that the extent of lateral rotation is then greater than that of medial rotation.

The movements around the **transverse axis** are **extension** (dorsiflexion, retroversion) and **flexion** (anteflexion, anteversion).

Abduction and **adduction** occur about a **sagittal axis**.

Lateral rotation (A) is produced by
– Gluteus maximus (red, inferior gluteal nerve)
– Quadratus femoris (blue, inferior gluteal nerve, sacral plexus)
– Obturator internus (yellow, inferior gluteal nerve, sacral plexus)
– Gluteus medius and gluteus minimus with their dorsal fibers (orange, superior gluteal nerve)
– Iliopsoas (green, lumbar plexus, femoral nerve)
– All the functional adductors except the pectineus muscle and the gracilis (violet, obturator nerve, tibial nerve, p. 242)
– Piriformis (gray, sacral plexus)
– Sartorius (see p. 248; not shown)

Medial rotation (B) is produced by
– Anterior fibers of the gluteus medius and the gluteus minimus (red, superior gluteal nerve)
– Tensor fasciae latae (blue, superior gluteal nerve)
– The part of the adductor magnus inserted into the adductor tubercle (yellow, tibial nerve)

In the same way, the pectineus muscle (not shown) acts as a medial rotator with the leg abducted.

The color of the arrows represents the order of importance of the muscles in each movement:

red
blue
yellow
orange
green
brown
violet
gray

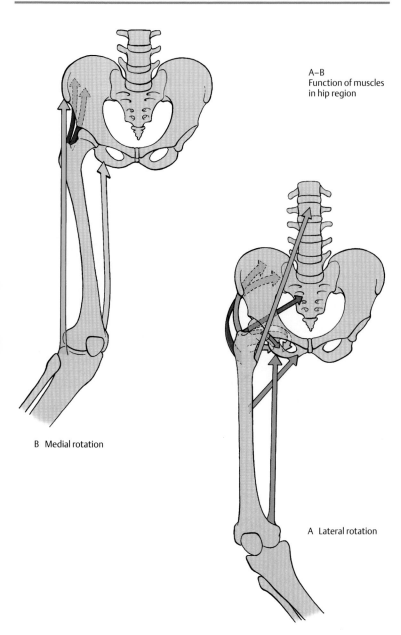

A–B
Function of muscles
in hip region

B Medial rotation

A Lateral rotation

Lower Limb

Function of the Hip Muscles and Adductors of Thigh, continued (A–D)

The **extensors** (A) of the hip joint are:
- Gluteus maximus (red, inferior gluteal nerve)
- Dorsal fibers of the gluteus medius and gluteus minimus (blue, superior gluteal nerve
- Adductor magnus (green, obturator nerve and tibial nerve, p. 242)
- Piriformis (brown, sacral plexus)

The following thigh muscles (hamstring muscles) also function as extensors of the hip:
- Semimembranosus (yellow, tibial nerve, p. 250)
- Semitendinosus (orange, tibial and common peroneal nerve, p. 250)
- Long head of the biceps femoris (violet, tibial nerve, p. 250)

Clinical tip: If the most important extensor, the gluteus maximus, is put out of action, an active standing up from a sitting position is not possible, although standing and walking on a level plane can be done.

The **flexors** (B) of the hip joint are
- Iliopsoas (red, lumbar plexus, femoral nerve)
- Tensor fasciae latae (orange, superior gluteal nerve)
- Pectineus (green, femoral and obturator nerve)
- Adductor longus (brown, obturator nerve)
- Adductor brevis (brown, obturator nerve)
- Gracilis (brown, obturator nerve)

The following thigh muscles are flexors at the hip joint:
- Rectus femoris (blue, femoral nerve, p. 248)
- Sartorius (yellow, femoral nerve, p. 248)

Clinical tip: If the iliopsoas is put out of action, flexion is no longer possible across the horizontal plane when in the sitting position.

Abduction (C) is carried out by
- Gluteus medius (red, superior gluteal nerve)
- Tensor fasciae latae (blue, superior gluteal nerve)
- Gluteus maximus with its attachment at the fascia lata (yellow, inferior gluteal nerve)
- Gluteus minimus (orange, superior gluteal nerve)
- Piriformis (green, sacral plexus)
- Obturator internus (brown, inferior gluteal nerve)

Clinical tip: If the abductors are paralyzed, the pelvis cannot be fixed on the unaffected side when standing on the affected leg. The pelvis falls on the healthy side (unilateral positive **Trendelenburg test**). When abductor function is impaired on both sides (as in congenital dislocation of the hip), the patient develops a waddling gait (bilateral positive **Trendelenburg sign**).

Adduction (D) is produced by
- Adductor magnus with the adductor minimus (red, obturator and tibial nerve)
- Adductor longus (blue, obturator nerve)
- Adductor brevis (blue, obturator nerve)
- Gluteus maximus with its attachment at the gluteal tuberosity (yellow, inferior gluteal nerve)
- Gracilis (orange, obturator nerve)
- Pectineus (brown, obturator nerve)
- Quadratus femoris (violet, inferior gluteal nerve and sacral plexus)
- Obturator externus (not illustrated)

Of the thigh muscles, especially involved is the
- Semitendinosus (green, tibial nerve)

The color of the arrows in the following series indicates the importance of the muscles in the individual movements:

red
blue
yellow
orange
green
brown
violet

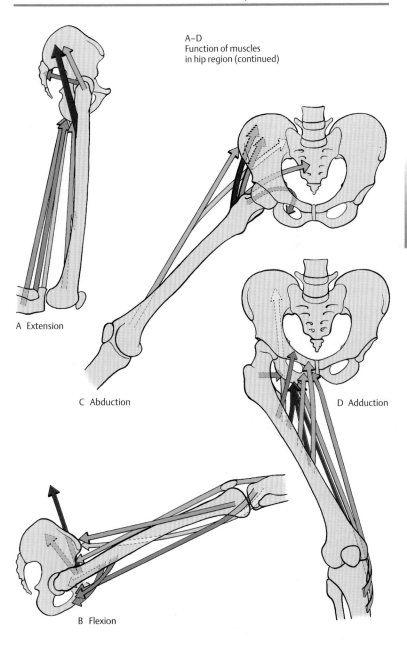

A–D
Function of muscles
in hip region (continued)

A Extension

C Abduction

D Adduction

B Flexion

Anterior Thigh Muscles (A–D)

The **quadriceps femoris** consists of **four parts**, of which the straight part, the rectus femoris, acting on two joints, runs in a channel formed by the other three single joint muscles.

The straight head of the **rectus femoris muscle** (**1**) arises from the *anterior inferior iliac spine* (**2**), and the reflected head from the *upper margin of the socket of the hip joint in the supra-acetabular groove.*

The **vastus intermedius** (**3**) *arises from the anterior and lateral surface of the femur* (**4**). It is easily distinguished from the vastus lateralis but is more difficult to separate from the vastus medialis. It covers the *articular muscle of the knee*, which arises distal to it and radiates into the capsule of the knee joint.

The **vastus medialis** (**5**) *arises from the medial lip of the linea aspera* (**6**).

The **vastus lateralis** (**7**) *arises* (**8**) *from the lateral surface of the greater trochanter, the intertrochanteric line, the gluteal tuberosity, and the lateral lip of the linea aspera.*

The four muscles join to form a *common tendon which is inserted into the patella* (**9**). Distal to the patella, the tendon is continued as the *patellar ligament* (**10**) and is *inserted into the tibial tuberosity* (**11**). Superficial fibers run across the patella, while the deep tendon fibers insert into its upper and lateral margins.

Mainly fibers of the vastus medialis and few fibers of the rectus femoris form the *medial patellar retinaculum*, and fibers of the vastus lateralis and rectus femoris form the *lateral patellar retinaculum*. Fibers from the iliotibial tract also radiate into the lateral patellar retinaculum. The retinacula extend distally around the patella to the tibial condyles.

The quadriceps femoris is *the* extensor at the knee joint. The rectus femoris also flexes at the hip joint. The articular muscle of the knee protects the capsule of the knee joint from being nipped during extension. Nerve supply: femoral nerve (L2–L4).

■■ **Variants:** The part of the rectus femoris which normally takes its origin from the upper margin of the acetabulum may be missing, and the articular muscle of the knee may also be absent.

The **sartorius** (**12**) *arises from the anterior superior iliac spine* (**13**) and runs obliquely over the thigh in its fascial investment *to the pes anserinus superficialis* (**14**), by which it *is attached to the crural fascia* (**15**) and *is medial to the tibial tuberosity.* The sartorius acts on two joints as a flexor at the knee joint and, if the knee is flexed, together with the other muscles of the pes anserinus, it functions as medial rotator of the leg. In addition, it brings about flexion at the hip joint. Due to its course it also functions as a lateral rotator at the hip joint.
Nerve supply: femoral nerve (L2–L3).

16 Gracilis
17 Adductor longus
18 Adductor brevis
19 Pectineus
20 Iliopsoas
21 Tensor fasciae latae
22 Cut edge of fascia lata
23 Vasto-adductor membrane = anteromedial intermuscular septum = subsatorial fascia

Lower Limb

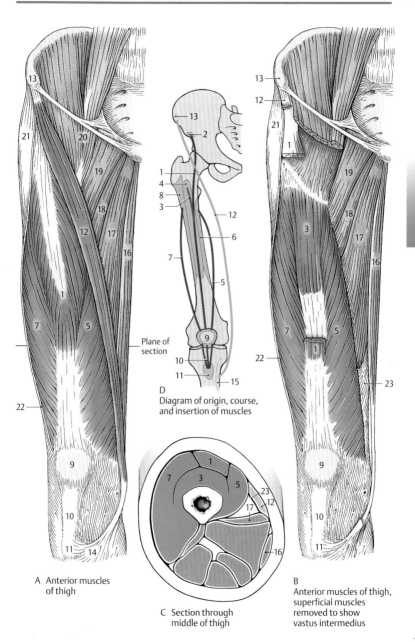

D Diagram of origin, course, and insertion of muscles

A Anterior muscles of thigh

C Section through middle of thigh

B Anterior muscles of thigh, superficial muscles removed to show vastus intermedius

Posterior Thigh Muscles (A–D)

The **biceps femoris** (**1**) has a **long head** and a **short head**. The **long head** (**2**), which acts over two joints, *arises from the ischial tuberosity* (**3**) in common with the semitendinosus (**4**). The **short head** (**5**), acting only over one joint, *originates from the middle third of the lateral lip of the linea aspera* (**6**) *and the lateral intermuscular septum*. The heads unite to form the biceps femoris (**1**), which is *inserted into the head of the fibula* (**7**). Between the muscle and the fibular collateral ligament of the knee joint is the inferior subtendinous bursa of biceps femoris. The long head produces extension (retroversion) of the hip joint. The biceps femoris flexes at the knee joint and laterally rotates the flexed leg. It is the only lateral rotator at the knee joint and thus opposes all the medial rotators.
Nerve supply: long head, tibial nerve (L5–S2); short head, common peroneal nerve (S1–S2).

■■ **Variants:** The short head may be absent; there may also be additional bundles of muscle fibers.

The **semitendinosus** (**4**) *arises by a common head* (see above) *from the ischial tuberosity* (**3**) *and runs toward the medial surface of the tibia* together with the gracilis (**9**) and sartorius (**10**) *to join the pes anserinus superficialis* (**8**). There is a large tibial intertendinous bursa (anserine bursa) between the surface of the tibia and the attachment to the pes anserinus. The muscle acts on two joints, being involved in extension at the hip joint, flexion at the knee joint and medial rotation of the leg.
Nerve supply: tibial nerve (L5–S2).

■■ **Variant:** Within its muscle belly there may be an oblique tendinous intersection.

The **semimembranosus** (**11**) *arises from the ischial tuberosity* (**3**). It is closely related to the semitendinosus. Below the medial collateral ligament, *its tendon divides into*

three parts; the **first** runs anteriorly to the *medial tibial condyle*, the **second** *goes into the fascia of the popliteus*, and the **third** part *continues into the posterior wall of the capsule as the oblique popliteal ligament*. This tripartite division may also be called the "deep" **pes anserinus** ("goose's foot").
The muscle acts on two joints and has a function similar to the semitendinosus. It produces extension at the hip joint and flexion with the medial rotation at the knee joint. Between its tendon (before the division) and the medial head of the gastrocnemius lies the semimembranosus bursa, which is sometimes continuous with the medial subtendinous bursa of gastrocnemius (see p. 210).
Nerve supply: tibial nerve (L5–S2).

■■ **Variants:** The muscle may sometimes be absent or may be completely fused with the semitendinosus. The oblique popliteal ligament need not always be present.

12 Adductor magnus
13 Adductor longus
14 Vastus medialis
15 Vastoadductor membrane = anteromedial intermuscular septum = subsatorial fascia

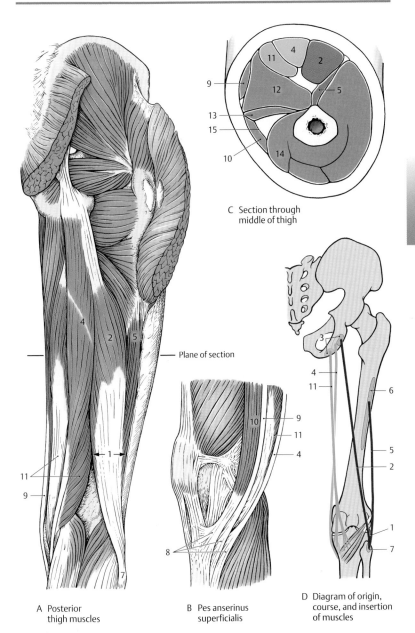

C Section through middle of thigh

Plane of section

Lower Limb

A Posterior thigh muscles

B Pes anserinus superficialis

D Diagram of origin, course, and insertion of muscles

Function of the Knee Joint Muscles (A–D)

Only a few muscles act exclusively on the knee joint, the majority act also on the ankle and subtalar joint.

We distinguish **extension**, and **flexion** around **transverse axes** which run through the femoral condyles (p. 194). Around the **long axis of the leg** there are the rotary movements of **medial** and **lateral rotation**. Rotation is only possible when the collateral ligaments are not tensed (see p. 212), i.e., in the extended position active rotation is impossible. Passively, in maximal extension, there is some lateral rotation of the leg on the non-weight-bearing side and medial rotation of the thigh of the weight-bearing limb of about 5°; the so-called "*closure rotation*" possible when the joint is "locked" or "screwed home" (see p. 212). This rotation is produced by the anterior cruciate ligament helped by the shape of the medial femoral condyle and the iliotibial tract (p. 254).

Extension (**A**) is carried out almost exclusively by the quadriceps femoris, with the tensor fasciae latae providing an insignificant assistance. The action of the quadriceps is better when the hip joint is extended since then the rectus femoris (red) and the vasti muscles (blue) come into full action.

Clinical tip: The power of the quadriceps femoris exceeds all other flexors very substantially. When this muscle is paralyzed, rising from the sitting position is not possible. Standing is only possible when the line of gravity of the body occurs in front of the transverse axis of movement.

Flexion (**B**) is produced by
- Semimembranosus (red, tibial nerve)
- Semitendinosus (blue, tibial nerve
- Biceps femoris (yellow, tibial and common peroneal nerve)
- Gracilis (orange, obturator nerve)
- Sartorius (green, femoral nerve)
- Popliteus (brown, tibial nerve)
- Gastrocnemius (violet, tibial nerve)

Clinical tip: The gastrocnemius has only a slight action in flexion. Nevertheless, when there is a supracondylar fracture of the femoral shaft, it pulls the distal fragment dorsally and distally.

The **medial rotators** (**C**) are
- Semimembranosus (red, tibial nerve)
- Semitendinosus (blue, tibial nerve)
- Gracilis (yellow, obturator nerve)
- Sartorius (orange, femoral nerve)
- Popliteus (green, tibital nerve)

Lateral rotation (**D**) is carried out by
- biceps femoris (red, tibial and common peroneal nerve)

The biceps femoris is almost the only lateral rotator of the thigh and counterbalances all muscles acting as medial rotators. When the leg is taking no weight, it can receive insignificant support (at the end of rotation) from the tensor fasciae latae (not illustrated).

The color of the arrows in the following series indicates the importance of the muscles in the individual movements.

red
blue
yellow
orange
green
brown
violet

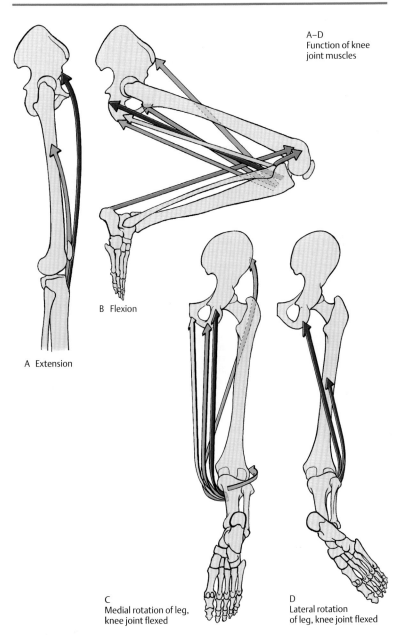

A–D
Function of knee
joint muscles

B Flexion

A Extension

C
Medial rotation of leg,
knee joint flexed

D
Lateral rotation
of leg, knee joint flexed

Lower Limb

Fascias of the Hip and Thigh (A—C)

The muscles of the hip region are invested by various fascias; for instance the iliopsoas muscle is covered by the **iliopsoas fascia**, which begins with the *psoas fascia* at the medial arcuate ligament as a sturdy fascial tube covering the psoas major and continues together with *iliac fascia* as far as the inguinal ligament. It forms the *iliopectineal arch*, which separates the muscular space (see p. 100) from the vascular space.

On the anterior surface, below the inguinal ligament, the pectineus is enclosed in a strong **pectineal fascia**, which is the pubic portion of the fascia lata (called also the Cowper ligament). The pectineal fascia combines with the iliac fascia to form the connective-tissue lining of the iliopectineal fossa. The latter is limited proximally by the inguinal ligament.

The gluteal region contains the delicate **gluteal fascia** (**1**) which covers the gluteus maximus and gives rise to septa that penetrate deeply between the individual muscle bundles. Between the gluteus maximus and the underlying gluteus medius lies the firm, strong **gluteal aponeurosis** (p. 236) from which portions of the gluteus maximus take origin. In the region of the gluteal sulcus, the superficial gluteal fascia merges with the fascia lata (**2**), the fascia of the thigh.

On the lateral side of the thigh, the **fascia lata** forms a dense connective tissue layer of parallel fibers which becomes weaker medially. A band of fibers, the **iliotibial tract** (**3**; pp. 236 and 422) is conspicuous on the lateral side. The gluteus maximus and tensor fasciae latae radiate into this iliotibial tract. The iliotibial tract is several centimeters wide and extends distally on the lateral side to the lateral tibial condyle. In this region the lateral patellar retinaculum is intimately blended with it. On the anterior surface of the thigh, the sartorius (**4**) possesses its own fascial covering. It overlies the *vasto-adductor membrane* (**5**). Similarly, the gracilis (**6**) is enclosed in its own fascial sheath which can be separated from the other fascias. All the thigh muscles have their own loose, delicate coverings which enable them to move against each other. From the fascia lata deep intermuscular septa project laterally and medially in the direction of the linea aspera. The *lateral intermuscular septum* (**7**) is relatively broad and provides an origin for several muscles. It divides the vastus lateralis (**8**) from the short head of the biceps femoris (**9**). The *medial intermuscular septum* (**10**) separates the vastus medialis (**11**) from the adductor canal (**12**).

On the anterior surface of the thigh below the inguinal ligament, in the region of the iliopectineal fossa which is covered superficially by the fascia lata, there is in the latter a porous area occupied by the **cribriform fascia**. This is pierced by vessels and nerves. Removal of this loose fascia reveals the **saphenous opening** (**13**), whose lateral margin, *the falciform margin*, or *Hey's* or *Burn's ligament* (**14**) forms a sharply defined border. The falciform margin extends medially with a *superior horn* (**15**, called also the *Scarpa ligament*) and an *inferior horn* (**16**).

The femoral canal and femoral hernias are described on page 100.

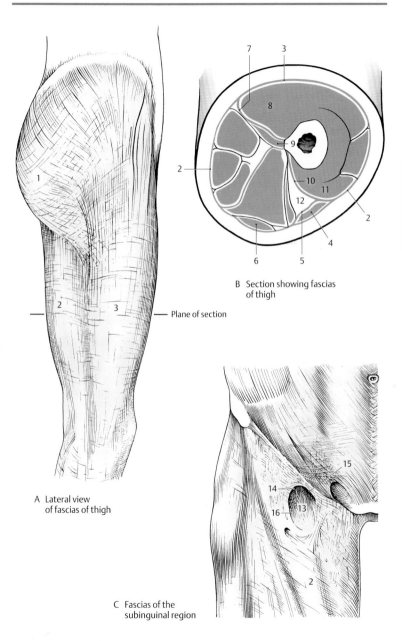

B Section showing fascias
   of thigh

Plane of section

A Lateral view
   of fascias of thigh

C Fascias of the
   subinguinal region

Long Muscles of the Leg and Foot

Classification of the Muscles (A–D)

All but one of the muscles which arise in the leg are attached to the bones of the foot. The only exception is the popliteus, which is inserted in the leg and must be classified with the thigh muscles. The muscles of the leg can only be classified according to their location, principally into anterior and posterior groups. They are separated by the tibia and fibula and the interosseous membrane.

The two main groups are divided in turn into subgroups or layers. The anterior muscle group consists of the anterior extensors and the lateral subdivision of the peroneal group. The flexors on the posterior side of the leg are subdivided into the superficial or calf muscles and the deep muscles.

Functionally, the leg muscles can be subdivided into the extensors, lying on the anterior surface and responsible for dorsiflexion of the foot, and the flexors, which lie posteriorly and produce plantar flexion of the foot.

On the basis of their innervation, however, the muscles may be divided into those which receive nerves from the dorsal division of the plexus and those which are supplied by the ventral division.

For practical purposes the muscles of the leg, like those of the forearm, are best discussed according to their location.

Anterior Muscles of the Leg

Extensor Group (see p. 258)
– Tibialis anterior (**1**)
– Extensor digitorum longus (**2**)
– Extensor hallucis longus (**3**)

Fibular (Peroneal) Group (see p. 260)
– Peroneus longus (**4**)
– Peroneus brevis (**5**)

Posterior Muscles of the Leg

Superficial Layer (see p. 262)
– Triceps surae (**6**; with Achilles tendon) consisting of
– Soleus (**7**)
– Gastrocnemius (**8**)
– Plantaris (**9**)

Deep Layer (see p. 264)
– Tibialis posterior (**10**)
– Flexor hallucis longus (**11**)
– Flexor digitorum longus (**12**)

13 Popliteus
14 Semimembranosus
15 Sartorius
16 Gracilis
17 Semitendinosus
18 Popliteal artery and vein
19 Tibial nerve
20 Common peroneal (fibular) nerve
21 Great saphenous vein
22 Small saphenous vein
23 Saphenous nerve
24 Superficial peroneal (fibular) nerve
25 Deep peroneal (fibular) nerve
26 Lateral sural cutaneous nerve
27 Sural nerve
28 Peroneal (fibular) artery
29 Anterior tibial artery and vein
30 Posterior tibial artery and vein
31 Tibia
32 Fibula

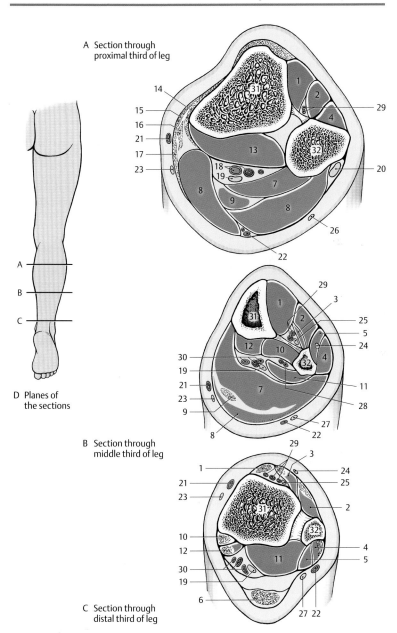

A Section through
proximal third of leg

D Planes of
the sections

B Section through
middle third of leg

C Section through
distal third of leg

Lower Limb

Lower Limb (side tab)

Anterior Leg Muscles

Extensor Group (A–C)

The **tibialis anterior** (**1**) *arises from a wide area* (**2**) *of the lateral surface of the tibia, the interosseous membrane, and the crural fascia.* Its three-sided belly ends in a tendon which extends beneath the superior extensor retinaculum (**3**) and the inferior extensor retinaculum (**4**) surrounded by a synovial sheath. *It is inserted in the plantar surface of the medial cuneiform bone* (**5**) *and the first metatarsal* (**6**). The subtendinous bursa of the tibialis anterior lies between its tendon and the medial cuneiform bone.

When the leg is not bearing any weight, the tibialis anterior flexes the foot dorsally and at the same time lifts the medial edge of the foot (supination). When the leg is weighted, it approximates the leg to the back of the foot as, for example, in rapid walking, or in skiing. A slight participation in pronation has also been described.
Nerve supply: deep peroneal (fibular) nerve (L4–L5).

> **Clinical tip:** Under great stress the tibialis anterior may become fatigued resulting in pain along the muscle.

The **extensor digitorum longus** (**7**) *arises from* a large area (**8**), namely from *the lateral condyle of the tibia, the head and anterior crest of the fibula, the deep fascia of the leg, and the interosseous membrane.* In the region of the ankle the tendon in which the muscle ends is divided into four parts and extends to the second–fifth digits.

These tendons are enclosed in a common synovial sheath and *run* under the superior extensor retinaculum (**3**) and the inferior extensor retinaculum (**4**), lateral to the tendon of the tibialis anterior; they extend over the dorsum of the foot *into the dorsal aponeuroses of the second–fifth digits.*

In the non-weight-bearing leg, the muscle produces dorsiflexion of the digits and the

foot. In the weight-bearing leg its function is the same as that of the tibialis anterior.
Nerve supply: deep peroneal (fibular) nerve (L5–S1).

■ **Variants:** The extensor digitorum longus may have an additional tendon which extends to the base of the fifth metatarsal and sometimes also to the base of the fourth metatarsal. This additional tendon is called the **peroneus tertius** (**9**), and as part of the extensor digitorum longus it may have a separate origin from the distal third of the anterior edge of the fibula. It acts as a pronator and abductor of the subtalar and talocalcaneonavicular joints.

The **extensor hallucis longus** (**10**) *arises from the medial surface of the fibula and the interosseous membrane* (**11**). It continues as a tendon which runs in its own synovial sheath between the sheath for the tendon of the tibialis anterior and that for the extensor digitorum longus beneath the superior extensor retinaculum (**3**) and inferior extensor retinaculum (**4**). It reaches across the first metatarsal to the dorsal aponeurosis of the great digit and *is inserted into the terminal phalanx* (**12**).
The extensor hallucis longus flexes the great toe dorsally and in the unstressed leg it aids dorsiflexion of the foot. In the weight-bearing leg its function resembles that of the tibialis anterior, since it brings the leg nearer to the dorsum of the foot. To a small extent it also aids in pronation and supination of the foot.
Nerve supply: deep peroneal (fibular) nerve (L4–S1).

■ **Variants:** An independent muscle or tendon bundle can frequently be split off and attach itself to the first metatarsal or in the region of the metatarsophalangeal joint as the **extensor hallucis accessorius** (**13**). This muscle is found primarily at the medial side of the main tendon.

14 Tibia
15 Fibula

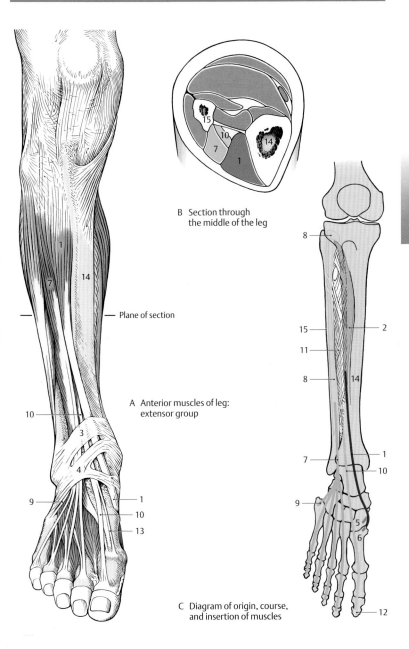

B Section through
the middle of the leg

Plane of section

A Anterior muscles of leg:
extensor group

C Diagram of origin, course,
and insertion of muscles

Lower Limb

Anterior Leg Muscles, continued

Fibular (Peroneal) Group (A–D)

The peroneal muscles act as plantar flexors, a function they attained only secondarily, due to their displacement behind the lateral malleolus. Originally they lay in front of the malleolus, as can still be seen in predators.

The **fibularis (peroneus) longus** (**1**) *arises* (**2**) *from the capsule of the tibiofibular joint, the head of the fibula, and the proximal region of the fibula.*

It ends in a long tendon which runs behind the lateral malleolus which passes in the malleolar groove behind the lateral malleolus in a common synovial sheath with the tendon of the *peroneus brevis* (**3**) underneath the *superior peroneal retinaculum* (**4**). The tendon of the peroneus longus *extends distally* from the peroneal trochlea of the calcaneus in an evagination of the common synovial sheath (fixed by the *inferior peroneal retinaculum* [**5**]), *across the plantar surface to the tuberosity of the first metatarsal* (**6**) *and the medial cuneiform bone* (**7**). Its tendon reaches the site of insertion by coursing through the tendon groove of the *cuboid* (**8**) in a special fibrous canal, which runs from the lateral side behind the tuberosity of the fifth metatarsal obliquely to the medial margin of the foot. Within this canal, on the sole of the foot, another synovial sheath encloses the tendon.

Due to this course its function is similar to that of a bow string (*Kummer*) and it braces the transverse arch of the foot. It depresses the medial edge of the foot and, together with the peroneus brevis, it is the strongest pronator. It also aids plantar flexion.
Nerve supply: superficial peroneal (fibular) nerve (L5–S1).

The **fibularis (peroneus) brevis** (**3**) *arises from the lateral surface of the fibula* (**9**). Its tendon, together with that of the peroneus longus, runs in a synovial sheath in the groove for the tendon of the peroneus longus, beneath the superior peroneal retinaculum (**4**). On the lateral surface of the calcaneus, the tendon becomes fixed proximally, i.e., above the peroneal trochlea of the calcaneus, by the inferior peroneal retinaculum (**5**) where an evagination of the common synovial sheath surrounds the tendon. *This is attached to the tuberosity of the 5th metatarsal* (**10**). The muscle acts like the peroneus longus.
Nerve supply: superficial peroneal (fibular) nerve (L5–S1).

■ **Variants:** The **peroneus quartus** is rarely present. It arises from the fibula and is attached to the lateral surface of the calcaneus or to the cuboid. It is closely associated with the tendons of the extensor digitorum longus. It may also send a small tendon to the fifth digit.

11 Tibia
12 Fibula
13 Soleus
14 Gastrocnemius
15 Interosseous membrane

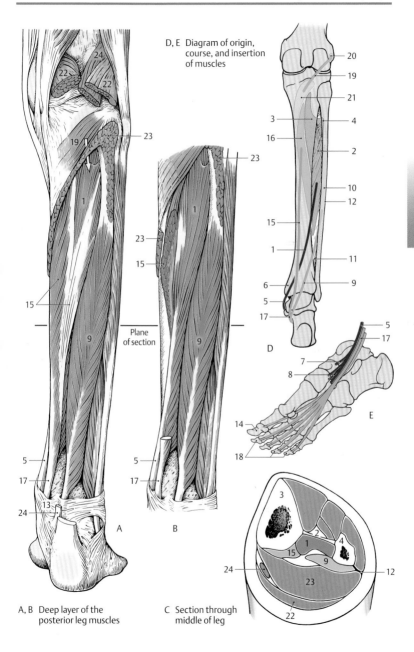

D, E Diagram of origin, course, and insertion of muscles

Plane of section

D

E

A, B Deep layer of the posterior leg muscles

C Section through middle of leg

Function of the Ankle, Subtalar and Talocalcaneonavicular Joint Muscles (A–D)

All the muscles act on several joints, but only their actions on the talocrural, subtalar, and talocalcaneonavicular joints will be described.

Dorsiflexion (extension) and **plantar flexion** (flexion) occur around the **transverse axis** of the talocrural (ankle) joint (see p. 222), which runs through the tip of the medial malleolus and the lateral malleolus.

Pronation, or eversion (elevation of the lateral margin of the foot), and **supination**, or inversion (elevation of the medial margin of the foot), occur around the **oblique axis** of the subtalar joint. The axis runs upwards extending outward from the back and below and inward toward the front.

Dorsiflexion (A) is produced by
– Tibialis anterior (red, deep peroneal nerve)
– Extensor digitorum longus (blue, deep peroneal nerve)
– Extensor hallucis longus (yellow, deep peroneal nerve)

Plantar flexion (B) is carried out by
– Triceps surae (red, tibial nerve)
– Peroneus longus (blue, superficial peroneal nerve)
– Peroneus brevis (yellow, superficial peroneal nerve)
– Flexor digitorum longus (green, tibial nerve)
– Tibialis posterior (brown, tibial nerve)

The triceps surae is the most important muscle in plantar flexion, whereas the remaining muscles contribute only a very slight action.

Pronation (C) is produced by
– Peroneus longus (red, superficial peroneal nerve)
– Peroneus brevis (blue, superficial peroneal nerve)
– Extensor digitorum longus (yellow, deep peroneal nerve)
– Peroneus tertius (orange, deep peroneal nerve)

Supination (D) is brought about by
– Triceps surae (red, tibial nerve
– Tibialis posteior (blue, tibial nerve)
– Flexor hallucis longus (yellow, tibial nerve)
– Flexor digitorum longus (orange, tibial nerve)
– Tibialis anterior (green, deep peroneal nerve)

The colors of the arrows show the order of importance of the muscles in each movement:

red
blue
yellow
orange
green
brown

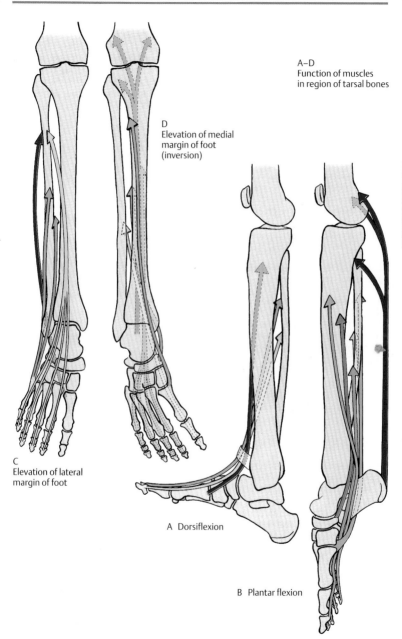

A–D
Function of muscles
in region of tarsal bones

D
Elevation of medial
margin of foot
(inversion)

C
Elevation of lateral
margin of foot

A Dorsiflexion

B Plantar flexion

Lower Limb

Intrinsic Muscles of the Foot

As in the hand, only the tendons of the extrinsic muscles of the foot extend into the foot; the muscle bellies of these tendons lie in the leg. In addition to these tendons there are the intrinsic muscles of the foot, which lie either on the dorsum or the sole of the foot. Apart from this topographical classification, the intrinsic muscles may be classified according to their innervation, the muscles of the dorsum of the foot being innervated by the dorsal division of the plexus and those of the sole of the foot by the ventral division. Like the muscles of the hand, the muscles of the sole of the foot may be divided into three groups; those of the middle plantar eminence and those which form the medial plantar eminence.

Muscles of the Dorsum of the Foot (A–C)

The tendons of the **extensor digitorum longus** (**1**; see p. 258) and the **extensor hallucis longus** (**2**; see p. 258) lie superficial to the intrinsic muscles of the dorsum of the foot. They are held in position by the *superior extensor retinaculum* (**3**; see p. 276) and the *inferior extensor retinaculum* (**4**; see p. 276). The tendons of the long extensors form the **dorsal aponeurosis** of the toes into which the short extensors of the digits and the *plantar and dorsal interossei* also radiate (**5**; see p. 274).
Nerve supply: deep peroneal nerve (L5-S1).

The **extensor digitorum brevis** (**6**) *arises from the calcaneus* (**7**), near the entrance to the tarsal sinus, and *from one side of the inferior extensor retinaculum* (**4**). *It extends with three tendons to the dorsal aponeurosis* (**8**) *of the second to fourth digits.* It is responsible for dorsiflexion of these digits.
Nerve supply: deep peroneal (fibular) nerve (S1–S2).

■■ **Variants:** Individual tendons may be absent. The tendon for the fifth toe is only occasionally present.

The **extensor hallucis brevis** (**9**), *which extends into the dorsal aponeurosis of the first digit, splits off from the extensor digitorum brevis, with which it has a common origin from the calcaneus.* Like the latter muscle it serves to dorsiflex the first digit.
Nerve supply: deep peroneal (fibular) nerve (S1–S2).

10 Tibialis anterior
11 Peroneus tertius

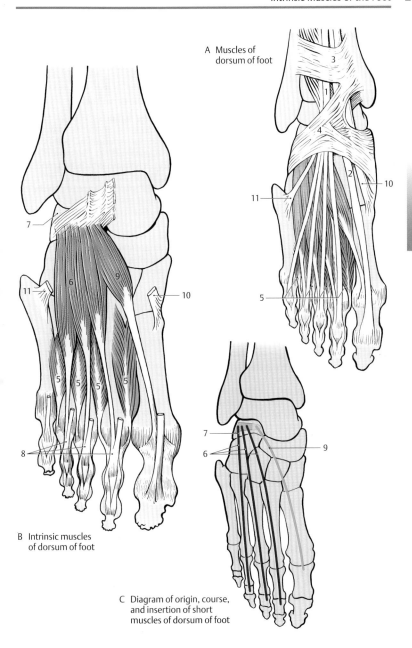

A Muscles of dorsum of foot

B Intrinsic muscles of dorsum of foot

C Diagram of origin, course, and insertion of short muscles of dorsum of foot

Lower Limb

Muscles of the Sole of the Foot (A–C)

Three muscles groups may be distinguished in the sole of the foot—the muscles in the regions of

- **The great toe**
- **The little toe**
- **The middle region**

The abductor hallucis and the flexor hallucis brevis belong to the region of the big digit. In a wider sense it also includes the adductor hallucis, which originally formed a separate system.

The abductor digiti minimi, the flexor digiti minimi brevis, and opponens digiti minimi belong to the region of the little toe.

The middle muscle group consists of the lumbricales, quadratus plantae, interossei, and flexor digitorum brevis.

All the muscles of the sole of the foot are covered by the dense and strong **plantar aponeurosis** (**1**), which is derived from the superficial fascia. The plantar aponeurosis consists of **longitudinal fiber bundles** (**2**), which arise from the tuber calcanei and radiate into the digits. **Transverse fascicles** (**3**) interconnect these longitudinal fiber bundles. On the medial and lateral borders of the foot, the plantar aponeurosis merges into the thin dorsal fascia of the foot. Two tough septa extend deeply from the surfaces as the *medial* and *lateral plantar septa* (**4**). The former is attached to the first metatarsal, the medial cuneiform bone, and the navicular, and the latter to the fifth metatarsal and the long plantar ligament.

The three connective tissue spaces formed by these septa and the plantar aponeurosis each contain the three muscle groups referred to above, and fatty tissue. These cushions, formed by the muscles and fat, transmit the weight of the body to the underlying substrate. *The plantar aponeurosis, septa, muscles, fatty tissues, and skeleton of the foot form a functional entity.* Thus, the plantar aponeurosis makes an important contribution to maintenance of the longitudinal arch (see p. 226). In addition, the plantar aponeurosis acts to protect the vessels and nerves against damage from pressure.

Muscles of the Great Toe

The **abductor hallucis** (**5**) *arises from the medial process of the tuber calcanei* (**6**), *from the flexor retinaculum, and from the plantar aponeurosis* (**7**). Its origin makes a tendon arch beneath which the tendons of the long flexors of the digits run in the tarsal canal. *The muscle is inserted into the medial sesamoid bone* (**8**) *and the base of the proximal phalanx* (**9**). There is usually a synovial bursa between its tendon of insertion and the metatarsophalangeal joint. It acts as an abductor and a weak flexor and helps to maintain the arch of the foot.
Nerve supply: medial plantar nerve (L5–S1).

The **flexor hallucis brevis** (**10**) *arises from the medial cuneiform bone* (**11**), *the long plantar ligament, and the tendon of the tibialis posterior.* It has **two heads**; the **medial head** (**12**) is combined with the abductor hallucis and *extends to the medial sesamoid bone* (**13**) *and the proximal phalanx* (**14**), while the **lateral head** (**15**) joins the adductor hallucis and *is inserted into the lateral sesamoid bone* (**16**) *and the proximal phalanx* (**17**). It is an important plantar flexor and is needed particularly in ballet dancing.
Nerve supply: medial plantar nerve (L5–S1).

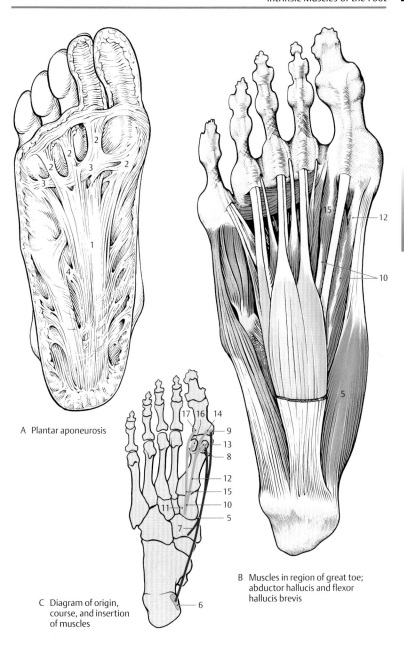

A Plantar aponeurosis

B Muscles in region of great toe;
abductor hallucis and flexor
hallucis brevis

C Diagram of origin,
course, and insertion
of muscles

Muscles of the Sole of the Foot

Muscles of the Great Toe, continued (A–C)

The **adductor hallucis** (**1**) has **two heads**. It only becomes visible after the flexor digitorum longus and the flexor digitorum brevis (**2**) have been removed (**A**). The strong **oblique head** (**3**) *arises from the cuboid* (**4**) *and lateral cuneiform* (**5**) *bones, and from the bases of the second and third metatarsals* (**6**). Other surfaces of origin may include the fourth metatarsal, the plantar calcaneocuboidal ligament, the long plantar ligament (**7**), and the plantar tendinous sheath (**8**) of the peroneus longus. The **transverse head** (**9**) *arises from the capsular ligaments of the metatarsophalangeal joints of the third–fifth digits* (**10**) *and also from the deep transverse metatarsal ligament.* **Both heads** *are inserted into the lateral sesamoid bone* (**11**) *of the great toe.* The muscle acts especially as a tensor of the plantar arches. In addition it adducts the great toe and may then plantar flex the proximal phalanx.
Nerve supply: deep branch of the lateral plantar nerve (S1–S2).

Intrinsic Muscles of the Little Toe (A–C)

The **opponens digiti minimi** (**12**) *arises from the long plantar ligament* (**7**) *and from the plantar tendinous sheath of peroneus longus* (**13**). *It is inserted into the fifth metatarsal* (**14**). Its functions are to plantar flex the fifth metatarsal and to support the plantar arch. It is quite often absent.
Nerve supply: lateral plantar nerve (S1–S2).

The **flexor digiti minimi** (**15**) *arises from the base of the fifth metatarsal* (**16**), *from the long plantar ligament* (**7**), *and from the plantar tendinous sheath of peroneus longus. It extends to the base of the proximal phalanx* (**17**) *of the fifth digit* and *usually merges with* the abductor digiti minimi. It acts as a plantar flexor of the little toe.
Nerve supply; lateral plantar nerve (S1–S2).

The **abductor digiti minimi** (**18**) is the largest and longest of the muscles of the little toe. In the main it actually forms the lateral margin of the foot. *It arises from the lateral process of the tuber calcanei* (**19**), *from the lower surface of the calcaneus* (**20**), *the tuberosity of the fifth metatarsal* (**21**) *and the plantar aponeurosis and extends to the proximal phalanx* (**22**) *of the fifth digit.* Like the other muscles it supports the arch of the foot. In addition it plantar flexes the fifth digit and, to a small extent, it acts also as an abductor.
Nerve supply: lateral plantar nerve (S1–S 2).

23 Quadratus plantae

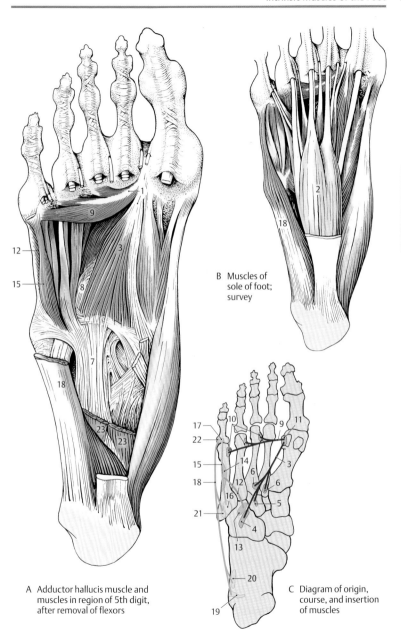

Lower Limb

B Muscles of sole of foot; survey

A Adductor hallucis muscle and muscles in region of 5th digit, after removal of flexors

C Diagram of origin, course, and insertion of muscles

Muscles of the Sole of the Foot, continued

Intrinsic Muscles in the Center of the Sole of the Foot (A–C)

The **four lumbricales** (**1**) *arise from the medial surfaces of the individual tendons* (**2**) *of the flexor digitorum longus. They extend to the medial margin of the proximal phalanges of the second–fifth digits and radiate into the extensor (dorsal) aponeurosis.* The muscles are involved in plantar flexion and movements of the four lateral digits toward the great toe. They also help to reinforce the plantar arch.

Nerve supply: medial plantar nerve to the first, second, and third lumbricales, and lateral plantar nerve to the fourth lumbricalis (L5–S2).

▬▬ **Variants:** In contrast to the lumbricales of the hand, those of the foot are quite variable. They may be absent or there may be more than four. They are inserted on the articular capsules of the metatarsophalangeal joints as well as to the proximal phalanges.

The **quadratus plantae** (**3**) is also known as the plantar head of the flexor digitorum longus (flexor accessorius). *It arises with two slips from the medial and lateral margins of the plantar surface of the calcaneus and projects into the lateral margin of the tendon* (**4**) *of the flexor digitorum longus.*

Nerve supply: lateral plantar nerve (S1–S2).

▬▬ **Variants:** It may extend into the common tendon of the flexor digitorum longus or into the four divisions of this tendon, in which case it only extends to the two lateral tendons.

The **interossei** may be divided into **plantar** (**5**; blue) and **dorsal** (**6**; red) parts. They are arranged with respect to the second digit as the longitudinal axis of the foot.

The **three plantar interossei** each arise by a **single head** *from the medial side of the third to fifth metatarsals* (**7**) *and may receive additional fibers from the long plantar liga-*

ment. They extent to the medial side of the base of the proximal phalanx of the third to fifth digits (**8**).

The **four dorsal interossei** arise by **two heads** *from the opposing surfaces of all the metatarsals* (**9**) *and from the long plantar ligament. They are attached to the bases of the proximal phalanges of the second to fourth digits* (**10**).

The plantar interossei act as adductors and pull the third, fourth, and fifth digits toward the second digit. The dorsal interossei are abductors. The first and second are inserted into the proximal phalanx of the second digit and the third and fourth are inserted into the proximal phalanx of the third and fourth digits.

In contrast to the interossei of the hand, they usually do not reach the extensor aponeurosis. In addition to their functions as abductor and adductor, they work together as plantar flexors at the metatarsophalangeal joints.

Nerve supply: deep branch of the lateral plantar nerve (S1–S2).

The **flexor digitorum brevis** (**11**) *arises from the undersurface of the tuber calcanei and from the proximal part of the plantar aponeurosis. Its tendons, which are inserted into the middle phalanx of the second to fourth digits, are divided near their termini* (**12**). The tendons of the flexor digitorum longus (**2**) run between these divided tendons. Thus, the flexor digitorum brevis is also called the perforatus. In this region the tendons together with the tendons of the flexor digitorum longus are surrounded by a tendinous sheath. This muscle plantar flexes the middle phalanges.

Nerve supply: medial plantar nerve (L5–S1).

▬▬ **Variants:** The tendon to the fifth digit (little toe) is often absent. In some cases the entire muscle may be absent.

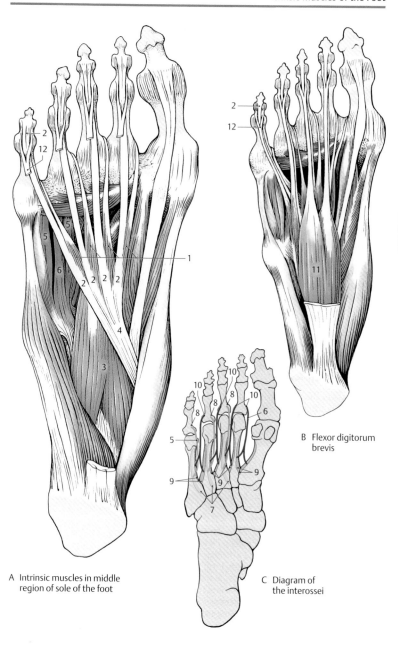

A Intrinsic muscles in middle region of sole of the foot

B Flexor digitorum brevis

C Diagram of the interossei

Fascias of the Leg and the Foot (A–D)

The superficial fascia of the leg, the **crural fascia** (**1**), is the continuation of the fascia lata and its special popliteal fascia. It encloses the superficial muscle layers of the leg. Strengthening fibers are interwoven into the crural fascia and delineate certain particular features. Thus, over the extensors in the distal anterior part of the leg there are transverse strengthening fibers, forming the *superior extensor retinaculum* (**2**), and in the tarsal region on the dorsum of the foot as the *inferior extensor retinaculum* (**3**), which are visible due to reinforcing fibers within the fascia. The retinacula can be demonstrated with care in the fascia.

On the lateral side there is an intermuscular septum, both in front of and behind the peroneal muscles, which extends from the crural fascia deeply to the fibula. These are the *anterior* (**4**) and *posterior* (**5**) *intermuscular septa of leg*. At the distal end, in the region of the lateral malleolus, strong fiber tracts are woven into the fascia, and form the *superior* and *inferior peroneal retinacula* (**6**). Both can only be demonstrated by dissection.

The fascia over the dorsal crural muscles is thin. It is only strengthened distally, so that between the medial malleolus and the calcaneus there is a dense fibrous structure, the *flexor retinaculum* (**7**), the superficial layer of which serves as the boundary of the tendons of the deep muscles of the tibia.

The musculature of the calf may be divided into a superficial and a deep layer of muscles. Between the two groups lies the **deep fascia of leg** (**8**), which arises proximal to the *tendinous arch of the soleus*. Part of the soleus also arises from it. At the distal end it has thicker fibers, and these form the *deep layer of the flexor retinaculum* on the medial side, and on the lateral side they contribute to the *superior peroneal retinaculum*. The four different muscle groups in the leg are separated in this way by these connective tissue layers and the interosseous membrane.

On the dorsum of the foot, the superficial **dorsal fascia of foot** (**9**) lies distal to the *inferior extensor retinaculum* (**3**). It is very delicate and thin. It forms the immediate continuation of the crural fascia and extends distalward into the extensor aponeurosis of the digits. Laterally it is attached to the sides of the foot.

Proximally, at the attachments of the superior extensor retinaculum, it forms the cross-shaped *inferior extensor retinaculum*, which, however, can be demonstrated only by careful dissection, and in which laterally the proximal crus is often absent. In this case these reinforcing fiber bundles within the fascia appear Y-shaped.

Deep to the tendons of the extensor digitorum longus is a connective tissue layer, the **deep dorsal fascia of foot,** which is dense and tight and is also attached to the borders of the foot.

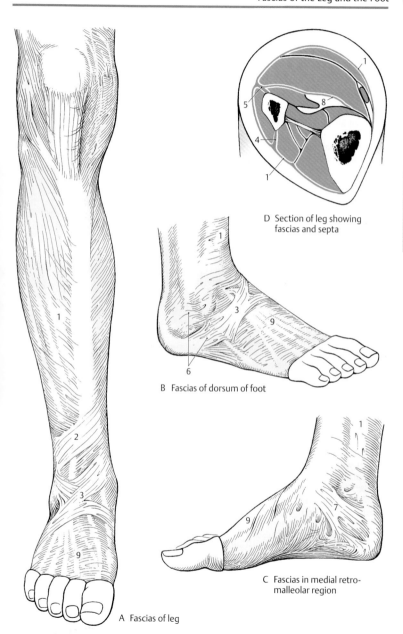

D Section of leg showing
   fascias and septa

B Fascias of dorsum of foot

C Fascias in medial retromalleolar region

A Fascias of leg

Tendinous Sheaths in the Foot (A–C)

As in the region of the hand, different **tendinous sheaths** are distinguished in the foot.

On the **dorsum of the foot, tendinous sheaths** are found for the tendons of
- Tibialis anterior (**1**)
- Extensor hallucis longus (**2**)
- Extensor digitorum longus (**3**)
- Fibularis (peroneus) tertius (when present)

The tendons or tendinous sheaths in this area are held in position by the *superior* (**4**) and *inferior* (**5**) *extensor retinacula.* On the lateral side of the tarsals in the region of the peroneal trochlea of the calcaneus is found the *common peroneal tendinous sheath* of the *peroneus* (**6**). The tendon of the peroneus longus (**7**) leaves this common synovial sheath and continues across the plantar region within its own sheath, the *plantar tendinous sheath* of the *peroneus longus.* The common tendon sheath for the peroneal muscles is fixed in position laterally by the *superior* (**8**) and *inferior* (**9**) *peroneal retinacula.*

The flexor tendons lie on the medial side of the foot directly behind the medial malleolus. Their tendinous sheaths course below the *flexor retinaculum of the foot* which comprises a *superficial layer* (**10**) of reinforced crural fascia, and a *deep layer* (**11**). Below this deep layer pass three tendons each of which is enclosed within its own synovial sheath, those of the tibialis posterior (tendinous sheath of tibialis posterior, **12**), flexor digitorum longus (tendinous sheath of flexor digitorum longus, **13**), and flexor hallucis longus (tendinous sheath of flexor hallucis longus, **14**) muscles (see also p. 436).

On the **plantar aspect of the foot** are found **five tendon sheaths** corresponding to the individual toes (**15**). As a rule, these **synovial sheaths** do not communicate with each other and are strengthened by stout **fibrous sheaths** (**16**), each of which consists of an anular and cruciform part. The *anular part* (**17**) consists of circular bundles of fibers and are located in the region of a joint. The *cruciform part* (**18**) is found between the joints and is composed of decussating connective tissue fibers. In contrast to the hand, no tendon sheaths are found in the middle compartment of the plantar surface of the foot. Only the two previously mentioned tendon sheaths, that for the flexor hallucis longus (**14**) and that for the flexor digitorum longus (**13**), extend into the metatarsal region.

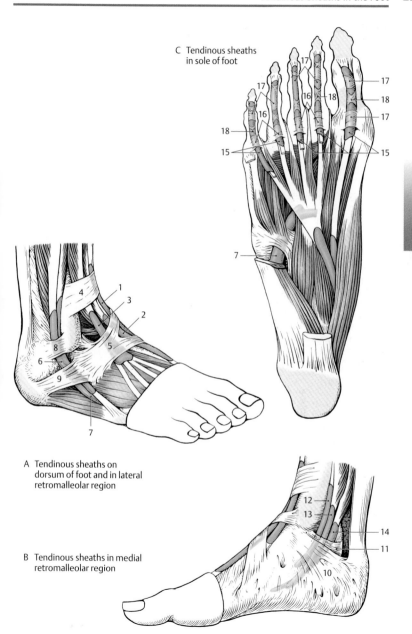

C Tendinous sheaths in sole of foot

A Tendinous sheaths on dorsum of foot and in lateral retromalleolar region

B Tendinous sheaths in medial retromalleolar region

Lower Limb

Anatomical Terms and their Latin Equivalents

Lower Limb	Membrum inferius
Acetabulum margin	Limbus acetabuli
Acetabulum notch	Incisura acetabuli
Ankle joint	Articulatio talocruralis
Anteromedial intermuscular septum	Septum intermusculare vastoadductorium
Bones of the toes	Ossa digitorum pedis
Free part of lower limb	Pars libera membri inferioris
Hip bone	Os coxae
Infrapatellar fat pad	Corpus adiposum infrapatellare
Intermediate zone	Linea intermedia
Knee joint	Articulatio genus
Lunate surface	Facies lunata
Obturator externus (internus)	M. obturatorius externus (internus)
Obturator groove	Sulcus obturatorius
Pecten pubis	Pecten ossis pubis
Pubic crest	Crista pubica
Sciatic nerve	N. ischiadicus
Symphysial surface	Facies symphysialis
Tendinous sheath	Vagina tendinum
Wing of ilium	Ala ossis ilii

Systematic Anatomy of the Locomotor System

Head and Neck

Skull (A, B)

The bony part of the head, the skull or **cranium**, forms the upper end of the trunk. It acts as the box for the brain and the sense organs, forms the substructure of the face, and also contains the initial portions of the gastrointestinal and respiratory tracts. The variety of its tasks determines the differentiation in the construction of the skull.

Subdivision of the Skull

The skull consists of two parts:
- The **neurocranium**, the brain box
- The **viscerocranium**, the facial skeleton

The boundary between the two lies in the region of the root of the nose and extends along the upper margin of the orbits to the external auditory meatus.

The shape of the skull is partly determined by the muscles, which may produce certain changes due to their functions, and in part by the contents of the skull. Thus, there is a correlation between the neurocranium and the brain contained within it. The influence here is reciprocal, as excessive expansion of the brain may produce enlargement of the neurocranium, e.g., as in hydrocephalus (see p. 310). On the other hand, premature cessation of neurocranial growth may result in malformation of the brain. There is not only a reciprocal effect within the neurocranium but also a close relationship to the facial skeleton. Thus the development of the muscles and of the supporting system of the dura mater within the skull capsule are also interrelated.

Ossification of the Skull

Fundamentally there are two developmental processes in the skull, distinguishable by the type of bone formation. One is the **chondrocranium** and the other the **desmocranium**. In the chondrocranium there is replacement bone formation, while in the desmocranium the individual bones develop as membranous bones directly from condensations in the connective tissue. Both types of development occur in the two functional parts (the neurocranium and viscerocranium). However, portions of either desmal or chondral origin may fuse together to form a single bone, as, for example, in the temporal bone.

The neurocranium (**A**; orange) consists of the occipital bone (**1**), sphenoid bone (**2**), squamous (**3**) and mastoid portion of the petrous (**4**) parts of the temporal bone, the parietal bones (**5**), and the frontal bone (**6**).

The **viscerocranium** (**A**; violet) is composed of the ethmoid bone (**7**), the inferior nasal conchae, the lacrimal bones (**8**), the nasal bones (**9**), the vomer, the maxillae (**10**) with the incisive bone, the palatine bones, the zygomatic bones (**11**), the tympanic parts (**12**) and the styloid processes (**13**) of the temporal bones, the mandible (**14**), and the hyoid bone.

Bones preformed in cartilage (**B**; blue) include the occipital bone (**1**; with the exception of the upper part of its squama, **15**), the sphenoid bone (**2**; with the exception of the medial lamella of the pterygoid process), the temporal bone with its petrous part (**4**) and the auditory ossicles, the ethmoid bone (**7**), the inferior nasal concha, and the hyoid bone.

The following bones are formed by **ossification in connective tissue** (**B**; green): the upper part of the squama of the occipital bone (**15**), the sphenoidal concha, the medial lamella of the pterygoid process, the tympanic part (**12**), the squamous part of the temporal bone (**3**), the parietal bone (**5**), the frontal bone (**6**), the lacrimal bone (**8**), the nasal bone (**9**), the vomer, the maxilla (**10**), the palatine bone, the zygomatic bone (**11**), and the mandible (**14**).

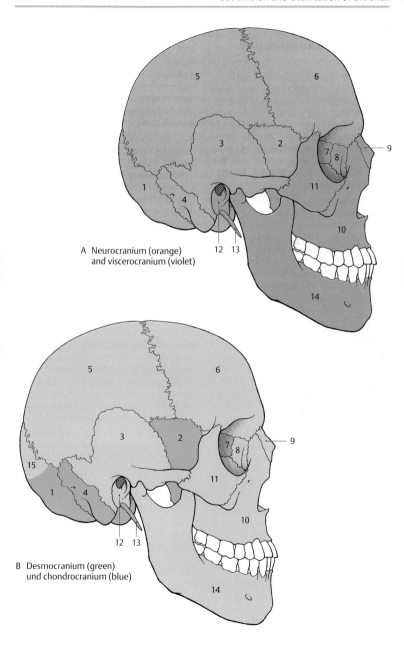

A Neurocranium (orange)
and viscerocranium (violet)

B Desmocranium (green)
und chondrocranium (blue)

Special Features of Intramembranous Ossification (A–D)

The skull cap develops in connective tissue and has several ossification centers from which bone formation radiates in all directions. In this way paired protuberances develop—*two frontal eminences* (**1**) and two *parietal eminences* (**2**). The bones develop from these eminences. At birth large connective tissue areas, the **fontanelles** or fonticuli, are still left between the individual bones.

The *anterior fontanelle* (**3**) is an unpaired opening closed by connective tissue, which is almost square and at birth has a diagonal length of 2.5–3 cm. The smaller, unpaired *posterior fontanelle* (**4**) is also closed by connective tissue and is triangular in shape. The anterior fontanelle lies between the two frontal bone anlagen and both parietal anlagen. The posterior fontanelle lies between the two parietal bone anlagen and the anlage of the upper squama of the occipital bone. The paired fontanelles lie laterally, of which the *sphenoidal fontanelle* (**5**), closed by connective tissue, is the larger and should be distinguished from the small *mastoid fontanelle* (**6**), which is occluded by cartilage (corresponding to a synchondrosis). The sphenoidal fontanelle lies between the frontal, parietal and sphenoid bones, and the mastoid fontanelle lies between the splenoid, temporal and occipital bones.

The fontanelles only become closed after birth, the first being the posterior fontanelle in the 3rd month, the sphenoidal fontanelle follows in the 6th month, the mastoid fontanelle in the 18th month, and the anterior fontanelle in the 36th month.

> **Clinical tip:** In the newborn and in infants the anterior fontanelle can be used for taking blood samples from the dural sinuses. Venepuncture is also possible through the great, anterior fontanelle.

Sutures and Synchondroses

The remnants of connective tissue between the cranial bones form cranial fibrous joints, cranial syndesmoses, the **sutures** (see p. 22), which permit continued growth of the bones. Only when the bones are completely fused as synostoses does growth cease.

Between some of the bones preformed in cartilage (chondrocranium) there are cranial cartilaginous joints, the **cranial synchondroses**. The *spheno-occipital synchondrosis*, which ossifies at about the 18th year, is of practical interest. In the region of the sphenoid body, the *intersphenoidal synchondrosis* is found, which ossifies early, while between the sphenoid and ethmoid bones is the *spheno-ethmoidal synchondrosis*, which does not ossify until maturity. In addition, cartilage remnants are retained throughout life between the petrosal part of the temporal bone and the adjacent bones, the *sphenopetrosal synchondrosis* and the *petro-occipital synchondrosis*.

Growth of the skull, as already stated, is dependent on the function and the contents of the skull. The neurocranium and viscerocranium do not grow at equal rates, but only in the first years of life is there more rapid growth of the viscerocranium which initially lagged behind.

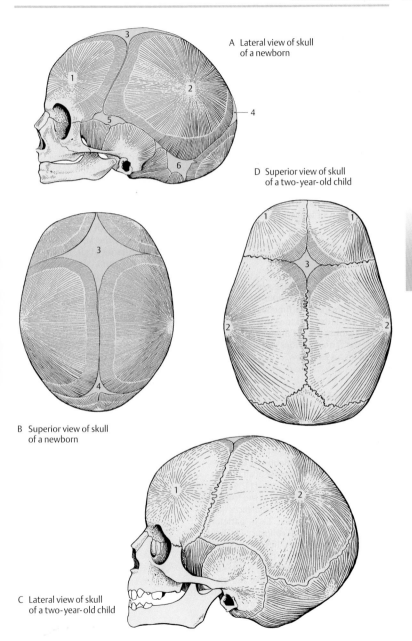

A Lateral view of skull
   of a newborn

D Superior view of skull
   of a two-year-old child

B Superior view of skull
   of a newborn

C Lateral view of skull
   of a two-year-old child

Head and Neck

Structure of the Cranial Bones

Each of the flat bones of the skull consists of
 – A compact **external table** (lamina externa)
 – A compact **internal table** (lamina interna)

and between the two lies
 – The **diploë** (spongy layer), in which there are numerous veins within the diploic canals

Within other bones of the skull are certain air-filled spaces associated with the nasal sinuses. The temporal bones contain the sensory organs of hearing and balance.

On the outside the skull is covered by the **pericranium**, and the inner surface of the skull is covered by the **endocranium** or **dura mater**.

It is useful first of all to take a unified view of the skull from its various aspects, in order to recognize the functional associations of the latter and to comprehend the special features of the individual cranial bones. The various cavities within the skull are also discussed below.

Calvaria (A–C)

The vault of the cranium, the calvaria, consists of a **frontal bone** (yellow), **parietal bones** (light brown), parts of the **temporal bones** (red), and the uppermost part of the **occipital bone** (orange). Examination of the outside of the skull will show first of all the sutures, e.g., the *coronal suture* (**1**), which separates the *squamous part* of the frontal bone (**2**) with the *frontal eminences* (**3**) from the parietal bones. Each parietal bone, also, has a *parietal eminence* (**4**). Between the parietal bones lies the *sagittal suture* (**5**), which runs from the coronal suture to the *lambdoid suture* (**6**), i.e., the suture between the parietal bone and the *squamous part* of the occipital bone (**7**). Laterally, in the parietal region, are the *in-ferior* (**8**) and *superior* (**9**) *temporal lines*. In close relationship to the sagittal suture, immediately in front of the lambdoid suture, lie the *parietal foramina* (**10**). Special features are described on p. 290.

The sutures are also visible *on the inner surface of the adult cranial vault.* On the cut surface the *external table* (**11**), the *diploë* (**12**), and the *internal table* (**13**) are exposed. In the most anterior part of the squamous part of the frontal bone lies the *frontal crest* (**14**) which extends toward the parietal bones. In the region of the sagittal suture is the shallow *groove for the superior sagittal sinus* (**15**). The *arterial grooves* (**16**), which contain the branches of the middle meningeal artery and its accompanying vein, ascend from the lateral toward the midline and posterior areas. Lateral to the groove for the superior sagittal sinus and lateral to the frontal crest there are a variable number of indentations of different size (*granular foveolae;* **17**) into which the arachnoidal granulations extend.

On the internal and external surfaces of the parietal bone in the vault are the *frontal* (**18**) and *occipital* (**19**) *angles*, while the sphenoid and mastoid angles are found only at the base of the skull.

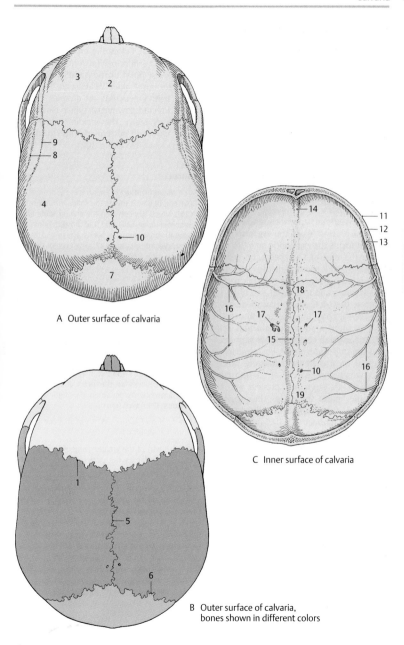

A Outer surface of calvaria

C Inner surface of calvaria

B Outer surface of calvaria,
bones shown in different colors

Lateral Aspect of the Skull (A–C)

In the orbitomeatal plane, which runs through the inferior margin of the orbit and the superior margin of the external acoustic meatus, the **neurocranium** shows the *temporal fossa* (**1**), which includes which includes part of the **temporal bone** (salmon), the **parietal bone** (brown), portions of the **frontal bone** (yellow), and the **sphenoid bone** (brick red).

The temporal fossa is limited above by the somewhat more prominent *inferior temporal line* (**2**) and the less obvious *superior temporal line* (**3**). From the *squamous part of the temporal bone* (**4**) the *zygomatic process* (**5**) extends anteriorly, and with the *temporal process* (**6**) of the **zygomatic bone** (blue) it forms the *zygomatic arch* (**7**). Inferior to the root of the zygomatic process lies the *external acoustic meatus* (**8**) which is bordered mainly by the **tympanic part** (**9**; **C**, light blue), and to a lesser extent by the **squamous part** (**4**; **C**, salmon) of the **temporal bone** (**B**, salmon). Immediately above this there is often a small *suprameatal spine* (**10**) and a small cavity, *foveola suprameatica = suprameatal triangle*. Posterior to the external meatus lies the *mastoid process* (**11**), which originated as a muscular apophysis. Between this process and the tympanic part there is the variably developed *tympanomastoid fissure* (**12**). The *mastoid foramen* (**13**) lies at the root of the mastoid process. Below the tympanic part (**9**) there is the *styloid process* of variable size (**C**, light green).

On examining the **viscerocranium** we see above the orbit the *supraciliary arch* (**14**) as a prominent ridge. Below it is the *supraorbital margin* (**15**) with the *supra-orbital notch*. The supra-orbital margin is continued over the anterolateral margin of the orbital opening into the *infra-orbital margin* (**16**). The latter is formed by the **zygomatic bone** and the *frontal process of the maxilla* (**17**). Medially is a depression, the fossa for the lacrimal sac (**18**); (orbit, see p. 306).

There are one (or two) small foramina in the zygomatic bone, the *zygomaticofacial foramen* (**19**). Below the infra-orbital margin lies the *infra-orbital foramen* (**20**). At the lowest point of the nasal opening the *anterior nasal spine* (**21**) is seen. The **maxilla** (light green) has an *alveolar process* (**22**) directed downward, which carries the maxillary teeth. The *maxillary tuberosity* (**23**) *bulges out posterior to this* (for details of the mandible, see p. 302).

Sutures

The *coronal suture* (**24**) separates the frontal and parietal bones. It meets the *sphenofrontal suture* (**25**), which lies between the *greater wing of the sphenoid bone* (**26**) and the frontal bone. The frontal and zygomatic bones are joined by the *frontozygomatic suture* (**27**). The *zygomaticomaxillary suture* (**28**) lies between the zygomatic bone and the maxilla, and the *temporozygomatic suture* (**29**) is found between the zygomatic and temporal bones. The *frontomaxillary suture* (**30**) lies between the frontal bone and the maxilla, and the *nasomaxillary suture* (**31**) is between the maxilla and the nasal bone (dark green). The *sphenosquamous suture* (**32**) forms the boundary between the greater wing of the sphenoid bone and the temporal squama. The temporal bone (light red) joins the parietal bone at the *squamous suture* (**33**). It may extend into the mastoid process as the *petrosquamous suture* (**34**) between its squamous (**C**, light red) and petrous (**C**, brown) parts.

The *lambdoid suture* (**35**) separates the parietal from the occipital bone (orange).

A small part of the greater wing of the sphenoid extends as far as the parietal bone, so that a *sphenoparietal suture* (**36**) can be described. Between the mastoid process and the parietal bone on the one hand and the occipital bone on the other lie the *parietomastoid* (**37**) and *occipitomastoid* (**38**) sutures.

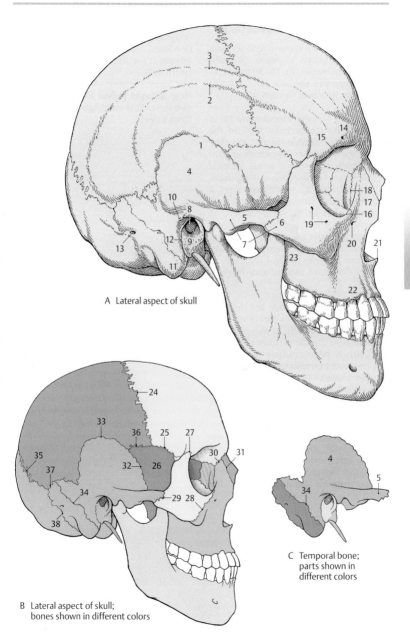

A Lateral aspect of skull

B Lateral aspect of skull;
   bones shown in different colors

C Temporal bone;
   parts shown in
   different colors

Posterior Aspect of the Skull (A, B)

In the dorsal view it is possible to see both **parietal bones** (brown, **1**), which are joined by the *sagittal suture* (**2**). The *lambdoid suture* (**3**) separates the two parietal bones from the **occipital bone** (orange, **4**).

The *external occipital protuberance* (**5**) is prominent on the occipital bone in the midline and is palpable through the skin. The *highest nuchal line* (**6**) extends upward and laterally from the external occipital protuberance. The line below is the *superior nuchal line* (**7**), which represents a transverse ridge lateral to the protuberance, and below it is the *inferior nuchal line* (**8**), which extends roughly in the center between the external occipital protuberance and the foramen magnum. The *inferior nuchal* line may begin at the, more or less well developed, *external occipital crest* (**9**).

Lateral to the occipital bone lies the *mastoid process* (**11**), which is part of the temporal bone, but which is joined to the occipital bone by the *occipitomastoid suture* (**10**). A petrosquamous suture (**12**) may be present completely or in part in the mastoid process. This suture shows that the mastoid process is formed from both the squamous and the petrous parts of the temporal bone. In the region of the *occipitomastoid suture* (**10**) is the *mastoid foramen* (**13**), through which the mastoid emissary vein passes. On the medial side of the mastoid process lies the *mastoid notch* (**14**), medial to which is the *occipital groove* (**15**). *Parietal foramina* (**16**) are situated in the region of the parietal bones.

■■ Variants: Sometimes the external occipital protuberance is particularly well developed. The upper squama may be present as a separate bone, the **incarial bone** (see p. 314).

The parietal foramina may be particularly large (**enlarged parietal foramina**) and may give rise to false conclusions in radiographs (bore holes).

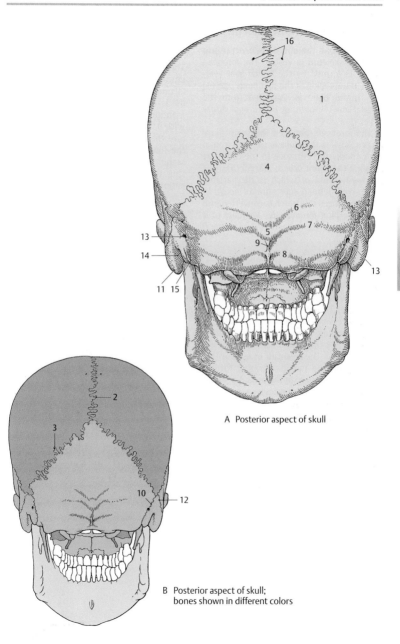

A Posterior aspect of skull

B Posterior aspect of skull;
    bones shown in different colors

Anterior Aspect of the Skull (A, B)

From the front, the entire **viscerocranium** or facial skeleton is visible. The forehead region is formed by the **frontal bone** (yellow). In the region of the *squamous part* (**1**) the frontal bone is separated from the **parietal bones** (brown) by the *coronal suture* (**2**).

In the forehead, between the *supraciliary arches* (**3**), lies the *glabella* (**4**). The frontal bone marks the entrance to the orbits by forming the *supra-orbital margin* (**5**), near the medial end of which is the variably sized, well-defined *supra-orbital notch*. In some instances this notch is converted into a *supra-orbital foramen* (**6**). Medially to it may lie a small *frontal notch* (**7**) or a frontal foramen.

Between the orbits the frontal bone is separated from the **nasal bones** (dark green) by the *frontonasal sutures* (**8**), and from the **maxillae** (light green) by the *frontomaxillary sutures* (**9**). The two nasal bones are joined by the *internasal suture* (**10**). Lateral to the orbital opening, the *frontozygomatic suture* (**11**) separates the frontal bone from the zygomatic bone. The **zygomatic bone** (blue) together with the maxilla forms a further part of the boundary of the orbital opening (for details of the orbital cavity, see p. 306).

The *infraorbital foramen* (**14**) is located in the **maxilla**, just below the *infraorbital margin* (**12**) and adjacent to the *zygomatico-maxillary suture* (**13**). It transmits a branch of the maxillary nerve, the infra-orbital nerve, an artery and a vein. Inferior to the orbit, in the region of the *maxillary body*, there is a deep depression, the *canine fossa* (**15**).

The *zygomatic process* (**16**) runs laterally from the maxillary body. The maxilla is attached to the frontal bone by the *frontal process* (**17**) which ascends from the maxillary body and connects with the nasal bone by the *nasomaxillary suture* (**18**). The *palatine process* (see p. 294) is directed medially and forms one of the foundation of the hard palate. Finally, in the tooth-bearing upper jaw, there is the downward-facing *alveolar process* (**19**).

The continuation of the infra-orbital margin on the frontal process is the *anterior lacrimal crest* (**20**). The center of the maxilla is formed by the *body of the maxilla* mentioned above. The latter demarcates with its *nasal notch* (**21**) the *piriform aperture*, the entrance into the nasal cavities. At the lower margin of the aperture in the region of the *intermaxillary suture* (**22**), a spur, the *anterior nasal spine* (**23**), projects anteriorly. In the zygomatic bone there are one or two *zygomaticofacial foramina* (**24**).

In the lower jaw, the **mandible** (light violet), the *body* (**25**), the *alveolar part* (**26**), and the *ramus* (**27**) are visible from the front. In the region of the body of the mandible, the *mental foramen* (**28**) lies vertically below the second premolar tooth. The *mental protuberance* (**29**) is found in the midline of the body of the mandible (see p. 302).

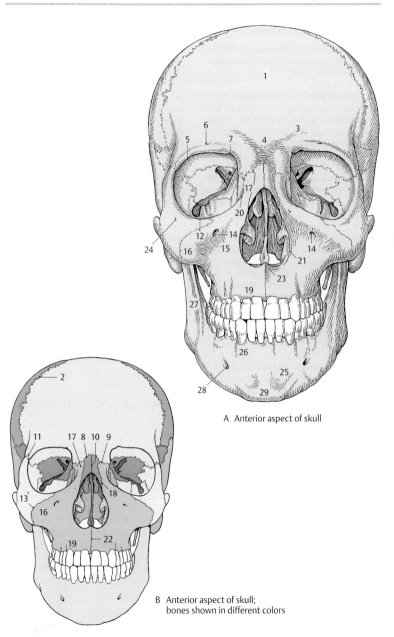

A Anterior aspect of skull

B Anterior aspect of skull;
bones shown in different colors

Inferior Aspect of the Skull (A–B)

The external surface of the base of the skull consists of an anterior visceral part and a posterior neural part.

The **anterior part** is formed on each side by the *palatine process of the maxilla* (**1**, light green), the *horizontal plate of the palatine bone* (**2**, green), the *alveolar process* and *tuber of the maxilla* (**3**) and the **zygomatic bone** (**4**, light blue). The **vomer** (dark blue) borders the *choanae* (**5**) medially. The two palatine processes are fused at the *median palatine suture* (**6**), the anterior end of which is indicated by the *incisive fossa* (**7**) housing the incisive canals. An *incisive suture* (**8**), which is often preserved, passes from the fossa up to the second incisor. The horizontal plate of the palatine bone contains the *greater* (**9**) and the *lesser* (**10**) *palatine foramina*. *Palatine grooves* pass anteriorly from the greater palatine foramen and are bordered by ridges, the *palatine spines*. The *transverse palatine suture* (**11**) is found between the **maxilla** (light green) and the **palatine bone** (medium green).

The **posterior part** of the base of the skull consists of the **sphenoid bone** (brick red), the **temporal bones** (salmon), and the **occipital bone** (orange). The pterygoid processes form the lateral borders of the choanae. We distinguish a *medial plate* (**12**), with its *hamulus*, and a *lateral plate* (**13**). Between them lies the *pterygoid fossa*. At the root of the medial plate is the *scaphoid fossa* (**14**) and next to it the *foramen lacerum* (**15**).

In the center lies the *body of the sphenoid bone* (**16**) and laterally its *greater wing* (**17**) with the *infratemporal crest* (**18**). The greater wing bears the *sphenoid spine* (**19**), whose base is pierced by the *foramen spinosum* (**20**). Between the foramen spinosum and the foramen lacerum opens the *foramen ovale* (**21**), and between the sphenoid bone and the petrous part of the temporal bone we find the *sphenopetrosal fissure* (**22**). From the latter the groove of the

auditory tube (**23**) extends posterolaterally. The *external opening of the cochlear canaliculus* is found on the side of the *jugular fossa* (**25**) and adjacent to the *external opening of the carotid canal* (**24**). This is limited laterally by the *jugular and occipital processes*. Between the jugular fossa and the external opening of the carotid canal is a small depression, the *petrosal fossula*, in which the canaliculus for the tympanic nerve opens. Next to this are the *tympanic part* (**26**) of the temporal bone and the *styloid process* (**27**) within its sheath. Immediately posterior to the process is the *stylomastoid foramen* (**28**). On the *mastoid process* (**29**) is the *mastoid notch* (**30**), and medial to it is the *occipitomastoid suture* (**31**) with the **occipital groove** for the occipital artery (**32**). Anterior to the mastoid process lies the opening of the *external acoustic meatus* (**34**), which is bounded by the *tympanic part* (**26**) and the *squamous part* (**33**).

The tympanic and squamous parts, as well as a small ridge of the petrous part, the *tegmental crest* bounded by the *petrotympanic* and *petrosquamous fissures*, form the *mandibular fossa* (**35**). This is limited anteriorly by the *articular tubercle* (**36**). The *zygomatic process of the temporal bone* (**37**) extends anterolaterally.

The *basilar part* (**38**) of the occipital bone, which bears the *pharyngeal tubercle* (**39**), fuses with the *body of the sphenoid bone* (**16**). The *petro-occipital fissure* runs between the petrosal part of the temporal and the occipital bone. The jugular fossa (**25**) is widened by the notch in the adjacent occipital bone to form the *jugular foramen*. The *foramen magnum* (**40**) is bordered laterally on each side by an *occipital condyle* (**41**) behind which lies the condylar fossa perforated by a *condylar canal* (**42**). Beginning directly behind the foramen magnum, the *external occipital crest* (**43**) passes upward to the *external occipital protuberance* (**44**).

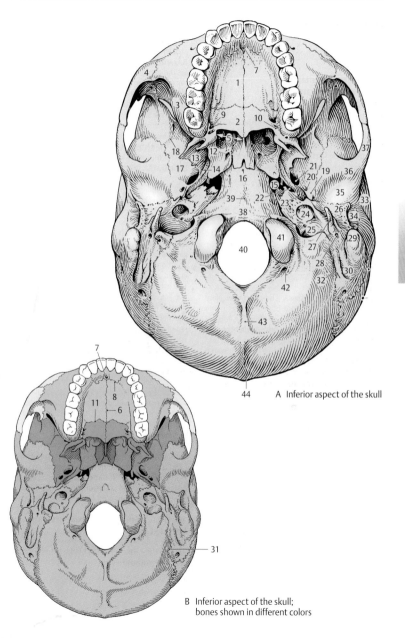

A Inferior aspect of the skull

B Inferior aspect of the skull;
bones shown in different colors

Internal Surface of Cranial Base (A, B)

The base of the skull is divided into three fossae:

The **anterior cranial fossa**
The **middle cranial fossa**
The **posterior cranial fossa**

The following bones form the inner surface of the base of the skull: the **ethmoid bone** (blue-violet), the **frontal bone** (yellow), the **sphenoid bone** (brick red), the **temporal bones** (salmon), the **occipital bone** (orange), and the **parietal bones** (brown).

The anterior cranial fossa is separated from the middle fossa by the *lesser wings of the sphenoid* (**1**) and the *jugum sphenoidale* (**2**). The middle and posterior cranial fossae are separated from each other by the *superior borders* (**3**) of the petrosal portions of the temporal bones and the *dorsum sellae* (**4**).

The anterior cranial fossa. The *cribriform plate* (**5**) formed by the ethmoid bone contains many small holes and bears in the midline the vertical *crista galli* (**6**) with its *ala of crista galli*. Anterior to the crista galli is the *foramen caecum* (**7**) and laterally lie the *orbital plates* (**8**) of the frontal bone with their *impressiones digitatae*. The cribriform plate is joined to the sphenoid bone by the *spheno-ethmoidal suture* (**9**). In the middle, the *prechiasmatic groove* (**11**) lies between the *optic canals* (**10**). The *anterior clinoid processes* (**12**) border the optic canals.

In the center of the **middle cranial fossa** there is the *sella turcica* with the *hypophysial fossa* (**13**) and lateral to the sella the *carotid sulcus* (**14**), which is the prolongation of the carotid canal. The carotid canal, which lies on the anterior wall of the petrous part of the temporal bone, is split open in its medial portion near the *foramen lacerum* (**15**). The medial end of the canal is bounded by the *sphenoidal lingula* (**16**). Lateral to the carotid groove is the *foramen ovale* (**17**), in front the *foramen rotundum* (**18**) and lateral the *foramen spinosum* (**19**). The *groove for the middle meningeal artery* (**20**) runs laterally from the foramen spinosum.

Near the apex of the petrous part, the *trigeminal impression* (**21**) can be seen, and lateral and somewhat posterior to it is the *hiatus for the greater petrosal nerve* (**22**), which continues toward the sphenopetrosal fissure as the *groove for the greater petrosal nerve* (**23**). The *hiatus for the lesser petrosal nerve* (**24**) lies immediately anterolateral to that of the greater petrosal nerve. The *superior border of the petrous part* (**3**) carries the more or less well developed *groove of the superior petrosal sinus* (**25**). A prominent swelling, the *arcuate eminence* (**26**), is produced by the anterior semicircular canal. The squamous part of the temporal bone is joined to the sphenoid bone by the *sphenosquamous suture* (**27**).

The *foramen magnum* (**28**) lies in the middle of the **posterior cranial fossa**. The *clivus* (**29**) ascends anteriorly and ends in the *dorsum sellae* (**4**) and its *posterior clinoid processes* (**30**).

Between the occipital bone and the petrous part of the temporal lies the *groove for the inferior petrosal sinus* (**31**) and also the petro-occipital synchondrosis, which may be seen in the macerated skull as the *petro-occipital fissure* (**32**). The groove for the inferior petrosal sinus ends in the *jugular foramen* (**33**). The *internal acoustic meatus* (**34**) opens onto the posterior surface of the petrous bone. Lateral to it, hidden under a small bony ridge, lies the *external opening of the vestibular aqueduct*.

The jugular foramen (**33**) is formed by the apposition of the jugular notches in the temporal and occipital bones. The *jugular notch in the occipital bone* is limited anteriorly by the projection of the *jugular tubercle*, and the jugular foramen is partly divided by the *intrajugular process of the temporal bone* (**35**). On its lateral side the jugular foramen is reached by the *groove of the sigmoid sinus* (**36**), which continues posteriorly into the *groove for the transverse sinus* (**37**). This extends to the *internal occipital protuberance* (**38**), from which the *internal occipital crest* (**39**) runs toward the foramen magnum (**28**). On either side of the anterior rim of the foramen magnum is the opening of the *hypoglossal canal* (**40**).

The clivus is formed by the body of the sphenoid bone and the basilar part of the occipital bone. During puberty they fuse (**os tribasilare**) but previously they are connected by the spheno-occipital synchondrosis.

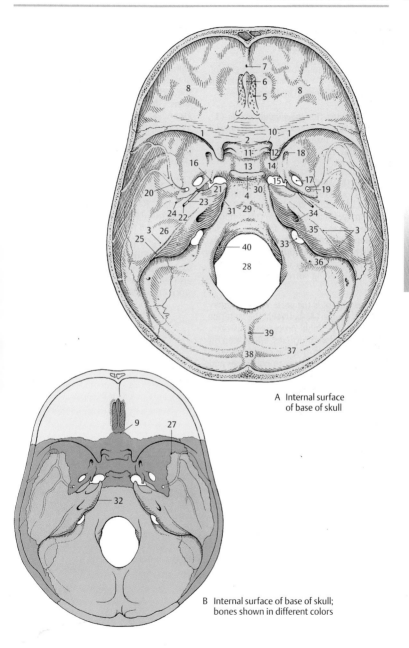

A Internal surface of base of skull

B Internal surface of base of skull; bones shown in different colors

■ Variants of the Internal Surface of cranial base (A–E)

In the middle cranial fossa, in the region of the sella turcica, a number of variants can be seen in radiological imaging studies.

In some cases the *sphenoidal lingula* (**1**), which is directed toward the temporal bone, may be fused with it. This distinctly demarcates the internal opening of the carotid canal.

Between the anterior and posterior clinoid processes there may be an additional process, the *middle clinoid process* (**2**). The latter may then fuse with the anterior clinoid process, when it forms a special opening, the *caroticoclinoid foramen* (**3**). Through this, the carotid notch, which lies medial to the anterior clinoid process, becomes an opening surrounded by bone on all sides.

Another variant is the presence of an *interclinoidal bridge* (**4**) between the anterior and posterior clinoid processes. This bony fusion of the two processes, when seen on radiographs, is termed the *sella bridge* (**4**). It may be present on one or both sides and can fuse (**5**) with the middle clinoid process if it is present.

A very rare variant is the presence of a *craniopharyngeal canal* (**6**) in the hypophysial fossa.

Between the foramen ovale and the body of the sphenoid bone, there is sometimes an aperture, which serves as the exit for a vein. This opening, the *foramen venosum* (**7**) is also called the sphenoidal emissarium or the foramen of Vesalius. It is not very uncommon and it permits communication between the cavernous sinus and veins on the outside of the skull. The foramen of Vesalius may be present on one or both sides.

In some cases the dorsum sellae may be so eroded laterally by more extensive looping of the internal carotid artery that it no longer has any bony connection with the clivus. In that case, the dorsum sellae will be absent from the macerated skull (**D**).

Sometimes the internal occipital crest is divided into two and between the parts is the well-developed *groove of the occipital sinus*. This may extend into a *marginal groove* (**8**), running lateral to the *foramen magnum* (**9**), to the *jugular foramen* (**10**). The *condylar canal* (**11**) may empty with a particularly large opening into the sigmoid sinus.

The jugular foramina may be unequal in size, more often the left being smaller than the right. Rarely is the *groove for the inferior petrosal sinus* (**12**) very deep. *The hypoglossal canal may be divided into two* (**13**).

The apex of the petrous part of the temporal bone may have a bony connection with the dorsum sellae. This bony bridge is also known as the *abducent bridge* (**14**), since the abducent nerve runs beneath it.

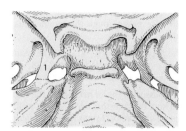

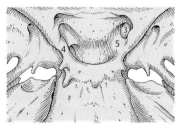

A Sella turcica; right sphenoidal lingula fused with temporal bone

C Sella turcica; interclinoid bridge, right caroticoclinoid foramen

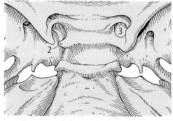

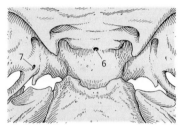

B Sella turcica; left middle clinoid process, right caroticoclinoid foramen

D Sella turcica; craniopharyngeal canal, foramen venosum, absence of dorsum sellae

Head and Neck

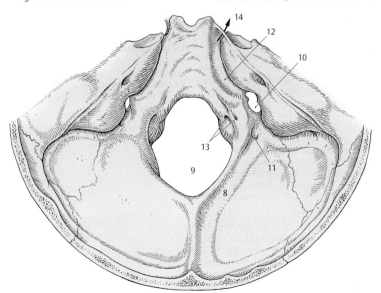

E Groove of right occipital sinus, divided canal for hypoglossal nerve

Sites for Passage for Vessels and Nerves (A, B)

The openings in the base of the skull transmit vessels and nerves.

In the region of the anterior cranial fossa the *olfactory nerves* (**1**) and the *anterior ethmoidal artery* (**2**) pass through the **cribriform plate** to the nasal cavity.

The *optic nerve* (**3**) and the *ophthalmic artery* (**4**) run through the **optic canal**.
Apart from the optic canal, the **superior orbital fissure** also forms a communication between the skull and the orbit. The *superior ophthalmic vein* (**5**), the *lacrimal nerve* (**6**), the *frontal nerve* (**7**), and the *trochlear nerve* (**8**) run in its lateral part. The *abducent nerve* (**9**), the *oculomotor nerve* (**10**), and the *nasociliary nerve* (**11**) pass through it more medially.

The *maxillary nerve* (**12**) passes through the **foramen rotundum**, while the *mandibular nerve* (**13**), together with a *venous plexus of the foramen ovale* which joins the cavernous sinus to the pterygoid plexus, runs through the **foramen ovale**. A recurrent branch of the mandibular nerve, the *meningeal branch* (**14**), together with the *middle meningeal artery* (**15**), reaches the cranial cavity through the **foramen spinosum**. The largest structure in the middle cranial fossa, the *internal carotid artery* (**16**) passes through the **carotid canal** into the cranial cavity. The internal carotid artery is surrounded by the *sympathetic carotid plexus* (**17**) *and internal carotid venous plexus*. The *greater petrosal nerve* (**18**) becomes visible at the **hiatus for greater petrosal nerve**, and the *lesser petrosal nerve* (**19**) runs through the **hiatus for lesser petrosal nerve** together with the *superior tympanic artery* (**20**).

In the posterior cranial fossa, the *medulla oblongata* (**21**), and on each side of it the *spinal part of the accessory nerve* (**22**), pass through the **foramen magnum**. Two large *vertebral arteries* (**23**), the small *anterior spinal artery* (**24**), the paired small *poste-rior spinal arteries* (**25**), and the *spinal vein* (**26**) also pass through the foramen magnum.

The *hypoglossal nerve* (**27**) and the *venous plexus of the hypoglossal canal* (**28**) pass through the **hypoglossal canal**.

The *glossopharyngeal nerve* (**29**), the *vagus* (**30**) and the *accessory nerve* (**31**), as well as the *inferior petrosal sinus* (**32**), the *internal jugular vein* (**33**), and the *posterior meningeal artery* (**34**) all pass through the **jugular foramen**.

The **internal acoustic meatus** transmits the *labyrinthine artery and vein* (**35**), the *vestibulocochlear nerve* (**36**), and the *facial nerve* (**37**).

On the *outer surface of the base of the skull* the *facial nerve* (**37**) becomes visible as it emerges from the **stylomastoid foramen,** through which the *stylomastoid artery* (**38**) enters the skull.

The *anterior tympanic artery* (**39**) and the *chorda tympani* (**40**) traverse the **petrotympanic fissure**.

The *greater palatine artery* (**41**) and the *greater palatine nerve* (**42**) pass through the **greater palatine foramen** in the hard palate, and the *lesser palatine arteries and nerves* (**43**) run through the **lesser palatine foramina**. The *nasopalatine nerve* and an artery (**44**) run through the **incisive canal** toward the palate.

The *condylar emissary vein* (**45**) runs through the **condylar canal**.

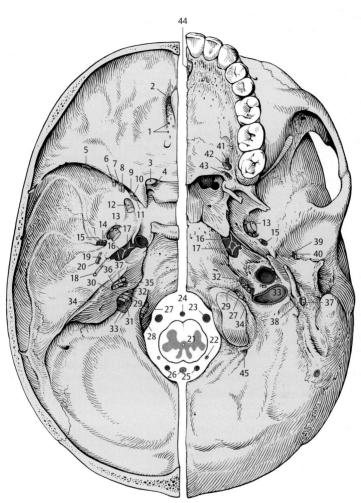

A Left side of diagram:
   Internal view of left base of skull

B Right side of diagram:
   External view of left base of skull

A, B Sites for passage for vessels and nerves in base of skull

Head and Neck

Mandible (A–C)

The lower jaw (mandible) is only connected with the other bones of the skull by synovial joints. It is preformed in connective tissue and consists of the **body (1)** with its ascending **ramus of the mandible (2)** on each side.

In the adult the **body of the mandible bears** the *alveolar part* (**3**), which is marked on its outer surface by the bulging *alveolar yokes* (**4**). In old age, i.e., after loss of the teeth, the alveolar part undergoes regression (see p. 304). On the front of the body of the mandible lies the *mental protuberance* (**5**), which is elevated on each side to form the *mental tubercle*. On the outer surface, on a vertical line through the second premolar, there is an opening, the *mental foramen* (**6**). The inferior surface of the mandible is called the base of the mandible. The *oblique line* (**7**) ascends from the body to the ramus of the mandible. Posteriorly the body of the mandible merges at the *mandibular angle* (**8**) with the ramus.

The **ramus of the mandible** has two processes, the anterior *coronoid process* (**9**) for insertion of a muscle, and the posterior *condylar process* (**10**) for the joint surface.

Between the processes lies the *mandibular notch* (**11**). The condylar process has a *neck* (**12**) and supports the *head of the mandible* with its *articular surface* (**13**). The mandibular head is also known as the *mandibular condyle* because of its cylindrical shape. On the inner aspect of the head of the mandible, below the articular surface, a small pit, *the pterygoid fovea* (**14**), for the insertion of part of the lateral pterygoid muscle is seen. Near the angle of the mandible there is sometimes a roughened area, the *masseteric tuberosity* (**15**) for the insertion of the masseter muscle. On the inner surface of the mandible in the region of the ramus lies the *mandibular foramen* (**16**), which is the entrance to the *mandibular canal*. The opening is partly concealed by a delicate spur of bone, the *lingula of the mandible* (**17**). The *mylohyoid groove* (**18**) begins directly at the mandibular foramen and runs obliquely downward. Below the mylohyoid groove, at the angle of the mandible, is the *pterygoid tuberosity* (**19**), which serves for the insertion of the medial pterygoid muscle.

The inner surface of the body of the mandible is divided by an oblique ridge, the *mylohyoid line* (**20**). Below this line, from which the mylohyoid muscle arises, we find the *submandibular fossa* (**21**), while above it and somewhat more anterior, is the *sublingual fossa* (**22**).

The dental alveoli are separated by the *interalveolar septa* (**23**). Within the alveoli of the molars, *interradicular septa* may be seen. Posterior to the last molar there is the variably developed large *retromolar triangle*.

Anteriorly, on the inner surface of the body, lies the *mental spine* (**24**), from which muscles arise (also called genial spines), and laterally, somewhat lower, are the *digastric fossae* (**25**), the points of insertion of the digastric muscles.

■■■ **Variants:** Two mental spines are sometimes present, one situated above the other.

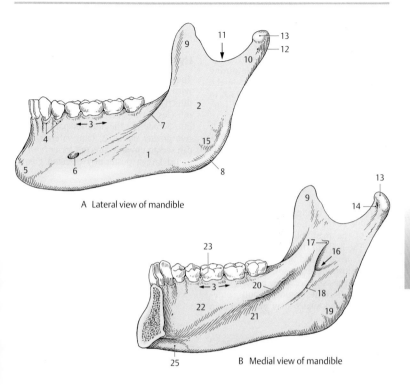

A Lateral view of mandible

B Medial view of mandible

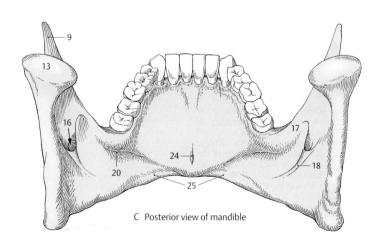

C Posterior view of mandible

Shape of Mandible (A–E)

The *angle of the mandible* differs at various stages of life. In the newborn (**A**) it is still relatively large, about 150°, while during childhood (**B**) it becomes smaller. In the adult (**C**) it is reduced to about 120–130°. In old age (**D**) it again increases to about 140°.

The change in the angle of the mandible is dependent on the presence of the alveolar part with its alveolar arch and the teeth. With eruption of the teeth there is an alteration in the mandibular angle of the infant, and it changes again in old age when the teeth are lost.

Apart from the change in the angle of the mandible at the various stages of life, the body of the mandible also shows variations. The body of the mandible bears the alveolar process, and in old age, after the teeth are lost, this regresses. During this regression the size of the body of the mandible becomes reduced and sometimes flattened, which may push the chin forward.

> **Clinical tip:** Modern dentistry can reduce age-related changes in the jaw with **dental implants**. Metal posts are surgically implanted in the mandible or maxilla to serve as abutments for dental crowns. This eliminates the need for a denture, which always constitutes a foreign body. However, dental implantation requires a highly experienced surgeon.

The alveolar part may vary in its orientation. In some instances, particularly among the primates, there may be an alveolar part protruding outward and the position of the teeth differs from that in modern humans.

Ossification: As noted on p. 282, the mandible is preformed in connective tissue. It appears on both sides in the first visceral arch as intermembranous bone, formed on *Meckel's* cartilage (*Meckel's jun. 1781 – 1833*). In the region of the symphysis, i.e., anteriorly, parts of *Meckel's* cartilage form the basis of those parts of the ossicula mentalia which develop in cartilage. These fuse with the mandible. The first bone cells appear in the 6th intrauterine week. Together with the clavicle, it is the first bone in the body to develop.

The synostosis of the two parts of the mandible begins in the 2nd month of life.

Hyoid Bone (F)

The hyoid bone, which may be included with the bony skeleton of the skull, is not directly connected but is joined to it by muscles and ligaments. It may be divided into a *body* (**1**), the anterior part, and the two *greater horns* (**2**) lying laterally. One can see an upward-directed *lesser horn* (**3**) and a larger, posteriorly directed *greater horn* (**2**).

Ossification: In the body and the greater horn of the hyoid bone, ossification centers develop in cartilage just before birth, while in the lesser horn the center develops much later, at about the 20th year. The lesser horn need not ossify but may remain cartilaginous. Like the mandible, the hyoid bone develops from the skeleton of the visceral arches.

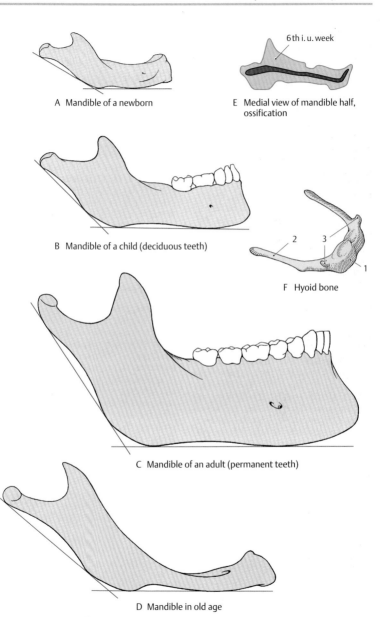

A Mandible of a newborn

E Medial view of mandible half, ossification

6th i. u. week

B Mandible of a child (deciduous teeth)

F Hyoid bone

C Mandible of an adult (permanent teeth)

D Mandible in old age

Head and Neck

Orbit (A, B)

Each **orbital cavity** is shaped like a four-sided pyramid, the apex lying deep inside and the base forming the orbital opening. It is demarcated by various bones.

Roof: The roof of the orbit is formed anteriorly by the *orbital plate of the frontal bone* (**1**) and posteriorly by the *lesser wing of the sphenoid* (**2**).

Lateral wall: The lateral wall consists of the *zygomatic bone* (**3**) and the *greater wing of the sphenoid* (**4**).

Floor: The anterior part of the floor is formed by the orbital surface of the *body of the maxilla* (**5**) and posteriorly by the *orbital process of the palatine bone* (**6**). Along the infra-orbital margin, the floor is completed anteriorly by the zygomatic bone (**3**).

Medial wall: The thin medial wall is formed by the *orbital plate of the ethmoid bone* (**7**), the *lacrimal bone* (**8**), and the *sphenoid* (**9**). In addition, the frontal bone (**1**) and the *maxilla* provide smaller contributions to this wall.

Orbital openings: The *supra-orbital* and *infra-orbital margins* of the entrance to the orbit have already been described (see p. 292). Medially and laterally they are joined together by the *medial* and *lateral margins*. Posteriorly there are two converging fissures, the *superior orbital fissure* (**10**) which opens into the cranial cavity, and the *inferior orbital fissure* (**11**) for the communication with the pterygopalatine fossa. The fissures converge medially and immediately above the junction lies the *optic canal* (**12**). From the inferior orbital fissure runs the *infra-orbital groove* (**13**) which becomes the *infra-orbital canal* to open below the infra-orbital margin as the *infra-orbital foramen* (**14**). On the lateral wall the zygomatic nerve passes through the *zygomatico-orbital foramen* (**15**). On the medial wall, where the ethmoid bone meets the frontal bone, are the *anterior* (**16**) and *posterior* (**17**) *ethmoidal foramina*. The nerves and arteries of the same name leave through these foramina. The anterior ethmoidal foramen opens into the cranial cavity, while the posterior one leads into the ethmoidal cells. Near the entrance into the orbit lies the *fossa for the lacrimal sac* (**18**) which is bounded anteriorly and posteriorly by the *anterior* (**19**) and the *posterior* (**20**) *lacrimal crests*. It leads into the *nasolacrimal canal*, which opens into the nasal cavity (see p. 308).

In the immediate neighborhood of the orbits are the **paranasal sinuses.** The variably sized orbital recess of the *frontal sinus* (**21**) extends into the roof of the orbit. Medially lie the ethmoid cells and dorsally the sphenoidal sinus. Inferiorly, the orbit is separated from the *maxillary sinus* (**22**) by a thin plate of bone.

Pterygopalatine Fossa (B, C)

The **pterygopalatine fossa** may be approached from the lateral side through the *pterygomaxillary fissure* (**23**). Anteriorly to it lies the *maxilla* (**24**), posteriorly the *pterygoid process* (**25**), and medially the *perpendicular plate of the palatine bone* (**26**). It is an important junction area for vessels and nerves. It is connected with the cranial cavity by the *foramen rotundum* (**27**), and with the lower surface of the base of the skull by the *pterygoid canal* (**28**). The *greater palatine canal* (**29**) and the lesser palatine canal lead to the palate, the *sphenopalatine foramen* (**30**) to the nasal cavity, and the inferior orbital fissure (**11**) into the orbital cavity.

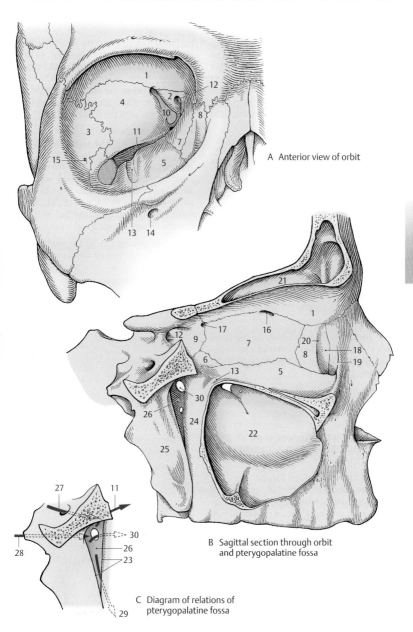

A Anterior view of orbit

B Sagittal section through orbit and pterygopalatine fossa

C Diagram of relations of pterygopalatine fossa

Nasal Cavity (A–C)

We distinguish a right and a left **bony nasal cavity** separated medially by the **nasal septum**. The septum often deviates from the midline. The nasal cavities open anteriorly into the **piriform aperture** (see p. 292) and posteriorly each opens via the **choana**, the posterior nasal aperture, into the pharynx (see vol. 2).

The **nasal septum** (**A**) consists of **cartilaginous** and **bony elements**. The **cartilaginous septum** (**1**) with its *posterior process* (**2**) completes the bony partition between the two nasal cavities. The **medial crus of the major alar cartilage** (**3**) is superimposed on each side on the septal cartilage as the medial border of the anterior opening of the nose. The bony partition, the **bony nasal septum**, is formed by the *perpendicular plate of the ethmoid* (**4**), the *sphenoidal crest* (**5**), and the *vomer* (**6**).

Bottom: The **floor** of the nasal cavity is formed by the *maxilla* (**7**) and *the palatine bone* (**8**).

The **roof** is formed anteriorly by the *nasal bone* (**9**), and further posterior and superior thereto by the *cribriform plate of the ethmoid* (**10**).

The **lateral wall** (**B**, **C**) of each nasal cavity is made irregular by the **three** turbinate bones, the **conchae nasales** and the underlying ethmoidal cells. The *superior* (**11**) and *middle* (**12**) *conchae* belong to the ethmoid bone, while the *inferior nasal concha* (**13**) is a separate bone of the skull.

Behind the superior concha lies the *spheno-ethmoidal recess* (**14**) into which the sphenoidal sinuses open. The *sphenopalatine foramen* (**15**) lies in the lateral wall of the recess. It connects it to the pterygopalatine fossa (p. 306). After removal of the three conchae, the *superior, medial*, and *inferior nasal meati* are revealed, and *the perpendicular plate of the palatine bone* (**16**) is fully exposed. The openings (**17**) of the posterior ethmoidal cells can be seen in the superior nasal meatus.

In the middle nasal meatus, the *uncinate process* (**18**) partly covers the *maxillary hiatus* (**19**) which connects the maxillary sinus with the nasal cavity. Superior to this process is the *ethmoidal bulla* (**20**), a particularly large anterior ethmoidal cell. Above and below the bulla the middle and the anterior ethmoidal cells open into the middle meatus of the nasal cavity.

Between the ethmoidal bulla and the uncinate process is the *ethmoidal infundibulum* (**21**), across which the *frontal sinus* (**22**), the *maxillary sinus* (**23**), and the anterior ethmoidal cells are connected with the nasal cavity. The uncinate process also partly covers the *lacrimal bone* (**24**), which forms the lateral wall together with the maxilla (**7**) and the ethmoid bone.

The *nasal opening* (**25**) *of the nasolacrimal canal* lies in the inferior nasal meatus.

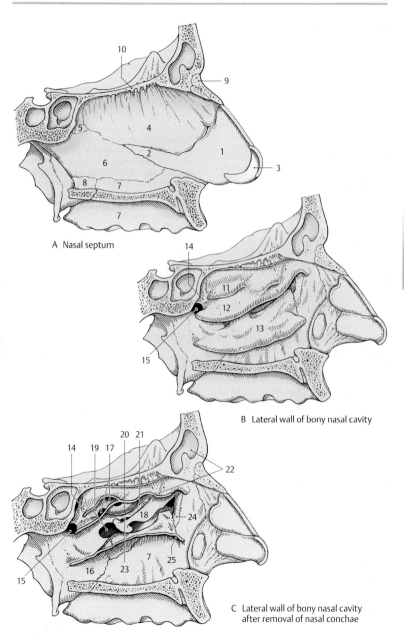

A Nasal septum

Head and Neck

B Lateral wall of bony nasal cavity

C Lateral wall of bony nasal cavity
after removal of nasal conchae

Cranial Shapes (A–C)

Anatomy and anthropology recognize a number of craniometric points, lines, and angles which permit comparison of the various types of normal skull (**A**) and also permit recognition of abnormal forms (**B**, **C**).

Some of the important points for measurement include: the *glabella* (**1**) = the smooth area between the eyebrows; the *opisthocranion* = the most posterior protruding point of the occipital bone in the midline sagittal plane; the *basion* = the anterior margin of the foramen magnum; the *bregma* (**2**) = the point of contact between the sagittal suture and the coronal suture; the *nasion* (**3**) = the crossing point of the nasofrontal suture with the median sagittal plane; the *gnathion* (**4**) = that point on the base of mandible in the median sagittal plane which protrudes furthest downward; the *zygion* (**5**) = the most laterally protruding point of the zygomatic arch. Also of interest are the *gonion* (**6**) = the widest, downward, backward and laterally directed point at the angle of the mandible; the *vertex* = the highest point of the skull in the midsagittal plane when oriented to the orbitomeatal plane; the *inion* = the most prominent point (center) of the external occipital protuberance.

Other points of measurement, lines, and angles may be found in textbooks of anthropology.

The most important indices based on a comparison of the distances between the individual points of measurement are presented below.

Length–Breadth Index of the Neurocranium

$$\frac{\text{greatest width of the skull}}{\text{greatest length of the skull}} \times 100 \ (=I)$$
(glabella-opisthocranion)

Long head (dolichocephaly) $I < 75$
Normal head (mesocephaly) $I = 75-80$
Short head (brachycephaly) $I > 80$

Length–Height Index of the Neurocranium

$$\frac{\text{height of the skull}}{\text{(basion–bregma)}} \times 100 \ (=I)$$
greatest length of the skull
(glabella–opisthocranion)

Wide head (platycephaly) $I < 70$
Normal head (orthocephaly) $I = 70-75$
Steeple head (hypsicephaly) $I > 75$

Facial Index

$$\frac{\text{height of the face}}{\text{(nasion–gnathion)}} \times 100 \ (=I)$$
width of the zygomatic arch

Wide face (euryprosop) $I < 85$
Medium face (mesoprosop) $I = 85-90$
Narrow face (leptoprosop) $I > 90$

Basically there is reciprocity between the growth of the brain and the skull. If there is a pathological increase in the volume of the contents of the skull, this will result simultaneously in marked enlargement of the bony skull. Pathological enlargement of the brain is due to enlargement of the cerebral cavities, which are filled with cerebrospinal fluid, and it may be associated with overproduction of cerebrospinal fluid (see also vol. 3).

Clinical tip: Malformations. In **hydrocephalus** (**B**), the cranial vault (neurocranium) is abnormally large in relation to the facial skeleton (viscerocranium). The cranial bones are thin. There is delayed closure of the enlarged fontanelles, and frontal and parietal bossing is present. The orbits are small and shallow.

Premature closure of the cranial sutures leads to **microcephaly** (**C**). The premature closure may result, for instance, from reduced brain growth. In microcephalus there are deep orbits and strong zygomatic arches.

Other malformations include the **scaphocephalus**, in which there is premature synostosis of the sagittal suture, and **oxycephalus**, in which the coronal suture ossifies prematurely.

These various malformations must be distinguished from artificially deformed skulls.

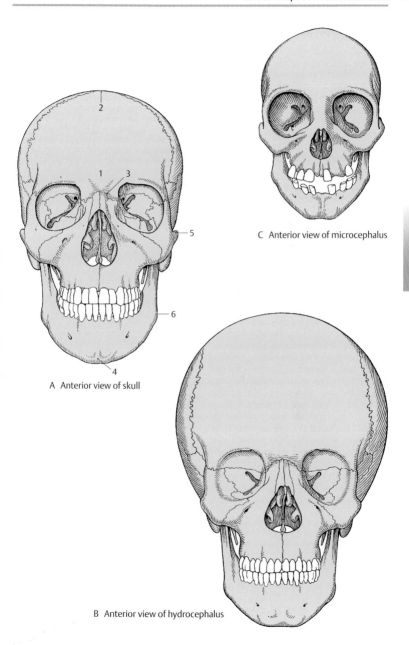

C Anterior view of microcephalus

A Anterior view of skull

B Anterior view of hydrocephalus

Special Cranial Shapes and Sutures (A–D)

The size and shape of the neurocranium depends on the growth of the brain, and the size of the viscerocranium will be substantially influenced by the activity of the masticatory apparatus. The influence of other elements, such as the supporting system of the dura mater, must also be taken into account. The various forms of the cranial sutures are also of interest in this regard.

In the skull, in the region of the intramembranous bones, there are three different types of sutures:
  – **Sutura plana**
  – **Sutura serrata**
  – **Sutura squamosa** (p. 22)

During development all the sutures are at first fairly straight and could be termed simple. It is only during the course of development that their shapes alter. Occasionally, subforms are seen, such as the *sutura limbosa*, which is a special form ot the sutura squamosa. There are also more sutures in the newborn than in adults; for example, because of the paired anlagen of the frontal bones there is *a frontal = metopic suture* (**1**), which usually closes between the 1st and 2nd years of life. If it persists (**A**) the skull is termed a **"crossed skull"**, *as there is a cruciform suture where the coronal (**2**), frontal (**1**), and sagittal (**3**) sutures meet. Remnants of the frontal suture may often be seen near the root of the nose* (**4**). If the frontal suture does persist, the forehead may become particularly prominent because of the more marked growth of both parts of the frontal bone.

> **Clinical tip:** Atypical bony anlagen may produce **additional sutures**. An incarial bone (p. 314) produces a transverse occipital suture. A *horizontal parietal suture* (**5**) is a special feature produced by the anlage of a *superior parietal bone* (**6**) and an *inferior parietal bone* (**7**). The atypical sutures may result in mistaken diagnoses on radiographs (fractures).

At the age of roughly 30 years, the individual sutures synostose and bone growth ceases. The first to fuse is usually the sagittal suture, but less frequently it is the coronal suture.

> **Clinical tip:** If there is an early general fusion of sutures, microcephalus results (see p. 310). If only one suture synostoses, the skull becomes abnormal in shape, e.g., scaphocephalus or oxycephalus. If only one part of a suture fuses prematurely, as may happen in the coronal suture, **plagiocephalus** or "crooked skull" (**C**, **D**) results. A plagiocephalic skull should be distinguished from an artificially deformed skull.

8 Outline of a plagiocephalic skull
9 Outline of a normally developed skull

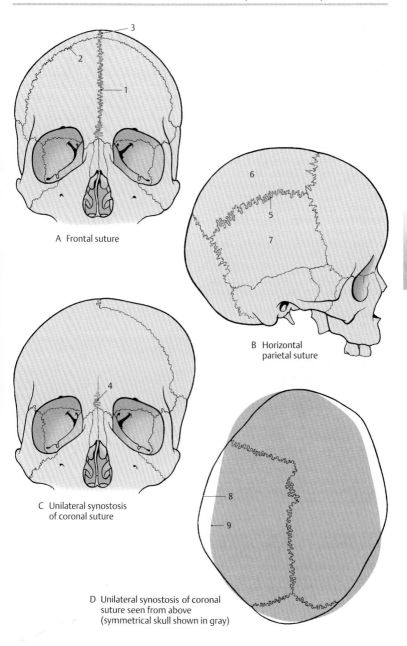

A Frontal suture

B Horizontal parietal suture

C Unilateral synostosis of coronal suture

D Unilateral synostosis of coronal suture seen from above (symmetrical skull shown in gray)

Head and Neck

Accessory Bones of the Skull (A–E)

Quite often there are supernumerary independent bones between or within the other bones of the skull. They are either called **epactal bones** or, if they lie between the other bones of the skull, wormian or **sutural bones**. These supernumerary bones, the majority of which develop in connective tissue, can be divided into two groups.

One group consists of bones that arise at typical sites and occasionally may be symmetrical. These may be bones which have specific anlagen during development but fail to unite with the other bones. They are of considerable practical interest, as the sutures between these bony parts may be confused with artificial fissures in radiographs. The second group of supernumerary bones are those which are completely irregular in number, shape, and location, and commonly show individual variations.

To the first group belongs particularly the **incarial bone** (**1**). This term is derived from the word Inca, as the bone has frequently (20%) been found in old Peruvian skulls. *It corresponds to the superior part of the interparietal bone, which developed from connective tissue,* and forms the upper squama of the occipital bone.

The lower part of the interparietal bone (*triangular plate*) fuses as a connective tissue component with the part which develops by chondral ossification (*supra-occipital bone*) and forms the lower squama. The incarial bone is bounded by both parietal bones (**2**) and by the lower squama (**3**) of the occipital bone. The suture between the incarial bone and the lower squama of the occipital bone corresponds to the *sutura mendosa* of the fetus, and is called the *transverse occipital suture* (**4**). The incarial bone may also be divided into two or three parts.

Other bones which occur in a typical position are those in the fontanelle region. Immediately adjacent to the incarial bone, in the posterior fontanelle, is the **apical bone** (**5**), which may persist as an independent bone. In the region of the greater fontanelle the **bregmatic bone** (**6**), also

called the frontoparietal bone, occurs less commonly. It is an epactal bone, either circular or rhomboidal in shape, and is uncommon.

Another typical epactal bone is the **epipteric bone** (**7**) or pterion ossicle, in which we distinguish *anterior* and *posterior parts.* It is found in the sphenoidal fontanelle, where it is bounded by the frontal bone (**8**), the parietal bone (**2**), the squamous part of the temporal bone (**9**), and the sphenoid bone (**10**). An anterior epipteric bone may not always extend to the parietal bone, and a posterior epipteric bone may not always reach the frontal bone. An undivided epipteric bone may occur, or both types mentioned above may be present, or only one of them. Lastly, in the region of the posterior lateral fontanelle there may be a separate bony anlage (**11**).

The second group comprises specifically the sutural wormian bones, which are particularly common. They occur in the region of the lambdoid, sagittal, and coronal (**12**) sutures. In addition, they may be found in the transverse occipital suture (see above).

Rarely an independent bony anlage (**13**) may be found within a bone. Epactal bones appear occasionally in the parietal bone (**2**) and very rarely in the frontal bone.

> **Clinical tip:** Intercalated and wormian bones may extend through the full thickness of the skull; they may be seen only on the surface, or only in the interior of the vault.

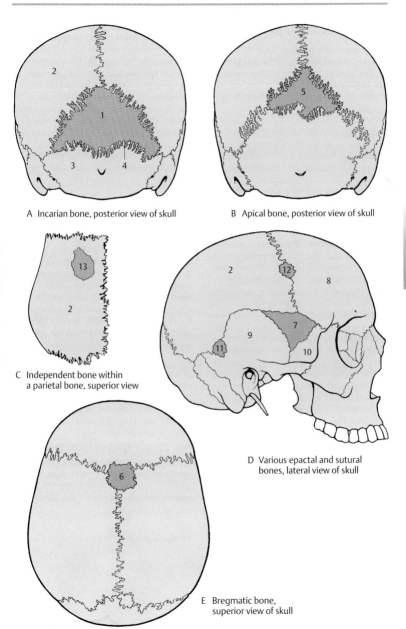

A Incarian bone, posterior view of skull

B Apical bone, posterior view of skull

C Independent bone within
   a parietal bone, superior view

D Various epactal and sutural
   bones, lateral view of skull

E Bregmatic bone,
   superior view of skull

Temporomandibular Joint (A–C)

The **temporomandibular joint** is divided into two compartments by the **articular disc** (**1**). The joint is formed, on the one side, by the **head of the mandible** (**2**) and, on the other side, by the **mandibular fossa** (**3**) with the **articular tubercle** (**4**).

The approximately cylindrical head of the mandible is so positioned that its longitudinal axis forms an angle, in the median plane just in front of the foramen magnum, of about 160° with the longitudinal axis of the joint of the opposite side. The head is covered by fibrocartilage and the mandibular fossa likewise possesses a lining of fibrocartilage.

The **articular disc** (**1**) represents a movable socket for the head of the mandible. Its anterior portion consists of fibrous material with interspersed chondrocytes; its posterior part is bilaminar. The upper portion (**5**), which is attached to the posterior wall of the mandibular fossa, consists of loose fibroelastic tissue, whereas the lower portion (**6**), which is fixed to the posterior margin of the head of the mandible, is composed of very taut fibrous tissue. Between these parts lies a retroarticular venous plexus which serves as a formative cushion (*Zenker*). Anteriorly, the articular disc is firmly united with the articular capsule and the *infratemporal head* of the *lateral pterygoid muscle* (**7**).

The **articular capsule** (**8**) is relatively loose and is reinforced by the *lateral ligament* (**9**), particularly on its lateral side. This ligament extends from the zygomatic arch to the condylar process directly below the head of the mandible, where it very frequently exhibits an eminence, sometimes a ridgelike elevation or, more rarely, a pitlike depression. In the older literature this was considered a condylar tubercle, a condylar crest, or a condylar fossa, respectively.

The **stylomandibular** (**10**) and **sphenomandibular** (**11**) **ligaments** act as guiding ligaments, although neither has a direct connection with the capsule. The sphenomandibular ligament extends from the *spine of the sphenoid* (**12**) to the *lingula of the mandible* (**13**), whereas the stylomandibular ligament stretches from the *styloid process* (**14**) to the *angle of the mandible* (**15**) and is in connection with the *stylohyoid ligament* (**16**). In addition, fibrous tracts extend from the angle of the mandible to the hyoid bone and are designated as the *hyomandibular ligament* (**17**).

Functionally, the temporomandibular joint represents a combination of two joints: an articulation between the articular disc and the head of the mandible and an articulation between the articular disc and the mandibular fossa. Active opening of the mouth always involves a **rotational movement** at the lower joint and a **sliding movement** anteriorly at the upper joint. The sliding movement is especially brought about by the lateral pterygoid muscle. Besides opening movements, lateral or **grinding movements** are produced.

The temporomandibular joint or the shape of its articular surfaces is dependent on the development of the dentition and, therefore, also on the age of the individual. With absent teeth (infants, elderly), the mandibular fossa is flat and the articular tubercle is inconspicuous.

The external acoustic meatus (**18**) lies directly behind the temporomandibular joint and the middle cranial fossa directly above it. The parotid gland (see vol. 2) and various vessels and nerves are also closely related to this joint.

19 Hyoid bone

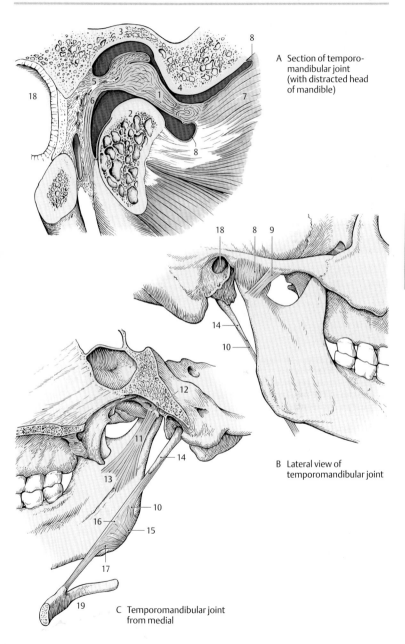

A Section of temporo-
mandibular joint
(with distracted head
of mandible)

B Lateral view of
temporomandibular joint

C Temporomandibular joint
from medial

Muscles and Fascias

Muscles of the Head

Mimetic Muscles

The mimetic muscles radiate into the skin of the face and the head, and their contraction causes displacement of the skin. This displacement, which takes the form of folds and wrinkles, is the basis of facial expression.

The expression is dependent on racial characteristics, intellectual capacity and the age of the individual. In youthful elastic skin these changes are reversible after muscle contraction, while in old age, when skin elasticity is diminished, wrinkles may remain. In the following section the function of each muscle will be described.

> **Clinical tip:** Facial expressions depend on the state of health. Various diseases of the heart, thyroid gland, stomach, and liver may have an effect on facial expression. Facial expressions may be especially affected by paralysis of the facial nerve.

The mimetic muscles are divided into:
  – **Muscles of the scalp**
  – **Muscles in the region of the eyelids**
  – **Muscles of the nasal region**
  – **Muscles of the mouth region**

Mimetic Muscles of the Scalp (A, B)

The muscles of the scalp constitute the **epicranius**. This is very loosely bound to the periosteum but very firmly to the scalp. Between the paired anterior and posterior bellies stretches a taut tendon, the **epicranial aponeurosis** (**1**), from which the fibers of the temporoparietal muscles also arise.

The **occipitofrontalis** consists of an *occipital belly* (**2**) and a *frontal belly* (**3**) on each side. *The former arises from the lateral two-thirds of the highest nuchal line and the latter* lacks a bony origin but instead *arises from the skin and the subcutaneous tissue of the eyebrow and the glabellar region.* The frontal belly is also closely related to the orbicularis oculi (**4**).

The **temporoparietalis** (**5**) *arises in the region of the galea aponeurotica and reaches the auricular cartilage.* The most posterior part of the muscle is also known as the *superior auricular muscle.*

The epicranius, particularly its anterior bellies, produces wrinkles in the forehead. In addition, contractions of both frontal bellies may lift the eyebrows and the upper eyelids. This produces the facial expression of astonishment.

Nerve supply: facial nerve.

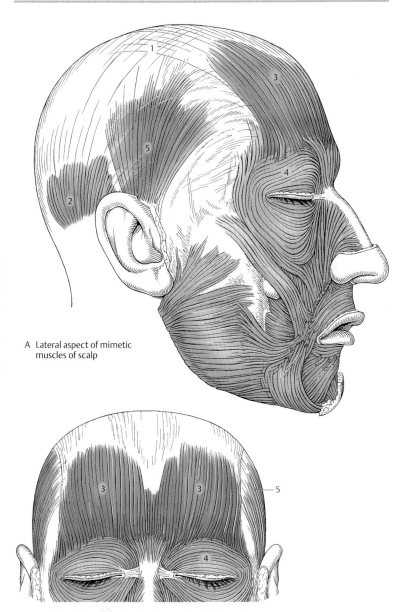

A Lateral aspect of mimetic muscles of scalp

B Anterior aspect of mimetic muscles of forehead

Muscles of the Head, continued

Mimetic Muscles in the Region of the Palpebral Fissure (A–F)

The **orbicularis oculi** consists of three parts: **orbital** (**1**), **palpebral** (**2**), and **lacrimal** (**3**); the latter is also regarded as deep part of the palpebral part. The thick **orbital part** (**1**) *is arranged circularly around the orbit and is attached to the palpebral ligament* (**4**), *the frontal process of the maxilla, and the anterior lacrimal crest.* In the upper lid the medial fibers of the orbital part fan out in the direction of the eyebrows. These fibers are also known as the *depressor supercilii.* The more delicate **palpebral part** (**2**) *lies immediately on the eyelids and extends also to the palpebral ligament.* The fibers lie partly on the tarsal plates (**5**) and partly on the orbital septum. The **lacrimal part** (**3**; *Horner's* muscle, deep part of the palpebral part*) lies medial to the deep crus of the palpebral ligament and arises chiefly from the posterior lacrimal crest* (**6**).

The orbital part is concerned with firm closure of the lid, while the palpebral part is primarily concerned with the blink reflex. The function of the lacrimal part is not fully understood. It is thought to expand the lacrimal sac or to expel its contents.

Through the close relationship of muscle fibers to the skin, radial folds in the region of the lateral angle of the eye are produced; these are called "crow's feet." The orbicularis oculi produces an expression of worry (**D**) and concern.

The **corrugator supercilii** (**7**) penetrates the orbicularis oculi and the frontal belly (**8**) of the epicranius. *It arises from the glabella and the supra-orbital margin and radiates into the skin of the eyebrows.*

It pulls the skin of the eyebrows downward and medially and produces a vertical furrow. It has a protective action in bright light and is called the muscle of pathetic pain. Its contraction produces the expression of a "thinker's brow" (**E**).

Mimetic Muscles in the Region of the Nose (A–F)

The **procerus** (**9**) *arises from the dorsum of the nose and radiates into the skin of the forehead. As a relatively thin muscle plate, it produces a transverse fold across the root of the nose.*

It produces a menacing expression. In old age these folds normally become permanent.

The **nasalis** consists of **transverse** (**10**) and **alar** (**11**) **parts**. *It arises from the alveolar yokes of the canine tooth and the lateral incisor, and reaches the skin on the side of the nose.* The transverse part is a thin, broad plate, which is joined by a flattened tendon to the transverse part of the muscle of the opposite side, while the alar part radiates into the skin on the nasal wing.

Contraction of this muscle pulls the nasal wing downward and backward and reduces the size of the nostril. It produces a happy, astonished expression and gives the impression of desiring, demanding, and sensuousness (**F**).

The **levator labii superioris alaeque nasi** (**12**) *arises from the infra-orbital margin and extends down into the skin of the upper lip and nasal wing.* It elevates not only the skin of the nasal wing but also that of the upper lip upward. Simultaneous bilateral contraction slightly lifts the tip of the nose.

It elevates the nasal wing and enlarges the nostrils. Stronger contractions produce a fold in the skin. The facial expression thus produced is one of displeasure and discontent (**G**).

In Figure **C**, the orbicularis oculi is folded over medialward, together with the tarsal plates. View of the posterior surface.

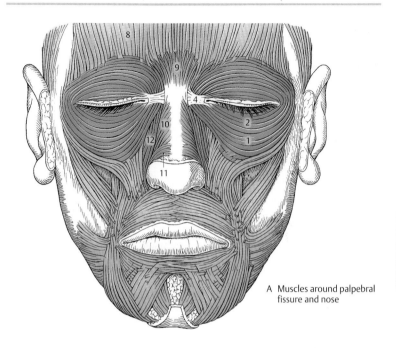

A Muscles around palpebral fissure and nose

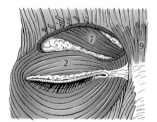

B Corrugator supercilii muscle

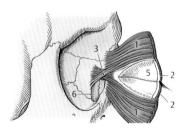

C Internal view of lacrimal part of orbicularis oculi

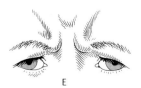

D E F G

D–F Effects of muscles on facial expression (from *Rouillé*)

Muscles of the Head, continued

Mimetic Muscles in the Region of the Mouth (A–L)

The **orbicularis oris** (**1**) appears like a circular muscle, but in fact it consists of four parts (**A**). It also has an inner **labial** and an outer **marginal part**. The shape of the mouth is determined by its tone and the shape of the underlying bone and teeth.

In weak contraction the lips are in contact or closed, while in strong contraction they pout forward and protrude in a sucking shape. The primary function of this muscle is seen in eating and drinking. Its contraction gives a facial expression of reserve (**D**).

The quadrilateral **buccinator** (**2**) *arises from the mandible in the region of the 1st and 2nd molars and from the pterygomandibular raphe* (**3**). *It extends to the angle of the mouth and forms the lateral wall of its vestibule.*

It enables air to be blown out of the mouth, pulls the angle of the mouth laterally and keeps the mucous membrane of the cheeks free of folds. It is involved in laughing and crying, and, when contracted, produces a facial expression of satisfaction (**E**).

The **zygomaticus major** (**4**) *arises from the zygomatic bone and extends toward the angle of the mouth.* Some of its fibers decussate with those of the depressor anguli oris.

It lifts the corner of the mouth upward and laterally. It produces the facial expression of laughter or pleasure (**F**).

The **zygomaticus minor** (**5**) *extends from the outer surface of the zygomatic bone to the nasolabial groove.*

The **risorius** (**6**) consists of superficial muscle bundles which *arise from the masseteric fascia and run to the angle of the mouth.*

Together with the zygomaticus major it produces the nasolabial folds. They are called, therefore, the laughing muscles. Contraction of the muscle produces an expression of action (**G**).

The **levator labii superioris** (**7**) is associated with the levator labii superioris alaeque nasi. *It arises from the infra-orbital margin and extends into the skin of the upper lip.*

The **levator anguli oris** (**8**) *arises below the infra-orbital foramen and runs to the angle of the mouth.*
It lifts the angle of the mouth and produces an expression of self-confidence (**H**).

The triangular **depressor anguli oris** (**9**) arises from the lower margin of the mandible and also extends to the angle of the mouth.
It pulls the angle of the mouth downward to produce an expression of sadness (**I**).

The **transversus menti** is only present as a specialization of the depressor anguli oris, a few fibers of which run transversely in the region of the chin and may be associated with the formation of a double chin.

The **depressor labii inferioris** (**10**) *arises from the mandible below the mental foramen and radiates into the skin of the lower lip.*
It pulls the lower lip down and produces an expression of perseverance (**K**).

The **mentalis** (**11**) *arises from the mandible in the region of the alveolar jugum of the lateral incisor and radiates into the skin of the chin.*
It produces the chin-lip furrow and is responsible for an expression of doubt and indecision (**L**).

The **platysma** (**12**) *radiates from the neck into the facial region* and is connected with the risorius and the depressors of the angle of the mouth and of the lower lip.

All mimetic muscles are innervated by the facial nerve.

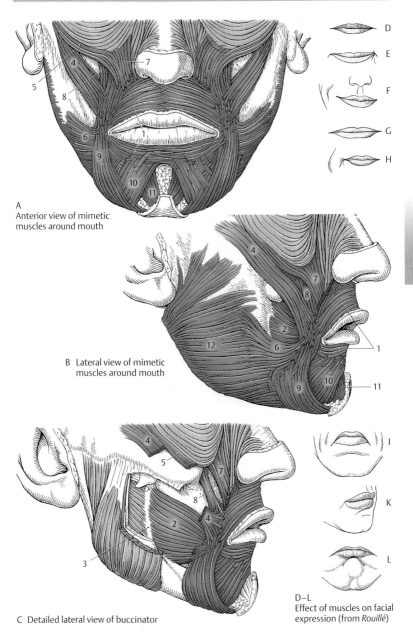

A
Anterior view of mimetic
muscles around mouth

B Lateral view of mimetic
muscles around mouth

C Detailed lateral view of buccinator

D–L
Effect of muscles on facial
expression (from *Rouillé*)

Muscles of the Head, continued

Muscles of Mastication (A–E)

The muscles of mastication are innervated by branches of the mandibular nerve. They develop phylogenetically from the first visceral arch.

In a strict sense they include the
– **Masseter** (**1**)
– **Temporalis** (**2**)
– **Lateral pterygoid** (**3**)
– **Medial pterygoid** (**4**)

The **masseter** (**1**) *arises from the zygomatic arch* (**5**) *and is inserted into the masseteric tuberosity* (**6**) on the angle of the mandible. The muscle is divided into a strong **superficial part** (**7**) with oblique fibers, and a **deep part** (**8**) whose vertical fibers arise from the inner surface of the zygomatic process of the temporal bone and from the temporal fascia. The masseter, like the temporalis, powerfully closes the jaws by elevating the mandible.
Nerve supply: masseteric nerve.

The **temporalis** (**2**) is the strongest elevator of the lower jaw. *It arises from the temporal fossa* (**9**) *as far as the inferior temporal line and from the temporal fascia* (**10**). It *is inserted* by a strong tendon *into the coronoid process* of the mandible (**11**). Its insertion also extends downward on the interior and anterior side of the mandibular ramus.
Nerve supply: deep temporal nerves.

The **lateral pterygoid** (**3**) is involved in all movements of the mandible. It serves as the guiding muscle of the mandibular joint. It consists of two parts: the **inferior head** (**12**) *arises from the lateral surface of the lateral plate of the pterygoid process*, and the **superior head** (**13**) *arises from the infratemporal surface* (**14**) *and the infratemporal crest of the greater wing of the sphenoid. The latter part extends to the articular disc, while the former part is inserted into the pterygoid fovea* (**15**).
Nerve supply: lateral pterygoid nerve.

The **medial pterygoid** (**4**) runs almost at right angles to the muscle just described. *It arises in the pterygoid fossa, i.e., the* **larger part** *from the medial surface of the lateral pterygoid plate* and the **smaller part** *from the lateral surface of that plate as well as with a few fibers from the maxillary tuberosity. It extends to the* angle of the mandible *where it is inserted into the pterygoid tuberosity*, so that the angle of the mandible lies in a sling formed by the masseter and medial pterygoid. It elevates the mandible and also pushes it forward. It may also be involved in lateral displacement of the lower jaw and participate in rotational movements.
Nerve supply: medial pterygoid nerve.

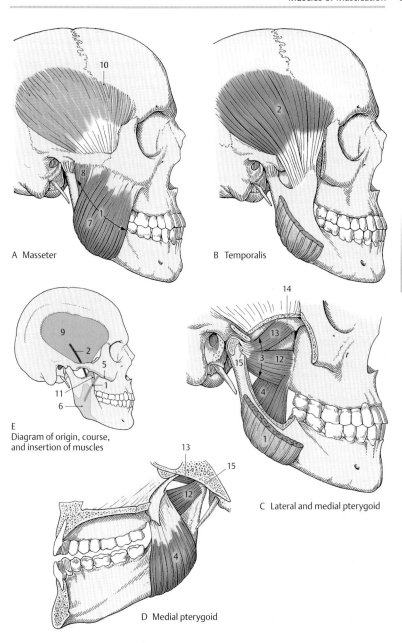

A Masseter

B Temporalis

E
Diagram of origin, course,
and insertion of muscles

C Lateral and medial pterygoid

D Medial pterygoid

Ventral Muscles of the Neck

Infrahyoid Muscles (A, B)

The infrahyoid muscles act on the hyoid bone and thus on the mandible, as well as on the cervical vertebral column.

The infrahyoid muscles include the
– **Sternohyoid**
– **Omohyoid**
– **Sternothyroid**
– **Thyrohyoid**

Phylogenetically, they belong to the great ventral longitudinal muscle system. The omohyoid is also included in the muscles of the shoulder girdle (see p. 146).

The **sternohyoid** (**1**) arises from *the posterior surface of the manubrium* (**2**), *from the sternoclavicular joint, and sometimes from the sternal end of the clavicle. It is inserted into the lateral region of the inner surface of the body of the hyoid bone* (**3**).

The **omohyoid** (**4**) has two bellies, a **superior** and an **inferior**, which are connected by an intervening tendon. The **inferior belly** *arises from the superior margin of the scapula*—adjacent to the scapular notch (**5**) and ascends obliquely. In the lateral region of the neck it is closely connected with the middle cervical fascia and it ends in an intermediate tendon which crosses the vascular-nerve cord of the neck. The **superior belly** arises from the intermediate tendon and ascends obliquely to reach the hyoid bone. *It is inserted,* usually without muscle fibers, *into the lateral third of the lower edge of the body of the hyoid* and with some fibers onto the inner surface of the body of the hyoid bone (**6**).

The **sternothyroid** (**7**) is wider than the sternothyroid which lies superficial to it. *It arises from the posterior surface of the sternal manubrium* (**8**) *and reaches the oblique line of the thyroid cartilage* (**9**). It closely invests the thyroid gland.

The **thyrohyoid** (**10**) is the continuation of the sternothyroid. *It arises from the oblique line of the thyroid cartilage* (**9**) *and is inserted onto the inner surface of the lateral third* (**11**) and *the lower margin of the median surface of the greater horn (Fischer).*

All the infrahyoid muscles work together, and specifically all together they may approximate the thyroid cartilage to the hyoid bone or, when the mouth is being opened, stabilize the laryngeal cartilages and the hyoid bone, or pull them downward. Because of its relationship to the neurovascular trunk and the middle cervical fascia, the omohyoid has the additional function of preventing pressure on the large underlying vein. It holds open the internal jugular vein and so aids return of blood from the head region to the superior vena cava.

The infrahyoid and the suprahyoid muscles (see vol. 2) can bend the head forward with the mouth shut. The omohyoid muscle is an accessory muscle in opening the mouth and in flexion, lateral flexion and rotation of the head (*Fischer* and *Ransmayr*).
Nerve supply: deep cervical ansa and thyrohyoid branch (C1, C2, and C3).

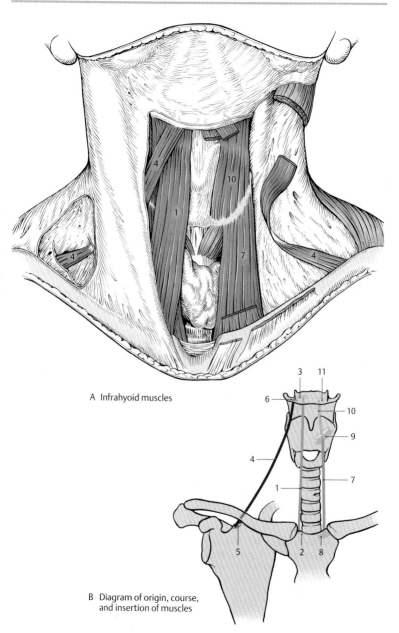

Head and Neck

A Infrahyoid muscles

B Diagram of origin, course,
and insertion of muscles

Head Muscles Inserted on the Shoulder Girdle (A–C)

The two muscles of the head which are inserted into the shoulder girdle are the trapezius and sternocleidomastoid.

The **trapezius** (**1**; see also p. 146) is divided into **descending** (**2**), **transverse** (**3**), and **ascending** (**4**) **parts**.

The **descending part** *arises from the superior nuchal line, the external occipital protuberance* (**5**) *and the ligamentum nuchae* (**6**; see p. 56) *and is inserted into the lateral third of the clavicle* (**7**). The **transverse part** *arises from the seventh cervical to the third thoracic vertebrae* (**8**; from the spinous processes and supraspinous ligaments) *and is inserted into the acromial end of the clavicle* (**9**), *the acromion* (**10**), *and part of scapular spine* (**11**). The **ascending part** *arises from the third to twelfth thoracic vertebrae* (**12**; from the spinous processes and the supraspinous ligaments) *and is inserted onto the spinal trigone and the adjacent part of the scapular spine* (**13**).

The primary function of the trapezius is a static one: it supports the scapula and thus stabilizes the shoulder girdle. Its contraction pulls the scapula and the clavicle backward and toward the vertebral column. The descending and ascending parts rotate the scapula. In addition to producing adduction, the descending part produces slight elevation of the shoulder, assisting the serratus anterior. If the latter muscle is paralyzed, the descending part is able to lift the arm to a little above the horizontal.
Nerve supply: accessory nerve and trapezius branch (C2–C4).

The **sternocleidomastoid** (**14**; see also p. 146) *arises by* **one head** *from the sternum* (**15**) *and by the* **other** *from the clavicle* (**16**). *It is inserted into the mastoid process and the superior nuchal line. There it has a tendinous connection with the origin of the trapezius.*

Unilateral action of the sternocleidomastoid turns the head to the opposite side and bends it to the ipsilateral side. **Bilateral contraction lifts the head.** This muscle is often incorrectly called the flexor of the head. Finally, the sternocleidomastoid can be an accessory muscle of respiration if the head is fixed and the intercostal muscles are paralyzed. If the intercostal muscles are still functioning, however, the sternocleidomastoid is not brought into action.
Nerve supply: accessory nerve and fibers C1–C2 from the cervical plexus.

Variants: Since the sternocleidomastoid and trapezius develop from the same material, they sometimes remain in a close relationship. The insertion of the trapezius to the clavicle may be considerably extended medially, and conversely the origin of the sternocleidomastoid may be displaced laterally. In this case the greater supraclavicular fossa, which is bordered by these two muscles and the clavicle, is reduced in size.

Clinical tip: Erb's point 2 (**17**) is located 2–3 cm above the clavicle and 1–2 cm past the posterior border of the sternocleidomastoid muscle. Stimulation applied at this point contracts various arm muscle by stimulating the upper part of the brachial plexus.

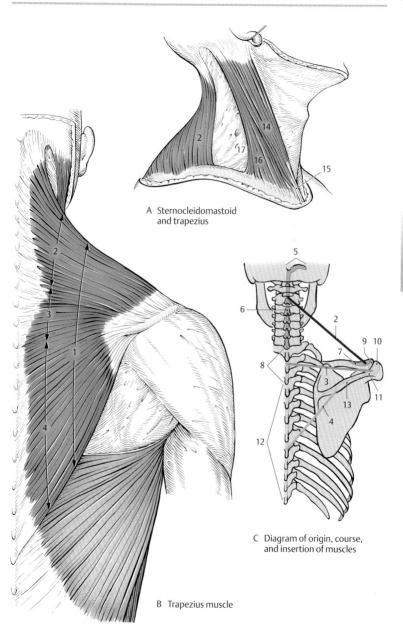

A Sternocleidomastoid
   and trapezius

B Trapezius muscle

C Diagram of origin, course,
   and insertion of muscles

Fascias of the Neck (A, B)

There are three layers of muscular fascias in the neck between the hyoid bone and the shoulder girdle.

The **superficial layer or investing layer** (**1**) **of the cervical fascia** (**1**) encloses all the structures of the neck except the platysma (**2**) and is continued dorsally into the nuchal fascia. The sternocleidomastoid (**3**) and trapezius (**4**) are embedded within. It extends from the mandible to the manubrium sterni and the clavicles. Between the hyoid bone and the mandible it is referred to as cervical fascia (see below).

Underneath lies the **middle or pretracheal layer** (**5**) **of the cervical fascia** into which the infrahyoid musculature is embedded (see p. 326). This fascia is closely applied in the region of the infrahyoid muscles (**6**). It does not, however, end at the lateral margins of the omohyoid muscles but continues laterally as a thin sheet. It comes into contact with the deep or prevertebral layer of the cervical fascia (**7**) and fuses with it. It is also connected with the connective tissue sheath around the neurovascular bundle (common carotid artery, internal jugular vein, vagus nerve) as the **carotid sheath** (fasciae cervicalis; **8**).

The pretracheal layer extends in a craniocaudal direction from the hyoid bone to the manubrium sterni and the clavicles. Cranial from the hyoid bone, it fuses with the superficial layer of the cervical fascia.

Between the superficial (**1**) and pretracheal (**5**) layers of the cervical fascia is the *suprasternal interfascial* space (**9**; see p. 354) in the region of the middle compartment of the neck.

The **deep or prevertebral layer** (**7**) **of the cervical fascia** covers the vertebral column and the deep cervical muscles associated with it. The deep muscles of the neck include the longus capitis, the longus colli (**10**), and the scalene muscles (**11**). The prevertebral layer arises from the base of the skull and extends into the thoracic cavity, where it is continuous with the endothoracic fascia.

The contents of the neck, larynx, esophagus (**12**), trachea (**13**), and thyroid gland (**14**), with the parathyroid glands, lie between the pretracheal and prevertebral layers.

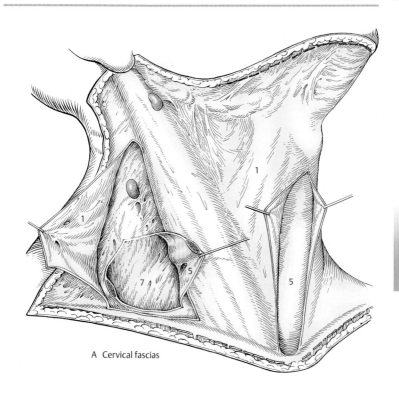

A Cervical fascias

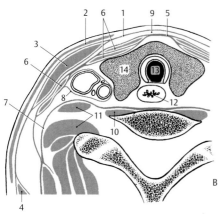

B Section through the neck
to show cervical fascias

Anatomical Terms and their Latin Equivalent

Head	Caput
Cribriform plate	Lamina cribrosa
Groove for the inferior petrosal sinus	Sulcus sinus petrosi inferioris
Groove for the lesser petrosal nerve	Sulcus nervi petrosi minoris
Hiatus for greater (lesser) petrosal nerve	
Highest nuchal line	Linea nuchalis suprema
Lesser (greater) wing of sphenoid	Ala minor (major) ossis sphenoidalis
Mastoid (frontal) notch	Incisura mastoidea (frontalis)
Occipital groove	Sulcus arteriae occipitalis
Prechiasmatic groove	Sulcus praechiasmaticus
Superior border of petrous part	Margo superior partis petrosac
Upper (lower) jaw	Maxilla (Mandibula)

Topography of Peripheral Nerves and Vessels

Head and Neck

Regions (A, B)

The head is separated from the neck by a line beginning at the chin continuing over the body of the mandible, the mastoid process and the superior nuchal line to reach the external occipital protuberance.

The neck is separable from the trunk by the jugular notch of the sternum and the clavicles. Dorsally no precise boundary line can be defined.

Regions of the Head

The **frontal region** (**1**) comprises the forehead up to the coronal suture. Adjacent to it, over the parietal bone on each side, is the **parietal region** (**2**), and over the squamous part of the temporal bone lies the **temporal region** (**3**). The **infratemporal region** (**4**) is covered by the zygomatic arch. Dorsally the **occipital region** (**5**) lies over the occipital bone.

The various **anterior fascial regions** are the **nasal region** (**6**), the **oral region** (**7**), and the **chin or mental region** (**8**). The **orbital region** (**9**) lies around the eyes, the **infra-orbital region** (**10**) is the area lateral to the nose, and the **buccal region** (**11**) is lateral to the oral region. The **zygomatic region** (**12**) lies about the zygomatic bone, and the **parotid region** (**13**) contains the masseter muscle and the parotid gland.

Regions of the Neck

The **neck** is divided into a **posterior region** (**14**) and ventrolateral regions. The latter is divided by the **sternocleidomastoid region** (**15**) into an unpaired **anterior triangle** and the paired lateral regions of the neck. The anterior triangle includes the area between the lower jaw and the anterior margins of both sternocleidomastoids. It can be further subdivided. In the center lies the **middle neck region** (**16**), which is limited by the hyoid bone, the omohyoids and sternocleidomastoids, and inferiorly by the jugular notch of the sternum. The depressed part of the middle neck region, which lies just above the sternal jugular notch, is designated the *suprasternal fossa* (**17**).

The submental triangle or submental region (**18**) extends between the hyoid bone and the chin region. Laterally it is separated from the **submandibular triangle** (**19**) by the anterior belly of the digastric muscle. This triangular area is limited cranially by the mandible. It might be helpful to use the angular tract of the cervical fascia to separate the submandibular triangle from its superoposterior part, the **retromandibular fossa** (**20**), which contains the cervical part of the parotid gland and the trunk of the facial nerve. The **carotid triangle** (**21**) is of great practical importance as it contains the bifurcation of the common carotid artery. It is limited cranially by the posterior belly of the digastric muscle, anteriorly by the superior belly of the omohyoid and dorsally by the sternocleidomastoid.

The **lateral cervical region** (**22**), or **posterior triangle of the neck**, ends anteriorly at the sternocleidomastoid, posteriorly at the trapezius and inferiorly at the clavicle. The omoclavicular triangle, or *greater supraclavicular fossa or triangle* (**23**), deserves special mention in this area. It is limited by the sternocleidomastoid, the inferior belly of the omohyoid and the clavicle. In thin individuals it may also be possible to see the *lesser supraclavicular (triangle) fossa* (**24**) between the two heads of the origin of the sternocleidomastoid.

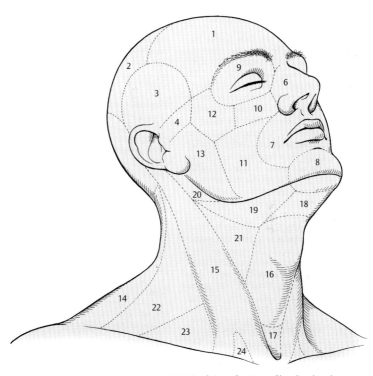

A Lateral view of regions of head and neck

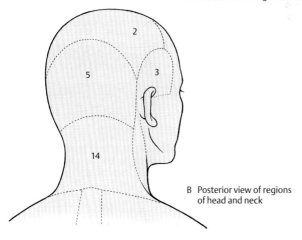

B Posterior view of regions of head and neck

Peripheral Pathways

Anterior Facial Regions (A, B)

The blood supply of the face comes primarily from branches of the external carotid artery and to a lesser extent from those of the internal carotid artery. On the anterior margin of the *masseter* (**1**), the *facial artery* (**2**) ascends and anastomoses via the *angular artery* (**3**) with the *dorsal nasal artery* (**4**), which stems from the ophthalmic artery. By way of larger branches in the facial region, the facial artery sends smaller branches to the lip region (see p. 340). The lateral region of the face is supplied either by the facial artery or by the *transverse facial artery* (**5**), which is a branch of the *superficial temporal artery* (**6**). The deep layers of the anterior facial region receive their blood supply from the *infra-orbital artery* (**7**), a terminal branch of the maxillary artery. The superficial temporal artery (**6**) supplies the temporal and parietal regions, and the forehead area proper is supplied by the *supratrochlear* (**8**) and *supra-orbital* (**9**) arteries, both being terminal branches of the ophthalmic artery. Among the larger superficial veins of the facial region only the *facial vein* (**10**), which anastomoses via the *angular vein* (**11**) with the *dorsal nasal vein* and the *superficial temporal vein* (**12**), lie superficially.

The mimetic muscles are supplied by branches of the facial nerve. These are the *temporal* (**13**), *zygomatic* (**14**), and *buccal* (**15**) *branches* and the *marginal mandibular branch* (**16**).

The sensory innervation to the skin of the face is derived from branches of the **trigeminal nerve**, the ophthalmic, the maxillary, and the mandibular nerves.

Ophthalmic nerve: The skin of the forehead is supplied by the frontal nerve with its *supratrochlear nerve* (**17**) and the *supra-orbital nerve* (**18**). Near the lateral corner of the eye the *lacrimal nerve* (**19**) penetrates the orbicularis oculi (**20**) with a few of its branches and innervates the skin in this region. The *external nasal nerve* (**21**), a branch of the nasociliary nerve, supplies the dorsum and tip of the nose.

Maxillary nerve: The lower eyelid, the cheek area, the lateral nasal region, the upper lip, and the anterior temporal region are innervated by branches of the *infra-orbital nerve* (**22**) and the *zygomaticofacial* and *zygomaticotemporal branches* of the zygomatic nerve.

Mandibular nerve: The skin of the lower lip, as well as that of the region of the body of the mandible (except its angle) and the chin area are supplied by the *mental nerve* (**23**), whereas the *auriculotemporal nerve* (**24**) innervates the skin of the region of the ramus of the mandible, the concha of the auricle, the largest portion of the external acoustic meatus, most of the external surface of the tympanic membrane, and the posterior temporal region. The mental nerve exits from the mental foramen; the auriculotemporal nerve ascends in front of the external ear together with the superficial temporal artery and vein.

Clinical tip: The anastomosis between the facial vein (**10**) and the dorsal nasal vein is important since it affords a direct connection to the cavernous sinus (see vol. 2), through which infection, e.g., from a furuncle on the lip, may be carried inside the skull.

Pressure Points of the Trigeminal Nerve (B)

The sensitivity of the three principal branches of the trigeminal nerve can be tested at the ramifications of these branches. The *supraorbital notch* (**25**) serves as a pressure point for the **supra-orbital nerve** (**18**), the *infra-orbital foramen* (**26**) as a pressure point for the **infra-orbital nerve** (**22**), and the *mental foramen* (**27**) for the **mental nerve** (**23**). All three pressure points lie along a roughly vertical line (**28**), running through the middle of pupil about 2—3 cm lateral to the midline.

The broken blue lines in Figure **B** indicate the boundaries between the regions supplied by the three branches of the trigeminal nerve.

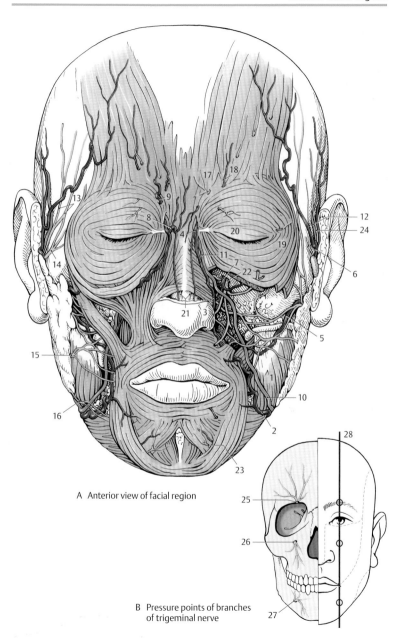

A Anterior view of facial region

B Pressure points of branches
of trigeminal nerve

Orbital Region (A, B)

In an anterior view the orbital region roughly corresponds to the region of the orbicularis oculi. In this area there are anastomoses between the facial vessels and vessels from the interior of the skull. These anastomoses are of practical importance, both as a source of collateral circulation and for the spread of bacteria from the skin of the face through the veins to the interior of the skull.

In the **orbital region** (A), the *orbital septum* (**1**) separates the superficial structures from the contents of the orbital cavity. Superficially the vessels are a continuation of *the facial artery and vein* (**2**), namely, the *angular artery and vein* (**3**). The *dorsal nasal artery and vein* (**5**) lie in front of the *palpebral ligament* (**4**). The dorsal nasal artery may branch from the *supratrochlear artery* (**6**) outside (see figure) or within the orbit. Together with the dorsal nasal artery, the *infratrochlear nerve* (**7**) also pierces the orbital septum. It often anastomoses with the *supratrochlear nerve* (**8**), which is only separated from it by the *trochlea* (B, **9**).

The supratrochlear nerve innervates the skin of the medial part of the forehead and the root of the nose and is accompanied by the *supratrochlear artery and veins* (**10**). Lateral to the supratrochlear nerve, the *medial branch* (**11**) of the supra-orbital nerve pierces the septum and adjacent to it is the *lateral branch* (**12**) of the supra-orbital nerve, accompanied by the *supra-orbital artery* (**13**). This artery and nerve leave an indentation in the bone, the supra-orbital notch, which is sometimes closed to form a supra-orbital foramen (see p. 292).

In the lateral angle of the eye, branches of the *lacrimal nerve* (**14**) pierce the orbital septum. The upper eyelid is innervated by these nerves and by branches of the frontal nerve. The lower eyelid is innervated by inferior palpebral branches of the *infra-orbital nerve* (**15**), which emerges from the infra-orbital foramen together with the *infra-orbital artery* (**16**).

Within the **orbit** (B), after removal of the orbital septum, the *superior oblique muscle of the eye* (**17**) becomes visible as it bends around the trochlea (**9**). The *levator palpebrae superioris* (**18**) and the *tarsal muscle* (**19**) can also be seen. A lateral tendon slip from levator palpebrae superioris divides the lacrimal gland into an *orbital part* (**20**), also termed the *Galen gland*, and a *palpebral part* (**21**), formerly called the *Rosenmüller* or *Cloquet gland*. Below the eyeball the *inferior oblique muscle of the eye* (**22**) arises from the infra-orbital margin.

In the medial corner of the eye, after the outer limb of the (medial) palpebral ligament has been divided, the *lacrimal sac* (**23**) with the *lacrimal canaliculi* (**24**) which open into it become visible.

25 Cut edge of the lateral part of the tendon of the levator palpebrae superioris
26 Outer limb of the (medial) palpebral ligament, divided and reflected

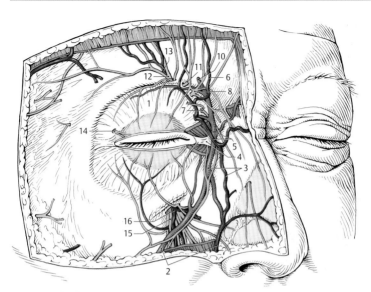

A   Orbital region, orbital septum

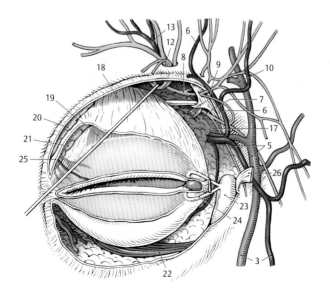

B   Orbital region, lacrimal apparatus,
vessels and nerves in orbit

Peripheral Pathways

Lateral Facial Regions

Parotid Region (A)

The **parotid region** is the most important part of the lateral facial region. In it lies the parotid gland (see vol. 2), which is differentiated into a superficial and a deep part. Anteriorly the *parotid gland* (**1**) lies on the *masseter muscle* (**2**) and posteriorly it occupies the retromandibular fossa. At the anterior margin of the parotid gland the *parotid* or *Stensen's duct* (**3**) leaves the gland and turns deeply down in front of the *buccal fat pad* (**4**). It is accompanied by the somewhat variably developed *transverse facial artery* (**5**), a branch of the *superficial temporal artery* (**6**). This supplies blood to parts of the face.

Between the superficial and deep parts of the gland lies the parotid plexus of the facial nerve, whose branches, as *temporal* (**7**) *zygomatic* (**8**), *buccal* (**9**), and *marginal mandibular* (**10**), become visible on the superior and anterior border of the gland and run to the mimetic muscles. At the inferior border of the parotid gland, the *cervical branch of the facial nerve* (**11**) is seen, which sometimes runs for a distance together with the marginal mandibular branch and which forms the superficial ansa cervicalis with the transverse cervical nerve (see p. 358).

At the inferior margin of the parotid gland the *retromandibular vein* (**12**) runs with the cervical branch of the facial nerve or with the marginal mandibular branch. This vein is joined by the *facial vein* (**13**) as it runs along the anterior border of the masseter muscle (**2**). Usually the *facial artery* (**14**) passes in front of the facial vein around the mandible (**bony pressure point**). It extends as the angular artery (see p. 336) to the medial corner of the eye and gives off the *inferior* (**15**) and *superior* (**16**) *labial arteries.*

The superficial temporal artery (**6**) lies at the superior margin of the parotid gland, directly in front of the external ear, where it gives off *anterior auricular branches* to

the external ear, as well as the *zygomatico-orbital artery*. Finally, after providing a *middle temporal artery*, it divides into a *frontal* (**17**) and *parietal* (**18**) *branch*. It can take a very tortuous course and is accompanied by the *superficial temporal vein* (**19**). The *auriculotemporal nerve* (**20**), a twig from the mandibular nerve, follows the parietal branch (**18**) and innervates the skin of the posterior temporal region. *Superficial parotid lymph nodes* (**21**) are found in variable numbers usually directly in front of the external ear.

Parotid Plexus (B)

Upon removal of the superficial part of the parotid gland there is usually a *superior* (**22**) and an *inferior branch* (**23**) of the facial nerve. The superior branch sends out the temporal branches (**7**) and the zygomatic branches (**8**), while the inferior branch gives off the buccal branches (**9**), the marginal mandibular branch (**10**), and the cervical branch (**11**). Both branches and their ramifications usually connect with one another by anastomoses, thus creating the parotid plexus.

Parallel to the inferior branch runs the retromandibular vein (**12**). An accessory parotid gland, which is sometimes present (**24**), may be small and is then covered by the superficial part of the parotid gland. If it is larger, it adheres to the parotid duct in front of the parotid gland.

Clinical tip: Malignant tumors of the parotid gland may cause damage to the facial nerve and its branches.
The superficial temporal artery **pulse** is palpable at the superior border of the parotid gland, just in front of the external auditory canal. The facial artery pulse is palpable at the anterior border of the masseter muscle at the base of the mandible.

25 Great auricular nerve
26 Platysma

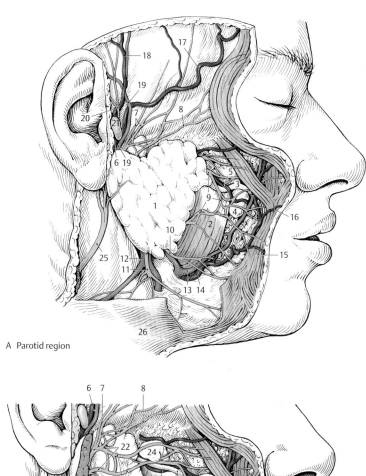

A Parotid region

B Parotid plexus

Infratemporal Fossa (A–G)

First Layer (A)

Access to the infratemporal fossa is gained by removal of the zygomatic arch and the coronoid process of the mandible. The *lateral* (**1**) and *medial* (**2**) *pterygoid muscles* then become visible. Anteriorly, the infratemporal fossa is limited by the *maxillary tuberosity* (**3**) and the *pterygomandibular raphe* (**4**).

The *maxillary artery* (**5**) may run between the two heads of the lateral pterygoid muscle. In this region it gives off the *buccal artery* (**6**) and the *superior posterior alveolar artery* (**7**) in addition to branches to the masticatory muscles, before descending into the pterygopalatine fossa. The maxillary artery is surrounded by a venous plexus, the *pterygoid plexus*, which is continuous with the *maxillary veins*.
The *buccal nerve* (**8**) also runs between the two heads of the lateral pterygoid muscle. Below the lateral pterygoid muscle the *lingual* (**9**) and *inferior alveolar* (**10**) *nerves* become visible, and above the muscle the *masseteric nerve* (**11**) is seen.

Second Layer (B)

The vessels and nerves of the infratemporal fossa only become fully visible after removal of the lateral pterygoid muscle and the condylar process of the mandible. The maxillary artery (**5**) lies lateral to the *sphenomandibular ligament* (**12**) and to the large branches of the *mandibular nerve* (**13**) and may be followed throughout its entire length. In its mandibular part it gives off the *anterior tympanic artery* (**14**), the *deep auricular artery* (**15**), and the *middle meningeal artery* (**16**), which reaches the interior of the skull through the foramen spinosum.

The middle meningeal artery passes between the two roots of the *auriculotemporal nerve* (**17**) which can frequently receive still additional fibers (**18**) from the inferior alveolar nerve (**10**). The auriculotemporal nerve (**17**) anastomoses with

communicating branches (**19**) from the *facial nerve* (**20**). By means of this anastomosis, which can wind around the *superficial temporal artery* (**21**), parasympathetic fibers pass from the otic ganglion to the facial nerve which then carries them to the parotid gland (see vol. 3).

Before it reaches the mandibular canal, the inferior alveolar nerve (**10**) gives off the *mylohyoid nerve* (**22**), which is accompanied by the *mylohyoid artery* (**23**), a branch of the *inferior alveolar artery* (**24**). The *chorda tympani* (**25**), which carries parasympathetic and sensory fibers, descends to join the lingual nerve. From the anterior part of the mandibular nerve (**13**), the buccal nerve (**8**) arises to innervate the mucous membrane of the cheek and to supply parasympathetic fibers from the otic ganglion to the glands of the cheek. Purely motor branches, such as the masseteric nerve (**11**), the medial and lateral pterygoid nerves, and the *deep temporal nerves* (**26**) arise also from the anterior part.

Special Features (C–G)

The maxillary artery has a very variable course because of its development. Thus, the maxillary artery (**5**) often lies laterally to the lateral pterygoid muscle (**C**) and less often medially to it (**A, D**). When it does lie medially, the artery usually runs to the pterygopalatine fossa, laterally (**E**) to the inferior alveolar nerve (**10**) and the lingual nerve (**9**), but medially to the buccal nerve (**8**). However, the artery may run between the branches (**F**) or, more rarely, medially to the trunk of the mandibular nerve (**G**).

Clinical tip: The infratemporal fossa provides clinical access to the trigeminal ganglion. **Trigeminal neuralgia** can be treated with injections and other procedures on the trigeminal ganglion, which is reached through the foramen ovale.

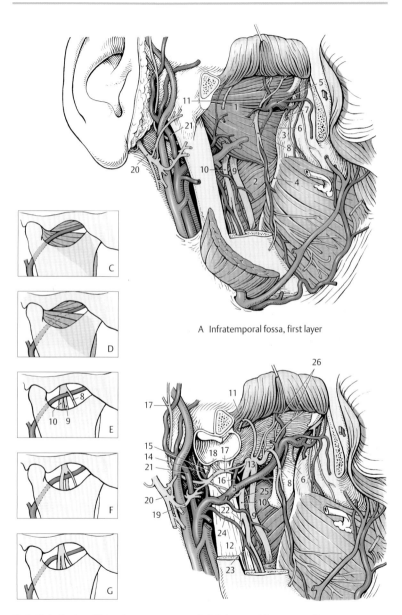

A Infratemporal fossa, first layer

C–G Variants of maxillary artery

B Infratemporal fossa, second layer

Superior View of the Orbit (A, B)

Only a few of the vessels and nerves of the orbit can be seen in an anterior approach and a clear view of their relationships can be gained only by removal of the roof of the orbit.

First Layer (A)

After removal of the orbital roof and the periorbita, it is possible to see the nerves which run through the lateral part of the superior orbital fissure; the most medial is the *trochlear nerve* (**1**), which innervates the *superior oblique muscle of the eyeball* (**2**). Alongside runs the relatively thick *frontal nerve* (**3**), which lies on the *levator palpebrae superioris* (**4**). The *supra-orbital artery* (**5**) accompanies its lateral branch, the *supra-orbital nerve* (**6**), while the medial branch, the *supratrochlear nerve* (**7**), runs along with the *supratrochlear artery* (**8**). The furthest lateral is the *lacrimal nerve* (**9**), which innervates the *lacrimal gland* (**10**) with the fibers received from the zygomatic nerve, and the skin at the lateral corner of the orbit.

The *superior ophthalmic vein* (**11**) also passes through the lateral part of the superior orbital fissure. One of its tributaries crosses below the *superior rectus muscle* (**12**) having anastomosed with the external facial veins (see p. 336) in the region of the *trochlea* (**13**); the other branch runs together with the *lacrimal artery* (**14**), which may give off small branches to muscles, and the *short posterior ciliary arteries* (**B**, **15**). Covered by the superior oblique (**2**) on the medial side lie the *anterior ethmoidal artery and nerve* (**16**), and superior to this muscle and more posteriorly run *the posterior ethmoidal artery and nerve* (**17**).

Second Layer (B)

After division and reflexion of the levator palpebrae superioris (**4**) and the superior rectus (**12**), the *optic nerve* (**18**), the *ophthalmic artery* (**19**), and the nerves which pass through the medial part of the superior orbital fissure become visible.

The *abducens nerve* (**20**), which innervates the *lateral rectus* (**21**), is the most lateral of them. Immediately medial to it runs the *oculomotor nerve* (**22**), which divides into two branches. The *superior branch* (**23**) supplies the levator palpebrae superioris (**4**) and the superior rectus (**12**). The *inferior branch* (**24**) innervates the *medial rectus* (**25**) and the inferior rectus and inferior oblique. In addition, the inferior branch sends the *oculomotor root* (**26**) to the *ciliary ganglion* (**27**), which lies on the optic nerve (**18**). The ganglion is connected with the *nasociliary nerve* (**29**) via a *nasociliary root* (**28**). From the ganglion the *short ciliary nerves* (**30**), which contain postganglionic parasympathetic fibers for innervation of the ciliary muscle and the sphincter pupillae, run to the *eyeball* (**31**). The short ciliary nerves also carry sensory and sympathetic fibers, the latter reach the ganglion from a sympathetic network (not shown) around the ophthalmic artery as sympathetic root of the ciliary ganglion. Sensory fibers from the nasociliary nerve also run to the eyeball through the *long ciliary nerves* (**32**). The nasociliary nerve, which gives off the ethmoidal nerves, is continued as the *infratrochlear nerve* (**33**).

> **Clinical tip:** The superior ophthalmic vein is important, as it anastomoses with the facial veins and opens into the sinus cavernosus. It provides a route by which infection in the facial region may spread to the sinus cavernosus.

■■ **Variant:** There is sometimes a *meningo-orbital artery* (**34**) joining the middle meningeal and the lacrimal arteries (anastomotic branch with the lacrimal artery).

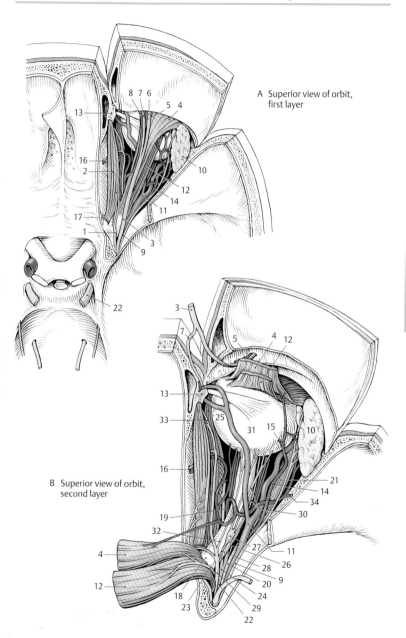

A Superior view of orbit, first layer

B Superior view of orbit, second layer

Occipital Region and Posterior Cervical (Nuchal) Region (A)

The vessels and nerves which supply the skin lie subcutaneously. The *occipital artery* (**1**) penetrates the nuchal fascia above the tendon arch (**2**) which extends between the area of attachment of the *sternocleidomastoid* (**3**) and the *trapezius* (**4**). The occipital artery is accompanied by an *occipital vein* (**5**) of variable caliber, which is sometimes absent and may be replaced completely by a large median vessel, the "*nuchal azygos vein*" (**6**).

In the immediate neighborhood of the occipital artery and vein, the *greater occipital nerve* (**7**) becomes subcutaneous. This nerve is the dorsal branch of the second cervical spinal nerve. Together with the *lesser occipital nerve* (**8**) from the cervical plexus, it innervates the skin on the back of the head. There are almost always anastomoses between branches of the greater and lesser occipital nerves. Immediately behind the ear the skin is also supplied by the posterior branch of the *great auricular nerve* (**9**). In addition, segmental dorsal branches, of which the third *occipital nerve* (**10**) is the more strongly developed, are involved in the cutaneous innervation of this region. *Occipital lymph nodes* (**11**) are found at the points where the vessels and nerves pass through the nuchal fascia.

Suboccipital Triangle (B)

The suboccipital triangle only becomes visible after removal of all the superficial muscles (**A**; sternocleidomastoid [**3**], trapezius [**4**], *splenius capitis* [**12**], and *semispinalis capitis* [**13**]). The *vertebral artery* (**14**) lies in this region. It passes through the foramina transversaria (cervical part) of the upper six cervical vertebrae, then, as the atlantic part lies in the groove for the vertebral artery on the *posterior arch of the atlas* (**15**) and enters the cranial cavity by piercing the posterior atlanto-occipital membrane.

The triangle is bordered by the *rectus capitis posterior major* (**16**), the *obliquus capitis superior* (**17**) and the *obliquus capitis inferior* (**18**). In this area the vertebral artery gives off a branch (**19**) to the surrounding muscles. Between the artery and the posterior arch of the atlas lies the *suboccipital nerve* (**20**) which, as the dorsal branch of the first cervical spinal nerve, innervates the muscles mentioned above and the *rectus capitis posterior minor* (**21**).

> **Clinical tip: Suboccipital puncture** is performed in these regions, using a needle to withdraw cerebrospinal fluid from the cerebellomedullary cistern (see Vol. 3). The needle is inserted in the midline between the external occipital protuberance and the spinous process of the axis. The needle tip is aimed directly at the root of the nose and is advanced between the recti capitis posteriores minores, piercing the posterior atlanto-occipital membrane and the dura mater. A firm resistance is felt as the needle pierces the dura. The cerebellomedullary cistern lies directly beneath the dura mater. The depth of needle insertion should **not** exceed **4–5 cm** in adults!
> If *contraindications* exist, suboccipital puncture should be withheld in favor of lumbar puncture (see p. 42).

22 Parotid gland
23 Mastoid lymph node

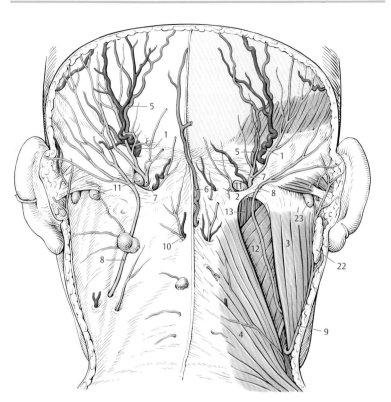

A Occipital and posterior cervical regions
Left: subcutaneous layer
Right: subfascial layer

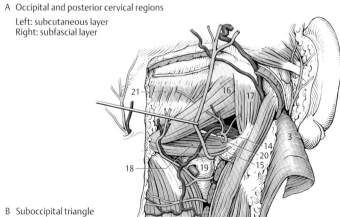

B Suboccipital triangle

Lateral Pharyngeal and Retropharyngeal Spaces (A)

Lateral to and behind the pharynx, the vessels and nerves between the head and the trunk run through the neck.

Furthest dorsally lies the *sympathetic trunk* (**1**), which divides at the *superior cervical ganglion* (**2**), into the *jugular nerve* (**3**) and the *internal carotid nerve* (**4**). While the carotid nerve follows the *internal carotid artery* (**5**), the jugular nerve turns toward the *inferior ganglion* (**6**) of the *vagus nerve* (**7**). In addition, there are connections to the *hypoglossal nerve* (**8**) and to the *carotid body* (**9**), which also receives fibers from the *nerve to the carotid sinus*, the *carotid branch* (**10**). Furthermore, the superior cervical ganglion sends out delicate descending branches, *external carotid nerves* (not illustrated) to the external carotid plexus and laryngopharyngeal branches and the superior cervical cardiac nerve.

The vagus nerve (**7**) passes through the jugular foramen and develops a superior and inferior ganglion (**6**). It descends between the internal carotid artery (**5**) and the *internal jugular vein* (**11**). In addition to small branches and anastomoses, the vagus nerve running medial to the internal carotid artery gives off the *superior laryngeal nerve* (**12**) which divides into an *external* (**13**) and an *internal* (**14**) *branch*. Other branches include the auricular branch and the *pharyngeal rami* (**15**), which run along with the pharyngeal branches (**16**) of the *glossopharyngeal nerve* (**17**) to supply the muscles of the pharynx and the pharyngeal mucous membrane.

The glossopharyngeal nerve (**17**), separated from the vagus nerve (**7**), and from *the external branch of the accessory nerve* (**19**) by a bridge of dura (**18**), transverses the jugular foramen and, after giving off pharyngeal branches and the nerve to the carotid sinus, *carotid branch* (**10**), runs caudalward and anteriorly between the internal carotid (**5**) and *external carotid* (**20**) *arteries.*

The external branch of the accessory nerve (**19**) usually takes a course dorsal to the *superior bulb* (**21**) of the internal jugular vein (**11**). Then it runs laterally and passes through the *sternocleidomastoid* (**22**), or medial to it in the lateral cervical region, also called posterior triangle of the neck (see p. 360).

The hypoglossal nerve (**8**) passes toward the front lateral to both carotid arteries. Immediately below the base of the skull it receives fibers (**23**) from the first and second cervical segments. It gives off most of its fibers in the *superior (anterior) root of the "deep" cervical ansa* (**24**; p. 362).

The external carotid artery gives off its dorsal branch, the *ascending pharyngeal artery* (**25**), which ascends alongside the pharynx and reaches the interior of the base of the skull passing through the jugular foramen by its branch, the posterior meningeal artery.

26 Pharyngobasilar fascia
27 Pharyngeal raphe
28 Superior constrictor
29 Middle constrictor
30 Inferior constrictor
31 Stylopharyngeus
32 Facial nerve
33 Thyroid gland
34 Right superior parathyroid gland

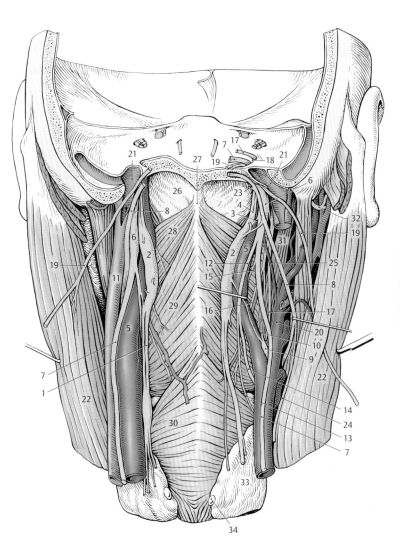

A   Lateral pharyngeal and retropharyngeal spaces

Submandibular Triangle (A, B)

The submandibular triangle (**A**) is bounded by the *base of mandible* (**1**), the *anterior belly* (**2**) of the *digastric*, and by the *angular tract of the cervical fascia* (**3**) with the interglandular septum. Deep down, starting from the tractus angularis, the interglandular septum divides the submandibular space from the parotid space. If it is removed, the submandibular triangle and the retromandibular fossa become continuous (**B**).

Submandibular Triangle, Superficial Layer (A)

The *submandibular gland* (**4**) lies superficial to the *mylohyoid* (**5**), around the posterior margin of which winds the *submandibular duct* (**6**) accompanied by a more or less well developed *uncinate (deep) process*.

In addition, the mylohyoid divides the submandibular triangle into a superficial and a deep compartment. The *facial artery and vein* (**7**) pass through the gland. The facial artery gives off the *submental artery* (**8**), which runs to the chin superficial to the mylohyoid (**5**), accompanied by the submental vein. The *mylohyoid nerve* (**9**), which arises from the inferior alveolar nerve lies in the same plane and innervates the mylohoid muscle and the anterior belly (**2**) of the digastric.

One or more *submental lymph nodes* (**10**) adhere externally to the mylohyoid and collect lymph from the chin and lower lip regions. Deep and medial to the mylohyoid, the *lingual nerve* (**11**) runs in an arch toward the tongue and is connected to the *submandibular ganglion* (**12**) by *ganglionic branches*. *Glandular branches* run from the ganglion to the submandibular gland. The submandibular duct (**6**) runs in the immediate vicinity of the ganglion together with the *hypoglossal nerve* (**13**) and a *vena comitans of the hypoglossal nerve*.

Submandibular Triangle, Deep Layer (B)

The *geniohyoid* (**14**) and *hyoglossus* (**15**) are seen after bending back the anterior belly of the digastric (**2**) and the mylohyoid (**5**). The styloglossus radiates forward into the tongue. Inferior to the hypoglossal nerve (**13**), the fibers of the hyoglossus (**15**) may be separated to demonstrate the *lingual artery* (**16**), in the depth, sometimes accompanied by a small lingual vein. The area where the artery is found is called the **triangle of the lingual artery**. It is formed by the hypoglossal nerve, the anterior belly of the digastric and the posterior border of the mylohyoid muscle (see Fig. **A**).

Medial to the hyoglossus, the *glossopharyngeal nerve* (**17**) descends from the retromandibular fossa and is crossed by the *ascending palatine artery* (**18**), a branch of the facial artery. The *stylohyoid ligament* (**19**) runs parallel to the glossopharyngeal nerve.

20 External carotid artery
21 Facial nerve
22 Masseter
23 Sternocleidomastoid
24 External jugular vein

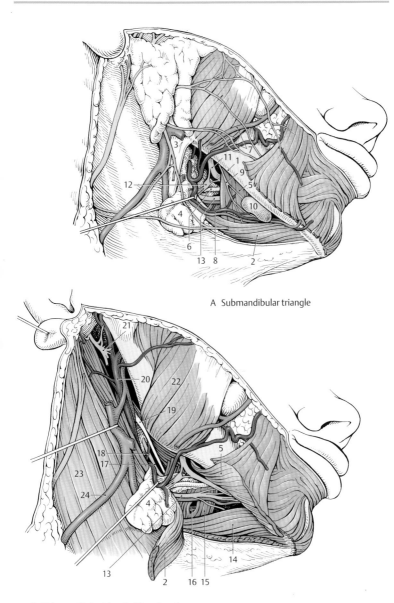

A Submandibular triangle

B Submandibular triangle (deep layer)
and retromandibular fossa

Retromandibular Fossa (A)

The retromandibular fossa is limited by the *ramus of the mandible* (**1**), the posterior belly of the digastric, and a narrow band of strong fibers of the *angular tract of the cervical fascia* (**2**). It contains the deep portion of the parotid gland.

After removal of the parotid gland, the *facial nerve* (**3**), emerging from the stylomastoid foramen and dividing into its branches, is visible. The first branch to be given off outside the skull is the *posterior auricular nerve* (**4**), which supplies the occipital belly of the occipitofrontal muscle with the occipital branch and the posterior muscles of the ear with the auricular branch. The next branches to leave the trunk of the facial nerve are the *digastric* (**5**) and *stylohyoid* (**6**) *branches*. The facial nerve then splits up into the *parotid plexus* (**7**), which lies between the superficial and deep parts of the parotid gland. This plexus also forms loops around the neighboring vessels and sends branches to the mimetic muscles, i.e., the *temporal* (**8**), *zygomatic* (**9**), and *buccal* (**10**) *branches and the marginal mandibular branch* (**11**). The *cervical branch of the facial nerve* (**12**) also arises from the parotid plexus. It innervates the platysma and forms the "superficial ansa cervicalis" with the transverse cervical nerve.

Deep in the retromandibular fossa is the *external carotid artery* (**13**), which divides into the *maxillary artery* (**14**) and the *superficial temporal artery* (**15**). The first branch of the superficial temporal artery is usually the *transverse facial artery* (**16**), which, however, may arise as a direct branch from the external carotid artery (see figure). The external carotid artery is accompanied by the *retromandibular vein*, which is formed from the *superficial temporal* (**18**) and the *maxillary* (**19**) *veins*.

When the retromandibular vein runs superficially, it anastomoses with the *facial vein* (**20**) and continues into the *external jugular vein* (**21**). In this case we find deep accompanying veins (**22**) of the external carotid artery. The *posterior auricular artery* (**23**) ascends dorsal to the retromandibular vein. At the superior margin of the retromandibular fossa, the superficial temporal artery and vein cross the *auriculotemporal nerve* (**24**), which emerges from the infratemporal fossa and innervates the skin of the posterior temporal region.

25 Great auricular nerve
26 Anastomosis with transverse cervical nerve ("superficial ansa cervicalis")
27 Parotid duct (cut)
28 Buccal nerve
29 Facial artery
30 Masseter
31 Buccinator

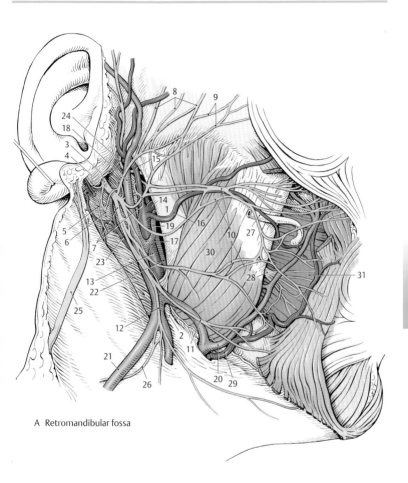

A Retromandibular fossa

Middle Region of the Neck (A, B)

In the middle region of the neck the division into layers produced by the cervical fascias is particularly clear.

Interfascial Space (A)

The *platysma* (**1**) is of variable size and lies directly beneath the skin. After this integumentary muscle is removed, the *superficial layer of the cervical fascia* (**2**) becomes visible, and if this is divided it reveals the *pretracheal layer of the cervical fascia* (**3**) covering the infrahyoid muscles. Caudally the region is limited by the *sternocleidomastoids* (**4**). Just above the jugular notch, in the suprasternal space, the *jugular venous arch* (**5**) joins the *right anterior* (**6**) to the *left anterior jugular vein*. These veins may also receive blood from deep structures through the middle or pretracheal layer of the cervical fascia (**3**).

Deep Layer (B)

After the pretracheal layer of the cervical fascia has been removed, the infrahyoid muscles and the *thyroid gland* (**7**) become visible. To obtain a better view of the thyroid gland and the entire region, certain muscles must be cut. Most medially and superficially lies the *sternohyoid* (**8**) and lateral to it is the *omohyoid muscle* (**9**). Deep to them lie the *thyrohyoid* (**10**) and *sternothyroid* (**11**). All the infrahyoid muscles are innervated on their respective sides by the *"deep" ansa cervicalis* (**12**) and by fibers which arise from the superior (anterior) root (thyrohyoid branch).

The thyroid gland (**7**) lies in front of the cricoid cartilage and the *trachea* (**13**). Its lateral lobes (see p. 356) reach the *thyroid cartilage* (**14**). Between the thyroid and the cricoid cartilages extends the *median cricothyroid ligament* (**15**), which is covered laterally by the *cricothyroid muscles* (**16**). On each side these muscles are innervated by the *external branch* (**17**) of the *superior laryngeal nerve* (**18**). The *internal branch* (**19**) of the superior laryngeal nerve perforates the *thyrohyoid membrane* (**21**). It is accompanied by the superior laryngeal artery, which arises from the *superior thyroid artery* (**20**).

The drainage of blood from the thyroid gland (p. 356) takes place via different veins, of which the *superior thyroid vein* (**22**) and the *unpaired thyroid plexus* (**23**) are evident in this region. This plexus passes in front of the trachea as "inferior thyroid vein" which as a general rule drains into the left brachiocephalic vein. The *brachiocephalic trunk* (**24**), which is situated directly in front of the trachea, proceeds obliquely upward. Lateral to the trachea and in front of the esophagus, the *recurrent laryngeal nerve* (**25**) courses toward the larynx.

▆▆▆ **Variants:** The jugular venous arch can occur at any level between the hyoid bone and the jugular notch. When it occupies the position directly below the hyoid bone, it is designated as the **subhyoid venous arch**. In rare cases, a vein is found which ascends from the thyroid gland, penetrates the pretracheal layer of the cervical fascia, and opens into the anterior jugular vein. In many cases, a thyroidea ima artery is present which arises from the brachiocephalic trunk or the aorta.

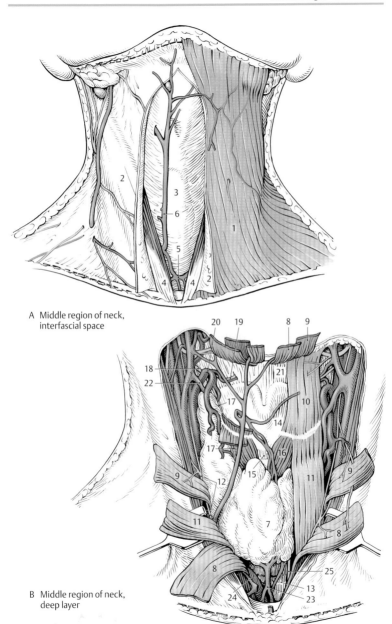

A Middle region of neck, interfascial space

B Middle region of neck, deep layer

Thyroid Region (A–G)

The **thyroid gland** consists of an *isthmus* (**1**), a *right lobe* (**2**), and a *left lobe* (**3**). Each lobe has a *superior* (**41**) and an *inferior pole* (**5**). The superior poles of both lobes reach the *thyroid cartilage* (**6**), while the isthmus lies in front of the cricoid cartilage and the trachea. Thus, the *median cricothyroid ligament* (**7**), which connects the cricoid with the thyroid cartilage, remains free, provided there is no *pyramidal lobe*. Such a lobe may sometimes ascend from the isthmus (remnant of the thyroglossal duct).

The thyroid gland receives its blood bilaterally from the *superior* (**8**) and *inferior* (**9**) *thyroid arteries*. The superior thyroid artery originates from the *external carotid artery* (**10**) and reaches the thyroid gland at its superior pole where it divides into *anterior, posterior,* and *lateral glandular branches*. The anterior glandular branch gives off a variably developed *cricothyroid branch* which reaches the median cricothyroid ligament. The inferior thyroid artery (**9**) is a branch of the *thyrocervical trunk* (**11**), which arises from the *subclavian artery* (**12**); it reaches the thyroid gland at its posterior surface. Of special significance is the relationship of this artery to the *recurrent laryngeal nerve* (**13**; B–D).

The blood returns through the *superior thyroid veins* (**14**), which open into the *internal jugular veins* (**16**) by the *common facial veins* (**15**). A *middle thyroid vein* (**17**) runs from the lateral margin of the thyroid gland directly to the internal jugular vein. At the lower end of the thyroid gland is the *unpaired thyroid venous plexus* (**18**) which, as the inferior thyroid vein, sends blood to the *left brachiocephalic vein* (**19**). Sometimes another vein may extend from the cranial margin of the isthmus to the anterior jugular vein (see p. 355, Fig. B).

Clinical tip: In the event of respiratory obstruction, **coniotomy** is performed as an emergency measure. The (elastic) median cricothyroid ligament (**7**), the free portion of the elastic cone of larynx, is severed **transversely**. This causes gapping of the incision. **Tracheotomy** is performed as an emergency operation. The trachea is split **longitudinally**. We distinguish between *superior tracheotomy* above the isthmus of the thyroid gland, *middle tracheotomy* through the isthmus, and *inferior tracheotomy* below the isthmus. The latter type is performed in children because they exhibit a sufficiently large distance between isthmus and sternum. The two other ways of access are used in adults. Great care should be taken with the jugular venous arch, and the unpaired thyroid plexus (**18**) should be taken care of, once the pretracheal lamina of the cervical fascia has been severed. Furthermore, the **brachiocephalic trunk** (**20**) which ascends from left to right may cross the trachea at a very high level. During thyroid gland surgery, care should also be taken of the *thoracic duct* (**21**), because it passes the thyroid at the lower left pole and opens into the *left venous angle* (**22**).

Variable Position of the Recurrent Laryngeal Nerve (B–D): In addition to innervating the mucous membrane of the subglottic space, the recurrent laryngeal nerve (**13**) innervates all laryngeal muscles other than the cricothyroid. Except in special cases its position is with approximately equal frequency (according to *Lanz*) either ventral to (**B**, 27%), dorsal (**C**, 36%), or in between (**D**, 32%) the branches of the inferior thyroid artery (**9**). In the drawing forward of the thyroid gland during surgery, great care must be taken, as even pulling on the nerve may produce paralysis of the laryngeal muscles.

Variants of the Inferior Thyroid Artery (E–G): The inferior thyroid artery is particularly variable both as to its site of origin and its course. The inferior thyroid artery (**9**) may run dorsal to the *vertebral artery* (**23**) toward the middle (**E**). Sometimes (**F**) the artery may divide immediately after it leaves the thyrocervical trunk. One branch may then lie ventral and the other dorsal to the *common carotid artery* (**24**) and the internal jugular vein (**16**). Finally (**G**), the inferior thyroid artery (**9**) may arise directly from the subclavian artery as the first branch (in 8% of the population). In rare cases, the inferior thyroid artery may arise either from the vertebral artery of from the internal thoracic artery. It may be absent in about 3% of the population, in which case its area of supply is taken over by the superior thyroid artery and/or by the thyroid ima artery. The latter may arise directly from the aortic arch or from the brachiocephalic trunk.

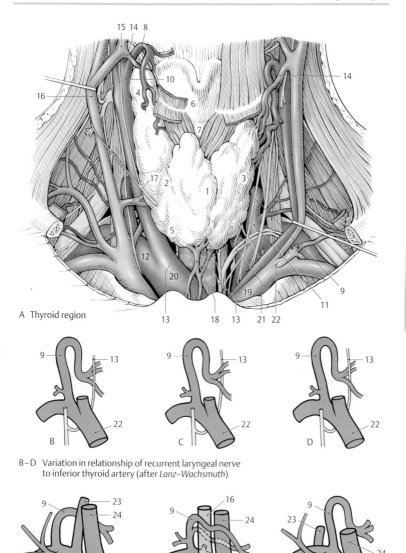

A Thyroid region

B–D Variation in relationship of recurrent laryngeal nerve
to inferior thyroid artery (after *Lanz–Wachsmuth*)

E–G Variants of branches of subclavian artery (personal observations)

Ventrolateral Cervical Regions (A, B)

The ventrolateral cervical regions may be divided into a superficial subcutaneous region with the nerve point, the lateral cervical region (posterior triangle of the neck), the carotid triangle, and the sternocleidomastoid region.

The Ventrolateral Subcutaneous Cervical Region (A)

Its boundaries are superiorly the *mandible*, anteriorly the median sagittal plane, posteriorly the palpable margin of the *trapezius*, and inferiorly the *clavicle* (**1**). The subcutaneous layer contains a cutaneous muscle, the platysma, large veins, and the cutaneous branches of the cervical plexus. The area in which these cutaneous branches penetrate the superficial layer of the cervical fascia is also called the **nerve point**. It lies roughly where the posterior border of the platysma crosses the sternocleidomastoid. After the platysma has been removed, all the superficial vessels and nerves become visible.

The *lesser occipital nerve* (**2**), which runs subcutaneously parallel to the posterior border of the sternocleidomastoid muscle, is the most cranial. This nerve, which takes part in the sensory innervation of the skin of the back of the head, may divide into two branches immediately after it has perforated the superficial layer of the cervical fascia. The largest caliber nerve is the *great auricular nerve* (**3**), which gives off an *anterior* (**4**) and a *posterior* (**5**) *branch* that ascend obliquely across the sternocleidomastoid muscle and take part in sensory innervation of the external ear. At about the same place as this nerve, the *transverse cervical nerve* (**6**) perforates the superficial layer of the cervical fascia, runs deep to the *external jugular vein* (**7**) and, together with the *cervical branch of the facial nerve* (**8**), forms the "superficial ansa cervicalis" (**9**). The platysma and the overlying skin are innervated by this ansa. Caudally, at different

levels, the *medial* (**10**), *intermediate* (**11**), and *lateral* (**12**) *supraclavicular nerves* perforate the superficial layer of the *cervical-fascia* to innervate the skin of the shoulder region.

> **Clinical tip:** Eiselsberg's phenomenon occurs on the right side of the shoulder as a so-called "false projection", i.e., pain may radiate into the right shoulder due to disease of the liver or gallbladder. Pain spreads into dermatomes (C3–C5; see vol. 3). Diseases of the pancreas may produce pain in the left shoulder region.

Lateral Cervical Region, First Layer (B)

After removal of the superficial layer of the cervical fascia, the posterior border of the *sternocleidomastoid* (**13**) and the anterior border of the *trapezius* (**14**) become visible. The *pretracheal layer of the cervical fascia* (**15**), which merges with the prevertebral layer of the cervical fascia in the lateral region of the neck, separates the first layer from the others. In addition to the structures already described above, the *external branch of the accessory nerve* (**16**) and the *trapezius branch* (**17**) of the cervical plexus, both of which supply the trapezius, run in this layer. Here we also find the *superficial cervical vein* (**18**), which joins the external jugular vein, and the *superficial cervical artery* (**19**). If the superficial cervical and dorsal scapular arteries arise together from the thyrocervical trunk, the stem is called the transverse artery of the neck. Several *superficial cervical lymph nodes* (**20**) lie alongside the veins.

Cervical plexus

- Roots: ventral rami C1–C4
- Branches: Lesser occipital nerve
            Great auricular nerve
            Transverse cervical nerve
            Supraclavicular nerves
            Phrenic nerve

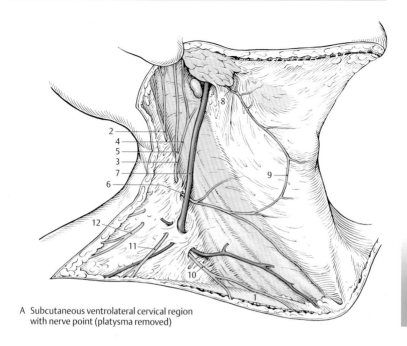

A Subcutaneous ventrolateral cervical region with nerve point (platysma removed)

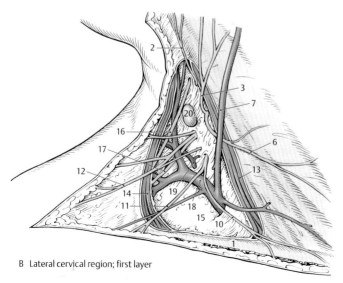

B Lateral cervical region; first layer

Ventrolateral Cervical Regions, continued (A, B)

Lateral Cervical Region, Second Layer (A)

After removal of the *pretracheal layer of the cervical fascia* (**1**), the *omohyoid muscle* (**2**), which is embedded by it, becomes visible. Cranial and dorsal to the omohyoid, the pretracheal layer of the cervical fascia merges with the *prevertebral layer of the cervical fascia* (**3**). It has only a firm texture in the **omoclavicular triangle**, which is formed by the *inferior belly* (**2**) *of the omohyoid*, the *sternocleidomastoid* (**4**), and the *clavicle* (**5**).

In the omoclavicular triangle the *external jugular vein* (**6**) and the *superficial cervical vein* (**7**) combine with the *subclavian* (**8**) and *internal jugular* (**9**) *veins* at the right venous angle to form the *brachiocephalic vein*. The *suprascapular vein* (**10**) also reaches the venous angle. The order in which the veins join shows marked variability. The *suprascapular artery* (**11**) runs with the vein of the same name just above the clavicle. The trunk of the *superficial cervical artery* (**12**) becomes visible cranial to the inferior belly of the omohyoid.

Lateral Cervical Region, Third Layer (B)

After the prevertebral layer of the cervical fascia (**3**) has been removed, the deep cervical muscles, the *scalenus anterior* (**13**), *scalenus medius* (**14**), *scalenus posterior* (**15**), *levator scapulae* (**16**), and *splenius cervicis* (**17**; one of spinotransversales), can be seen. Within the **"scalene gap"**, formed between the scalenus anterior and scalenus medius and the 1st rib, run the *brachial plexus* (**18**) and the *subclavian artery* (**19**). In the area of the scalene gap the subclavian artery gives off the *dorsal scapular artery* (**20**), which becomes visible behind the scalenus medius. This artery may also arise from the transverse artery of the neck

(p. 364). The *phrenic nerve* (**21**), a branch of the cervical plexus from segment C4, obliquely crosses the scalenus anterior muscle (**13**). The brachial plexus (**18**) gives off its supraclavicular branches, of which the *suprascapular* (**22**), *long thoracic* (**23**), and *dorsal scapular* (**24**) *nerves* become visible.

The *cervical lymph nodes* (**25**) together form a lymphatic chain, the *jugular trunk*, that extends to the venous angle. The right venous angle receives lymph vessels from the right side of the head and neck, the right arm (*right subclavian trunk*) and the right half of the thorax (*right bronchomediastinal trunk*). Lymph vessels from the other body regions run to the left venous angle (see vol. 2).

Brachial plexus

Roots: ventral rami C5–T1
- Superior trunk (C5, C6)
- Middle trunk (C7)
- Inferior trunk (C8, T1)

Branches: Supraclavicular part:
- Dorsal scapular nerve
- Long thoracic nerve
- Subclavian nerve
- Suprascapular nerve
- Subscapular nerves
- Thoracodorsal nerve
- Medial pectoral nerve
- Lateral pectoral nerve
- Muscular branches

(Infraclavicular part: see p. 372)

Clinical tip: Lesions of the brachial plexus may have various causes (obstetric trauma, cervical rib, extrinsic pressure). They are classified as upper or lower brachial plexus lesions (see p. 370).

Upper brachial plexus paralysis (*Erb-Duchenne paralysis*), caused by lesions of the C5 and C6 nerve roots, leads to weakness of the abductors and external rotators of the shoulder joint, the flexors of the elbow joint, and the supinator. It also causes mild sensory disturbances affecting the shoulder and radial surface of the forearm.

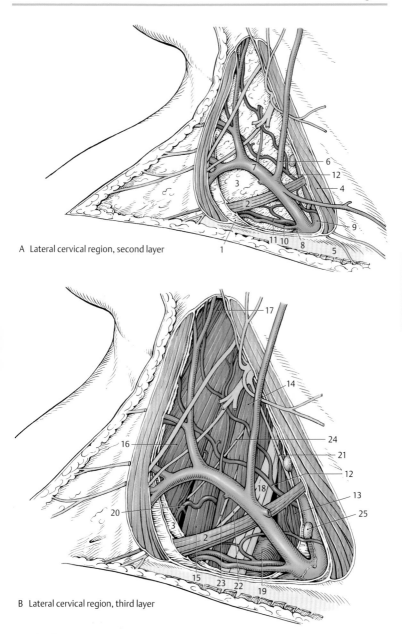

A Lateral cervical region, second layer

B Lateral cervical region, third layer

Ventrolateral Cervical Regions, continued (A–F)

Carotid Triangle (A)

The boundaries of the carotid triangle are the *sternocleidomastoid* (**1**), the *omohyoid* (**2**), and the *posterior belly* (**3**) of the *digastric*. The latter is fixed by the *stylohyoid* (**4**) to the *hyoid bone* (**5**).

The *common facial vein* (**6**) runs superficially; it receives the *vena comitans of hypoglossal nerve* (**7**) and the *superior thyroid vein* (**8**) before joining the *internal jugular vein* (**9**). Ventral to the latter lies the *common carotid artery* (**10**) with the *carotid sinus* (**11**; see vol. 2).

In 67 % of cases, at the level of the fourth cervical vertebra, the common carotid artery divides into the *internal carotid artery*, (**12**), which runs posteriorly, and the *external carotid artery* (**13**), which runs anteriorly. In about 20 % of cases the division occurs one vertebra higher, and in 11 % one vertebra lower, while in the remaining 2 % there are particularly high or low divisions, perhaps even completely outside the carotid triangle.

The internal carotid artery (**12**) as a rule has no branches. The first ventral branch of the external carotid artery (**13**) is the *superior thyroid artery* (**14**) which supplies blood to the *thyroid gland* (**15**) and to the larynx through the *superior laryngeal artery* (**16**). Sometimes the superior thyroid artery also gives off a *sternocleidomastoid artery* (**17**), which more often arises directly from the external carotid artery and loops over the *hypoglossal nerve* (**18**). The *lingual artery* (**19**) is another ventral branch which extends to the tongue, medial to the *hyoglossus* (**20**). The last branch within the carotid triangle is the *facial artery* (**21**), which arises medial to the posterior belly (**3**) of the digastric muscle and runs toward the face. The *carotid body* (**22**) lies in the angle of the carotid bifurcation. It is a paraganglion (see vol. 2) which is reached by sympathetic fibers and parasympathetic fibers. Parasympathetic fibers also run in the *nerve of the carotid sinus*

(**23**), a branch of the glossopharyngeal nerve, which extends to the carotid sinus (**11**), as well as to the carotid body.

The hypoglossal nerve (**18**) runs lateral to both carotid arteries and at the beginning of its arch it gives off the *superior root of the "deep" ansa cervicalis* (**24**). The fibers of this root arise from the first two cervical segments, like those of the *thyrohyoid branch* (**25**) which supplies the thyrohyoid muscle. Descending along the common carotid artery, the superior root joins the *inferior root of the "deep" ansa cervicalis* (**26**) from C2 and C3, which extends laterally or medially across the internal jugular vein to form the "*deep" ansa cervicalis* (**27**). This innervates the remaining infrahyoid muscles.

Medial to the external carotid artery lies the *superior laryngeal nerve*, whose *internal branch* (**28**) reaches the larynx together with the superior laryngeal artery (**16**). The superior laryngeal nerve is a branch of the *vagus nerve* (**29**), which runs between the internal carotid artery and the internal jugular vein and which is only separated by the prevertebral layer of the cervical fascia from the *sympathetic trunk* (**30**) and its *superior cervical ganglion* (**31**). In the superoposterior angle of the triangle we find the *external branch of the accessory nerve* (**32**).

■ **Variants (B–F):** Only the position of the external and internal carotid arteries and the origin of their three ventral branches are discussed here.

According to *Faller*, in 49 % of cases the internal carotid artery may arise dorsolateral (**B**) to the external carotid artery from the common carotid artery, and in 9 % it is ventromedial (**C**). All intermediate positions are possible.

A thyrolingual trunk (**D**) may be found in 4 % of cases, a linguofacial trunk (**E**) in 23 %, and a thyrolinguofacial trunk (**F**) in 0.6 %.

> **Clinical tip:** The common carotid artery can be pressed against the anterior tubercle of the C6 vertebra (Chassaignac tubercle) to palpate the carotid pulse or introduce a needle into the vessel.

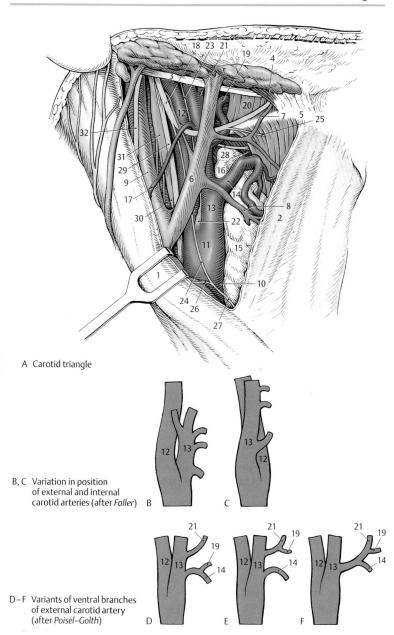

A Carotid triangle

B, C Variation in position
of external and internal
carotid arteries (after *Faller*)

D–F Variants of ventral branches
of external carotid artery
(after *Poisel–Golth*)

Ventrolateral Cervical Regions, continued (A)

Sternocleidomastoid Region (A)

The sternocleidomastoid region only becomes visible after removal of the *sternocleidomastoid* (**1**) and *omohyoid* (**2**) muscles. It joins the carotid triangle to the lateral region of the neck. When the sternocleidomastoid region is exposed, the large vessels and nerves which run through the neck can be seen.

The largest artery, the *common carotid artery* (**3**), ascends obliquely. It divides into the *external* (**4**) and *internal* (**5**) *carotid arteries*. The level of the division and variations in its position are described on page 362.

The arched *inferior thyroid artery* (**6**) running to the *thyroid gland* (**7**) is covered by the common carotid artery. This artery arises from the *thyrocervical trunk* (**8**), which branches off the *subclavian artery* (**9**) just before it enters the scalene gap. The thyrocervical trunk also gives off the *suprascapular artery* (**11**), which crosses ventral to the *scalenus anterior* (**10**), the *superficial cervical artery* (**12**), which lies quite superficially, and the *ascending cervical artery*. The *vertebral artery* (**13**) is the first ascending branch of the subclavian artery. After the subclavian artery has entered the scalene gap, in about 60% of people it gives off the *dorsal scapular artery* (**14**), which runs behind the *scalenus medius* (**15**) and in front of the *scalenus posterior* (**16**), and may divide into ascending and descending branches. In the remainder the dorsal scapular artery arises with the superficial cervical artery (**12**) from the thyrocervical trunk. The common origin is then called the *transverse cervical artery*.

Dorsal to the common carotid artery, the large *internal jugular vein* (**17**), into which the *facial* (**18**) and *middle thyroid* (**19**) *veins* open, is seen to descend. It joins the *subclavian vein* (**20**) to form the *right brachiocephalic vein* (**21**). The *external jugular vein* (**22**), which joins the transverse *cervical vein* (**23**), and the *suprascapular vein* (**24**) also reach the right venous angle.

Lymph vessels (**25**) from the right half of the head and neck and from the right upper limb and the right half of the thorax also run into the right venous angle.

The *"deep" cervical ansa* (**26**), which innervates the infrahyoid muscles, lies on the common carotid artery (**3**). It is formed from a *superior root* (**27**), which, at its origin, runs together with the *hypoglossal nerve* (**28**) and the *inferior root* (**29**). Dorsal to the internal jugular vein runs the *phrenic nerve* (**30**), which stems from the fourth cervical segment and uses the scalenus anterior as a guiding muscle. The *vagus nerve* (**31**), which gives off a *superior* (**32**) and an *inferior cervical cardiac branch* (**33**), also forms part of the neurovascular bundle.

The *sympathetic trunk* (**34**) with its *superior cervical ganglion* (**35**), the sometimes absent *middle cervical ganglion* (**36**), and *inferior cervical ganglion* are separated from the vagus nerve by the prevertebral layer of the cervical fascia. The inferior cervical ganglion is usually fused with the first thoracic ganglion, forming the *stellate ganglion* (**37**), which lies on the head of the 1st rib medial to the vertebral artery (**13**). The sympathetic trunk (**34**) forms the *thyroid loop* (**38**) around the inferior thyroid artery (**6**) and gives off the *cervical cardiac nerves* (**39**). Deeply, the *recurrent laryngeal nerve* (**40**) lies on the trachea.

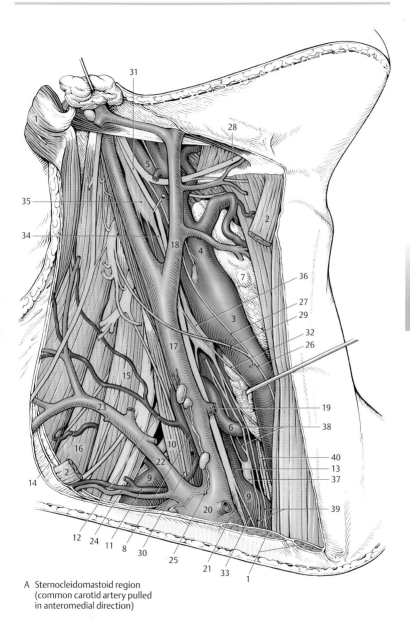

A Sternocleidomastoid region
(common carotid artery pulled
in anteromedial direction)

Scalenovertebral Triangle (A)

The margins of the scalenovertebral triangle are the *longus colli* (**1**), the *scalenus anterior* (**2**), and the cupula of the pleura. The prevertebral layer of the cervical fascia covers the triangle and its contents can be seen only after removal of the fascia.

The *subclavian artery* (**3**) lies on the cupula of the pleura, from which connective tissue fiber bands (the costopleural ligament) run to the 1st rib. Its first ascending branch is the *vertebral artery* (**4**), which crosses ventrally the roots of the *brachial plexus from T1* (**5**) and *C8* (**6**), to reach the vertebral column at the transverse foramen of the sixth cervical vertebra. Dorsal to the vertebral artery (**4**) runs the *vertebral vein* (**7**) which leaves the vertebral column at the transversarium foramen of the seventh cervical vertebra. Adjacent to the vertebral artery, the *thyrocervical trunk* ascends (see p. 364), followed by the *costocervical trunk* (**8**), which gives off the *deep cervical artery* (**9**), the *highest intercostal artery*, and, rarely, a *dorsal scapular artery* (**10**) of abnormal origin. The *internal thoracic artery* (**11**) extends caudally, running parasternally with the *internal thoracic vein* (**12**) to reach the rectus sheath (see p. 398).

Ventrally, the subclavian artery and its branches on the left side are crossed by the *thoracic duct* (**13**), which forms a cranially convex arch. The thoracic duct opens into the *left venous angle* (**14**), which is formed by the junction of the *internal jugular* (**15**) and *subclavian veins* (**16**).

The roots of the brachial plexus out of C5–T1 run deep down, while the *sympathetic trunk* (**17**) runs superficial to them. At the level of the sixth cervical vertebra, the sympathetic trunk often contains a *middle cervical ganglion* (**18**) lying on the scalenus anterior (**2**). Caudal to the ganglion, the sympathetic trunk together with the *superior cardiac nerve* (**19**) form the *ansa thyroidea* (**20**), through which passes the inferior thyroid artery. The sympathetic trunk gives off the *ansa subclavia* (**21**), which winds around the subclavian artery (**3**). This ansa subclavia extends to the inferior cervical ganglion which fuses with the first thoracic ganglion to form the *stellate (cervicothoracic) ganglion* (**22**). The latter lies on the head of the first rib. The *inferior cardiac nerve* (**23**) arises from it. It runs in a groove formed by the *trachea* (**25**) and the *esophagus* (**26**).

Clinical tip: The presence of a cervical rib may lead to **cervical rib syndrome (Naffziger syndrome)**. This is associated with pain coming from the brachial vessels and from the branches of the three fascicles, in particular, in the region supplied by the ulnar nerve. In addition, one should palpate in the greater supraclavicular fossa.

However, the pain coming from vessels and nerves may also occur in the absence of a cervical rib. This is called the **scalenus anticus syndrome**. The pain is caused by hypertrophy and hypertonicity of the scalenus anterior muscle.

The supraclavicular lymph nodes, whose efferents drain directly into the junction of the left subclavian and internal jugular veins, may harbor distant lymphogenous metastases from gastric carcinoma. They are known as the **Virchow-Troisier sentinel nodes** for this type of cancer.

A sentinel node (older term: "signal node") is the first node that receives lymphatic drainage from a tumor. It is useful for confirming or excluding lymphogenous metastasis in certain types of cancer.

---

27 Phrenic nerve
28 Left brachiocephalic vein
29 Scalenus medius
30 Scalenus posterior
31 Levator scapulae
32 Trapezius
33 Clavicular part of the pectoralis major
34 Left common carotid artery
35 Left vagus nerve

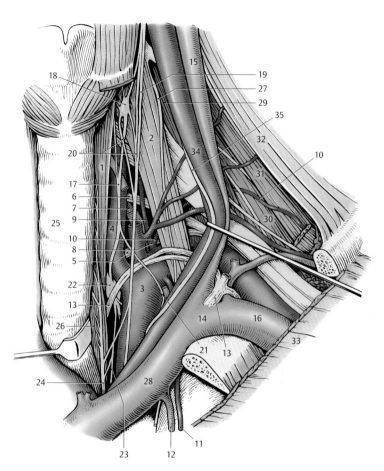

A Scalenovertebral triangle
(common carotid artery, subclavian vein,
and vagus nerve pulled in lateral direction)

Upper Limb

Regions (A–C)

Superficially, there is no clear demarcation between the free upper limb or its root and the thorax, but by dissection it is possible to separate the mainly muscular connection of the arm together with its root from the thorax. The free limb and its root must be considered together for proper understanding of the topography of the peripheral neurovascular pathways. The following regional subdivisions are made for practical purposes and are not founded on development.

Regions around the Shoulder

Anteriorly there is the **infraclavicular fossa** (**1**) with the *deltopectoral triangle* (**2**) through which the peripheral pathways extend to the arm, i. e., the central part of the **axillary region** (**3**) with the *axillary fossa* (**4**). Lateral to the shoulder joint is the **deltoid region** (**5**), onto the dorsal side of which adjoins the **scapular region** (**6**).

Regions of the Arm

The arm is organized into an **anterior region of arm** (**7**), the basic component of which is the flexor muscles, and a **posterior region of arm** (**8**), occupied by the extensors. Within the anterior brachial region, the *medial bicipital groove* (**9**) deserves special attention because it lies in front of the medial intermuscular septum and corresponds to the main pathway taken by the brachial vessels and nerves passing from the axilla to the cubital fossa. A *lateral bicipital groove* is described in front of the lateral intermuscular septum; in it the cephalic vein courses superficially (subcutaneously).

Regions of the Elbow

The **anterior cubital region** (10), the center of which is represented by the *cubital fossa*, adjoins the anterior brachial region on the flexor side. Within the cubital fossa the vascular and nerve bundles divide. The **posterior cubital region** (**11**), which lies dorsally, contains muscles and only smaller vascular networks.

Regions of the Forearm

The **anterior region of forearm** (**12**) lies distal to the cubital fossa and contains the large vessels and nerves between the flexors. The dorsal part is formed by the **posterior region of forearm** (**13**).

Regions of the Hand

In the wrist, there is the transition to the **palm** (**14**), which extends from the midcarpal joint to the metacarpophalangeal joints. The **dorsum of the hand** (**15**) has the same limits. Laterally, between the dorsum of the hand and the palm is the **radial fovea** (**16**) containing the radial artery.

Regions of the Carpus

The **anterior region of wrist** (**17**) lies on the palmar plane between the anterior antebrachial region and the palm of the hand. The **posterior region of wrist** (**18**) lies on the dorsal plane.

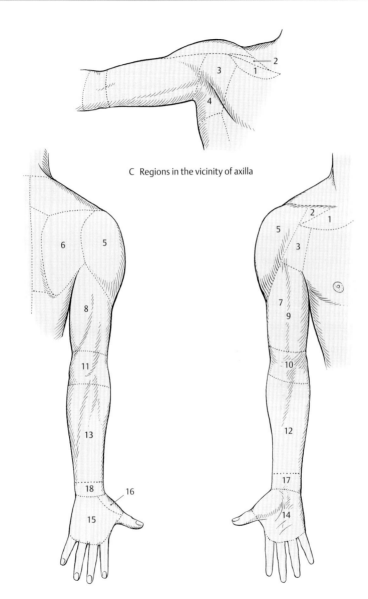

C Regions in the vicinity of axilla

B Posterior view of regions
   of upper limb

A Anterior view of regions
   of upper limb

Peripheral Pathways

Deltopectoral Triangle (A, B)

The *clavicle* (**1**), the *deltoid* (**2**), and the *pectoralis major* (**3**) form the proximal, lateral, and medial boundaries of the deltopectoral triangle. Distally, it merges into the deltopectoral groove. Since the width of the base of the triangle is quite variable, it is possible to separate the *clavicular part* (**4**) *of the pectoralis major* from the clavicle and to reflect it downward.

Superficial Layer (A)

Superficially, the pectoral fascia in the region of the triangle shows a slight depression. Between the clavicle (**1**), the *coracoid process* (**B 5**), and *the pectoralis minor* (**B 6**), the *clavipectoral fascia* (**7**) stretches from the deep surface of the deltoid to the deep surface of the pectoralis major. This fascia divides the triangle into two compartments.

In the superficial layer the *cephalic vein* (**8**) reaches the triangle through the deltopectoral groove. It penetrates the clavipectoral fascia to end in the *axillary vein* (**B 9**). The cephalic vein is joined by branches from the surrounding areas. Lateral to the cephalic vein, the *thoraco-acromial artery* (**B10**), which stems from the axillary artery pierces the clavipectoral fascia (**7**). It divides into *clavicular* (**11**), *acromial* (**12**), *deltoid* (**13**), and *pectoral* (**B 14**) *branches*. *The pectoral nerves* run together with the latter vessels and may penetrate the fascia clavipectoralis as a common trunk (**15**).

Deep Layer (B)

The deep layer contains the vessels and nerve bundles that supply the upper limb. Distal to the *subclavius* (**16**) from medial to lateral are the axillary vein (**9**), *axillary artery* (**17**), and three nerve cords, which are the infraclavicular portion of the brachial plexus. They are the superficially situated *lateral cord* (**18**), which may already have divided into its branches, the *posterior cord* (**19**), and the *medial cord* (**20**). At the upper border of the pectoralis

minor (**6**) the vessels and nerves lie more deeply. The *suprascapular artery, vein and nerve* (**21**) can be seen lying very deep in the lateral part.

The superficial compartment sometimes contains lymph nodes (not shown in the diagram). They drain lymph from the lymph vessels that run along the cephalic vein. They are in continuity with the deep infraclavicular nodes (not shown).

■■ **Variants:** It is common to find a vein (**22**) looping superficially around the clavicle interconnecting the axillary vein with the subclavian vein, producing a venous ring. The cephalic vein may sometimes be poorly developed.

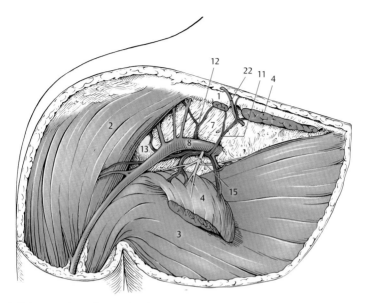

A   Deltopectoral triangle, superficial layer

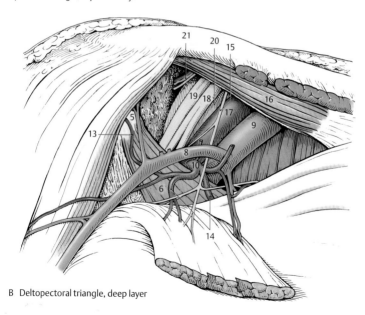

B   Deltopectoral triangle, deep layer

Axillary Region (A)

The vessels and nerves to the upper limb run through the axilla. The boundaries of the axilla are the *pectoralis major* (**1**) and *pectoralis minor* (**2**) anteriorly and the *latissimus dorsi* (**3**) posteriorly. The thoracic wall with the *serratus anterior* (**4**) lies medially, and laterally there is the humerus with the *short head of the biceps brachii* (**5**) and the *coracobrachialis* (**6**).

Most medial of all is the *axillary vein* (**7**) formed from the brachial veins. It runs centrally, receiving a larger number of small veins. It is joined in the deltopectoral triangle (see p. 370) by the *cephalic vein* (**8**). The *axillary artery* (**9**), which lies lateral to the vein, gives off the *thoraco-acromial artery* (**10**), with its *pectoral* (**11**), *acromial* (**12**), and *deltoid* branches. A *lateral thoracic artery* (**13**) arises from the thoraco-acromial artery in 10% of cases (see figure), or directly from the axillary artery. Another branch of the axillary artery, the *subscapular artery* (**14**), gives off the *thoracodorsal* (**15**) and *circumflex scapular arteries* (**16**). The last branches of the axillary artery are the *anterior* (**17**) and *posterior circumflex humeral arteries* (**18**).

At the tendinous insertion of the latissimus dorsi (**3**), the axillary artery continues as the *brachial artery* (**19**) and gives off the *profunda brachii artery* (**20**) as its first branch.

The three cords of the brachial plexus lie in the axillary region medial, lateral and posterior to the axillary artery, and there divide into various branches. The posterior cord gives off the *axillary* (**21**) and *radial* (**22**) nerves. Accompanied by the posterior circumflex humeral artery and vein (**18**), the axillary nerve (**21**) passes through the quadrangular space (see p. 374) toward the *deltoid* (**23**) and *teres minor*. The radial nerve (**22**) runs in the medial bicipital sulcus accompanied by the profunda brachii artery (**20**) with which it runs into the sulcus for the radial nerve. The *medial* (**24**) and *lateral cords* (**25**) form the (often du-

plicated) median bifurcation (*medial and lateral roots*), from which the *median nerve* (**26**) continues superficial to the axillary artery. The median nerve, accompanied by the brachial artery, then enters the medial bicipital groove. Other branches of the medial cord, the *ulnar nerve* (**27**), the *medial antebrachial cutaneous nerve* (**28**) and the *medial brachial cutaneous nerve* (**29**) also reach this groove. Branches of intercostal nerves 1–3 join the medial cutaneous brachial nerve as *intercostobrachial nerves* (**30**).

The lateral cords give off, apart from the lateral root of the median nerve (here duplicated), the *musculocutaneous nerve* (**31**), which pierces the coracobrachialis.

On the wall of the thorax, the *long thoracic nerve* (**32**), arising from the supraclavicular part of the brachial plexus, descends on the lateral surface of the serratus anterior and innervates it. The *subscapular nerve* (**34**) lies on the *subscapularis* (**33**) and may give off the *thoracodorsal nerve* (**35**) to innervate the latissimus dorsi (**3**).

> **Clinical tip:** Lower brachial plexus paralysis (*Dejerine-Klumpke paralysis*) is caused by lesions of the C8 and T1 nerve roots. It presents with paralysis of the short hand muscles and long digital flexors, accompanied by sensory losses on the ulnar surface of the hand and forearm.

Brachial plexus

(Roots and supraclavicular part, see p. 360)
- Infraclavicular part
  - Lateral cord
    - Musculocutaneous nerve
    - Lateral root of median nerve
  - Medial cord
    - Medial root of median nerve
    - Ulnar nerve
    - Medial brachial cutaneous nerve
    - Medial antebrachial cutaneous nerve
  - Posterior cord
    - Axillary nerve
    - Radial nerve

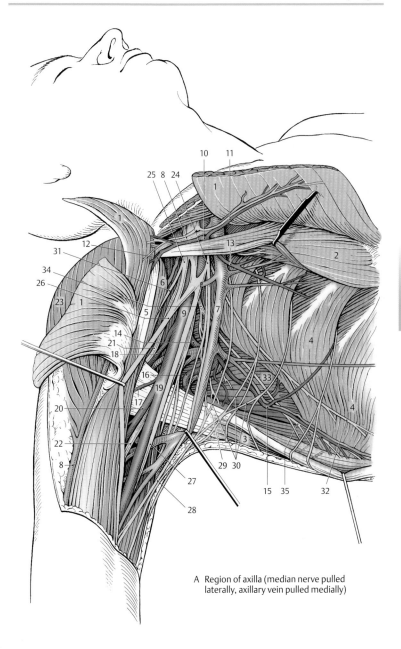

A Region of axilla (median nerve pulled laterally, axillary vein pulled medially)

Axillary Spaces (A–D)

The slitlike opening between the *teres minor* (**1**) and *teres major* (**2**) and the *humerus* (**3**) is divided by the *long head of the triceps brachii* (**4**) into a **quadrangular space** and a **triangular space.**

Through the **quadrangular space** the *axillary (circumflex) nerve* (**5**) reaches the dorsal side. This nerve provides a branch (**6**) to the teres minor and then buries itself in the *deltoid* (**7**). It also innervates the upper lateral skin area via the *superior lateral brachial cutaneous nerve* (**8**). The axillary nerve is usually accompanied by the *posterior circumflex humeral artery* (**9**), and the commonly paired *posterior circumflex humeral veins*. The artery supplies the deltoid, the long head of the triceps brachii (**4**) and the *lateral head of the triceps brachii* (**10**).

The *circumflex scapular artery* (**11**) runs through the **triangular space** to the dorsal surface of the scapula on which it anastomoses with the suprascapular artery. The artery is accompanied by the *circumflex scapular vein*. Deeply a twig (**12**) from the subscapular nerve, which innervates the teres major (**2**) can be seen. It does not run through the triangular space.

■■ **Variants (B–D):** The posterior circumflex humeral artery (**9**), which usually (**B**) runs through the quadrangular space, arises as one of the terminal branches of the axillary artery. It often has a common origin with the subscapular artery. Distal to the teres major tendon, the *profunda brachii artery* (**13**) arises as the first branch of the *brachial artery* (**14**). In about 7% of cases, according to *Lanz–Wachsmuth*, the profunda brachii artery (**13**) arises (**C**) from the posterior humeral circumflex artery (**9**). In these cases the profunda brachii artery runs distalward dorsal to the tendon of the teres major. In 16% of cases (**D**) the origin of the posterior circumflex humeral artery (**9**) is from a typical profunda brachii artery (**13**), and in those cases the posterior circumflex humeral artery does not traverse the quadrangular space.

15 Radial nerve

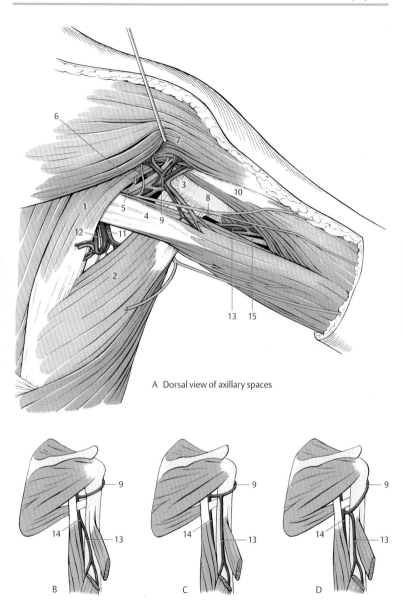

A Dorsal view of axillary spaces

B–D Variants of arteries (after *Lanz–Wachsmuth*)

Anterior Region of Arm

Subcutaneous Layer (A)

The coarse, firm *brachial fascia* (**1**) surrounds the muscles of the arm. On the medial and lateral side from the humerus, the intermuscular septum radiates into it (see p. 180) to form two compartments, the anterior and posterior compartment of arm. The subcutaneous veins, nerves and lymph vessels run superficially to the brachial fascia. In inflammatory conditions the lymph vessels may be seen through the skin as fine red lines.

The *cephalic vein* (**2**) runs on the lateral border of the biceps brachii. It carries blood from the radial side of the hand and the forearm via the deltopectoral groove to the deltopectoral triangle (see p. 370). The veins are accompanied by the *lateral superficial lymph vessels* (not shown) which transport lymph from the two radial digits, the radial part of the palm, and the forearm (see p. 370).

The medial bicipital groove shapes the brachial fascia on the medial side of the biceps brachii, and in its distal half the usually well-developed *basilic vein* (**3**) runs subcutaneously. This vein pierces the brachial fascia at the **basilic hiatus** (**4**) and runs deep to become one of the veins accompanying the brachial artery. In the subcutaneous part of its course in the arm it is accompanied by the *medial antebrachial cutaneous nerve* and its branches; the *anterior branch* (**5**) runs lateral to the vein and closely adheres to it, while the *posterior branch* (**6**) lies medial and a short distance away from it.

Near the basilic hiatus, in about one-third of cases, *cubital* (some of them named *supratrochlear*) *lymph nodes* (**7**) are found which act as the first filtration point for lymph from the three ulnar digits. The *medial superficial lymph vessels* run along the medial bicipital groove; they may accompany the basilic vein, or they may reach subcutaneously to the axilla. They are usually more numerous and larger than those that accompany the cephalic vein.

Branches of the *medial brachial cutaneous nerve* (**8**) innervate the skin from the axilla downward. In addition, they are joined by the *intercostobrachial nerves* (**9**) from T1 and T3, which innervate a small cutaneous area on the inner surface of the arm.

▪▪▪ **Variants:** The position of the basilic hiatus is very variable. It may lie immediately at the transition to the cubital region. The cephalic vein is sometimes absent.

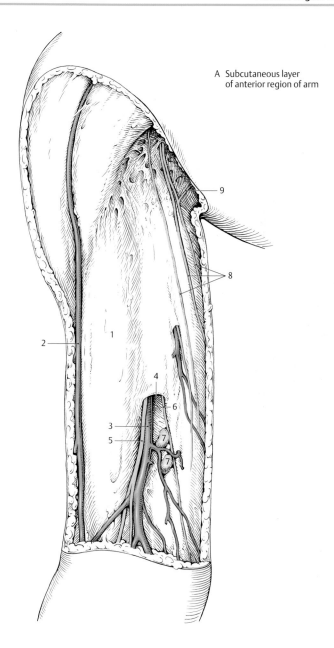

A Subcutaneous layer
   of anterior region of arm

Anterior Region of Arm, continued (A–E)

Medial Bicipital Groove (A, B)

The medial bicipital groove is bounded on one side by the *biceps brachii* of the arm (**1**) and on the other by the *medial intermuscular septum* (not shown) and the *triceps brachii* (**2**). It contains the blood vessels and nerves to the upper limb. The *medial antebrachial cutaneous nerve* (**3**) is the most superficial structure, and its anterior branch lies on the *basilic vein* (**4**). Both leave the medial bicipital groove at the basilic hiatus, which may lie at various levels. The basilic vein may drain into the *brachial veins* (**5**), or it may only join the axillary vein in the axilla (see Fig. A).

Furthest medially runs the *ulnar nerve* (**6**), lying on the medial intermuscular septum. At the border between the middle and the distal third of the arm, the ulnar nerve penetrates the medial intermuscular septum and runs dorsally from the septum to the dorsal side of the medial epicondyle of the humerus.

The *median nerve* (**7**) runs lateral to the basilic vein and crosses the *brachial artery* (**8**) from the lateral to the medial side. The brachial artery, which is the deepest structure throughout the entire length of the medial bicipital groove, gives off a series of branches.

In addition to muscular branches (**9**), the brachial artery gives off the *profunda brachii artery* (**10**) in the proximal region of the medial bicipital groove. Here it joins the *radial nerve* (**11**) and leaves the medial bicipital sulcus with it at the level of the margin between the proximal and middle third of the arm. Then the profunda brachii artery runs with the radial nerve in the radial groove on the dorsal surface of the humerus and ends as the *radial collateral artery* after giving off the *medial collateral artery*. Other branches of the brachial artery include the *superior ulnar collateral artery* (**12**), which accompanies the ulnar nerve (dorsal to it) and the *inferior ulnar collateral artery* (not visible).

■ **Variants (C–E):** The relationship between the median nerve (**7**) and brachial artery (**8**) and its branches may be variable. Although, according to *Lanz*, the median nerve follows a typical course in 74% of cases, a *superficial brachial artery* (**13**), which arises from the brachial artery, may run superficial to the median nerve. In that case the brachial artery may be completely rudimentary (in 12% of cases according to *Lanz*), or it may divide into two arteries at variable levels (14%). The profunda brachii artery may arise together with the posterior circumflex humeral artery (see p. 374).

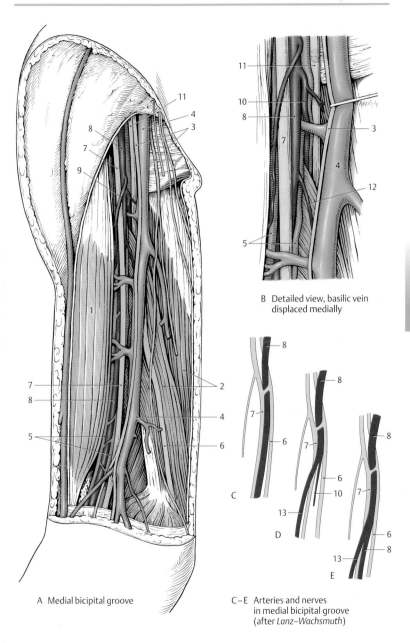

B Detailed view, basilic vein
displaced medially

A Medial bicipital groove

C–E Arteries and nerves
in medial bicipital groove
(after *Lanz–Wachsmuth*)

Posterior Region of Arm (A, B)

Subcutaneous Layer (A)

The *deltoid fascia* (1) and the *brachial fascia* (2) invest the muscles. Subcutaneously, there are mainly the cutaneous nerves in addition to small arterial branches and delicate veins. Branches of the *superior lateral cutaneous nerve of arm* (3), which arises from the axillary nerve, pass at the inferior margin of the deltoid muscle through the fascia. The branches predominantly supply the skin covering the deltoid muscle. However, the demarcation against the area supplied by the *inferior lateral cutaneous nerve of arm* (4) varies.

The inferior lateral cutaneous nerve of arm (4), which branches from the *radial nerve* (**B** 5), is often accompanied by a smaller artery and vein where is passes through the fascia. It supplies the distal skin region on the lateral side up to the elbow. The *branches* (6) *of the posterior cutaneous nerve of arm* (**B** 7), which arises proximally from the radial nerve (**B** 5), reach the dorsal surface of the upper arm and supply it.

Subfascial Layer (B)

After removal of the brachial fascia the *long head* (8) and the *lateral head* (9) of the *triceps brachii* (10) can be severed. This permits demonstration of the radial groove and the structures lying in it. The radial nerve (5) runs from medioproximal to laterodistal.

Its first proximal branch is the posterior cutaneous nerve of arm (7). In the region of the radial groove the radial nerve gives off the *muscular branches* (11) and, distally to these, the inferior lateral cutaneous nerve of arm (4).

Together with the radial nerve runs the *deep artery of arm* (12), which is usually associated with two accompanying veins. Right after branching off the brachial artery (see p. 378), this artery often gives off a small branch to the deltoid muscle, as do the nutrient arteries of humerus. The *middle collateral artery* (13) branches off in the radial groove; it is accompanied by a muscular branch of the radial nerve (11). This artery, like the terminal branch of the deep brachial artery, the *radial collateral artery* (14), reaches the articular rete of elbow. A branch of the radial collateral artery becomes visible at the anterior aspect between the brachialis and brachioradialis muscles, together with the radial nerve, and anastomoses with the radial recurrent artery (see p. 384).

> **Clinical tip:** Fractures of the humeral shaft endanger the radial nerve. When repositioning the fragments, one should take special care of this nerve (see also p. 148).

15 Anterior and posterior branches of the medial cutaneous nerve of forearm
16 Basilic vein
17 Middle head of triceps muscle

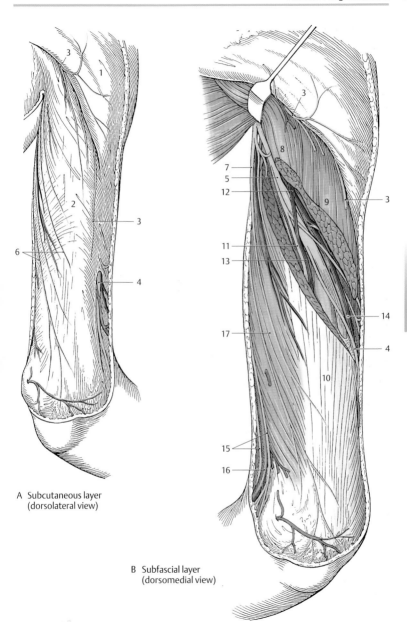

A Subcutaneous layer
(dorsolateral view)

B Subfascial layer
(dorsomedial view)

Cubital Fossa (A–G)

Subcutaneous Layer (A)

The anterior cubital region at the bend of the elbow is not sharply demarcated from the anterior brachial region and it is just as poorly demarcated from the forearm. Normally the term cubital fossa refers to an area 2–3 fingers in breadth proximal and distal to the articular space.

Subcutaneously there is a variable amount of well-developed fatty tissue containing veins, nerves, lymphatics, and lymph nodes. The cutaneous veins of the subcutaneous layer are very important clinically, as the cubital fossa as a rule is the region for intravenous injections and for taking blood samples, etc.

According to the development of the venous system, the course taken by the veins, as well as their caliber, fluctuates widely.

The *basilic vein* (**1**), which is commonly well-developed and easy to see beneath the skin, runs medially. It is usually continuous with the *antebrachial basilic vein*, (**2**, basilic vein of forearm), but it may come from the *median antebrachial vein*. Many other variants (**B–G**) are possible.

In the region of the *basilic hiatus* (**3**) the basilic vein becomes subfascial. It is accompanied by branches of the *medial antebrachial cutaneous nerve* (**4**). Often (33% of cases) there are lymph nodes near the basilic hiatus (see p. 376). The *cephalic vein* (**5**) runs along the lateral margin of the cubital fossa. It is always palpable but not always visible, and in many instances it is not as well developed as the basilic vein. The cephalic vein in the distal part of the region accompanies the *lateral antebrachial cutaneous nerve* (**6**), which is the terminal branch of the musculocutaneous nerve.

A *median cubital vein* (**7**) normally unites the basilic and cephalic veins. There is almost always a *deep median cubital vein* (**8**), which joins the superficial and deep veins.

▬ **Variants (B–G):** There are numerous variants of the subcutaneous veins. Thus, the cephalic vein (**5**) and the basilic vein (**1**) may continue from a median antebrachial vein. There is also a considerable range in size of the two main cutaneous veins. The median cubital vein may sometimes be absent (**E**).

Clinical tip: Intravenous injections in the cephalic vein are less painful, as it is not closely related to any nerve. The basilic vein is closely related to the branches of the medial antebrachial cutaneous nerve.
In some individuals, particularly those with poorly developed subcutaneous fatty tissue, the veins are easily displaced and are known clinically as "rolling veins" because they have to be secured in place for injections.
Indwelling cannulas are usually placed in a dorsal hand vein to facilitate arm movements at the elbow joint.

9 Cubital lymph nodes

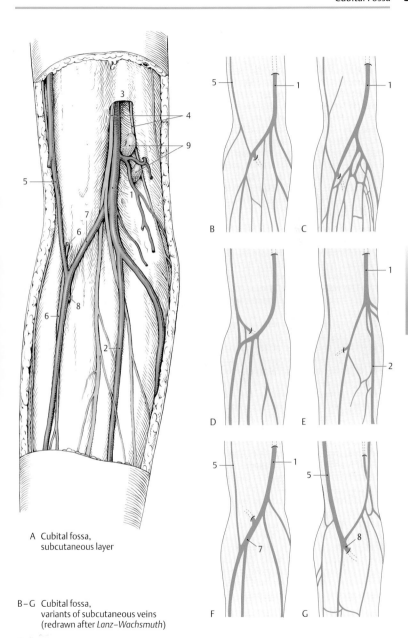

A Cubital fossa,
   subcutaneous layer

B–G Cubital fossa,
     variants of subcutaneous veins
     (redrawn after *Lanz–Wachsmuth*)

Cubital Fossa, continued (A—E)

Deep Layer 1 (A)

After removal of the fascia, the muscles which border the cubital fossa become visible. From the proximal margin the *biceps brachii* (**1**) with its tendon runs toward the radial tuberosity, and with its *bicipital aponeurosis* (**2**) toward the antebrachial fascia. It partly covers the *brachialis* (**3**), which is inserted into the ulnar tuberosity. On the medial side, arising from the medial epicondyle, the *pronator teres* (**4**) and the superficial flexors of the hand run distally, and on the lateral side the fossa is bounded by the *brachioradialis* (**5**).

The neurovascular bundle, which descends from the medial bicipital groove (see p. 378), splits up within the cubital fossa. The *brachial artery* (**6**), covered by the bicipital aponeurosis (**2**) gives off the radial artery. The *radial artery* (**7**) runs distally superficial to the flexors of the forearm.

In the cubital fossa the *median nerve* (**8**) leaves the brachial artery and runs distally between the two heads of the pronator teres, which it also innervates. The *ulnar nerve* (**9**) leaves the medial bicipital groove before it reaches the cubital fossa and runs dorsal to the medial epicondyle. The *radial nerve* (**10**) becomes visible between the brachialis (**3**) and the brachioradialis (**5**) and divides into a smaller, sensory, *superficial branch* (**11**) and a larger, predominantly motoric, *deep branch* (**12**). The superficial branch supplies cutaneous fibers to the radial half of the dorsum of the hand, the thumb, and the dorsal surface of the proximal phalanges of the second and third digits. The deep branch penetrates the *supinator* (**13**), winds laterally around the neck of radius, innervates the radial and dorsal muscles of forearm, and terminates as posterior interosseous nerve. This nerve provides sensory supply to the wrist joints, the interosseous membrane, and parts of the periosteum of radius and ulna.

Deep Layer 2 (B)

After severing the bicipital aponeurosis (**2**), the division of the brachial artery (**6**) becomes visible. Its first branch is the radial artery (**7**). The *radial recurrent artery* (**14**) branches off either from this artery or already from the brachial artery and runs along the radial nerve (**10**) in proximal direction. It anastomoses with the anterior branch of the radial collateral artery. At the level of the proximal margin of the supinator (**13**), the brachial artery gives off the *ulnar recurrent artery* (**15**). Thereafter, the brachial artery divides into the *common interosseous artery* (**16**) and the *ulnar artery* (**17**). The latter passes behind the median nerve (**8**) and the pronator teres (**4**). The individual arteries are accompanied by veins that are paired in most cases.

■■ **Variants (C–E):** The median nerve usually (approx. 95%) runs between the two heads of the pronator teres (**C**). Occasionally it pierces the *humeral head* (**18**) of the pronator teres (barely 2%; **D**). In about 3% of cases, the median nerve lies directly on the bone and runs deep to the two heads of the pronator teres (**E**). In such cases a fracture of the proximal part of the radius and ulna may endanger the nerve.

Variants of the brachial artery and its branches in this region have been reported, although infrequently, e.g., the brachial artery may run dorsal to the supracondylar process when present.

The current nomenclature divides the brachial artery into a radial and an ulnar artery, the latter giving off the common interosseous artery. This nomenclature is not consistent with the embryological development of the arteries of the arm and should be avoided, e.g., because of diverse variants, such as a higher origin of the radial artery. For this reason the developmentally based classification has been retained (p. 390).

> **Clinical tip:** The deep branch of the radial nerve is endangered in cases of dislocation, lesions of the capsular ligaments, and fractures in the region of the neck of radius.

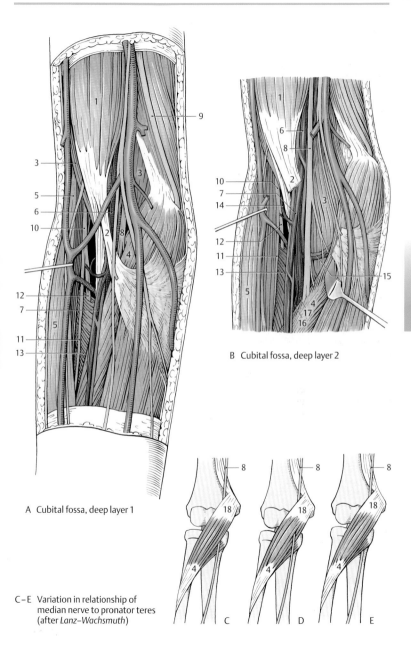

A Cubital fossa, deep layer 1

B Cubital fossa, deep layer 2

C–E Variation in relationship of
median nerve to pronator teres
(after *Lanz–Wachsmuth*)

Anterior Region of forearm (A, B)

Subcutaneous Layer (A)

In the subcutaneous adipose tissue are the well-developed cutaneous veins, which, to be sure, are subject to great variations in their courses. The cutaneous arteries are small and unimportant. The cutaneous nerves run independently of the veins and are very constant both in location and size.

On the radial side there is the *cephalic antebrachial vein* (**1**), which mostly *anastomoses* (**2**) distally with the other veins of the forearm. Proximally it often gives off the *median cubital vein* (**3**), which sometimes may arise from the median antebrachial vein. The *lateral antebrachial cutaneous nerve* (**4**), the terminal branch of the musculocutaneous nerve, crosses beneath the cephalic vein in the cubital fossa. In the distal part of the forearm the *superficial branch of the radial nerve* (**5**) lies in close proximity to the cephalic vein.

The *antebrachial basilic vein* (**6**) passes at the medial side of the anterior region of forearm and is accompanied medially and laterally by twigs (**7**) from the *medial antebrachial cutaneous nerve.*

In the distal third of the forearm, the *palmar branch* (**8**) of the ulnar nerve lies subcutaneously. Radially from it and just proximal to the anterior carpal region, the *palmar branch* (**9**) of the median nerve pierces the fascia.

Subfascial Layer (B)

After cutting through the firm antebrachial fascia which is reinforced proximally and medially by the bicipital aponeurosis, the deep-lying vessels and nerves come into view. These vessels and nerves are arranged essentially into three bundles or routes and, indeed, into a radial, a middle, and an ulnar bundle.

The **radial neurovascular bundle**, consisting of the *radial artery* (**10**) and *radial veins* (**11**), proceeds distally between the bra-chioradialis (**12**) and *flexor carpi radialis* (**13**) and is accompanied in the proximal segment by the *superficial branch of the radial nerve* (**14**). The *deep branch of the radial nerve* (**15**), which gives off the *posterior interosseous nerve* in the forearm, penetrates the *supinator* (**16**) within the cubital fossa.

The **middle neurovascular bundle**, which is situated between the superficial and deep flexors, houses the *median nerve* (**17**), sometimes accompanied by a *median artery* (variant, p. 390). The median nerve usually travels between the two heads of the *pronator teres* (**18**) and, in the region of the wrist, lies radial to the tendons of the *flexor digitorum superficialis* (**19**). The *anterior interosseous artery* and the *anterior interosseous nerve*, a branch of the median nerve, reside in a deep compartment of the middle bundle between the deep flexors and the interosseous membrane.

The **ulnar neurovascular bundle** lies in the middle and distal third of the forearm between the flexor digitorum superficialis (**19**) and *flexor carpi ulnaris* (**20**). It consists of the *ulnar nerve* (**21**), the *ulnar artery* (**22**), and the *ulnar veins* (cut off in the illustration, **23**). After its exit from the brachial artery, the ulnar artery crosses proximally under the median nerve (**17**), the pronator teres (**18**), and the common head of the superficial flexors. The flexor carpi ulnaris (**20**) serves as a guide for the location of the ulnar nerve (**21**).

> **Clinical tip:** The **pulse** is palpated at a typical site (see also p. 164) on the distal forearm. The radial artery runs on the palmar side, medial to the brachioradialis tendon, passing just in front of the radial styloid process.
> *Note:* If occlusive vascular disease is suspected, the pulse should be taken at additional sites such as the dorsal pedal artery (see p. 438), superficial temporal artery, facial artery (see p. 340), and common carotid artery (see p. 364).

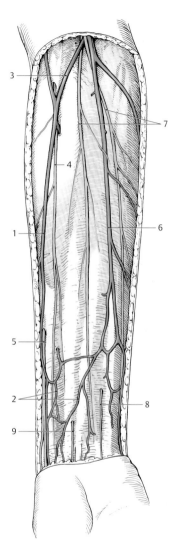

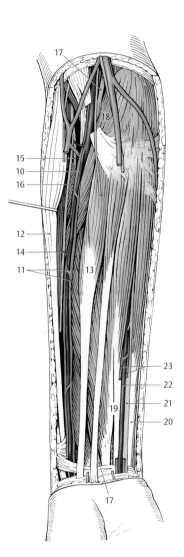

A Anterior region of forearm,
   subcutaneous layer

B Anterior region of forearm,
   subfascial layer

Anterior Region of wrist (A)

The distal margin of the wrist is the flexor retinaculum. The proximal margin is visible on the skin only as the proximal skin crease of the wrist.

Proximal to the *flexor retinaculum* there are strong fiber strands in the *antebrachial fascia* (**1**), which also form a deep layer (**2**) and which are connected to the bones of the forearm. Superficially run the veins and nerves as described previously on page 386, as well as the tendon of the *palmaris longus* (**3**). Deeply, the most radial structure is the *radial artery* (**5**) and its accompanying veins lying on the *pronator quadratus* (**4**).

On the ulnar side of the artery lies the tendon of the *flexor carpi radialis* (**6**) within its own tendon sheath, followed next by the tendon sheath of the *flexor pollicis longus* (**7**). Between this muscle and the common tendon sheath (**8**) for the *flexor digitorum superficialis* and the *flexor digitorum profundus* runs the *median nerve* (**9**). The structures run through the carpal tunnel (canalis carpi, see p. 124) to the palm of the hand.

> **Clinical tip: Carpal tunnel syndrome** often results from a "transligamentous" thenar branch (23%), which passes through the carpal ligament on arising from the median nerve. In all cases a disproportion exists between the carpal tunnel and its contents, causing severe pain in the thenar region as well as hypo- and paresthesias.

The *ulnar artery* (**10**) with its accompanying veins and the *ulnar nerve* (**11**) lie radial to *the flexor carpi ulnaris* (**12**) and run to the palm of the hand superficial to the flexor retinaculum. They lie between the deep (**2**) and superficial layers of the antebrachial fascia. The superficial layer is usually strengthened by tendinous fiber bands of the flexor carpi ulnaris muscle (see p. 160) so that the ulnar artery and nerve reach the palm in their own fascial ulnar channel (**Guyon's box**).

Palm of Hand

Superficial Layer (B)

The palm of the hand is subdivided into three regions: the thenar eminence, the central compartment (metacarpal region), and the hypothenar eminence. The fascia encloses these lateral regions, while the central compartment is covered by the coarse, firm *palmar aponeurosis* (**13**). This represents the continuation of the palmaris longus (**A 3**) and on its ulnar border it radiates into the rather variably developed *palmaris brevis* (**14**).

The palmar aponeurosis is divided into longitudinal (**15**) and transverse (**16**; see p. 178) *fascicles*. At the radial, ulnar and distal margins of the palmar aponeurosis, the *common palmar digital arteries* (**17**) and the nerves of the same name become subcutaneous. The arteries divide into the *proper palmar digital arteries* (**18**), which, accompanied by the *proper palmar digital nerves* (**18**), extend to the terminal phalanges of the digits. The *proper palmar digital veins* reach the *superficial palmar venous arch*, which lies superficially at the root of the digits.

In the forearm (p. 386) the ulnar nerve gives off the *palmar branch* to supply the skin of the ball of the little finger.

> **Clinical tip:** The nerves at the sides of the digits can be anesthetized by the **Oberst anesthetic method** of neural blockade. It is important to remember that the skin of the terminal phalanx of the thumb and the middle and terminal phalanges of the index and middle digits is also innervated on the dorsal surface by the *proper palmar digital branches* of the median nerve.

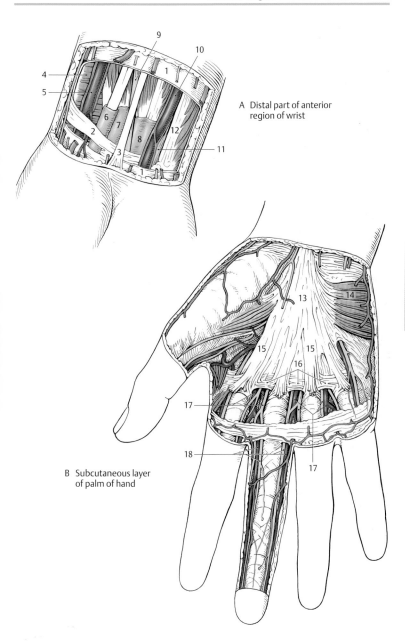

A Distal part of anterior region of wrist

B Subcutaneous layer of palm of hand

Palm of Hand, continued (A–H)

Deep Layer, Superficial Palmar Arch (A)

After removal of the fascia and the palmar aponeurosis, the superficial palmar arch (**1**) and the muscles of the thenar and hypothenar eminences become visible. The *superficial palmar arch* (**1**) is mainly formed by the *ulnar artery* (**2**), which runs superficial to the *flexor retinaculum* (**3**). It is connected with the *superficial palmar branch of the radial artery* (**4**). The superficial palmar arch gives off the common *palmar digital arteries* (**5**) which run at first superficial to the tendons of the long flexors (**6**) and at the roots of the digits between these tendons.

The ulnar artery, which gives off a *deep palmar branch* (**7**), accompanies the *ulnar nerve* (**8**), which with its *superficial branch* (**9**) medial to the artery reaches the palm of the hand. The superficial branch of the ulnar nerve innervates the skin of the ulnar two and a half digits. It is often connected to the branches of the *median nerve* (**11**) by an *anastomotic branch* (**10**). In the region of the flexor retinaculum (**3**), the *deep branch* (**12**) becomes separated from the *ulnar nerve* and penetrates deeply between the *abductor digiti minimi* (**13**) and the *flexor digiti minimi brevis* (**14**).

Already in the carpal tunnel (see p. 124) the median nerve has often divided into the *common palmar digital nerves* (**15**). It gives off branches to the thenar muscles (excluding the deep head of the flexor pollicis brevis and the adductor pollicis).

Deep Palmar Arch (B)

When the tendons of the flexors of the digits (**6**) are removed, the *deep palmar arch* (**18**) appears lying on the *interossei and usually running* (**16**) proximal to the *transverse head* (**17**) *of the adductor pollicis*. This arch is formed by the deep palmar branch of the ulnar artery (**7**) and the radial

artery and gives off the *palmar metacarpal arteries* (**19**). It is accompanied by the deep branch of the ulnar nerve (**12**).

Variants of the Superficial Palmar Arch (C–H)

The superficial palmar arch may be very variably developed. The typical palmar arch (**C**) is present in only 27% of cases (*Lanz–Wachsmuth*). In the same proportion of subjects (27%) the arch is formed solely by the ulnar artery (**D**).

In some cases, the "comitans artery of the median nerve" is retained as the "original" median artery and may, either by anastomosing with the ulnar artery or without formation of the arch (**E**), together with the ulnar artery, give off the artery to the digits. During embryonic development of the blood supply to the hand, the "original" median artery takes over from the common interosseous artery which develops beforehand. In lower mammals this stage of development persists longer, while in primates the radial and ulnar arteries arise from the median artery. Embryologically, a persistent median artery is an atavism.

Sometimes (6%) not all the digital arteries arise from a superficial palmar arch, which is formed only by the ulnar artery (**F**). A superficial palmar arch may be completely absent and then the arteries of the digits are given off by the radial artery as well as by the ulnar artery (4.5%, **G**) or (12%) the arteries of the digits arise from the deep palmar arch and the ulnar artery (**H**).

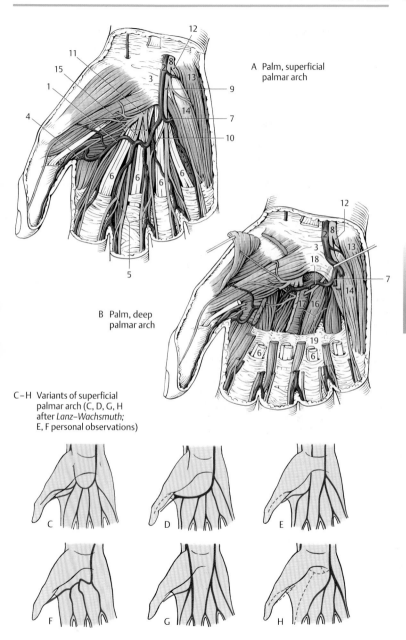

A Palm, superficial
   palmar arch

B Palm, deep
   palmar arch

C–H Variants of superficial
      palmar arch (C, D, G, H
      after *Lanz–Wachsmuth;*
      E, F personal observations)

Peripheral Pathways

Dorsum of the Hand (A, B)

Subcutaneous Layer (A)

The proximal boundary of the dorsum of the hand is the *extensor retinaculum* (**1**), a part of the fascia which is strengthened by a large number of transverse fibers.

Subcutaneously the veins coming from the digits (usually two joined by anastomoses) are continued in the *dorsal metacarpal veins* (**2**) of which three are usually particularly well developed. The largest are the dorsal metacarpal veins at the root of the fourth digit which, after combining, runs as the *accessory cephalic vein* (= vena salvatella, **3**) to the forearm. The *dorsal metacarpal vein of the fifth digit* (**4**) represents the beginning of the basilic vein, while the first dorsal metacarpal vein is called the *cephalic vein of the thumb* (**5**). A large number of anastomoses interconnect all the veins to form the *venous network of the dorsal hand* (**6**). On the ulnar side, covered by veins, runs the *dorsal branch of the ulnar nerve* (**7**), while radially the terminal parts of the *superficial branch of the radial nerve* (**8**) are found.

Subfascial Layer (B)

After removal of the fascia, the extensor tendons and the branches of the *radial artery* (**9**) become visible. In the region of the radial fovea, the radial artery gives off the *dorsal carpal branch* (**10**) and runs between the heads of the *first dorsal interosseous* (**11**) into the palm of the hand. The dorsal carpal branch gives off the *dorsal metacarpal arteries* (**12**), which again divide into the *dorsal digital arteries* (**13**).

Radial Fovea, "Anatomical Snuff Box" (C)

The triangular radial fovea, or anatomical snuff box, is limited dorsally by the tendon of the *extensor pollicis longus* (**14**) and on the palmar side by the tendon of the *extensor pollicis brevis* (**15**) and the tendon of the abductor pollicis longus (**16**). The scaphoid and trapezium bones form the floor. Proximally the extensor retinaculum (**1**) completes the depression.

It contains the tendons of the *extensor carpi radialis longus* (**17**), the *extensor carpi radialis brevis* (**18**), and the radial artery (**9**). In the fovea, the radial artery gives off its dorsal carpal branch (**10**). The branches of the superficial part (**8**) of the radial nerve cross the radial fovea superficially.

> **Clinical tip:** The term "anatomical snuffbox" is a misnomer.

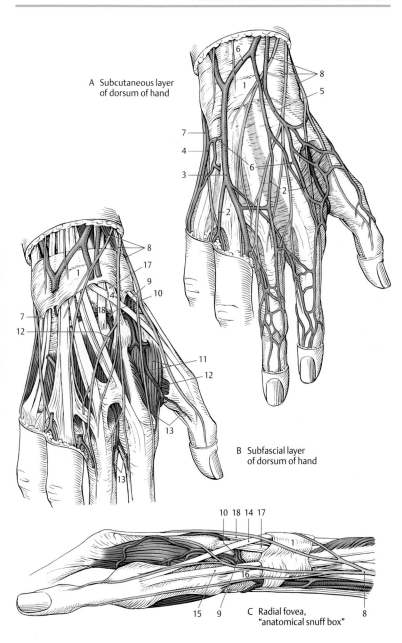

A Subcutaneous layer
of dorsum of hand

B Subfascial layer
of dorsum of hand

C Radial fovea,
"anatomical snuff box"

Peripheral Pathways

Trunk

Regions (A, B)

Superficially, there are no distinct demarcations between the trunk and the upper and lower limbs. The subdivision into regions has a purely practical purpose and has no developmental basis. The lack of demarcation results in some overlap in the transitional regions between trunk and limbs. The trunk regions are subdivided into the regions of the thorax and those of the abdomen.

Regions of the Thorax

The *deltoid region* (**1**), the *infraclavicular fossa* (**2**) with the *clavipectoral triangle* (**3**), and the *axillary region* (**4**) are described on p. 368 as transitional regions of the free upper limb.

The **mammary region** (**5**) includes the area of the mammary gland. The **inframammary region** (**6**) lies caudally, and the **lateral pectoral region** (**7**) lies laterally. These three regions are collectively known as **pectoral region**. The lateral pectoral region connects with the axillary region. The **presternal region** (**8**) connects the left and right mammary and inframammary regions.

In the median on the back there is the **vertebral region** (**9**), and laterally to it are the **suprascapular region** (**10**), the **interscapular region** (**11**), the **scapular region** (**12**), and the **infrascapular region** (**13**).

Regions of the Abdomen

The transitional region between thorax and abdomen, the **hypochondrium** (**14**) lies laterally. Between the two hypochondriac regions, in the area of the infrasternal angle, is the **epigastric region** (**15**). These three regions are caudally delimited by the *transpyloric plane*, which is the transverse plane through the midpoint between the jugular notch of the sternum and the upper

edge of the symphysis. The **umbilical region** (**16**) includes the area between the two midclavicular lines, the transpyloric plane, and the plane running through the anterior superior iliac spines. The latter plane, *interspinous plane*, contains the *interspinous distance* (see p. 190).

On both sides of the umbilical region lie the **lateral abdominal regions** (**17**). Following in caudal direction, the **inguinal regions** (**18**) adjoin laterally to the inguinal sulcus, and the **pubic region** (**19**) adjoins medially to the upper edge of the symphysis and the pubic crests.

In the median on the back, below the vertebral region, lies the **sacral region** (**20**), which includes the area over the sacrum. On both sides of these regions lie the **lumbar regions** (**21**), which merge into the gluteal regions at the iliac crests.

Adjacent to the pubic region is the urogenital region (not illustrated), which adjoins the anal region (not illustrated). These two regions are collectively known as **perineal region**; they connect the regions of the abdomen with those of the back.

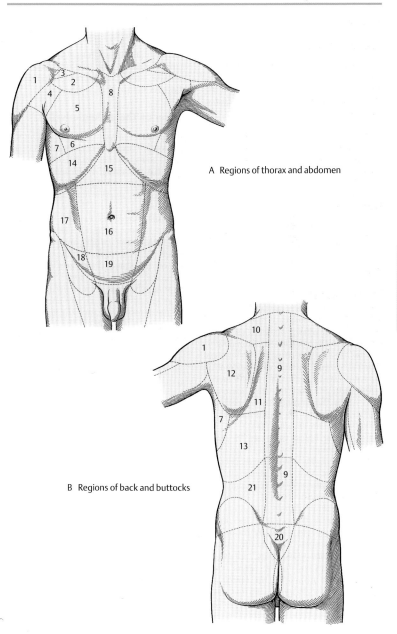

A Regions of thorax and abdomen

B Regions of back and buttocks

Regions of the Thorax (A, B)

Anterior Thorax Regions (A)

Of special importance in the female are the tissues in the subcutaneous layer of the mammary region. The breast rests on the *pectoral fascia* (**1**). It consists of the mammary gland, fibrous connective tissue, and adipose tissue, which are collectively known as the *body of breast* (**2**). A process of various size, the *axillary process* (**3**), may extend into the axilla. The fibrous tissue forms the suspensory ligaments of the breast, which connect the pectoral fascia with the skin and are located between the lobes of the gland.

Around the *areola of the mammary gland* (**4**) there is a delicate venous plexus, the *areolar venous plexus* (**5**). From this plexus the blood drains via the *anterior cutaneous branches* (**6**) to the anterior intercostal veins and, laterally, to the *thoraco-epigastric vein* (**7**) and *lateral thoracic vein* (**8**). Blood is supplied both laterally and medially. Branches of the lateral thoracic artery, the *lateral mammary branches* (**9**) penetrating the *axillary fascia* (**10**), extend laterally to the body of breast. The internal thoracic artery gives off perforating branches which reach the subcutaneous layer through the 1st–6th intercostal spaces near the sternum. Larger perforating branches reach the breast medially as *medial mammary branches* (**11**).

Lateral to the breast there are the paramammary lymph nodes, and in the axilla there are the *axillary lymph nodes* (**12**).

Crossing the clavicle from above, the *medial* (**13**) and *intermediate* (**14**) *supraclavicular nerves* from the cervical plexus reach the clavipectoral triangle and the infraclavicular fossa, respectively. The mammary region is innervated by the *medial mammary branches* (**15**) from the *anterior cutaneous branches* (**16**) of the 2nd–4th intercostal nerves and by the *lateral mammary branches* (**17**) from the *lateral cutaneous branches* (**18**) of the 2nd–4th intercostal nerves. One or two *intercostobrachial nerves* (**19**), usually from the 2nd (and 3rd)

intercostal nerve, extend to the upper arm through the axillary region.

The pectoralis major muscle with its three parts is visible in the subfascial layer. The cephalic vein runs laterally through the clavipectoral triangle (see p. 370).

Posterior Thorax Regions (B)

In the subcutaneous layer on the thoracic fascia there are cutaneous branches of arteries, veins, and nerves. It is important to note that the scapular line represents the boundary between the supply areas of the posterior and anterior branches of the spinal nerves.

The following muscles can be demonstrated in the subfascial layer: *trapezius* (**20**), *latissimus dorsi* (**21**), and *rhomboideus major* (**22**). The *infraspinatus muscle* (**23**) lies on the scapula, the *teres minor* (**24**) originates from the lateral margin of scapula, while the *teres major* (**25**) originates inferior to the teres minor. Between the two teres muscles and the *long head of the triceps muscle* (**26**) is the medial axillary foramen (see p. 374) with the *circumflex vein and circumflex artery of scapula* (**27**). From the *scapular spine* (**28**), the *spinal part of the deltoid muscle* (**29**) extends to the upper arm.

> **Clinical tip:** Lymph drainage of the mammary gland is of special importance because of the high incidence of **breast cancer**. The lymph drains via several vessels, usually four, into the venous angle. One lymphatic vessel reaches the axillary lymph nodes either directly or via the paramammary lymph nodes. From there it drains into the venous angle via infraclavicular and supraclavicular lymph nodes.
> The second vessel extends from the parammary lymph nodes directly to the infraclavicular lymph nodes and finally into the venous angle via the supraclavicular lymph nodes.
> The third vessel reaches the infraclavicular and supraclavicular lymph nodes, frequently involving also the interpectoral lymph nodes.
> The fourth vessel comes from the medial portions of the gland and runs through the parasternal lymph nodes alongside the internal thoracic arteries and veins to the venous angle.
> The first lymph node affected by metastasis is called the **sentinel node** (see p. 366).

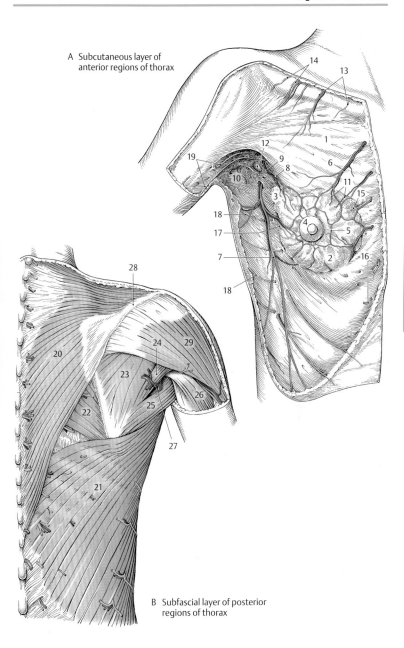

A Subcutaneous layer of
   anterior regions of thorax

B Subfascial layer of posterior
   regions of thorax

Peripheral Pathways

Regions of the Abdomen (A)

Upon removal of the subcutaneous fascia of abdomen (see p. 92), the subcutaneous vessels and nerves become visible on the delicate *(superficial) abdominal fascia*. Especially noteworthy are the *para-umbilical veins* surrounding the navel; they anastomose with the *superficial epigastric veins* (**1**) and with the *thoraco-epigastric veins*.

The superficial epigastric vein, which is accompanied by a delicate artery of the same name, crosses the inguinal ligament and joins the femoral vein in the saphenous opening (see p. 416). The thoraco-epigastric vein ascends from the navel in latero-superior direction and reaches the axillary vein. The *superficial circumflex iliac artery and vein* (**2**) ascend in the lateral area of the inguinal ligament.

In the paramedian region, the *anterior cutaneous branches* (**3**) of the *8th–12th intercostal nerves* (**4**) penetrate the rectus sheath and the fascia. The *lateral cutaneous branches* (**5**) of the *9th–12th intercostal nerves* are visible laterally to them.

Just superior to the superficial inguinal ring, the *anterior branch of the iliohypogastric nerve* (see p. 400) becomes subcutaneous. The *lateral branch of the iliohypogastric nerve* (**6**) penetrates the fascia in the area of the anterior superior iliac spine.

Upon removal of the fascia and subsequent incision of the anterior layer of the rectus sheaths (see p. 88), the *rectus abdominis* (**7**) becomes visible on both sides. Posterior to the rectus abdominis, but inside the rectus sheath, run the *inferior epigastric artery and vein* (**8**) which anastomose above the navel with the *superior epigastric artery and vein* (**9**).

The rectus sheath contains the rectus abdominis, which adheres at the *tendinous intersections* (**10**) to the anterior layer. The inferior and superior epigastric arteries and veins also run inside the rectus sheath, and so do the 8th–12th intercostal nerves, which enter through the *posterior layer* (**11**) *of the sheath of the rectus abdominis.*

Clinical tip: The para-umbilical veins extend alongside the *round ligament of the liver* (see vol. 2) to the left branch of the portal vein; they connect with the superficial epigastric veins and the thoraco-epigastric veins. This creates a subcutaneous portosystemic anastomosis. If there is a backflow of blood due to liver disease, these veins become dilated and are then visible underneath the skin. This condition is referred to as **"caput medusae"** (head of Medusa).

Other portosystemic anastomoses of clinical importance are the submucosal plexus in the inferior third of the esophagus and the submucosal plexus in the rectum.

Retroperitoneal anastomoses are also present. Note, however, that the subcutaneous anastomosis described here is the *only* anastomosis that communicates directly with the left branch of the portal vein; all the others drain into the portal vein trunk. **The presence of a "Medusa head"** (caput medusae) **generally indicates congestion in the left hepatic lobe.**

12 Linea alba
13 Pyramidalis
14 External oblique
15 Transversalis fascia
16 Arcuate line
17 Anterior layer of the rectus sheath

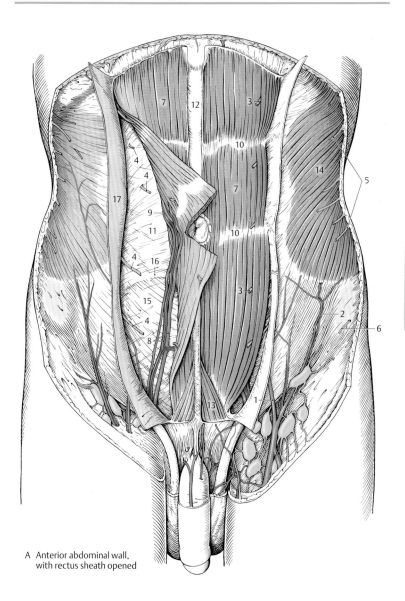

A Anterior abdominal wall,
with rectus sheath opened

Inguinal Region

Inguinal Canal (A–C)

First Layer (A)

The inguinal region and the pubic region are superficially covered by the subcutaneous fascia of abdomen (see p. 92). Only upon removal of the connective tissue membrane is it possible to view the subcutaneous vessels and nerves. Running over the *(superficial) abdominal fascia* (**1**) and crossing the inguinal canal are the *superficial epigastric artery and vein* (**2**), while the *superficial circumflex iliac artery and vein* (**3**) run laterally.

Both vascular bundles extend to the saphenous hiatus in the subinguinal region (see p. 416). The *external pudendal artery and vein* (**4**), which are frequently duplicated, also connect to the saphenous hiatus. After crossing the *spermatic cord* (**5**), they reach the pudendal region.

Superior to the *superficial inguinal ring* (**6**) the *anterior cutaneous branch of the iliohypogastric nerve* (**7**) can be viewed, while the *ilio-inguinal nerve* (**8**) runs together with the spermatic cord (or round ligament of uterus, respectively) and gives off sensory branches to supply the proximal inner surface of thigh, the mons pubis, the scrotal skin in the male, and the labium majus in the female.

> **Clinical tip:** Of special importance are the *superficial inguinal lymph nodes* (**9**); in the female, they are reached through the inguinal canal by lymph vessels **from the fundus** and **body of the uterus**. They play a major role in the lymphogenous spread of **endometrial carcinoma**. (See also "sentinel node," p. 366.)
> Other lymphatics drain to the interiliac lymph nodes and directly to the aortic lymph nodes. The **cervix** never (!) drains to the inguinal nodes. It drains to the iliac, interiliac, gluteal, sacral, and rectal lymph nodes and directly to the aortic nodes.

Second Layer (B, C)

After precise delimitation of the superficial inguinal ring (**6**) in the male, the outer sheath of the spermatic cord (**5**), the *external spermatic fascia* (**10**) is opened. This exposes the external inguinal ring with the *lateral crus* (**11**), the *medial crus* (**12**), the *intercrural fibers* (**13**), and the *reflected ligament* (**14**).

Upon severing the aponeurosis of the *external oblique* (**15**), the *internal oblique* (**16**) can be viewed. Its inferior fibers extend as *cremaster muscle* (**17**) on the spermatic cord and form its middle sheath, the *cremasteric fascia and muscle* (**18**). It is accompanied by the *genital branch* (**19**) of the genitofemoral nerve, which supplies the cremaster muscle and also participates in the sensory supply of the ilio-inguinal nerve. The delicate cremasteric artery and vein are embedded in the muscle and, therefore, hardly visible.

Resting on the internal oblique, the *iliohypogastric nerve* (**20**) extends medially and penetrates with its anterior cutaneous branch (**7**) the external oblique aponeurosis and the fascia above the external inguinal ring. Sometimes the nerve splits into two branches before it penetrates. It provides sensory supply to the skin in the inguinal region.

After precise delimitation of the superficial inguinal ring (**6**) in the female, the round ligament of uterus becomes visible. It radiates into the connective tissue of the labium majus. Closely adjoining this band are the delicate artery and vein of the round ligament of uterus and the genital branch of the genitofemoral nerve. The round ligament of uterus is accompanied by the ilio-inguinal nerve.

When opening the inguinal canal, some fibers of the internal oblique are revealed; they merge with the round ligament of uterus. They are referred to as the round ligament part of the internal oblique and correspond to the cremaster muscle in the male.

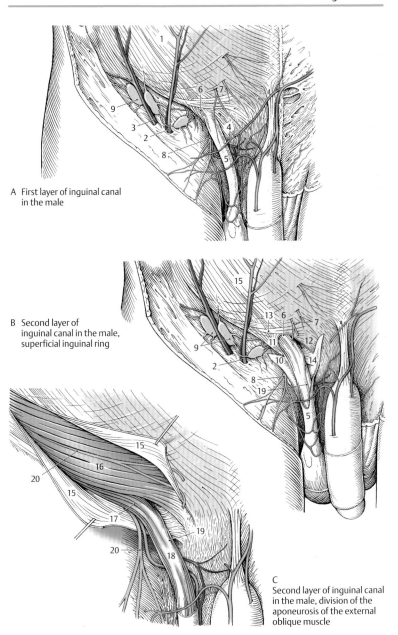

A First layer of inguinal canal in the male

B Second layer of inguinal canal in the male, superficial inguinal ring

C Second layer of inguinal canal in the male, division of the aponeurosis of the external oblique muscle

Inguinal Region

Inguinal Canal, continued (A–C)

Third Layer (A, B)

After severing the *cremasteric fascia and muscle* (**1**) the last and very thin sheath of the spermatic cord, the *internal spermatic fascia* (**2**), becomes visible. Further cutting of the *internal oblique* (**3**) exposes the roof of the inguinal canal, the *transverse abdominis* (**4**), and also the posterior wall, the *transversalis fascia* (**5**). The internal spermatic fascia (**2**) evaginates as a continuation of the transversalis fascia, thus making it possible to determine the position of the *deep inguinal ring* (**6**). The variably developed *interfoveolar ligament* (**7**) lies medial to the deep inguinal ring (see also p. 98).

Fourth Layer (C)

Cutting the internal spermatic fascia (**2**) exposes the content of the spermatic cord and also opens the deep inguinal ring. The spermatic cord contains the white, round *ductus deferens* (**8**), the *testicular artery* (**9**), and the *pampiniform plexus* (**10**).

The ductus deferens (**8**) is the continuation of the *duct of epididymis* and extends through the inguinal canal into the lesser pelvis. Here it unites, together with its ampulla of ductus deferens, with the *excretory duct* of the *seminal gland (seminal vesicle)* to form the *ejaculatory duct*. The testicular artery (**9**) originates directly from the abdominal aorta. The pampiniform plexus (**10**) continues as *testicular vein*. On the left side, the testicular vein extends across the *left renal vein* to the inferior vena cava. The right testicular vein drains directly into the inferior vena cava.

If parts of the transversalis fascia are removed when the internal spermatic fascia is opened, the preperitoneal structures are exposed: the *inferior epigastric artery and*

vein (**11**) and the *cord of umbilical artery* (**12**). The weak sites in this region of the abdominal wall also become visible. These are the peritoneal fossae: Lateral to the inferior epigastric artery and vein there is the *lateral inguinal fossa* (**13**); the deep inguinal ring projects into it. The *medial inguinal fossa* (**14**) lies between the chorda of umbilical artery and the inferior epigastric artery and vein, while the *supravesical fossa* (**15**) lies medial to the chorda of umbilical artery. The superficial inguinal ring projects into the latter two fossae.

> **Clinical tip:** The three fossae constitute areas of weakness in the abdominal wall, creating sites of predilection for inguinal hernias (see p. 100). Three types of inguinal hernia are distinguished based on the location of the internal opening:
> a) **Indirect (lateral) inguinal hernia:** pulsation of the inferior epigastric artery medial to the hernia.
> b) **Direct (medial) inguinal hernia:** pulsation lateral to the hernia.
> c) **Supravesical hernia:** no pulsations because the hernial opening is medial to the lateral umbilical ligament.
> The hernial opening can be quickly identified by endoscopic examination, which aids in classifying the hernia.

16 Aponeurosis of the external oblique
17 Inguinal ligament
18 Iliohypogastric nerve
19 Reflected ligament
20 Ilio-inguinal nerve

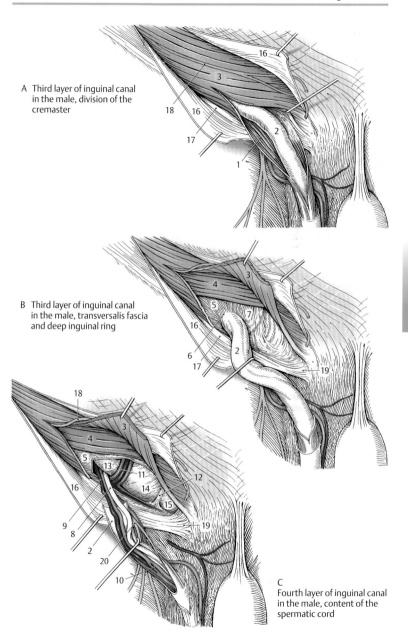

A   Third layer of inguinal canal in the male, division of the cremaster

B   Third layer of inguinal canal in the male, transversalis fascia and deep inguinal ring

C   Fourth layer of inguinal canal in the male, content of the spermatic cord

Lumbar Region (A, B)

First Layer (A)

Upon removal of the intestines, the parietal abdominal fascia can be peeled off. This exposes primarily the branches of the lumbar plexus.

At the inferior margin of the 12th rib (**1**) runs the *subcostal nerve* (**2**) as the last of the anterior branches of the thoracic nerves. It is partially covered by the portion of the *lumbar part of the diaphragm* (**4**) originating from the *lateral arcuate ligament* (**3**). The *quadratus lumborum* (**5**) is visible underneath the lateral arcuate ligament, while the portion of the *psoas major* (**7**) originating from the 12th thoracic vertebra is visible underneath the *medial arcuate ligament* (**6**).

The first branch of the lumbar plexus, the *iliohypogastric nerve* (**8**), is visible at the lateral margin of the psoas major. It crosses the quadratus lumborum and penetrates the abdominal muscles above the iliac crest. Almost parallel to it and penetrating the psoas major runs the *ilio-inguinal nerve* (**9**), which extends to the deep inguinal ring. Next, the *genitofemoral nerve* (**10**) penetrates the psoas major and divides at varying levels into the *genital branch* (**11**) and the *femoral branch* (**12**). The former extends to the inguinal canal, while the latter passes through the vascular space to reach the subinguinal region.

At the lateral margin of the psoas major and near the iliac fossa there is another branch of the lumbar plexus, the *lateral femoral cutaneous nerve* (**13**). It extends laterally, near the anterior superior iliac spine, to the muscular space. The most prominent branch, the *femoral nerve* (**14**), runs in the groove between the *iliacus muscle* (**15**) and psoas major (**7**) and passes through the muscular space (lacuna musculorum) to reach the thigh. The last branch, the *obturator nerve* (**16**), is the only one running medial to the psoas major; after crossing the *external iliac artery and vein* (**17**), it reaches the *obturator canal*.

Second Layer (B)

Removal of the superficial part of the psoas major exposes the *anterior branches* (**18**) of the first four lumbar nerves. These lie on the *deep part* (**19**) of the psoas major and form the lumbar plexus. The branch of the 4th lumbar nerve divides into a *superior* and an *inferior branch* (**20**). The latter unites with the anterior branch of the 5th lumbar nerve to form the *lumbosacral trunk*, which participates in the formation of the sacral plexus.

Medial to the emerging anterior branches runs the *sympathetic trunk* (**21**) and, on the right side, also the *inferior vena cava* (**22**). The segmental *lumbar arteries and veins* (**23**) adhere to the vertebral column. They pass underneath the anterior branches and deep portion of the psoas major.

24 Internal iliac artery
25 Inferior epigastric artery
26 Deep circumflex iliac artery and vein

(The sacral plexus and the lumbar plexus can be considered a unit that is called the **lumbosacral plexus.**)

Lumbar plexus

– Roots: Ventral rami (L1 – L4)
– Branches: – Iliohypogastric nerve
  – Ilio-inguinal nerve
  – Genitofemoral nerve
  – Lateral femoral cutaneous nerve
  – Obturator nerve
  – Femoral nerve

Sacral plexus

– Roots: Ventral rami (L4 – S3)
– Branches: – Gluteal nerves
  – Muscular branches
  – Inferior clunial nerves
  – Posterior femoral cutaneous nerve
  – Pudendal nerve
  – Coccygeal nerve
  – Sciatic nerve

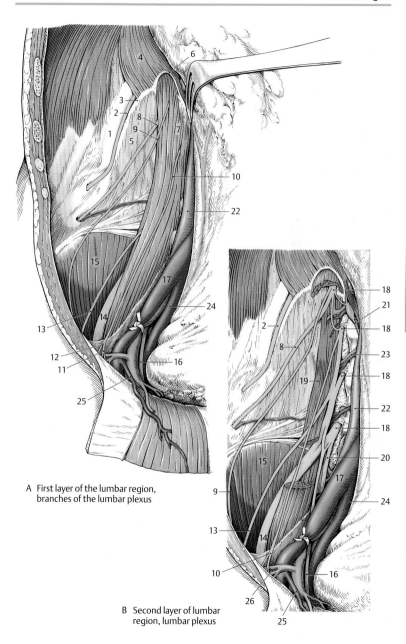

A First layer of the lumbar region, branches of the lumbar plexus

B Second layer of lumbar region, lumbar plexus

Perineal Region of the Female (A, B)

The perineal region is divided into the urogenital region in anterior direction and the anal region in posterior direction. Fasciae and muscles allow definition of several structural layers.

Superficial and Middle Layers (A)

Urogenital region: In the lateral area along the inferior pubic ramus and the ramus of the ischium, the *superficial perineal fascia* (**1**) is divided into two layers, a fatty *outer layer* and a membranous *inner layer* (right side of the preparation). The two layers unite near the *vestibule of vagina* (**2**). Removal of the superficial perineal fascia exposes the *superficial perineal space* (left side of the preparation).
Posterior labial branches (**3**), which originate from the *perineal artery* (**4**) and are accompanied by veins of the same name, extend to the vestibule of vagina and the *perineal body* (**5**). The perineal artery often penetrates the inner layer of the superficial perineal fascia. The *perineal nerves* (**6**) cross the posterior margin of the urogenital diaphragm (p. 106) and extend together with the arterial branches to the vestibule of vagina and the perineal body.
The superficial perineal space contains the following muscles: the *bulbospongiosus* (**7**) medially, the *ischiocavernosus* (**8**) laterally, and the *transversus perinei superficialis* (**9**) posteriorly.

Anal region: The *obturator fascia* (**10**) borders laterally on the *ischio-anal (ischiorectal) fossa.* This fossa extends to the front and lies then between the urogenital diaphragm and the pelvic diaphragm with the *inferior fascia of the pelvic diaphragm* (**11**). It contains plenty of abdominal fat, the *fat body of the ischioanal fossa.* In a fold of the obturator fascia (**10**) lies the *pudendal canal* (**12**). The *inferior rectal artery* (**13**) and the *inferior rectal nerve* (**14**) supply the *sphincter ani externus* (**15**) and the anal skin. There may be additional perineal branches (not shown) for the labial skin and a perforating cutaneous nerve for the anal skin. Both originate from the posterior cutaneous nerve of thigh. Numerous *inferior rectal veins* (**16**), which anastomose with the medial rectal veins, extend to the internal pudendal vein.

Removal of the inferior fascia of the pelvic diaphragm (**11**) exposes the sphincter ani externus (**15**) and the *levator ani* (**17**) (left side of the preparation). Posterior to the *anus* (**18**) in the median plane there is the *anococcygeal ligament* (**19**); parts of the levator ani muscles radiate into it. The *internal pudendal arteries and veins* (**20**) and the *pudendal nerve* (**21**) pass through the lesser sciatic foramen and then run inside the pudendal canal (*Alcock's canal*).

Deep Layer (B)

Urogenital region: Removal of the bulbospongiosus and ischiocavernosus muscles (**8**) with the inferior fascia of the urogenital diaphragm (perineal membrane) opens the deep perineal space. In addition to muscles, it contains the *crura of the clitoris* (**22**); they unite to form the *body of the clitoris* (**23**) which terminates in the *glans of the clitoris* (**24**).

On each side lateral to the vestibule of the vagina (**2**) lies an erectile body, the *bulb of vestibule* (**25**); the two bulbs are connected by the *commissure of the bulbs* (**26**) between the crura of the clitoris. On both sides lies the *great vestibular gland* (**27**) covered by the bulb of vestibule inside the urogenital diaphragm; it opens via a secretory duct between the labium minus and the vaginal orifice into the vestibule of the vagina (**28**).

> **Clinical tip:** The inner layer of the superficial perineal fascia is also known as deep perineal fascia.
> Unfortunately the term "urogenital diaphragm" has been dropped from modern anatomical (but not clinical!) usage, although it is technically correct.

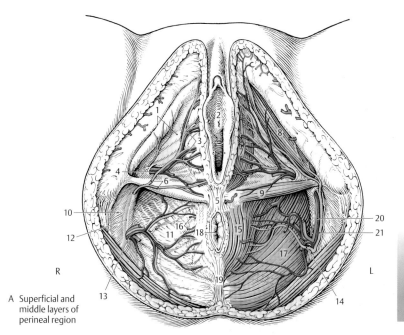

A Superficial and
   middle layers of
   perineal region

R

L

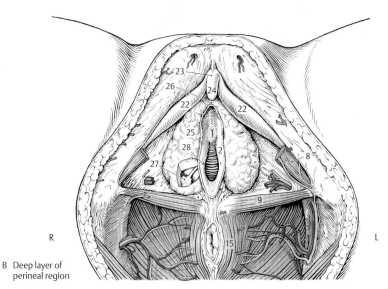

B Deep layer of
   perineal region

R

L

Perineal Region of the Male (A)

Superficial Layer (Right Side of Specimen)

Urogenital region: The *superficial perineal fascia* (**1**) with its outer layer and inner layer (deep perineal fascia or Colles fascia) continues on the thigh as *fascia lata* (**2**) and on the *penis* (**3**) as *superficial fascia of the penis* (**4**). Together with the superficial abdominal fascia it also forms the tunica dartos.

The *perineal artery* (**5**), which originates from the internal pudendal artery, often penetrates the urogenital diaphragm near its posterior margin and gives off *posterior scrotal branches* (**6**). These are accompanied by *posterior scrotal veins* (**7**). *Scrotal* and *muscular branches* (**8**) from the pudendal nerve extend to the scrotum and to the skin and muscles of the urogenital region. *Perineal branches* (**9**) from the posterior cutaneous nerve of thigh also extend to the scrotum, while the *inferior cluneal nerves* (**10**) reach the skin in the inferior part of the gluteal region.

Anal region: The *obturator fascia* (**11**) delimits the region laterally, the *gluteus maximus* (**12**) with the *gluteal fascia* in posterior direction, and the *perineal body* (**13**), the *anus* (**14**), and the *anococcygeal ligament* (**15**) medially. The deep ischio-anal fossa is filled by fatty tissue, the *fat body of ischio-anal fossa*. Its roof is formed by the *inferior fascia of the pelvic diaphragm* (**16**).

Middle Layer (Left Side of Specimen)

Urogenital region: Removal of the superficial perineal fascia opens the superficial perineal space. Medially, the *bulbospongiosus* (**17**) lies on the spongy body of penis (spongy body of male urethra) and the cavernous body of penis. The *ischiocavernosus* (**18**), which originates from the ramus of the ischium, lies laterally. In posterior direction, the *superficial transverse perineal* (**19**) delimits the space, while the *perineal membrane* (*inferior fascia of the urogenital diaphragm*) (**20**) forms the roof.

The *internal pudendal artery and vein* (**21**) penetrate the urogenital diaphragm and give off the above-mentioned branches. The *pudendal nerve* (**22**) extends to the superficial perineal space (*Colles' space*) at the posterior margin of the urogenital diaphragm.

Anal region: Removal of the inferior fascia of the pelvic diaphragm (**16**) exposes the *levator ani* (**23**) and the *coccygeus* (**24**) *muscles*.

Inside the *pudendal canal* (*Alcock's canal*) (**25**), the internal pudendal artery gives off the *inferior rectal artery* (**26**), which often divides into two branches. It is accompanied by the *inferior rectal veins* (**27**), which extend to the pudendal vein. *Inferior rectal nerves* (**28**) supply the *sphincter ani externus* (**29**) and the anal skin.

> **Clinical tip:** The posterior urethra is usually approached surgically through the perineum, especially in the treatment of strictures. The perineal approach is also used for radical prostatectomy. In all cases the central tendon of the perineum, the **perineal body**, must be divided.

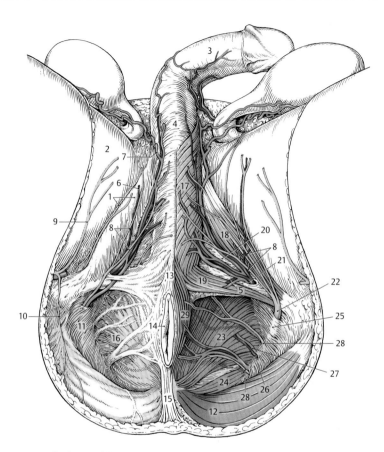

A Superficial and middle layers
of perineal region

Perineal Region of the Male, continued (A, B)

Deep Layer (A, B)

Urogenital region: Removal of the perineal membrane (inferior fascia of the urogenital diaphragm; right side of specimen) opens the deep perineal space. The *deep transverse perineal* (**1**) extends to the urogenital hiatus and, with its most posterior fibers, to the *perineal body* (**2**). The *ischiocavernosus* (**3**), which originates from the ramus of the ischium, radiates into the tunica albuginea of the *crus of penis* (**4**).

The *internal pudendal artery* (**5**) gives off the *perineal artery* (**6**) at the posterior margin of the urogenital diaphragm. Covered by the crus penis, it extends to the front and gives off the urethral artery where the crura of the penis unite. The artery is accompanied by the *internal pudendal vein* (**7**), which receives the *posterior scrotal veins* (**8**).

Removal of the *bulbospongiosus muscle* (**9**) exposes the *spongy body of the penis* (**10**; left side of specimen). Posterior to the *bulb of the penis* (**11**), the posterior end of the spongy body, there is the pea-sized *bulbourethral gland* (**12**) on both sides.

Anal region: Removal of the *obturator fascia* (**13**) opens the pudendal canal and exposes the internal pudenda artery and vein and also the *pudendal nerve* (**14**). Alongside the *internal obturator* (**15**) extends the *tendinous arch of levator ani* (**16**) to the *ischial tuberosity* (**17**). The *sacrospinal ligament* (**18**) reaches from here to the sacrum and forms together with the lesser sciatic notch the lesser sciatic foramen.

The *levator ani* (**19**) extends together with the *puborectalis* (**20**), *pubococcygeus* (**21**), and *iliococcygeus* (**22**) to the external anal sphincter and *anococcygeal ligament* (**23**). The most anterior fibers of the puborectal muscle, the *prerectal fibers = puboperineal muscle* (**24**), demarcate the *urogenital hiatus* (**25**) on both sides and radiate into the perineal body (**2**). The *prostate* (**26**) is visible inside the urogenital hiatus. The *external anal sphincter* (**27**) surrounds the *anus* (**28**) with three parts. The *coccygeus* (**29**) forms the pelvic diaphragm together with the levator ani muscle.

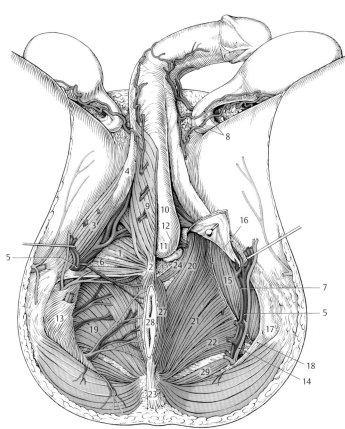

A Deep layer
of perineal region

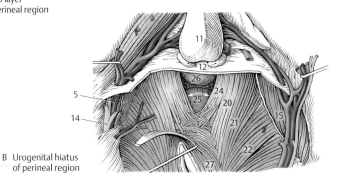

B Urogenital hiatus
of perineal region

Lower Limb

Regions (A, B)

As in the upper limb, the boundaries between the regions of the lower limb are
somewhat arbitrary and have been drawn
from a practical viewpoint.

Regions of the Hip

Anteriorly the regions around the hip joint
also represent subdivisions of the thigh.
We distinguish a *subinguinal region* (**1**),
which is bounded by the inguinal ligament
and the sartorius and pectineus muscles as
part of the large femoral triangle. The
femoral triangle (**2**) extends further distally
and is limited by the inguinal ligament, the
sartorius, and the adductor longus. Dor-
sally there is the **gluteal region** (**3**), which almost corresponds to the region of the gluteus maximus and extends to the gluteal
sulcus.

Regions of the Thigh

The **anterior region of the thigh** (**4**) adjoins
the femoral triangle. It extends distally to
the region of the knee and laterally to the
tensor fasciae latae. Dorsally, the **posterior
region of the thigh** (**5**) lies next to the gluteal
region and ends above the popliteal fossa.

Regions of the Knee

In front, the **anterior region of the knee** (**6**) extends from the lower margin of the ante-
rior thigh region to the tibial tuberosity.
The **posterior region of the knee** (**7**) lies dorsally. The middle part of this region is also
called the **popliteal fossa**.

Regions of the (Lower) Leg

The **anterior region of the leg** (**8**) extends
from the tibial tuberosity to the malleoli.
Medially this region, at the part of the tibia
palpable through the skin, continues into
the **posterior region of the leg** (**9**), which has
its proximal and distal borders at the same
level as those of the anterior region. Behind
the medial malleolus lies the **medial retromalleolar region**, and behind the lateral malleolus lies the **lateral retromalleolar region**
(**10**).

Regions of the Foot

The **heel region** (**11**) lies dorsal to the retromalleolar regions. Anteriorly and superiorly is the **dorsum (dorsal region) of the foot**
(**12**), and inferiorly the **sole (plantar region)
of the foot** (**13**).

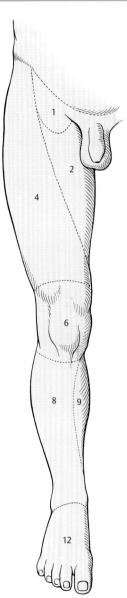

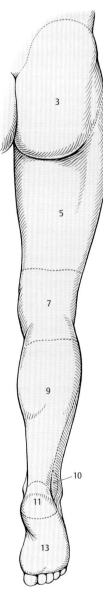

A Anterior view
   of regions of lower limb

B Posterior view
   of regions of lower limb

Subinguinal Region

Subcutaneous Layer (A, B)

The abundant subcutaneous fatty tissue is divided by dense *connective tissue lamellae* = *membranous layer* (**1**) into two layers. The connective tissue lamellae, which were formerly known as the superficial femoral fascia or *Scarpa's fascia*, partly cover the subcutaneous vessels and nerves and extend below the saphenous opening. Only after removal of all the subcutaneous fatty tissue and connective tissue lamellae can the *fascia lata* (**2**) be seen. Most of the fascia lata is generally of an aponeurotic character, except in the region of the saphenous opening, where there is a looser, reticular structure, called the *cribriform fascia* (**3**; see p. 254).

The subcutaneous veins, which reach this region in a stellate pattern, pierce the cribriform fascia. The largest and the most regularly occurring vessel is the great *saphenous vein* (**4**). It runs from the thigh to the cribriform fascia (**3**). Often a *lateral accessory saphenous vein* (**5**) accompanies it. The *external pudendal veins* (**6**) run from the pubic region and the *superficial epigastric vein* (**7**) runs from the umbilical region to the cribriform fascia. The *superficial circumflex iliac vein* (**8**) runs parallel to the inguinal ligament. The junction of all these veins is very variable and will be discussed on page 416. The smaller arteries are the *external pudendal artery* (**9**), the *superficial epigastric artery* (**10**), and the *superficial circumflex iliac artery* (**11**) accompany the veins of the same names.

The *superficial inguinal lymph nodes* (p. 400), which can be divided into two groups, lie on the cribriform fascia. One group, the *horizontal tract*, lies parallel to the inguinal ligament, whereas the other group, the *vertical tract*, is situated parallel to the great saphenous vein. The horizontal tract is organized into the *superomedial* (**12**) and the *superolateral* (**13**) *superficial inguinal lymph nodes*. The lymph nodes of the vertical tract are designated as *inferior superficial inguinal lymph nodes* (**14**).

The cutaneous nerves in this region arise from the *femoral branch* (**15**) of the *genitofemoral nerve*. In the male, the *spermatic cord* (**16**), accompanied by the *ilio-inguinal nerve* (**17**), courses in the inguinal region above the inguinal ligament and reaches the scrotum. The skin lateral to the cribriform fascia is innervated by anterior cutaneous rami of the femoral nerve.

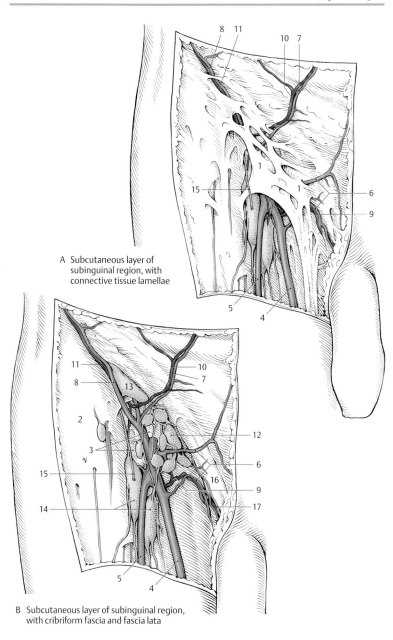

A Subcutaneous layer of
   subinguinal region, with
   connective tissue lamellae

B Subcutaneous layer of subinguinal region,
   with cribriform fascia and fascia lata

Peripheral Pathways

Saphenous Opening (A–R)

The **saphenous opening**, delineated by the *falciform margin* (**1**) with its *superior* (**2**) and *inferior* (**3**) *horns*, becomes visible after removal of the cribriform fascia. Within the opening lie medially the *deep inguinal lymph nodes* (**4**), next to them the *femoral vein* (**5**), and most laterally the *femoral artery* (**6**). In or lateral to the saphenous opening, the *femoral branch* (**7**) of the genitofemoral nerve becomes subcutaneous. Still further laterally, the *anterior cutaneous branches* (**8**) *of the femoral nerve* perforate the fascia lata.

According to *Lanz-Wachsmuth*, in the region of the saphenous opening in 37% of cases the following veins open into the femoral vein (**A**): the *great saphenous vein* (**9**), the *lateral accessory saphenous vein* (**10**), the *superficial circumflex iliac vein* (**11**), the *superficial epigastric vein* (**12**), and one or more *external pudendal veins* (**13**). Therefore, the so-called **"venous star"** shows many variations, which are shown in the various detailed diagrams.

Variants (B–R)

Lateral Accessory Saphenous Vein (B–E). In 1% of cases this vein may join the femoral vein proximal to the opening (**B**). In 9% of cases there is a common junction with a trunk consisting of the superficial circumflex iliac vein and the superficial epigastric vein (**C**). In the same proportion there is a common terminal of the lateral accessory saphenous vein and the superficial circumflex iliac vein (**D**). Rarely, the lateral accessory saphenous vein and the superficial epigastric vein (**E**) join at their termination.

The **great saphenous vein (F–G)** may receive a *medial accessory saphenous vein* (**14**). Either it perforates the fascia (**F**) distal to the saphenous opening (in 1%), or it reaches the femoral vein (**G**) in the saphenous opening.

In 1% of cases the **external pudendal veins** (**H–I**) join a medial accessory saphenous vein (**H**), while in 2% of cases they combine with the superficial epigastric vein (**I**).

The position of the **superficial epigastric vein** (**J–N**) is particularly variable. It may join with the superficial external pudendal vein before the great saphenous vein (**J**). Sometimes (1%) it opens proximal to the saphenous opening into the femoral vein (**K**). In 9% of cases it may form a common trunk with the superficial circumflex iliac vein and this opens into the lateral accessory saphenous vein (**L**), which reaches the great saphenous vein in the saphenous opening. Sometimes the superficial epigastric and the superficial circumflex iliac veins join the superficial external pudendal vein and the lateral accessory saphenous vein to form a common trunk, which joins the great saphenous vein within the saphenous opening (**M**). In 6% of cases, the superficial epigastric vein runs into the superficial circumflex iliac vein and this trunk opens directly into the femoral vein (**N**).

As has already been described, in 9% of cases the **superficial circumflex iliac vein** (**O–R**) may open with the superficial epigastric vein and the lateral accessory saphenous vein into the great saphenous vein (**O**), and in a further 9% the lateral accessory saphenous vein also opens into it (**P**). Sometimes the superficial circumflex iliac vein opens into the great saphenous vein together with the superficial epigastric vein (**R**).

The variants described above represent a summary of the author's many observations, as well as those of *Lanz-Wachsmuth*.

Clinical tip: Intra-arterial injections in the femoral artery are performed at a site approximately 1 cm below the inguinal ligament. Locate the midpoint of a straight line between the anterior superior iliac spine and pubic tubercle. Measure approximately 0.5 cm lateral from that point, and insert the needle vertically. Vertical movement of the needle will be noted when the needle tip comes in contact with the pulsating artery. When the needle pierces the artery wall, a pulsatile surge of blood will enter the syringe.

Peripheral Pathways

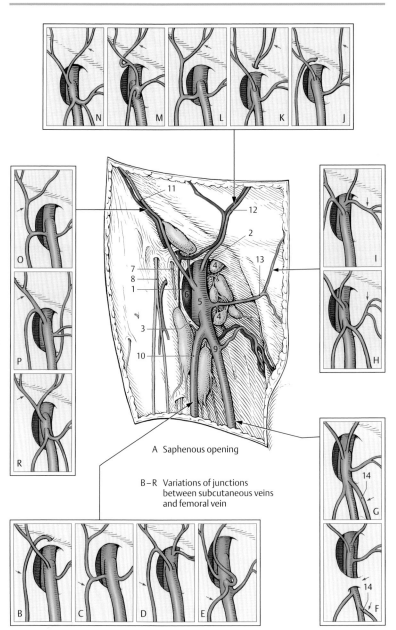

A   Saphenous opening

B–R   Variations of junctions
between subcutaneous veins
and femoral vein

Gluteal Region (A, B)

Subcutaneous Layer (A)

The *gluteal fascia* (**1**) becomes evident after removing the skin and the fat-rich subcutaneous tissue. At the upper margin of the gluteus maximus, this fascia becomes continuous with the firm *gluteal aponeurosis* (**2**).

The skin is innervated by the clunial nerves and by the *lateral cutaneous branch* (**3**) *of the iliohypogastric nerve.* The upper portion is supplied by the *superior clunial nerves* (**4**) which are the dorsal rami of spinal nerves L1–L3. The middle area of the skin of the gluteal region is innervated by the *middle clunial nerves* (**5**), which are the dorsal rami of spinal nerves S1–S3. *Inferior clunial nerves* (**6**), which arise directly or indirectly from the sacral plexus, loop around the lower margin of the gluteus maximus; indirectly, insofar as we can be dealing with twigs from the posterior femoral cutaneous nerve.

The blood supply of the skin is essentially from branches of the superior and inferior gluteal arteries. In the medial region it involves a twig from the lumbar arteries, whereas laterally, in the region of the greater trochanter, the arterial branches arise from the first perforating artery (from the deep artery of thigh).

Subfascial Layer (B)

The *gluteus maximus* (**7**) and the ischiocrural muscle group at its lower margin become visible after removal of the gluteal fascia. The latter muscle group comprise muscles originating from the ischial tuberosity: the *adductor magnus* (**8**), *semimembranosus* (**9**), *semitendinosus* (**10**), and the *long head of the biceps* (**11**). The *posterior femoral cutaneous nerve* (**12**) courses laterally to the biceps and crosses over it superficially.

Deeply lies the *sciatic nerve* (**13**), which extends distally and can be tracked relatively easily if one draws a line from the ischial tuberosity to the greater trochanter and divides it into thirds. The sciatic nerve can then be found at the lower margin of the gluteus maximus between the prolonged border of the medial and middle third of this line. Lateral to the sciatic nerve, the *first perforating artery* (**14**) and its accompanying veins descend obliquely while crossing over the *adductor minimus* (**15**).

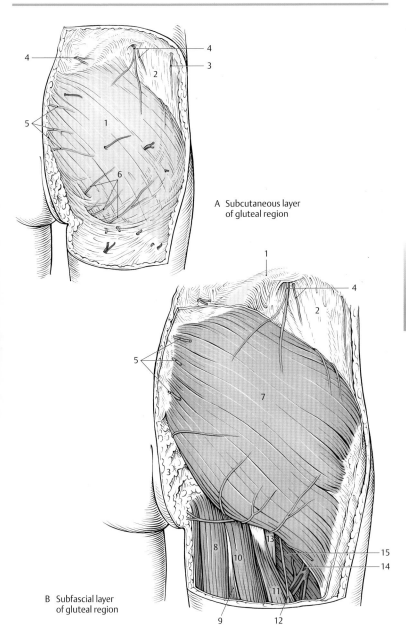

A Subcutaneous layer
of gluteal region

B Subfascial layer
of gluteal region

Gluteal Region, continued (A–C)

Deep Layer (A)

After the *gluteus maximus* (**1**) has been divided, the vessels and nerves which traverse the suprapiriform and infrapiriform foramina come into view.

The two foramina are formed by the *piriformis* (**2**), which subdivides the **greater sciatic foramen**. The *superior gluteal artery and vein* (**3**) and the *superior gluteal nerve* (**4**) pass through the **suprapiriform foramen** laterally. The artery sends a branch (**5**), accompanied by a vein, to the gluteus maximus (**1**), and then, together with a vein and the nerve, it runs between the *gluteus medius* (**6**) and the *gluteus minimus* (**7**). The superior gluteal nerve innervates the gluteus medius and minimus and the tensor fasciae latae.

The *inferior gluteal artery and vein* (**8**) and the *inferior gluteal nerve* (**9**) run through the **infrapiriform foramen** to the gluteus maximus (**1**). The *internal pudendal artery and vein* (**10**) and the *pudendal nerve* (**11**) arch posterior to the ischial spine and reach the ischiorectal (ischio-anal) fossa through the lesser sciatic foramen. They run dorsal to the *superior gemellus* (**12**) and then adhere to the *obturator internus* (**13**). The *posterior femoral cutaneous nerve* (**14**) and the *sciatic nerve* (**15**) leave the lesser pelvis through the infrapiriform foramen and reach the thigh by passing dorsal to the *superior gemellus* (**12**), the *obturator internus* (**13**), the *inferior gemellus* (**16**), and the *quadratus femoris* (**17**).

The posterior cutaneous femoral nerve (**14**) gives off the *inferior clunial nerves* (**18**) and then *a perineal branch* (**19**) soon after it emerges from the infrapiriform foramen. It then passes superficial to the *long head of the biceps muscle* (**20**), while the sciatic nerve (**15**) runs between this muscle and the *adductor magnus* (**21**).

▓▓ **Variants:** In about 85% of cases the sciatic nerve runs through the infrapiriform foramen (**A**) as a trunk. In about 15% of cases, the sciatic nerve already divides within the pelvis into its two branches, the tibial nerve and the common peroneal nerve. In about 12% the common peroneal nerve perforates the piriform muscle, while in 3% it even leaves the pelvis through the suprapiriform foramen.

Clinical tip (B, C): The gluteal region is an ideal site for **intramuscular (intragluteal) injections**. Intragluteal injections are usually given into the superolateral quadrant (cross-hatched in blue) of the gluteal region (**B**) into the gluteus maximus (**1**) or the gluteus medius (**6**). There is, however, danger of injecting too superficially, i.e., subcutaneously, or too deep between the gluteus maximus and the gluteus medius into the intermuscular fat, thus endangering the superior gluteal nerve (**4**). Injury to this nerve causes paralysis of the gluteus medius, gluteus minimus, and tensor fasciae latae.

A. v. Hochstetter has recommended injecting from the side (**C**) in a triangular field (hatched in red), behind the anterior superior iliac spine, into the gluteus medius and gluteus minimus. The muscles should be in a relaxed state (aided by slight anteversion of the hip and slight flexion of the knee), as this allows for a painless injection.

22 Sacrotuberous ligament
23 Trochanteric bursa of gluteus maximus

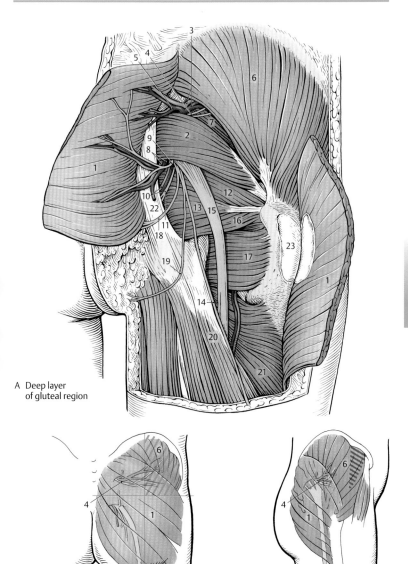

A Deep layer
of gluteal region

B Diagram of vessels and nerves potentially
endangered by intragluteal injections

C Intragluteal injection site as
recommended by *A. v. Hochstetter*

Peripheral Pathways

Anterior Region of the Thigh

Subcutaneous Layer (A)

The various areas of the subcutaneous tissue of the anterior thigh region differ in their structure. The proximal part, in the subinguinal region, has strong connective tissue lamellae = membranous layer (see p. 414), which divide the subcutaneous fatty tissue into two layers. In addition, the **saphenous opening** (**1**) is covered by a loose connective tissue layer, the cribriform fascia.

When the cribriform fascia is removed, the sharp margin of the saphenous opening, the falciform margin, becomes visible. The falciform margin merges into the fascia lata medially in the superior and inferior horns (p. 254). The **fascia lata** (**2**), which is continuous but for the saphenous opening, is also variable in structure. In the lateral thigh it is taut and kept stretched by the tensor fasciae latae which radiates into it. This part of the fascia is also called the *iliotibial tract* (**3**). The fascia is looser in the medial part of the thigh.

The *great saphenous vein* (**4**) runs subcutaneously and is often joined by the *lateral accessory saphenous vein* (**5**) and less often by the *medial accessory saphenous vein* (**6**). The other veins which enter the saphenous opening have already been described on page 416.

Laterally, near the junction between the proximal and middle thirds, the *lateral femoral cutaneous nerve* (**7**), becomes epifascial, while the *anterior cutaneous branches of the femoral nerve* (**8**) perforate the fascia at various levels. The *femoral branch* (**9**) *of the genitofemoral nerve* either runs through the saphenous opening or lateral to it through the fascia lata. A small area of skin on the medial upper side of the thigh is innervated by the *ilio-inguinal nerve* (**10**).

11 Superolateral and inferior superficial inguinal lymph nodes
12 Deep inguinal lymph nodes
13 Femoral vein
14 Femoral artery
15 Superficial epigastric artery and vein
16 Superficial circumflex iliac artery and vein
17 External pudendal artery and vein

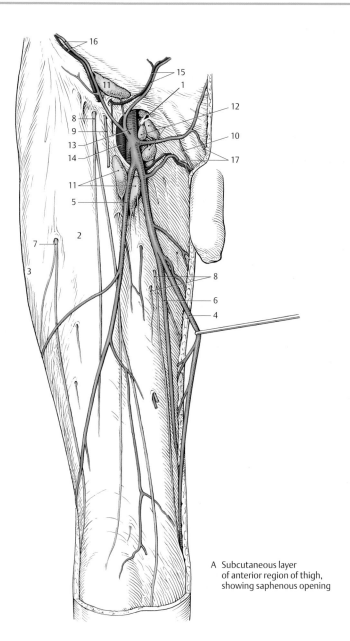

A Subcutaneous layer
of anterior region of thigh,
showing saphenous opening

Anterior Region of the Thigh, continued (A–H)

Deep Layer (A)

The large vessels and nerves are seen after removal of the fascia lata. Within the **femoral triangle**, which is limited by the *inguinal ligament*, the *sartorius* (**1**), and the *adductor longus* (**2**), lymphatics, the *femoral vein* (**3**), and *the femoral artery* (**4**) reach the thigh through the vascular space, and the *femoral nerve* (**5**) and the *iliopsoas* (**6**) through the muscular space.

After having given off its superficial branches (see p. 414), the femoral artery (**4**) gives rise to muscular branches, and a particularly large one, the *profunda femoris artery* (**7**), is buried deeply in the muscles. In 58% of cases the profunda femoris artery gives off the *medial circumflex femoral artery* (**8**) to the adductors and the head of the femur, and the *lateral circumflex femoral artery* (**9**), which sends an *ascending branch* (**10**) to the head of the femur and a *descending branch* (**11**) to the *quadriceps femoris* (**12**). The profunda femoris artery usually ends in three *perforating arteries* (**13**) which reach the adductor muscles and the dorsal muscles of the thigh. Medial to the femoral artery, the femoral vein (**3**) enters the vascular space. It collects, in addition to the subcutaneous veins (see p. 416), the veins which accompany the arteries.

The femoral nerve (**5**) passes through the muscular space into the thigh and, after giving off the anterior femoral cutaneous branches, it innervates the sartorius (**1**), the quadriceps femoris (**12**), and the *pectineus* (**14**). Its longest, purely sensory branch is the *saphenous nerve* (**15**), which runs lateral to and together with the femoral artery (**4**) and femoral vein to reach the **adductor canal**. These structures lie on the adductor longus (**2**), which takes part in forming the anteromedial intermuscular septum (= vasto-adductor membrane), and the posterior wall of the adductor canal. Apart from the adductor longus,

the *vastus medialis* (**16**), the *adductor magnus* (**17**), and the *anteromedial intermuscular septum* (= *vasto-adductor membrane*; **18**) are involved in formation of the adductor canal. The saphenous nerve usually (62%) perforates this membrane together with the *descending genicular artery* (**19**) to extend onto and innervate the medial surface of the leg. It gives off an *infrapatellar branch* (**20**).

Variants (B–H)

There is great variability on the origin of the saphenous nerve (**15**) from the femoral nerve and its course in the thigh (*Sirang*). Very often it arises from the femoral nerve (**5, B**) proximal to the lateral circumflex femoral artery (**9**). It may embrace the lateral circumflex femoral artery (**C**) with two roots. Somewhat less commonly it only arises from the femoral nerve after crossing the lateral circumflex femoral artery (**D, E**). It reaches the adductor canal, perforates the anteromedial intermuscular septum (= vasto-adductor membrane; **18**) and may give off its infrapatellar branch, either medial (**B, C**) or lateral (**D**) to or through the sartorius (**E**). In rare cases (**E**), the infrapatellar branch also receives fibers from the cutaneous branch of the *anterior branch of the obturator nerve* (**21**).

The branches from the femoral artery (**4**) are also very variable. Most commonly (58% according to *Lippert*) the medial (**8**) and lateral (**9**) circumflex femoral arteries arise from the profunda femoris artery (**F 7**). In 18% of cases (according to *Lippert*, **G**) the lateral circumflex femoral artery (**9**) arises from the profunda femoris artery (**7**), while, according to the same author, the medial circumflex femoral artery (**8**) arises from the profunda femoris artery (**7**) in only 15% of cases (**H**). The remaining 8% are distributed among much rarer variants.

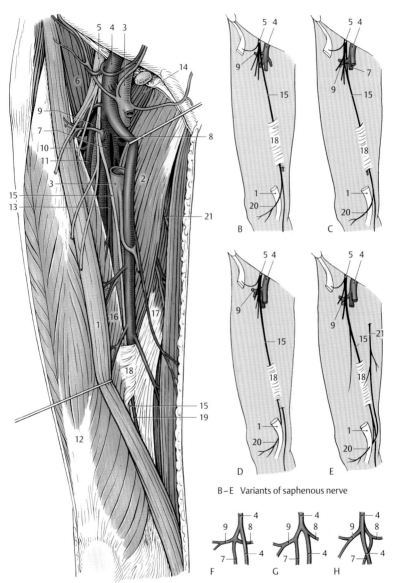

B – E Variants of saphenous nerve

A Subfascial layer of anterior region of thigh, with femoral artery displaced medially

F – H Variation in branching of femoral artery in subinguinal region (after *Lanz–Wachsmuth*)

Posterior Region of the Thigh (A, B)

After removal of the fascia, leaving the *ilio-tibial tract* (**1**) intact, at the lower margin of the *gluteus maximus* (**2**) the subfascial part of the *posterior femoral cutaneous nerve* (**3**) becomes visible as it runs superficial to the *long head of the biceps femoris* (**4**).

Between the *long head* (**4**) and the *short head* (**5**) *of the biceps femoris*, the *sciatic nerve* (**6**) runs distally. At variable levels it divides into the *tibial* (**7**) and the *common fibular (peroneal) nerves* (**8**). Before this division, the sciatic nerve gives off another branch (**9**) to the biceps femoris. The tibial nerve runs between the heads of the *gastrocnemius* (**10**), giving off various branches (see p. 430). The common fibular nerve follows the posterior margin of the *biceps femoris* (**11**).

The *primary perforating artery* (**12**), a branch of the deep femoral artery, reaches the posterior side of the thigh. It passes between the pectineus and adductor brevis muscles and then pierces the adductor minimus and magnus muscles. With its accompanying veins, it crosses the sciatic nerve ventrally (but dorsally to the adductor minimus and adductor magnus) and gives off branches to the long head of the biceps femoris (**4**) and the *semitendinosus* (**13**). On the dorsal surface of the adductor magnus, the primary perforating artery anastomoses with branches of the *secondary perforating artery* (**14**) and the latter anastomoses with branches of the *tertiary perforating artery*. The tertiary perforating artery is the end artery of the deep artery of thigh and penetrates the adductor magnus near to the hiatus of the adductor tendon. It supplies the semimembranosus and the short head of the biceps muscle.

After displacement of the *semimembranosus* (**15**), the *adductor hiatus* (**16**) comes into view. The adductor hiatus (**B**) is bounded by the two parts of the *adductor magnus* (**17**). One part is inserted into the medial lip of the linea aspera and the other into the adductor tubercle of the medial epicondyle. The femoral artery, which runs through the adductor canal, passes through the adductor hiatus to reach the popliteal fossa and becomes the *popliteal artery* (**18**) on the dorsal side of the thigh. In addition to muscular branches, it also gives off the medial and lateral superior genicular arteries. The popliteal artery is generally accompanied by the usually paired *popliteal veins* (**19**).

▬ **Variant:** Very occasionally there is one *sciatic artery* which developmentally is the primary vascular supply to the leg. Remnants remain as the *comitans artery* of the *sciatic nerve*.

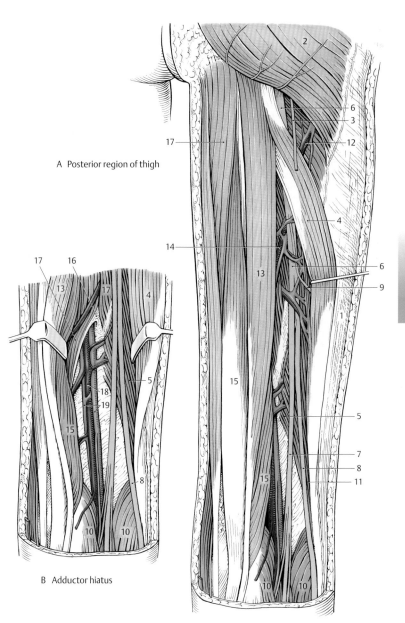

A Posterior region of thigh

B Adductor hiatus

Peripheral Pathways

Posterior Region of the Knee (A–K)

Subcutaneous Layer (A)

The *great saphenous vein* (**1**) lies in the sub-cutaneous layer at the medial margin of the posterior knee region. In the leg it is ac-companied by the *saphenous nerve* (**2**), which becomes subcutaneous at the lower margin of the popliteal fossa. The *small saphenous vein* (**3**) sometimes (see below) perforates the fascia at the lower margin of the popliteal fossa. It is accompanied by the *medial sural cutaneous nerve* (**4**) which is continued as the sural nerve (see p. 434). In addition, the *posterior femoral cutaneous nerve* with its branches (**5**) terminates in the popliteal fossa.

Variations in the Course of the Small Saphenous Vein (B–E)

The small saphenous vein, which is very important in phlebology, runs a variable course in relation to the crural fascia. Ac-cording to *Moosmann* and *Hartwell* the small saphenous vein (**3**) perforates the crural fascia in the distal third of the leg in 7% of cases (**B**), runs subfascially to the popliteal fossa and then turns deep to join the *popliteal vein* (**6**). Most commonly (51.5%) the small saphenous vein (**3**) per-forates the fascia in the middle third of the leg (**C**).

The second most common site (32.5%) for the small saphenous vein (**3**) to perforate the fascia is in the proximal third (**D**). It perforates the fascia within the posterior knee region (**E**) in only 9% of cases.

Variations in the Site of Union of the Small Saphenous Vein with a Larger Vein (F–K)

Mercier et al. also reported great variability in the manner in which the small saphenous vein (**3**) opens into the larger veins. In addition to its typical opening (**F**) into the popliteal vein (**6**), the small saphenous vein (**3**) may also give off a branch to the great saphenous vein (**1, G**). In the presence of this branch, the small saphenous vein (**3**) may also open directly into the *femoral vein* (**7, H**). Further vari-ants include either an opening solely into the great saphenous vein (**I**) or into the femoral vein (**J**), in which the latter union also may be delta-shaped (**K**).

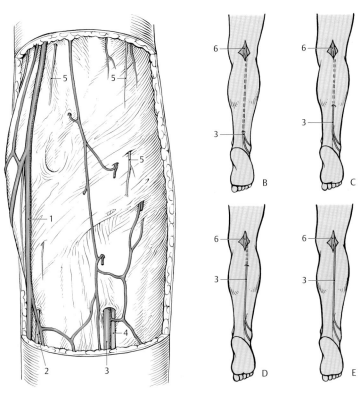

A Subcutaneous layer
   of popliteal fossa

B–E Sites of perforation of fascia
     by small saphenous vein
     (after *Moosmann* and *Hartwell*)

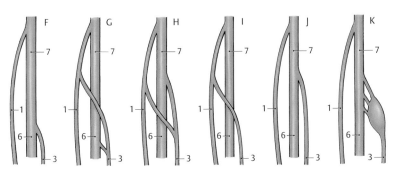

F–K Various ways in which small saphenous vein opens into larger veins (after *Mercier* et al.)

Popliteal Fossa (A–G)

Deep Layer (A)

After removal of the fascia, the rhomboidal popliteal fossa bounded by muscles is seen. The popliteal fossa is bounded medially and proximally by the *semimembranosus* (**1**), laterally and proximally by the *biceps femoris* (**2**), and distally by the *lateral* (**3**) and the *medial* (**4**) *heads of the gastrocnemius*. The sciatic nerve and its branches can be seen proximally between the semimembranosus and the biceps femoris.

The *common fibular (peroneal) nerve* (**5**) descends superficially along the posterior border of the biceps femoris, while the second branch, the *tibial nerve* (**6**), extends distally between the two heads of the gastrocnemius. The tibial nerve gives off *muscular branches* (**7**) and a *medial sural cutaneous nerve* (**8**), which, together with the communicating peroneal branch, forms the sural nerve (see p. 434).

Deep in the popliteal fossa we find the *popliteal artery* (**10**) accompanied by the *popliteal veins* (**9**). At a variable level (see below) this artery gives off the *anterior tibial artery* (**11**). The small saphenous vein usually reaches the popliteal vein but, as in the preparation illustrated, it may not open into a larger vein until it is proximal to the popliteal fossa.

Variants of the Arterial Branches (B–G)

In 90% of cases (**B**) the popliteal artery (**10**) gives off as its first branch the anterior tibial artery (**11**) dorsal to the *popliteus muscle* (**12**), dividing further distally into the *posterior tibial* (**13**) and *fibular (peroneal)* (**14**) *arteries*. In about 4% of cases (**C**) the arteries arise together. It is unusual (1%) for the anterior tibial artery and the peroneal artery (*anterior peroneotibial trunk*; **15**) to originate together at the distal edge of the popliteus (**D**).

In 3% of cases the popliteal artery (**10**) gives off the anterior tibial artery just proximal to the popliteus (**E**, see also Fig. **A**).

In 1% of individuals the anterior tibial artery (**11**) arises at the same high level with the presence of an anterior peroneotibial trunk (**F 15**) or, another variant, the course of the anterior tibial artery (**11**) runs ventral to the popliteus (**12 G**).

Clinical tip: Atypical or additional origins of muscle fibers of the gastrocnemius muscle from the popliteal fascia, from the medial lip of the linea aspera and from the connective tissue covering of the popliteal vessels can lead to a **"popliteal compression syndrome"**. This syndrome can also appear in those rare instances in which the anterior tibial artery courses ventrally to the popliteus muscle (**G**).

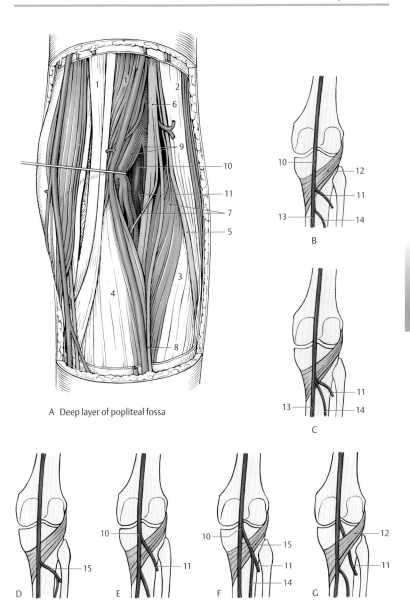

A Deep layer of popliteal fossa

B

C

D   E   F   G

B–G Variants of arterial branches of popliteal artery (after *Lanz–Wachsmuth*)

Anterior Region of the Leg (A, B)

The subcutaneous neurovascular bundles run essentially on the medial side of the leg.

The *great saphenous vein* (**1**) collects blood from the medial side and the dorsum of the foot and ascends to the triceps surae with the *saphenous nerve* (**2**). This nerve innervates the skin on the medial surface of the leg as far as the medial margin of the foot, and with its *infrapatellar branch* (**3**) it innervates the skin of the *infrapatellar region*. Later it gives off the *medial cutaneous branches of the leg* (**4**).

After removal of the fascia of the leg in the lateral region, the *tibialis anterior* (**5**) is seen proximal to the *tibia* (**6**). The *extensor digitorum longus* (**7**) lies lateral to the tibialis anterior and deeply in between them is the *extensor hallucis longus* (**8**). Laterally, the *fibularis (peroneus) longus* (**9**) and the *fibularis (peroneus) brevis* (**10**) may also be seen.

The *superficial fibular (peroneal) nerve* (**11**) runs distally between the extensor digitorum longus (**7**) and the fibular muscles and branches on the dorsum of the foot. It perforates the fascia of the distal half of the leg. Deep between the tendon of the tibialis anterior (**5**) and the extensor hallucis longus muscle (**8**) runs the *anterior tibial artery* (**12**) with its accompanying veins, the *anterior tibial veins* (**13**), and the *deep fibular (peroneal) nerve* (**14**), which together with its motor fibers also carries sensory fibers from the area of skin between the first and second digits.

Clinical tip: The stress of prolonged marching may cause the **"anterior tibial syndrome"**. This produces sharp pain lateral to the tibia due to damage to the anterior tibial artery and the tibialis anterior muscle. There is usually also associated damage to the deep fibular (peroneal) nerve, which may be misdiagnosed as a peroneal paralysis.

15 Fibularis tertius

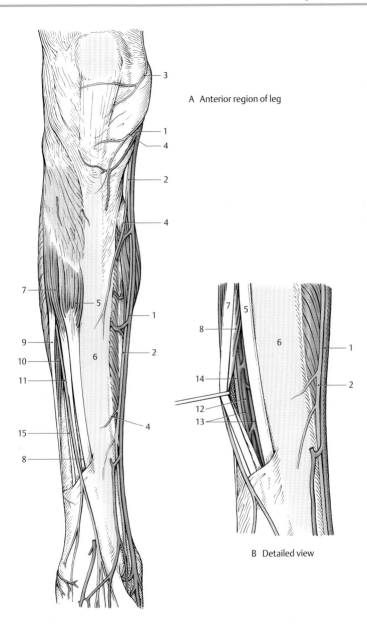

A Anterior region of leg

B Detailed view

Posterior Region of the Leg (A–E)

Of the larger structures, only veins and nerves are visible subcutaneously. The region is supplied with blood deeply through branches of the posterior tibial artery. The appearance is not fundamentally altered by removal of the fascia of the leg, although the *triceps surae* (**1**) does become visible with the two heads of the *gastrocnemius* (**2**) and the *soleus* (**3**). The triceps surae is attached to the calcaneus by the *calcaneal tendon* (**4**).

The *saphenous nerve* (**5**) and the *great saphenous vein* (**6**) are visible medially. The largest structure is the *small saphenous vein* (**7**), which begins at the lateral margin of the foot and ascends toward the popliteal fossa. Its relationship to the fascia is described on p. 428. The great and small saphenous veins are connected by numerous anastomoses. There are also the *perforating veins* (**8**), which join the subcutaneous veins to the deep veins (anterior and posterior tibial and fibular = peroneal veins). Valves direct the flow of blood from the superficial to the deep veins.

The *medial cutaneous sural nerve* (**9**) is accompanied by the small saphenous vein and usually perforates the fascia in the middle of the leg. It joins the *peroneal communicating branch* (**10**) to form the *sural nerve* (**11**), which innervates the skin of the posterior region of the leg. With its continuation, the *lateral dorsal cutaneous nerve* (**12**), it innervates the lateral margin of the dorsum of the foot, and with the *lateral calcaneal branches* (**13**) it innervates the lateral calcaneal area. *Medial calcaneal branches* (**14**) arise directly from the tibial nerve and innervate the skin in the medial region of the calcaneal area. Immediately posterior to the head of the fibula, the *common fibular (peroneal) nerve* (**15**) descends. It is always in danger of injury because of its superficial position.

After removal of the *medial head of the gastrocnemius* (**16**), the *popliteus* (**17**) becomes visible; it is covered by the fascia.

This way the *popliteal artery* (**18**), the *popliteal veins* (**19**), and the *tibial nerve* (**20**) can be viewed until they enter the *tendinous arch of the soleus muscle* (**21**). The entrance may be hidden by the *plantar muscle* (**22**). Deep in the posterior region of the leg, covered by the soleus (**3**), run the *posterior tibial artery* (**23**) and the *fibular (peroneal) artery* (**24**). The posterior tibial artery is the continuation of the *popliteal artery* (**18**) after it has given off the *anterior tibial artery* (**25**).

▆▆ **Variants (C–E):** As at other sites, the arteries show a number of variants, knowledge of which is important for clinical purposes (arteriography, ligations, etc.). As a rule (**C**) the posterior tibial artery (**23**) descends on the posterior surface of the tibia, reaches the medial retromalleolar region (see p. 410) and divides into the plantar arteries. The fibular (peroneal) artery (**24**) descends near the fibula, giving off a *perforating branch* (**26**) which pierces the interosseous membrane and ends in the region of the lateral malleolus. Sometimes (**D**) the phylogenetically older fibular (peroneal) artery (**24**) may replace a poorly developed posterior tibial artery (**23**). In rare cases (**E**), the posterior tibial artery is completely absent and the fibular (peroneal) artery (**24**) takes over the blood supply for the entire region usually supplied by this artery.

Clinical tip: A practical distinction is drawn between **communicating veins** and **perforator veins** in the leg. Communicating veins establish a direct connection between the superficial (epifascial) and deep (subfascial) venous systems, while perforator veins establish an indirect connection via muscular veins.
All the veins have valves that normally direct blood flow from the superficial veins to the deep veins. When the valves are incompetent, the flow direction is reversed and **varicose veins** develop. **Thrombosis** occurs exclusively in the deep veins (!) and may lead to varicosity, edema, and crural ulcer.

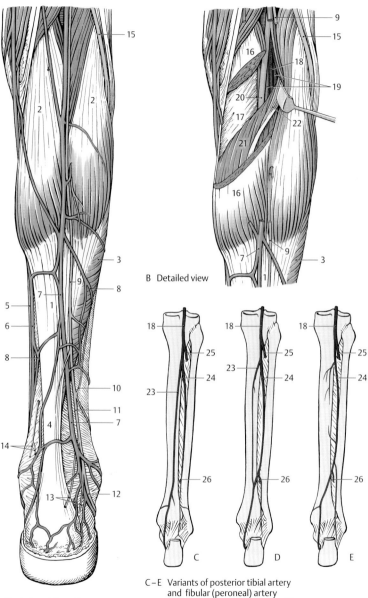

B Detailed view

C–E Variants of posterior tibial artery
and fibular (peroneal) artery
(redrawn after *Lanz–Wachsmuth*)

A Posterior region of leg

Medial Retromalleolar Region (A, B)

The medial retromalleolar region includes the area between the medial malleolus and the calcaneal tendon. It is limited distally by the **flexor retinaculum** (laciniate ligament), which consists of a *superficial* and a *deep layer* (see below).

The *superficial layer* (**1**) is a thickening of the *fascia of the leg* (**2**). It extends from the medial malleolus to the posterior surface of the calcaneal tendon and the calcaneal tuberosity. Neither proximally nor distally is it clearly demarcated.

Subcutaneous Layer (A)

This layer contains veins, cutaneous nerves and small cutaneous arteries (not illustrated). The *great saphenous vein* (**3**) runs near the malleolus and is readily visible through the thin skin. It receives blood from the cutaneous venous network and from deep veins (**4**). The *saphenous nerve* (**5**) branches in this region to supply sensory innervation to the skin.

Subfascial Layer (B)

After removal of the fascia of the leg, the neurovascular bundle and the long muscles of the sole to the foot can be seen proximal to the flexor retinaculum. Also visible is the *deep layer* (**6**) of the flexor retinaculum, which extends from the medial malleolus to the calcaneus and complements the bone grooves in creating osteofibrous canals for the long muscles of foot.

Immediately behind the medial malleolus runs the tendon of the *tibialis posterior* (**7**) and adjacent to it the tendon of the *flexor digitorum longus* (**8**). The tendon of the *flexor hallucis longus* (**9**) lies deeper and is displaced somewhat backward by the medial tubercle of the posterior process of the talus. All three muscles have their own tendon sheaths (see p. 279), which are not illustrated here.

Between the superficial (**1**) and deep (**6**) layers runs the neurovascular bundle for the sole of the foot. Adjacent to the tendon of the flexor digitorum longus (**8**) runs the *posterior tibial artery* (**10**) with its accompanying *posterior tibial veins* (**11**). Posterior to these veins lies the *tibial nerve* (**12**), which usually divides between the two layers into its terminal branches, the *medial* and *lateral plantar nerves*.

Sometimes this division may occur proximal to the flexor retinaculum and then the medial plantar nerve lies immediately posterior to the flexor digitorum longus.

Clinical tip: The loose, highly mobile skin here permits tissue fluid to accumulate, and **edema** may occur. Finger pressure will then produce lasting indentations (pitting), which indicate fluid retention in the body. The pulse of the posterior tibial artery may also be felt in this region.

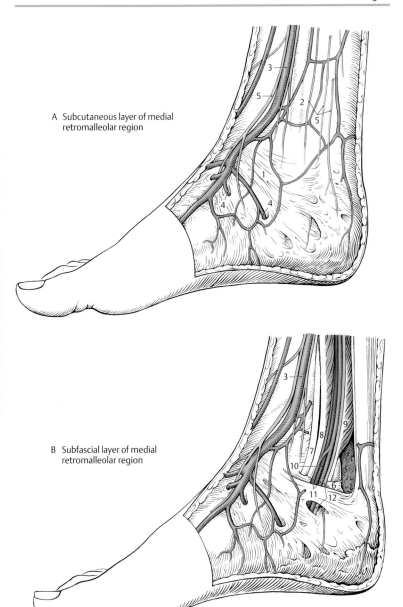

A Subcutaneous layer of medial retromalleolar region

B Subfascial layer of medial retromalleolar region

Dorsum of the Foot (A–G)

Subcutaneous Layer (A)

A dense network of veins, the *dorsal venous network of foot* (**1**), forms a *dorsal venous arch* (**2**) in the region of the metatarsal bones. Into these superficial veins not only the *superficial dorsal metatarsal veins* (**3**) open, but also deep veins, the *perforating veins* (**4**) and the *intercapitular veins* (**5**). The blood is drained mainly through the *great saphenous vein* (**6**) and only a smaller proportion travels via the *lateral malleolar network* (**7**) to the small saphenous vein.

Small branches only from the deep arteries reach the subcutaneous layer and the *first dorsal metatarsal artery* (**8**), which has a variable origin (see below), is the only one that is visible.

The *medial dorsal cutaneous nerve* (**9**) innervates the skin on the medial side of the dorsum of the foot, in many cases supplemented by the *saphenous nerve* (**10**), which innervates the medial margin of the foot. Sometimes the saphenous nerve (**10**) ends in the region of the medial malleolus. Only the adjacent regions of the skin of the first and second digits are innervated by the *deep fibular (peroneal) nerve* (**11**), which may anastomose with branches of the *medial dorsal cutaneous nerve* (**12**). The *intermediate dorsal cutaneous nerve* (**13**) supplies the lateral half of the skin of the dorsum of the foot, supplemented at its lateral margin by the final branch of the sural nerve, the *lateral dorsal cutaneous nerve* (**14**).

Subfascial Layer (B)

After removal of the fascia and retention of the inferior extensor retinaculum, the *dorsalis pedis artery* (**15**) becomes visible. It runs onto the dorsum of the foot, accompanied by the deep fibular (peroneal) nerve (**11**). With the tendon of the *tibialis anterior* (**16**) passing beneath the medial ends of the inferior extensor retinaculum, the dorsalis pedis artery and accompanying veins and nerve lie between the tendons of the *extensor hallucis longus* (**17**) and the *extensor digitorum longus* (**18**). The dorsalis pedis artery gives off the lateral tarsal artery in the region of the retinaculum and forms an *arcuate artery* (**19**) from which arise the *dorsal metatarsal arteries* (**20**). These give origin not only to the *dorsal digital arteries* (**21**), but also to the perforating branches to the sole of the foot, of which the *deep plantar branch* (**22**) to the first interosseous space is particularly important. The dorsalis pedis artery is accompanied by veins which communicate with the superficial veins.

> **Clinical tip:** The **pulse** is palpable in the dorsalis pedis artery lateral to the tendon of the extensor hallucis longus. The loose subcutaneous tissue on the dorsum of the foot becomes filled with fluid if there is a disturbance of the circulation, thus producing **edema**.

■■ **Variants of the Arteries (C–G):** The dorsal metatarsal arteries, and therefore also the arcuate artery, are very variable. Only in 20% of cases (**C**) do the dorsal metatarsal arteries arise from the dorsalis pedis artery, while in 6% (**D**) the fourth metatarsal artery is supplied by a perforating branch from the sole of the foot. In 40% (**E**) only the first metatarsal artery originates from the dorsalis pedis artery, and the remainder of the dorsal metatarsal arteries stem from plantar arteries. In 10% (**F**) all the dorsal metatarsal arteries come from the sole of the foot, and in 5% of cases (**G**) the first dorsal metatarsal artery alone arises from a plantar artery.

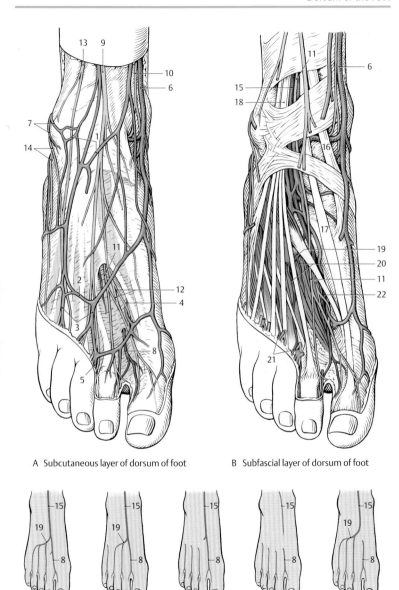

A Subcutaneous layer of dorsum of foot

B Subfascial layer of dorsum of foot

C–G Variants of arteries of dorsum of foot (after *Lippert*)

Sole of the Foot (A—G)

Superficial Layer (A)

With the exception of the margins of the foot the *plantar aponeurosis* (**1**) covers the deep structures of the sole, including the principal trunks of the peripheral pathways. As the skin of the sole of the foot has a particularly rich blood supply, there are a large number of *plantar cutaneous arteries* (**2**) and *plantar cutaneous veins* (**3**). In the calcaneal region, the arteries form a network, the *rete calcaneum (calcaneal anastomosis)*, which is supplied by branches from the *posterior tibial* and *fibular arteries*. Additional branches stem from the *medial plantar* and the *lateral plantar arteries*. The *medial plantar artery* gives off a *superficial branch* (**4**), which becomes visible at the medial margin of the plantar aponeurosis, accompanied by the *first proper plantar digital nerve* (**5**). Lateral to the aponeurosis there is often a subcutaneous *branch* (**6**) *of the lateral plantar artery* accompanied by the *proper plantar digital nerve* (**7**) for innervation of the outer margin of the little digit.

Between the longitudinal bundles of the aponeurosis (**1**), the *common plantar digital arteries* (**8**) and the *common plantar digital nerves* (**9**) become subcutaneous. The common plantar digital arteries, which divide into *proper plantar digital arteries* (**10**), usually represent a continuation of the plantar metatarsal arteries (see p. 442), but may (very uncommonly) arise from a **"superficial" plantar arch**. Often the superficial branch (**4**) of the medial plantar artery can take over the blood supply to the medial side of the great digit as the *first proper plantar digital artery* (**11**). The common plantar digital nerves (**9**) divide subcutaneously into the *proper digital nerves* (**12**).

Variants of the Deep Plantar Arch (B–G)

In 27% of cases (**B**) the four plantar metatarsal arteries are supplied by the *deep plantar branch* (**13**) of the dorsalis pedis artery, while in 26% (**C**) the *deep plantar arch* (**14**) is formed entirely by the deep plantar branch. In 19% (**D**), the fourth plantar metatarsal artery arises from the *deep branch* (**15**) of the lateral plantar artery, and in 13% (**E**) the third plantar metatarsal artery does so as well, while the others stem from the deep plantar branch (**13**). In only 7% of cases (**F**) do all the plantar metatarsal arteries arise from a deep plantar arch (**14**) that is formed entirely from the deep branch (**15**) of the lateral plantar artery. In 6% (**G**) the second to fourth plantar metatarsal arteries arise from a deep plantar arch (**14**), while the first plantar metatarsal artery arises from the deep plantar branch (**13**).

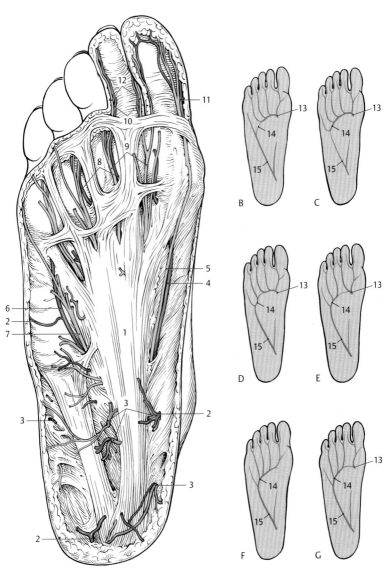

A Superficial layer
of sole of foot

B–G Variants of arteries
of sole of foot (after *Lippert*)

Sole of the Foot, continued (A, B)

Deep Layer (A)

After removal of the *plantar aponeurosis* and the *flexor digitorum brevis* (**1**), the medial and lateral neurovascular bundles of the sole of the foot are revealed. Medially, lying next to the *abductor hallucis* (**2**), the *medial plantar artery* (**3**), its accompanying veins and the *medial plantar nerve* (**4**) reach the sole of the foot. The medial plantar artery (**3**), which may run laterally (more frequently) or medially (less frequently) to the nerve, divides into a *superficial branch* (**5**), which runs superficially to the *flexor hallucis brevis* (**6**), and a *deep branch. The superficial branch may (uncommonly) continue as the first proper plantar digital artery* (**7**), accompanied by the *first proper plantar digital nerve* (**8**), which may have divided proximally from the *medial plantar nerve* (**4**). The medial plantar nerve divides in sequence into the *first, second, and third common plantar digital nerves* (**9**), which give off branches (**10**) to the lumbricals. The first to third common plantar digital nerves continue as the *proper plantar digital nerves* (**11**). Sometimes, the *proper plantar digital nerve* (**12**) to the lateral side of the fourth digit may stem from the medial plantar nerve. Usually, this region is innervated by branches of the *lateral plantar nerve* (**13**).

The lateral neurovascular bundle, which extends toward the digits medial to the *abductor digiti minimi* (**14**), consists (from medial to lateral) of the lateral plantar nerve (**13**) and the *lateral plantar artery* (**15**) and its *accompanying veins* (**16**). The lateral plantar artery divides into a *superficial* (**17**) and a *deep* (**18**) *branch*. The superficial branch supplies the lateral margin of the foot and the little digit, while the deep branch takes part in formation of the *deep plantar arch* (**19**).

The lateral plantar nerve (**13**) gives off muscular branches to the muscles which arise from the calcaneus, and also cutaneous branches to the lateral margin of

the foot. It divides into a *superficial* (**20**) and a *deep* (**21**) *branch*. The superficial branch innervates via muscular branches the *flexor digiti minimi brevis* (**22**) and the *fourth lumbricalis* (**23**), as well as areas of skin above them. The skin of the little digit and usually the lateral surface of the fourth digit are innervated by the *common plantar digital nerves* (**24**), which divide into *proper plantar digital nerves* (**25**). The deep branch (**21**) accompanies the deep plantar arch and innervates the *adductor hallucis longus* and the *opponens digiti minimi* as well as the interossei.

Deep Plantar Arch (B)

After removal of the *quadratus plantae* (**26**) and the tendons of the *flexor digitorum longus* (**27**) as well as the *oblique head* (**28**) of the adductor hallucis, the deep plantar arch (**19**) is revealed.

It runs deep in the foot, adheres closely to the interossei muscles, and anastomoses with the *deep plantar branch* (**29**) of the dorsal artery of the foot. Three to four *metatarsal plantar arteries* (**30**) arise from the plantar arch; they usually give off the *common plantar digital arteries* (**31**), which divide into the *proper plantar digital arteries* (**32**).

For variants of the deep plantar arch, see p. 440.

33 Interossei plantar muscles
34 Transverse head of the adductor hallucis

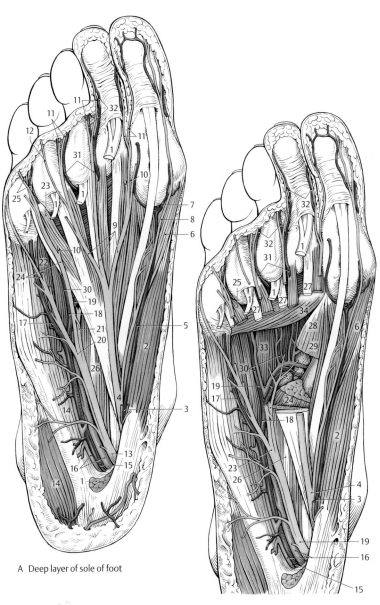

A Deep layer of sole of foot

B Deep plantar arch

Anatomical Terms and their Latin Equivalents

Topography of Peripheral Nerves and Vessels	
Anterior (posterior) region of leg	Regio cruris anterior (posterior)
Anterior (posterior) region of thigh	Regio femoralis anterior (posterior)
Arm	Brachium
Artery (vein) of round ligament of uterus	A.(V.) ligamenti teretis uteri
Buccal fat pad	Corpus adiposum buccae
Cord (lateral, etc.)	Fasciculus (lateralis, etc.)
Deltopectoral (clavipectoral) triangle	Trigonum clavipectorale
Falciform margin	Margo falciformis (arcuatus)
Fat body of ischio-anal fossa	Corpus adiposum fossae ischioanalis
Forearm	Antebrachium
Heel region	Regio calcanea
Hip joint	Articulatio coxae
Medial (lateral) bicipital groove	Sulcus bicipitalis medialis (lateralis)
Muscular space	Lacuna musculorum
Parotid plexus	Plexus intraparotideus
Parotid region	Regio parotideomasseterica
Quadrangular space	Foramen axillare laterale
Region of knee	Regio genus
Region of wrist	Regio carpalis
Saphenous opening	Hiatus saphenus
Seminal gland	Glandula vesiculosa
Sole of foot	Planta pedis
Suboccipital triangle	Trigonum a. vertebralis
Triangular space	Foramen axillare mediale
Upper limb	Membrum superius (Extremitas superior)
Vascular space	Lacuna vasorum

For Those Who Want to Learn More

There is a centuries-old tradition in medicine of naming a structure, disease, diagnostic method, or condition after the person who first described it. Unfortunately, an ignorance of history has resulted in a tendency to use the name of the second, third, or even fourth describer rather than the discoverer. For example, some 15 scientists described the inguinal ligament over the centuries, and their pupils honored them by assigning various regional names to the ligament. This resulted in terms such as the Poupart ligament and Cooper ligament, even though Vesalius and his pupil Fallopio actually discovered the ligament in the 15th century.

Failure to apply the first-describer rule has led to a chaotic situation in which some terms have even been associated with the wrong names. By the mid-20th century, this led European anatomists to *dispense with eponyms* and use only Latin terms for descriptions and findings. Unfortunately this practice was not adhered to, nor was it adopted in the U.S., and so the author has appended a list of the proper names that

Index of Proper Names

ALCOCK, Thomas (1784–1833). Surgeon, London (p. 406, Alcock canal = pudendal canal).

BELLINI, Lorenzo (1643–1704). Anatomist, Pisa (p. 200, Bellini ligament = iliofemoral ligament).

BERTIN, Exupere (1712–1781). Anatomist, France (p. 200, Bertini ligament = iliofemoral ligament).

BIGELOW, Henry (1818–1890). Surgeon, Boston (p. 200, Bigelow ligament = iliofemoral ligament).

CHASSAIGNAC, Charles Marie Edouard (1804–1879). Surgeon, France (p. 362, Chassiagnac tubercle = anterior tubercle of the C6 vertebra).

CHOPART, Francois (1743–1795). Surgeon, France (p. 222, Chopart ligament = bifurcate ligament; Chopart joint line = transverse tarsal joint).

CLOQUET, Jules Germain (1790–1883). Anatomist and surgeon, Paris (p. 100, Cloquet node = Rosenmüller lymph node = deep inguinal lymph node; p. 338, Cloquet or Rosenmüller gland = palpebral part of lacrimal gland).

COLLES, Abraham (1773–1843). Surgeon, Dublin (p. 96, Colles ligament = reflex inguinal ligament; p. 122, Colles fracture = distal radial fracture; p. 408, Colles membrane = perineal membrane).

COOPER, Sir Astley Paston (1768–1841). Surgeon and anatomist, London (p. 98, Cooper fascia = cremasteric fascia; p. 100, Cooper ligament = pectineal ligament).

COWPER, William (1666–1709). Anatomist and surgeon, London (p. 254, Cowper ligament = pectineal fascia = pubic part of fascia lata).

DEJERINE-KLUMPKE, Augusta (1859–1927). Neurologist, Paris (p. 372, lower brachial plexus paralysis).

DUCHENNE, Guillaume (1806–1875). Neurologist, Paris (p. 360; Duchenne-Erb paralysis = upper brachial plexus paralysis).

EISELSBERG, von Anton (1860–1939). Surgeon, Königsberg and Vienna (p. 358, Eiselberg phenomenon = pain projecting to the right or left side of the shoulder).

ERB, Wilhelm (1840–1921). Neurologist, Heidelberg (p. 70, Erb's point 1 = left parasternal auscultation point in the cardiac valvular plane (see Vol. 2) in the third intercostal space; p. 328, Erb's point 2 = supraclavicular point approximately 3 cm above the clavicle and 1–2 cm posterior to the sternocleidomastoid muscle = electrical stimulation point for the upper brachial plexus; p. 360, Duchenne-Erb paralysis = upper brachial plexus paralysis).

FICK, Rudolf (1866–1939). Anatomist, Innsbruck and Berlin (p. 26, Fick vacuum phenomenon = radiographic lucencies caused by intra-articular tissue gas; p. 82, internal intercostal muscles = muscles of expiration).

GALEN (129–199 AD). Physician, Pergamon (p. 338, Galen gland = orbital part of lacrimal gland).

GOLGI, Camillo (1843–1926). Pathologist (1906 Nobel Prize in Medicine), Pavia (p. 4, Golgi apparatus = organelle present in every nucleated cell).

GUYON, Jean (1831–1920). Surgeon and urologist, Paris (pp. 180 and 388, Guyon canal = ulnar tunnel = ulnar canal).

HAVER, Clopton (1650–1702). Anatomist, London (p. 14, Haversian system = osteon).

HAYEK, von Heinrich (1900–1969). Anatomist, Shanghai, Würzburg, and Vienna (p. 80, Hayek ligament = transverse cupular ligament).

HENLE, Friedrich G. J. (1809–1885). Anatomist, Zurich, Heidelberg, and Göttingen (p. 92, Henle ligament = inguinal falx).

HESSELBACH, Franz (1759–1816). Anatomist and surgeon, Würzburg (p. 92, Hesselbach ligament, called also Blumberg ligament or Heymann ligament = internal inguinal ligament = interfoveolar ligament; p. 98, Hesselbach triangle = inguinal triangle).

LISFRANC, Jacques (1790–1847). Surgeon, Paris (Lisfranc joint line = tarsometatarsal joint line).

LUSCHKA, von Hubert (1820–1875). Anatomist, Tübingen (p. 58, Luschka joints = uncovertebral joints).

NAFFZIGER, Howard (1884–1956). Surgeon, San Francisco (p. 36, Naffziger syndrome = cervical rib triad).

NELATON, Auguste (1807–1873). Surgeon, Paris (p. 196, Roser-Nelton line = imaginary line between anterior superior iliac spine, tip of greater trochanter, and ischial tuberosity).

OBERST, Maximilian (1849–1925). Surgeon, Halle, Saale (p. 388, Oberst nerve block = anesthesia of the fingers).

ROSENMÜLLER, Johann (1771–1820). Surgeon and anatomist, Leipzig (see under CLOQUET).

ROSER, Wilhelm (1817–1888). Surgeon, Marburg, Lahn (see under NELATON).

SCARPA, Antonio (1752–1832). Anatomist and surgeon, Modena (p. 92, Scarpa fascia = membranous layer of subcutaneous abdominal fascia; p. 254, Scarpa ligament = superior horn of falciform margin).

SCHMORL, Christian Georg (1861–1932). Pathologist, Dresden (p. 54, Schmorl nodes = protrusions of intervertebral disk material into adjacent vertebrae).

THOMSON, A. (1809–1884). Anatomist, Glasgow (p. 92, Thomson ligament = rough correspondence with iliopubic tract).

TRENDELENBURG, Friedrich (1844–1924). Surgeon, Rostock, Bonn and Leipzig (p. 246, Trendelenburg sign = pelvic tilt in one-legged stance, waddling gait).

TROISIER, Charles Emile (1844–1919). Physician, Paris (p. 366, Troisier nodes = Virchow glands = enlarged left supraclavicular lymph nodes due to metastasis from gastric malignancies).

VESALIUS, Andreas (1514–1564). Anatomist, Padua, Basel and Madrid (pp. 84 and 188, Vesalius ligament = inguinal ligament; first described by Vesalius and his pupil Gabriele FALLOPIO (1523–1562), anatomist, Ferrara, Pisa and Padua).

VIRCHOW, Rudolf (1821–1902). Pathologist, Würzburg and Berlin (p. 366, see under TROISIER).

VOLKMANN, Alfred (1800–1879). Physiologist, Halle, Saale (p. 14, Volkmann canals = oblique vascular canals in bone).

References

Textbooks, Handbooks

Bardeleben, K.: Handbuch der Anatomie des Menschen, Bd. II. Fischer, Jena, 1908 – 1912

Benninghoff: Makroskopische Anatomie, Embryologie und Histologie des Menschen, 15. Aufl., Bd. I, hrsg. von D. Drenckhahn u. W. Zenker, Urban & Schwarzenberg, München – Wien – Baltimore 1994

Braus, H.: Anatomie des Menschen, 3. Aufl., Bd. I, hrsg. von C. Elze. Springer, Berlin 1954

Bucher, O., H. Wartenberg: Cytologie, Histologie und mikroskopische Anatomie des Menschen, 11. Aufl. Huber, Bern 1989

Feneis, H.: Anatomisches Bildwörterbuch, 7. Aufl. Thieme, Stuttgart 1993

Figge, F. H. J., W. J. Hild: Atlas of Human Anatomy. Urban & Schwarzenberg, München 1974

Frick, H., H. Leonhardt, D. Starck: Taschenlehrbuch der gesamten Anatomie, Bd. 1 u. 2, 3. Aufl., Thieme, Stuttgart 1987

Gardner, E., J. D. Gray, R. O'Rahilly: Anatomy, 4. Aufl. Saunders, Philadelphia 1975

Grosser, O.: Grundriß der Entwicklungsgeschichte des Menschen, 7. Aufl., hrsg. von R. Ortmann, Springer, Berlin 1970

Hafferl, A.: Lehrbuch der topographischen Anatomie, 3. Aufl., hrsg. von W. Thiel. Springer, Berlin 1969

Hollinshead, W. H.: Functional Anatomy of the Limbs and Back, 4. Aufl. Saunders, Philadelphia 1976

Kremer, K., W. Lierse, W. Platzer, H. W. Schreiber, S. Weller (Hrsg.): Chirurgische Operationslehre. Vol. 1 – 10. Thieme, Stuttgart 1987 – 1999

Lang, J., W. Wachsmuth: Praktische Anatomie, Bein und Statik, Bd. I/4, 2. Aufl. Springer, Berlin 1972

Langmann, J.: Medizinische Embryologie, 8. Aufl. Thieme, Stuttgart 1989

von Lanz, T., W. Wachsmuth: Praktische Anatomie, Bd. I/2: Hals. Springer, Berlin 1955

von Lanz, T., W. Wachsmuth: Praktische Anatomie, Bd. I/3: Arm, 2. Aufl. Springer, Berlin 1959

Leonhardt, H.: Histologie, Zytologie und Mikroanatomie des Menschen, 8. Aufl. Thieme, Stuttgart 1990

Mc Gregor, A. L., J. du Plessis: A Synopsis of Surgical Anatomy, 3. Aufl. Wright, Bristol 1969

Montgomery, R. L., M. C. Singleton: Human Anatomy Review. Pitman Medical, London 1975

Nishi, S.: Topographical Atlas of Human Anatomy, Bd. I – IV. Kanehara Shuppan, Tokyo 1974 – 1975

Pernkopf: Anatomie, Bd. 1 u. 2, hrsg. von W. Platzer, 3. Aufl., Urban u. Schwarzenberg, München – Wien – Baltimore 1987 – 1989

Rauber/Kopsch: Lehrbuch und Atlas der Anatomie des Menschen, Bd. I: Bewegungsapparat, hrsg. von B. Tillmann, G. Töndury. Thieme, Stuttgart 1987

Reiffenstuhl, G., W. Platzer, P.-G. Knapstein: Die vaginalen Operationen, 2. Aufl., Urban & Schwarzenberg, München – Wien – Baltimore 1994

Saegesser, M.: Spezielle chirurgische Therapie, 10. Aufl. Huber, Bern 1976

Sobotta: Atlas der Anatomie, Bd. 1 u. 2, 20. Aufl. hrsg. von R. Putz, u. R. Pabst, Urban und Schwarzenberg, München-Wien-Baltimore 1994

Starck, D.: Embryologie, 3. Aufl. Thieme, Stuttgart 1975

Tischendorf, F.: Makroskopisch-anatomischer Kurs, 3. Aufl. Fischer, Stuttgart 1979

Tittel, K.: Beschreibende und funktionelle Anatomie des Menschen, 8. Aufl. Fischer, Stuttgart 1978

Töndury, G.: Angewandte und topographische Anatomie, 5. Aufl. Thieme, Stuttgart 1981

Williams, P. L., R. Warwick, M. Dyson, L. H. Bannister: Gray's Anatomy, 37. Aufl. Churchill, Livingstone, Edinburgh 1989

General Anatomy

Barnett, C. H.: The structure and functions of synovial joints. In: Clinical Surgery, hrsg. von Rob, C., R. Smith: Butterworth, London 1966 (S. 328 – 344)

Barnett, C. H., D. V. Davies, M. A. Mac Conaill: Synovial Joints, Their Structure and Mechanics. Longmans, London 1961

Basmajian, J. V.: Muscles Alive, 3. Aufl. Williams & Wilkins, Baltimore 1974

Bernstein, N.: The Coordination and Regulation of Movements. Pergamon Press, Oxford 1967

Bourne, G. H.: Biochemistry and Physiology of Bone, 2. Aufl., Bd. I: Structure. Academic Press, New York 1972

Bourne, G. H.: The Structure and Function of Muscle, 2. Aufl., Bd. I: Structure. Academic Press, New York 1972

Brookes, M.: The Blood Supply of Bone. Butterworth, London 1971

Dowson, D., V. Wright, M. D. Longfield: Human joint lubrication. Bio-med. Engng 4 (1969) 8–14, 160–165, 517–522

Freeman, M. A. R.: Adult Articular Cartilage. Pitman, London 1973

Haines, R. W., A. Mohiudin: The sites of early epiphyseal union in the limb girdles and major long bones of man. J. Anat. (Lond.) 101 (1967) 823–831

Hancox, N. M.: Biology of Bone. Cambridge University Press, London 1972

Jonsson, B., S. Reichmann: Reproducibility in kinesiologic EMG-investigation with intramuscular electrodes. Acta morphol. neerl.-scand. 7 (1968) 73–90

Joseph, J.: Man's Posture: Electromyographic Studies. Thomas, Springfield/Ill. 1960

Kapandji, I. A.: The Physiology of Joints, 2. Aufl., Bd. I–III. Longman, London 1970/71/74

MacConaill, M. A., J. V. Basmajian: Muscles and Movements. Williams & Wilkins, Baltimore 1969

Mysorecar, V. R.: Diaphyseal nutrient foramina in human long bones. J. Anat. (Lond.) 101 (1967) 813–822

Rasch, P. J., R. K. Burke: Kinesiology and Applied Anatomy, 5. Aufl. Lea & Febiger, Philadelphia 1974

Russe, O. A., J. J. Gerhardt, O. J. Russe: Taschenbuch der Gelenkmessung mit Darstellung der Neutral-Null-Methode und SFTR-Notierung. 2. Aufl. Huber, Bern 1982

Serratrice, G., J. Eisinger: Innervation et circulation osseuses diaphysaires. Rev. Rhum. 34 (1967) 505–519

Smith, D. S.: Muscle. Academic Press, New York 1972

Trunk

Beck, A., J. Killus: Mathematisch statistische Methoden zur Untersuchung der Wirbelsäulenhaltung mittels Computer. Biomed. Techn. 19 (1974) 72–74

Bowden, F., H. El-Ramli: The anatomy of the oesophageal hiatus. Brit. J. Surg. 54 (1967) 983–989

Cavallotti, C.: Morfologia del trigoni lombocostali del diaframma umano. Acta med. Rom 6 (1968) 21–29

Condor, R. E.: Surgical anatomy of the transversus abdominis and transversalis fascia. Ann. Surg. 173 (1971) 1–5

Danburg, R.: Functional anatomy and kinesiology of the cervical spine. Manu. Med. 9 (1971) 97–101

Diaconescu, N., C. Veleanu: Die Wirbelsäule als formbildender Faktor. Acta anat. (Basel) 73 (1969) 210–241

Donisch, E. W., W. Trapp: The cartilage endplates of the human vertebral column (some considerations of postnatal development). Anat. Rec. 169 (1971) 705–716

Doyle, J. F.: The superficial inguinal arch. A reassessment of what has been called the inguinal ligament. J. Anat. (Lond.) 108 (1971) 297–304

Drexler, L.: Röntgenanatomische Untersuchungen über Form und Krümmung der Halswirbelsäule in den verschiedenen Lebensaltern. Hippokrates, Stuttgart 1962

Epstein, B. S.: The Vertebral Column. Year Book Medical Publishers, Chicago 1974

François, R. J.: Ligament insertions into the human lumbar body. Acta anat. (Basel) 91 (1975) 467–480

Groeneveld, H. B.: Metrische Erfassung und Definition von Rückenform und Haltung des Menschen. Hippokrates, Stuttgart 1976

Helmy, I. D.: Congenital diaphragmatic hernia (A study of the weakest points of the diaphragm by dissection and a report of a case of hernia through the right foramen of Morgagni. Alexandria med. J. 13 (1967) 121–132

Hesselbach, A. K.: Die Erkenntnis und Behandlung der Eingeweidebrüche, Bauer u. Raspe, Nürnberg 1840

Johnson, R. M., E. S. Crelin, A. A. White et al.: Some new observations on the functional anatomy of the lower cervical spine. Clin. Orthop. 111 (1975) 192–200

Kapandji, I. A.: L'Anatomie fonctionelle du rachis lombo sacre. Acta orthop. belg. 35 (1969) 543–566

Krämer, J.: Biomechanische Veränderungen im lumbalen Bewegungssegment. Hippokrates, Stuttgart 1973

Krmpotic-Nemanic, J., P. Keros: Funktionale Bedeutung der Adaption des Dens axis beim Menschen. Verh. anat. Ges. (Jena) 67 (1973) 393–397

Langenberg, W.: Morphologie, physiologischer Querschnitt und Kraft des M. erector spinae im Lumbalbereich des Menschen. Z. Anat. Entwickl.-Gesch. 132 (1970) 158–190

Liard, A. R., M. Latarjet, F. Crestanello: Precisions anatomiques concernant la partie superieure du muscle grand droit de l'abdomen et de sa gaine. C. R. Ass. Anat. 148 (1970) 532–542

Ludwig, K. S.: Die Frühentwicklung des Dens epistrophei und seiner Bänder beim Menschen. Morphol. Jb. 93 (1953) 98–112

Ludwig, K. S.: Die Frühentwicklung des Atlas und der Occipitalwirbel beim Menschen. Acta anat. (Basel) 30 (1957) 444–461

Lytle, W. J.: The inguinal and lacunar ligaments. J. Anat. (Lond.) 118 (1974) 241–251

MacVay, C. B.: The normal and pathologic anatomy of the transversus abdominis muscle in inguinal and femoral hernia. Surg. Clin. N. Amer. 51 (1971) 1251–1261

Mambrini, A., M. Argeme, J. P. Houze, H. Isman: A propos de l'orifice aortique du diaphragme. C. R. Ass. Anat. 148 (1970) 433–441

Nathan, H., B. Arensburgh: An unusual variation in the fifth lumbar and sacral vertebrae: a possible cause of vertebral canal narrowing. Anat. Anz. 132 (1972) 137 – 148

Niethard, F. U.: Die Form-Funktionsproblematik des lumbosakralen Überganges. Hippokrates, Stuttgart 1981

Okada, M., K. Kogi, M. Ishii: Endurance capacity of the erectores spinae muscles in static work. J. Anthrop. Soc. Nippon 78 (1970) 99 – 110

Pierpont, R. Z., A. W. Grigoleit, M. K. Finegan: The transversalis fascia. A practical analysis of an enigma. Amer. Surg. 35 (1969) 737 – 740

Platzer, W.: Funktionelle Anatomie der Wirbelsäule. In: Erkrankungen der Wirbelsäule, hrsg. von R. Bauer. Thieme, Stuttgart 1975 (S. 1 – 6)

Platzer, W.: Die zervikokraniale Übergangsregion in Kopfschmerzen, hrsg. von H. Tilscher et al. Springer, Berlin 1988

Prestar, F. L., R. Putz: Das Lig. longitudinale posterius – Morphologie und Funktion. Morphol. Med. 2 (1982) 181 – 189

Putz, R.: Zur Manifestation der hypochordalen Spangen im cranio-vertebralen Grenzgebiet beim Menschen. Anat. Anz. 137 (1975) 65 – 74

Putz, R.: Charakteristische Fortsätze – Processus uncinati – als besondere Merkmale des 1. Brustwirbels. Anat. Anz. 139 (1976) 442 – 454

Putz, R.: Zur Morphologie und Rotationsmechanik der kleinen Gelenke der Lendenwirbel. Z. Orthop. 114 (1976) 902 – 912

Putz, R.: Funktionelle Anatomie der Wirbelgelenke. Thieme, Stuttgart 1981

Putz, R., A. Pomaroli: Form und Funktion der Articulatio atlanto-axialis lateralis. Acta anat. (Basel) 83 (1972) 333 – 345

Radojevic, S., E. Stolic, S. Unkovic: Le muscle cremaster de l'homme (Variations morphologiques et importance partique). C. R. Ass. Anat. 143 (1969) 1383 – 1386

Reichmann, S., E. Berglund, K. Lundgren: Das Bewegungszentrum in der Lendenwirbelsäule bei Flexion und Extension. Z. Anat. Entwickl.-Gesch. 138 (1972) 283 – 287

Schlüter, K.: Form und Struktur des normalen und des pathologisch veränderten Wirbels. Hippokrates, Stuttgart 1965

Shimaguchi, S.: Tenth rib is floating in Japanese. Anat. Anz. 135 (1974) 72 – 82

de Sousa, O. M., J. Furlani: Electromyographic study of the m. rectus abdominis. Acta anat. (Basel) 88 (1974) 281 – 298

Steubl, R.: Innervation und Morphologie der Mm. levatores costarum. Z. Anat. Entwickl.-Gesch. 128 (1969) 211 – 221

Takebe, K., M. Vitti, J. v. Basmajian: The functions of semispinalis capitis and splenius capitis muscles. An electromyographic study. Anat. Rec. 179 (1974) 477 – 480

Taylor, A.: The contribution of the intercostal muscles to the effort of respiration in man. J. Physiol. (Lond.) 151 (1960) 390 – 402

Taylor, J. R.: Growth of human intervertebral discs and vertebral bodies. J. Anat. (Lond.) 120 (1975) 49 – 68

Töndury, G.: Entwicklungsgeschichte und Fehlbildungen der Wirbelsäule. Hippokrates, Stuttgart 1958

v. Torklus, D., W. Gehle: Die obere Halswirbelsäule, 3. Aufl. Thieme, Stuttgart 1987

Veleanu, C., U. Grun, M. Diaconescu, E. Cocota: Structural peculiarities of the thoracic spine. Their functional significance. Acta anat. (Basel) 82 (1972) 97 – 107

Witschel, H., R. Mangelsdorf: Geschlechtsunterschiede am menschlichen Brustbein. Z. Rechtsmed. 69 (1971) 161 – 167

Zaki, W.: Aspect morphologique et fonctionnel de l'annulus fibrosus du disque intervertebral de la colonne cervicale. Bull. Ass. Anat. 57 (1973) 649 – 654

Zukschwerdt, L., F. Emminger, E. Biedermann, H. Zettel: Wirbelgelenk und Bandscheibe. Hippokrates, Stuttgart 1960

Upper Limb

Basmajian, J. V., W. R. Griffin jr.: Function of anconeus muscle. An electromyographic study. J. Bone Jt. Surg. 54-A (1972) 1712 – 1714

Basmajian, J. V., A. Travill: Electromyography of the pronator muscles in the forearm. Anat. Rec. 139 (1961) 45 – 49

Bearn, J. G.: An electromyographical study of the trapezius, deltoid, pectoralis major, biceps and triceps, during static loading of the upper limb. Anat. Rec. 140 (1961) 103 – 108

Bojsen-Møller, F., L. Schmidt: The palmar aponeurosis and the central spaces of the hand. J. Anat. (Lond.) 117 (1974) 55 – 68

Christensen, J. B., J. P. Adams, K. O. Cho, L. Miller: A study of the interosseous distance between the radius and ulnar during rotation of the forearm. Anat. Rec. 160 (1968) 261 – 271

Čihák, R.: Ontogenesis of the Skeleton and the Intrinsic Muscles of the Hand and Foot. Springer, Berlin 1972

Clarke, G. R., L. A. Willis, W. W. Fish, P. J. R. Nichols: Assessment of movement at the glenohumeral joint. Orthopaedics (Oxford) 7 (1974) 55 – 71

Dempster, W. T.: Mechanisms of shoulder movement. Arch. phys. Med. 46 (1965) 49 – 70

Doody, S. G., L. Freedman, J. C. Waterland: Shoulder movements during abduction in the scapular plane. Arch. phys. Med. 51 (1970) 595 – 604

Dylevsky, I.: Ontogenesis of the M. palmaris longus in man. Folia morphol. (Prague) 17 (1969) 23 – 28

Franzi, A. T., E. Spinelli, G. Ficcarelli: Variazione del muscolo palmare lungo: Contributo alla casistica. Quad. Anat. prat. 25 (1969) 71 – 76

Garn, S. M., C. G. Rohman: Variability in the order of ossification of the bony centers of the hand and wrist. Amer. J. phys. Anthropol. (N.S.) 18 (1960) 219 – 230

Glasgow, E. F.: Bilateral extensor digitorum brevis manus. Med. J. Aust. 54 (1967) 25

Hohmann, G.: Hand und Arm, ihre Erkrankungen und deren Behandlung. Bergmann, München 1949

Jonsson, B., B. M. Olofsson, L. C. Steffner: Function of the teres major, latissimus dorsi and pectoralis major muscles. A preliminary study. Acta morphol. neerl.-scand. 9 (1972) 275 – 280

Kaneff, A.: Über die wechselseitigen Beziehungen der progressiven Merkmale des M. extensor pollicis brevis beim Menschen. Anat. Anz. 122 (1968) 31 – 36

Kapandji, A.: La rotation du pouce sur son axe longitudinal lors de l'opposition. Rev. chir. Orthop. 58 (1972) 273 – 289

Kauer, J. M. G.: The interdependence of carpal articulation chains. Acta anat. (Basel) 88 (1974) 481 – 501

Kauer, J. M. G.: The articular disc of the hand. Acta anat. (Basel) 93 (1975) 590 – 605

Kiyosumi, M.: New ligaments at articulationes manus. Kumamoto Med. J. 18 (1965) 214 – 227

Krmpotic-Nemanic, J.: Über einen bisher unbeachteten Mechanismus der Fingergrundgelenke. Gegenseitige Längsverschiebung der Finger bei der Flexion. Z. Anat. Entwickl.-Gesch. 126 (1967) 127 – 131

Kuczynski, K.: Carpometacarpal joint of the human thumb. J. Anat. (Lond.) 118 (1974) 119 – 126

Landsmeer, J. M. F.: Atlas of the Hand. Churchill, Livingstone, Edinburgh 1976

Lewis, O. J., R. J. Hamshere, T. M. Bucknill: The anatomy of the wrist joint. J. Anat. (Lond.) 106 (1970) 539 – 552

Long, C.: Intrinsic-extrinsic muscle control of the fingers. Electromyographic studies. J. Bone Jt. Surg. 50-A (1968) 973 – 984

McClure, J. G., R. Beverly: Anomalies of the scapula. Clin. Orthop. 110 (1975) 22 – 31

Metha, H. J., W. U. Gardner: A study of lumbrical muscles in the human hand. Amer. J. Anat. 109 (1961) 227 – 238

Mrvaljevic, D.: Sur les insertions et la perforation du muscle coracobrachial. C. R. Ass. Anat. 139 (1968) 923 – 933

Murata, K., K. Abe, G. Kawahara et al.: The M. serratus anterior of the Japanese. The area of its origin and its interdigitation with the M. obliquus externus abdominis. Acta anat. Nippon. 43 (1968) 395 – 401

Neiss, A.: Sekundäre Ossifikationszentren. Anat. Anz. 137 (1975) 342 – 344

Pauly, J. E., J. L. Rushing, L. E. Scheving: An electromyographic study of some muscles crossing the elbow joint. Anat. Rec. 159 (1967) 47 – 54

Poisel, S.: Die Anatomie der Palmaraponeurose. Therapiewoche 23 (1973) 3337

Ravelli, A.: Die sogenannte Rotatorenmanschette, Öst. Ärzteztg. 13/14 (1974)

Renard, M., B. Brichet, A. Fonder, P. Poisson: Rôle respectif des muscles sous-épineux et petit rond dans l cinématique de l'humerus. C. R. Ass. Anat. 139 (1968) 1266 – 1272

Renard, M., A. Fonder, C. Mentre, B. Brichet, J. Cayotte: Contribution à l'étude de la fonction du muscle sousépineux. Communication accompagnée d'un film. C. R. Ass. Anat. 136 (1967) 878 – 883

Roche, A. F.: The sites of elongation of the human metacarpals and metatarsals. Acat. anat. (Basel) 61 (1965) 193 – 202

Schmidt, H.-M.: Die Guyon'sche Loge. Ein Beitrag zur klinischen Anatomie der menschlichen Hand. Acta anat. 131 (1988) 113 – 121

Schmidt, H.-M., U. Lanz: Chirurgische Anatomie der Hand. Hippokrates Verlag, Stuttgart 1992

Shrewsbury, M. M., R. K. Johnson: The fascia of the distal phalanx. J. Bone Jt. Surg. 57 A (1975) 784 – 788

Shrewsbury, M. M., M. K. Kuczynski: Flexor digitorum superficialis tendon in the fingers of the human hand. Hand 6 (1974) 121 – 133

Shrewsbury, M. M., R. K. Johnson, D. K. Ousterhout: The palmaris brevis. A reconstruction of its anatomy and possible function. J. Bone Jt. Surg. 54-A (1972) 344 – 348

Soutoul, J. H., J. Castaing, J. Thureau, E. De Giovanni, P. Glories, M. Jan, J. Barbat: Les rapports tête humérale-glène scapulaire dans d'abduction du membre supérieur. C. R. Ass. Anat. 136 (1967) 961 – 971

Stack, H. G.: The Palmar Fascia. Churchill, Livingstone, London 1973

Strasser, H.: Lehrbuch der Muskel- und Gelenkmechanik, Bd. IV: Die obere Extremität. Springer, Berlin 1917

Weston, W. J.: The digital sheaths of the hand. Aust. Radiol. 13 (1969) 360 – 364

Lower Limb

Ahmad, I.: Articular muscle of the knee: articularis genus. Bull. Hospit. Dis. (N. Y.) 36 (1975) 58 – 60

Altieri, E.: Aplasia bilaterale congenita della rotula. Boll. Soc. Tosco-Umbra Chir. 28 (1967) 279 – 286

Asang, E.: Experimentelle und praktische Biomechanik des menschlichen Beins. Med. Sport (Berl.) 13 (1973) 245 – 255

Aumüller, G.: Über Bau und Funktion des Musculus adductor minimus. Anat. Anz. 126 (1970) 337–342

Basmajian, J. V., T. P. Harden, E. M. Regenos: Integrated actions of the four heads of quadriceps femoris: An electromyographic study. Anat. Rec. 172 (1972) 15–20

Bojsen Møller, F., V. E. Flagstadt: Plantar aponeurosis and internal architecture of the ball of the foot. J. Anat. (Lond.) 121 (1976) 599–611

Bowden, R. E. M.: The functional anatomy of the foot. Physiotherapy 53 (1967) 120–126

Bubic, I.: Sexual signs of the human pelvis. Folia med. (Sarajevo) 8 (1973) 113–115

Candiollo, L., G. Gautero: Morphologie et fonction des ligaments méniscofémoraux de l'articulation du genou chez l'homme. Acta anat. (Basel) 38 (1959) 304–323

Ching Jen Wang, P. S. Walker: Rotatory laxity of the human knee joint. J. Bone Jt. Surg. 56-A (1974) 161–170

Čihák, R.: Ontogenesis of the Skeleton and Intrinsic Muscles of the Human Hand and Foot. Springer, Berlin 1972

Dahhan, P., G. Delephine, D. Larde: The femoropatellar joint. Anat. Clin. 3 (1981) 23–39

Detenbeck, L. C.: Function of the cruciate ligaments in knee stability. J. Sports Med. 2 (1974) 217–221

Didio, L. J. A., A. Zappalá, W. P. Carney: Anatomico-functional aspects of the musculus articularis genu in man. Acta anat. (Basel) 67 (1967) 1–23

Emery, K. H., G. Meachim: Surface morphology and topography of patello-femoral cartilage fibrillation in Liverpool necropsies. J. Anat. (Lond.) 116 (1973) 103–120

Emmett, J.: Measurements of the acetabulum. Clin. Orthop. 53 (1967) 171–174

Gluhbegovic, N., H. Hadziselimovic: Beitrag zu den vergleichenden anatomischen Untersuchungen der Bänder des lateralen Meniskus. Anat. Anz. 126 Suppl. (1970) 565–575

Goswami, N., P. R. Deb: Patella and patellar facets. Calcutta med. J. 67 (1970) 123–128

Heller, L., J. Langman: The menisco-femoral ligaments of the human knee. J. Bone Jt. Surg. 46-B (1964) 307–313

Hoerr, N. L., S. J. Pyle, C. C. Franciss: Radiographic Atlas of Skeletal Development of Foot and Ankle. Thomas, Springfield/Ill. 1962

Hohmann, G.: Fuß und Bein, ihre Erkrankungen und deren Behandlung. 5. Aufl. Bergmann, München 1951

Hooper, A. C. B.: The role of the iliopsoas muscle in femoral rotation. Irish J. med. Sci. 146 (1977) 108–112

Jacobsen, K.: Area intercondylaris tibiae: osseous surface structure and its relation to soft tissue structures and applications to radiography. J. Anat. (Lond.) 117 (1974) 605–618

Janda, V., V. Stará: The role of thigh adductors in movements patterns of the hip and knee joints. Courrier, Centre internat. de l'Enfance 15 (1965) 1–3

Jansen, J. C.: Einige nieuwe functioneelanatomische aspecten von de voet. Ned. T. Geneesk. 112 (1968) 147–155

Johnson, C. E., J. V. Basmajian, W. Dasher: Electromyography of sartorius muscle. Anat. Rec. 173 (1972) 127–130

Joseph, J.: Movements at the hip joint. Ann. R. Call. Surg. Engl. 56 (1975) 192–201

Kaplan, E. B.: The iliotibial tract, clinical and morphological significance. J. Bone Jt. Surg. 40-A (1958) 817–831

Kaufer, H.: Mechanical function of the patella. J. Bone Jt. Surg. 53-A (1971) 1551–1560

Kennedy, J. C., H. W. Weinberg, A. S. Wilson: The anatomy and function of the anterior cruciate ligament. As determined by clinical morphological studies. J. Bone Jt. Surg. 56-A (1974) 223–235

Knief, J.: Materialverteilung und Beanspruchungsverteilung im coxalen Femurende. Densitometrische und spannungsoptische Untersuchungen. Z. Anat. Entwickl.-Gesch. 126 (1967) 81–116

Kummer, B.: Die Biomechanik der aufrechten Haltung. Mitt. Naturforsch. Ges. Bern 22 (1965) 239–259

Kummer, B.: Funktionelle Anatomie des Vorfußes. Verh. dtsch. arthop. Ges. 53 (1966) 483–493

Kummer, B.: Die Beanspruchung der Gelenke, dargestellt am Beispiel des menschlichen Hüftgelenks. Verh. dtsch. Ges. orthop. Traumatol. 55 (1968) 302–311

Lesage, Y., R. Le Bars: Etude electromyographique simultanée des differents chefs du quadriceps. Ann. Méd. phys. 13 (1970) 292–297

Loetzke, H. H., K. Trzenschik: Beitrag zur Frage der Varianten des M. soleus beim Menschen. Anat. Anz. 124 (1969) 28–36

Marshall, J. L., E. G. Girgis, R. R. Zelko: The biceps femoris tendon and its functional significance. J. Bone Jt. Surg. 54-A (1972) 1444–1450

Martin, B. F.: The origins of the hamstring muscles. J. Anat. (Lond.) 102 (1968) 345–352

Menschik, A.: Mechanik des Kniegelenkes. I. Z. Orthop. 112 (1974) 481–495

Menschik, A.: Mechanik des Kniegelenkes. II. Z. Orthop. 113 (1975) 388–400

Mörike, K. D.: Werden die Menisken im Kniegelenk geschoben oder gezogen? Anat. Anz. 133 (1973) 265–275

Morrison, J. B.: The mechanics of the knee joint in relation to normal walking. J. Biochem. 3 (1970) 51–61

Novozamsky, V.: Die Form der Fußwölbung unter Belastung in verschiedenen Fußstellungen. Z. Orthop. 112 (1974) 1137–1142

Novozamsky, V., J. Buchberger: Die Fußwölbung nach Belastung durch einen 100-km-Marsch. Z. Anat. Entwickl.-Gesch. 131 (1970) 243–248

Oberländer, W.: Die Beanspruchung des menschlichen Hüftgelenks. Z. Anat. Entwickl.-Gesch. 140 (1973) 367–384

Ogden, S. A.: The anatomy and function of the proximal tibiofibular joint. Clin. Orthop. 101 (1974) 186–191

Olbrich, E.: Patella emarginata – Patella partita. Forschungen und Forscher der Tiroler Ärzteschule 2 (1948–1950) 69–105

Pauwels, F.: Gesammelte Abhandlungen zur funktionellen Anatomie des Bewegungsapparates. Springer, Berlin 1965

Pheline, Y., S. Chitour, H. Issad, G. Djilali, J. Ferrand: La région soustrochantérienne. C. R. Ass. Anat. 136 (1967) 782–806

Platzer, W.: Zur Anatomie des Femoropatellargelenks. In: Fortschritte in der Arthroskopie, hrsg. v. H. Hofer. Enke, Stuttgart 1985

Platzer, W.: Zur funktionellen und topographischen Anatomie des Vorfußes. In: Hallux valgus, hrsg. von N. Blauth. Springer, Berlin 1986

Raux, P., P. R. Townsend, R. Miegel et al.: Trabecular architecture of the human patella. S. Biomech. 8 (1975) 1–7

Ravelli, A.: Zum anatomischen und röntgenologischen Bild der Hüftpfanne. Z. Orthop. 113 (1975) 306–315

Renard, M., B. Brichet, J. L. Cayotte: Analyse fonctionelle du triceps sural. C. R. Ass. Anat. 143 (1969) 1387–1394

Rideau, Y., P. Lacert, C. Hamonet: Contribution à l'etude de l'action des muscles de la loge postérieure de la cuisse. C. R. Ass. Anat. 143 (1969) 1406–1415

Rideau, Y., C. Hamonet, G. Outrequin, P. Kamina: Etude électromyographique de l'activité fonctionelle des muscles de la loge postérieure de la cuisse. C. R. Ass. Anat. 146 (1971) 597–603

Rother, P., E. Luschnitz, S. Beau, P. Lohmann: Der Ursprung der ischiokruralen Muskelgruppe des Menschen. Anat. Anz. 135 (1974) 64–71

Sick, H., P. Ring, C. Ribot, J. G. Koritke: Structure fonctionelle des menisques de articulation du genou. C. R. Ass. Anat. 143 (1969) 1565–1571

Sirang, H.: Ein Canalis alae ossis illii und seine Bedeutung. Anat. Anz. 133 (1973) 225–238

Stern jr., J. T.: Anatomical and functional specializations of the human gluteus maximus. Amer. J. phys. Anthropol. 36 (1972) 315–339

Strasser, H.: Lehrbuch der Muskel- und Gelenkmechanik, Bd. III: Die untere Extremität. Springer, Berlin 1917

Strauss, F.: Gedanken zur Fuß-Statik. Acta anat. (Basel) 71 (1971) 412–424

Suzuki, N.: An electromyographic study of the role of muscles in arch support of the normal and flat foot. Nagoya med. J. 17 (1972) 57–79

Takebe, K., M. Viti, J. V. Basmajian: Electromyography of pectineus muscle. Anat. Rec. 180 (1974) 281–284

Tittel, K.: Funktionelle Anatomie und Biomechanik des Kniegelenks. Med. Sport (Berl.) 17 (1977) 65–74

von Volkmann, R.: Wer trägt den Taluskopf wirklich, und inwiefern ist der plantare Sehnenast des M. tibialis post. als Bandsystem aufzufassen? Anat. Anz. 131 (1972) 425–432

von Volkmann, R.: Zur Anatomie und Mechanik des Lig. calcaneonaviculare plantare sensu strictiori. Anat. Anz. 134 (1973) 460–470

Zivanovic, S.: Menisco-meniscal ligaments of the human knee joint. Anat. Anz. 135 (1974) 35–42

Head and Neck

Bochu, M., G. Crastes: La selle turcique normale etude radiographique. Lyon méd. 231 (1974) 797–805

Buntine, J. A.: The omohyoid muscle and fascia; morphology and anomalies. Aust. N. Z. J. Surg. 40 (1970) 86–88

Burch, J. G.: Activity of the accessory ligaments of the mandibular joint. J. prosth. Dent. 24 (1970) 621–628

Campell, E. J. M.: The role of the scalene and sternomastoid muscles in breathing in normal subjects. An electromyographical study. J. Anat. (Lond.) 89 (1955) 378–386

Carella, A.: Apparato stilo ioideo e malformazioni della cerniera atlo occipitale. Acta neurol. (Napoli) 26 (1971) 466–472

Couly, G., C. Brocheriou, J. M. Vaillant: Les menisques temporomandibulaires. Rev. Stomat. (Paris) 76 (1975) 303–310

Fischer, C., G. Ransmayr: Ansatz und Funktion der infrahyalen Muskulatur. Anat. Anz. 168 (1989) 237–243

Fortunato, V., St. D. Bocciarelli, G. Auriti: Contributo allo studio della morfologia ossea dell'area cribrosa dell'etmoide. Clin. otorinolaring. 22 (1970) 3–15

Hadziselimovic, H., M. Cus, V. Tomic: Appearance of the sigmoid groove and jugular foramen in relation to the configuration of the human skull. Acta anat. (Basel) 77 (1970) 501–507

Honee, G. L. J. M.: The Musculus pterygoideus lateralis. Thesis, Amsterdam 1970 (S. 1–152)

Ingervall, B., B. Thilander: The human sphenooccipital synchondrosis. 1. The time of closure appraised macroscopically. Acta odont. scand. 30 (1972) 349–356

Isley, C. L., J. V. Basmajian: Electromyography of human cheeks and lips. Anat. Rec. 176 (1973) 143–148

Lang, J.: Structure and postnatal organization of heretofore uninvestigated and infrequent ossifications of the sella turcica region. Acta anat. (Basel) 99 (1977) 121–139

Lang, J., S. Niederfeilner: Über Flächenwerte der Kiefergelenkspalte. Anat. Anz. 141 (1977) 398–400

Lang, J., K. Tisch-Rottensteiner: Lage und Form der Foramina der Fossa cranii media. Verh. anat. Ges. (Jena) 70 (1976) 557–565

Melsen, B.: Time and mode of closure of the spheno-occipital synchondrosis determined on human autopsy material. Acta anat. (Basel) 83 (1972) 112–118

Oberg, T., G. E. Carlsson, C. M. Fajers: The temporomandibular joint. A morphologic study on human autopsy material. Acta odont. scand. 29 (1971) 349–384

Platzer, W.: Zur Anatomie der „Sellabrücke" und ihrer Beziehung zur A. carotis interna. Fortschr. Röntgenstr. 87 (1957) 613–616

Pomaroli, A.: Ramus mandibulae. Bedeutung in Anatomie und Klinik. Hüthig, Heidelberg 1987

Porter, M. R.: The attachment of the lateral pterygoid muscle to the meniscus. J. prosth. Dent. 24 (1970) 555–562

Proctor, A. D., J. P. de Vincenzo: Masseter muscle position relative to dentofacial form. Angle Orthodont. 40 (1970) 37–44

Putz, R.: Schädelform und Pyramiden. Anat. Anz. 135 (1974) 252–266

Shapiro, R., F. Robinson: The foramina of the middle fossa. A phylogenetic, anatomic and pathologic study. Amer. J. Roentgenol. 101 (1967) 779–794

Schelling, F.: Die Emissarien des menschlichen Schädels. Anat. Anz. 143 (1978) 340–382

Stofft, E.: Zur Morphometrie der Gelenkflächen des oberen Kopfgelenkes (Beitrag zur Statik der zerviko-okzipitalen Übergangsregion. Verh. anat. Ges. (Jena) 70 (1976) 575–584

Vitti, M., M. Fujiwara, J. V. Basmajian, M. Lida: The integrated roles of longus colli and sternocleidomastoid muscles: an electromyographic study. Anat. Rec. 177 (1973) 471–484

Weisengreen, H. H.: Observation of the articular disc. Oral. Surg. 40 (1975) 113–121

Wentges, R. T.: Surgical anatomy of the pterygopalatine fossa. J. Laryngol. 89 (1975) 35–45

Wright, D. M., B. C. Moffett jr.: The postnatal development of the human temporomandibular joint. Amer. J. Anat. 141 (1974) 235–249

Zenker, W.: Das retroartikuläre plastische Polster des Kiefergelenkes und seine mechanische Bedeutung. Z. Anat. Entwickl.-Gesch. 119 (1956) 375–388

Peripheral Nerves and Vessels

Beaton, L. E., B. J. Anson: The relation of the sciatic nerve and of its subdivisions to the piriformis muscle. Anat. Rec. 70 (1937) 1

Fasol, P., P. Munk, M. Strickner: Blutgefäßversorgung des Handkahnbeins. Acta anat. (Basel) 100 (1978) 27–33

Hilty, H.: Die makroskopische Gefäßvariation im Mündungsgebiet der V. saphena magna des Menschen. Schwabe, Basel 1955

Lahlaidi, A.: Vascularisation arterielle des ligaments intra-articulaires du genou chez l'homme Folia angiol. (Pisa) 23 (1975) 178–181

Lauritzen, J.: The arterial supply to the femoral head in children. Acta orthop. scand. 45 (1974) 724–736

Lippert, H.: Arterienvarietäten, Klinische Tabellen. Beilage in Med. Klin. 1967–1969, 18–32

May, R.: Chirurgie der Bein- und Beckenvenen. Thieme, Stuttgart 1974

May, R., R. Nißl: Die Phlebographie der unteren Extremität, 2. Aufl. Thieme, Stuttgart 1973

Mercier, R., Ph. Fouques, N. Portal, G. Vanneuville: Anatomie chirurgicale de la veine saphene externe. J. chir. 93 (1967) 59

Miller, M. R., H. J. Ralston, M. Kasahara: The pattern of innervation of the human hand. Amer. J. Anat. 102 (1958) 183–218

Moosmann, A., W. Hartwell jr.: The surgical significance of the subfascial course of the lesser saphenous vein. Surg. Gynec. Obstet. 118 (1964) 761

Ogden jr. A.: Changing patterns of proximal femoral vascularity. J. Bone Jt. Surg. 56-A (1974) 941–950

Poisel, S., D. Golth: Zur Variabilität der großen Arterien im Trigonum caroticum. Wien. med. Wschr. 124 (1974) 229–232

Schmidt, H.-M.: Topographisch-klinische Anatomie der Guyon'schen Loge an der menschlichen Hand. Acta anat. 120 (1984) 66

Sirang, H.: Ursprung, Verlauf und Äste des N. saphenus. Anat. Anz. 130 (1972) 158–169

Tillmann, B., K. Gretenkord: Verlauf des N. medianus im Canalis carpi. Morphol. Med. 1 (1981) 61–69

Wallace, W. A., R. E. Coupland: Variations in the nerves of the thumb and index finger. J. Bone Jt Surg. 57-B (1975) 491–494

Weber, J., R. May: Funktionelle Phlebologie. Thieme, Stuttgart 1989

Wladimirov, B.: Über die Blutversorgung des Kniegelenkknorpels beim Menschen. Anat. Anz. 140 (1976) 469–476

Index

Boldface page numbers indicate extensive coverage of the subject.